Students with Emotional and Behavioral Problems

Assessment, Management, and Intervention Strategies

Joyce Anderson Downing

Central Missouri State University

PEARSON

Merrill
Prentice Hall

Upper Saddle River, New Jersey
Columbus, Ohio

Library of Congress Cataloging-in-Publication Data

Downing, Joyce Anderson.

   Students with emotional and behavioral problems : assessment, management, and
intervention strategies / Joyce Anderson Downing.

     p. cm.

   Includes bibliographical references and index.

   ISBN 0-13-039476-9 (pbk.)

   1. Teachers of problem children—Training of—United States. 2. Problem
children—Education—United States. 3. Behavior disorders in children—United States.
4. Classroom management—United States. 1. Title.

LC4802.D69 2007

371.93—dc22   2006045143

Vice President and Executive Publisher: Jeffery W. Johnston
Senior Editor: Ann Castel Davis
Editorial Assistant: Penny Burleson
Production Editor: Sheryl Glicker Langner
Production Coordination: Kathy Glidden, Stratford Publishing Services
Design Coordinator: Diane C. Lorenzo
Cover Design: Thomas Borah
Cover Image: Super Stock
Photo Coordinator: Valerie Schultz
Production Manager: Laura Messerly
Director of Marketing: David Gesell
Marketing Manager: Autumn Purdy
Marketing Coordinator: Brian Mounts

Photo Credits: Laura Bolesta/Merrill, p. 2; Scott Cunningham/Merrill, p. 20; Anne Vega/Merrill, p. 42; Anthony Magnacca/Merrill, p. 66, 82, 244; Liz Moore/Merrill, p. 98; Susan Oristaglio/PH College, p. 122; Tony Freeman/PhotoEdit Inc., p. 138; Gail Meese/Merrill, p. 164; Roy Ramsey/PH College, p. 196; Laimute E. Druskis/PH College, p. 226; Mary Kate Denny/PhotoEdit Inc., p. 260; Richard Hutchings/PhotoEdit Inc., p. 276.

Pearson Prentice Hall™ is a trademark of Pearson Education, Inc.
Pearson® is a registered trademark of Pearson plc.
Prentice Hall® is a registered trademark of Pearson Education, Inc.
Merrill® is a registered trademark of Pearson Education, Inc.

Pearson Education Ltd.   Pearson Education Australia Pty. Limited
Pearson Education Singapore Pte. Ltd.   Pearson Education North Asia Ltd.
Pearson Education Canada, Ltd.   Pearson Educación de Mexico, S.A. de C.V.
Pearson Education–Japan   Pearson Education Malaysia Pte. Ltd.

ISBN: 0-13-039476-9

For my parents, Floyd and Helen Anderson,
who taught their four daughters
to believe that anything is possible.

PREFACE

I developed this book in response to the need for an updated textbook addressing methodology and best practices for instruction and management of students with emotional and behavioral problems. Designed primarily for preservice training of special educators, the text provides all educators with practical, hands-on information about interventions that work with the most challenging students. I selected the content to explore the life span from early childhood education through the unique needs of adolescents and on to transition to adulthood.

Many state teacher certification programs require knowledge and skills concerning characteristics and teaching methods specific to students with emotional and behavioral disorders (EBD). This text is a valuable resource in states moving toward cross-categorical programming (i.e., for a cross-categorical methods course), or for advanced behavior management courses offered to general educators working with students with emotional and behavioral problems in inclusive school settings.

This text can be used at either the undergraduate or graduate level. Instructors can select appropriate extension and application activities to fit the needs of their course.

While grounded in research on best practice, many of the materials and activities used in this text have been drawn from direct experiences in classrooms and clinical settings. The text includes information and resources from a variety of philosophical and theoretical perspectives. However, the author admits to certain beliefs, preferences, and predispositions related to the provision of a free and appropriate public education for all students with EBD in the least restrictive environment:

1. This textbook includes interventions for children with conduct disorders and other disruptive behaviors.
2. No single theoretical perspective or intervention model works with all students all the time.
3. Well-prepared teachers are willing to extend themselves beyond their comfort zone to meet the needs of individual students.

4. Education is a collaborative process; the best outcomes are achieved through mutual respect and power sharing among all stakeholders.

ORGANIZATION OF THE BOOK

The book has been organized into four distinct parts to allow instructors to easily match content to the knowledge and skill needs of students in their particular course.

Part I: Foundations provides the context of special education for students with special needs, including those with EBD. Chapter 1 (written by Linda M. Bigby) provides a brief review of history, culture, philosophical approaches, and special education law as these areas relate to students with EBD. Chapter 2 (written by Judith K. Carlson) overviews the diagnostic assessment process and legal requirements for evaluation under IDEA, with a specific focus on evaluating students with emotional and behavioral problems.

Part II: Effective Classroom Practices covers assessment for eligibility and instructional planning and management, and best practices in the prevention and positively focused management of student problem behavior at the school, classroom, and individual level. The chapters in this section span diagnostic categories, and include background information, as well as concepts and approaches commonly used to educate students with EBD.

Part III: Interventions for Specific Populations examines the subgroups of students with severe emotional and behavioral challenges that teachers are likely to encounter in the classroom: disorders of attention, disruptive behavior disorders, autism spectrum disorders (contributed by Theresa L. Earles-Vollrath, Katherine Tapscott Cook, and Jennifer B. Ganz), anxiety and mood disorders, and other disorders of childhood and adolescence. Each chapter includes information concerning characteristics and practical intervention strategies for addressing the unique needs of each diagnostic grouping. While chapters are organized by DSM-IV diagnostic criteria to allow readers to construct manageable schema, approaches to intervention are not limited to the medical model.

Part IV: Consultation and Collaboration provides resources related to the role of the EBD teacher as a collaborative partner, working with families and other professionals in planning for students with emotional and/or behavioral problems. Chapters in this section cover effective collaborative communication skills for working effectively with parents and other professionals, strategies for working with community mental health professionals (written by Bill J. McHenry), and crisis intervention techniques.

FEATURES

Each chapter in the text includes pedagogical features designed to provide students with opportunities to interact with chapter content in several different ways. The **Connecting to the Classroom** vignettes provide a brief introduction to the chapter via a real-world scenario. **Check Your Understanding** questions at the end of each chapter provide ten true/false, multiple choice, and short essay questions that allow students to test their grasp of major concepts and terminology. **Application Activities** provide a variety of ways to extend learning beyond the classroom with individual and small-group assignments; most relate to case studies or to community or national resources associated with the chapter topic.

* I have structured this text to facilitate development of course syllabi that correspond directly to Council for Exceptional Children (CEC) standards for special educators, and Praxis II™ content areas. Appendix C provides a crosswalk for each chapter that identifies the relevant standard and facilitates development of extension and case study activities directly tied to competencies.
* A number of chapters provide multidisciplinary **Perspectives**, which draw on the expertise of professionals from the field of mental health, as well as from various educational settings. These **Perspectives** are provided to expand upon chapter content and encourage reflection and discussion.
* **Appendix A: Connecting to Teaching** features four in-depth case studies (authored by Lynda Nelson Day, Jerry Neal, and Theresa Earles-Vollrath) that allow students to apply knowledge and skills in a simulated setting. Each case focuses on a specific age group and cluster of diagnostic features.

* End-of-chapter activities prompt students to interact with each case repeatedly throughout the course, integrating and extending their understanding of the content.

ACKNOWLEDGMENTS

Completion of this project would not have been possible without the labors and supportive efforts of professional colleagues, family, and friends. Judith Carlson and Frankie Dissinger from University of Missouri–Kansas City were involved in the initial stages of envisioning, outlining, and pitching the concept for the book to Merrill/Prentice Hall. Judi also spent endless hours working with me to expand the outline and refine the first few chapters, and contributed Chapter 2 to this effort. Linda Bigby provided her expertise on the history of special education law to Chapter 1. Theresa Earles-Vollrath, Katie Cook, and Jeni Ganz brought their years of experience in autism spectrum disorders to Chapter 9. Bill McHenry, my colleague in counselor education, provided Chapter 12. The wonderful case studies in Appendix A were developed by three of my colleagues at Central Missouri State University (CMSU): Jerry Neal, Theresa Earles-Vollrath, and Lynda Nelson Day. Valuable **Perspectives** were provided by Alex Thompson (Chapter 2), Mary Magee Quinn (Chapter 5), Alice-Ann Darrow (Chapter 6), Eleanor Guetzloe (Chapter 8), Rich Simpson (Chapter 9), Avis Smith (Chapter 10), and Fred Overton and Jon Bair (Chapter 14).

I also must acknowledge the research assistance of several graduate students over the past few years, particularly Mary Jane Acrea, Krista Brewster, April Harris, and Tim Weil. Elizabeth Hicks assisted with conceptualizing the graphic design of several of the figures. A number of my colleagues at CMSU graciously agreed to critique rough drafts of chapters, including Sandy Hutchinson, David Sundberg, Gregory Turner, Patricia Antrim, Theresa Earles-Vollrath, and Jim Machell (now at University of Central Oklahoma). Avis Smith, from Crittenton Behavioral Health, and John Maag, from the University of Nebraska–Lincoln, provided further clinical expertise by reviewing the affective disorders chapter.

I would be remiss if I did not acknowledge the flexibility and support provided by all my coworkers in the Department of Educational Leadership and Human Development at CMSU, particularly my special education colleagues. As well as providing direct assistance in writing the book, they allowed me to juggle my teaching load, course times, and other professional responsibilities so that I could stay on track with my writing schedule. They provided the warm, collegial environment in which creative efforts thrive. Without Barb Hicks, Helen Mills, Jim Machell, Jerry Neal, and everyone else, I could not have managed. Dean Richard Sluder was also very gracious about letting my responsibilities as Associate Dean slide a bit when I had deadlines looming.

Priceless preproduction assistance was provided by my family: my parents, Helen and Floyd Anderson, my sisters, Carol Havenner, Jennifer Mitchell, and Julie Squire, and my nephews Andrew and Aaron Mitchell. They encouraged, proofread, checked references, filed, and helped haul things back and forth. My husband Michael Downing was a critical part of the entire writing process, helping me keep things in perspective. When I became too obsessive, he encouraged me to take breaks, eat something healthy, or get out of the house. When he thought I was slacking, he asked subtle questions like, "How's the book coming?"

A million thanks to the incredible editorial staff at Merrill/Prentice Hall—Ann Davis, who believed in the process and got us off to a great start; Allyson Sharp, whose enthusiasm and supportive hand-holding was priceless; and Kathy Burk, whose eagle eye and attention to detail averted many potential problems. Thanks also to Kathy Glidden, at Stratford Publishing Services, Inc., who beat every self-imposed deadline she established and to Simone Payment for her careful copyediting.

The unsung heroes and heroines of every new textbook are the peer reviewers who generously give of their time and expertise to help shape the content of the book for its intended consumers. For this text, those reviewers included Martin Agran, University of Northern Iowa; Ellyn Arwood, University of Portland; Roger F. Bass, Carthage College; Gerlinde G. Beckers, Louisiana State University; Dawn J. Behan, Upper Iowa University; Lisa Bloom, Western Carolina University; Nettye R. Brazil, University of Louisville; Jim Burns, The College of St. Rose; Frances M. Butler, Weber State University; Sandy Devlin, Mississippi State University; Barbara K. Given, George Mason University; Philip Gunter, Valdosta State University; Karen S. Harris, Fayetteville Technical Community College; Joan Henley, Arkansas State University; Kristine Jolivette, Georgia State University; Cindy Marble, Arizona State University Polytechnic; and Sheila Saravanabhavan, Virginia State University.

DISCOVER THE MERRILL RESOURCES
FOR SPECIAL EDUCATION WEBSITE

Technology is a constantly growing and changing aspect of our field that is creating a need for new content and resources. To address this emerging need, Merrill Education has developed an online learning environment for students, teachers, and professors alike to complement our products—the *Merrill Resources for Special Education* Website. This content-rich website provides additional resources specific to this book's topic and will help you—professors, classroom teachers, and students—augment your teaching, learning, and professional development.

Our goal with this initiative is to build on and enhance what our products already offer. For this reason, the content for our user-friendly website is organized by topic and provides teachers, professors, and students with a variety of meaningful resources all in one location. With this website, we bring together the best of what Merrill has to offer: text resources, video clips, web links, tutorials, and a wide variety of information on topics of interest to general and special educators alike. Rich content, applications, and competencies further enhance the learning process.

The *Merrill Resources for Special Education* Website includes:

* Video clips specific to each topic, with questions to help you evaluate the content and make crucial theory-to-practice connections.

* Thought-provoking critical analysis questions that students can answer and turn in for evaluation or that can serve as basis for class discussions and lectures.
* Access to a wide variety of resources related to classroom strategies and methods, including lesson planning and classroom management.
* Information on all the most current relevant topics related to special and general education, including CEC and Praxis™ standards, IEPs, portfolios, and professional development.
* Extensive web resources and overviews on each topic addressed on the website.
* A search feature to help access specific information quickly.

To take advantage of these and other resources, please visit the *Merrill Resources for Special Education* Website at

http://www.prenhall.com/downing

Teacher Preparation Classroom

TEACHER PREP

MERRILL
PRENTICE HALL

Your Class. Their Careers. Our Future. Will your students be prepared?

We invite you to explore our new, innovative and engaging website and all that it has to offer you, your course, and tomorrow's educators! Organized around the major courses pre-service teachers take, the Teacher Preparation site provides media, student/teacher artifacts, strategies, research articles, and other resources to equip your students with the quality tools needed to excel in their courses and prepare them for their first classroom.

This ultimate on-line education resource is available at no cost, when packaged with a Merrill text, and will provide you and your students access to:

Online Video Library. More than 150 video clips—each tied to a course topic and framed by learning goals and Praxis-type questions—capture real teachers and students working in real classrooms, as well as in-depth interviews with both students and educators.

Student and Teacher Artifacts. More than 200 student and teacher classroom artifacts—each tied to a course topic and framed by learning goals and application questions—provide a wealth of materials and experiences to help make your study to become a professional teacher more concrete and hands-on.

Research Articles. Over 500 articles from ASCD's renowned journal *Educational Leadership*. The site also includes Research Navigator, a searchable database of additional educational journals.

Teaching Strategies. Over 500 strategies and lesson plans for you to use when you become a practicing professional.

Licensure and Career Tools. Resources devoted to helping you pass your licensure exam; learn standards, law, and public policies; plan a teaching portfolio; and succeed in your first year of teaching.

How to ORDER *Teacher Prep* for you and your students:

For students to receive a *Teacher Prep* Access Code with this text, instructors **must** provide a special value pack ISBN number on their textbook order form. To receive this special ISBN, please email **Merrill.marketing@pearsoned.com** and provide the following information:

- Name and Affiliation
- Author/Title/Edition of Merrill text

Upon ordering *Teacher Prep* for their students, instructors will be given a lifetime *Teacher Prep* Access Code.

CONTRIBUTORS

CHAPTERS

Linda Bigby, Ed.D., author of Chapter 1, is an associate professor in the Department of Educational Leadership and Human Development at Central Missouri State University, where her areas of expertise include school leadership and special education administration. Previously, she served as a public school special education administrator for 28 years, and worked for the state education agency. She is an active member of the Council for Exceptional Children and is a past president of the Missouri Council for Administrators of Special Education.

Judith K. Carlson, Ph.D., author of Chapter 2, is an assistant professor of special education at the University of Missouri–Kansas City. Her research interests are urban education and teacher preparation. She has published numerous articles on autism, Asperger Syndrome, and related disorders. Dr. Carlson is active in the Council for Exceptional Children, and has served as president of the Kansas Federation.

Theresa L. Earles-Vollrath, Ph.D., coauthor of Chapter 9, is an assistant professor of special education at Central Missouri State University. She has been working in the field of special education for 16 years as a teacher for children with autism, as director of an autism resource center located at the University of Kansas Medical Center, and as an autism specialist for a public school district. In addition to teaching at the college level, Dr. Earles-Vollrath serves as a consultant to local school districts.

Katherine Tapscott Cook, coauthor of Chapter 9, is a program coordinator and consultant for the Kansas City Regional Professional Development Center at the University of Missouri–Kansas City. Her principal research interests include sensory integration and social skill instruction for students with autism spectrum disorders.

Jennifer B. Ganz, coauthor of Chapter 9, is an assistant professor of special education at the University of Texas at San Antonio. She previously worked as a general and special education teacher and an educational consultant. Her research interests include strategies to improve social and communication skills in individuals with autism spectrum disorders.

Dr. Bill McHenry, author of Chapter 13, is an assistant professor in the Department of Counseling and College Student Personnel at Shippensburg University of Pennsylvania. He is a national certified counselor, licensed professional counselor (in Pennsylvania and Missouri), and a certified school counselor (in Pennsylvania and Missouri). He has worked as a professional school counselor, mental health counselor, community agency counselor, coordinator of rehabilitation services, and group home supervisor.

CASE STUDIES

Lynda Nelson-Day, Ed.D., teaches early childhood special education courses at Central Missouri State University. Over the years, she has been involved in policy-making decisions and advocacy for early intervention and early childhood programs. She is committed to the establishment of quality programs for young children with special needs and their parents.

Jerry Neal, Ed.D., is an associate professor and special education program coordinator at Central Missouri State University. His current research interests include making technology available to persons with disabilities in public schools and college libraries and assisting business and industry in developing ways to train employees in assistive technologies.

BRIEF CONTENTS

CONTENTS

Chapter 4
BEST PRACTICES FOR PREVENTING PROBLEM BEHAVIORS: SCHOOLWIDE STRATEGIES   66

Chapter 5
BEST PRACTICES FOR PREVENTING PROBLEM BEHAVIORS: CLASSWIDE STRATEGIES AND INTERVENTIONS   82

Chapter 6
BEST PRACTICES FOR ADDRESSING PROBLEM BEHAVIORS: INDIVIDUAL AND SMALL-GROUP STRATEGIES AND INTERVENTIONS   98

APPENDICES 291

Note: Every effort has been made to provide accurate and current Internet information in this book. However, the Internet and information posted on it are constantly changing, so it is inevitable that some of the Internet addresses in this textbook will change.

PART

FOUNDATIONS

LEGAL, HISTORICAL, AND CULTURAL PERSPECTIVES

Linda Bigby

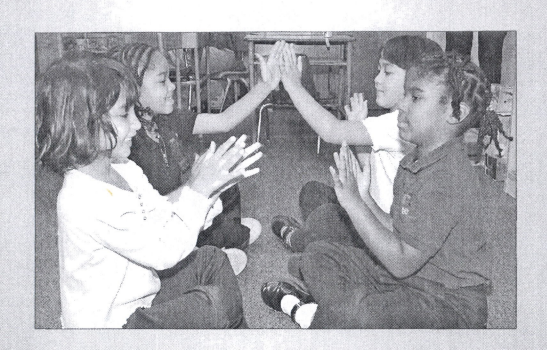

CHAPTER PREVIEW

CONNECTING TO THE CLASSROOM: *A Vignette*

Desmond is a 13-year-old enrolled in the seventh grade in an urban school system. His district's early childhood screening program identified him as a child in need of special education assistance. Desmond participated in a noncategorical special education program offered by his district, receiving articulation services from the speech-language pathologist and participating in weekly social-skills groups offered by a therapist from a neighborhood agency. When Desmond entered kindergarten, he continued to receive speech services and was transitioned into Part B special education services as a student with a learning disability in reading and written language. During his early elementary years, Desmond's articulation improved and the school system took speech goals off his **individualized education program (IEP)**; he received 300 minutes per week of special education services focused on his reading and writing.

In fourth and fifth grade, Desmond continued to struggle academically. School discipline records show that he was increasingly involved in conflicts with his peers that Desmond attributed to being teased and bullied.

Unfortunately, Desmond's move to middle school in the sixth grade appeared to exacerbate his existing problems, both academically and socially. His grades were mostly Cs and Ds. Despite spending 45 minutes each day in the resource room, he did not meet any of his sixth-grade IEP goals. Further, Desmond's teachers reported that he frequently was sullen and noncompliant, and that he often "overreacted" to teasing by peers. As part of his scheduled reevaluation, Desmond's IEP team conducted a functional behavioral assessment in addition to reevaluating his reading and writing skills. They found that, while Desmond still lagged behind his peers in reading and written language, he now also met the Individuals with Disabilities Education Act (IDEA) criteria for the category of emotional disturbance (ED). The team proposed adding a behavioral goal to Desmond's IEP to address his difficulties complying with teacher requests. Desmond's parents objected to the ED label, and felt the IEP failed to address his educational or emotional and behavioral needs adequately. They asked the district to provide more intensive special education services and counseling for Desmond. The district feels their IEP is adequate without the additional services. Desmond's parents are considering exercising their due process rights to initiate a request for mediation.

AMERICAN EDUCATION AND STUDENTS WITH DISABILITIES

As the timeline in Figure 1-2 illustrates, the early history of the education of children with disabilities is largely a story of neglect. National acknowledgement and protection of the educational rights of children with disabilities did not come quickly or without struggle. Special education programs developed slowly in public schools for a number of reasons. Financial resources for such programs were minimal. Little was known about the origins of disabilities or how to address them in an educational setting. The combination of meager financial resources and public apathy hindered early efforts to extend educational opportunities to individuals with disabilities (Alexander & Alexander, 2001).

Prior to the middle of the 20th century, educational programs for students with disabilities were localized, inconsistent, and voluntary. Some states or local districts established programs to serve students who were hearing or visually impaired, mentally ill, mentally retarded, or physically disabled. However, little distinction was made between mental retardation and mental illness. Officials often placed students with severe handicaps and those who exhibited extreme deviance in the same institutional or residential settings. Conditions in these facilities were frequently deplorable and rarely included formal educational services.

Impact of the Civil Rights Movement

The Civil Rights Movement in the United States provided the critical momentum needed for parents and professional advocates to secure educational rights for students with disabilities. Based on the equal protection clause of the 14th Amendment, the landmark *Brown v. Board of Education* case in 1954 addressed inequities in educational opportunity for African-American students. The case moved through several levels of appeals and was finally resolved by the U.S. Supreme Court. Chief Justice Warren wrote the unanimous decision, stating:

> We conclude that in the field of public education the doctrine of "separate but equal" has no place. Separate educational facilities are inherently unequal.

This landmark school desegregation case established the foundation upon which advocates for students with disabilities built their legal claim for equal educational rights. During the years following the 1954 *Brown v. Board of Education* decision, parents and advocates increased their efforts to secure equal access for children with disabilities, both through the courts and the legislature. Two federal class action suits were decided in 1972: *Pennsylvania Association for Retarded Citizens (PARC) v. Commonwealth of Pennsylvania* and *Mills v. Board of Education*. Both had profound effects on the education of children with disabilities and paved the way for the passage of the *Education for All Handicapped Children Act* passed in 1975 as Public Law 94-142. The most

---

We declare the following principles to be the Code of Ethics for educators of persons with exceptionalities. Members of the special education profession are responsible for upholding and advancing these principles. Members of The Council for Exceptional Children agree to judge and be judged by them in accordance with the spirit and provisions of this Code.

A. Special education professionals are committed to developing the highest educational and quality of life potential of individuals with exceptionalities.

B. Special education professionals promote and maintain a high level of competence and integrity in practicing their profession.

C. Special education professionals engage in professional activities which benefit individuals with exceptionalities, their families, other colleagues, students, or research subjects.

D. Special education professionals exercise objective professional judgment in the practice of their profession.

E. Special education professionals strive to advance their knowledge and skills regarding the education of individuals with exceptionalities.

F. Special education professionals work within the standards and policies of their profession.

G. Special education professionals seek to uphold and improve where necessary the laws, regulations, and policies governing the delivery of special education and related services and the practice of their profession.

H. Special education professionals do not condone or participate in unethical or illegal acts, nor violate professional standards adopted by the Delegate Assembly of CEC.

FIGURE I–I The Council for Exceptional Children (CEC) Code of Ethics for Educators of Persons with Exceptionalities
Source: Council for Exceptional Children. (2003). *What every special educator must know: Ethics, standards and guidelines for special educators.* Arlington, VA: Author.

Year	Event	Issue/Impact
1787	Northwest Ordinance	Established land grants for educational institutions[1]
1867	Department of Education Act	Established federal office/department of education[1]
1868	14th Amendment to the U.S. Constitution	Equal protection under the law cannot be denied by states, right to due process
1933	Formation of the Cuyahoga County Ohio Council for the Retarded Child	First parent advocacy group formed to protest exclusion of children from school[3,4]
1954	*Brown v. Board of Education*	Segregation by race violated equal protection, denied equal educational opportunity
1958	Education of Mentally Retarded Children Act P.L. 85-926	Supplied funding for training of teachers in area of mental retardation (MR)
1964	Civil Rights Act of 1964 P.L. 88-352	Provided support for teacher in-service training addressing the impact of desegregation[1]
1964	Economic Opportunity Act of 1964 P.L. 88-452	Established college work-study, Job Corps, Head Start, Follow Through, Upward Bound, and Volunteers in Service to America (VISTA)[1]
1965	The Elementary and Secondary Education Act—Title I (ESEA) P.L. 89-10	Provided funding for the improvement of K–12 education, focus on disadvantaged students
1965	ESEA Amendments of 1965 P.L. 89-313	Created the Bureau of Education for the Handicapped, supplied funding to states operating state schools[2]
1966	ESEA Amendments of 1965—Title VI P.L. 89-750	Added funding for education of students with disabilities at local level, not restricted to state schools
1972	*Pennsylvania Association for Retarded Citizens (PARC) v. Pennsylvania*	Established right of children with MR to a free public education (FAPE)
1972	*Mills v. Board of Education* 348 F. Supp. 866 (D.D.C.)	Affirmed right to FAPE, specified procedural safeguards
1973	Rehabilitation Act of 1973 P.L. 93-112	Section 504 of the Act protected rights of individuals with disabilities by any agency receiving federal financial assistance, prohibits discrimination
1974	ESEA Amendments of 1974 P.L. 93-380	Created Bureau of Education for the Handicapped, National Advisory Council for Handicapped Children, required states receiving federal funding for special education to set goals for full participation of students with disabilities, specified due process procedures, described least restricted environment, addressed gifted and talented[4]
1974	Family Education Rights and Privacy Act (FERPA, also known as Buckley Amendment) §513 of P.L. 93-380	Established rights of parents to view and confirm accuracy of student educational records, established privacy safeguards
1975	The Education for All Handicapped Children Act (EAHCA) P.L. 94-142	Educational bill of rights for students with disabilities, including nondiscriminatory testing and placement, LRE, procedural due process, and FAPE[4]

(continued)

FIGURE 1–2   Timeline of Significant Events for Education of Students with Disabilities

Year	Event	Issue/Impact
1980	Department of Education Organization Act P.L. 96-88	Made ED a cabinet-level department, reaffirmed state control of education and national commitment to equal access to education[1]
1983	Education of the Handicapped Act Amendments of 1983 P.L. 98-199	Addressed architectural barriers, clarified participation of students with disabilities in private schools[1]
1984	Carl D. Perkins Vocational Education Act P.L. 98-377	Replaced 1963 Vocational Education Act, making funding available to make vocational education accessible to all people, including handicapped and disadvantaged[1]
1986	Handicapped Children's Protection Act of 1986 P.L. 99-372	Established the rights of parents to recover costs and attorney fees if they prevail in a due process action under EHA
1986	Education of the Handicapped Amendments of 1986—Part H (Infants and Toddlers with Disabilities Act) P.L. 99-457	Provided federal financial incentives for states providing programs for infants and toddlers with disabilities
1990	Americans with Disabilities Act (ADA) P.L. 101-336	Established protection from discrimination for all individuals with disability, reasonable accommodations, expanded 504 mandate to include all public services and public accommodations
1990	Individuals with Disabilities Education Act (IDEA), Amendments to EAHCA P.L. 101-476	Included person-first language, added autism and TBI as separate categories, addressed discipline, and required transition plan by age 16[4]
1994	Safe Schools Act of 1994 Part of P.L. 103-227	Established grants to LEAS to implement violence-prevention activities[1]
1997	The Individuals with Disabilities Education Act Amendments of 1997 P.L. 105-17	Consolidated IDEA, emphasized parental role, encouraged mediation, and changed funding formulas[4]
2002	No Child Left Behind Act of 2001 (NCLB) P.L. 107-110	Reauthorized ESEA with new provisions in areas of testing, accountability, parental choice, and early reading[1]
2004	Individuals with Disabilities Education Improvement Act of 2004 P.L. 108-446	Reauthorized IDEA, aligned IDEA with NCLB, made changes in IEP process and content requirements, discipline/manifestation procedures, defined highly qualified special educator

[1]NCES, 2003
[2]Trohanis, 2002
[3]Turnbull, 1993
[4]Yell, 1998

FIGURE 1-2   Timeline of Significant Events for Education of Students with Disabilities (*continued*)

significant outcome of *PARC v. Pennsylvania* (1972) was recognition of educational rights for children with disabilities under the Constitution. The *PARC* decision required that students with mental retardation age 6 through 21 should be provided access to a free public education, and specified that children with disabilities should be educated in regular classrooms whenever possible. The findings in *Mills v. Board of Education* expanded the earlier *PARC v. Pennsylvania* decision to include all school-age children with disabilities in a free public education, regardless of the severity of disability. The plaintiffs in the class action included students with behavior problems, emotional disturbance, hyperactivity, and mental retardation who had previously been suspended, expelled, or transferred without due process because of their disruption in the classroom. In addition, the *Mills* decision outlined due process and procedural safeguards, defining the rights of children and families.

LEGAL ENTITLEMENTS IN SPECIAL EDUCATION

It was in the 1970s that the major efforts to secure equal educational access converged, involving all three branches of the government. During this time period, particularly during the Johnson presidency, a pervasive concern for the equality of educational opportunity swept the nation (Alexander & Alexander, 2001). Although much of the public discussion still focused on racial desegregation, the concern for equity also included students with disabilities. Parents and advocacy groups played a significant role in the drafting and passage of the federal special education laws and served as the primary watchdogs for the enforcement of the new federal special education mandates (Rothstein, 1990).

Civil Rights Legislation Affecting Persons with Disabilities in the Community

Congress passed P.L. 93-112, the Rehabilitation Act of 1973, prohibiting discrimination against persons with disabilities in programs receiving federal funds.

Section 504 is an important provision of the act that states, in part:

> No otherwise qualified disabled individual in the United States shall, solely by the reason of his handicap, be excluded from the participation in, be denied the benefits of, or be subject to discrimination under any program or activity receiving federal financial assistance. (Section 504, 29 U.S.C. § 794 [a])

Congress passed the Americans with Disabilities Act (ADA, P.L. 101-336) in 1990. This law expanded the civil rights and discrimination protections of Section 504 in public institutions to many private sector areas, including employment, public accommodations, transportation, and telecommunications. The enforcement agency for disability rights in schools under both the Rehabilitation Act and ADA is the Office of Civil Rights (OCR) in the U.S. Department of Education. (See Sidebar 1–1 for a guide to reading federal law citations.)

Educational Legislation Directly Affecting Special Education

Public Law 94-142. It was not until 1975 that the federal government finally required all states to provide special education to students with disabilities. The major legislative landmark affecting American special education was introduced as the Education of the Handicapped Amendments of 1974, but the 93rd Congress did not act on it prior to adjournment (Yell, 1998). It was reintroduced and passed by the 94th Congress and signed into law on November 29,

SIDEBAR 1–1

Understanding Law Citations

Federal statutes and regulations are published by the U.S. Government Printing Office. They are organized in volumes or titles, and divided into sections and subsections. Interpreting the abbreviations will allow you to identify and locate the source. For example, IDEA is published in *United States Code* Title 20; the IDEA regulations are contained in the *Code of Federal Regulations* Title 34. The IDEA citation 20 U.S.C. § 1401(a) refers to *United States Code*, Title 20, Section 1401, Subsection a. If a citation indicates § 1401 *et seq.*, it means that the text is in Section 1401 and those that follow. The citation for IDEA regulations 34 C.F.R. § 300.13 can be found in the *Code of Federal Regulations*, Title 34, Section 300.13. Laws are also referred to by their Public Law designations. These indicate which Congress passed the law, and the number it was assigned when signed. Thus, the Education for All Handicapped Children Act (1975) is P.L. 94-142, or the 142nd law enacted by the 94th Congress.

1975, as the Education for All Handicapped Children Act (EAHCA), or P.L. 94-142. EAHCA was the first federal legislation to mandate a free, appropriate public education for all handicapped children between the ages of 3 and 21.

Meyen (1978) described the passage of the EAHCA as noteworthy because of the concept of perpetuity embedded in the law. Goodman (1976) describes the act as "the Bill of Rights for the Handicapped" because it was designed to correct inequalities on behalf of individuals with disabilities. Rothstein (1990) reported that in 1975 about 3 million children with disabilities were not receiving appropriate programming in public schools and another 1 million were excluded totally from public education. Thus, more than half of the estimated 8 million American children with disabilities were receiving either an inappropriate education or no educational service at that time. This federal legislation mandated for the first time in history that all children with disabilities in the United States had a right to a free and appropriately designed public education in the environment least restrictive for them (McIntire, 2000). Turnbull and Turnbull (1978) presented a contemporary view of P.L. 94-142, identifying six major principles inherent in EAHCA:

- **Zero reject**—No child, regardless of disability, may be excluded from a free appropriate public education.
- **Testing, classification, and placement**—All children with disabilities must be assessed in a fair and nondiscriminatory fashion.
- **Individualized and appropriate education**—All children must be provided with meaningful educational services, based on their individual needs.
- **Least restrictive environment**—Children with disabilities may not be segregated inappropriately from their nonhandicapped peers.
- **Procedural due process**—Parents of a child with disabilities have the right to have input into the educational decisions about their child, and the right to protest those decisions when they disagree with the school's recommendations.
- **Parent participation and shared decision-making**—Parents have the right to participate in the Individualized Education Program (IEP) team, and to have access to relevant student information.

Early Amendments to P.L. 94-142. Congress has made amendments to EAHCA periodically since 1975 (see Figure 1-1). Some of the more significant early revi-

sions included P.L. 99-372, the Handicapped Children's Protection Act, which authorized attorneys' fees for prevailing parents, and P.L. 99-457, which created Part H to provide funds for early intervention services for infants and toddlers with disabilities (Yell, 1998).

1990 Amendments. In 1990, P.L. 101-476, another amendment to the EAHCA, resulted in a number of significant changes. Reflecting changes in prevailing philosophy and terminology, Congress renamed the statute the Individuals with Disabilities Education Act (IDEA). The new language placed the emphasis on the individual first, rather than on the disability. Therefore, the terminology "handicapped children" used in the original law was changed to "individuals with disabilities" in IDEA 1990. (See Sidebar 1-2: Examples of People-First Language.)

Content changes to the 1990 IDEA included expanding the definition of disabling conditions to include traumatic brain injury and autism as separate categories. The importance of transition planning was stressed, requiring the IEP to include a transition plan for all students at 16 years of age.

1997 Amendments. On May 13, 1997, the House of Representatives passed H.R. 5, the Individuals with Disabilities Education Act of 1997, by a 420-to-3 vote. The following day, the Senate passed S. 717, the companion bill, by a margin of 90-to-1 (NADSE, 1997; Peper, Martin, Jensen, Maichel, & Hetlage, 1998). On June 4, President Clinton signed the bill into law as P.L. 105-17, the Amendments to the Individuals with Disabilities Education Act of 1997.

The 1997 Reauthorization built on the basic structure of IDEA, embracing the core concepts of **free appropriate public education (FAPE)** and **least restrictive environment (LRE)**. IDEA 1997 reflected the belief that special education for the majority of students with disabilities should not be a separate *place* for learning, but rather *a set of services and supports* designed to help them be involved in the general education environment and progress through the general education curriculum. The reauthorization of IDEA focused on modifications to improve education results, promote school safety, and reduce paperwork. A number of changes affected daily practice and created new procedures and new documentation requirements. These included changes in IEP content and team membership, introduction of a voluntary mediation system, and language concerning discipline of students with IEPs (Yell, 1998). Other changes were designed to

Examples of People-First Language

Many advocates for individuals with disabilities have emphasized the need to use language that respects each individual, placing the person first, instead of the disability. This language style often describes the needs and abilities of the individuals, rather than what they cannot do.

Examples of language that *does not* place people first or focuses on the *dis*ability:

> disabled children
> the autistic boy

> a nonverbal student
> the handicapped restroom

Examples of language that *does* place people first and focuses on ability:

> children with a disability
> the boy with autism
> a student who uses sign language to communicate
> the accessible restroom

---

increase parent participation and reverse the trend of increasingly antagonistic parent-school relationships.

No Child Left Behind.   George W. Bush described the No Child Left Behind Act of 2001 (NCLB) as the cornerstone of his administration. A reauthorization of the Elementary and Secondary Education Act (ESEA), the major principles of NCLB included: "increased accountability for States, school districts, and schools; greater choice for parents and students, particularly those attending low-performing schools; more flexibility for States and local educational agencies (LEAs) in the use of Federal education dollars; and a stronger emphasis on reading, especially for our youngest children" (U.S. Department of Education, 2001, para 4). NCLB required each state to establish a system of standards-based assessment, with results broken out in subgroups by income, race, ethnicity, disability, and level of English proficiency. States also had to establish timelines for improvement and corrective actions for districts and schools that did not make **adequate yearly progress (AYP)** toward statewide proficiency goals. For a school or district to meet the AYP goals, each of the subgroups (including special education) had to demonstrate AYP toward meeting state goals. Potential remedies for poor performance included parental choice and budgetary penalties. In exchange for increased accountability, the federal government gave states more flexibility in their allocation of federal funds. Another aspect of NCLB accountability required LEAs to ensure that all their teachers were **"highly qualified"** in the core academic subjects taught. A final provision of NCLB required states

to "allow students who attend a persistently dangerous school, or who are victims of violent crime at school, to transfer to a safe school" (U.S. Department of Education, 2001, Other Major Program Changes, para 3). Although NCLB was not conceptualized as a special education law, proponents of the new standards hypothesized that accomplishing the goals of NCLB would reduce the need for referrals to special education.

IDEA 2004.   After two years of bipartisan wrangling, and a fair amount of professional dissent, the legislature passed the Individuals with Disabilities Education Improvement Act of 2004 in November, 2004, as H.R. 1350. President George W. Bush signed it into law on December 3, 2004, making it P.L. 108-446. A major focus of this reauthorization was to align IDEA with the goals established by NCLB, increasing accountability of schools for the progress of students with disabilities. According to the White House press release citing President Bush's remarks at the signing of the bill, IDEA 2004 would:

- raise expectations for students,
- hold schools accountable for teaching every child,
- assure that special education teachers are qualified to teach special education and their subject area,
- provide tutoring programs in schools that need improvement,
- make the system less litigious, and
- provide parents and schools with more flexibility to meet the needs of students with special needs. (Bush, 2004)

IDEA 2004 also made procedural changes concerning participation of parents in IEP meetings, the content of IEPs, due process procedures and timelines, and discipline.

NOTE: At the time this chapter is being written, the final regulations for IDEA 2004 have not been published by the Department of Education; therefore, final interpretive guidance is still forthcoming on implementation of the changes contained in the law.

EDUCATION OF STUDENTS WITH EMOTIONAL/BEHAVIORAL DISORDERS

Individual values and personal experiences form the framework for our beliefs about human behavior in general, and determine how we answer important questions about students who are perceived to have emotional and/or behavioral problems. What kind of behavior is acceptable or unacceptable? How do we determine when a student's problem behavior can be ignored or requires a teacher response? How do we influence or change the behavior of others? Why do students misbehave? How do students develop emotional or behavior disorders (EBDs) that require special education and focused interventions? As a society evolves, so do the answers to these underlying questions about the origins and treatment of EBD.

Emergence of Conceptual Models Related to EBD

During the second half of the 20th century, a number of clearly defined **conceptual models** emerged related to human behavior. Each of these philosophical approaches has been reflected in general educational programming, as well as in development of strategies and interventions for students whose behavior is problematic. The matrix in Figure 1–3 briefly overviews each approach, describing its perspective on etiology and highlighting examples of representative strategies and interventions. During the 1950s, 1960s, and 1970s, many educational programs adhered strictly to one specific model. Some of those special programs and schools are still in existence. However, in current practice, a comprehensive program for students with EBD is likely to include integrated aspects of several models. In integrated programs, teachers select and implement interventions validated by clinical and classroom research that are the "best fit" for the teacher and individual students in that classroom environment.

Students with "serious emotional disturbance" have been included as eligible students with disabilities since the passage of EAHCA in 1975. The 1997 IDEA amendments included changes in the label—dropping the word "serious" and making minor changes in the eligibility criteria for ED. The current federal definition of emotional disturbance is contained in Figure 1–4.

Both the definition and terminology of ED have been problematic from the outset. Some educators have described the language as subjective and vague. For example, verbiage related to characteristics being exhibited "to a marked degree" and "over a length of time" required subjective interpretation by school teams. States, districts, and IEP teams have, therefore, implemented the eligibility criteria differently, leading to the rather odd phenomenon that a student who is eligible for special education as ED in one state may move across the state line and be found ineligible under that state's guidelines. To many, the inclusion of students with schizophrenia and the exclusion of students who are socially maladjusted (unless they are also emotionally disturbed) seems contradictory and unnecessary. Why single out two specific clinical diagnoses? What is the rationale for including one, while excluding the other? For that matter, why use clinical nomenclature at all to describe an educational disability? To address these difficulties, the National Mental Health and Special Education Coalition (NMHSEC), a collaborative task group comprised of the major professional organizations whose members work with students who have EBD, formulated an alternative definition (Forness & Knitzer, 1992). (See Figure 1–5.) However, to date, this alternative definition has not gained the support of legislators or of many school administrators.

ONGOING ISSUES AND CHALLENGES

During the 30-year implementation of federal special education law, researchers and educators have grappled with several thorny issues that directly affect EBD practice. These issues include (a) the number and types of students being found eligible for special education services in the various categories, (b) continuing disproportionate overrepresentation in special education of students of color and those for whom English is a second language, (c) the likelihood that students with EBD will be served in more restrictive placements than students with other mild-moderate disabilities, and (d) the need to balance school safety with the individual due process rights of students with EBD.

Model	Etiology of Behavior and Behavior Problems	Intervention Approaches
Behavioral	Determined and maintained by external forces, essentially behavior is learned	• Manipulation of stimuli including antecedents and consequences based on principles of reinforcement (e.g., contingency contracts, token economies) • Positive behavioral supports (PBS) • Applied behavior analysis (ABA) • Behavior reduction procedures (e.g., differential reinforcement) • Extinction procedures
Biophysical or Medical	Within the individual, a biological or physical deficit, defect, or malfunction	• Psychopharmacology • Nutritional supplements and dietary interventions • Training based on biofeedback, sensory integration • Highly structured classroom with limited environmental stimulation or distraction • Psychiatric treatment programs
Ecological or Environmental	In the relationship between the student and the physical, educational, and social environment	• Eclectic interventions tailored to the unique situation and based on ecological analysis • Manipulating variables in the physical environment (e.g., lighting, noise level, proximity to the window) • Manipulating variables in the educational environment (e.g., pacing, frequency of breaks, difficulty of task demands) • Manipulating variables in the social environment (e.g., peer coaching, cooperative learning)
Humanistic	Mismatch between the individual student and the educational system, excessive regimentation and restriction	• Programs based on individual student choices, focus on self-fulfillment with the teacher as facilitator of learning (e.g., open schools, alternative) • Holistic education • Socially relevant curriculum (e.g., women's studies, Afrocentric programs)
Psychodynamic or Psychoanalytic	Within the individual, an internal psychic problem or conflict	• Psychotherapy, focused on resolution of intrapsychic conflict and development of healthy relationships
Psychoeducational	Within the individual, an internal psychic problem that manifests in conflicts with others in the school environment	• Insight-based counseling focused on why the student misbehaves in the educational context (e.g., life space crisis intervention) • Development of healthy relationships in a therapeutic milieu • Stress reduction and coping strategies • Expressive therapies
Social Learning or Social Cognition	Learned through social interactions, problems related to inadequate or inappropriate models, or to the student's irrational beliefs	• Counseling focused on identifying and correcting irrational thoughts or belief systems (e.g., locus of control interventions, rational emotive therapy, reality therapy, developmental therapy) • Cognitive behavioral techniques (e.g., self-monitoring, problem-solving strategies) • Social-skills training that involves observation of models, role playing, and evaluation

FIGURE 1–3   Features of Major Conceptual Models of EBD

(i) The term means a condition exhibiting one or more of the following characteristics over a long period of time and to a marked degree that adversely affects a child's educational performance:

(A) An inability to learn that cannot be explained by intellectual, sensory, or health factors.

(B) An inability to build or maintain satisfactory interpersonal relationships with peers and teachers.

(C) Inappropriate types of behavior or feelings under normal circumstances.

(D) A general pervasive mood of unhappiness or depression.

(E) A tendency to develop physical symptoms or fears associated with personal or school problems.

(ii) The term includes schizophrenia. The term does not apply to children who are socially maladjusted, unless it is determined that they have an emotional disturbance.

FIGURE 1–4   Federal Definition of Emotional Disturbance
Source: 34 C.F.R. § 300.7 (b) (4).

I. The term emotional or behavioral disorder means a disability characterized by behavioral or emotional responses in school programs so different from appropriate age, cultural, or ethnic norms that they adversely affect educational performance, including academic, social, vocational or personal skills, and which:

a. is more than a temporary, expected response to stressful events in the environment;

b. is consistently exhibited in two different settings, at least one of which is school-related; and

c. persists despite individualized interventions within the education program, unless, in the judgment of the team, the child's or youth's history indicates that such interventions would not be effective.

Emotional or behavioral disorders can co-exist with other disabilities.

II. This category may include children or youth with schizophrenic disorders, affective disorders, anxiety disorders, or other sustained disturbances of conduct or adjustment when they adversely affect educational performance in accordance with section I.

FIGURE 1–5   Proposed Alternative Definition of EBD
Source: Forness & Knitzer, 1992, p. 13.

Number and Characteristics of Students Being Served under IDEA

Since its enactment in 1975, EAHCA (P.L. 94-142) has had a tremendous impact on public education, specifically on special education. The number and proportion of students ages 6 through 21 served under IDEA has grown steadily, and in 1999–2000 was increasing at more than twice the rate of both the resident population and school enrollment estimates. According to the U.S. Department of Education, the number of students ages 3 through 21 served under IDEA rose from 4.7 million in 1990–91 to 6.2 million in 1999–2000 (U.S. Department of Education, 2000). In the *Twenty-third Annual Report to Congress*, the Department of Education also indicated that the number of students with disabilities served under IDEA reached 5,683,707 in 1999–2000, a 30.3% increase in only 10 years. Specific learning disabilities were the most prevalent disability during that decade. Speech or language impairments, mental retardation,

and emotional disturbance were the next most commonly diagnosed disabilities—often termed "high incidence" special education categories. Of the students served under IDEA, almost 9 out of 10 students were classified under one of these four labels. The largest increase of students during this time period was in the 12- to 17-year-old age range. Tables 1–1 and 1–2 reflect the changes in number of students by disability category and by age.

The *Twenty-third Annual Report* indicated that graduation rates were on the increase for most students; however, that has not been true for students in special education. The lowest graduation rates were within the disability categories of mental retardation, 41.7%, and emotional disturbance, 41.9%. While drop-out rates were also reported as declining overall, the highest drop-out rates occurred among students with EBD. Approximately half of the students identified with EBD quit school in 1998–99. The *Twenty-third Annual Report* also indicated that when students with EBD leave

TABLE 1–1 Changes in Number of Students Ages 6 through 21 Served under IDEA by Disability Category, 1990–91 and 1999–2000

	1990–91	1999–2000	Difference	Change (%)
Specific Learning Disabilities	2,144,017	2,871,966	727,949	34.0
Speech or Language Impairments	987,778	1,089,964	102,186	10.3
Mental Retardation	551,457	614,433	62,976	11.4
Emotional Disturbance	390,764	470,111	79,347	20.3
Multiple Disabilities	97,629	112,993	15,364	15.7
Hearing Impairments	59,211	71,671	12,460	21.0
Orthopedic Impairments	49,340	71,422	22,082	44.8
Other Health Impairments	56,349	254,110	197,761	351.0
Visual Impairments	23,682	26,590	2,908	12.3
Autism	—	65,424	—	[a]
Deaf-Blindness	1,524	1,845	321	21.1
Traumatic Brain Injury	—	13,874	—	[a]
Developmental Delay	—	19,304	—	[b]
All Disabilities	4,361,751	5,683,707	1,321,956	30.3

[a]Reporting on autism and traumatic brain injury was first required in 1992–93.
[b]Optional reporting on developmental delay for students ages 3 through 7 was first allowed in the 1997–98 school year.
Source: U.S. Department of Education, Office of Special Education Programs, Data Analysis System (DANS) as reported in the *Twenty-third Annual Report to Congress on the Implementation of the IDEA* (2000).

TABLE 1–2 Percentage and Number of Children Served under IDEA by Disability and Age Group During the 1999–2000 School Year: High-Incidence Disabilities

	Ages 6–11		Ages 12–17		Ages 18–21	
	Number	Percentage	Number	Percentage	Number	Percentage
Specific Learning Disabilities	1,118,152	39.9	1,608,645	61.9	145,169	51.1
Speech or Language Impairments	958,182	34.2	126,724	4.9	5,058	1.8
Mental Retardation	238,714	8.5	308,802	11.9	66,917	23.5
Emotional Disturbance	159,879	5.7	283,934	10.9	26,298	9.3
Multiple Disabilities	51,312	1.8	47,010	1.8	14,671	5.2
All Disabilities	2,802,385	100.0	2,597,134	100.0	284,188	100.0

Source: U.S. Department of Education, Office of Special Education Programs, Data Analysis System (DANS) as reported in the *Twenty-third Annual Report to Congress on the Implementation of the IDEA* (2000).

school, they often lack the social skills necessary to be successfully employed.

The number of students with disabilities being educated in the regular classroom has continued to increase during the past decade. By 1998-99, nearly half (47%) of identified students spent at least 80% of their school day in a regular class. However, students with EBD, mental retardation, or multiple disabilities continue to be more likely to receive services *outside* the regular classroom for more than 60% of the school day (U.S. Department of Education, 2000).

Overrepresentation of Ethnic and Low-English Proficient Students in Special Education

IDEA specifies that, as part of the process for determining students eligible to be served in a special education category, the team must also determine that the disability is not *primarily* the result of environmental, cultural, or economic disadvantage, or limited English proficiency. This distinction can be a difficult one for school teams to make, however, given the lack of definitive research concerning causality or etiology of most disabilities, and the complex and interactive nature of poverty and other risk factors.

An area of particular concern since the passage of the EAHCA has been the disproportionate overrepresentation of minority students, particularly African Americans, and those with limited English proficiency in special education (Yell, 1998). As reported in the *Twenty-third Annual Report to Congress* (U.S. Department of Education, 2000), African-American students with disabilities exceeded their representation in the general student population across all disability categories (see Table 1-3).

TABLE 1-3 Percentage of Students Ages 6 through 21 Served by Disability and Race/Ethnicity, 1999–2000 School Year [a, b, c]

Disability	American Indian/ Alaska Native	Asian/Pacific Islander	Black (non-Hispanic)	Hispanic	White (non-Hispanic)
Specific Learning Disabilities	1.4	1.6	18.4	16.6	62.1
Speech or Language Impairments	1.2	2.4	16.1	12.7	67.6
Mental Retardation	1.1	1.8	34.2	9.1	53.8
Emotional Disturbance	1.1	1.2	27.3	8.9	61.5
Multiple Disabilities	1.5	2.3	20.0	11.5	64.8
Hearing Impairments	1.3	4.6	16.4	17.9	59.8
Orthopedic Impairments	0.8	3.0	14.7	14.8	66.8
Other Health Impairments	1.1	1.4	14.9	8.0	74.7
Visual Impairments	1.1	3.5	18.6	14.0	62.9
Autism	.07	4.8	20.5	9.2	64.9
Deaf-Blindness	2.0	7.5	24.8	11.2	54.6
Traumatic Brain Injury	1.6	2.4	16.9	10.5	68.5
Developmental Delay	0.9	0.8	30.5	4.1	63.7
All Disabilities	1.3	1.8	20.3	13.7	62.9
Resident Population	1.0	3.8	14.5	16.2	64.5

[a]Due to rounding, rows may not sum to 100%.

[b]Race/Ethnicity distributions exclude Outlying Areas because current population estimates by race/ethnicity were not available for those areas.

[c]Population counts are July 1999 estimates from the U.S. Census Bureau.

Source: U.S. Department of Education, Office of Special Education Programs, Data Analysis System (DANS) as reported in the *Twenty-third Annual Report to Congress on the Implementation of the IDEA* (2000).

During the 1998–99 school year, 20.2% of all students in special education were African American, compared to 14.8% of the general school-age population (20 U.S.C. § 1400 [c] [12] [d]). This pattern was particularly evident in schools with predominantly white students and teachers (20 U.S.C. § 1400 [c] [12] [e]). The proportion of American Indian/Alaska Native students with disabilities also slightly exceeded their representation in the resident population in most disability categories. Graduation rates also have varied by race/ethnicity, ranging from 63.4% among White students to 43.5% among Black students.

In contrast, students from ethnic minorities and limited-English backgrounds are much less likely to be served in programs for the gifted and talented. Research studies concerning disproportionate representation have examined a variety of potential causes, including poverty; discrimination or cultural bias in teacher referral, or in the assessment process; cultural differences between minority students and their teachers; and limited teacher preparation in cultural competence. These factors will be discussed further in Chapters 2, 3, 12, and 14 as they relate to assessment, placement, teacher collaboration, and crisis intervention, respectively.

The Office of Civil Rights estimated that 174,530 students with disabilities needed services for limited English proficiency (LEP) in 1997 (U.S. Department of Education, 2000). The LEP students served in U.S. schools come from a variety of national, cultural, and linguistic backgrounds. The majority of LEP students were from Spanish-speaking homes with Spanish being the first language for nearly 73% percent of LEP students.

As mentioned previously, the number of minority and LEP children living in poverty may partially explain their overrepresentation in special education. The *Twenty-third Annual Report to Congress* (U.S. Department of Education, 2000) found that poverty was the single greatest predictor of academic and social failure in America's schools. However, poverty alone does not account for the disproportionality. As Patton and Townsend (2001) and others have pointed out, the complex interaction of economic, political, and social realities has resulted in a school system that works to the advantage of some students and to the disadvantage of others.

> It is spurious to deny that every aspect of schooling is layered by race, social relationships, ability grouping, tracking, special education labeling and classification, discipline referrals, suspensions and expulsions, dropout rates, composition of the teaching force. The social structure in schools sustained by instructional arrangements, pedagogy, content in textbooks, and a predominantly white teaching force raises serious moral/ethical questions that should be opened to interrogation and reflective thinking. (Ewing, 2001, p. 13)

Placement Issues

Serving students in the least restrictive environment (LRE) has been a legal requirement since the passage of EAHCA in 1975. However, the law also requires that a full **continuum of services** be afforded to students with disabilities. This continuum or cascade of service-delivery options may range from full inclusion in the regular classroom to a special-purpose school or residential facility for students with special needs. Along the continuum are such options as teacher consultation, pull-out services from a special educator or related service provider, and self-contained classes in a regular school building. The IEP team is responsible for making the placement recommendation, based on the individual needs of the child. The determination of what constitutes the LRE for a specific child will vary, based on present level of performance, needs for special education and related services, need for accommodations and modifications, and the resources available. The LRE placement is likely to change or evolve over the duration of the student's career in special education. According to Kauffman (2004), the LRE is the most inclusive setting in which the student's needs can be met, with the fewest restrictions. However, as noted earlier, students with EBD tend to be served in more restrictive settings than their special-education peers in other categories.

Special-education advocates have long stressed the need for high academic expectations and the importance of access to the **general education curriculum** for students with special needs. IDEA 1997 provided for changes and additions to the IEP content, team membership, and team procedures. These changes were intended to encourage greater access for students to the general education curriculum, as well as a greater level of participation in the IEP decision-making process by parents and students. While progress toward IEP goals has traditionally been an important method for determining the success of a student in special education, recent legislation (e.g., NCLB) has emphasized the concurrent responsibility of schools to demonstrate that students with special needs are making adequate yearly progress (AYP) on high-stakes assessment measures correlated with the general education curriculum and state education goals. Balancing the individual needs of the student for a functional curriculum with the requirements of high-stakes testing presents an increasing challenge for teachers and administrators.

Discipline-Related Issues

Discipline and suspension issues related to students with disabilities have been, and continue to be, a source of controversy both within professional education and at the national level. Critics have charged that IDEA essentially created a double standard for students with disabilities, requiring educators to determine the extent to which discipline problems are a manifestation of (i.e., caused by) the student's disabilities. Some administrators feel the dual system has led to diminished behavioral expectations for students with disabilities (Allee, 2002). Congress and the courts have continued to further define disciplinary rules for students with IEPs and to balance the safety and control needs of the school with the due process rights of students with disabilities. Discipline issues reportedly were the most emotional and most difficult issues Congress faced during the 1997 IDEA reauthorization (Jones & Aleman, 1997). A substantial portion of the 2004 IDEA changes also related to disciplinary issues.

IDEA 2004 contains specific language regarding the process of imposing disciplinary sanctions on students who bring weapons or drugs to school, who commit crimes on school property, or who are believed to be dangerous. The need for school administrators to provide a safe environment for all students has to be balanced with the due process rights of students with disabilities. See Figure 1-6 for the legal requirements regarding suspension and expulsion, determining an **alternative placement**, conducting a **manifestation determination**, and sharing information with the criminal justice system.

(k) PLACEMENT IN ALTERNATIVE EDUCATIONAL SETTING.—
  (1) AUTHORITY OF SCHOOL PERSONNEL.—
    (A) CASE-BY-CASE DETERMINATION.—School personnel may consider any unique circumstances on a case-by-case basis when determining whether to order a change in placement for a child with a disability who violates a code of student conduct.
    (B) AUTHORITY.—School personnel under this subsection may remove a child with a disability who violates a code of student conduct from their current placement to an appropriate interim alternative educational setting, another setting, or suspension, for not more than 10 school days (to the extent such alternatives are applied to children without disabilities).
    (C) ADDITIONAL AUTHORITY.—If school personnel seek to order a change in placement that would exceed 10 school days and the behavior that gave rise to the violation of the school code is determined not to be a manifestation of the child's disability pursuant to subparagraph (E), the relevant disciplinary procedures applicable to children without disabilities may be applied to the child in the same manner and for the same duration in which the procedures would be applied to children without disabilities, except as provided in section 612 (a) (1) although it may be provided in an interim alternative educational setting.
    (D) SERVICES.—A child with a disability who is removed from the child's current placement under subparagraph (G) (irrespective of whether the behavior is determined to be a manifestation of the child's disability) or subparagraph (C) shall—
      (i) continue to receive educational services, as provided in section 612 (a) (1), so as to enable the child to continue to participate in the general education curriculum, although in another setting, and to progress toward meeting the goals set out in the child's IEP; and
      (ii) receive, as appropriate, a functional behavioral assessment, behavioral intervention services and modifications, that are designed to address the behavior violation so that it does not recur.
    (E) MANIFESTATION DETERMINATION.—
      (i) IN GENERAL.—Except as provided in subparagraph (B), within 10 school days of any decision to change the placement of a child with a disability because of a violation of a code of student conduct, the local educational agency, the parent, and relevant members of the IEP Team (as determined by the parent and the local educational agency) shall review all relevant information in the student's file, including the child's IEP, any teacher observations, and any relevant information provided by the parents to determine—
        (I) if the conduct in question was caused by, or had a direct and substantial relationship to, the child's disability; or
        (II) if the conduct in question was the direct result of the local educational agency's failure to implement the IEP.

FIGURE 1–6 IDEA 2004: Disciplinary Procedures

(ii) MANIFESTATION.—If the local educational agency, the parent, and relevant members of the IEP Team determine that either subclause (I) or (II) of clause (i) is applicable for the child, the conduct shall be determined to be a manifestation of the child's disability.

(F) DETERMINATION THAT BEHAVIOR WAS A MANIFESTATION.—If the local educational agency, the parent, and relevant members of the IEP Team make the determination that the conduct was a manifestation of the child's disability, the IEP Team shall—

    (i) conduct a functional behavioral assessment, and implement a behavioral intervention plan for such child, provided that the local educational agency had not conducted such assessment prior to such determination before the behavior that resulted in a change in placement described in subparagraph (C) or (G);

    (ii) in the situation where a behavioral intervention plan has been developed, review the behavioral intervention plan if the child already has such a behavioral intervention plan, and modify it, as necessary, to address the behavior; and

    (iii) except as provided in subparagraph (G), return the child to the placement from which the child was removed, unless the parent and the local educational agency agree to a change of placement as part of the modification of the behavioral intervention plan.

(G) SPECIAL CIRCUMSTANCES.—School personnel may remove a student to an interim alternative educational setting for not more than 45 school days without regard to whether the behavior is determined to be a manifestation of the child's disability, in cases where a child—

    (i) carries or possesses a weapon to or at school, on school premises, or to or at a school function under the jurisdiction of a State or local educational agency;

    (ii) knowingly possesses or uses illegal drugs, or sells or solicits the sale of a controlled substance, while at school, on school premises, or at a school function under the jurisdiction of a State or local educational agency; or

    (iii) has inflicted serious bodily injury upon another person while at school, on school premises, or at a school function under the jurisdiction of a State or local educational agency.

(H) NOTIFICATION.—Not later than the date on which the decision to take disciplinary action is made, the local educational agency shall notify the parents of that decision, and of all procedural safeguards accorded under this section.

(2) DETERMINATION OF SETTING.—The interim alternative educational setting in subparagraphs (C) and (G) of paragraph (1) shall be determined by the IEP Team.

(3) APPEAL.—

(A) IN GENERAL.—The parent of a child with a disability who disagrees with any decision regarding placement, or the manifestation determination under this subsection, or a local educational agency that believes that maintaining the current placement of the child is substantially likely to result in injury to the child or to others, may request a hearing.

(B) AUTHORITY OF HEARING OFFICER.—

    (i) IN GENERAL.—A hearing officer shall hear, and make a determination regarding, an appeal requested under subparagraph (A).

    (ii) CHANGE OF PLACEMENT ORDER.—In making the determination under clause (i), the hearing officer may order a change in placement of a child with a disability. In such situations, the hearing officer may—

        (I) return a child with a disability to the placement from which the child was removed; or

        (II) order a change in placement of a child with a disability to an appropriate interim alternative educational setting for not more than 45 school days if the hearing officer determines that maintaining the current placement of such child is substantially likely to result in injury to the child or to others.

(4) PLACEMENT DURING APPEALS.—When an appeal under paragraph (3) has been requested by either the parent or the local educational agency—

(A) the child shall remain in the interim alternative educational setting pending the decision of the hearing officer or until the expiration of the time period provided for in paragraph (1)(C), whichever occurs first, unless the parent and the State or local educational agency agree otherwise; and

(B) the State or local educational agency shall arrange for an expedited hearing, which shall occur within 20 school days of the date the hearing is requested and shall result in a determination within 10 school days after the hearing.

(5) PROTECTIONS FOR CHILDREN NOT YET ELIGIBLE FOR SPECIAL EDUCATION AND RELATED SERVICES.—

(A) IN GENERAL.—A child who has not been determined to be eligible for special education and related services under this part and who has engaged in behavior that violates a code of student conduct, may assert any of the protections provided for in this part if the local educational agency had knowledge (as determined in accordance with this paragraph) that the child was a child with a disability before the behavior that precipitated the disciplinary action occurred.

(continued)

(B) BASIS OF KNOWLEDGE.—A local educational agency shall be deemed to have knowledge that a child is a child with a disability if, before the behavior that precipitated the disciplinary action occurred—

    (i) the parent of the child has expressed concern in writing to supervisory or administrative personnel of the appropriate educational agency, or a teacher of the child, that the child is in need of special education and related services;

    (ii) the parent of the child has requested an evaluation of the child pursuant to section 614 (a) (1) (B); or

    (iii) the teacher of the child, or other personnel of the local educational agency, has expressed specific concerns about a pattern of behavior demonstrated by the child, directly to the director of special education of such agency or to other supervisory personnel of the agency.

(C) EXCEPTION.—A local educational agency shall not be deemed to have knowledge that the child is a child with a disability if the parent of the child has not allowed an evaluation of the child pursuant to section 614 or has refused services under this part or the child has been evaluated and it was determined that the child was not a child with a disability under this part.

(D) CONDITIONS THAT APPLY IF NO BASIS OF KNOWLEDGE.—

    (i) IN GENERAL.—If a local educational agency does not have knowledge that a child is a child with a disability (in accordance with subparagraph (B) or (C)) prior to taking disciplinary measures against the child, the child may be subjected to disciplinary measures applied to children without disabilities who engaged in comparable behaviors consistent with clause (ii).

    (ii) LIMITATIONS.—If a request is made for an evaluation a child during the time period in which the child is subjected to disciplinary measures under this subsection, the evaluation shall be conducted in an expedited manner. If the child is determined to be a child with a disability, taking into consideration information from the evaluation conducted by the agency and information provided by the parents, the agency shall provide special education and related services in accordance with this part, except that, pending the results of the evaluation, the child shall remain in the educational placement determined by school authorities.

(6) REFERRAL TO AND ACTION BY LAW ENFORCEMENT AND JUDICIAL AUTHORITIES.—

  (A) RULE OF CONSTRUCTION.—Nothing in this part shall be construed to prohibit an agency from reporting a crime committed by a child with a disability to appropriate authorities or to prevent State law enforcement and judicial authorities from exercising their responsibilities with regard to the application of Federal and State law to crimes committed by a child with a disability.

  (B) TRANSMITTAL OF RECORDS.—An agency reporting a crime committed by a child with a disability shall ensure that copies of the special education and disciplinary records of the child are transmitted for consideration by the appropriate authorities to whom the agency reports the crime.

(7) DEFINITIONS.—In this subsection:

  (A) CONTROLLED SUBSTANCE.—The term 'controlled substance' means a drug or other substance identified under schedule I, II, III, IV, or V in section 202(c) of the Controlled Substances Act (21 U.S.C. 812 (c)).

  (B) ILLEGAL DRUG.—The term 'illegal drug' means a controlled substance but does not include a controlled substance that is legally possessed or used under the supervision of a licensed health-care professional or that is legally possessed or used under any other authority under that Act or under any other provision of Federal law.

  (C) WEAPON.—The term 'weapon' has the meaning given the term 'dangerous weapon' under section 930 (g) (2) of title 18, United States Code.

  (D) SERIOUS BODILY INJURY.—The term 'serious bodily injury' has the meaning given the term 'serious bodily injury' under paragraph (3) of subsection (h) of section 1365 of title 18, United States Code.

(l) RULE OF CONSTRUCTION.—Nothing in this title shall be construed to restrict or limit the rights, procedures, and remedies available under the Constitution, the Americans with Disabilities Act of 1990, title V of the Rehabilitation Act of 1973, or other Federal laws protecting the rights of children with disabilities, except that before the filing of a civil action under such laws seeking relief that is also available under this part, the procedures under subsections (f) and (g) shall be exhausted to the same extent as would be required had the action been brought under this part.

FIGURE 1–6 IDEA 2004: Disciplinary Procedures (*continued*)

Source: IDEA 2004, 20 U.S.C. § 1414 (k-l).

CHAPTER SUMMARY

- This chapter has depicted the legal and historical stages through which services for school-age children with disabilities have progressed. It also reviewed landmark legal cases and federal legislation. Specific emphasis was given to The Education for All Handicapped Children Act of 1975 and the amendments to this act, leading up to the 2004 reauthorization of IDEA. Also discussed were the conceptual models from which programming for students with EBD developed, the confusion regarding the current federal definition of ED, and the ongoing issues that confront the field.

CHECK YOUR UNDERSTANDING

1. *True or False.* Federal involvement has been minimal and contributed little to the evolution of special education.
2. *True or False.* IDEA establishes obligations and responsibilities of schools to consider placing students in the general education classrooms with supplementary aids and services first, before considering other alternative placements that may be more restrictive.
3. Identify the three separate powers/branches of government and what each branch does.
4. Which of the following is the amendment in the U.S. Constitution that extends equal rights and equal protections to individuals? (a) First, (b) Fourth, (c) Tenth, (d) Fourteenth
5. Which of the following public laws did Congress enact in 1975 to ensure that all students with disabilities have access to a free appropriate public education? (a) Section 504, (b) Education of the Handicapped Act, (c) American Disabilities Act, (d) Family Educational Rights and Privacy Act
6. The 1990 Reauthorization of the Education of the Handicapped Act (EHA) added which of the following disability categories? (a) Hyperactivity and Emotional Disturbance, (b) Autism and Traumatic Brain Injury, (c) Emotional Disturbance and Autism, (d) Autism and Hyperactivity
7. Which of the following is the more common name of the Education of the Handicapped Act (EHA)? (a) The IDEA Amendments, (b) Handicapped Children's Protection Act, (c) Individuals with Disabilities Education Act (IDEA), (d) Education of the Handicapped Amendments Act
8. Briefly explain how the rights of children with disabilities emerged from a history of neglect.
9. Token economies and contingency contracts are examples of interventions from which conceptual model of EBD? (a) behavioral, (b) biophysical or medical, (c) ecological or environmental, or (d) psychoeducational
10. Moving a student with ADHD to a seat near the front of the room but away from the windows and computer station is an example of an intervention based on which conceptual model of EBD? (a) behavioral, (b) biophysical or medical, (c) ecological or environmental, or (d) psychoeducational

APPLICATION ACTIVITIES

1. Educational practitioners (teachers and administrators) need to know how to locate and utilize sources of information related to special education laws, regulations, legislation, and compliance, as well as stay current in the field. Information from Web sites and the Internet serve as resources to keep current. The following activities should assist in accessing several sources of information related to the area of special education pertinent to your state, and specific aspects that affect local school-district operations.

   - Find the department of education Web site for your state.
   - From your state's Web site, find the link for school laws and legislation. Find the laws related to special education.
   - From your state's Web site, find the link for special education compliance. Find the state plan for your state.
   - Review your state plan for special education. Find your state's definition and eligibility criteria for emotional disturbance.
   - From your state department of education's Web site, find other links that are available as resources in the field of special education.

2. Compare and contrast the current federal definition of ED, the proposed alternative definition of EBD, and your state's definition and eligibility criteria for this category. Discuss the advantages and disadvantages of each in terms of facilitating (a) referral, (b) eligibility decisions, and (c) classroom programming.

CHAPTER 2

ASSESSMENT FOR DIAGNOSIS AND INTERVENTION

Judith K. Carlson

CHAPTER PREVIEW

CONNECTING TO THE CLASSROOM: *A Vignette*

Ms. Steiner had heard reports that Jamilla, a second-grade transfer student, had experienced both academic and behavioral problems in her previous school. Jamilla's grades and standardized test scores were abysmal. She was in the lowest reading group for her age, frequently had been sent to the principal, and usually was in the "time-out box" on the playground during recess. Ms. Steiner read the many disciplinary reports in Jamilla's file, and found she had repeatedly used profanity and shoved other students in the hallways and in the lunchroom. However, there was no evidence that positive behavior strategies had been attempted with Jamilla, and no anecdotal information about the girl's strengths or interests. In the first week of classes in Ms. Steiner's room, Jamilla had demonstrated general noncompliance with teacher instructions, grumbled and complained about every assignment, and appeared unable—or unwilling—to work independently at her desk. Ms. Steiner's attempts to verbally encourage and redirect Jamilla had resulted in a full-blown temper tantrum, complete with crying, screaming, and ripping up notebook papers. In a previous year, Ms. Steiner might have lapsed into thinking "Jamilla is not appropriate for my classroom. She never listens, is disrespectful and uncooperative, and is a total distraction to the other students. She belongs in special education!" However, just last summer, Ms. Steiner had taken a course in designing data-based classroom interventions and now she was armed with a plan. First, she would observe Jamilla to identify her major problem areas and determine how often and under what conditions these problems occurred. She would talk to Jamilla and to her parents to find out more about her history, her strengths, and her interests. Then she would look at what tests and informal measures might be appropriate to assess Jamilla's strengths and weaknesses in academics, behavior, and social skills. With this data, and the help of her general and special education colleagues on the student assistance team, Ms. Steiner would determine appropriate academic and behavioral interventions for Jamilla, and design an evaluation plan to measure success. If those interventions didn't work, then—and only then—would she consider making a referral for special education evaluation. Ms. Steiner was determined to do everything she could to make this a great year for Jamilla and for the whole class.

ASSESSMENT: DEFINITION AND BASIC ASSUMPTIONS

Assessment is the engine that drives decision-making in a quality special education program. Many similar and overlapping terms are associated with the assessment process, including measurement, testing, evaluation, formative and summative data collection, and probing. Although these terms may be used interchangeably in conversations among teachers and other professionals, each term has a separate and distinct meaning. Figure 2–1 defines how these terms will be used in the context of this chapter.

Why Assess?

For students suspected of having emotional or behavioral disorders (EBD), assessment serves one or more of the following six purposes:

- **Screening and referral**—to identify students at high risk for school failure or who may need specially designed education and related services as a result of a disability
- **Diagnosis and eligibility determination**—to assess whether a student meets the federal guidelines established under IDEA for identification as EBD or another category
- **IEP development**—to provide detailed information about the student's present level of educational performance, so that an individualized program may be created with specific special education and related services

- **Placement decision making**—to identify the least restrictive environment in which the student's individual IEP goals can be accomplished, and to determine the degree to which the student will be exposed to the general education curriculum
- **Instructional planning**—to design and implement day-to-day academic, behavioral, and social-skill activities based on IEP goals and objectives, as well as on the general education curriculum
- **Ongoing progress evaluation**—to provide formative and summative data concerning progress toward IEP goals and objectives and in the general education curriculum

This chapter will address special education evaluation through the first step of screening and referral, as well as provide an overview of the general components of the diagnostic assessment process. Some assessment strategies and measures discussed in this chapter will go beyond the scope of the traditional classroom teacher, requiring specialized training to administer, score, and interpret. Other techniques will be used daily by teachers and other educational professionals in student instruction and progress monitoring. Whether acting as an examiner, a diagnostician, a consultant, or a classroom teacher, it is critical that special educators understand the basic language, purposes, and interpretation of assessment used with students identified with emotional/behavioral disorders (EBD).

Term	Definition/Use in This Chapter
Assessment	A process designed to collect and analyze data for decision-making purposes.
Evaluation	The process of analyzing data to make informed judgments.
Formative data	Information that is collected over time, designed to study progress or growth of knowledge and skills.
Measurement	A variety of formal and informal activities designed to describe individual performance in quantifiable terms.
Probes	A brief, informal set of questions or activities designed to demonstrate student mastery or nonmastery of specific information or skills, or to test hypotheses concerning learning or reinforcement preferences.
Summative data	Information collected at the end of an instructional period to determine mastery of knowledge and/or skills.
Testing	The process of administering a structured set of questions/items designed to elicit specific responses from individuals or groups.

FIGURE 2–1   Definitions of Assessment Terminology

Basic Assumptions

All assessment is governed by basic assumptions that act as guidelines in the selection of tests or measures and in the interpretation of assessment results. Basic assumptions reveal both the conditions under which a test was developed and how those conditions must be followed when administering, scoring, and interpreting the test. Basic assumptions outline the circumstances under which the specific test may or may not be appropriate or useful in a given situation. It is the ethical responsibility of special educators to make sure that they: (a) know the legal requirements for assessment of students with disabilities, (b) are familiar with the use and limitations of assessment measures, and (c) administer and interpret assessment instruments in a way that is unbiased (CEC, 2003).

With commercially published tests and assessment instruments, the basic assumptions of the developer should be provided in the accompanying user or technical manual. Reading the manual allows the examiner to decide if the test is an appropriate measure for an individual student in a specific situation. The manual will also indicate whether a test may be administered by an educator, or if specialized training and qualifications are required. If tests are from noncommercial sources, such as district-developed or teacher-made measures, it is important that the examiner identify the basic assumptions of the test developer and determine appropriateness of that test for the situation before selecting or administering the instrument.

TYPES OF ASSESSMENT

Many assessment tools and techniques are available for use with students at risk for, or identified with, EBD. The range of assessment options is broad and varied. To select the appropriate assessment battery for a specific student, it is important to understand the differences among some basic types of assessment strategies.

Formal and Informal Assessment

Both formal and informal assessment techniques are used when evaluating students with EBD. **Formal assessment** generally refers to published assessment instruments that come with specific rules for administration, scoring, and interpretation (McLoughlin & Lewis, 2001). These commercially published tests include both standardized and norm-referenced tests and give the

examiner the opportunity to evaluate a student's performance relative to others at similar chronological or developmental ages. Formal assessment techniques often yield standard scores, percentile ranks, age- and grade-level scores, and other statistically derived information about a student's performance. Using the information provided in the test manuals and interpretation guides, the user can answer many valuable questions about a student's learning.

Informal assessment commonly refers to those assessment procedures with less rigid administration, scoring, and interpretation rules (McLoughlin & Lewis, 2001). Informal assessment includes published instruments, as well as measures or techniques developed by school districts, teachers, and other professionals specifically for use with an individual student or group of students. Informal assessment strategies can range from screening measures used to identify students ready to enter kindergarten to teacher-made probes examining the student's skills in a specific skill area (e.g., a series of activities designed to elicit peer-related social skills).

Standardized and Norm-Referenced Tests

Educators often use commercial tests to identify students with disabilities, including EBD, and then design an IEP or intervention plan. Many of these commercial tests are standardized or norm-referenced tests. **Standardization** refers to the process of constructing a test in such a way that raw scores or student responses can be statistically manipulated to produce scores that conform to specific predetermined scales of measurement. Two types of standardized measures commonly used in educational settings are achievement tests and aptitude (i.e., intelligence quotient, or IQ) tests. A test becomes **normed** by administering the test to a large group of people and examining their performance. Those individuals and their scores determine the norm for that test, often by age or grade level. Scores on standardized tests are not interpreted by comparison to an absolute mastery criterion, such as 8 out of 10 correct, but by comparing the individual student's performance to a similar group of students in the norming sample.

For example, on a test standardized by age group, 10-year-old Barbara from Chicago achieves a standard score of 90 on a test with a mean of 100 and a standard deviation of 15. This score can be compared to the reference group of all 10-year-olds who took the test as part of the norming sample. This norm referencing provides a benchmark against which the student's level of performance can be evaluated as being typical, below, or above the level expected for her age group. In Barbara's case, her score of 90 falls within one standard deviation of the mean (i.e., 100 +/− 15) and her performance could be considered within the average range of scores.

Norming groups can be categorized by a variety of demographic variables including age, grade level, gender, ethnicity, geographical region, and socioeconomic status. The additional stratification allows comparison to students who most closely resemble the target student, as well as to the national norms as a whole. For example, in addition to comparing Barbara to all 10-year-olds, she also could be compared to other 10-year-old females from Midwest urban areas, if her test provided that information.

It is important that the norming sample include a large number of students who are proportionately representative of all the children in the general population on the variables listed above. In some tests normed prior to the 1990 amendments to the Individuals with Disabilities Education Act (IDEA), test creators excluded students with disabilities from the norming sample. Other tests may have used a norming sample that was outdated, geographically restricted, or that undersampled students from specific groups. The less similar the student being tested is to the test's sample, the less valuable the results of testing generally will be (Waterman, 1994). Conversely, the more closely the norming sample reflects the general population and includes students similar to the one being tested, the more confidence evaluators can have that the resulting score is meaningful.

When administering, scoring, or interpreting a standardized test, it is essential that the examiner honor the basic assumptions and requirements of the test as published in the administration and interpretation manuals for the test. Some tests require that examiners possess specific qualifications or complete supervised training. Even when this is not the case, the examiner must be prepared to give the test correctly, having thoroughly studied the manual. For most standardized tests, multiple practice administrations are necessary to become fluent with the materials and procedures. Generally, items must be presented to the student in a specific order, in a specific way, frequently using scripted language or directions. Many standardized tests are used with children and youth of varying ages and ability levels; they often establish guidelines to determine the starting point and ending point for students on each subtest (i.e., basals and ceilings). Tests used to make important educational decisions about students should be administered individually by qualified personnel, in a setting that is conducive to putting forth optimal concentration and effort. In general, examiners must administer the test under standardized conditions that replicate the way the test was taken by the individuals in the norming sample. If standardized tests are not selected and administered correctly, the scores obtained from these tests will not be accurate, and may result in inappropriate educational decisions.

Reliability and Validity.   Two concerns in selection of standardized tests are the instrument's reliability and validity. Although there are many types of reliability and validity, the basic idea behind each concept is relatively simple. **Reliability** means that the test yields similar results every time it is given. This does not mean that a student would necessarily answer the same questions correctly if given the test more than once, but that the overall outcome of the test would be very similar if administered to the same student, under the same conditions, at the same point in time. Reliability is established by the test's developer using statistical procedures during the norming process.

Validity is the extent to which the test measures what it claims to measure. For example, an aptitude or IQ test proposes to measure a person's ability or potential to learn whereas an achievement test proposes to measure a person's current level of knowledge or learning. For a test to be valid, it must yield results that fit within the concepts or constructs around which the test was designed. Validity is also established using statistical procedures during the norming process. To maintain validity, students should not be given the same standardized test, or the same version of a test, too frequently or they will become "test-wise" and the results will show how well they have learned the test, rather than measuring their actual aptitude, ability, or skills.

Information on the reliability and validity of a standardized test must be provided by the publishers in the test manual. Salvia and Ysseldyke (2001) suggest that a minimum reliability standard of .80 be used for screening devices and a higher standard of .90 be used for making important educational decisions.

Decisions about validity must be made by an informed evaluator who is confident that the measure is appropriate for answering specific questions about students. Responsibility for the selection of assessment instruments varies from state to state and district to district. A team of qualified individuals, a school psychologist or psychometrist, a school counselor, a special educator, or a general educator may select the assessment battery. The National Information Center for Children and Youth with Disabilities (NICHCY) (Waterman, 1994) provides a list of questions to guide educators in selecting tests:

* According to the publisher or expert reviewers, what, specifically, is the test supposed to measure? Is its focus directly relevant to the skill area(s) to be assessed? Will student results on the test address the educational questions being asked?
* Is the test reliable and valid?
* Is the content/skill area being assessed by the test appropriate for the student, given his or her age and grade?
* Is the test norm-referenced, does the norm group resemble the student?
* Is the test intended to evaluate students, to diagnose the specific nature of a student's disability or academic difficulty, to inform instructional decisions, or will it be used for research purposes?
* Is the test administered in a group or individually?
* Does the examiner need specialized training in order to administer the test, record student responses, score the test, or interpret results?
* Will the student's suspected disability impact upon his or her taking of the test?
* How similar to actual classroom tasks are the tasks the child is asked to complete on the test? (pp. 8–9)

In addition to considering the reliability and validity of the instrument and its administration, examiners working with students with EBD must address special issues related to the student's disability. Three common concerns relate to compliance, effort, and interfering behaviors. First, did the student participate willingly in the assessment and comply with examiner instructions? If not, the examiner must evaluate the degree to which reluctance, negativity, or refusal affected the results of the assessment. Second, did the student put forth her best effort so that results are an actual reflection of her knowledge and skills? If the student was easily frustrated, or gave up when questions became difficult, then the result may reflect typical classroom performance rather than an optimal score on the measure. In some cases, "test-wise" students may realize that several wrong answers in a row will result in a swifter

end to testing and deliberately provide incorrect responses to avoid further assessment. Finally, did the student exhibit behaviors that interfered with or interrupted the administration of the standardized test? It may be possible for the examiner to ignore self-stimulatory or distracting behaviors if the student continues to respond appropriately to test stimuli (e.g., rocking back and forth, nose-picking). However, more extreme behaviors may make it necessary to redirect the student or stop the examination (e.g., running around the room, throwing test materials). As part of the evaluation summary, the examiner must describe the extent to which any of the student's EBD characteristics interfered with the potential reliability and validity of assessment results.

Criterion-Referenced Tests

A **criterion-referenced test** determines whether or not a student meets a specific, preset criteria or mastery level. Criterion-referenced tests are scored according to a predetermined standard for content mastery established by the test developer, a national group of content-area experts, the state, the local school district, or the teacher.

Criterion-referenced tests can be formal or informal. They can assess a student's performance across a variety of subjects (e.g., language arts) or cover a specific topic area in greater depth (e.g., phonemic awareness). Unlike standardized tests, criterion-referenced tests do not allow comparisons to norming samples. The student answers each item either correctly or incorrectly, resulting in a final score that can be compared only to the criterion (i.e., pass/fail) or to their previous score (i.e., progressing/not progressing). For example, The National Council of Teachers of Mathematics (2000) has established standards and grade-level expectations for skill mastery in K–12 math classes. The Carlson Consolidated School District has developed a test based on those skills, and decided to offer small-group remedial math tutoring after school to second graders who have mastered fewer than 80% of the expectations for kindergarten through second grade. Jimmy has only mastered 12 (27%) of the 45 expectations, and therefore qualifies for the new program. Belinda has mastered 43 (96%) of the skills, and does not.

Curriculum-Based Measures

Curriculum-based measures (CBM) allow for assessment of a student's abilities directly related to a specific curriculum or scope and sequence of skills. Many schools have designed CBM to test how well their students perform from year to year in the district-selected curriculum. Classroom teachers use CBM to determine whether a lesson or series of lessons has been understood by individual learners. Technically, any teacher-designed test that evaluates a student's performance on a specific set of academic or social skills that has been taught in her classroom would qualify as a curriculum-based measure.

The primary advantage of CBM is that the information can be easily translated into classroom instructional planning (McLoughlin & Lewis, 2001). CBM is drawn directly from the student's learning experiences and, therefore, is a highly authentic form of assessment. Additionally, some researchers believe use of CBM data may aid in addressing issues related to the assessment of students from minority populations who are frequently overrepresented in EBD programs (Plasencia-Peinado & Alvarado, 2001). Another advantage of CBM is that it offers information not only about the accuracy of a student's performance but also about efficiency or fluency. Fluency is often overlooked in classroom assessment, but is an integral component when designing intervention strategies to address student concerns (Waterman, 1994). This is particularly true for children with emotional and behavioral problems, who may know *how* to perform a necessary social skill but be unable to do it quickly, fluently, and in a way that appears socially competent to adults and peers.

An increasingly common application of CBM in the classroom setting is portfolio assessment. **Portfolio assessment** is a form of authentic assessment in which artifacts such as work products, presentations, or other examples of skills, knowledge, and dispositions are displayed in a collection, traditionally accompanied by reflective essays describing the artifacts and the rationale for selecting them. Much like an artist's portfolio, student portfolios can incorporate many types of exemplars, from paper copies of classroom work products to full-blown multimedia presentations. Using portfolio assessment allows students to demonstrate both progress and competency in a unique and individual fashion. Portfolios also allow teachers to collect work products in a purposeful fashion, to facilitate error-pattern analysis, and to evaluate progress on individual goals and objectives. It is also a form of assessment that is easily shown to—and understood by—parents.

Commercially produced curriculum-based measures have long accompanied specific programs such as basal reading series and other subject-area textbooks. More recently, test publishers have released tools marketed as curriculum-based measures that actually represent a composite of the skills required by several major textbooks or curricula for a specific age or grade level, rather than corresponding to material contained in one specific textbook. Although these measures may not fit the technical definition of CBM, teachers can still use these measures to evaluate student performance, provided the items are a good match for the classroom's actual curriculum.

Many states have instituted statewide assessment based on an agreed-upon set of competencies or a scope and sequence of skills for a specific grade level or on their state educational standards. These are often called **high-stakes tests** because their results are used to determine important consequences for individual students (e.g., graduation from high school), individual teachers (e.g., merit pay based on student performance), individual schools (e.g., being identified as a school in need of improvement), and school districts (e.g., programmatic funding). These high-stakes tests represent yet another application of CBM.

Behavior Rating Scales and Inventories

Behavior rating scales provide a way to formally organize and quantify intuitive or perceptual information about student behavior. These tools provide contextual clues about difficult-to-measure constructs related to the diagnosis of EBD, such as interpersonal and intrapersonal skills and feelings. Rating scales and inventories assist in soliciting and interpreting inference or judgments from parents, teachers, and clinicians about the presence, severity, or frequency of a given behavior. Most take relatively little time to complete, require no special training to administer, and are easy to score. In recent years, however, some of these scales and inventories have become much more complex analyses of data collected on a range of emotional and social variables (Bullock, Wilson, & Campbell, 1990; Hosp, Howell, & Hosp, 2003). To assist in determining eligibility for special education or the need for related services (e.g., counseling), some measures have been designed to align with specific educational or clinical diagnostic criteria for emotional disturbance.

Rating scales and behavior inventories utilize information obtained from teachers, parents, caregivers, or others involved in the daily life of the student. Rating scales that include a component of self-evaluation, where the student provides input or rates her own behavior, give additional utility to the measure. Because rating scales reflect secondhand recall and judgments about behavior that occurred in the past, they can sometimes lack adequate reliability and validity (Salvia & Ysseldyke, 2001). At best, the scores represent others' perceptions of student behavior, which can be subjective and reflect factors other than the individual child's actual behavior. For this reason, it is important that rating scales and behavior inventories be used in combination with other forms of assessment (e.g., structured interviews and direct observation) and not as the sole determiner of an eligibility, placement, or intervention decision. Comparing several different ratings on an individual student may help confirm or disconfirm the utility of the information. Figure 2–2 lists some of the most common behavior rating scales, checklists, and inventories.

Although the questions posed on many rating scales focus on undesirable or inappropriate behaviors, those scales that include the rating of student strengths and adaptive behaviors provide a more comprehensive profile and facilitate instructional planning and ongoing monitoring of intervention progress. In a study comparing 14 forms of 9 commonly used behavior rating scales, Hosp, Howell, and Hosp (2003) found that most scales had a high percentage of items measuring negative behaviors (e.g., hitting, refusal to follow directions). They pointed out that a score based on the presence of those behaviors might be useful for diagnostic and planning purposes, and would provide a measure for monitoring reduction of undesirable behaviors, but not for determining whether prosocial behaviors had improved. "Using these scales, an educator would not be able to determine if the decreasing negative action is being replaced with a positive one or no behavior at all" (p. 204). For example, Jamilla's current score on a behavior rating scale might indicate that her aggressive behavior toward peers is less of a concern now than when her previous teacher had filled out the same rating scale a year ago. However, the difference in scores might reflect that Jamilla has shifted from overtly hitting and kicking peers—behaviors measured on that particular rating scale—to more covert verbal threats, bullying, and intimidation that are not tapped by items on the scale.

Some behavior inventories take the form of **sociometric measures**. These types of measures examine how a student is viewed by peers on a set of variables, or how the student views herself in relation to peers on those same variables. Sociograms and peer rating scales are two such measures. **Sociograms** are diagrams that visually represent student relationships and social choices, based on observation or information solicited from students (e.g., Who would you most/least like to work with on a project?). **Peer rating scales** provide students with an opportunity to rate or rank their peers on a list of skills, behaviors, or characteristics (e.g., Would you say Jamilla is friendly all of the time, some of the time, or none of the time?). While these techniques do not directly assess the student, classmates' input on the desirability or undesirability of a student's behavior or social status can be a powerful predictor of future social outcomes. These techniques can help teachers identify potential allies for peer tutoring interventions or target social skill deficits to address with intervention. Sociometric techniques lend insight into the social structure of a classroom and can be especially important in the assessment of young children with EBD (Brown, Odom, & Buysee, 2002).

Direct Observation

Direct observation is considered to be one of the essential best practices in the field of assessment (Merrell, 2001). Whether a structured observation designed to collect specific data (e.g., counting how many times Jamilla verbalizes a profanity during a recess period) or an informal observation resulting in a written narrative or anecdotal report (e.g., a transcript of ongoing events during a seatwork period), direct observation can provide insight into the many complex factors that affect student emotional, behavioral, and social development. It is important that behavioral observation involve multiple measures, multiple observers, and multiple observation settings. It is also critical that evaluators conduct their observations at different times during the day. The ability to recognize and record behavior, select the most appropriate places to observe the student, and find efficient and clear means of interpreting results are all essential components of effective direct observation. Although contrived situations can be used to elicit a specific behavior, direct observation is best completed in authentic settings where students commonly interact with peers, teachers, or others. This means that the classroom, the playground, the lunchroom, and so on are all prime locations for conducting direct observation.

Teacher Observation and Classroom Record-Keeping. Just as IDEA requires that specific records be maintained during the referral, screening, and identification

Rating Scale Name	Characteristics	Population
Behavior Assessment System for Children (BASC)	Comprehensive rating scale including teacher, parent, and self-rating scales; Student Observation System; and Structured Developmental History. Measures adaptive and problem behaviors in school, home, and community settings.	Ages 4–18; self-report ages 8–18; teachers, parents, or caregivers ages 4–18
Behavior Rating Profile—2nd edition (BRP-2)	Six norm-referenced instruments that evaluate student behavior at home and school, as well as interpersonal relationships. Factors include: deviant behavior, specific settings of problem behaviors, and others' perception of behavior that is different.	Ages 6–18; completed by target student, teachers, parent, or caregiver
Behavioral and Emotional Rating Scale: A Strength-Based Approach to Assessment (BERS)	Norm-referenced, standardized measure. Includes 52 items covering 5 factors: interpersonal strengths, family involvement, intrapersonal strengths, school functioning, and affective strengths.	Ages 5–18; completed by parent, teacher, or caregiver
Behavior Dimensions Rating Scale	Rating scale with bimodal choices (e.g., agreeable/quarrelsome). Yields four subscale scores: aggressive/acting out, irresponsible/inattentive, socially withdrawn, and fearful/anxious.	Ages 5–adult; completed by teachers, parents, or counselors
Burks' Behavior Rating Scales	110 item, 5-point response scale to identify how often behavior occurs on a 19-problem behavior list.	1st–9th grade; completed by parent, teacher, or caregiver
Child Behavior Checklist (CBCL)	Thorough assessment of behavioral problems, emotional disturbance, and psychopathology. Scores include specific emotional, behavioral, and somatic problems, as well as competence scales such as academic and adaptive functioning.	Ages 6–18; completed by target student, parent, teacher, or caregiver
Revised Behavior Problem Checklist (RBPC)	89-item scale that evaluates behavior problems. Subscales include: conduct disorder, socialized aggression, attention problems, anxiety, psychotic behavior, and motor tension.	Ages 5–18; completed by teacher, parent, or caregiver
Social Emotional Dimension Scale (SEDS)	Norm-referenced, standardized, 21-item rating scale. Subscales include: peer avoidance, aggressive interaction, teacher avoidance, inappropriate behavior, depressive reaction, and physical reaction.	Ages 5–18; completed by teachers, counselors, psychologists
Social Skills Rating System (SSRS)	Standardized series of questionnaires with subscales that include: social skills, problem behaviors, and academic competence.	Ages 3–18; completed by teachers, parents, or caregivers
Teachers Report Form (TRF)	The teacher form of Child Behavior Checklist that assesses the behavior problems, emotional disturbance, and psychopathology of students. (See CBCL.)	Ages 6–18; completed by teacher
Walker–McConnell Scale of Social Competence and School Adjustment	43-item scale with two primary domains of adaptive behavior and interpersonal social competence. Subscales include: teacher-preferred social behavior, peer-preferred social behavior, and school adjustment.	School-aged children; completed by teachers

[1]Publisher information for these measures is included in Appendix B, and was compiled from publisher Web sites and the *Mental Measurements Yearbook* database.

FIGURE 2–2   Commonly Used Behavior Rating Scales and Checklists[1]

processes, classroom records detailing when, how often, and how long a behavior occurred should be part of the ongoing assessment record as well. Classroom record keeping assists teachers in making an accurate evaluation of: (a) the student's present level of performance, (b) how a support system or modification plan is working, (c) the impact of a new instructional method, or (d) a student's progress toward IEP goals and objectives. When these classroom records are displayed in a visual format (e.g., a table, chart, or graph), the student, parents, and other professionals can easily view progress on these goals.

Describing Behavior. How upset was she? How often did you sneeze yesterday? Most people do not remember such details unless they have been cued to the importance of a specific event or behavior and take notes or collect data. A doctor often deals with statements such as "it hurts all the time" or "my stomach gets really upset." The physician probably would be elated if the patient brought in a chart or list of symptom frequency with indications of the time, place, and situation in which the symptom occurred.

Educators frequently refer to student behaviors using similarly vague descriptions: "Jamilla comes in angry most every morning" or "she never turns her work in on time." However, what does "comes in angry" look like? How often is "most every morning"? When *does* she turn in her assignments? Is the problem with all assignments, or just with her math seatwork? By keeping detailed records, the teacher develops a clear picture of the target behavior. Instead of saying, "She never turns in work on time," the teacher can make the simple data-based statement "Jamilla completed less than 25% of assigned work on 7 of the last 10 in-class math assignments." The teacher's perception that Jamilla was angry could be clarified as: "Four of the last five mornings, Jamilla has walked into the room with a frown on her face, avoided eye contact with teacher or peers, and muttered unintelligibly under her breath when greeted by the teacher." Describing behavior in a language that makes it concrete and measurable is an essential component of successful behavioral assessment. Using specific descriptive language can lead to a clear definition of the target behavior, and more productive discussions on how to design appropriate interventions. Clear definitions allow everyone on the team—including parents, teachers, and the student—to quantify and discuss target behaviors in the same way.

Figure 2–3 describes some of the more common methods of recording and coding behavior during classroom observation and provides examples for

Technique	Purpose	Instructions/Example
Anecdotal Record	To identify and describe problem behaviors that occur in a specific environment, or to determine what events precede and follow a specific target behavior	Take general notes to develop a narrative description of specific incidents or behaviors observed in a particular setting in concrete, factual terms. *Example:* Mrs. Griffith, concerned about Amanda's off-task behavior, asks you to watch her during seatwork time to see what gets her off track, what she does instead of working on the assignment, and what seems to get her to return to work.
Frequency Count	To provide data on how often a behavior of interest occurs; may be used multiple times to compare frequency before, during, and after an intervention to measure its effectiveness	Count the number of times a behavior occurs within a given period of time. Use tally marks to record data, and graphs to compare data from several observations. *Example:* The kindergarten teacher has observed Rafaela grabbing toys from other children during afternoon free-play time. You watch her and determine that she grabbed toys 3 times during the 15-minute play time. The teacher plans to start a sticker chart with Rafaela tomorrow and asks you to return in a week to take data on this behavior again.

(continued)

FIGURE 2–3 Common Data-Collection Techniques

Technique	Purpose	Instructions/Example
Time Sampling	To provide an estimate of the frequency and duration of a behavior when continual observation is not feasible or when multiple behaviors or students are being observed in the same time period	Divide the observation period into equal time periods and make a grid or table listing the times you will observe. Use a stopwatch or set a timer to prompt you to look at the student. Put down a plus if the behavior is observed and a minus if the behavior is not observed at that time. Usually this data is reported as a percentage or ratio, found by dividing the number of plusses by the number of intervals. This method may underestimate because the observer may miss some behaviors that occur between observation times._Example:_ Mr. Hawkins is concerned that Jeff and Ron are off task during his woodworking class. He makes a chart on a sheet of graph paper with times in 5-minute increments across the top (9:00, 9:05, 9:10, etc.) and the boys' names (Jeff, Ron) down the side. He sets his watch to go off every five minutes, beginning at 9:00. Each time the watch alarm beeps, he looks at Jeff and Ron, and puts either a plus or a minus in the box by their names. He discovers that Jeff was on task 60% of the time (6 out of 10) and Ron was on task 40% of the time (4 out of 10).
Duration Recording	To determine how long a behavior of interest lasts; may be conducted multiple times to determine the impact of an intervention	Using a watch or clock with a second hand, write down the time the target behavior starts and stops. Subtract to find the duration. (Could also use a stopwatch.)_Example:_ At least once a day, Barbara engages in verbal tirades or tantrums, yelling about how she hates school, how stupid the teacher is, how hard the work is, etc. She frequently calls other students names, tears up her work, and throws objects from her desk around the room. The teacher wants to try self-calming techniques with Barbara that might reduce the amount of time she spends throwing tantrums. To determine the baseline, she takes data for one week by timing each episode, and finds that the average length of Barbara's tantrums is 6.5 minutes. After teaching Barbara to use a stress ball when she feels frustrated, she will continue timing the episodes to see if the length decreases.
Latency Recording	To measure the length of time between two behaviors of interest	Use the same technique as duration recording, but start timing at the end of behavior #1 and stop timing at the beginning of behavior #2._Example:_ Jaquitha seems to take a long time complying with teacher requests to begin her seatwork. The teacher times the interval beginning with the teacher request to get out her spelling book and ending with Jacquitha having the book on her desk. This technique could also be used with Barbara, to see if the length of time between her tantrums increased after implementation of the stress-ball intervention.

FIGURE 2–3 Common Data-Collection Techniques (*continued*)

each. Alex Thompson's Perspective (Box 2-1) describes unintrusive data-collection techniques for classroom teachers. For more information concerning use of direct observation techniques as a part of functional behavioral assessment, see Chapter 3.

Interview Techniques

Essentially, an **interview** is a purposeful conversation designed to gather information about a student's present level of performance in academic, behavioral, or

Thompson Perspective

PERSPECTIVE: ALEX THOMPSON, Ph.D. (Senior Research Statistician)
Easy-to-Use Teacher Data-Collection Techniques

Data collection brings to mind difficult tasks requiring the juggling and memory of an on-air baseball announcer. Add to that the fact that the teacher is trying to instruct a class and maintain a balance between enthusiastic educational inquiry and total chaos and you have the elements of a nightmare or a new television reality show.

Fortunately, data collection can be relatively simple and fit right in with the normal flow of the classroom. Here are some simple ways to get the data a concerned teacher needs to make and measure interventions without being tied to a desk.

For counting how many times a behavior occurs:

* Put a bunch of rubber bands on one wrist. Move them to the other wrist as a counter.
* Place paper clips or other small objects in one pocket. Move them to another pocket to keep track of your count.
* Move chalk in the chalk tray, push pins on a corkboard, or books on a shelf from a starting position to a second position.
* Walk past your desk and move items from one jar to another.

For knowing how long a behavior lasts:

* Start and stop a stopwatch or on a watch with stopwatch capability.
* Count slowly: one-one thousand, two-one thousand, three-one thousand, etc. This counting method approximates seconds.
* Silently sing the alphabet song and remember the letter when the behavior stops.
* Move rubber bands, chalk, or other items to remember total time.

Write your data on a collection sheet when you have a moment. Have more than one student to observe? Use different colors of rubber bands. Get a watch for both wrists. Get creative. Find what works best for you. Make it as easy and fun as possible. Just make sure the student doesn't know what the rubber bands or whatever mean. You wouldn't want to bias your data!

Alex Thompson, Ph.D., is a senior research statistician with Hallmark Cards in Kansas City, Missouri.

social-skill activities. Interviews are highly adaptable. They can be presented in a structured format, with questions designed to examine specific areas, or as a relaxed, open conversation. Interview answers and the issues they raise can help determine additional avenues of assessment.

Information provided in an interview setting directly reflects the experiences and views of individual participants and, therefore, is subjective. Information gained from interviews should be confirmed by historical records, direct observation, or interviews with additional informants. Figure 2–4 contains a sample interview protocol designed to gather background information on a student with emotional or behavioral problems.

Preparation for the interview is a critical component in gathering useful and accurate information. Providing informants with a list of sample questions in advance will cue them to think about relevant history and organize relevant documentation to bring to the meeting. A careful review of the student's school records or work samples may help identify patterns or areas of specific concern and can assist in determining who should be interviewed and some of the questions to be asked. Parents or primary caregivers, for example, may be able to provide detailed information about the student's family, school, and medical history: "It is especially important that they contribute their unique, 'insider' perspective on the child's functioning, interests, motivation, difficulties,

```
Name of Student:
Name of Person Interviewed:
Relationship to Student:
Name of Interviewer:
Date, Time, and Location of Interview:
Reason for Interview:
```

Family, Home, and Health

- Who else lives in the home?
- Does the student have regular contact with extended family? If so, with whom?
- Any recent changes or losses in family status? If so, please describe.
- Who in the family is the student closest to?
- Does the student have any significant conflicts with any family members?
- Does the student do anything at home that concerns you?
- How do you manage the student's behavior problems at home?

- Describe the student's typical routine on a school day.
- What does the student like to do in his/her spare time?
- Describe the student's hobbies or special interests.
- Describe the student's responsibilities around the house.
- How would you describe the student's health during the developmental years?
- Has the student ever been hospitalized?
- Does the student have any current health problems?
- Does the student take any medications?
- Any other concerns related to family, home, or health?

School History

- List the schools previously attended and years.
- How does the student do academically? Grades? Test scores?
- How does the student get along with peers?
- How does the student get along with teachers and other authority figures?
- What is the student's favorite/easiest/best subject?

- What is the student's least favorite/most difficult/worst subject?
- Does the student participate in extracurricular activities? If so, which?
- Does the student's behavior interfere with his/her learning, or that of classmates?
- Describe the student's school disciplinary history.
- Any other concerns related to school?

FIGURE 2–4 Sample Interview Protocol for Gathering Information About a Student with Emotional/Behavioral Problems
Source: Adapted from Downing & Smith, 1999.

and behavior in the home or community" (Waterman, 1994, p. 6).

Teachers can offer perspectives about current interaction between the student and others in the classroom or school environment. Teachers can also provide insight into the types of environmental factors and task demands that seem to trigger problem behaviors, as well as what type of reinforcement seems to work well. An interview with the student provides insight into how she views difficult situations, her strategies for problem solving, and what type of concrete and social reinforcers she finds most attractive.

Diagnostic Teaching

Diagnostic teaching, sometimes called diagnostic probes or dynamic assessment, involves the systematic manipulation of instructional material and conditions to determine the most appropriate or effective strategy to teach a specific skill or concept to a student (Feuerstein, 1979; McLoughlin & Lewis, 2001). Diagnostic teaching is designed with an individual student in mind, driven by her specific areas of concern. In diagnostic teaching, the evaluator/teacher uses informal measures to determine how the student learns best; that is, how she responds to particular teaching modes or techniques.

For example, to determine how Jamilla best learns spelling words, Ms. Steiner would select a list of 30 spelling words that were all similar in rule-base, structure, and difficulty (i.e., at Jamilla's instructional reading level). Ms. Steiner would print the words on individual flash cards, to serve as the stimulus for her practice spelling sessions. After making sure that Jamilla could read all of the words, Ms. Steiner would divide the flash cards into three random groups of 10 words. To practice the first group of spelling words, Jamilla would write each word 10 times on a piece of notebook paper. Jamilla would practice the second group of words by spelling each word 10 times aloud to a peer or dictating them into a tape recorder. For the third group of words, Jamilla would draw each word 10 times in a box of damp sand. When the three different practice sessions had been completed, Ms. Steiner would test Jamilla on the list of 30 words—following the usual classroom format for spelling tests—and then examine her performance on each set of words to see if there was a difference between the number of words learned in the written, verbal/auditory, and tactile practice sessions. Ms. Steiner could then use this information to select the most effective mode of instruction for Jamilla to practice her spelling words in the future.

Diagnostic probes incorporate teaching into the assessment process, making it performance-based and linking it directly to a specific classroom or district curricula. This type of assessment may be particularly useful with students from varied cultural backgrounds who may not have been exposed to the types of problems or tasks found on many standardized tests, or for students who typically do not perform well on high-stakes tests. Combining diagnostic teaching with a student interview can contribute substantially to developing an understanding of the way a student thinks and processes information, as well as understanding different problem-solving approaches used by the student.

THE ASSESSMENT PROCESS

As discussed at the beginning of this chapter, teachers and other professionals use assessment for a variety of purposes. Regardless of its purpose, however, the assessment process is comprised of a series of equally important steps that must be considered when completing any evaluation. Figure 2-5 shows the steps involved in the assessment process, as it is described in this book; Figure 2-6 reproduces the language of IDEA 2004 regarding the procedural requirements related to the special education evaluation process.

The assessment process should have an "outcomes-based" focus. **Outcomes-based measurement** means that the assessment itself must be meaningful and directly related to the information needed for the desired end product or outcome (i.e., student learning). Outcomes-based assessment involves probing, teaching and evaluating the skills that are important to real-life situations for the student (Waterman, 1994).

Step	Description
1	Clarify the referral question(s)
2	Use multiple information sources
3	Develop a list of preliminary strengths and concerns
4	Collect/design the assessment package
5	Collect and analyze data
6	Synthesize and interpret results

FIGURE 2–5   Steps in the Diagnostic Assessment Process

Determining Eligibility for Special Education Services

Diagnostic assessment is part of the complete special education referral process mandated by IDEA. While the initial referral by the parents or teachers may include a variety of concerns, diagnostic assessment illuminates and clarifies the student's strengths and deficiencies and provides the data necessary to make an eligibility determination. By law, the assessment phase of an EBD referral must include the following elements: (a) informed parental consent for the evaluation; (b) a variety of tests designed not only to focus on the specific educational concerns in the referral but also on any cognitive, behavioral, emotional, or physical limitations that affect a diagnosis of a disability; (c) competent test examiners; (d) full interpretation of the test results and observations by the evaluation team; and (e) a meeting between the students, parents, teachers, and evaluators to discuss programming options.

IDEA describes the procedural safeguards required as part of the diagnostic assessment process. The tests must be evaluated as being (a) relevant to the student and to the student's situation, (b) culturally and racially unbiased, and (c) provided in the student's native language or the language most likely to yield useful performance data. Test administrators must understand not only how to administer the test, but also must be familiar with the testing background of the student. It should also be noted that parental consent for the assessment does not imply parental consent for the recommended placement/outcome from the results of the diagnostic assessment. Educators must obtain parental consent for initiation of services separately.

Evaluation Procedures

(1) NOTICE—The local education agency shall provide notice to the parents of a child with a disability, in accordance with subsections (b) (3), (b) (4), and (c) of section 615, (1415) that describes any evaluation procedures such agency proposes to conduct.

(2) CONDUCT OF EVALUATION—In conducting the evaluation, the local educational agency shall—
    (A) use a variety of assessment tools and strategies to gather relevant functional, developmental, and academic information, including information provided by the parent, that may assist in determining—
        (i) whether the child is a child with a disability, and
        (ii) the content of the child's individualized education program, including information related to enabling the child to be involved in and progress in the general education curriculum, or for preschool children, to participate in appropriate activities;
    (B) not use any single measure or assessment as the sole criterion for determining whether a child is a child with a disability or determining an appropriate educational program for the child; and
    (C) use technically sound instruments that may assess the relative contribution of cognitive and behavioral factors, in addition to physical or developmental factors.

(3) ADDITIONAL REQUIREMENTS—Each local agency shall ensure that—
    (A) assessments and other evaluation materials used to assess a child under this section—
        (i) are selected and administered so as not to be discriminatory on a racial or cultural basis;
        (ii) are provided and administered in the language and form most likely to yield accurate information on what the child knows and can do academically, developmentally, and functionally, unless it is not feasible to so provide or administer;
        (iii) are used for purposes for which the assessments or measures are valid and reliable;
        (iv) are administered by trained and knowledgeable personnel; and
        (v) are administered in accordance with any instructions provided by the producer of such instruments;
    (B) the child is assessed in all areas of suspected disability;
    (C) assessment tools and strategies that provide relevant information that directly assists persons in determining the educational needs of the child are provided; and
    (D) assessments of children with disabilities who transfer from one school district to another school district in the same academic year are coordinated with such children's prior and subsequent schools, as necessary and expeditiously as possible, to ensure prompt completion of full evaluations.

(4) DETERMINATION OF ELIGIBILITY AND EDUCATIONAL NEED—Upon completion of the administration of assessments and other evaluation measures—
    (A) the determination of whether the child is a child with a disability as defined in section 602(3) (1401(3)) and the educational needs of the child shall be made by a team of qualified professionals and the parent of the child in accordance with paragraph (5); and
    (B) a copy of the evaluation report and the documentation of determination of eligibility shall be given to the parent.

(5) SPECIAL RULE FOR ELIGIBILITY DETERMINATION—In making a determination of eligibility under paragraph (4)(A), a child shall not be determined to be a child with a disability if the determinant factor for such determination is—
    (A) lack of appropriate instruction in reading, including the essential components of reading instruction (as defined in section 1208(3) of the Elementary and Secondary School Act of 1965);
    (B) lack of instruction in math; or
    (C) limited English proficiency.

FIGURE 2–6 IDEA 2004: Evaluation Procedures
Source: IDEA 2004, 20 U.S.C. § 1414 (b) (1–5).

Steps in the Diagnostic Assessment Process

The diagnostic assessment process is complex, and often involves the participation of multiple team members to gather and synthesize information, and to administer and interpret test results. It is, therefore, important for all members of the assessment team to follow a consistent, agreed-upon sequence of steps to make sure all necessary activities are carried out in a systematic, timely fashion.

Clarifying the Referral Question(s). The first step in the diagnostic assessment process is to determine what question or questions the evaluation plan will be designed to answer. The more refined and targeted the referral questions, the more efficient and effective the results of the assessment will be. It is essential to spend some time up front determining what skills/areas will be examined during the assessment, and how the information will be ultimately used. If, for example, the main focus of the diagnostic assessment is to determine whether a student is eligible for special education services in *any* of the mild-moderate categorical areas, broad questions about the student's academic performance and behavior in a classroom setting may be appropriate. If the question is whether the student qualifies as EBD, the question—and therefore the assessment strategy—is more focused. On the other hand, to obtain information the classroom teacher might use to determine where the student should begin in the grade-level math curriculum, the diagnostic assessment questions will address the scope and sequence of developmental math skills.

Using Multiple Information Sources. IDEA requires that special education eligibility decisions be based on more than one information source. This means that a student cannot be identified as having EBD based on the results of a single test or one individual's professional opinion. When conducting observations, administering tests, or interviewing critical stakeholders, it is essential to include a variety of individuals, settings, and sources in the design and implementation of the assessment process.

Developing a List of Preliminary Strengths and Concerns. Once the referral questions and information sources have been determined, it is time to develop a preliminary list of strengths and concerns for the student. This list should be related to the type of information desired from the assessment battery and should list specific facts about positive and negative aspects of the student's performance or abilities.

Selecting/Designing the Assessment Package. A multitude of commercially published tests and rating scales are available for inclusion in an assessment battery. In addition, as discussed previously, informal diagnostic probes and examiner-developed measures can enhance the quality of the assessment.

Guided by the referral questions, and using the preliminary list of strengths and concerns as a framework, select individual instruments to become part of the assessment battery. A variety of books can help evaluators identify the measures that will best address the needs of their individual student. Four useful references

for published assessment instruments are *Tests in Print VI* (Murphy, Plake, Impara, & Spies, 2002); *The Fifteenth Mental Measurements Yearbook* (Plake, Impara, & Spies, 2003); *A Consumer's Guide to Tests in Print* (Hammill, Brown, & Bryant, 1992); and *Test Critiques, Volumes I–X* (Sweetland & Keyser, 1984–1994).

When compiling an assessment battery, it is important to investigate how suitable a given test is for answering the particular referral questions, as well as its match with the characteristics of the specific student. (See the list of questions from the National Information Center for Children and Youth with Disabilities earlier in this chapter.) Give consideration to how similar the assessment formats are in relation to actual classroom tasks. Whenever assessment is being used to guide eligibility or placement decisions, instruments must be individually, not group, administered.

Collecting and Analyzing Data. This phase of the diagnostic assessment process involves administering and scoring tests, conducting observations and interviews, and implementing diagnostic teaching or other informal assessment strategies. Once data collection has begun, it is important to follow a predetermined schedule to avoid confounding factors such as a change in the student's instructional environment, maturation due to the passage of time, changes in the home environment, and/or other unknown circumstances. During data collection and analysis, the examiner simply gathers information and records the results. Results should not be interpreted and predictions should not be made about a student's performance until administration of the assessment package is completed.

Synthesizing and Interpreting Results. The synthesis and interpretation of assessment results depends heavily upon the experience and skills of those involved in the diagnostic assessment process. Collaboration is essential at this point in the process and how well examiners work together as a team—pooling findings and discussing implications—will determine the success or failure of the process. A case manager or team leader should oversee the diagnostic assessment process and compile the relevant data into a final report detailing the results of the evaluation. All professionals responsible for any aspect of the assessment should prepare a written report on their findings or be prepared to present this information orally to the case manager for inclusion in the final diagnostic summary. During the interpretation phase, results should be discussed not simply in terms of numbers and scores but also should include the implications that can be drawn from these data. Educational recommendations and insights of the team should also be discussed in objective, practical language. According to Waterman (1994),

> It is very important that each report be stated in a way that allows others on the team, including parents and teachers, to understand what was found, what the results mean, and what the professional recommends. The use of specialized, technical vocabulary—jargon—often obscures meaning and should be avoided or explained in lay terms. (p. 22)

Once compiled, the final evaluation summary should be accompanied by relevant copies of the test protocols and observation notes to allow professionals encountering this data in the future to clearly understand the scores, context, and interpretation.

Assessment for Instructional Planning

When assessment is used for instructional planning, the focus of the process shifts from diagnostic to prescriptive. **Prescriptive measurement** is evaluation designed to be translated directly into classroom practice. The teacher is often the primary examiner in this type of assessment, with the purpose of gaining detailed information about student performance that can be incorporated into weekly goals and objectives. The teacher can use the resulting objectives to develop daily lesson plans and student activities. While diagnostic assessment for eligibility determination may include measures that yield information applicable to classroom interventions, the use of assessment data in daily instruction will be covered in greater detail in Chapter 3.

OTHER CONSIDERATIONS IN THE ASSESSMENT PROCESS

Whether assessment is intended to be diagnostic or for instructional planning, IEP team members must consider individual student characteristics in selecting, administering, and interpreting formal and informal measures. These considerations include student learning traits and preferences as well as cultural factors that may influence assessment. Special care must also be taken when assessing very young children suspected of having EBD or students who may have both EBD and a developmental delay. In all cases, the team must follow the ethical standards of the profession as established by the Council for Exceptional Children (2003).

Identifying Student Learning Traits

Student learning traits are those individual characteristics that provide "insight into the manner in which facts, information, and concepts are acquired and used" (Myles, Constant, Simpson, & Carlson, 1989, p. 11). Examining these factors as part of the assessment process allows a unique look into *how* a student learns and performs in addition to determining *what* the student knows. Learning traits assessment involves the creation of examiner-designed probes to look at specific areas of performance and problem solving. These areas include: (a) how the student approaches tasks and uses information from her environment (learning styles); (b) interpersonal skills and stressors that affect the student's behavior (behavioral patterns); (c) the way a student manipulates, stores, and retrieves information from memory (strategies); (d) the student's need for structure in academic and social situations (environmental predictability); and (e) the individual regulation of behavior/emotional issues (Myles & Adreon, 2001).

Analysis of the various environmental factors and learner characteristics that influence performance provides a valuable addition to information gained from formal and informal assessment. According to the National Information Center for Children and Youth with Disabilities (NICHCY), many of these factors should be considered during the assessment process. Sample questions include:

* In what physical environment does the student learn best?
* What is useful, debilitating, or neutral about the way the student approaches a task?
* Can the student hold multiple pieces of information in memory and then act upon them?
* How does increasing or slowing the speed of instruction impact upon the students accuracy?
* What processing mechanisms are being taxed in any given task?
* How does this student interact with a certain teacher style?
* With whom has the student been successful? What about this person seems to have contributed to the student's success?
* What is encouraging to the student? What is discouraging?
* How does manipulating the mode of teaching (e.g., visual or auditory presentation) affect the student's performance? (Waterman, 1994, pp. 9–10)

Assessing Students from Diverse Backgrounds

IDEA provides guidelines for nondiscriminatory testing that, along with careful selection of appropriate assessment measures, can assist in reducing the possibility of biased referrals, assessment results, and eligibility decisions. However, although eliminating all bias from assessment is impossible, the likelihood of bias increases when the student in question is from a different culture than the majority, the referring teacher, or the examiner, or when the student has limited proficiency in English. This is particularly true when using measures that are, by their very nature, subjective (e.g., interviews, rating scales, sociometric measures), or when professional judgment is a component of the eligibility decision, such as it is for EBD. Teachers may interpret student behaviors and academic performance through the lens of their own experiences, rather than through comparison to the norms of the student's cultural or racial identity. As a result of the ongoing concerns regarding the overrepresentation of minority students in special education, IDEA 2004 included a requirement that states must implement "policies and procedures designed to prevent the inappropriate overidentification or disproportionate representation by race and ethnicity" (20 U.S.C. § 1412 [24]).

Townsend (2002) recommends the following strategies for culturally responsive teaching and assessment:

- Interpret standardized test scores in conjunction with authentic assessments, such as portfolios and curriculum-based measures.
- Employ a strengths-based model of assessment that is linked closely to the classroom instructional process.
- Establish academic expectations and instructional strategies that are consistent with students' actual abilities (e.g., critical thinking skills), rather than based on stereotypical assumptions regarding the impact of the students' ethnicity, gender, and social class (e.g. assuming that all African-American males need direct, remedial instruction in basic academic subjects or that girls will do more poorly in upper-level math courses).
- Become familiar with the process of racial identity development for the children with whom you work.
- Employ strategies that minimize test preoccupation and anxiety.

Assessing Young Children with Emotional/Behavioral Problems

As alluded to earlier in this chapter, the assessment of young children with emotional and behavioral problems is particularly difficult. Drotar (2002) describes several challenges to early identification and intervention. First, although it has long been accepted that early intervention provides the best potential for preventing serious disorders later in life, or for limiting their impact on functioning, there is a general reluctance to identify young children's behavior as problematic. Second, there is a dearth of empirical studies focused on addressing behavior and emotional problems during the early childhood years; most early intervention research has focused on addressing cognitive and academic delays. Third, the types of behavioral and emotional problems exhibited by young children do not fit into existing typologies or diagnostic systems (e.g., *The Diagnostic and Statistical Manual of Mental Disorders, DSM-IV-TR*).

Assessing Students with Lower Cognitive Skills

Some students served under the diagnostic category of EBD may have concomitant cognitive skill deficits, such as severe learning disabilities, autism, Rett syndrome, childhood disintegrative disorder, or mental retardation. Assessing these students may require using specialized tools, such as discrete trial training, nonverbal assessment, or evaluation of adaptive behavior skills. These types of assessment will be covered in more detail in Chapter 9 as part of the discussion of pervasive developmental disorders.

Standards and Ethics of Assessment

In all areas of special education, specific legal and professional standards for viable and ethical intervention exist to protect both the student and her family. Assessment is no exception. Plans for assessment, as well as the results of the assessment, must be kept confidential. These materials and the subsequent information gained from the assessment fall under the legal and ethical ordinances for confidentiality. Multicultural factors must also be addressed with attention paid to such issues as linguistic diversity, and testing students in their primary language and over culturally appropriate content. Additional precautions should be considered, including the following factors:

1. Educational assessment is a quasi-science. As with all social service fields, there are no specific, empirical tests that tell conclusively how smart a student is or what the potential achievement of that student might be. Unlike a medical blood test that can specifically determine the percentage of red blood cells in a person's body, an IQ test can be interpreted only within the bounds of knowledge held by experts in the field who developed the test. Although these test results are accepted as well-supported hypotheses, note that the scores are based on a statistical interpretation of the data and must be perceived with that element of uncertainty in mind.

2. Educational assessment involves a certain amount of inference, often referred to as clinical judgment. Clinical judgment adds an external, subjective dimension to the results of the assessment. How the examiner or observer reports and interprets a situation can and does influence the result. Although still important in the overall picture of a student's performance, this type of data is affected by the perspective and experience of the examiner.

3. All assessment involves error in measurement. This error is often taken into consideration for standardized or norm-referenced tests but may not be as clearly identified in other assessment tools. Whenever possible, scores from tests should be reported in ranges, rather than specific numbers, and data that are not comparable in status or method of collection should not be compared to one another.

> It is important to remember that all assessment involves error. What emerges from the assessment process is not a "true" picture of the student but, rather, a patchwork of pictures that have captured the student at various moments in time. The more comprehensively the assessment was conducted—sampling or observing student behavior in different settings at different times, consultation with the family, interviewing those involved with the student, administering tests, ecologically assessing the student's environments, and so on—the more comprehensive the picture of the student should be and the more informed decision making will be as well. (Waterman, 1994, p. 22)

CHAPTER SUMMARY

* Assessment is a vital component in the identification, diagnosis, and education of students with EBD. The process of assessment contributes to a multitude of decisions made on a daily basis regarding everything from a diagnosis of EBD to the content of tomorrow's social studies lesson. Governed by basic assumptions and driven by time-honored standards and ethics, the field of assessment continues to grow and contribute to the quality of service for students with exceptional learning needs. Techniques of record keeping, test administration, observation, interviewing, and rating behavioral and academic data are the job of many professionals involved in the education of students with EBD. Each practitioner has a duty to understand the basic types of assessment, the components that comprise a valid and reliable assessment package, and the importance of accurate interpretation of assessment results. The application of diagnostic assessment is a challenge requiring additional training and extensive practice going well beyond the scope of this chapter. The knowledge gained in this ongoing pursuit will benefit both teachers and students, raising the standard of quality educational services and outcomes-based instruction.

CHECK YOUR UNDERSTANDING

1. *True or False.* Basic assumptions in assessment outline the circumstances under which the test may or may not be appropriate or useful in a given situation.
2. *True or False.* Standardized or norm-referenced tests are scored by comparing a student's performance against an absolute criteria preset by the test publisher, school district, or teacher.
3. List three individuals who may be asked to complete a behavior rating scale during the course of a diagnostic assessment for a student with EBD.
4. According to Merrell (2001), which type of assessment is considered to be an "essential" best practice when developing a diagnostic assessment package?
5. Why would it be desirable to have direct observation data collected by more than one individual?
6. *True or False.* Interviews are an easy assessment tool to administer, as they may be conducted with little or no preparation.

7. *True or False.* Educators must receive specialized training to administer most common behavior rating scales.
8. What are two additional names used for the assessment process called "diagnostic teaching"?
9. List the six steps involved in the diagnostic assessment process.
10. *True or False.* All assessment involves error in measurement.

APPLICATION ACTIVITIES

1. In your own words, briefly describe each of the six steps in a quality diagnostic assessment.
2. Examine three of the commonly used behavior rating scales. Compare the norming samples, validity, and reliability information provided in the manuals.
3. Select a case study from Appendix A. Applying what you have learned about the types of assessment commonly used with students with EBD, describe which strategies and instruments you would consider in creating an assessment package for this student. Provide a brief rationale for the types you selected and eliminated.
4. Explore your state's policies and practices designed to reduce disproportionate referral and placement of ethnic and language minority students in special education.
5. Interview an evaluation team member about beliefs on "ethical practice" and "multicultural concerns" related to assessment. Provide examples of practices that demonstrate each of these concepts.
6. Using the form in Figure 2–4, interview a parent. Discuss the results with a peer.
7. Go to the Council for Exceptional Children's Web site at http://www.cec.sped.org/. Find the Code of Ethics and Standards of Practice page. Read the Code and summarize the responsibilities of special educators that relate to assessment and instruction of students with disabilities.

PART 2 EFFECTIVE CLASSROOM PRACTICES

3

TRANSLATING ASSESSMENT DATA INTO INDIVIDUALIZED INSTRUCTION

CHAPTER PREVIEW

CONNECTING TO THE CLASSROOM: *A Vignette*

Mrs. Findlay looked around the room from her seat at the small table. Jim's teacher Mr. Roberts was there, as was the counselor. They both said hello when Mrs. Findlay arrived, then went back to talking about a conference they both attended recently. Three other people came into the room as a group and sat down across the table. Two of the three smiled at Mrs. Findlay, then started talking quietly to each other; the third started leafing through a catalog. They all looked like teachers, and carried notebooks or stacks of important-looking papers, pencils, and coffee cups or soft drinks. Mrs. Findlay felt strange; she had brought only her purse. When the principal arrived a few minutes later, everyone sat at the table to start the conference. They went around the table, said their name, and identified their role on "the team." Mrs. Findlay wondered what team they were talking about. She just knew that Jim had been in trouble a lot this year, and his grades had dropped. A month or so back, she had received a letter saying they wanted to give Jim some tests to see what his problem was. The next thing she got was an invitation to this meeting. In addition to Jim's teacher, counselor, and the principal, the other three people were a special education teacher, the district's special education director, and the school psychologist. The school psychologist went over the list of tests that Jim had taken and the scores he had received, using a lot of numbers and professional-sounding words that Mrs. Findlay had never heard before. Then he said, "After reviewing the information gathered during the assessment process, the team has determined that Jim is eligible for special education in the category of emotional disturbance." After that, Mrs. Findlay hardly heard anything he said, but it had something to do with an IEP. (What is an IEP? Emotional disturbance? Were they saying Jim was crazy?) She thought he was just having a bad year; it had never occurred to Mrs. Findlay that her son might have a disability.

TRANSLATING ASSESSMENT DATA INTO INSTRUCTIONAL PRACTICE: THE IEP AND THE BIP

The process that began in Chapter 2 with referral and assessment of students for special education evaluation continues in this chapter with determining eligibility, conducting functional behavioral assessment, writing the IEP, and making placement decisions. This chapter includes information concerning the legal requirements for those topics. However, because the purpose of this book is to prepare teachers to work with students who have emotional/behavioral disorders (EBD), the strategies and techniques described focus primarily on addressing the affective and behavioral needs of this population of students rather than on identifying and remediating academic skill deficits.

Determining Eligibility

Based on the results of a special education evaluation, a team of qualified professionals must determine whether the student is eligible for special education. The eligibility process includes examining the student's records and work samples, the results of formal and informal assessments, data from classroom observations, and information from interviews with parents, teachers, and the student. The team may find the student eligible if he meets the criteria for one or more categories of special education as defined in the Individuals with Disabilities Education Act (IDEA, 1997, 2004), *and* the team believes he requires special education and related services. However, if the team believes the disability is primarily a result of lack of instruction in reading or math, or lack of proficiency in English, he cannot be found eligible. See Figure 3-1 for the federal definition of EBD contained

in the IDEA 1997 regulations (published in 1999). Figure 3-2 describes the process of determining eligibility for special education specified in the IDEA 2004 reauthorization.

As discussed at length in Chapter 1, the IDEA definition of emotional disturbance (ED) uses language that requires professional judgment or interpretation. For example, what is "a long period of time" or "to a marked degree"? Does the adverse educational impact mean that the student must be receiving failing grades or functioning below grade level?

Many states and local districts have provided additional guidance for school teams making eligibility decisions. Therefore, it is necessary that at least one member of the team be familiar with the federal, state, and local regulations regarding special education eligibility. The most recent federal description of an IEP team's composition is contained in Figure 3-3, and the requirements for team member attendance are listed in Figure 3-4.

If, after careful consideration of all the evidence, the team members agree that a student is eligible under the IDEA category of emotional disturbance, they must schedule a meeting to develop an individualized education program (IEP). The 1997 IDEA federal timeline required that this initial IEP meeting be conducted within 30 days of the determination of eligibility. The 2004 reauthorization of IDEA specifies that the eligibility determination decision be made within 60 days of the initial referral for assessment, or within the guidelines established by the state (20 U.S.C. § 1414 [C] [i] [II]). Thus, depending on state guidelines, this may allow school teams up to 90 days to gather additional data necessary to determine the student's present level of performance; conduct formal and informal assessments, observations and interviews; and complete a functional behavioral assessment (FBA). Often, the team may need the additional time because the data needed to determine

---

(i)　The term means a condition exhibiting one or more of the following characteristics over a long period of time and to a marked degree that adversely affects a child's educational performance:

　　(A)　An inability to learn that cannot be explained by intellectual, sensory, or health factors.

　　(B)　An inability to build or maintain satisfactory interpersonal relationships with peers and teachers.

　　(C)　Inappropriate types of behavior or feelings under normal circumstances.

　　(D)　A general pervasive mood of unhappiness or depression.

　　(E)　A tendency to develop physical symptoms or fears associated with personal or school problems.

(ii)　The term includes schizophrenia. The term does not apply to children who are socially maladjusted, unless it is determined that they have an emotional disturbance.

FIGURE 3–1　IDEA Regulations § 300.7: Child with a Disability—Emotionally Disturbed
Source: 34 C.F.R. § 300.7 [b] [4].

(4) DETERMINATION OF ELIGIBILITY AND EDUCATIONAL NEED—Upon completion of the administration of assessments and other evaluation measures—

    A. the determination of whether the child is a child with a disability as defined in section 602 (3) (1401 (3)) and the educational needs of the child shall be made by a team of qualified professionals and the parent of the child in accordance with paragraph (5); and

    B. a copy of the evaluation report and the documentation of determination of eligibility shall be given to the parent.

(5) SPECIAL RULE FOR ELIGIBILITY DETERMINATION—In making a determination of eligibility under paragraph (4) (A), a child shall not be determined to be a child with a disability if the determinant factor for such determination is—

    A. a lack of appropriate instruction in reading, including in the essential components of reading instruction (as defined in section 1208 (3) of the Elementary and Secondary Education Act of 1965);

    B. lack of instruction in math; or

    C. limited English proficiency.

FIGURE 3–2   IDEA 2004: Eligibility Determination

Source: IDEA 2004, 20 U.S.C. § 1414 (b) (4–5).

---

(1) DEFINITIONS—In this tittle:

  (A) INDIVIDUALIZED EDUCATIONAL PROGRAM—

    (i) IN GENERAL—The term 'individualized education program' or 'IEP' means a written statement for each child with a disability that is developed, reviewed, and revised in accordance with this section and that includes—

      (I) a statement of the child's present levels of academic achievement and functional performance, including—

        (aa) how the child's disability affects the child's involvement and progress in the general education curriculum;

        (bb) for preschool children, as appropriate, how the disability affects the child's participation in appropriate activities; and

        (cc) for children with disabilities who take alternate assessments aligned to alternate achievement standards, a description of benchmarks or short-term objectives;

      (II) a statement of measurable annual goals, including academic and functional goals, designed to—

        (aa) meet the child's needs that result from the child's disability to enable the child to be involved in and make progress in the general education curriculum; and

        (bb) meet each of the child's other educational needs that result from the child's disability;

      (III) a description of how the child's progress toward meeting the annual goals described in subclause (II) will be measured and when periodic reports on the progress the child is making toward meeting the annual goals (such as through the use of quarterly or other periodic reports, concurrent with the issuance of report cards) will be provided;

      (IV) a statement of the special education and related services and supplementary aids and services, based on peer-reviewed research to the extent practicable, to be provided to the child, or on behalf of the child, and a statement of the program modifications or supports for school personnel that will be provided for the child—

        (aa) to advance appropriately toward attaining the annual goals;

        (bb) to be involved in and make progress in the general education curriculum in accordance with subclause (I) and to participate in extracurricular and other nonacademic activities; and

        (cc) to be educated and participate with other children with disabilities and nondisabled children in the activities described in this subparagraph;

      (V) an explanation of the extent, if any, to which the child will not participate with nondisabled children in the regular class and in the activities described in subclause (IV) (cc);

      (VI) (aa) a statement of any individual appropriate accommodations that are necessary to measure the academic achievement and functional performance of the child on State and districtwide assessments consistent with section 612 (a) (16) (A); and

        (bb) if the IEP Team determines that the child shall take an alternate assessment on a particular State or districtwide assessment of student achievement, a statement of why—

      (VII) the projected date for the beginning of the services and modifications described in subclause (IV), and the anticipated frequency, location, and duration of those services and modifications.

FIGURE 3–3   IDEA 2004: Individualized Education Programs

Source: IDEA 2004, 20 U.S.C. § 1414 (1) (A).

(A) INDIVIDUALIZED EDUCATIONAL PROGRAM TEAM—The term 'individualized education program team' or 'IEP Team' means a group of individuals composed of—

    (i) the parents of a child with a disability;

    (ii) not less than 1 regular education teacher of such child (if the child is, or may be, participating in the regular education environment

    (iii) not less than 1 special education teacher, or where appropriate, not less than 1 special education provider of such child;

    (iv) a representative of the local education agency who—

        (I) is qualified to provide, or supervise the provision of, specially designed instruction to meet the unique needs of children with disabilities;

        (II) is knowledgeable about the general education curriculum; and

        (III) is knowledgeable about the availability of resources of the local educational agency;

    (v) an individual who can interpret the instructional implications of evaluation results, who may be a member of the team described in clauses (ii) through (vi);

    (vi) at the discretion of the parent or the agency, other individuals who have knowledge or special expertise regarding the child, including related services personnel as appropriate; and

    (vii) whenever appropriate, the child with a disability.

(B) IEP TEAM ATTENDANCE—

    (i) ATTENDANCE NOT NECESSARY—A member of the IEP Team shall not be required to attend an IEP meeting, in whole or in part, if the parent of a child with a disability and the local educational agency agree that the attendance of such member is not necessary because the member's area of the curriculum or related services is not being modified or discussed in the meeting.

    (ii) EXCUSAL—A member of the IEP Team may be excused from attending an IEP meeting, in whole or in part, when the meeting involves a modification to or discussion of the member's area of the curriculum or related services, if—

        (I) the parent and the local educational agency consent to the excusal; and

        (II) the member submits, in writing to the parent and the IEP Team, input into the development of the IEP prior to the meeting.

    (iii) WRITTEN AGREEMENT AND CONSENT REQUIRED—A parent's agreement under clause (i) and consent under clause (ii) shall be in writing.

FIGURE 3–4   IDEA 2004: IEP Teams and Attendance
Source: IDEA 2004, 20 U.S.C. § 1414 (1) (B–C).

eligibility and arrive at a categorical label of EBD does not provide sufficient information to develop an appropriate, individualized program. "A multimillion dollar testing industry has developed around the simple decision of whether a student is or is not eligible for services within the federal or state definition of EBD. Yet such data, painstakingly gathered by school psychologists and others on the multidisciplinary team, tell us nothing about the instructional or social-emotional needs of a student" (Cessna & Skiba, 1996, p. 118).

Establishing the Present Level of Performance

For students identified with EBD, the team must determine the present level of performance in academic and functional areas that are affected by the disability. This information is often available from results of special education evaluation, schoolwide assessments, and from classroom records and work samples. The 2004

Amendments to IDEA specified additional areas, called special factors, that must be considered during IEP development for students with exceptional needs. For students whose behavior interferes with their own education, or that of other students, IDEA requires implementation of positive behavioral strategies, supports, and interventions (see Figure 3-5).

Functional Behavioral Assessment (FBA). For students with EBD, functional behavioral assessment (FBA) can be an important part of assessing the present level of performance, as well as the response to different types of intervention. Information gained from a thorough FBA allows IEP teams to develop interventions that are data-driven and more likely to succeed. Although success of FBA has been well documented with students with severe disabilities and in clinical settings, it is relatively new to public school educators. Few studies have been conducted with milder, high-frequency behaviors, or with low-frequency, high-intensity behaviors in

(3) DEVELOPMENT OF IEP—
(A) In general—In developing each child's IEP, the IEP Team, subject to subparagraph (C), shall consider—
    (i)   the strengths of the child;
    (ii) the concerns of the parents for enhancing the education of their child;
    (iii) the results of the initial evaluation or most recent evaluation of the child; and
    (iv) the academic, developmental, and functional needs of the child.
(B) CONSIDERATION OF SPECIAL FACTORS—The IEP Team shall—
    (i)   In the case of a child whose behavior impedes the child's learning or that of others, consider the use of positive behavioral interventions and supports, and other strategies, to address that behavior.

FIGURE 3–5   IDEA 2004: Development of IEP and Special Factors

Source: IDEA 2004, 20 U.S.C. § 1414 (d) (3) (A–Bi).

SIDEBAR 3–1

Defining FBA

Functional behavioral assessment (FBA) is the process of gathering information, identifying patterns of behavior, and generating hypotheses about the functions of behavior.

Functional analysis is the process of hypothesis testing, and manipulating antecedents and consequences to determine the impact on the target behavior.

general education classroom settings (Doggett, Edwards, Moore, Tingstrom, & Wilczynski, 2001; Lewis & Sugai, 1996; Nelson, Roberts, Mathur, & Rutherford, 1999). A review of 100 articles published between 1980 and 1999 (Ervin et al., 2001) found that FBA had successfully identified variables that predicted high-frequency problem behaviors. However, very few of those studies used FBA to examine academic behaviors. The interventions and studies were generally conducted by clinicians or consultants rather than school personnel, and minimal information was provided concerning how acceptable the interventions were to teachers, parents, and students.

A more recent review (Reid & Nelson, 2002) specifically focused on FBA use with students exhibiting high-incidence problem behaviors in school settings. The authors found 14 articles and summarized the results as follows:

- Utility/Effectiveness—Most problem behaviors were related to attention or escape, and often to difficulty of academic demands. Two studies demonstrated only slight improvements; the remainder showed pronounced improvements, and seven (50%) of the projects reduced inappropriate

behavior to nearly zero, and increased appropriate behavior to nearly 100%.
- Acceptability—Only 4 of the 14 studies reported social validity data, which was a concern for the authors. "If the results of FBA in terms of behavior change are not viewed as meaningful improvements or if the FBA process itself is viewed as intrusive, aversive, or impractical, then it is unlikely to be widely accepted or practiced" (p. 17).
- Practicality—Teacher participation was limited in the 14 studies. The interventions were generally developed and implemented by clinicians or consultants.

Teachers have expressed some resistance to trying FBA due to the perception that it is a complicated and extremely time-consuming process (Conroy & Davis, 2000; Quinn, 2000). Therefore, if teachers are expected to implement FBA and develop appropriate interventions, they will need simple, easy-to-follow procedures and systematic training. Teachers and team members serving as behavior analysts need to be familiar with the techniques associated with applied behavioral assessment, direct and indirect assessment, data analysis, behavior management strategies, and curricular strategies to teach functionally equivalent replacement behaviors (Shellady & Stichter, 1999).

In the school-based FBA process, parents have been a forgotten group of stakeholders. Peterson, Derby, Berg, & Horner (2002) point out that parents seldom have been involved in FBA. When parents were consulted, it was usually at the hypothesis-generation phase; however, their assistance in hypothesis and intervention testing should be considered as well. This may be particularly true if the problem behavior occurs at home, with the parent providing the stimulus and/or consequence. When this is the case, it seems logical to implement the intervention at home, as well as at school.

Rationale for Using FBA in Developing IEPs. Three aspects of FBA make it useful for teams that want to develop effective classroom strategies: (1) FBA can identify important variables that explain why a target behavior occurs or does not occur in specific circumstances; (2) FBA can identify antecedents and consequences that appear to control the expression of the target behavior; and (3) FBA can identify the function or purpose a target behavior or class of behaviors serves for a specific individual (Reid & Nelson, 2002). Thus, according to Sterling-Turner, Robinson, and Wilczynski (2001), "FBAs eliminate 'shot-in-the-dark' (or trial-and-error) interventions that are based solely upon the topography of the problem without regard to function and may reduce the number of components in treatment packages needed to resolve the problem" (p. 221). Focusing strictly on the form or topography of the behavior—what the behavior looks or sounds like—is unlikely to lead to effective interventions. Research has demonstrated that interventions based on an FBA are more likely to be effective and durable over time (Asmus, Vollmer, & Borrero, 2002; Quinn, Gable, Rutherford, Nelson, & Howell, 1998). Ervin and colleagues (2001) found that FBA interventions were even more durable if they were paired with instruction of replacement behaviors.

Functional behavioral assessment is also a legal requirement for certain students. The 1997 amendments to IDEA require FBAs for students whose behavior impedes the learning of self or others; for students with IEPs who are suspended in excess of 10 school days, constituting a change of placement; or for students placed in an interim alternate educational setting because of behavior that is dangerous to self and others or is related to weapons or drugs (IDEA, 20 U.S.C. § 1414 [d] [3] [B] [i]). This would include: (a) disruptive behaviors that interfere with teaching and learning, (b) noncompliant behaviors, (c) verbal and physical aggressive or abusive behaviors, and (d) behaviors resulting in the destruction of property (Drasgow & Yell, 2001; Drasgow, Yell, Bradley, & Shriner, 1999).

Various definitions and procedures have been published to guide practitioners through a systematic, step-by-step FBA process, linking assessment to intervention (e.g., Conroy & Davis, 2000; Dunlap & Kern, 1993; Dunlap et al., 1993; Kaplan, 2000; Quinn et al., 1998). Although this chapter advocates using FBA proactively, as part of the IEP-development process, the same sequence and procedures would be appropriate for an FBA conducted as part of a disciplinary action.

FBA Step I: Conduct Environmental Assessment and Review Existing Data. The first task in conducting an FBA is to assess the ecology of the student's problem behaviors. First, examine the physical classroom setting. How is the classroom organized? Where and by whom is the student seated? How does the seating arrangement allow student access to the teacher and teacher supervision of the target student?

Second, consider the instructional management aspects of the room. Is the schedule clearly defined and followed? Are rules and routines taught, practiced, prompted, and enforced? Is unstructured or "down" time kept to a minimum? Does the teacher provide a higher rate of positively reinforcing statements than punishing? How are instructional activities paced and sequenced?

Next, review classroom records. Can you discern a pattern in the student's appropriate or inappropriate behavior? Do behavior problems tend to occur at specific times of day, during specific activities, or when specific adults or peers are present? What happens when specific demands or requests are made? Do specific antecedent events trigger the student's behavior in a predictable fashion (Axelrod, 2003)? Finally, conduct interviews with significant individuals—including teachers, parents, and the student—to determine whether they see patterns of behavior.

A number of published instruments are available to assist teachers in collecting data. They can be classified into two general groups: indirect or informant assessment (e.g., interviews and checklists) and direct or descriptive assessment (e.g., direct observation and data collection). Figure 3-6 provides a representative sample of measures used in recent FBA studies.

FBA Step II: Identify and Define Prioritized Behavior. Once the initial data has been gathered, the team must next define specific target behaviors, and prioritize them

Center for Effective Collaboration and Practice. This Web site features a miniweb focused on functional behavioral assessment. Resources include a three-part series available as downloadable pdf files: (I) An IEP team's introduction to functional behavioral assessment and behavior intervention plans, (II) Conducting a functional behavioral assessment, and (III) Creating positive behavioral intervention plans and supports. Low-cost videos are also available, and a trainer's guide and discussion board are planned. Available at http://cecp.air.org/fba/default.asp.

Center for Evidence-Based Practice: Young Children with Challenging Behavior. This Web site, hosted by the University of South Florida, provides information and links to resources of a variety of evidence-based practice. For young children with challenging behavior, this site provides instructions and data-collection forms designed to conduct FBA. Available at http://challengingbehavior.fmhi.usf.edu/fba.htm.

Chandler, L. K., & Dahlquist, C. M. (2002). *Functional assessment strategies to prevent and remediate challenging behavior in school settings*. Upper Saddle River, NJ: Merrill/Prentice Hall. This book provides detailed information on the use of functional assessment and intervention strategies for use with individual or class-wide behavioral challenges. It includes numerous case examples.

Kaplan, J. S. (2000). *Beyond functional assessment: A social-cognitive approach to the evaluation of behavior problems in children and youth*. Austin, TX: Pro-Ed. The book provides information to supplement traditional environmental analysis and assist teachers in developing more effective behavior intervention plans and IEPs. Includes assessment strategies, performance objectives, and forms for data collection.

Liaupsin, C. J., Scott, T. M., & Nelson, C. M. (2001). *Functional behavior assessment: An interactive training module*. These CD-ROM–based training materials provide instruction in FBA using a slide-show format, case studies, reproducible documents, and self-assessments. Available from Sopris West, at http://www.sopriswest.com.

McConnell, M. E. (2001). *Functional behavioral assessment: A systematic process for assessment and intervention in general and special education classrooms*. This book discusses team roles and responsibilities in the FBA process. It includes numerous forms for data collection and analysis, as well as for development of behavioral intervention plans.

O'Neill, R. E., Horner, R. H., Albin, R. W., Storey, K., & Sprague, J. R. (1997). *Functional assessment and program development for problem behavior—A practical handbook* (2nd ed.). Pacific Grove, CA: Brooks/Cole Publishing. This book includes detailed information on strategies for conducting FBA, as well as for developing behavior support and intervention plans. It includes forms for interviews, observation, data collection, and summarization.

FIGURE 3–6   Sample FBA Resource List

to determine where to begin. The first part of the task is to identify the behaviors that interfere with student learning. These are the behaviors the team can target for decreasing or extinguishing. It is also important to identify those student behaviors that would be considered strengths and that the team would like to support or increase. The behaviors should be defined in terms that are clear, observable, and measurable. For example, calling a student aggressive is vague; describing the behavior as "kicking and hitting peers" is much more useful. In the vignette at the beginning of this chapter, the teacher might have said, "Jim mopes around all day, is as slow as molasses, and doesn't complete his work." While this is a colorful description, two different observers might not agree about what "moping" looked like, or how slow molasses really is. Does Jim's teacher really mean that he never completes his work? It would be difficult to go into the classroom and take data on this behavior. A better set of descriptors for Jim's behavior might be, "Several times each afternoon, Jim puts his head down on his desk, hides his face, and does not participate for 5 to 15 minutes at a stretch. When the teacher gives oral instructions, it takes Jim longer to start than his classmates. In the past two weeks, Jim has turned in 14 out of 24 assignments; 5 of the 14 he turned in were incomplete."

Once the student's problem behaviors and positive behaviors have been identified and defined, the next task is to rank the target behaviors in priority order. It is important not to target so many problems at once that the student or the teacher feels overwhelmed. Keep in mind that IEPs are generally written to cover one-year periods of time. Implementing several interventions at the same time also makes it difficult to tell which strategy resulted in any subsequent change in behavior.

There are several ways to think about structuring behavioral targets. Most teams choose to begin with behaviors that represent a safety risk or are dangerous to the student or others. The following five-point rubric provides teams with a simple way to weight the severity or relative disruption of a student's behavior:

Level 1: Behavior is confined only to the observed student. May include such behaviors as: refusal to follow directions, scowling, crossing arms, pouting, or muttering under his/her breath.

Level 2: Behavior disrupts others in the student's immediate area. May include: slamming textbook closed, dropping book on the floor, name calling, or using inappropriate language.

Level 3: Behavior disrupts everyone in the class. May include: throwing objects, yelling, open defiance of teacher directions, or leaving the classroom.

Level 4: Behavior disrupts *other* classrooms or common areas of the school. May include: throwing objects, yelling, open defiance of school personnel's directions, or leaving the school campus.

Level 5: Behavior causes or threatens to cause physical injury to student or others. May include: display of weapons, assault on others. (Gable, Quinn, Rutherford, Howell, & Hoffman, 1998, p. 13)

Sometimes the behaviors selected will fall into a logical hierarchy or sequential order. If one skill or behavior is a prerequisite for another, then it should be addressed first. The team may also want to determine whether behaviors are a skill deficit (i.e., the student doesn't possess the skill or know how to perform the required task), or a performance deficit (i.e., the student has the skill but does not use it consistently or appropriately).

Another way to rank behaviors is to determine the degree of impact each behavior has on the student's ability to be successful and select the ones that are likely to make the most significant improvement in the student's status. Kennedy (2002) has suggested a list of nine questions that teams may wish to consider in selecting and prioritizing behaviors for intervention:

1. Is behavior change demonstrated in typical settings?
2. Does the intervention promote movement into the least restrictive environment?
3. Is the intervention conducted by families and/or school and community personnel?
4. Is the person's entire day/week impacted by the intervention?
5. Is the intervention maintained over time?
6. Is the intervention enabling and skill building?
7. Is the recipient of the intervention happier?
8. Do secondary customers [parents, teachers] value the intervention?
9. Will taxpayers view the intervention as worthy of public funding? (pp. 145-150)

FBA Step III: Form Initial Functional Hypothesis and Identify Establishing Operations, Triggers, and Consequences. Developing a functional hypothesis involves making an informed guess, based on data, regarding the relationship between the target behavior and the most common environment or conditions under which it occurs. First, look back over the environmental assessment and classroom data. Determine when and where the target behavior is most likely or least likely to occur and what is going on when the behavior occurs or is absent. Identify critical environmental or setting variables. Try to identify antecedent events or triggers that typically precede the target behavior and consequences, reinforcers, and/or responses that generally occur immediately after the behavior. Antecedents or triggers can be a single event (e.g., a teacher request) or can include multiple factors, including environmental, interactional, or internal factors (sometimes called establishing operations). See Sidebar 3-2 for examples of potential triggers for common problem behaviors. If the team is not certain what factors are serving as triggers, set up a series of at least three systematic observations when the student is most likely to exhibit the target behavior and use the list in Sidebar 3-2 as a checklist.

ABC worksheets (A = Antecedent, B = Behavior, C = Consequence) and scatterplots provide a systematic, visual way to display your data. **ABC worksheets** allow an observer to describe what happened immediately before or after the target behavior, putting it in a context that allows patterns to emerge under visual examination. ABC analysis often serves as a prelude to more targeted or refined behavior observation procedures. The team can use a **scatterplot** to find patterns of behavior by identifying how often, and under what conditions, target behaviors occur in a series of targeted observations. Observers can record scatterplot data using frequency-count or time-sampling techniques (described in Chapter 2, Figure 2-3, pp. 29-30). Figures 3-7, Figure 3-8, and Figure 3-9 (pp. 52-57) provide examples of ABC observation forms and scatterplots.

In addition to visually examining scatterplots and ABC charts to identify patterns, frequency count data obtained from these data collection sheets can be used to compute the probability that a behavior will occur in a given situation. To do this with the ABC chart data, divide the total number of target behaviors (B) that occur with specific antecedents (A) or consequences (C) by the total number of target behaviors (B) observed. For example, the team has selected Jim's off-task behavior (putting head on arms, hiding face, not working) as the first intervention target. You observe Jim

Potential Triggers for Problem Behavior

Environmental Factors:

* Crowded space
* Uncomfortable temperature
* Lack of organization
* Change in schedule

Interactional Factors:

* Demand delivered in hostile tone
* Denial or delay of reinforcer
* Student's behavior is ignored

* Another student's behavior is reinforced
* Boring or difficult tasks
* Teacher reprimand or correction

Internal/Individual Factors (Establishing Operations):

* Illness
* Hunger
* Pain
* Exhaustion

Source: Based on Axelrod, S. (2003). Adapted with permission.

---

for 30 minutes on three different days during different subjects and count the number of times he puts his head down, using ABC charting to note what happens just before and after this action. The results are 16 observed instances of the target behavior, 11 during pencil-paper tasks. Compute the probability that this setting demand is a trigger for Jim's off-task behavior:

$$11 \div 16 = .69 \times 100 = 69\%$$

So there is about a 69% or two-thirds probability that the function of Jim's behavior is related to something about the pencil-paper tasks. You can use a similar formula and process for duration or ratio data, as follows: divide the duration of the target behavior exhibited with specific antecedents or consequences by the total duration that the target behavior was displayed. This time, the team selected Jim's off-task behavior (putting head on arms, hiding face, not working), but was interested in the amount and percent of time Jim was off task. Jim was observed for three 30-minute periods. He was off task a total of 52 minutes, all during pencil-paper tasks.

$$52 \div 90 = .58 \times 100 = 58\%$$

However, Jim was sitting up in his seat and appeared to be participating for the remaining 38 minutes of the observation, which consisted of direct instruction and guided practice activities. Therefore, Jim was off task 58% of the time during the observation, but 100% of the time that was devoted to pencil-paper tasks.

To use scatterplot data, compute the percentage of the target behavior that occurred during each setting or demand condition. For example, using the scatterplot in Figure 3–8b (p. 55), you could determine the percentage of time that disruptions occurred on various days of the week or in specific classes. Using 3-9b (p. 57), you could determine how likely aggressive behavior was during reading activities compared to other situations, such as use of manipulatives.

Once the team has reached agreement on the pattern or patterns evident in the data, it is time to formulate the hypothesis about what function the behavior is serving for the student in that specific situation. Most behavior can be classified into two broad functional areas: behavior designed to *get* something or behavior designed to *avoid* something (Carr, 1977; Scott & Nelson, 1999). Carr (1977) proposed three underlying operant mechanisms that explained most problem behaviors: (1) positive reinforcement (the student gets something perceived as positive), (2) negative reinforcement (the student avoids something perceived as negative), and (3) sensory reinforcement (the student enjoys the sound, smell, taste, sight, or feel of something—also a form of positive reinforcement). The underlying function of behavior may also be a combination of more than one function, or an effort to communicate (for example, "I don't understand!") (Jolivette, Barton–Arwood, & Scott, 2000).

One way to format a functional behavioral hypothesis is as follows: "*[The behavior]* tends to occur when *[describe situation]*. It is less likely to occur when *[describe situation]*. It appears that the function of the behavior is to *[gain/avoid]*." Figure 3–10 (p. 58)

ABC OBSERVATION FORM

Student Name: _____   Observation Date: _____

Observer: _____   Time: _____

Activity: _____   Class Period: _____

Behavior: _____

ANTECEDENT	BEHAVIOR	CONSEQUENCE

FIGURE 3–7a   Sample ABC Observation Form

Source: © 1998, CECP. From Gable, R.A., Quinn, M. M., Rutherford, R. B., Howell, K. W., & Hoffman, C. C. (1998). *Addressing Student Problem Behavior Part II: Conducting a Functional Behavioral Assessment* (3rd ed.). Washington, DC: The Center for Effective Collaboration and Practice. (Reprinted with permission.) Available online at: http://www.air.org/cecp/fba/problembehavior2/Appendix%20B.pdf.

ABC OBSERVATION FORM

Student Name: _Trish_	Observation Date: _10/5_
Observer: _Ms. Pasillas_	Time: _9:40-9:55 a.m._
Activity: _disruptive behavior on the playground_	Class Period: _3_

ANTECEDENT	BEHAVIOR	CONSEQUENCE
Trish joins group of 4 girls playing catch.		
	Trish waits for ball to be thrown to her.	Girls do not throw ball to Trish.
	Trish yells "Throw it to me!"	Girls throw ball to her, she misses it and another girl, LuAnne catches it and throws it to Sandy.
Ball is again thrown to Karen.	Trish yells "I said throw it to me you jerk!"	
Karen begins to walk away with the ball.	Trish runs up behind Karen and kicks her saying "Give it to me damn it!"	Karen cries. Trish takes the ball.

FIGURE 3–7b Completed ABC Observation Form

Source: © 1998, CECP. From Gable, R. A., Quinn, M. M., Rutherford, R. B., Howell, K.W., & Hoffman, C. C. (1998). *Addressing Student Problem Behavior Part II: Conducting a Functional Behavioral Assessment* (3rd ed.). Washington, DC: The Center for Effective Collaboration and Practice. (Reprinted with permission.) Available online at: http://www.air.org/cecp/fba/problembehavior2/Appendix%20B.pdf.

Functional Assessment Scatterplot

Student: _____ Grade: _____ School: _____

Date(s): _____ Observer(s): _____

Behavior(s) of concern: _____

Setting: _____

ACTIVITY	TIME	DAY OF THE WEEK					TOTAL
		Monday	Tuesday	Wednesday	Thursday	Friday	
Total							

FIGURE 3–8a Sample Scatterplot

Source: © 1998, CECP. From Gable, R. A., Quinn, M. M., Rutherford, R. B., Howell, K. W., & Hoffman, C. C. (1998). *Addressing student problem behavior part II: Conducting a functional behavioral assessment* (3rd ed.). Washington, DC: The Center for Effective Collaboration and Practice. (Reprinted with permission.) Available online at: http://www.air.org/cecp/fba/problembehavior2/appendixa.htm.

Functional Assessment Scatterplot

Student: _Myree_   Grade: _6th_   School: _John B Lynn_

_10/4/97 to 10/8/97_   Observer(s): _Dennis_

Behavior(s) of concern: _disrupts class w/ inappropriate comments and verbal threats directed at peers._

Setting: _____

ACTIVITY	TIME	DAY OF THE WEEK					TOTAL
		Monday	Tuesday	Wednesday	Thursday	Friday	
Math	9:20-10:10	II	I ЖЖ ЖЖ	ЖЖ III	III	ЖЖ	29
Science	10:10-11:00	II	I	I	I		4
Social Studies	11:00-11:50		I				1
English	11:50-12:30	I	I ЖЖ	I ЖЖ		II	15
Lunch	12:30-1:00						0
Health/P.E.	1:00-1:50						0
Art	1:50-2:40						0
Total		5	18	15	4	7	49

FIGURE 3–8b   Completed Scatterplot Form

Source: © 1998, CECP. From Gable, R. A., Quinn, M. M., Rutherford, R. B., Howell, K. W., & Hoffman, C. C. (1998). *Addressing student problem behavior part II: Conducting a functional behavioral assessment* (3rd ed.). Washington, DC: The Center for Effective Collaboration and Practice. (Reprinted with permission.) Available online at: http://www.air.org/cecp/fba/problembehavior2/appendixa.htm.

Classroom Scatterplot

Student _____ Teacher _____ Observer(s) _____

Activity _____

No. of Students _____ Start Time _____ End Time _____ Date _____ Total _____

Observation Interval: 10 sec ____ 15 sec ____ 20 sec ____

Time Sampling Procedure: 1. Continuous Recording: ____ 2. Non-Continuous Recording (every ____ min.): ____ 3. Other: ____

Instructional Conditions	Appropriate Responses									Inappropriate Responses							
Phase *baseline*	Acad Talk	Answer Ques	Ask Ques	Atten	Task Partic	Read Aloud	Read Silent	Write	Other Appro.	Total	Aggress./ Disruptive	Off Task	Out of Seat	Non Compliance	Talk Out	Other Inappro.	Total Inappro.	Grand Total
Paper/Pencil																		
Listen-Lecture																		
Teacher-Pupil Discussion																		
Manipulatives																		
Inst. Games																		
Worksheets Workbook																		
Readers																		
Student-Student																		
Media/Tech Other																		
Transition																		
Other																		
Total																		

FIGURE 3–9a Sample Classroom Scatterplot

Source: © 1998, CECP. From Gable, R. A., Quinn, M. M., Rutherford, R. B., Howell, K. W., & Hoffman, C. C. (1998). *Addressing student problem behavior part II: Conducting a functional behavioral assessment (3rd ed.).* Washington, DC: The Center for Effective Collaboration and Practice. (Reprinted with permission.) Available online at: http://www.air.org/cecp/fba/problembehavior2/appendixa.htm.

Classroom Scatterplot

Student __Charles__   Teacher __Miller__   Observer(s) __Evans__

Activity _____

No. of Students __21__   Start Time __9:10__   End Time __9:55__   Date _____   Total __45 min.__

Observation Interval: 10 sec ____ 15 sec ____ 20 sec __X__

Time Sampling Procedure: 1. Continuous Recording: ____   2. Non-Continuous Recording (every ____ min.): __X__   3. Other: ____

Instructional Conditions (Phase baseline)	Appropriate Responses										Inappropriate Responses							
	Talk Acad	Answer Quea	Ask Quea	Atten	Task Partic.	Read Aloud	Read Silent	Write	Other Appro.	Total	Aggrea./Disruptive	off Task	Out of Seat	Non Compliance	Talk Out	Other Inappro.	Total Inappro.	Grand Total
Paper/Pencil																		
Listen-Lecture			I							1								2
Teacher-Pupil Discussion		II		II						4	I				II		3	7
Manipulatives																		
Inst. Games																		
Worksheets Workbook																		
Readers											III	II		II	١١١١١	II	14	14
Student-Student																		
Media/Tech Other																		
Transition																		
Other																		
Total	0	2	1	2	0	0	0	0	0	5	4	2	0	2	7	2	17	22

FIGURE 3-9b Completed Classroom Scatterplot

Source: © 1998, CECP. From Gable, R. A., Quinn, M. M., Rutherford, R. B., Howell, K. W., & Hoffman, C. C. (1998). Addressing student problem behavior part II: Conducting a functional behavioral assessment (3rd ed.). Washington, DC: The Center for Effective Collaboration and Practice. (Reprinted with permission.) Available online at: http://www.air.org/cecp/fba/problembehavior2/appendixa.htm.

Target Behavior	Bobby's negative verbal outbursts: "I can't do this." "This is stupid." "I hate school."
Antecedents/Triggers/Circumstances	Mostly happens during math class, rarely occurs during reading or social studies, never during recess or specials
Consequences/Reinforcers	Teacher offers encouragement, most peers ignore, one or two laugh
Hypothesis	Bobby's verbal disruptions appear to be more frequent in math and result in gaining teacher and peer attention.

Target Behavior	Julia's frequent tardiness
Antecedents/Triggers/Circumstances	80% of tardies occur in fourth-hour Spanish, after lunch, the rest distributed through the school day, Julia only sees her boyfriend at noon, his lunch period is later than hers
Consequences/Reinforcers	Teacher verbally reprimands Julia and sends her to the office for a hall pass, which takes her back through the commons area and results in missing additional instruction
Hypothesis	Julia appears to be lingering in the commons area to see her boyfriend at lunch time and may be gaining additional socialization time when she goes to the office for a tardy slip.

Target Behavior	Raphael's teeth grinding and rocking back and forth in his seat
Antecedents/Triggers/Circumstances	Mostly happens when teacher is engaged with other students, rarely occurs during small-group instruction or art activities, never during one-on-one instruction
Consequences/Reinforcers	Teacher provides high level of verbal and token reinforcers during individual and small-group instruction, Raphael always picks the art center during free time, Raphael stops grinding his teeth and rocking when verbally prompted by teacher, paraprofessional, or peer, and starts again when left alone for more than a few minutes
Hypothesis	Raphael appears to engage in self-stimulatory behavior when he is not actively engaged in direct instruction or an activity he enjoys.

FIGURE 3–10   Examples of FBA Hypothesis Generation

contains several examples of functional behavioral hypotheses, each worded slightly differently.

FBA Step IV: Verify or Test Hypothesis.   (This hypothesis-testing phase may also be referred to as functional analysis.) As before, you should observe the student when existing conditions are likely to produce the target behavior, as well as when the student is more likely to exhibit acceptable behaviors. Take data under both conditions and compare to determine whether the hypothesis is supported or not. For example, Jim's initial on/off task and assignment-completion data suggested a function related to avoiding independent seatwork. Collecting additional data during independent seatwork time (demand condition) and during other scheduled activities (attention or play conditions) might help to verify whether avoiding seatwork is the best functional explanation of his behavior.

Some behaviors occur at such low rates that direct observation in natural settings may not be efficient (this includes some high-intensity behaviors, like fighting or throwing a tantrum). A similar technique, called **analogue assessment**, involves the teacher systematically manipulating variables to determine which ones are the most and least likely to produce the target behavior. This technique is called "analogue" because the conditions are contrived, rather than naturally occurring. In Jim's case, his team might try antecedent manipulation by modifying or shortening the task, providing choices about when and how to complete the task, removing a component of the task (e.g., writing), or changing the order of tasks within his daily schedule. They might also vary the consequences by not allowing Jim to escape (e.g., giving him one-on-one assistance), providing additional access to reinforcing activities for task completion, or allowing a break after a specified period of on-task behavior. The Center for Effective Collaboration and Practice recommends implementing a change for three to five lessons to rule out the novelty of the intervention as the cause of the behavior change (Quinn et al., 1998).

FBA Step V: Review Data, Identify Patterns, and Refine Hypothesis. Continue collecting and analyzing data until the results are fairly consistent and there is general agreement among team members that the hypothesis is correct. "Usually descriptive data are collected for up to five total hours or until multiple instances of the target behavior are observed" (Asmus et al., 2002, p. 79). If the behavior is a dangerous one, the team should consider proceeding directly to intervention once the hypothesis has been formulated.

FBA Step VI: Design an Intervention Based on Relevant Settings, Reinforcers, and Deterrents. IEP teams may take a variety of approaches to selecting an intervention and designing a behavior intervention plan (BIP). While these intervention techniques will be discussed at greater length in subsequent chapters, strategies might include:

- Modifying one aspect of the classroom environment,
- Implementing positive behavioral strategies designed to reinforce appropriate behavior,
- Manipulating an antecedent or consequence,
- Teaching the student to cope with a triggering event or circumstance,
- Teaching a functionally equivalent replacement behavior,
- Making a change in the curriculum or instructional strategy. (Quinn et al., 1998; Gable, Quinn, Rutherford, Howell, & Hoffman, 2000)

Many effective interventions use a combination of these approaches to address the ecology of the behavior. Kerr and Nelson (2002) suggest that, whenever an inappropriate behavior is targeted for reduction, another appropriate behavior must be identified that is functionally equivalent (i.e., meets the same need for the student). "The BIP must address two parallel intervention strategies: one to teach and support the replacement behavior, and one to correct or reduce the target behavior. The plan should insure that the target (undesired) behavior is no longer effective, efficient, or relevant to producing the outcomes it once did" (p. 62). For example, if a student's misbehavior was calling loudly for teacher assistance during independent seatwork (i.e., attention seeking), an antecedent intervention might increase the amount of teacher attention and monitoring during

those assignments. A consequence–based intervention might teach the student how to appropriately request teacher assistance and reinforce use of the new skill.

Writing the IEP and Behavior Intervention Plan (BIP)

IDEA specifies that an individualized education plan must be developed for each child found eligible for special education services. The initial IEP meeting must be held within 30 days of the eligibility determination; the multidisciplinary team and the parents of the student with a disability must be present. The student herself may participate at any age but *must* participate from the age of 14. Additionally, an **individualized transition plan (ITP)** must be in place by the time the student reaches age 16 to address post-secondary needs and goals.

The 2004 amendments to IDEA specify that the IEP team, including representation from general education, will be involved in developing both academic and social/behavioral goals and strategies, and in making the placement decision. Each individual brings a number of unique qualities to the meeting: (1) a perspective of the student based on experience, (2) a level of expertise related to the student's problems, (3) an agenda or level of commitment, and (4) a working style and interpretation of their role in the process (Jolivette et al., 2000).

Setting Annual Goals and Defining Measurable Objectives and Benchmarks

NOTE: In an effort to reduce the burdensome paperwork load involved in implementing IDEA, the 2004 reauthorization of IDEA eliminated the requirements for IEP objectives and benchmarks for many students. However, the authors consider them a key component of accountability for student progress; therefore, we included the process for developing quality objectives and benchmarks in this chapter. Further, under IDEA 2004, some states will be granted waivers to other procedural aspects of IEP development. Therefore, your state's procedures and requirements may be somewhat different than what is presented here.

Students whose behavior interferes with their own learning or that of other students must have measurable annual goals and short-term objectives or benchmarks to address that behavior. These goals should be based on the results of the FBA and should focus on reducing problem behaviors while simultaneously teaching replacement behaviors (Drasgow et al., 1999). **Annual goals** are the measurable learning outcomes that you would expect a specific student to achieve in a year, based on his present level of performance. **Benchmarks** are milestones that divide annual goals into component parts, often corresponding to the grading or reporting periods of a school year. **Short-term objectives (STOs)** are discrete skill components or measurable steps toward each goal. The IEP/BIP team must use task analysis to break down the annual goals into these logical, incremental steps and decide whether to use objectives or benchmarks for each step.

Goals should address every major area of concern that was discussed in the description of the present level of performance and the evaluation report. Students with EBD will, by federal definition, have academic as well as social, affective, and behavioral problems. In selecting goals, IEP/BIP teams must balance the student's need for academic progress in the general education curriculum with the parallel need for social competence, emotional well-being, and behavioral development that will lead to success in educational and community settings.

Well-written, measurable goals, objectives, and benchmarks have four essential components. See Figure 3–11 for examples.

* **Conditions**—Describe the stimulus or task being presented to the student, as well as any accommodations or positive behavioral supports to be provided.
* **Response mode**—Note what the student will do, using an action verb to describe an observable behavior. (For example, "write" or "verbally state," not "know" or "understand.")
* **Criteria for success**—Define the mastery level, how many times the student must achieve mastery

to be considered proficient, and the time frame for achieving mastery.

* **Measurement plan**—Determine the measure or technique you will use to confirm that the goal, objective, or benchmark has been met.

Determining Need for Special Education and Related Services

Once the goals and objectives have been written, the IEP team must decide which specific services the student will require to achieve his goals and objectives. The student may need intensive, individualized services from a special educator in specific goal areas, assistance from related services personnel, or both. Related services may include:

* Audiology
* Counseling services
* Early identification and assessment of disabilities in children
* Medical services
* Occupational therapy
* Orientation and mobility services
* Parent counseling and training
* Physical therapy
* Psychological services
* Recreation
* Rehabilitation counseling services
* School health services
* Social work services in schools
* Speech-language pathology services
* Transportation (IDEA 1999, 34 C.F.R., §300.24; Authority: 20 U.S.C. 1401 [22])

Conditions	Response Mode	Criteria for Success	Measurement Plan
Given 20 instructional-level sight words in a 1-second flashed presentation. . .	Billy will verbally state the word. . .	within 5 seconds of stimulus presentation and with 90% accuracy on three consecutive trials. . .	as recorded on data sheet.
At recess with a paraprofessional present to provide verbal precorrection. . .	Alonzo will participate in an organized recreational activity. . .	with no incidents of verbal or physical aggression against peers. . .	as observed by paraprofessional and reported on IEP progress data form.
When given a pencil-paper task to complete independently during class time. . .	Laurence will remain in his seat with eyes on task. . .	80% of the time. . .	as recorded by the paraprofessional using interval recording.

FIGURE 3–11 Examples of IEP Objectives

Once the team has identified the services necessary, they must determine the location, frequency, and duration of those services. IEP teams are also responsible for identifying positive behavioral supports, accommodations, and modifications needed for the student to meet his goals and participate with his general education peers to the maximum extent possible.

Identifying Positive Behavioral Supports (PBS). Historically, practitioners have relied on the utility of punishment-based procedures to reduce undesirable behavior because punishment often produces immediate results. However, intervention strategies based on FBA have typically focused on antecedent-based interventions, extinction, and differential reinforcement (Asmus et al., 2002). When the IEP/BIP process is used proactively with students who have EBD, it "will result in educational programming that does not rely on punitive reductive procedures to change behavior but, rather, will develop skill-based programming designed to improve the lives of students with problem behaviors" (Yell & Katsiyannis, 2000, p. 161). The goal of PBS is to implement systemic interventions that prevent most "garden variety" behavior problems. (For more specific information on PBS, see Chapter 4.) Positive behavioral supports are often directed toward the antecedents or triggers of the potential problem behavior. PBS may also involve teaching the student a replacement behavior that meets their perceived need, but is more acceptable to the teacher and peers.

Gartin and Murdick (2001) suggest the following positive behavioral strategies for altering the instructional setting or situation: changing the level of the task or demand, changing the noise level, changing the voice tone of the adult, changing the sequence of tasks, omitting an aversive activity, and enriching the environment with preferred tasks. They also suggest instructional strategies such as using explicit, direct instructional techniques and providing errorless learning opportunities.

For students whose behavior follows predictable antecedents, practice activities designed to prepare students or accustom them to potentially problematic situations can help prevent outbursts. Strategies for students seeking sensory input might include providing them with an alternative sensory stimulus to replace one that is disruptive, potentially harmful, or that causes them to stick out in the classroom environment. For students whose behaviors are an attempt to communicate or to avoid potentially aversive activity, positive behavioral supports provide students with acceptable alternative ways to communicate their wishes, or to request a break or a choice of activities.

Identifying Instructional Accommodations and Modifications. Byrnes (2000) defines **accommodation** as "an adjustment to an activity or setting that removes a barrier presented by a disability so that a person can have access equal to that of a person without a disability. An accommodation does not guarantee success or a specific level of performance. It should, however, provide the opportunity for a person with a disability to participate in a situation or activity" (p. 21). Accommodations in instruction or assessment are changes in the presentation of information or in the way a student responds, but they do not change the purpose of the assignment or the content knowledge being assessed. Frequently accepted accommodation categories include:

- **Presentation mode**—Reading instructions orally, providing a tape recording of a textbook, providing Braille or large-print version of materials
- **Response mode**—Tape recording or dictating responses, providing multiple choice rather than essay questions, keyboarding rather than handwriting responses
- **Schedule**—Providing more time or frequent breaks, "chunking" large tasks into smaller sessions, scheduling difficult tasks at preferred time of day
- **Setting**—Using a study carrel for privacy, allowing the student to take his test in separate room, providing preferential seating
- **Equipment/assistive technology**—Using a screen reader, providing software for spelling or grammar checks, or using a picture board to enhance communication

Modifications are changes in the actual curriculum itself, so that the student is being instructed with different goals, materials, and standards than the other students. Common types of modifications include using functional or parallel curriculum, reducing the difficulty or amount of work required, or grading with a modified scoring guide. For example, while the seventh-grade science class is conducting an experiment to precipitate salt from ocean water, Edgar (a student with autism) will work with his paraprofessional to identify food that tastes salty. A student mainstreamed into a high school geometry class may only be required to complete the even-numbered homework items, or might be graded using a scale that required only 85% for an A, 75% for a B, and so on. Accommodations and modifications are implemented with the intent of leveling the playing field for students with disabilities and minimizing the negative impact of the impairment. Many of these accommodations are appropriate for use in assessment situations as well; however, states and local school districts may have guidelines defining what types of accommodations and modifications are appropriate. IEP teams need to be knowledgeable about their local options to ensure students meet the qualifications for graduation.

Determining Placement

> It is crucial that the [special education] placement be based on each student's educational needs. Thus, the goals, benchmarks, STOs, special education and related services, and supplementary aids and services must be determined prior to making any placement decisions. This means that the IEP team decides the placement in which appropriate educational services should be provided after the program has been planned. (Drasgow, Yell, & Robinson, 2001, p. 364)

IDEA requires states and local education agencies to provide a continuum of services for students with EBD and other disabilities. Although the continuum provides a range of placement options, IDEA also requires that students be served in the least restrictive environment (LRE) that is consistent with their individual needs, as defined in the IEP. Students with EBD, like those with other disabilities, should be educated in the general education classroom, using the general education curriculum, and with their typically achieving peers to the maximum extent possible. However, experience has shown that students with EBD are identified later in their educational careers than students with other disabilities, and are frequently served in more restrictive settings. As student behavior escalates and classroom interventions fail, teachers, administrators, and parents come to believe that services cannot be provided in less restrictive environments (Hallenbeck, Kauffman, & Lloyd, 1993). The IEP team is responsible for making the placement decision; however, informed parental consent is required.

Evaluating Progress

Once the IEP is written, the IEP team's job is not finished; they should then begin formative evaluation, using data collection techniques described in the IEP goals, objectives, and benchmarks. The IEP must be implemented as written and should be reviewed and revised at least annually.

EARLY CHILDHOOD PLANNING AND THE INDIVIDUALIZED FAMILY SERVICES PLAN (IFSP)

Young children with disabilities ages three through five years old are covered by Part C of IDEA. However, unlike school-age students with disabilities, preschoolers may receive their special education and related services in an array of settings. These programs may include community-based preschools, privately operated child-care or day-care centers, Head Start programs, and early childhood special education programs operated by local school districts.

While preschool-aged children are seldom identified as eligible under IDEA specifically for emotional/behavioral problems, dealing effectively with students' challenging behaviors is a concern for many early childhood programs. The Division for Early Childhood (DEC) of the Council for Exceptional Children has issued a position statement concerning interventions for challenging behaviors based on three underlying principles:

- Many young children engage in challenging behavior in the course of early development. The majority of these children respond to developmentally appropriate management techniques.
- DEC believes strongly that many types of services and intervention strategies are available to address challenging behavior.
- DEC believes strongly that families play a critical role in designing and carrying out effective interventions for challenging behaviors. (Walsh, Smith, & Taylor, 2000, p. 6)

Young children whose behavior is extreme or atypical may be referred to their local school district for special education evaluation. If the school district finds the child eligible under Part C of IDEA, they must develop an **individualized family services plan (IFSP)** to provide the child with a free, appropriate public education (FAPE). Because of the family-focused nature of the IFSP for preschool-aged children with disabilities, the services often assist parents, as well as the student. These may include parent support groups and parenting training.

ADOLESCENT ISSUES AND INDIVIDUAL TRANSITION PLANNING (ITP)

As discussed in Chapter 1, students identified as EBD often drop out before completing high school and experience a variety of problems in the community as adults (e.g., lower rates of employment). For students with disabilities age 16 and older, IDEA requires that IEPs address transition planning in terms of course selection. From age 16, the IEP must also specifically address postgraduation planning, and representatives of relevant community agencies and services must participate in planning. This plan is called an individualized transition plan (ITP) and may be included within the body of the IEP, or as an attachment to it. However, reviews of practice have found that transition planning for students with EBD is often neglected, and IEP teams may overlook important areas (Shearin, Roessler, & Schriner, 1999). Ideally, the ITP describes a three-stage process including goal setting, needs assessment, and planning.

The ITP: Setting Goals

The first step in developing an ITP is determining the student's postsecondary goals. This may be accomplished by administering an aptitude/interest inventory, or interviewing the student, parents, and teachers to identify his likes and dislikes, skills, strengths, and aspirations. Goals may address postsecondary training or education, employment options, living arrangements, and types of community participation, including recreation and leisure.

It is important that the goals selected reflect both the desire for the highest quality of life possible for the student and a realistic appraisal of his skills and potential for success in various environments. For example, Mitchell says he wants to be a veterinarian. If he is a student with at least an average intelligence who demonstrates an aptitude for math and science and is likely to complete a bachelor's degree in a related field, that would be a realistic goal. If, however, Mitchell is a student with pervasive developmental disorder who is functioning academically on the 2nd-grade level in 10th grade, it may be more realistic to discuss other options that involve working with animals (e.g., grooming dogs, working in a stable or a veterinarian's office).

The ITP: Conducting the Needs Assessment

The **needs assessment** may be a formal or informal process designed to identify the skills and knowledge the student needs to achieve his life goals and determine his present level of performance on relevant tasks. Assessment measures may involve review of records and work products, administration of standardized tests,

curriculum-based measures, interviews, or practical activities related to goal areas. Examples include:

- **Academic**—What courses has the student taken related to his postsecondary goals, and what were his grades? What additional courses would he need to take to achieve his goals? If he is planning to attend college, is he aware of the choices available and the entrance and application requirements for those institutions?
- **Career/vocational**—What are the skills required by the student's choice of future employment? What type of supports or working environments will he need to be successful (e.g., working for himself, competitive employment, a job coach, sheltered workshop)?
- **Transportation**—Is obtaining a driver's license a realistic option? If not, will he be able to use public transportation? If not, what other options are available in the community?
- **Socialization and relationships**—Does the student have friends and a desire for an intimate relationship? If so, what resources are needed to support those relationships (e.g., family planning, child-development information)? If not, what resources are needed to assist in forming and developing relationships (e.g., social-skills training, enrollment in a community program)?
- **Community participation and self-advocacy**—To what degree will the individual function as a citizen in the community (e.g., register to vote, attend church)? What decisions will he be able to make for himself on a daily basis (e.g., what clothes to wear, which television programs to watch)? What types of support will be necessary for him to participate in the activities he likes?
- **Housing**—Will the student continue to live at home after graduation? Would he prefer to live alone, or with roommates? What other housing options are available in the community (e.g., group homes, supervised apartments, residential facilities)?
- **Financial/income/resources**—Will the student be eligible for continued aid or social services after high school? Will he need assistance applying for programs such as social security, food stamps, or housing subsidies? Can he manage his own finances, balance a checkbook, manage credit, and pay taxes?
- **Health and medical**—Does the student need support for ongoing health concerns? Does he have health insurance and understand how to manage

his benefits? Is he able to identify symptoms of common illnesses and make responsible decisions about taking over-the-counter medications or calling the doctor? Does he understand his medical condition and the medications he is currently taking? If the answer to any of these questions is no, what supports will he need?

- **Legal and support services**—Will the student be able to assume responsibility for his own affairs when he reaches the age of majority, or will he need a legal guardian to assist with some or all areas of decision making? Will other community and government agencies be involved in making decisions regarding the student's future housing, educational, and medical needs?

The ITP: Planning for the Future

The final step of the ITP process is to identify the general strategies and specific activities that will be used to bridge the gap between the student's present level of performance and those skills required to achieve the desired goals. In *Strengthening the Safety Net* (2001), Ryan describes promising transition-focused programs for adolescents with EBD. The programs reviewed use a variety of strategies including: relationship building, social-skills training, academic/vocational training, student goal setting, accessing other agencies, involving families, and forming community partnerships. Because resources and requirements vary, it is necessary to familiarize yourself with the resources in the local community and state in which the student resides.

CHAPTER SUMMARY

- IDEA regulations describe the process whereby a student may be found eligible for services as EBD. Following that determination, a multidisciplinary team that includes the parents of the student must meet to devise an individualized education program (IEP) and behavior intervention plan (BIP). The IEP for a student with EBD must begin with a description of the present level of performance. The IEP team then writes measurable goals and short-term objectives or benchmarks to address major areas of concern. Hypotheses generated during the functional behavioral assessment (FBA) process are used to develop goals, objectives, and benchmarks, and to guide implementation of positive behavioral supports, accommodations, and modifications. Based on the needs of the individual

student and the goals to be met, the IEP specifies the need for special education and related services. The final step of the IEP/BIP process is to determine placement in the least restrictive environment.

CHECK YOUR UNDERSTANDING

1. *True or False*. Children under the age of 5 are not covered by IDEA.
2. *True or False*. If the IEP team believes that the primary disability is a result of lack of instruction in reading or math, the student may not be found eligible for special education services.
3. *True or False*. A team is allowed to write a BIP without completing a functional behavioral assessment if a student's behaviors are considered dangerous to self and/or others.
4. When selecting behavioral targets for the BIP, which of the following behaviors would be considered to be a "Level 5" behavior? (a) display of a weapon, (b) refusal to follow directions, (c) leaving school or campus, or (d) none of the above
5. Which of the following conditions would prohibit a student from being eligible for special education services under the label of emotional disturbance? (a) school phobia, (b) depression, (c) poor peer relationships, or (d) social maladjustment
6. Students with disabilities must have an ITP in place by what age?
7. Describe what should be included on the IEP in a statement of present level of performance?
8. Define the concept of a "continuum of alternative placements."
9. List the four components required in the hypothesis-generation stage of FBA.
10. What are the basic differences between a "short-term objective" and a "benchmark?"

APPLICATION ACTIVITIES

1. Reread the IEP vignette that appeared at the beginning of the chapter. Identify at least four ways the team could have helped Jim's mother feel better prepared to participate in this meeting.
2. In small groups, select a case study from Appendix A. Assign the roles of each team member (general educator, special educator, school psychologist, parent, etc.). Role-play an

IEP meeting for your selected student, to include the following steps: (a) determine eligibility, (b) describe present level of performance and prioritize concerns, (c) generate functional hypotheses for interfering behaviors, (d) write measurable IEP/BIP goals and short-term objectives or benchmarks for each prioritized concern, (e) determine special education and related services needed, and (f) determine placement.

3. In small groups, examine the data in Figure 3-8b. Identify patterns and develop at least one hypothesis for the function of this behavior.

4. In small groups, examine the data in Figure 3-9b. Identify patterns and develop at least one hypothesis for the function of this behavior. Describe potential positive behavioral supports that might reduce the likelihood this behavior would recur.

5. Observe a student with emotional/behavioral problems in a classroom setting. In collaboration with the teacher, select and define a target behavior, and design a procedure for collecting FBA data. Using a scatterplot or ABC observation form, conduct the FBA. Generate a hypothesis and discuss an appropriate intervention goal with the teacher.

BEST PRACTICES FOR PREVENTING PROBLEM BEHAVIORS
Schoolwide Strategies

CHAPTER PREVIEW

CONNECTING TO THE CLASSROOM: *A Vignette*

Mr. Hawkins, the principal of Belleview High School, walked down the hall toward the school's commons area. He could hear the murmur of voices as he rounded the corner. Students were sitting and standing in small groups, laughing and talking in reasonable conversational tones. Some were eating lunch; others had already finished. He admired the new posters outlining the Belleview Beliefs—the expectations for student behavior in the commons area. The students in the print shop had done a very professional job on them.

Mr. Hawkins noticed that two or three teachers were providing active supervision, circulating, talking quietly to students. As Mr. Hawkins passed the coach talking to Donna and Jenny, he inwardly braced himself, expecting that those two were up to no good, as usual. To his surprise, Coach was handing each student a "Belleview Buck" and saying, "You girls have provided a great example of rule one—respecting others. I noticed that you gave up your seats when you finished eating to let two students with lunch trays sit down. Thanks." Jenny and Donna smiled shyly and quickly looked at Mr. Hawkins to see if they were in trouble. He grinned back at them, gave them each a high five, and walked on toward the lunch line. Remembering the chaos that had reigned in the commons area just a few short weeks ago, he thought, "This positive behavior support stuff really works! I'm glad we tried it instead of shutting down the commons and confining the students to the cafeteria during lunch period. Now, if those two young ladies will just stay out of my office for a few days . . ."

SCHOOL REFORM AND STUDENTS WITH EMOTIONAL AND BEHAVIORAL DISORDERS (EBD)

The role of the public school in the latter part of the 20th century expanded to include a wide variety of purposes and activities that were previously the domain of the family and other community institutions (e.g., churches, health centers). Sex education and family-living courses, substance-abuse education, and access to direct health services became increasingly commonplace on school grounds. At the same time, public concerns about school safety and an increased emphasis on accountability for student outcomes required schools to do more with less, stretching limited resources to include the new initiatives without abandoning any of their previous scope of responsibility.

Students with emotional and behavioral disorders pose a particular dilemma for schools wanting to increase test scores and graduation rates while reducing disciplinary problems. This chapter will provide an overview of major school reform efforts with implications for students with EBD, and introduce schoolwide positive behavioral supports (PBS) as a model that addresses the needs of all students, teachers, and the community for safer and more effective schools. In addition, PBS can act as the first level of prevention activities for students at risk for EBD, potentially decreasing the need for more targeted and intensive individual interventions.

The Increasingly Challenging School Environment

The general public school population—and their teachers—contend with an increasing number of risk factors related to poor academic, social, and behavioral outcomes. The student body includes more children of teenage parents; a higher proportion of students with developmental delays; an increasing number of latchkey children; a more varied ethnic and cultural composition; and students with daily exposure to alcohol, drugs, and gangs (Stephens, 1998). Another risk factor for students with behavior problems is disorganized families characterized by poor parenting skills and management practices (Hawkins, Farrington, & Catalano, 1998; Stephens, 1998). In urban areas, added challenges include extreme levels of poverty and unemployment, socially disorganized communities with high levels of crime and mobility, and low levels

of neighborhood attachment (Hawkins, Farrington, & Catalano, 1998). With all of these challenges, perhaps it is not surprising that teacher recruitment and retention issues have gained national attention, especially in special education.

Disturbing Outcomes for Students with EBD

Students with EBD, by IDEA definition, have difficulty with educational performance as well as problems with interpersonal relationships, inappropriate feelings and behavior under normal circumstances, mood disorders, or physical symptoms or fears (see the Determining Eligibility section in Chapter 3).

According to Jolivette, Stichter, Nelson, Scott, and Liaupsin (2000), "Individuals with emotional and behavior disorders (EBD) experience the least favorable outcomes of any group of individuals with disabilities" (p. 1). They are likely to have long-term problems with academics, employment, and social relationships. As a result, they receive their services in more restrictive environments, as compared to students with other disabilities. Between 1984 and 1995, slightly more than half of students with EBD were placed in special classes, day schools, or residential facilities (Office of Special Education Programs, 1998). These issues also apply to students from minority ethnic or cultural backgrounds who are suspended, expelled, and excluded from general education programs in disproportionate numbers (Markey, Markey, Quant, Santelli, & Turnbull, 2002; Utley, Kozleski, Smith, & Draper, 2002).

The poor school and postschool outcomes of students with EBD suggests a failure of the public schools to adequately address their needs. (See Figure 4-1.) In response to overwhelming evidence that existing programs for students with EBD were unsuccessful, an expert panel developed the *National Agenda for Achieving Better Results for Children and Youth with Serious Emotional Disturbance* (the term used for EBD prior to IDEA 1997). The panel identified seven strategic targets, based on the existing research base on best practices:

Target #1: Expand Positive Learning Opportunities and Results—To foster the provision of engaging, useful, and positive learning opportunities. These opportunities should be result-driven and should acknowledge as well as respond to the experiences and needs of children and youth with serious emotional disturbance.

- **Academic Outcomes**—Students with EBD have lower grades than any other group of students with disabilities. They fail more courses and they more frequently fail minimum competency examinations than do other students with disabilities; they also are retained at grade level more often at the end of the school year. High school students with EBD have an average grade point average of 1.7 (on a four-point scale), compared to 2.0 for all students with disabilities and 2.6 for all students. Forty-four percent received one or more failing grades in their most recent school year (compared to 31% for all students with disabilities). Of those who took minimum competency tests (22% were exempted), 63% failed some part of the test.
- **Graduation Rates**—Forty-two percent of youth with EBD earn a high school diploma, as opposed to 50% of all youth with disabilities and 76% of similarly aged youth in the general population.
- **School Placement**—Eighteen percent of students with EBD are educated outside of their local schools, compared to 6% of all students with disabilities. Of those in their local schools, fewer than 17% are educated in regular classrooms, in contrast to 33% of all students with disabilities.
- **Dropout Rates**—Forty-eight percent of students with EBD drop out of grades 9 through 12, as opposed to 30% of all students with disabilities and only 24% of all high school students. (Another 8% of students with disabilities, including students with EBD, drop out before grade 9.)
- **School Absenteeism**—Students with EBD miss more days of school per year (an average of 18 days) than do students in any other disability category.
- **Encounters with the Juvenile Justice System**—Twenty percent of students with EBD are arrested at least once before they leave school as opposed to 9% of students with disabilities and 6% of all students. Fifty-eight percent of youth with EBD are arrested within five years of leaving school, as opposed to 30% of all students with disabilities. Of those students with EBD who drop out of school, 73% are arrested within five years of leaving school.
- **Identification Rates of Students of Varying Socioeconomic Backgrounds**—The rates of identification of children and youth with EBD vary across racial, cultural, gender, and socioeconomic lines. Although African-American and White students represent 16% and 68% of the school-age enrollment respectively, they represent 22% and 71% of the students classified as EBD. On the other hand, Hispanic Americans and Asian Americans represent 12% and 3% of the school-aged population respectively, but only 6% and 1% of the students classified as EBD. Data also suggest that students from low socioeconomic backgrounds are overrepresented and female students underrepresented among those identified with serious emotional disturbance.
- **Compared to all students with disabilities:** (1) students with EBD are more likely to be placed in restrictive settings and are more likely to drop out of school; (2) their families are more likely to be blamed for the student's disability and are more likely to make tremendous financial sacrifices to secure services for their children; and (3) their teachers and aides are more likely to seek reassignment or leave their positions.

FIGURE 4–I   Likely Outcomes for Students with EBD*

Source: Chesapeake Institute. (1994, September).

*The term SED (serious emotional disturbance) was used rather than EBD prior to the 1997 amendments to IDEA. For consistency, SED was replaced with EBD in this figure.

Target #2: Strengthen School and Community Capacity—To foster initiatives that strengthen the capacity of schools and communities to serve students with serious emotional disturbance in the least restrictive environments appropriate.

Target #3: Value and Address Diversity—To encourage culturally competent and linguistically appropriate exchanges and collaborations among families, professionals, students, and communities. These collaborations should foster equitable outcomes for all students and result in the identification and provision of services that are responsive to issues of race, culture, gender, and social and economic status.

Target #4: Collaborate with Families—To foster collaborations that fully include family members

on the team of service providers that implements family focused services to improve educational outcomes. Services should be open, helpful, culturally competent, accessible to families, and school- as well as community-based.

Target #5: Promote Appropriate Assessment—To promote practices ensuring that assessment is integral to the identification, design, and delivery of services for children and youth with SED. These practices should be culturally appropriate, ethical, and functional.

Target #6: Provide Ongoing Skill Development and Support—To foster the enhancement of knowledge, understanding, and sensitivity among all who work with children and youth with and at risk of developing serious emotional disturbance. Support and development should be ongoing and aim at strengthening the capacity of families, teachers, service providers, and other stakeholders to collaborate, persevere, and improve outcomes for children and youth with SED.

Target #7: Create Comprehensive and Collaborative Systems—To promote systems change resulting in the development of coherent services built around the individual needs of children and youth with and at risk of developing serious emotional disturbance. These services should be family-centered, community-based, and appropriately funded. (Chesapeake Institute, 1994, Figure 2)

The Focus on Prevention

The growing expectation is that schools will deliver socially acceptable, effective, and efficient interventions to ensure safe, productive environments where norm-violating behavior is minimized and prosocial behavior is promoted. (OSEP Center on Positive Behavioral Interventions and Supports, 2000, p. 133)

When behavioral difficulties are dangerous or harmful to others or property, the first reaction is a call for dramatic school reform that includes installation of metal detectors, hiring security guards, conducting random drug tests, and instituting school uniform policies. Because of the tragic nature of recent violent school acts, these kinds of reactions are predictable and understandable. The immediate and natural response is to remove the source of the discomfort and to use structural modifications to prevent similar acts from recurring. Unfortunately, these reactive approaches do not provide positive and preventative measures that are based on careful and ongoing assessment of multiple school systems and for changes in the ways in which teachers behave and school systems operate. (Sugai, Sprague, Horner, & Walker, 2000, Discussion section, paragraph 2)

Prevention of misbehavior is both efficient and effective. Research on effective instruction has emphasized that taking a proactive, rather than reactive, approach to management of student behavior maximizes learning time (Brophy, 1988; Brophy & Good, 1986; Wyne & Stuck, 1982). That is, rather than dealing with management problems on a case-by-case basis, the effective school has a plan that encompasses many common student behaviors and misbehaviors and is implemented consistently by all school personnel from the first day of school. "Classroom management is best construed not as a process of compelling conformity from students who know what to do but refuse to do it, but

instead as a process of being clear and consistent in teaching students desired rules and procedures" (Brophy, 1988, p. 241). In a more recent article, Brophy reported: "Research on classroom management suggests that successful managers approach management as a process of establishing an effective learning environment rather than emphasizing their roles as disciplinarians" (1998, p. 1). Thus, by establishing and consistently following clear behavioral expectations and intervention guidelines at the schoolwide level, teachers and school administrators can minimize the time needed to deal with disruptive behaviors, and maximize the time students spend actually engaged in learning activities. The increased classroom time devoted to active teaching and learning will result in greater student achievement, lower rates of problem behavior, and higher levels of satisfaction for students, teachers, and administrators alike. The same premise can be extended beyond the individual classroom to the general school population to promote prosocial norms and behavior (Hawkins et al., 1998).

During the past two decades, many schools have found it useful to borrow preventative intervention approaches based on a public health or mental health model for students whose problems are primarily emotional or behavioral. In health-related fields, prevention strategies have generally focused on three identified levels of intensity. **Primary prevention** activities are those designed for the general population and intended to educate and to prevent the later development of a disease, condition, or problem. Prime-time television ads discouraging tobacco and drug use are examples of primary prevention activities. **Secondary prevention** strategies target high-risk individuals and groups and provide information and services specific to them. The goals of secondary prevention programs may be to monitor or minimize the impact of risk factors, to provide information concerning the benefits and risks of certain behaviors or lifestyle choices, to teach coping skills, or to slow or arrest the development of a potential problem. For example, information concerning the warning signs and symptoms of HIV/AIDS would be distributed through clinics and community-service agencies serving high-risk populations (e.g., intravenous drug users). Individuals who had recently lost a loved one might be invited to a grief and loss support group. The third level—**tertiary prevention**—often called treatment, generally consists of focused individualized interventions designed to limit the impact and development of an existing condition or problem. For example, many communities require participation in counseling or anger management classes as a condition of probation following a domestic violence conviction.

Problems with Existing Prevention Research Base

Unfortunately, efficacy research on prevention activities and programs has been less than rigorous, making claims of success questionable. Although Gottfredson and Gottfredson (2001) cited two dozen generally positive reviews of prevention research, they found a general weakness in research design that raised questions about reliability of results: "When stringent standards for the quality of the research evidence are applied, only a handful of prevention programs meet them" (p. 314). The Center for the Study and Prevention of Violence (2003) has identified only 11 programs nationwide that meet the Center's "National Blueprints" standards that evaluate program effectiveness in terms of deterrent effect and strong research design. They have identified an additional 21 as "Promising Programs," meeting some—but not all—of the criteria for selection as a blueprint.

The Center for the Study and Prevention of Violence also examined the data concerning several well-known prevention initiatives. They found there was no convincing support for student profiling (CSPV, 2000), or for the D.A.R.E. Program (CSPV, 1998a) and inconsistent data concerning the impact of positive peer programs (CSPV, 1998b).

In a national survey of public and private schools, Gottfredson and Gottfredson identified prevention activities and disciplinary practices of more than 600 schools (2001). They found that schools were implementing a wide variety of prevention activities, especially in the middle schools. The most common activities involved setting and enforcing rules and policies (100%), and providing isolated information (e.g., brochures, assemblies) to students, families, or staff on specific prevention topics (90%). Only about half of the schools reported implementing the kinds of activities most similar to the positive behavior supports model—improving classroom organization and management or practices (57%), or school planning or structural/process change (57%). Gottfredson and Gottfredson (2001) also pointed out that 81% of the prevention effectiveness studies have focused on instructional programs, rather than on the many other kinds of activities schools have implemented: "The field lacks a sufficient research base to characterize the effectiveness of most types of activities in schools intended to reduce or prevent delinquency or problem behavior" (p. 315).

Characteristics of Effective Programs for All Students

The U.S. Department of Education's Safe and Drug Free Schools and Office of Special Education Programs undertook an effort to identify prevention programs that were both well-designed and successful in the winter of 1997–1998. They collaborated to study several schools that had achieved positive outcomes for all students, including those with EBD. Through focus groups and site visits, the expert panel identified eight characteristics that the programs had in common, as follows:

1. **Safe schools are everybody's business.** Administrators, staff, and students must all understand the rules and their consequences. The first step to a safe, drug-free, and effective learning environment is a schoolwide commitment to good behavior.

2. **Safe schools are one family.** Regular and special educators and students are all part of the school family. Discipline and positive behavior supports and activities should involve all staff and students.

3. **Safe schools are caring schools that value and respect all students.** Safe schools build and support staff capacity to be caring and to address the diverse needs of all students.

4. **Safe schools have high academic standards and provide students with the support to achieve these standards.** Children who learn well, behave well. Many behavior problems are partly the result of academic failures and frustrations.

5. **Safe schools have high behavioral standards and provide students with positive support to achieve these standards.** Well-trained teachers with administrative support can create positive environments that promote appropriate behavior and development.

6. **Safe schools are strategic schools.** They assess needs, develop and implement research-based strategies, and coordinate services to address the needs of all students.

7. **Safe schools combine three approaches.** Schoolwide prevention efforts for all students; early intervention for students who are found to be at risk of behavioral problems; and targeted individualized interventions for students with severe behavior problems.

8. **Safe schools view the school as part of the larger community.** They bring in the parents, mental health and other social service agencies, businesses, youth and juvenile justice workers, and other community services and players to build safe schools and communities. (Quinn, Osher, Hoffman, & Hanley, 1998, Executive Summary, Qualities Shared by Successful Schools section)

THE SCHOOL COMMUNITY AS A POSITIVE CLIMATE FOR LEARNING

The recommendations regarding characteristics that make schools safe also describe schools that have a vibrant, demanding, and inclusive school culture in which every student, teacher, administrator, and parent provides input and is held accountable for putting forth their best effort. Therefore, the culture of a school begins at the top, and at the bottom. Every individual who enters the building brings unique experiences, values, and expectations that add variety and interest to the school.

Effective schools rely on consistently enforced policies and procedures to assure smooth functioning and minimize disruptions. Most districts and schools have attempted to codify their policies and procedures into teacher, student, and parent handbooks, identifying expectations, rules, and consequences. Often, however, recipients of these efforts perceive them negatively, rather than viewing them as a positive resource. That is particularly true when rules and regulations are unclear, or enforced inconsistently or in a punitive fashion, and when student accountability is emphasized without the necessary positive culture and behavioral supports.

Researchers have proposed a variety of approaches for building community. Schaps (2003) suggests four strategies: (1) actively cultivate respectful, supportive relationships among students, teachers, and parents; (2) emphasize common purposes and ideals; (3) provide regular opportunities for service and cooperation; and (4) provide developmentally appropriate opportunities for autonomy and influence. These strategies are similar to the "Three C's" that *Cooperative Discipline* calls the "building blocks of self-esteem" (Albert, 1996, p. 172). Esteem-building activities build a sense of community while helping students feel *Capable*, *Connected*, and *Contributing*.

Stephens (1998) observes that safe, inclusive school communities display an overall climate of ownership and school pride, including community-service projects, exciting extracurricular programs, high levels of cultural and social awareness, and respect for diversity. For students whose cultural and ethnic background differs from the majority of their peers and teachers, the level of cultural competence is an important factor in their feelings of belonging and acceptance. "The essential elements of a culturally competent system include (a) valuing diversity, (b) having the capacity for cultural self-assessment, (c) recognizing the dynamics inherent in cross-cultural interactions, (d) having cultural knowledge, and (e) developing adaptations to interventions and service delivery options that reflect an understanding of cultural diversity" (Utley et al., 2002, p. 204). Since the majority of classroom teachers in America are female, and of Western European descent—and an increasing number of our students are not—this requires a commitment by teachers to learn and grow to be successful in diverse classrooms (Townsend, 2003). Utley and colleagues suggest that

> General and special educators must examine their expectations, broaden their knowledge base, and develop skills so that behavior problems are not based on unidimensional or deficit perspectives. Culturally responsive teaching must be multidimensional and encompass curriculum content, learning context, classroom climate, student-teacher relationships, instructional strategies, and performance assessments that are based on cultural knowledge, experiences, contributions, and perspectives of urban multicultural youth. (p. 206)

POSITIVE BEHAVIORAL SUPPORTS

As we discussed in Chapter 3, positive behavioral supports (PBS) were mentioned in IDEA 1997 for the first time as a preferred intervention strategy for developing individual student behavior plans based on functional behavioral assessment. Additionally, elements of the PBS model address virtually all of the goals of the Chesapeake Institute's *National Agenda*, the characteristics of safe schools, and the purposes of prevention, while building a caring community. Individual intervention strategies based on PBS can be used effectively to address the needs of individual students with EBD by providing the external structure many of them need to be successful. However, there is a growing body of evidence that PBS has great potential for improving school outcomes and climate for *all* stakeholders, not just for students with special needs. The remainder of this chapter will discuss the PBS model as it applies to the entire school system; subsequent chapters will focus on classroom and individual applications.

Definitions and Key Characteristics

PBS is a broad range of systemic and individualized strategies for achieving important social and learning outcomes while preventing problem behavior. (The Center for Innovation in Special Education, 2002, slide 55)

Positive behavioral interventions and supports involve the whole school, and successful implementation emphasizes the identification, adoption, and sustained use of effective policies, systems, data-based decision making, and practices. (OSEP, 2000, p. 131)

At the core, PBS is the integration of (a) behavioral science, (b) practical interventions, (c) social values, and (d) a systems perspective. (OSEP, 2000, p. 134)

PBS has evolved into a process for supporting the achievement of socially and educationally important outcomes for all students. It is not a static curriculum and does not look the same in every behavior intervention plan, classroom, school, family, and community. PBS is for all students, with or without disabilities, their families, and educators. (Sugai & Horner, 2002, p. 133)

Positive behavior includes all those skills that increase the likelihood of success and personal satisfaction in normative academic, work, social, recreational, community, and family settings. *Support* encompasses all those educational methods that can be used to teach, strengthen, and expand positive behavior and all those systems change methods that can be used to increase opportunities for the display of positive behavior. (Carr et al., 2002, pp. 4–5)

The positive behavioral supports (PBS) model introduced in the previous chapter employs a three-tiered framework—similar to the three-tiered prevention model—to address student behavioral issues proactively. Primary prevention efforts are designed and implemented schoolwide, involving all staff and students. The second level of strategies targets classrooms as instructional and management units. Finally, the tertiary interventions target those students whose behavior violates the established norms and who require additional structure and support, either as individuals or in small groups. This generally includes students with EBD, for whom structure, consistency, and predictability are essential.

Many of the assessment and intervention strategies of PBS have their roots in applied behavior analysis (Carr et al., 2002). However, implementing PBS in a school melds the values and technology of behaviorism, humanism, and ecology (see conceptual models in Chapter 1). PBS *cannot* be implemented strictly as a behavioral intervention, because it also requires an ecological analysis of natural settings and social validity of outcomes. "Behav-ior change is not simply the result of applying specific techniques to specific challenges. The best technology will fail if it is applied in an uncooperative or disorganized context" (Carr et al., 2002, p. 8). Implementing PBS requires a philosophical shift for some teachers, and most will need ongoing staff development training. "The ability to implement PBS may require schools to undergo both personnel training and systems change" (Turnbull, Wilcox, Stowe, & Turnbull, 2001, p. 16).

The Process: Components of Systems Change

Lewis and Sugai (1999) identified the following six essential components of a schoolwide effective behavior support plan:

1. A statement of purpose that is worded positively and describes student academic and behavioral outcomes
2. Schoolwide behavioral rules and expectations that provide clearly stated, age-appropriate replacement behaviors for identified school problems
3. Procedures for teaching expected behavior that use research-validated procedures for explicit instruction in the desired social skills and behaviors
4. Procedures for encouraging expected behavior that initially includes token and tangible incentives paired with social recognition and natural reinforcers and fades concrete incentives as students master the new skills
5. Procedures for discouraging problem behavior that provide a continuum of consequences that are applied schoolwide, based on a written code or policy
6. Procedures for record keeping that support making data-based instructional decisions

Ideally, a buildingwide system of positive behavioral supports would be developed by a collaborative team including representatives of all stakeholder groups (administrators, teachers, parents, students, and other building staff). The team would identify, in advance of implementation, responsibilities for teaching, monitoring, and record keeping. All staff members would be responsible for developing rules and correction procedures, for teaching them to students, and for actively monitoring student behavior. Administrators should be active participants in the process; part of their responsibility is to monitor and reinforce teacher/staff implementation of the components in classrooms and in nonclassroom areas.

We will discuss each of the PBS components in the following section; examples are also provided. Some of the specific interventions mentioned in this section (e.g., token economy, reinforcement) will be covered at length in chapters 5 and 6.

A Statement of Purpose That Is Worded Positively and Describes Student Academic and Behavioral Outcomes. Most schools use mission statements, creeds, slogans, mascots, and others symbols to represent their vision and purpose, and promote positive values, group identification, and unity. "Special rituals, stories, and events define a school community's core values and ensure their perpetuation" (Glickman, 2003, p. 34). Many schools begin the day with a special homeroom period or "morning circle," begin assemblies with the school song or pledge, and develop ceremonies unique to their mission statement. **Examples:** Students at Downing High School are Capable, Caring, and Connected to the Community (this statement is based on principles of *Cooperative Discipline* by Albert [1996]). The Wilmore Wildcats are respectful, responsible, and ready to learn. The Belleview Tigers are gracious, respectful, and responsible (GRR).

Schoolwide Behavioral Rules and Expectations That Provide Clearly Stated, Age-Appropriate Replacement Behaviors for Identified School Problems. Because statements of purpose are necessarily vague, they must be actualized or broken down into clearly stated rules or expectations. Rules should be succinct, few in number, and worded positively. (See Chapter 5, Establishing Rules and Routines.) Each rule should correspond to the behavior desired, replacing the behavior that is problematic. **Examples:** Come to class prepared to learn (to address students arriving late without needed materials). Keep hands and feet to self (to respond to pushing in line). An elementary school in the Pacific Northwest identified their expectations as "Be Kind. Be Safe. Be Responsible" (Lewis-Palmer, Sugai, & Larson, 1999, p. 5). The High Five Program developed by Fern Ridge Middle School (Taylor-Greene & Kartub, 2000) is another example of a PBS-based set of expectations:

1. Be Respectful
2. Be Responsible
3. Follow Directions
4. Keep Hands and Feet to Self
5. Be There—Be Ready (p. 233)

Belleview Tigers are:

Gracious

Respectful

Responsible

FIGURE 4–2 Schoolwide Expectations Example: Belleview Beliefs

Figure 4-2 shows another example of schoolwide expectations for the fictitious Belleview Tigers.

Procedures for Teaching Expected Behavior That Use Research-Validated Procedures for Direct Instruction in the Desired Social Skills and Behaviors. It is not sufficient to state expectations and post them in visible places around school. Rules and routines must be explicitly taught to students with EBD. Effective direct instructional techniques must also be used to teach replacement behaviors that involve new social skills. (see Chapter 5, Teach Social Skills). To implement PBS consistently and schoolwide, staff must teach and reinforce expectations in all environments. An efficient way to coordinate this is to develop and disseminate lesson plans. For example, the Belleview Tigers have identified their expectations as "Be Gracious, Be Respectful, Be Responsible." The PBS team needs to specifically describe what behaviors these three rules mean, and provide guidance for teachers on how to teach being gracious, respectful, and responsible. A social skills lesson on graciousness might include saying "please" and "thank you" and waiting your turn.

Procedures for Encouraging Expected Behavior That Initially Include Token and Tangible Incentives Paired with Social Recognition and Natural Reinforcers and Fade Concrete Incentives as Students Master the New Skills. The team must identify a reinforcement strategy that encourages students who exhibit the desired behaviors. The rewards may be tangible, social, or token, and earned by individuals or groups (e.g., the 3rd grade, the 1st lunch period, or the Blue Team). For example, the Belleview Tigers are working on being responsible in the lunchroom, which means not taking food you won't eat, throwing trash away, and returning dishes and trays to the conveyor belt. Each day, each class that has 100% of students demonstrating responsibility receives a tiger sticker on the lunchroom chart. As soon as the class has received 15 stickers, they earn a pizza party with the principal. The team and building administration may also wish to develop a reinforcement strategy for teachers who actively participate in the schoolwide implementation of PBS. This means that when each Belleview classroom earns their pizza party, the teacher earns a gift certificate at a local restaurant. For more options, see Chapter 6, Reinforcement Strategies.

Procedures for Discouraging Problem Behavior That Provide a Continuum of Consequences That Are Applied Schoolwide, Based on a Written Code or Policy. Each building needs an individualized code of conduct or discipline policy that outlines the potential consequences for serious rule infractions. A continuum of graduated options should be available, based on the type and severity of behavior. The five-level system described in Chapter 3 as a way of prioritizing behavioral targets could also be used to guide selection of consequences. Behaviors on levels 1 and 2 would most likely result in consequences within the classroom (e.g., loss of privileges), while levels 3 through 5 might necessitate removal or administrative intervention (e.g., restitution, in-school suspension). For example, Melissa frequently interrupts her peers and speaks without raising her hand in class, in violation of the "Be Respectful" expectation. Her teacher decides this is a Level 2 behavior, reminds Melissa of the expectation to take turns and listen when others are speaking, and takes away 5 token economy points each time Melissa exhibits this behavior. However, when Melissa refuses to follow the paraprofessional's instructions during recess, her teacher recognizes a Level 4 behavior, reminds Melissa that being respectful means following instructions, and requires Melissa to spend her next recess period writing an apology to the recess monitor. Again, schoolwide consistency is the key to successful implementation.

Procedures for Record Keeping That Support Making Data-Based Instructional Decisions.

Where to Begin? The team's first task is to conduct a functional behavioral assessment in the schoolwide setting. What are the problems identified by teachers? Where are the most common trouble spots? What data is available to support teacher perceptions? Additional questions to guide data collection and analysis include: "(a) What is the nature of recent behavioral incidents (e.g., number of referrals per day per month, type of behavioral incidents, location of behavioral incidents)? and (b) What behavior supports are in place and to what degree must they be improved?" (Lewis-Palmer et al., 1999, p. 2).

Schools collect mountains of data; the team's job is to determine which data will be useful in developing the PBS plan and what additional information is needed. Common activities include reviewing existing data and permanent products from teachers and administration, using rating scales or surveys to identify concerns and priorities, interviewing stakeholders, and directly observing and recording student behavior (Lewis-Palmer et al., 1999). For example, the Belleview teachers have identified trash on the floor as a problem in the lunchroom and hallways. For a week, the custodian and lunchroom manager keep track of how many items of trash they pick up in those two locations to serve as baseline data for the team.

Using Data to Identify Priorities. One strategy for identifying trouble spots is to use office discipline referrals as a critical indicator. (See Figure 4-3 for a sample data collection form.) "Administrators and faculty committed to improving the schoolwide discipline systems in their school may find value in examining: (a) the total number of office discipline referrals for a school year; (b) the number of students enrolled during the school year; (c) the number of school days in the year; and (d) the allocation of office discipline referrals by student, location, and date. . . . For school faculty members to use their information to the best advantage, multiple years of information should be compared" (Sugai et al., 2000, p. 96). **Example:** Sugai and colleagues (2000) examined data from 20 elementary and middle schools from seven districts (for

STUDENT BEHAVIOR REFERRAL

Student: _____ Date: _____ Time: _____

Grade Level: _____ Referred by: _____ Location of Incident: _____

REASON(S) FOR REFERRAL

Aggressive Behavior
[ ] Destruction of property
[ ] Throwing objects
[ ] Physical aggression
[ ] Self-damaging behaviors
[ ] Verbal abuse or threats
[ ] Fighting
Insubordination/Disrespect
[ ] Leaving area without permission
[ ] Arguing with teacher
[ ] Persistent intentional disruption
[ ] Persistent cursing/sexual language
[ ] Explicit sexual behavior
Contraband
[ ] Possession of _____
Other Serious Infraction
[ ] Describe:
Comments:

[ ] Student may return to class when de-escalated, finished processing, and ready to work.
[ ] Student may return to class at the end of this period—time _____. (Please send classwork.)
[ ] Other _____.

CLASSROOM INTERVENTIONS

[ ] Modified instructional methods/demands
[ ] Review rules/clarify expectations
[ ] Offer choices/alternatives
[ ] Verbal redirection—# of times _____
[ ] Physical redirection
[ ] Teacher/student conference
[ ] Conference with _____
[ ] Changed placement within the classroom
[ ] Classroom consequences/loss of privileges
[ ] Required restitution
[ ] Brief time-out in classroom (5–10 minutes)
[ ] Time-out in the buddy/recovery room
[ ] Other—describe: _____

_____
Teacher signature

INTERVENTIONS WHILE OUT OF ROOM

[ ] Demonstrated de-escalation by following instructions, talking quietly, etc.
[ ] Completed think sheet (copy attached).
[ ] Verbally processed behavior with staff.
[ ] Completed other therapeutic worksheet or assignment: _____
[ ] Demonstrated on-task behavior by working on assignment for _____ minutes.
[ ] Agreed-upon consequence/required restitution _____
[ ] Other _____

Comments/Follow-up Plan:

_____
Support Staff Signature

Time student returned to class: _____

FIGURE 4–3 Sample Office Referral Sheet

multiple years, where available), and used it to calculate the following statistics:

1. The mean number of office discipline referrals per student attending school.
2. The mean number of office referrals per student who received at least one referral.
3. The average number of office discipline referrals per school day.
4. The proportion of students with 1+ (one or more) and 10+ (10 or more) referrals, and
5. The proportion of all referrals accounted for by the 5% of students with the most office discipline referrals. (p. 97)

The Missouri PBS Initiative (CISE, 2002) suggests the following rubric for decision making based on office referral data:

- Implement universal, schoolwide interventions when more than 35% of students receive referrals in a year.
- Use universal interventions targeting specific nonclassroom settings when many problems occur in a specific area.
- Focus on classroomwide interventions when more than 50% of office referrals come from the classroom.
- Develop small group and individual interventions for the worst repeat offenders (approximately 5%).

Implementing PBS in Nonclassroom Settings. While PBS components (e.g., rules, expectations) should be taught and modeled in every classroom, the schoolwide focus is often on behaviors in specific nonclassroom settings, such as hallway, cafeteria, auditorium, restroom, and bus. The team must identify which nonclassroom settings to target, and then prioritize them. There is no need to implement PBS on the bus if the school has few problems with student bus-riding behaviors. Figure 4–4 demonstrates how the Belleview Tigers defined their key beliefs to address student behaviors in the halls.

Lewis and Sugai (1999) have identified a general strategy for addressing nonclassroom problems:

> Because nonclassroom settings tend to involve larger numbers of students than classroom contexts and focus on supervision instead of academic instruction, attention is directed toward (a) features of the environment, (b) establishing predictable routines, (c) teaching students appropriate setting-specific behaviors, and (d) focusing staff on the effective use of active supervision strategies. (p. 10)

Similarly, Sugai and Horner (2002) suggest that interventions in nonclassroom settings include "(a) active

In the halls, Belleview Tigers are:

Gracious
- **Walk quietly**
- **Keep hands and feet to self**
- **Stay to the right**

Respectful
- **Use quiet voices**
- **Admire displays of student work**

Responsible
- **Follow directions**
- **Stay with your group**

FIGURE 4–4   Nonclassroom Example: Hallway Expectations

supervision, (b) high rates of positive reinforcement, (c) clearly taught consequences for rule violations, and (d) precorrections (preteaching) for problem situations" (p. 132).

If error correction is necessary in nonclassroom settings, White, Algozzine, Audette, Marr, and Ellis (2001) recommend a four-step correction procedure. In a friendly but firm tone:

1. State the behavior.
2. State the violated rule or expectation.
3. State the agreed-upon consequence.
4. Offer encouragement to prevent future violations. (p. 5)

Figure 4–5 illustrates a "Belleview Buck" used to reinforce student behavior in the hallway, and an "Oops" slip used as a consequence for a first infraction.

$ Belleview Buck $

_____ (name) was

awarded a Belleview Buck on _____ (date)

by _____ (name) for

being ☐ Gracious ☐ Respectful ☐ Responsible

Oops!

_____ (name) forgot to be

☐ Gracious ☐ Respectful ☐ Responsible today.

Remember to _____.

_____ (date) _____ (name)

FIGURE 4–5 Reward and Consequence Examples: Belleview Buck and Oops Slip

The Emerging PBS Research Base

Turnbull, Wilcox, Stowe, and Turnbull (2000) point out that a sufficient research base existed in 1997 for Congress to identify PBS as the intervention of choice for students with problematic behaviors. In addition, there was substantial prior support for the elements of PBS in law and public policy. This section will provide brief overviews of a sampling of recent research studies examining the efficacy of PBS interventions.

One study, conducted by Lewis, Sugai, and Colvin (1998) in a public elementary school, examined the impact of social-skills instruction and implementation of PBS strategies in the school cafeteria, at recess, and in the halls during transition. The interventions studied included use of social praise and tangible incentives for compliant behavior and an error-correction procedure for inappropriate behavior. The investigators found that targeted problem behaviors were reduced in all three settings.

In a similar study at another elementary school implementing PBS, direct social-skills instruction and a group contingency intervention reduced problem behavior across three recess periods (Lewis, Powers, Kelk, & Newcomer, 2002).

A study using precorrection and active supervision to reduce problem behaviors on the playground (Lewis, Colvin, & Sugai, 2000) found that problem behaviors declined although teacher supervision activities actually did not increase measurably.

Nelson and Martella (1998) investigated the impact of two PBS components—establishing, teaching, and reinforcing schoolwide rules and routines; and consistently responding to disruptive behavior—in an elementary school. They found that office referrals and disciplinary actions decreased over the four-year duration of the study.

Kartub, Taylor-Greene, March, and Horner (2000) studied the impact of a middle school intervention that used PBS strategies (teaching, monitoring, and rewarding appropriate behavior) to reduce hallway noise. They found that the initial time invested in teaching appropriate behavior was warranted, given the improvement in lunch transitions. As they observed, "If many students (say, more than 3%) engage in the same disruptive behavior, it is not the students but the environment that needs to change" (p. 179).

One school district implemented a comprehensive prevention program in seven elementary schools in one district (Nelson, Martella, & Marchand-Martella, 2002). The five intervention components were: schoolwide discipline based on the PBS model, one-to-one reading tutoring, conflict resolution, family management training using videotapes, and individualized functional behavior intervention plans for disruptive students. During the two-year study, researchers observed positive effects on the number of disciplinary referrals, overall academic performance, and social adjustment and academic performance of targeted students with disruptive behaviors.

After one year of PBS implementation using the High Five Program, Taylor-Greene and Kartub (2000) observed that the Fern Ridge Middle School experienced a 47% reduction in office referrals. In 2000, after five years of High Fives, discipline referrals were down 68% from the 1994–1995 levels (Taylor-Greene & Kartub, 2000). They described other, more qualitative benefits of the PBS effort: "Today, all adults in the school operate from a positive team approach. Efforts are directed toward working with students—helping them to make appropriate choices and stay in school. Staff encourage students to be part of the solution rather than the problem, and they have learned the value of teaching and reinforcing students for appropriate behavior" (p. 234).

In reviewing the literature concerning implementation of PBS programs, Horner and Sugai (2000) identified consistent themes of successful schoolwide behavioral support initiatives:

1. Schoolwide behavior support procedures were designed by local teams.
2. Successful schools relied on clear administrative direction and support.
3. Schools identified a small number of behavioral expectations that defined the culture of the school.

4. The behavioral expectations were taught to all students.
5. Performing to the behavioral expectations was rewarded through an ongoing recognition system.
6. Dangerous and disruptive behavior resulted in corrections. Problem behaviors were neither ignored nor rewarded.
7. Information on student performance was collected continuously and summarized for decision making by local teams. (p. 231)

CHAPTER SUMMARY

- Prevention of misbehavior in schools may be addressed at three levels: schoolwide strategies, classroom strategies, and individual strategies. This chapter focused on the characteristics of successful schoolwide systems. At the individual school building level, a proactive system of structure and supports should include policies and procedures to encourage expected behaviors and discourage problem behaviors. The PBS model is a promising model, with the potential to improve school outcomes for all students, including those with EBD. Essential features of a schoolwide PBS system were described, along with a review of recent implementation studies. Although these interventions have proven effective with many students, they are typically not sufficient for those students with severe emotional and behavioral disorders. Chapter 5 will include strategies for structuring a classroom to support students with challenging behaviors. Chapter 6 will address the more challenging students who require individual or small-group interventions, often focused on consequences or contingent reinforcement. Additional strategies for use with specific clinical populations will be found in Part II of this text. However, it is important to remember that for individualized interventions to be most effective, the essential components of schoolwide and classroom prevention must also be in place.

CHECK YOUR UNDERSTANDING

1. *True or False*. Students with EBD have the least favorable postschool outcomes of any group of students with disabilities.
2. *True or False*. Positive behavior supports are recommended by IDEA 1997.

3. Describe the three levels of school-based prevention activities and provide an example of each.
4. Students with EBD are at risk for life-long problems in what areas?
5. School rules should be _____, _____, and _____.
6. What was your high school mascot? Motto? How were they used to promote unity and school spirit?
7. Name four common nonclassroom areas where behavior problems often occur.
8. According to Horner and Sugai (2000), what are the common themes of successful PBS programs?
9. How are PBS and FBA related at the schoolwide level?
10. When schoolwide interventions do not succeed in preventing the misbehavior of a small group of students, what is the next logical option?

APPLICATION ACTIVITIES

1. In a small group, design a PBS schoolwide plan for Downing High School that includes a statement of purpose and a list of expectations. Your office referral data indicates that most of your problems occur in the halls during transition time and in the cafeteria. The most common misbehaviors are yelling, running, and inappropriate physical contact. Define expectations for the halls and cafeteria and design a reward and consequence system.
2. Visit the OSEP Technical Assistance Center for Positive Behavior Interventions and Supports at http://www.pbis.org. Follow their links to visit a school implementing PBS.
3. Locate and read one of the articles cited under "The Emerging Research Base" and identify the critical features of PBS exemplified in that school or district's plan.

CHAPTER 5

BEST PRACTICES FOR PREVENTING PROBLEM BEHAVIORS
Classwide Strategies and Interventions

CHAPTER PREVIEW

CONNECTING TO THE CLASSROOM: *A Vignette*

Ms. Andrews took one last look around the classroom before going out into the hall to greet her new students. She reviewed her mental list of "things to do before school starts":

- Review records and organize students (and desks) into cooperative learning groups.
- Post class schedule and rules.
- Create an agenda of routines to teach prior to recess, lunch, and gym class.
- Organize lesson plans and materials so they are easily accessible.
- Decorate bulletin board for exemplary work and divide into areas labeled with each student's name.
- Get management-system materials and supplies ready to go.

Ms. Andrews put her hand into her pocket and, feeling the happy-face stickers, smiled to herself. "It's going to be a great year," she thought.

CREATING A POSITIVE CLASSROOM LEARNING ENVIRONMENT

In 1994, the U.S. Department of Education's Office of Special Education Programs disseminated the *National Agenda for Achieving Better Results for Children and Youth with Serious Emotional Disturbance* (Chesapeake Institute, 1994). The first of seven strategic targets identified in that document was to expand positive learning opportunities and results for students with serious emotional disturbance (SED) or EBD. But what are positive learning opportunities? Chapter 4 discussed preventing problem behavior through careful schoolwide planning and use of buildingwide positive behavioral strategies that have proven effective for many students with garden variety behavior problems. This chapter will look in greater detail at the teacher behaviors and management strategies that have been linked to higher levels of academic functioning and lower levels of problem behaviors. See Table 5-1 for a list of key indicators of effective programs for students with EBD. The scope of this book does not permit a detailed analysis of each of the desirable EBD program indicators. However, it is worth noting that effective programs and classrooms attend to environmental management as well as behavior management, to affective education as well as academic education, to the needs of the individual as well as to the needs of the group, and to planning for life-long success and satisfaction for students. The focus of this chapter will be on creating an effective classroom environment for all children, including those with EBD.

Viewpoints on Effective Classrooms

Now, more than ever, we must take a good look at what we are teaching our children by the way we treat

TABLE 5–1   Quality Program Indicators

I. Environmental Management: The systematic use of resources, physical factors and organizational and communication schema to structure students' total environment for the purpose of providing necessary support and control.

   a. Classroom organization and management support of functional behaviors.
   b. Resources are adequate, appropriate personnel with expertise in instruction, behavior and emotional needs are adequate and appropriate for program.
   c. Physical space/layout is used intentionally to support students' emotional/behavioral needs.
   d. The emotional climate is safe as demonstrated by students' willingness to initiate interactions or ask questions.
   e. Scheduling is done intentionally to support students' emotional/behavioral needs.
   f. Communication systems facilitate support for the student in the total environment.

II. Behavior Management: Systems, including classroom management, individual management, school rules, and crisis management systems to assist the student in obtaining and maintaining prerequisite behaviors for learning and to assume increasing responsibility for his/her own behavior.

   a. Systems for classroom management facilitate appropriate behaviors.
   b. Procedures and modifications are utilized to assist students in following the school and/or bus rules.
   c. Management systems are in place for atypical and crisis situations.
   d. There is a system for individual behavior management to facilitate appropriate behavior.
   e. Behavioral intervention or interactions are utilized to encourage students to be more responsible for their behavior.
   f. Behavior management systems involve key persons in the student's environment.

III. Affective Education: Systematic instruction, the primary purpose of which is to help students acquire information, attitudes and skills that will encourage appropriate behavior and mental health.

   a. Students are systematically provided with information and skills regarding behavior.
   b. Affective education covers personal, relationship, and life skills.
   c. Curriculum is selected on the basis of individual students' needs.
   d. Good instructional practices are employed to teach affective education.
   e. Transference and maintenance of skills is systematically planned and taught.

IV. Individuation and Personalization: Systematic assistance and support for which the primary purpose is to help the student with personalization and internalization about alternative ways to behaving and viewing one's beliefs, oneself, and the world.

   a. Students are systematically assisted in internalizing and personalizing new affective information and behavior skills.
   b. Good teaching/counseling strategies are employed to assist student in personalizing and internalizing information.

TABLE 5–1 *(continued)*

V. Academic: Systems that promote academic growth utilizing various techniques or curricula that is appropriate to the student's individual learning needs.

    a. A comprehensive academic curriculum is available for the student.
    b. Modifications/alternatives to the regular curriculum are provided when needed.
    c. Systems/structures accommodations are used to help maintain students in the least restrictive environment.
    d. Effective instruction is provided.

VI. Career/Life Skills/Transitions: Systems that develop skills necessary for productive, meaningful life outside of school. These systems provide the link between the skills a student gains in his/her school experience and application of those skills in the nonacademic setting.

    a. Students are systematically provided with information/skills necessary for life outside of school.
    b. Curriculum is appropriate in content, level, scope, and developmental sequence.
    c. Effective instruction is demonstrated.

Source: © 2003, CCBD/CEC. From Neel, R. S., Cessna, K. K., Borock, J., & Bechard, S. (2003, Spring). Quality program indicators for children with emotional and behavioral disorders. *Beyond Behavior,* Table 1, pp. 6–9. [Adapted with permission.]

- Power and classroom leadership are shared; many activities are collaborative
- Teacher has established rapport and made a personal connection with each student
- Emphasis is on establishing and meeting high, but reasonable, expectations
- High levels of positive teacher–student interactions are present
- High levels of appropriate and accurate student responses are in evidence
- Emphasis is on helping students do the right thing and preventing misbehavior, rather than waiting until an infraction occurs and then applying negative or punitive consequences
- A continuum of graduated consequences is matched to individual students and their problem behaviors
- Techniques are used to keep student negative feelings and behavior from escalating

FIGURE 5–1 Features of Positive Classrooms

them. Controlling their behavior is simply not enough. We must help them become decision makers and critical thinkers. We must help them feel that they can contribute to society, and we must enhance their joy for learning. (Curwin & Mendler, 1988, p. vii)

Views on good teaching and learning have shifted from a transmission view, in which teachers mostly explain and demonstrate and students mostly memorize or replicate, to a social construction or learning community view, in which teachers and students share responsibility for initiating and guiding learning efforts. (Brophy, 1998, p. 2)

Classroom management is complex: what constitutes a good management strategy depends (at least) upon the teacher's role, personality, goals, and strategies; characteristics of the management "problem"; and the role, personality, developmental level, and goals of the students. (McCaslin & Good, 1998, p. 172)

The traditional vision of a well-managed classroom featured an authoritarian teacher demanding and obtaining compliance, with students sitting quietly, hands folded, in straight rows of desks. However, this style of management does not fit with the current image of educators as facilitators of learning, helping students develop higher-order thinking skills in classes in which teachers and students work both independently and collaboratively to solve problems. Freiberg (1998) describes this more flexible, student-centered classroom as emphasizing caring, guidance, cooperation, and the building of self-discipline, while encouraging students to think for themselves and to help each other. Figure 5-1 lists common features of positive classrooms.

The behaviors required for all students to be successful in inclusive classrooms go beyond simply following the rules and completing assignments (see Box 5-1). Students must develop the skills needed to work independently, as well as to participate successfully in small groups and class discussions. Teachers, then, must determine which skills students need and create a positive environment in which students can learn and interact while facilitating positive work habits and social interactions. In doing so, teachers must first address their own attitudes and behaviors, which in turn may have a dramatic influence on students' classroom behaviors (Carpenter & McKee-Higgins, 1996). "Simply put, if the teacher is trying to create a trusting, cooperative learning environment for students, then the management system must also promote the same dispositions, behaviors, and skills—in part through opportunities for thinking and problem solving in the academic and social spheres" (McCaslin & Good, 1998, p. 173).

There is no one perfect management style that will fit every teacher and every classroom of students. This is especially true when the classroom includes students with emotional or behavioral problems. However, Traynor (2002) found that two groups of teachers have better outcomes, those who: (a) enforce a specific and reasonable set of classroom rules, or (b) focus on student self-control. These two management styles allow students to practice and develop higher-level thinking and learning skills, and maintain or contribute to self-esteem and emotional well-being.

The Role of Positive Teacher–Student Interactions

"When the teacher is defining consequences, a focus on positive consequences, not punishment, will ensure an environment that will promote positive interactions" (Hardman & Smith, 1999, p. 179). It may seem obvious that if teachers want to promote a positive, engaging classroom atmosphere, they should model and support the behaviors they want to see. However, the research on interactions between teachers and students with emotional and behavior problems suggests that this is not the approach many educators take with difficult-to-handle young people. Shores and Wehby (1999) reviewed a number of studies (e.g., Shores, Gunter, & Jack, 1993) that examined teacher interactions with students identified as EBD or as at-risk based on disruptive or aggressive classroom behavior. In their review, they found that, in general, teachers provided little praise or positive social reinforcement to these students when they exhibited desirable behaviors, with an average rate of only 2.5 positive interactions per hour in one study. They found that most teacher statements to the children were neutral commands, to which students generally complied, that were then followed by another teacher request rather than reinforcement. In these studies, responses to negative behavior could best be described as inconsistent, with teachers in one study responding to about every fifth infraction. One hypothesis formed by the

researchers about the underlying reasons for this data was that "teachers may engage in behavior to escape or avoid social contact with many of these difficult-to-teach children" (Shores & Wehby, 1999, p. 194).

In a study in which teachers deliberately tried to increase their rate of positive responses and decrease negative responses to 9th-grade students considered at risk for disruptive behavior, researchers found that time on task increased, more students completed their assignments, and the school experienced a 35.5% decrease in student suspensions (Mayer et al., 1993). Another study (Beyda, Zentall, & Ferko, 2002) demonstrated that in positive, student-centered instructional environments providing enhanced access to information, feedback, social stimulation, interest, and pacing, students with EBD exhibited higher rates of task-appropriate behavior and lower rates of negative behaviors, essentially looking very similar to their nondisabled peers. Not surprisingly, in classrooms in which teachers exhibited higher levels of control and negativity, students with EBD had higher levels of negative behavior as well. To facilitate an effective teaching and learning environment for both students and teachers, Gunter, Coutinho, and Cade (2002) recommend a ratio of three or four positive, desirable interactions to each undesirable or negative interaction.

The Use of Least-Intrusive Interventions

Writers associated with the psychoeducational model (introduced in Chapter 1) suggest that teachers focus on providing the support students need for success, intervening or interrupting in a way that redirects student behaviors while preserving dignity. This perspective would suggest that teachers "should only impose as much teacher or outside influence as is necessary to achieve desirable student behaviors and a positive learning climate" (Carpenter & McKee-Higgins, 1996, p. 198).

Most teachers find that they need a continuum of intervention strategies and techniques (Smith & Rivera, 1995) to be successful with a classroom of diverse students. For minor behaviors, such as talking quietly to a peer during instruction, something as simple as moving closer to the student may be sufficient to redirect the student's attention to the task at hand. This type of intervention can easily be accomplished with no interruption to the flow of instruction, and without calling unnecessary attention to a behavior you do not wish to encourage. For persistent or louder talking, a brief verbal redirection might be necessary. For major rule violations, especially those that pose a threat to safety,

BOX 5–1   Quinn Perspective

PERSPECTIVE: MARY MAGEE QUINN Multilevel Prevention for Classrooms

The three-tiered prevention model traditionally used by public health professionals has lately been applied to the prevention of antisocial behavior in schools. Much work has been done to show that this model is effective in preventing problem behaviors from occurring when implemented on a schoolwide basis. However, some teachers who believe in the value of this approach to prevention have reported that they have a difficult time convincing skeptics at the school level to buy into the model. For those teachers, I advocate implementing the model within their classrooms. Following are some suggestions for implementing the model in a classroom setting.

At the primary level the emphasis is on providing skills and supports that are needed by all students. In order to do this, ask yourself "What is it that *every* student needs in order to learn?" We know that students need predictability, such as being aware of behavioral expectations (or rules) and the consequences of meeting—or not meeting—those expectations. This is more than just listing the rules on the wall; this means teaching the rules and making sure everyone knows exactly what to do in each area of the classroom. It also means teaching routines, such as how you collect homework, sharpen pencils, are excused for the restroom, or line up. We may think this is understood, but don't take anything for granted; teach these routines and use them consistently.

It also is vitally important for all students to feel that they can be successful academically. Lessons must be relevant, well organized, and lead to mastery. Examine your lessons and ask yourself, "Is there any part of this lesson that will cause any of my students to be bored or frustrated?" If the answer is yes, make modifications to the overall lesson or to individual assignments to prevent this. Finally, make sure the environment is conducive to learning. Are there noises that might distract students (fish tank or humming lights)? Is there clutter? Examine the physical arrangement of your classroom to make sure that there is nothing distracting in areas where students are asked to concentrate. These universal approaches to insuring that the learning environment is conducive to the learning of every child will prevent many behavior problems.

At the secondary level, the emphasis is on providing skills and supports to those students who are at risk for academic failure or behavior problems. Identify those students who might benefit from social skills (e.g., listening, following directions) or academic support (e.g., tutoring, mentoring, curricular modification, more time to complete assignments, response modification or materials modification) and provide them in small-group settings. Also, pay special attention to the seating arrangements and scheduling (i.e., attention span) for these students. Are you expecting someone with an attention span of 10 minutes to concentrate on a lecture for more than 30 minutes? If this is the case, break presentations up into smaller segments.

At the tertiary level, the emphasis is on students who are already failing academically or who are having behavior problems. These students may need a functional assessment of their behavior (or learning problem) so you can identify more individualized ways to help them. At this level, it is important for you to include the services from others in the school (e.g., counselor, behavior specialist, peer mediator). It also is important to include the student and his or her parents in determining the function of the behavior and some potential interventions for making the student feel more successful in the classroom.

The three-tiered approach can easily be implemented at the classroom level and used as a model for prevention. If one of your goals is to advocate for schoolwide prevention, I suggest that you collect data on changes in academic achievement and behavior problems. This will help you in your efforts to convince skeptics of the power of prevention.

Mary Magee Quinn is a senior research analyst at the National Institutes of Research, and deputy director of the Center for Effective Collaboration and Practice.

teachers need preestablished consequences that can be applied swiftly and unemotionally. What is needed is a flexible system that allows teachers to match the intensity of intervention to the intensity of the problem behavior, always with the intent of minimizing instructional interruptions.

The remainder of this chapter provides well-established strategies for structuring a classroom for students with EBD. These techniques will be most effective in a classroom in which the buildingwide system of PBS preventative techniques is in place (as discussed in Chapter 4). The strategies may be used individually or in various combinations as teachers encourage development and maintenance of new appropriate behaviors to replace those that are not functional in the classroom.

Structuring the Physical Environment: Organizing for Student Success

Experienced teachers have found that one of the keys to managing academic activities is to consider the way the classroom is organized. Students with EBD, in particular, need a structured and consistent classroom environment (Wehby, Symons, Canale, & Go, 1998). The most effective classrooms are dynamic organisms, providing structure and needed support, yet able to adapt to meet the needs of individual students. The physical space in the classroom should suit the academic objectives and activities being addressed, provide for smooth teacher and student movement, and avoid problem traffic patterns and bottlenecks (Englert, 1984; Evertson, 1986). One method of addressing the issue of space usage and traffic flow is to create a paper scale model of the classroom and furniture to assist in planning the layout of the room. The classroom should be arranged to allow the teacher easy view of all students from various positions in the room, as well as quick and easy access to all students. Preferential or designated seating may be necessary for students who demonstrate the need for teacher proximity or are distracted easily by external stimuli, or to minimize the impact of sensory impairments.

While it may seem obvious, the degree to which furniture and desks match the size of the students is an important consideration. Students who are uncomfortable are more likely to be distracted and unable to sit still.

Another important consideration is how instructional materials are organized. For students who have attention and behavior problems, dangerous or seductive objects need to be stored securely out of sight. Although creating a warm and supportive learning atmosphere is important to many teachers, access to distractors should be limited. Give thought to how and where students store their materials, supplies, and backpacks.

Decide whether specific areas will be designated for use by individuals or small groups of students (e.g., computer area, "safe spot"). The desire for quiet and privacy must be balanced with the need for teacher access to, and supervision of, those areas during instruction. Identify areas that are off limits to students (e.g., the teacher's desk, the file cabinet) or that require permission to access (e.g., the computer, the storage cabinet). Provide labels and boundary markers to identify special areas, and to clarify any specific rules and expectations for activities that take place in those areas.

Structuring the Instructional Environment: Effective Instructional Techniques and Inclusive Strategies

In addition to structuring the EBD student's physical environment, it is important that instruction also be organized to maximize successful participation and minimize down time. This section will describe strategies for scheduling and time management, effective communication, and planning and managing instructional activities.

Scheduling and Time Management. The goal of an effective teacher is to maximize the time students are actively engaged in learning, and limit the time spent in noninstructional activities, such as waiting and transitioning (Brophy, 1998), or engaging in misbehavior. Many students with EBD experience their most problematic behaviors during "down time" in the classroom.

Research on time usage has demonstrated that the same amount of learning time can have different outcomes or consequences, depending both on student attention and appropriate instruction (Good, 1984). Careful scheduling can increase the time available for instruction and the opportunity to learn (Englert, 1984).

Teachers should consider both the time allocated to each subject, and how that time is used for various activities within each subject area, in an effort to provide the most time available to tasks that actively engage students (Berliner, 1984; Brophy, 1988). Although the proportion of time students spend actively engaged in learning will vary, depending on the task requirements and other factors, some general guidelines are needed to enable the teacher to determine whether student attention to task is at an appropriate level. For most classroom whole-group or small-group activities, such as discussion and guided practice, students should be actively engaged in the task 90% of the time. For independent practice activities with teacher monitoring, 80% is often the optimal level of engagement for students with special needs. For students with EBD, these engagement rates must be realistic goals; it is virtually impossible for anyone to stay totally focused for an entire class period, let alone an entire school day.

Communication. The techniques and strategies used to guide communication in the classroom can have a dramatic impact on student achievement, behavior, and self-esteem. For teachers of students with EBD, positive communication is often the key to development of rapport and healthy relationships with students. Three classroom communication techniques—attention signals, feedback and error correction, and student questioning and responding—are essential for establishing positive communication.

Attention Signals. Before attempting to deliver instruction, teachers must first gain or focus the attention of the students. This can be accomplished by using **attention signals**—a variety of verbal and nonverbal cues and signals—depending on the circumstances. Coaches may blow a whistle to interrupt a noisy sports activity, but that signal would be too intrusive in the classroom. Common nonverbal classroom signals include turning the lights on or off, ringing a small bell or chime, or raising a hand in the air. Verbal cues might include a warning or heads-up about an impending transition (e.g., "You have 10 seconds before we begin the film") or specific instructions (e.g., "Please open your textbook to page 42 and get ready to take notes"). Regardless of the signal chosen, the procedure must be explicitly taught and modeled for students (e.g., "When I hold my hand up, that means to stop what you are doing, be quiet, and listen for instructions"). It is critical to note that students with EBD may have difficulty following multistep directions. Brief instructions that are clear and concise will result in better student compliance.

Feedback. In general, students are most responsive to **feedback** that is immediate, constructive, relevant, and specific (Wood, Long & Fecser, 2001). For example, a paper returned a week later that says "Nice job!" at the top does not carry the same message as one returned immediately that says, "Nice job on this week's spelling test. You got 8 out of 10 words, now we just need to review that rule about CVCE words." Not surprisingly, most people respond better to positive feedback. Lewis and Sugai (1999) suggest a ratio of four positive statements for every negative or corrective teacher statement. Students with EBD, and those who have experienced long-term frustration and failure in school settings, may need even higher levels of reinforcement. Positive statements include both praise (e.g., "Tashia, I can tell you really worked hard on this assignment. Look at how many problems you finished correctly in 20 minutes!") and encouragement (e.g., "Carla, I know you are feeling frustrated, but I'm sure together we can figure this out. Let's give it one more try").

Some students with EBD may have experienced so much failure that they will initially respond negatively to praise statements. Students unaccustomed to success may require patience while they adjust to not always being in trouble. Some will respond less negatively if the praise is less public, written on the paper, or stated privately rather than in front of peers.

Questioning and Error Correction. In an effort to focus on core content knowledge, much of the drill-and-practice material used with students who have learning and behavior problems tends to rely on factual/recall questioning techniques. Students with EBD should be exposed to questions at the varying levels of Bloom's taxonomy of educational objectives (1979). However, they may need additional time, practice, and encouragement to generate confident responses to higher-level questions than do their typically achieving peers. Students with EBD may need increased **opportunities to respond (OTR)** as well. Unfortunately, research on effective teaching practices seems to suggest that teachers of students with EBD actually provide lower rates of instruction (Shores et al., 1993). In 1987, the Council for Exceptional Children published recommendations concerning rates of OTR for students with mild-moderate disabilities. Sutherland and Wehby (2001) summarized those guidelines as follows:

> During instruction of new material, teachers should elicit 4 to 6 responses per minute from students and students should respond with 80% accuracy. During practice or drill work, students should respond at a rate of 8 to 12 responses per minute, with 90% accuracy. (p. 114)

Teachers should handle incorrect student responses in a supportive, nonjudgmental manner. Madeline Hunter (1994) identified a process she called "dignifying errors," that provides an effective way to respond to incorrect answers without triggering the negative emotional response teachers often get from students with EBD. First, reframe the student's response as a correct answer by linking it to a different question, then provide the student with the correct answer, and finally hold the student accountable for providing the correct response, as shown in the following example:

Teacher: Who was the first president of the United States?
Jaime: Abraham Lincoln.
Teacher: You are remembering Abraham Lincoln, who served as our 16th president during the Civil War. I was looking for our first president, George Washington. I'll come back to you in a few minutes with that question. Our first president was. . . ?
Jaime: George Washington.

Planning for Academic Success.   One of the first things a teacher can do, even before the school year begins, is establish clear instructional goals. Classwide goals are generally set in terms of the curriculum involved, and the expectations or standards of the school and community in which the classroom is located. It may be useful for the beginning teacher to make an outline or calendar of the sequence of overall goals for the year, broken down into grading periods, before attempting to write daily and weekly lesson plans. Although experienced teachers know that long-range plans are always subject to change, establishing clear goals helps keep the teacher accountable for covering the content, and provides a yardstick against which to measure progress through the curriculum.

After long-range classroom goals have been established, teachers also must consider the demands of the curriculum in relation to the specific group of students in their classroom. Classwork that is too easy or too difficult for individual students is likely to result in an increase in behavior problems; therefore, determining the appropriate quantity, quality, and level of challenge in classroom activities is critical to preventing misbehavior. Students with EBD being served in inclusive settings may require modifications or accommodations to allow them to access the general education curriculum alongside their peers (Choate, 2000). Those receiving services in pull-out programs may need to work on IEP academic goals that

differ from the general education curriculum, or have objectives that are sequenced differently than those in the general education classroom. In addition, students with EBD are likely to have IEP goals focused on affect, behavior, or social skills that are outside the realm of traditional general education curriculum. It seems ironic that students who have been identified as educationally disabled often are responsible for mastering a more extensive set of behavioral and social competencies than their typically achieving peers. Scheduling and coordinating the activities of a diverse caseload of students with EBD is often the first challenge of a new school year.

Lesson Planning.   Educators have developed a number of models to guide effective lesson planning (e.g., Hunter, 1994). These rubrics have a number of common features that relate to the needs of students with EBD, as follows:

- **Preparation/advance organizer/anticipatory set**—Students with EBD often require additional assistance connecting instruction to previous experience in meaningful ways. They also are likely to challenge the relevance of curriculum (e.g., "Why do we have to do this anyway? I'm never going to use this stuff!"). Therefore, it is essential to provide an introduction to each lesson that relates it to prior knowledge and provides a clear rationale or motivational statement.
- **Direct instruction/model**—Students with EBD are often not good self-starters and may have difficulty with self-instructional materials—both in terms of resistance and poor strategies for seeking assistance when needed. Therefore, provide explicit, direct instruction and modeling when new curriculum involves unfamiliar concepts, vocabulary, or task requirements.
- **Opportunities for practice/generalization**—Teachers must provide students with EBD sufficient time to practice new skills and to achieve mastery and fluency. In addition, these students often need explicit instruction in how to discriminate the situations in which the new skills should be applied or generalized. Therefore, provide examples—when and where to use the skill—and nonexamples—when and where *not* to use the skill.
- **Evaluation**—Lesson evaluation has two important components as it relates to the student with EBD. First, how did the student perform relative to progress on IEP goals and objectives? Second, what modifications would make the lesson more effective? Lesson planning is a process of continuous

improvement. Effective teachers refine and modify their lesson plans based on student performance.

Figures 5-2, 5-3, and 5-4 provide an overview of lesson planning steps, a blank lesson plan form, and a completed sample lesson plan.

Student Monitoring. Another important classroom variable is the degree to which the teacher is able to stay on top of what all of the students are doing in the classroom. Englert (1984) used the terms "withitness" and "overlappingness" to describe the effective teacher who continuously monitors the entire room, whether engaged in whole-group, small-group, or individual instruction. Kea (1988) described three aspects of **instructional monitoring**. First, teachers watch groups and attend to what is happening in the entire room and judge how well the total activity system is functioning. Second, teachers observe student conduct or behavior, paying particular attention to any deviations from the prescribed program. Third, teachers monitor the pace, rhythm, and duration of classroom events. Thus, effective classroom managers are continuously monitoring everything going on in the room—including student attention, behavior, and progress. They accomplish this while circulating through the room providing individual assistance and feedback, directing small-group instruction, maintaining visual contact with all class members, and using nonverbal signals to prevent student misbehavior.

Grouping Students. Among the decisions a teacher makes when planning and scheduling classroom activities is whether presentation and practice will be

---

Step 1: Review. The review serves as a link to prior knowledge from previous lessons into the current lesson. The review should be brief and actively involve students whenever possible.

Step 2: Advance Organizer. The advance organizer sets the stage for the entire lesson. It serves several purposes. First, it gives the order in which the lesson will occur (e.g., "First we will see a video about icebergs, next we will measure the depth of some famous icebergs, and finally, we will take a little quiz about icebergs"). Second, it provides a rationale for why the lesson is important (e.g., "Why would it be important for a captain of a ship to know the location and depth of an iceberg?"). Next, explicitly state your instructional objective. Tell the students what they will know or be able to do at the conclusion of the lesson. Finally, it tells the student how long the lesson will last (e.g., "Let's begin with our video, which is 15 minutes long"). These components are critical for learners who have difficulty maintaining their focus during instructional time.

Step 3: Presentation. This is the most important step in an effective lesson. The teacher must *teach* the students something about the topic. It sounds obvious but, unfortunately, many teachers skip this portion of the lesson and go directly into practice. Even with individualized instruction, the teacher must present information directly to the student. Gear the presentation phase of a lesson to the cognitive abilities and patience levels of your class. Lower-functioning students or students who have short attention spans need minipresentations not lasting more than 5 to 7 minutes. Higher-functioning students may benefit from presentations lasting 30 to 45 minutes. Don't rely on a work folder to meet this step in the lesson. Share your expertise. Teach something.

Step 4: Guided Practice. During this phase of the lesson, students practice newly learned concepts in a structured way while the teacher can still catch and correct mistakes as they occur. Some guided practice activities include work at the whiteboard or chalkboard, peer teams, small-group discussions, games, or individual projects. Whenever possible, include a self-check component in which students can compare their work products to a model or answer key. Guided practice should continue until correct responses are in the 80% to 90% range.

Step 5: Independent Practice. This is the "test" portion of your lesson, when you determine whether a student has achieved mastery of the concept(s) taught or if you need to go back and reteach any lesson content. Independent practice should include three essential components: (a) a direct test of the objective(s) you have set for the lesson, (b) evidence of whether the student is having problems with any portion of the material, and (c) no teacher coaching or assistance, other than to keep the student focused on completing the task. Again, in special education, a mastery criterion of 80% correct responses is often used.

Step 6: Evaluation. Whenever possible, provide students with immediate feedback on the quality and accuracy of their work. If your lesson does not lend itself to instantaneous critique (e.g., reading an essay for content and structure), try to provide some specific feedback that is positive. Noting what a student has done well will lay the foundation for better acceptance of future corrective feedback.

Step 7: Recap. Go back over the highlights of the presentation. The recap should be brief and to the point. It is the executive summary of your lesson; it should help students get a firm grasp on the content that was most important.

Step 8: Preview. At the end of each lesson, use a "tickler" to get students interested in the content that will come next. The preview helps tie together how concepts are linked to provide greater knowledge about a subject. Keep the preview short and exciting. Leave your learners wanting more.

FIGURE 5–2 Steps in an Effective Lesson Plan

Objective(s) of this lesson

Review

Advance Organizer

Presentation

Guided Practice

Independent Practice

Evaluation

Recap

Preview

FIGURE 5–3   Sample Lesson Plan Form

Pragmatics and Social Skills: Keeping a Positive Attitude

Objective(s) of this lesson
When presented with a description of a typical classroom situation, the student will identify and verbally state one technique to manage a positive attitude relevant to the situation with 100% accuracy on 4 out of 5 trials.

Review
Remember last week when we talked about the differences between a positive and a negative attitude? We discussed different examples of each kind of attitude and did role-plays on how to replace a negative statement with a positive change statement. How many of you can think of a situation in which you were angry at one of your teachers? How many of you can think of a time when one of your teachers was upset with you? One thing that can help in these situations is to have the right attitude.

Advance Organizer
Today we are going to continue learning about techniques we can use to present a positive attitude in difficult situations. We are going to develop some ideas as a group, then practice those ideas in small-group teams. Finally, you are going to take a Positive Attitude Quiz and see if you can fix even the most difficult situations with your positive attitude. These skills will be helpful for you when dealing with teachers, principals, your parents, and even other kids in your class.

Presentation
* Have students brainstorm ways they can show teachers that they have a good attitude. List their responses on the board.
* Give each student a copy of "Wonderful Ways to Manage Your Classroom Attitude" and a marker. As each suggestion is read aloud, direct students to underline the main points. Allow time for discussion and elicit examples and nonexamples for each suggestion.
* Limit the time of this teacher-led presentation to allow each student to participate but not to exceed the attention span of the group.

Guided Practice
Place students in cooperative learning groups of about three members per group. Each group will be given one handout called "Taking Responsibility for Your Classroom Attitude." Assign each student a role as discussion leader, recorder, or presenter. As each situation is read by the presenter, the discussion leader will pose questions to help the group explore options for taking responsibility. The recorder will write the general answer/solution down. The teacher will provide both supportive and corrective feedback to the groups.

Independent Practice
Prepare classroom situation cards with a typical classroom scenario described on each card. There should be enough cards for each student to have a different scenario. Give each student the opportunity to present his/her scenario to the group and orally offer one suggestion to address this scenario using a positive attitude technique.

Evaluation
Score each student's response as Excellent, Adequate, or Probably Won't Work. Give the student his/her score, written on a notecard for privacy, immediately after responding. Give students who fail to provide a relevant response on the first trial at least one additional opportunity (without the use of teacher prompts).

Recap
Today we looked at techniques to use a positive attitude to help in situations that happen every day in the classroom. It makes sense to know these techniques because everyone gets into situations where a positive or negative attitude can make a difference.

Preview
Tomorrow we will talk about how our physical posture can change the meaning of what we are saying. It is like a secret language of our bodies that we can use to express our thoughts. You won't want to miss this one.

FIGURE 5–4 Sample Lesson

accomplished through whole-class, small-group, or individualized instruction. Consideration should be given to the specific content area involved, as well as the skills, needs, and preferences of the teacher and of individual students in the classroom. In general, whole-class instruction is used to provide review, to introduce new concepts, and to allow supervised practice of new skills. When possible, many teachers break the class into smaller groups for more intensive teacher instruction and supervised practice. The small-group approach is particularly appropriate for beginning reading instruction, and for highly heterogeneous classes. However, Brophy and Good (1986) caution that "the small-group approach requires well-chosen assignments that the students are willing to engage in and able to complete successfully, as well as rules and procedures that enable students to get help (if confused) or direction (about what to do when finished) without disrupting the momentum of the teacher's small-group lessons" (p. 361).

Research has found that small-group instruction has a number of advantages over whole-class instruction (D'Zamko & Raiser, 1986; Polloway, Cronin, & Patton, 1986; Sindelar, Rosenberg, Wilson, & Bursuck, 1984). These benefits include:

* Increased time on task
* Better use of teacher time (e.g., less preparation time)
* More efficient student management
* Minimization of the effect of economic limitations
* Increased instructional time
* Increased peer-to-peer interaction
* Increased overlearning and generalization of skills
* Enhanced observational learning
* Enhanced turn-taking and pragmatic skills
* Increased academic achievement
* More individual attention for each child
* Increased motivation and self-esteem

Research suggests that cooperative student grouping may provide many of the same advantages as teacher-supervised group instruction. Cooperative learning requires both individual and group accountability for successful completion of classroom projects and activities. Work by Johnson and Johnson (1999) and by Slavin (1992) demonstrated both social and academic gains for students of all ages and ability levels when using cooperative student grouping. However, an analysis of eight studies of using **cooperative learning** with students with EBD found mixed results and raised concerns that teachers may not be implementing the model as it was intended (Sutherland, Wehby, & Gunter, 2000). Berliner (1984) cautions that cooperative grouping assignments

should be flexible and subject to change to suit the needs of the curriculum and individual students: "The evidence suggests that the assignment of students to work groups is occasionally like a life-long sentence and always results in students in different groups learning different things while in school" (p. 12). This may be of particular concern for students with EBD and other disabilities who are pulled out of the general education environment and curriculum for small-group instruction. Teachers must deliberately select tasks that lend themselves to effective cooperative group work. Lotan (2003) suggests selecting tasks that have the following design features:

* They are open-ended and require complex problem solving.
* They provide students with multiple entry points to the task and multiple opportunities to show intellectual competence.
* They deal with discipline-based, intellectually important content.
* They require positive interdependence as well as individual accountability.
* They include clear criteria for the evaluation of the group's product. (p. 72)

Researchers have also suggested individual and peer tutoring as approaches that increase student engaged time, and therefore academic gains (e.g., Englert, 1984; Stevens, 1985).

Regardless of the instructional grouping chosen, all instruction should be tailored to accommodate the skills and needs of individual students within the classroom. Stevens and Rosenshine (1981) defined individualization as a characteristic of effective instruction and stated that the term implies helping each student (a) to succeed, (b) to achieve a high percentage of correct responses, and (c) to become confident of his own competence. They further noted that this type of instruction need not be provided on a one-on-one basis, but could be provided in group situations as well (Stevens & Rosenshine, 1981).

Proactive Behavior Management

As the title of this chapter suggests, the EBD teacher's goal is to prevent as many behavior problems as possible by careful planning, organization, and management. This section will discuss important, proactive behavior management strategies for students with EBD—explicit instruction in rules, routines, and social skills.

Establishing Rules and Routines. In addition to establishing long-term goals and academic standards, the proactive teacher sets clearly established expectations regarding student behavior and responsibility, enforces and reinforces those rules consistently, and monitors student progress through data collection. In general, and especially with younger children or those more likely to experience behavior problems, it is important to schedule sufficient time to address rule management during the first few weeks of school. Research suggests that the teacher establish a few simple rules (i.e., three to five) that are posted, taught, and modeled by the teacher, and that are overtly practiced by the students, with feedback from the teacher (Brophy, 1998; Christenson, Ysseldyke, & Thurlow, 1989; Englert, 1984; Stevens, 1985). With older students, soliciting their participation in the development of classroom rules may increase ownership and peer support, leading to improved compliance and fewer rule violations (Johns, Crowley, & Guetzloe, 2002).

Considerable lesson time is lost during transitions within lessons, and between activities and locations in the building. McCaslin and Good (1998) list five common times when misbehavior occurs:

* Before the lesson starts
* In the initial stages of a lesson
* During the transition from one lesson activity to another
* During the transition from teacher-directed to student-directed control of the lesson
* At the conclusion of the lesson

Establishing and practicing routines and transition behaviors for likely trouble spots will clarify expectations, facilitate movement, and minimize lost instructional time. Teachers should provide detailed instruction for each routine, accompanied by sufficient modeling, examples, and nonexamples; practice; and provide feedback to assure smooth transitions (Brophy, 1998; Christenson et al., 1989; Englert, 1984; Evertson, 1986; Stevens, 1985). Using cues, precorrection (anticipation of potential problems), and reminders before initiating a transition will lessen the need for corrective feedback. For example, it takes less time to say, "Don't forget our plan is to get in line quietly, keeping your hands and feet to yourself," than it requires to individually respond to several students who make errors during the lining-up process. Although the time required for transitions will vary according to age, grade level, and type of transition, many teachers use this general estimate for determining the appropriate length of transitions: 30 seconds for any in-seat transition between activities or lessons; 30 seconds plus actual time required to move from place to place for out-of-seat transitions. One strategy for reducing lost time during transition is to use a stopwatch and encourage students to equal or exceed their own best time.

Teach Social Skills. Students with EBD often have difficulty with **social competence**. They lack specific interpersonal skills that are valued by peers and teachers (e.g., sharing toys, taking turns in conversations), and/or they possess the skills but lack discrimination in when, where, and with whom to use them.

In the landmark study *At the Schoolhouse Door* (1990), Knitzer, Steinberg, and Fleisch found that many students with EBD possess social skill deficits; however, they also found that many schools do not offer the systematic training required to learn these skills or the ongoing practice required for maintenance and generalization. Although many teachers consider social competence to be one of the major factors in the successful integration of students with EBD, social-skills training (SST) has received limited support in the research to date. One review of the research base revealed that only about half of the students with EBD participating in social-skills programs demonstrated improvement, especially when the training was on a very general level (Quinn, Kavale, Mathur, Rutherford, & Forness, 1999). Gresham, Sugai, and Horner (2001) examined a number of such narrative reviews and meta-analyses looking at effect size (a standardized way of measuring treatment impact) in SST programs. They found a range of effect sizes from .20 to .87, and identified five potential reasons for the inconsistent results among studies: (1) differences in student population characteristics, including special education diagnoses, age of students, and resistance of behaviors to intervention; (2) poor match between specific social-skill deficits and targeted intervention strategies; (3) little evidence of treatment integrity (i.e., the accuracy and consistency of the intervention program); (4) little correspondence between behaviors taught and those assessed by various outcome measures; and (5) lack of evidence that skills taught in SST programs generalized to, or were maintained in, natural environments.

Recommendations for improving practice and achieving better outcomes of social-skills training have included: (a) focus training on specific skills in which students have identified deficits, (b) provide training programs of longer duration and higher intensity, (c) provide sufficient practice to assure skill acquisition, and (d) teach social skills in natural settings with nondisabled peers rather than expecting training in pull-out or clinical settings to generalize to the classroom (Kavale & Forness, 1996; Quinn et al., 1999; Scott & Nelson, 1998).

Gresham (2002) suggests that social-skills training must be based on assessment of the individual student's social-skill errors. The social-skill deficits or errors can then be classified into four categories upon which interventions can be planned (Gresham et al., 2001), as follows:

- **Skill-acquisition deficits**—The student does not know how to perform the required social behavior even under optimal circumstances, or does not discriminate when the situation calls for a specific social skill.
- **Skill-performance deficits**—The student knows how to perform the skill, but does not do so at acceptable levels.
- **Fluency deficits**—The student lacks sufficient models or practice to perform the skill consistently or at an appropriate rate.
- **Interfering or competing behaviors**—The student has failed to acquire the social skill because of the presence of internalizing or externalizing behaviors.

A number of commercially produced social-skills curricula have been published for students with a range of deficits. Many of those materials have been based on normal stages of child and adolescent development. Others have been constructed specifically for students with developmental delays, mental retardation, or other disabilities. When selecting social-skills materials for the classroom, it is important to match the content with the skills needed by the students in your class.

Class Meetings. Many teachers hold formal and informal class meetings; however, well-run class meetings can play a particularly important role in the EBD classroom. Advocates of class meetings point to numerous potential purposes for class meetings: creating a positive classroom environment (Nelsen, Lott, & Glenn, 2000), teaching role-playing and conflict resolution (Browning, Davis, & Resta, 2000), and building a sense of community while improving peer social relationships and problem-solving skills (Potter & Davis, 2003). Schaps (2003) suggests that "class meetings are useful for setting goals and norms, planning activities, and identifying and solving problems. They are essential for building peer relationships and fostering shared goals in the classroom" (p. 33).

Initially, the teacher will need to set norms and expectations for meetings, determine the agenda, and facilitate

discussions. However, allowing students to gradually take over responsibility for organizing and managing their class meetings increases their ownership of the process, and provides them with meaningful, authentic opportunities for leadership. One advocate of student-directed meetings says, "The meetings give students a safe venue for bringing up concerns, listening to others' points of view, sorting through possible options and outcomes, and deciding what's best for everyone" (Leachman & Victor, 2003, p. 64).

CHAPTER SUMMARY

- Prevention of misbehavior in schools may be addressed at three levels: schoolwide strategies, classroom strategies, and individual strategies. This chapter focused on classwide strategies and interventions for teachers of students with EBD. Within the classroom, teachers address prevention through a variety of techniques involving physical organization of the classroom, instructional planning and delivery, and proactive behavior management.

CHECK YOUR UNDERSTANDING

1. *True or False.* The effective teacher deals with management problems on a case-to-case basis.
2. For individualized interventions to be effective it is important for _____ to be in place.
3. What is the often the key to the development of rapport and healthy relationships with students with EBD?
4. Which type of instruction should be used to provide review, to introduce new concepts, and to allow supervised practice of new skills? (a) whole class, (b) small group, (c) individualized, or (d) none of the above
5. Students with EBD often need _____ to discriminate the situations in which new skills should be applied or generalized. (a) adequate thinking time, (b) additional preparation, (c) explicit instruction, or (d) none of the above
6. Many students with EBD possess deficits in what area of development, which makes it harder for them to establish bonds with other students?
7. What is meant by the concept "withitness"?
8. What are the two most important components of lesson evaluation as it relates to students with EBD?

9. What is meant by the term "dignifying errors" and why is it important to use this method in classroom instruction for students with EBD?

10. Name and describe the lesson plan model recommended for use with students with EBD.

APPLICATION ACTIVITIES

1. Select a grade level and design an ideal resource room for students with EBD. Your plan should accommodate up to 12 students at one time. Address potential problems by manipulating seating arrangement, traffic flow, storage, and special-activity areas.

2. Based on the BIP you developed in Chapter 3, design a lesson plan to address one of the short-term objectives or benchmarks you developed. Use the lesson-planning format provided in this chapter.

3. Develop a set of interview questions based on the effective characteristics of programs for students with EBD in Table 5-1. Interview a teacher who works with students who have EBD to determine (a) which of the effective practices are in place, and (b) what strategies the district uses to implement them.

4. Select a case study from Appendix A. Determine what proactive modifications and accommodations would be most effective for this student in the areas of (a) physical arrangement of the classroom, (b) instructional delivery, and (c) proactive behavior management.

CHAPTER 6

BEST PRACTICES FOR ADDRESSING PROBLEM BEHAVIORS

Individual and Small-Group Strategies and Interventions

CHAPTER PREVIEW

CONNECTING TO THE CLASSROOM: *A Vignette*

Mr. Jennings is always at his classroom door before the students come up the stairs—smiling, greeting them by name as they enter the room, giving some a quiet pat on the shoulder or a high-five. Inside the classroom, he reminds students of the morning routine, which is also written on the board in the front of the room: Turn in your homework, get settled, and see if you can solve the Daily Puzzler on your desk. There's a bonus for anyone who has it within the first 5 minutes of class. Don't forget to check your journal, and to write in it if there is anything I should know.

After the bell rings, Mr. Jennings closes his door and walks into the room. As he passes each desk, he leans over, puts his initials on the daily point sheet, and quietly says something to each student, "I appreciate how hard you're working on the Puzzler. I can practically hear the gears turning. I noticed how quickly you got to work this morning. Thanks." As he walks past Luanna's desk, she hands Mr. Jennings her journal and he quickly reads the note Luanna has written about her tough night at home, writes a sympathetic comment in response, and returns the journal with an extra pat on the shoulder for this young woman who has so many responsibilities.

As he looks around the room, at the students' intense expressions of concentration, Mr. Jennings wishes the principal would walk by and look in the door. You would never guess this was a classroom full of students diagnosed with emotional and behavioral problems!

INTERVENTION TECHNIQUES DESIGNED TO TEACH, INCREASE, OR MAINTAIN DESIRABLE BEHAVIORS

As we discussed in Chapter 5, teacher strategies for preventing misbehavior include structuring the physical and instructional environment and proactive behavior management. The next powerful set of prevention strategies involves avoiding behavioral triggers and teaching and reinforcing desirable behaviors in the classroom.

Antecedent Instruction-Related Strategies

Some students find certain academic tasks aversive and are likely to resist—either actively or passively—when presented with those tasks. Several strategies can boost student interest, tailor specific activities to individual students, and increase the likelihood of successful completion.

One strategy is to select instruction topics based on individual or group preferences. Provide students with an opportunity to choose between activities that meet the same instructional goal. For example, when studying the rainforest, the activity menu might include reading, writing, illustrating, mapping, graphing, or constructing dioramas. Allowing students to select preferred activities may increase student engagement and reduce resistance (Harding, Wacker, Barretto, & Rankin, 2002). For example, you could ask: "Would you prefer to write a book report, draw a picture, or dictate the story into the tape recorder? Would you rather use pencil and paper or the computer? You have your choice of doing the even- or odd-numbered problems."

Warm-up activities presented prior to a task associated with behavior problems can prevent or defuse frustration and avoidance responses (Kern, Choutka, & Sokol, 2002). Examples of warm-up activities include brainstorming, discussing vocabulary, or using graphic organizers before beginning a writing task. Not surprisingly, Gunter and Shores (1994) found that student disruptive behavior decreased when they were provided with instructional information needed to complete a task successfully prior to being asked to do so.

Another strategy, called **behavioral momentum**, pairs preferred and nonpreferred activities. Embedding tasks the student is less likely to perform within or immediately following tasks that have a high probability of completion increases the likelihood of compliance.

Reinforcement Strategies

Reinforcement is a powerful technique used to increase the rate of prosocial behaviors. Reinforcement involves delivering a consequence (C) that increases the probability that the target behavior (B) will occur again in the presence of a given antecedent (A). (See Figure 6-1 for a reminder of the ABC sequence.) Commonly used classroom reinforcement strategies include verbal praise, approving gestures (nods, smiles, winks, thumbs-up), positive physical touch (pat on shoulder, high five), individual feedback and recognition, positive individual attention, and individual and group tangibles.

Reinforcement may be positive—providing a consequence that is rewarding to the student—or negative—taking away an aversive stimulus or task, so long as the effect of the consequence is to increase or maintain target behavior. Figure 6-2 provides definitions and examples of positive and negative reinforcement, as well as other common terms associated with the behavioral model discussed in Chapter 1.

Selecting Reinforcers. Figure 6–3 provides a list of potential classroom reinforcers for students with EBD. However, these items only work as reinforcers if they

A	B	C
Antecedent	**Behavior**	**Consequences**
What occurs immediately preceding the target behavior? What are the setting characteristics and task requirements? Who else was present?	The specific behavior the team has targeted for study and/or intervention. Must be observable, measurable, and occur repeatedly.	What occurs just after the target behavior? How do others respond to the student? What does the student obtain or avoid by performing this behavior?

FIGURE 6–1   The ABCs of Behavior Management

Reinforcement terms	Definitions	Examples
Antecedent manipulation	Modify instructional environment to increase the likelihood of appropriate behavior	Review expectations before lining students up for lunch
Chaining	Reinforce successive approximations of a desired behavior	Break a long division problem down into steps; praise completion of each step
Contingency contract	Predetermined written agreement between teacher and student regarding a specific relationship between a contingency and a behavior	Award 10 minutes free time when spelling task is completed
Extrinsic reinforcement	Reward not directly connected to the behavior	Give sticker or praise for quiet listening
Extinction/ignoring	Remove all reinforcement or attention from undesirable behavior	Ignore student talking out, then reward student appropriate behavior
Intrinsic reinforcement	Pleasure derived from the natural consequences of a behavior	Demonstrate self-satisfaction or pride
Negative reinforcement	Removing an unpleasant consequence to increase a behavior	Restore recess privilege for assignment completion
Overcorrection	Requiring a student to make restitution or to practice the target behavior repeatedly	Require student to clean all the desks in the class for writing on classroom furniture
Positive reinforcement	Presentation of a pleasurable or desirable consequence for behavior	Praise student for satisfactory work
Response cost	Taking away a privilege, token, or reinforcement	Deduct points from student's daily sheet
Shaping	Selected reinforcement of successive approximations	Reward each instance of improvement in pronunciation
Tangible reinforcement	A reinforcer that the student can actually touch	Award sticker, edibles, gum or candy
Time-out	Removing the opportunity for reinforcement	Place child in a seat facing away from class for 30 seconds
Token economy	Predetermined system of specified behaviors and consequences with a systematic award plan	Award stickers that can be exchanged for various reinforcers for completion of math task

FIGURE 6–2 Behavior Management Terminology

Source: From J. A. Downing, M. R. Moran, B. S. Myles, and C. K. Ormsbee, 1991. Using Reinforcement in the Classroom. *Intervention in School and Clinic,* 27(2), 85–90. Copyright 1991 by PRO-ED, Inc. Adapted with permission.

increase the likelihood that the behavior you pair them with will be repeated. Students' individual preferences can be determined through interview, classroom discussion, or by conducting a survey. It is always desirable to have a menu or selection of different reinforcers available for individuals to work toward because their preferences are likely to be diverse, and to change from day to day. Remember that reinforcers don't have to be expensive—many of the social reinforcers (e.g., praise, recognition) only take a second and don't cost a penny.

Guidelines for Using Reinforcers. For maximum effect, reinforcers should be:

- Tied to positively stated classroom rules that have been explicitly taught and practiced (Hardman & Smith, 1999)

Social	Tangible	Token/Generalized
• Smiles	• School supplies (e.g., cool erasers and pencils)	• Points
• Positive gestures (e.g., thumbs-up, pat on the back)	• Baseball cards	• Stars, stickers
• Free time or computer time	• Small toys	• Play money
• Honor as student of the week on bulletin board	• Edibles (e.g., raisins, candy, popcorn, juice)	• Poker chips, marbles
• Play a game with a friend	• Pizza party for the class	• Coupon to skip one homework assignment
• Show the principal your paper or point sheet		
• Tutor a younger student		
• Take the gerbil home for the weekend		
• Sit in a preferred place at lunch		
• Pick a game the class will play at recess		

FIGURE 6–3   Potential Reinforcers

- Contingent on performance of the behavior (i.e., the student receives the reinforcer only if and when she exhibits the target behavior)
- Delivered immediately or with minimal delay
- Introduced at high levels—ideally a 1:1 ratio—to teach new or replacement behaviors, then decreased in frequency and/or quantity as those behaviors become part of the student's skill repertoire
- Paired—associating social reinforcers with tangibles, and then gradually weaning the student to a lower rate of social reinforcement alone for maintenance. (Quinn et al., 2000)

Negative Reinforcement.   The term *negative reinforcement* is often confused with punishment; however, it is essentially the *removal* of a negative or aversive stimulus or consequence with the result of *increasing* the likelihood a behavior will occur again. Teachers should avoid the unintentional negative reinforcement cycle described by Gunter and Coutinho (1997) that often happens when students are frustrated with a particular academic task and refuse to comply with a teacher request. The student's behavior is disruptive, so the teacher abandons the academic task to intervene (e.g., reprimand the student, send her to time-out). The student avoids the academic task and is reinforced by the interruption; the teacher is reinforced when the disruption stops. Unfortunately, this type of interaction may increase both the student's disruptions and the teacher's instructional interruptions.

Another common example of negative reinforcement occurs daily in grocery store checkout lines. The toddler fusses, begs, and cries because she wants the

Teach Appropriate Behaviors That Result in Escape or Avoidance

1. Teach students appropriate methods to indicate that they do not want to begin or participate in activities or tasks, use materials, or interact with peers.
2. Teach students appropriate methods to request alternative activities, tasks, materials, people, or locations.
3. Teach students appropriate methods to request breaks from aversive tasks or activities.
4. Teach students appropriate methods to request an end to activities, interactions, or tasks.

Change the Task, Activity, Materials, or Peers

1. Reduce the difficulty. Make the instructions easier to understand, make the task or activity easier to do, or make the materials easier to use.
2. Reduce or change task demands or expectations or shorten the duration of the activity or task.
3. Provide choice of tasks, activities, materials, and peers.
4. Make the task, activity, or materials more interesting.

Arrange for Incremental and Continued Success in Performing the Task or Using the Materials

1. Provide assistance during the task or activity.
2. Provide positive corrective feedback during the task or activity.
3. Model task-related behavior and appropriate behavior.
4. Provide prompts and cues prior to the task or activity.
5. Reinforce partial task completion.
6. Reinforce participation and successive approximations toward the behavioral objective.
7. Teach the student appropriate ways to request assistance.
8. Use small cooperative groups or peer tutoring.

Intersperse Activities, Tasks, and Materials

1. Alternate tasks, activities, and materials.
2. Use behavioral momentum.
3. Use preferred activities and tasks to reinforce participation in nonpreferred activities and tasks.
4. Provide breaks during the activity or task.

Other General Strategies

1. Provide presignals and safety signals to increase self-control.
2. Ignore challenging behavior.
3. End the task or activity on a positive, successful note.

FIGURE 6–4   Intervention Strategies Related to the Negative Reinforcement Function

Source: From Chandler, Lynnette K., and Dahlquist, Carol M., *Functional assessment: Strategies to prevent and remediate challenging behavior in school settings,* 1st Edition. © 2002, p. 124. Reprinted by permission of Pearson Education, Inc., Upper Saddle River, NJ.

candy placed enticingly within reach of her seat in the shopping cart. The parent initially may try ignoring or saying no, but eventually gives in and gives the toddler the treat (positively reinforcing the child). The child immediately stops fussing and is quiet (negatively reinforcing the parent by removal of the aversive behavior).

Teachers can use negative reinforcement deliberately to provide students with breaks in activities they find difficult. Avoiding or postponing the aversive activity reinforces the student. This tactic works well in combination with allowing access to preferred activities

(McComas, Goddard, & Hoch, 2002). Figure 6–4 provides a menu of intervention strategies based on the principle of negative reinforcement.

Other Encouragement Strategies

A variety of research-based strategies are available to teach students new behaviors and skills and to encourage students to use their new skills in the classroom and other environments. Those strategies include: modeling, shaping and chaining, proximity control and subtle signals, individualized self-discipline goals, contingency contracting, token economies, and therapeutic expressive activities. Teachers of students with EBD will need to select the strategy best suited to the needs of the student and the situation.

Modeling. Young children learn by observing and imitating those around them; modeling is how humans learn language, social values, and many behaviors. Unfortunately, not all models available to children are positive and they are just as likely to pick up undesirable behaviors from others as desirable ones—especially if their peers reinforce them. Some students may not spontaneously learn from models in the environment and may need explicit instruction in imitation. Modeling has become a formal part of many school-based youth development programs where at-risk students are exposed to motivational speakers, taught social skills using role-playing, or matched with mentors from local businesses. Teachers may also use it on a daily basis in the classroom or hallway, by calling student attention to positive examples and nonexamples of target behaviors.

Shaping and Chaining. Children do not learn complex or difficult skills overnight. In many instances, the demands of the general education classroom far exceed the ability of students with EBD to perform at the desired level. Tasks that are extremely difficult, or those with multiple steps or components, can be taught using two related strategies—shaping and chaining. Both shaping and chaining involve **task analysis**—breaking a complex or multi-step task down into small, manageable components or discrete steps.

Shaping is the process of reinforcing successive approximations of the desired behavior. Physical education teachers use shaping to train students to peform the high jump. Initially, the teacher sets the bar where every student can be successful and jump high enough to clear the bar. With instruction and encouragement, the teacher gradually raises the bar to a challenging level.

Many teachers use shaping in the classroom to encourage students to continue to progress toward a long-term goal. For example, if Lori can only stay focused on her math seatwork for 3 minutes, the teacher reinforces her every time she stays on task for 3 minutes for 5 consecutive days. Then she sets a slightly higher behavioral target and asks Lori to try for 4 minutes, then for 5, and so on. At each level, the teacher reinforces Lori each time she meets the higher criterion until the behavior is consistent and fluent;

then, the teacher raises the criterion again. Shaping can be used to alter any property of the desired student response (e.g., frequency, latency, duration, fluency).

Chaining uses task analysis to identify the discrete parts or steps involved in a complex behavior. The first step is modeled or taught in isolation and the student is reinforced for mastering it; next, the second step is taught and reinforced and so on, until the student has mastered the entire sequence. Chaining can be accomplished either forward—the student learns the first step first—or backward—the student learns the final step first. According to Walker, Shea, and Bauer (2004), both forms of chaining are useful in the classroom: "Their application depends on the particular task being taught, the individual being instructed, and other variables such as time and personnel availability" (p. 131).

Teaching shoe tying can illustrate the chaining process and can be accomplished in either direction. In forward chaining, the parent or teacher instructs the child to take one shoelace in each hand and cross the laces over one another. Once the child has accomplished that step, the adult reinforces the child and completes the process. In backward chaining, the adult performs the entire sequence of steps and leaves the last one—pulling the two loops tight—for the child, and reinforces performance of that step.

Proximity Control and Subtle Signals. Gunter and Shores (1995) found a positive relationship between teacher circulation in the classroom and students' learning and behavior. Active monitoring focuses student attention to task and provides a tacit reminder that the teacher is watching.

If simple proximity is not enough, a quick verbal or nonverbal signal may be sufficient to redirect a child who is off task or talking. For students who need a personal reminder, establishing a prearranged signal may be helpful. For example, "Chanel, I notice you seem to be having trouble paying attention during my math demonstrations. I don't want to embarrass you by saying something in front of the other students, but I really want you to hear what I'm saying. When I see you starting to fiddle with your papers or look around the room, I'm going to pull on my left earlobe like this. [Teacher demonstrates.] That will be our private signal that you need to refocus. Okay?"

If the classroom rules are posted and numbered, the teacher can nonverbally redirect students by reminding them of the rule they may be violating by simply signaling the number with her fingers, or by pointing to the relevant rule on the wall without interrupting instructional flow. Precorrection and other preventative measures can be used simply and efficiently with many minor, but irritating, classroom disruptive behaviors.

Setting Individualized Self-Discipline Goals. Educational researchers have raised concerns that classroom control based on strict adherence to rules is not sufficient if the goal is to help students become self-managing. McCaslin and Good (1998) point out three potential pitfalls of focusing on sheer compliance with behavioral rules. First, success depends on constant teacher monitoring. Second, if teachers obtain compliance through manipulation of rewards and consequences, it is unlikely that the appropriate behavior will generalize to other settings or situations. Third, working strictly on a compliance level does not give students the opportunity to experience and learn to value more the complex cooperative, interactive, and divergent kinds of learning that are the norm in many general education classrooms. Self-management procedures are preferred by teachers, and researchers have shown them to be related to increased student performance (McQuillan & DuPaul, 1996).

To become self-directed, students need opportunities to reflect on their behavior and the thinking underlying the behavior, discuss their options, form a plan that involves making good choices, and evaluate their progress. One strategy for helping students move beyond simply following the rules to self-managed behavior is to spend a few minutes at the beginning of every day or every class period negotiating and setting individual goals. The teacher then assists the student in monitoring and evaluating progress throughout the day, reinforcing desirable goal-related behaviors. Students can use this strategy for academic as well as behavioral tasks. For example, a student reluctant to participate in creative writing might be asked, "How many paragraphs (or sentences) do you want to write today?" A student with peer aggression problems might decide to focus on keeping her hands to herself today. Self-management and cognitive-behavioral strategies have been particularly effective with students who have attention problems; for more information on these techniques, see Chapter 7.

Contingency Contracts. "Grandma's Law" is familiar to most children: "Finish your homework, then you may play games on the computer." A **contingency contract**, sometimes called a behavior contract, is a more formalized version of this if/then statement that can be used to address social, academic, or behavioral goals with individual students. Potential uses of the contingency contract include:

- Introducing and teaching new (or replacement) behaviors,
- Increasing the rate of a desired behavior,
- Maintaining and supporting application or generalization of skills,
- Decreasing or extinguishing undesirable behaviors,
- Monitoring completion of academic tasks or objectives, and
- Documenting results of problem-solving or crisis-intervention sessions. (Downing, 2002, p. 168)

See Figure 6–5 for a contingency contract planning worksheet.

Token Economies. A **token** is a generalized reinforcer that can be traded in for a variety of rewards or reinforcers at a later time (i.e., the back-up reinforcer). A **token economy** is a system of dispensing and redeeming tokens. Token economies have been used effectively to manage behavior in elementary and secondary classrooms, as well as in treatment and institutional settings. They can be relatively simple or very complex to administer, generally corresponding to the difficulty of the behaviors being addressed and the cognitive and developmental levels of the student. In a 1993 review of the professional literature, Shores, Gunter, and Jack found that, appropriately implemented, token economy systems had substantial empirical support. Myles, Moran, Ormsbee, and Downing (1992) suggest a six-step implementation process:

1. Identify target behaviors to be reinforced, involving students to increase ownership.
2. Specify and select reinforcers, providing a menu or selection of items at varying levels of desirability and cost.
3. Identify token types and schedules, selecting something inexpensive, acceptable to the students, and not easily falsified. Determine the rate and ratio at which tokens will be awarded.
4. Plan token distribution and redemption procedures, taking into account students' age and ability to tolerate waiting.
5. Initiate and implement the system, giving students a mini-lesson on how the economy will function.
6. Plan for inflation as students become more self-motivated by gradually shifting to an economy with higher costs, longer intervals between reinforcement opportunities, etc. (p. 164)

Student name:	Teacher:
Priority area of concern:	
Circumstances under which behavior occurs:	
What triggers the behavior or increases the likelihood that it will occur?	
What inhibits the behavior or makes it less likely to occur?	
Hypothesis about the function of the behavior:	
Current level of performance/baseline:	
Expectation/objective:	
What positive behavioral supports, adaptations, or environmental modifications have been tried previously?	
What tangible and social reinforcers are effective with this student?	
Will there be a negative consequence for failure to fulfill the contract? What?	
Who needs to be included in the contract?	
Time frame for contract implementation and evaluation/follow-up conference:	

FIGURE 6–5 Contingency Contract Planning Worksheet

Source: From "Individualized Behavior Contracts" by J.A. Downing, 2002, *Intervention in School and Clinic, 37*(3), 168–172. Copyright 2002 by PRO-ED, Inc. Adapted with permission.

Therapeutic Expressive Activities. For the purposes of this section, we will define **therapeutic activities** as a wide range of activities that promote students' emotional well-being, coping skills, and self-concept. These activities may be directed or facilitated by a variety of individuals, including teachers, parents, older peers (e.g., camp counselors), or trained professionals from related fields (e.g., art therapists). On the other hand, **therapy** is a process that includes evaluation, treatment planning, treatment, and documentation of progress. Therapy is provided by individuals who have completed specialized training in the relevant field (e.g., music therapy, recreational therapy, psychology). Many states have certification standards for professional counselors and expressive therapists that require a master's degree or advanced clinical training.

Gladding (1992) advocates the use of both verbal (e.g., drama, literature) and nonverbal (e.g., music, movement, painting, sculpting) expressive arts in counseling. He indicates that participation in the expressive arts improves self-concept, enriches lives, and promotes flexibility and adaptation to change. The arts may also provide vehicles to address and redirect aggressive and impulsive behaviors into more socially acceptable creative activities (Gladding, 1992; Henley, 1999).

Expressive activities are commonly used to provide opportunities to reflect, develop insight, and resolve problems. However, some parents and public officials have raised concerns about what they characterize as the schools' intrusion into private and family matters. Specifically, they may object to school programs related to substance abuse, sex education, child development, and counseling activities that encourage students to discuss their feelings or personal experiences outside of school. Jenkinson (1994) suggests that before implementing counseling programs or other potentially sensitive activities, schools should proactively address concerns regarding confidentiality and invasion of privacy:

- Clearly identify the educational objectives of the activity or assignment and the student outcomes in terms of knowledge or understanding of the proposed topic.
- Determine how any information collected will be treated, who will have access to the information, and for what purpose.
- Consider the potential for harm that might occur as a result of a breach in confidentiality or misuse of the information resulting from the activity.

Journal Writing. Teachers use **journal writing** (or journaling) for a variety of classroom purposes (Cobine, 1995; Jackson & Owens, 1999; Kerka, 1996;

Staton, 1987). Teachers often use journals as an instructional tool, to provide a systematic opportunity for the student to record information and reflect on what they have read (e.g., a literature journal) or studied (e.g., a math journal). A dialogue journal consists of the student and teacher writing notes back and forth to each other on a regular basis. These notes may be structured (e.g., question and answer format) or unstructured (e.g., informal and conversational). Dialogue journals create a vehicle for students and teachers to engage in an authentic, interactive conversation about the students' experiences inside and outside of the classroom. For students in the EBD classroom, journals may also provide an important outlet to discuss concerns, address issues, and resolve problems.

When introducing journal-writing activities for the first time, clarify the purpose(s) for writing and the expectations regarding confidentiality and whether journal entries will be graded. For students who have difficulty with written language assignments, it may be helpful to make it clear that you are going to read for content, and not respond to errors in spelling and punctuation. See Figure 6–6 for a list of sample "starters" for journal writing.

Role-Playing and Social Stories. Many students with EBD have difficulty responding appropriately in novel situations; others require concrete, step-by-step instructions and repeated practice to master new social skills. For these students, drama-based activities provide both the schema needed for comfort in new situations and the positive practice required to develop fluency in new behaviors. Role-playing can be handled very much like putting on a class play, following these steps:

- Identify a topic or situation, either from an actual unsuccessful recent experience or based on something that is going to happen soon (e.g., what we do on a field trip to the zoo).
- Describe the scenario, or have students write one or more scripts.
- Determine who the characters will be and "cast" students in the parts.
- Identify a "director" who will be responsible for starting and stopping the action.
- Inform the audience members what their role will be and what they are to watch for.
- Perform the script.
- Discuss the scenario, identify possible changes or improvements, and replay as needed.

For younger students and students with communication problems including autism spectrum disorders, role-playing may not be successful. For these students, a more appropriate strategy might be to generate a picture or comic book depicting them engaging in the desired behavior. Information concerning developing social stories and comic-strip conversations with these students is in Chapter 9 of this book.

Bibliotherapy. **Bibliotherapy** is defined as the use of literature to provide guidance and support for students. Teachers may select issues related to the entire class, to small groups, or to individual students. Nola Kortner Aiex (1993) cites numerous reasons to use books as a therapeutic intervention. Bibliotherapy can help students:

- Develop self-concept
- Increase understanding of human behavior or motivations
- Develop honest self-appraisal
- Find interests outside of themselves
- Relieve emotional or mental pressure
- See they are not the first to experience a problem
- Identify multiple solutions to a problem
- Discuss a problem more freely
- Plan a course of action or solution to a problem

Bibliotherapy can also provide prevention or educational information about difficult topics, such as child abuse, substance abuse, death, divorce, illness, and discrimination (e.g., Hippie, Comer, & Boren, 1997; Kramer, 1999; Kramer & Smith, 1998; McDaniel, 2001;

My favorite thing to do in my spare time is . . .
My favorite animal is . . . because . . .
If I were a plant, I would be a . . . because . . .
If I were a car, I would be a . . . because . . .
The three best things about me are . . .
If I could change one thing about myself, it would be . . .
One time when I was really happy . . .
A time when I was really sad was when . . .
One of the things that really makes me mad is . . .
I'm really worried that . . .
The thing about girls/boys that makes me crazy is . . .
Something that really bugs me about adults is . . .
A good friend is someone who . . .
A good teacher is someone who . . .
My friends like me because . . .
A year from now (5 years, 10 years), I want to be . . .

FIGURE 6–6 Sample Topics for Journal Writing

Wolverton, 1988). Bibliotherapy has also been proposed to promote emotional intelligence (Sullivan & Strang, 2002), to celebrate individuality and diversity or to heighten sensitivity (Stroud, Stroud, & Staley, 1999), to draw out shy or socially withdrawn students (Brophy, 1996), to address behavior problems (Sridhar & Vaughn, 2000), and to enhance the respectful inclusion of students with disabilities in general education classrooms (Kramer, 1999; Myles, Ormsbee, Downing, Walker, & Hudson, 1992). Figure 6–7 provides criteria for selecting appropriate books for and about students with learning differences.

A classroom bibliotherapy sequence may be similar to other literature-based instructional routines, including: prereading activities (e.g., introducing vocabulary, predicting content from title and pictures); guided reading of the book or story; a facilitated postreading discussion; and problem-solving, practice, or homework activities (Forgan, 2002). Sridhar and Vaughn (2000) suggest a variety of follow-up and extension activities including creative writing, art, discussion, and role-playing.

While the classroom teacher certainly can use therapeutic literature in the classroom, it may be desirable to coteach or collaborate with the school counselor when implementing bibliotherapy activities on sensitive or clinical topics (Stringer, Reynolds, & Simpson, 2003).

Art Therapy.   Art teachers can use art as a therapeutic technique by talking with students about their art (Dunn-Snow & D'Amelio, 2000). However, Ullman (2001) cautions that art therapy is more than simply recreational use of art materials, and must include both components— artistic expression *and* therapy. Art therapists have completed a course of study specifically designed to develop skills in assessment, treatment, and progress evaluations using art as a medium. According to Fliegel (2000), "It is this knowledge of, and sensitivity to, the creative process that enables the art therapist to advocate for an understanding of the communicative value of symptoms and creative endeavors, and to promote a treatment response that supports the adolescent as a productive member of the community" (p. 88).

Music Therapy.   Over the past 20 years, researchers have made a number of expansive claims about the positive impact of music on intelligence, development, academic performance, and personality (Wilcox, 2000). Providing patients with self-selected music has become common in many doctors' and dentists' offices to assist patients with stress reduction and relaxation, and to provide simple distraction from the procedure that is taking place beyond the headphones. In clinical settings, researchers have found that calm music can reduce agitation in individuals with dementia (Lou, 2001), help manage anxiety and stress ("In Sync," 2001), and assist with pain control (Kwekkeboom, 2003; Wilcox, 2000).

Similarly, results in classroom studies have demonstrated that listening to music creates a relaxed state that may have a positive impact on acquisition of academic skills, including reading, writing, and math (Carlson, Hoffman, Gray, & Thompson, 2004; Smith, 2001) and

---

General Criteria for Selecting Books *for* Students with Learning Differences

- Does the story line respond to student interests?
- Does the material match students' language and background experiences?
- Does the material teach students about their world?
- Is the story line presented in a predictable, chronological format?
- Is the story line presented in a deductive format?

General Criteria for Selecting Books *about* Students with Learning Differences

- Does the material portray persons with learning differences realistically?
- Does the material portray persons with learning differences in a variety of settings and situations?
- Does the material encourage acceptance and respect of persons with learning differences?
- Does the story line respond to student interest?

FIGURE 6–7   Checklist: Selecting Literature for and about Students with Learning Differences

Source: From "Guidelines for Selecting Literature for and About Students with Learning Differences" by B. S. Myles, C. K. Ormsbee, J. A. Downing, B. L. Walker, and F. G. Hudson, 1992, *Intervention in School and Clinic,* 27(4), 215–220. Copyright 1992 by PRO-ED, Inc. Reprinted with permission.

improved retention of spelling words (Anderson, Henke, McLaughlin, Ripp, & Tuffs, 2000). Budge (1998) found that students who listened to calming music demonstrated improved memory for academic tasks and were more optimistic. Another study found that playing quiet music in the classroom in the morning reduced the frustration behaviors (i.e., head jerking and screaming) of an individual with autism (Orr, Myles, & Carlson, 1998).

Mills (1996) found that assertive behaviors increased with music that was faster paced, or had a rapid tempo. Accordingly, teachers wanting to increase the level of activity in the classroom (e.g., during clean-up time after an activity) might play a march or an upbeat pop song (with appropriate lyrics). To produce a relaxation or calming effect, teachers should select music that moves at a slower tempo. Hoffman (1995) suggests music with a meter between 50 and 60 beats per minute, similar to the rhythm of a relaxed heartbeat.

Music has also been used successfully to teach, by embedding academic or social content in the lyrics of songs (e.g., the alphabet song, the friendship song). Many individuals remember song lyrics more easily than verbal information learned in a different manner. In a study involving students with severe EBD, Cade and Gunter (2002) found that students were able to memorize division math facts set to music at a 100% mastery level after only two sessions.

It appears that the more actively involved students are in the exploration of music, the greater the potential for gains. Ella Wilcox (2000), associate editor of

Teaching Music, summarizes the research on music and learning as follows:

> Brain imagery has shown increases in parts of the cerebral hemisphere and in the thickness of neural fibers connecting the two sides of the brain in children who begin stringed-instrument or keyboard study before the age of seven compared to children who are not exposed to this kind of learning. (p. 1)

> Moving to music, dancing, playing instruments, and experimentation with materials that make sounds are all helpful to the development of toddlers. It is the doing, in addition to the listening, that offers the greatest positive benefit in all aspects of learning, especially in music. Studies that reveal significant changes in children's spatial and cognitive development almost all involve the child as actor, not spectator. (p. 11)

> So far, it's clear that listening to high-quality music is good, experimenting with musical sound is better, and studying music long-term is best. (p. 14)

Individual and group music instruction, as well as more clinically based music therapy, may include a variety of activities such as singing, playing instruments, rhythmic movements, and dance. Students with EBD will benefit from exposure to and instruction in music for all of the reasons listed above. However, an additional consideration for including students with EBD and other disabilities in music programs is that, provided the instruction taps their abilities and not their disabilities, students may experience lower stress levels and higher success levels in music than they do in the core academic subjects. (See Box 6–1.)

BOX 6–1   Darrow Perspective

PERSPECTIVE: ALICE-ANN DARROW Music Therapy for Students with Behavior Disorders

Music is a highly desirable activity for even the most challenging student. As a result of its desirability, the contingent use of music can be easily incorporated into behavioral management programs to reinforce appropriate behaviors. In addition, selected musical behaviors can be taught that are incompatible with inappropriate or negative behaviors. For example, a student cannot play a guitar while striking another student, or play the piano while walking around the room. Music can also be used to induce mood change and relaxation in students who are anxious or stressed. These techniques have been used successfully with children and adolescents in residential treatment centers, juvenile detention centers, and public schools (Epstein, Pratto, & Skipper, 1990; Saperston, 1989; Silverman, 2003; Wilson, 1975).

(continued)

Using music as a contingency. Much of the early music therapy research related to children and adolescents with behavioral or emotional problems was carried out in residential treatment facilities or hospitals (Mitchell, 1966; Wasserman, 1972). Since the mid 1970s, most children and adolescents with behavior disorders have attended public schools, although some students with severe emotional disorders are still enrolled in special out-patient or residential programs where they receive music therapy services. The use of music as a reinforcer has been used for many years by music therapists to effectively modify challenging behaviors. Music has been used contingently to modify inappropriate: bus behaviors (McCarty, McElfresh, Rice, & Wilson, 1978), verbal behaviors to parents (Madsen & Madsen, 1968), and disruptive classroom behaviors (West et al., 1995). Computer and electronic music is especially effective in managing the behaviors of adolescents (Krout, 1988). Such music, along with popular teen music, is particularly attractive to adolescents, and consequently can be used in relatively simple ways to encourage prosocial behaviors. Savan (1999) found that even the use of classical background music resulted in the reduction of students' aggressive behaviors. Periods of preferred listening are often an effective reward for students with behavior disorders to initiate or maintain appropriate classroom behaviors such as:

- staying in their seat
- completing work assignments
- being punctual
- raising their hand to speak, or
- participating in class activities

Music learning to modify inappropriate behavior. Learning music, such as a new instrument, requires many behavioral prerequisites—sitting still, holding an instrument, manipulating the instrument, and reading music. The process of music learning increases the likelihood that students with behavior disorders will engage in these adaptive behaviors, and that the musical product itself will motivate continued engagement (Gardstrom, 1987; Kivland, 1986). For students with behavior disorders, the positive sense of self that comes from learning a musical skill does much to enhance their confidence, and consequently, their willingness to socialize appropriately with others. While learning music, students can participate in various musical organizations that allow for rewarding social contacts with their peers. An additional benefit of participation in musical organizations is that they often require regular school attendance, satisfactory grades, and conduct reports. The development of performance skills can do much to enhance a student's sense of self. Participation in various musical activities supports the development of adolescent independence and nurtures a healthy self-concept.

The use of music to modulate mood. Depression is a frequent secondary condition of students with behavior disorders (Heward, 2003). According to researchers, one of the benefits of music for individuals with depression is its ability to induce or to alter mood states (Keneally, 1998; Mornhinweg, 1992; Silverman, 2003). Music has also been found to alter the behaviors and cognitive thought processes of depressed individuals (Williams & Dorow, 1983). Although music can be used to modify a student's affect or to elicit socially appropriate behaviors, it may also encourage inappropriate behaviors in certain situations (Durand & Mapstone, 1998). Furthermore, varying diagnoses such as ADD and ADHD have been shown to react differently to background music: some students may find that background music focuses their attention while others are distracted by it (Pratt, Abel, & Skidmore, 1995). Musical preferences of a student must be considered as well as the sedative or stimulative characteristics of the music itself. Listening to preferred music, regardless of style (heavy metal, rap), has been shown to induce positive changes in mood. Thus, adolescents who prefer heavy metal music may experience an increase in positive affect upon listening to their preferred kind of music. Although heavy metal music and rap are often blamed for encouraging aggressive and violent behaviors in teenagers, research does not support this myth (Took & Weiss, 1994). Research shows that, contrary to popular belief, adolescent listeners do not pay close attention to lyrics and are therefore not significantly influenced by them (Wanamaker & Reznikoff, 1989).

The use of music to modulate physical activity. Sedative or stimulative music can be used effectively to modulate students' physical activity (Harris, Bradley, & Titus, 1992; Skaggs, 1997). Students will often remain in their seat in order to listen to their preferred music. Music that sedates hyperactive or inappropriate behavior may be a quick, efficient, and noninvasive way to manage difficult behavior (Saperston, 1989). Although stimulative music such as rap and heavy metal may stimulate muscle activity, preferences for these kinds of music do not predict behavior problems (Epstein, Pratto, & Skipper, 1990).

The use of lyric analysis in counseling students with behavior disorders. Students with behavior disorders often choose inappropriate ways to express their emotions. Music therapy can provide these students with an alternative means of communication, and an opportunity to express their emotions through song writing or lyric analysis. Adolescents' preferred music can be used as a structure and impetus for discussing issues such as substance abuse, suicide, and coping with stress (Mark, 1987; Trzcinski, 1992). Lyric analysis relies on the text component of music. The music therapist or the student can select songs to use as the impetus for discussion. The music therapist can also write a song for a student to convey an emotion or message. Trained music therapists also have a variety of songwriting techniques that allow students to successfully write their own lyrics. The content of the song may describe relevant issues the student is dealing with in their life. It may also be a way to explore what is missing in a student's life, such as a parent, friends, or love.

Music therapy can facilitate the development of prosocial behaviors and the suppression of negative behaviors. In order to be successful, however, the music therapist must adapt the broad range of treatment techniques to the individualized needs of the student. As students practice and gradually acquire new relational and behavioral skills, the music therapist must facilitate the transfer of these skills outside the music therapy context and into the students' home and school environments.

The advantage of using music with students who have behavior disorders is that music is inherently non-threatening and an inviting medium. Music offers the reluctant student a safe environment in which to explore emotions. Music is extremely adaptable in ways such as style, age appropriateness, and sophistication; and as a result, is capable of targeting various problem behaviors across a wide age range of students. Nearly all students respond to music. Their response to music assists in establishing a strong foundation for engaging in therapeutic work. Students' natural interest in music is enhanced by the fact that they are occupied in activities associated more with play or fun than work or therapy (Hussey & Layman, 2005).

REFERENCES

Durand, V. M., & Mapstone, E. (1998). Influence of "mood-inducing" music on challenging behavior. *American Journal on Mental Retardation, 102,* 367–378.

Epstein, J. S., Pratto, D. J., & Skipper, J. K., Jr. (1990). Teenagers, behavioral problems, and preferences for heavy metal and rap music: A case study of a southern middle school. *Deviant Behavior, 11,* 381–394.

Gardstrom, S. C. (1987). Positive peer culture: A working definition for the music therapist. *Music Therapy Perspectives, 4,* 19–23.

Harris, C. S., Bradley, R. J., & Titus, S. K. (1992). A comparison of the effects of hard rock and easy listening on the frequency of observed inappropriate behaviors: Control of environmental antecedents in a large public area. *Journal of Music Therapy, 29,* 6–17.

Heward, W. L. (2000). *Exceptional children: An introduction to special education* (6th ed.). Upper Saddle River, NJ: Merrill/Prentice Hall.

Hussey, D. L., & Layman, D. (2003). Music therapy with emotionally disturbed children. *Psychiatric Times, 20,* Retrieved February 16, 2005, from http://www.psychiatrictimes.com/p030637.html.

Keneally, P. (1998). Validation of a music mood induction procedure: Some preliminary findings. *Cognition and Emotion, 2,* 11–18.

Kivland, M. J. (1986). The use of music to increase self-esteem in a conduct disordered adolescent. *Journal of Music Therapy, 23,* 25–29.

Krout, R. E. (1988). Using computer and electronic music resources in clinical music therapy with behaviorally disordered students, 12 to 18 years old. *Music Therapy Perspectives, 5,* 114–118.

Madsen, C. K., & Madsen, C. H., Jr. (1968). Music as a behavior modification technique with a juvenile delinquent. *Journal of Music Therapy, 5,* 72–76.

Mark, A. (1987). Adolescents discuss themselves and drugs through music. *Journal of Substance Abuse Treatment, 3,* 243–249.

McCarty, B. C., McElfresh, C. T., Rice, S. V., & Wilson, S. J. (1978). The effect of contingent background music on inappropriate bus behavior. *Journal of Music Therapy, 15,* 150–156.

Mitchell, G. C. (1966). Bedtime music for psychotic children. *Nursing Mirror, 122,* 452.

(continued)

Mornhinweg, G. C. (1992). Effects of music preference and selection on stress reducing. *Journal of Holistic Nursing, 10*, 101–109.

Pratt, R. R., Abel, H. H., & Skidmore, J. (1995). The effects of neurofeedback training with background music on EEG patterns of ADD and ADHD children. *International Journal of Arts Medicine, 4*, 24–31.

Saperston, B. M. (1989). Music-based individualized relaxation training (MBIRT): A stress-reduction approach for the behaviorally disturbed mentally retarded. *Music Therapy Perspectives, 6*, 26–33.

Savan, A. (1999). The effect of background music on learning. *Psychology of Music, 27*, 138–146.

Silverman, M. J. (2003). The influence of music on the symptoms of psychosis: A meta-analysis. *Journal of Music Therapy, 40*, 27–40.

Skaggs, R. (1997). Music-centered creative arts in a sex offender treatment program for male juveniles. *Music Therapy Perspectives, 15*, 73–78.

Took, K. J., & Weiss, D. S. (1994). The relationship between heavy metal and rap music and adolescent turmoil: Real or artifact? *Adolescence, 29*, 613–621.

Trzcinski, J. (1992). Heavy metal kids: Are they dancing with the devil? *Child and Youth Care Forum, 21*(1), 7–22.

Wanamaker, C. E., & Reznikoff, M. (1989). Effects of aggressive and nonaggressive rock songs on projective and structured tests. *The Journal of Psychology, 123*, 561–570.

Wasserman, N. M. (1972). Music therapy for emotionally disturbed in a private hospital. *Journal of Music Therapy, 9*, 99–104.

West, R. P., Young, K. R., Callahan, K., Fister, S., Kemp, K., Freston, J., & Lovitt, T. C. (1995). The musical clocklight: Encouraging positive classroom behavior. *Teaching Exceptional Children, 27*(2), 46–51.

William, C., & Dorow, L. G. (1985). Changes in complaints and noncomplaints of a chronically depressed psychiatric patient as a function of an interrupted music/verbal feedback package. *Journal of Music Therapy, 20*, 143–155.

Wilson, C. V. (1975). The use of rock music as a reward in behavior therapy with children. *Journal of Music Therapy, 13*, 39–48.

Alice-Ann Darrow, Ph.D., is the Irvin Cooper Professor of Music Therapy and Music Education at Florida State University. Her teaching and research interests are teaching music to special populations and the role of music in deaf culture. Related to these topics, she has been the recipient of eighteen university, federal, or corporate grants, and published numerous monographs, research articles, and book chapters.

Source: Darrow, A.-A. (2005). Music therapy for students with behavior disorders. In M. Adamek & A.-A. Darrow (Eds.) *Music in special education* (pp. 147–150). Silver Spring, MD: The American Music Therapy Association. Reprinted with permission.

Play Therapy.

> Play is to the child what verbalization is to the adult. It is a medium for expressing feelings, exploring relationships, describing experiences, disclosing wishes, and self-fulfillment. (Landreth & Bratton, 1999, Introduction)

> Play therapy is a well thought out, philosophically conceived, developmentally based, and research-supported approach to helping children cope with and overcome the problems they experience in the process of living their lives. (Landreth & Bratton, 1999, Play therapy research and results section, para. 1)

Play therapy is a systematic, interactive process between a child and a trained play therapist who guides the process to promote positive developmental growth and address problems. Researchers have found that play therapy can be an effective therapeutic approach for a variety of children's problems including, but not limited to, the following areas:

- Abuse and neglect
- Aggression and acting out
- Attachment difficulties
- Dissociation and schizophrenia
- Fear and anxiety
- Traumatization
- Withdrawal and isolation

Pet Therapy.

The goals of animal-assisted activities are similar to those of other expressive therapies:

- Promote socialization and effective communication
- Address areas of anxiety or concern (e.g., grief or loss)
- Improve self-esteem and self-confidence
- Increase student motivation and engagement
- Reduce disruptive and noncompliant behavior

Chandler (2001) suggests a wide variety of activities that can be facilitated with animals. Samples include:

- Learning information about the animal, its history, care, and/or training
- Teaching the animal a new skill or behavior
- Developing social awareness and empathy by discussing how animals might feel in certain situations, interpreting their behavior, and generalizing to human behavior

Therapeutic Recreation. In reviewing the literature on outdoor recreation programs, Berman and Davis-Berman (2000) found support for the notion that these programs can be used effectively to develop emotional strength and well-being. They point out that, while the primary purpose of recreation programs may be to provide enjoyable activity, participants can experience a variety of secondary affective benefits leading to improved socialization. The well-known adventure recreation program, Outward Bound, describes their participant outcome goals as developing "self-reliance, responsibility, teamwork, confidence, compassion, and environmental and community stewardship" (http://www.outwardbound.com). These goals correspond to deficits identified in many students with EBD. Wise (2001) has described similar goals and positive outcomes for community-based recreational programs for students with special needs.

INTERVENTION TECHNIQUES DESIGNED TO DECREASE OR ELIMINATE UNDESIRABLE BEHAVIORS

Despite the best efforts of teachers to prevent student misbehavior through careful planning and proactive, positive management strategies, some students—including many with EBD—may continue to exhibit problem behaviors. For these students, it may be necessary to target negative, disruptive, or potentially harmful behaviors for reduction.

Planned Ignoring/Extinction

According to Kerr and Nelson (2002), "behavior is weakened by withholding the consequences (usually social) that have maintained it" (p. 132). This process is called *extinction* by the behavioral model and *planned ignoring* in psychodynamic terminology. In either case, the process involves determining what has been reinforcing the undesirable behavior—most often attention—and withdrawing it. What the teacher does while ignoring inappropriate behavior will depend on the situation. She may simply not respond at all to the problem behavior, continuing instruction or her previous activity uninterrupted. At other times, she will need to avert her gaze or physically turn away to avoid the appearance of paying attention to the student who is misbehaving.

An equally important part of extinction is "catching the student being good." As soon as the student is exhibit-ing the desired behavior, the teacher should provide reinforcement without referring to the problem behavior.

Planned ignoring must be used carefully and with great patience. The teacher must ignore the behavior even though the child escalates in an attempt to regain the attention to which she had been accustomed. That is, the problem behavior will almost always get worse before it begins to go away. The increase in intensity will generally be temporary if the teacher and others in the environment are able to avoid paying attention to it.

In clinical settings, extinction procedures have been used successfully for some very extreme behaviors, such as self-injury or self-damaging (e.g., head banging, eye gouging). However, in the classroom, ignoring is most useful for addressing behaviors that are passive (e.g., student crosses arms, sticks out lip, refuses to begin assignment) or mildly disruptive (e.g., pencil-tapping). The technique should not be used for behaviors that might cause harm to the student or others without additional staff training and a carefully designed safety plan.

Restitution

Diane Chelsom Gossen (1992) defines **restitution** as "the action of repairing a damage done" (p. 47). Restitution must create opportunities for individuals to correct their mistakes, make amends to the victim, and become a stronger member of the group or community in the process (Gossen, 1998). Gossen (2004) describes key components of an effective restitution process as follows:

* Restitution is not a payback; it is a pay forward.
* Restitution restores relationships.
* Restitution is an invitation, not coercion.
* Restitution teaches the person to look inside.
* Restitution is looking for the basic need behind the problem.
* Self-restitution is the most powerful tool.
* Restitution is about "being," not "doing."
* Restitution strengthens.
* Restitution focuses on solutions.
* Restitution restores one to the group. (p. 72)

Restitution is a restorative act that may take the form of an apology, compensation, or some type of labor performed for a specific victim or in a symbolic way for the community as a whole. In the past decade, educators have given growing support to restitution as a component of both juvenile justice and school-based disciplinary systems (Chernoff & Watson, 2000; Nessel, 1998; Nessel, 1999; Wade, 1997; Yazzie, 2000). There has been a dramatic increase in teen courts in

- Is the proposed restitution seen by the victim as adequate compensation or amends?
- Will it require effort on the part of the offender?
- Does it reduce the incentives for further offenses?
- Is it relevant to the type of offense?
- Is it tied to a value statement that helps the student see it as part the big picture (e.g., how people treat each other with kindness or respect)?
- Does it strengthen the offender and help him/her develop into a more responsible individual?
- Was it created without criticism, guilt, or anger?
- Does it avoid stimulating feelings of resentment or being overextended on the part of the helping adult?

FIGURE 6–8   Effective Restitution Checklist

Source: Based on Gossen, D. C. (1992). *Restitution: Restructuring school discipline.* Chapel Hill, NC: New View Publications. Adapted with permission.

particular (including student courts). In those situations, the adolescent offenders adjudicate the case. "In 1991 there were over 50 teen courts in 14 states; by 1999, the number of teen courts had grown to more than 500 in 45 states and Washington, DC" (Nessel, 1999, p. 1).

According to Yazzie (2000), key components of effective restitutional interventions include breaking the cycle of violence, accepting responsibility, and offering symbolic amends or restitution. Program evaluations have demonstrated successful outcomes for restitutional interventions. Juvenile offenders involved in diversion programs involving restitution and/or community service have experienced lower recidivism rates than other youth (Chernoff & Watson, 2000). The National Consortium on Alternatives for Youth at Risk published a 1994 study of the PayBack program, and found that 90% of youth placed in community service work sites completed their restitution activities.

Schools that want to implement a schoolwide restitution program may wish to consider peer mediation or a youth tribunal to facilitate conflict resolution or resolve disciplinary issues. However, according to Gossen (1992), putting restitution into practice in the classroom can be as simple as asking an offending student, "What do you need to do to make it right?" You might also add a restitution component to your problem-solving procedures. The likelihood that a student's proposed restitution plan will be effective can be increased by using the checklist in Figure 6–8. Each question that cannot be answered positively represents a potential roadblock to successful restitution.

Punishment and Negative Interactions

According to Kazdin (2001), "**Punishment** is the presentation or removal of a stimulus or event after a response, which decreases the likelihood or probability of that response" (p. 56). Kazdin points out that this behavioral definition of punishment is at variance with the usual social use of the term as a penalty for a particular behavior. As with reinforcement, if the target behavior does not respond to a presumably punishing consequence as anticipated and begin moving in the desired direction, the intervention is not working. Some students seem to provoke negative interactions with their peers or teachers, perhaps in an effort to gain power, perhaps because negative attention may seem preferable to being ignored. In these cases, the interventions adults intend as "punishment" do not function that way.

Commonly used classroom punishment techniques include disapproving or negative statements, time-out, response cost, and overcorrection. Punishment techniques should be used with caution because of their potentially negative impact and the ethical concerns they raise for educators.

Kazdin (2001) describes common negative side effects of punishment:

- The student's emotional reaction to the punishment may interfere with the learning process, and be more disruptive than the original behavior.
- The student may react by escaping the situation (e.g., running away) or avoiding the punisher.
- The student may react with aggression toward the punisher, which is negatively reinforced if it results in the punisher retreating.
- Children raised in an environment where punishment is modeled and used to control them are likely to learn and use those techniques.
- If punishment results in immediate reduction of target behavior, it reinforces the punisher (making it more likely the cycle will recur). If there is not an immediate reduction, the punisher may escalate.

The Center for Effective Collaboration and Practice has suggested punishment only be used when: "(a) the behavior is dangerous to the student or others, and (b) every other intervention has been appropriately implemented and failed, or (c) when the student's behavior is so noxious that it prevents him from learning or forming meaningful social relationships" (Quinn et al., 2000, p. 28).

The decision to use punishment in classrooms for students with disabilities should be made at a district or programmatic level, based on research-guided policies and procedures. Information concerning the discipline plan should be clearly communicated to parents, students, and other stakeholders in advance. Some schools have chosen to establish a discipline committee, similar in function to human-subjects committees at universities, to review IEPs and behavior plans that include punishment or aversive consequences prior to implementation. Just like other IEP goals, progress toward behavioral goals must be monitored systematically and programs revised as needed.

Verbal Reprimands. Kauffman, Mostert, Trent, and Hallahan (2002) suggest that if teachers must use verbal reprimands, they keep them brief and to-the-point, make them as private as possible, and secure the student's attention (e.g., make eye contact, use her name). For example, "Mary, I need you to return to your seat."

Overcorrection. **Overcorrection** is the process of eliciting some kind of student effort as a penalty for misbehavior (Kazdin, 2001). One type of overcorrection, called positive practice, involves repetition of a task or skill the student has failed to demonstrate, to reinforce its correct application. For example, when Angie runs in the school hallway, the teacher says, "Angie, please go back to the top of the stairs and show me how you are supposed to walk down the hall." A common component of overcorrection may be some type of mandatory restitution—mentioned earlier—that requires the student to restore the environmental effects of the behavior. Positive practice and restitution may be used separately, or in combination (Kazdin, 2001).

Response Cost. **Response cost** occurs when a student loses a reinforcer or a privilege she had previously earned or anticipated earning. For example, Maria receives an allowance of $5.00 per week for making her bed, picking up her own things, and helping load the dishwasher Monday and Thursday. Today she oversleeps and leaves for school without making her bed; her dirty clothes from yesterday are left in a heap at the foot of her bed. Maria's mother deducts 50 cents from her next allowance payout.

Losing telephone or television privileges and being grounded are common response-cost strategies used by parents. In the classroom, response cost may be used in conjunction with a contract or token economy to provide a deterrent for failure, or to back up the reinforcer that the student will earn for being successful. For example, Beverly continues to talk to a peer during a social studies video after being signaled by the teacher to think about Rule #4: I will be the best student I can and encourage other students to do their best. The teacher quietly and unemotionally walks over and puts a check mark on Beverly's daily point sheet.

Time-Out. **Time-out** means the temporary removal of the student from the opportunity for reinforcement. As a punisher, time-out should result in a reduction of the unwanted behavior it is paired with as a consequence. If the student likes being in time-out or seems to be provoking the teacher into sending her to time-out, then it is functioning as a reinforcer by letting her avoid or escape something else she does not want to do.

Time-out, when effectively used, provides a student with a brief opportunity to de-escalate, regroup, engage in problem solving, and then return to class. Generally, 1 minute per year of the child's age will be sufficient to accomplish this (i.e., 5 minutes for a 5-year-old, 12 minutes for a 12-year-old).

Used inappropriately, time-out may become an opportunity for a power struggle between student and teacher. Figure 6-9 provides a set of procedures proposed by the Center for Effective Collaboration and Practice (Quinn et al., 2000) for using time-out effectively as a classroom intervention. Some teachers prefer the time-out space to be a sterile environment, with few distractions and nothing the student can easily destroy. Others make the time-out space a "safe spot" with a comfortable bean bag or rocker to sit on, a stuffed animal to hold, or a stress ball to squeeze.

FORMING AND FACILITATING PSYCHOEDUCATIONAL GROUPS*

School counselors and experienced teachers are often asked to facilitate psychoeducational or therapeutic groups to assist students experiencing problems with

---

*Content adapted from Downing, J. A., & Smith, A. H. (1999). *Counselor cadre training curriculum: Updating your clinical and consultative skills.* Unpublished manuscript.

- Consult school administration for district time-out policies.
- Discuss the use of time-out options and procedures with the student's parents. Include this on the student's IEP.
- Define which behaviors will earn time-out.
- Decide how long the time-out should last.
- Specify time-out procedures.
- Thoroughly discuss the time-out procedure with the students:
  - Specify the behaviors.
  - Specify warnings to be given.
  - Teach directions for going to time-out.
  - Teach proper time-out behavior.
  - Teach procedures for returning from time-out.
- Post time-out rules in the classroom.
- Warn students when their behavior may lead to time-out.
- Implement time-out without emotion or discussion.
- Begin timing the time-out only when the student begins to exhibit appropriate behavior.
- Discuss appropriate alternative behaviors in private upon student's return from time-out.
- Keep a time-out log for each incident that includes:
  - Child's name
  - Description of behavior or incident that resulted in time-out
  - Time of incident
  - Duration of time-out
  - Behavior during time-out
- Review the log regularly to evaluate effectiveness.

FIGURE 6–9 Guidelines for Implementing Time-Out

Source: From Quinn, M. M., Osher, D., Warger, C., Hanley, T., Bader, B. D., & Tate, R. et al. (2000). *Educational strategies for children with emotional and behavioral problems.* Washington, DC: American Institutes for Research, Center for Effective Collaboration and Practice (CECP). Copyright 2000 by CECP. Reprinted with permission.

social, emotional, or coping skills. According to Gladding (1994), these school-based counseling groups "deal with specific, nonpathological problems that members are aware of prior to joining and which do not involve major personality changes" (p. 1). Common focus areas include: social skills, relationships with peers and adults, anger management, grief and loss, substance abuse, adolescent sexuality, school attendance, and underachievement.

Identifying the Need or the Topic

Educators may identify the need for services informally (e.g., through conversations in the teachers lounge or with a student in the hallway) or formally (e.g., by the principal or parent group). In a school implementing positive behavioral supports, determine the need for group interventions by examining data collected by the school office regarding number of absences, tardies, office referrals, failing grades, and so on.

Identifying and Setting Goals

Group goals will depend on the topic and the type of students identified as needing assistance. For most ongoing groups, it is helpful to develop both long- and short-term goals. Long-term goals address the intended outcome of the experience (e.g., improving social skills, reducing at-risk status); short-term goals may be set on a daily or weekly basis and address a specific subskill or problem (e.g., giving positive feedback to a peer, being on time to class). Student involvement in goal-setting generally will increase ownership and participation, as well as teach the students how to set and monitor their own goals.

Getting Organized

The logistics of running a group need to be carefully considered in advance of the first meeting. Facilitators may want to address the following questions:

- Which students are being targeted for the group? Will the group composition be homogeneous (alike) or heterogeneous (varied) by problem, age, gender, etc.?
- When is it most convenient to hold the group, considering potential scheduling conflicts, time of day, preceding and following activities, etc.?
- Is there a location that can be used for the group each time to provide a sense of stability and to allow posting of rules and expectations, placing chairs in a circle, etc.?

- Will the selected location protect the confidentiality of the group?
- Will the group be facilitated by one person, or would cofacilitation be preferable? If only one adult will be present, will a back-up plan be necessary to handle disruptive/aggressive behavior?
- Is there a system in place to solicit informed parental consent for participation?
- How many sessions will you hold? Will the group be time-limited or ongoing? Will new students be added to the group after it starts or will they be put on a waiting list for the next group?

Session Format

The following format for group facilitation includes elements drawn from the counseling literature, as well as from what we know about effective instruction. It can serve as a general outline or framework to be varied based on the characteristics of each group and its facilitator(s). The amount of time devoted to each section may change over the course of the group's development. For example, establishing rules and rapport may receive a larger proportion of time during the initial sessions of a group, with the balance gradually shifting toward content and skill acquisition over time.

Starting the Group

Give some thought to how you plan to open the group, particularly at the first meeting. Think about getting acquainted, establishing rules, and determining participants' readiness to begin.

Icebreakers/Energizers/Focusers. Opening activities are particularly desirable when members of a group do not know each other well, to break the tension at the first meeting, or when a new student joins an established group. These activities may take various forms, including: an opening ritual/routine (e.g., saying the group motto, singing a special song), a noncompetitive game, a worksheet, a journaling topic, and so on.

Establishing Rules and Safety. To build rapport and trust within the group, take time during the first meeting to establish group norms. If possible, develop the expectations with the input of group members. Make sure confidentiality is addressed explicitly: "What is said in the group stays in the group." Other common expectations involve taking turns and listening to others (Gladding, 1994). Post the rules in the group room or make copies available to all group members; review them often.

Checking In. Establishing a triage or check-in routine provides an activity for the facilitator and group members to touch base before beginning the content. It also allows the counselor to adjust the activities and focus for the session as recent occurrences require.

Delivering the Content

Just like an academic lesson, the presentation is the "meat" of the group session. It is when new information and skills are presented and practiced.

Introducing the Topic/Advanced Organizer. Many students who experience academic, behavioral, or emotional problems also have difficulty organizing their thinking. Telling the group what the topic is in advance reduces anxiety and sets the stage for what is to come. If possible, provide a rationale for addressing the specific issue for the day by relating the topic to past, present, or future life experiences of the members.

Presentation. Address the various learning styles of the group by using a variety of techniques to introduce content and skill information. Some lecture, reading material, or audiovisual aids may be appropriate, but most students learn best by actively interacting with the content.

Application Activities. Practice and application activities may include paper-and-pencil tasks, group or dyadic discussions, role-playing, brainstorming, problem solving, and so on. If students are learning a new skill, they will need sufficient practice to achieve mastery and fluency before being expected to use the new skill in their natural environments (classrooms, at home, etc.).

Establishing Closure

Summing Up/Giving Assignments. At the end of a group session, it generally is helpful to summarize what students have done, learned, or agreed to try. If specific assignments will be given, check for understanding by having a student paraphrase or reexplain the expectations.

Checking Out. Just as checking in gives the counselor a chance to assess the group's mood and readiness at the beginning of a session, checking out provides an opportunity to make sure everyone is ready to leave the group. This may be particularly important if the topic was emotionally charged or sensitive.

Evaluation

Ideally, you should determine the techniques to assess the progress of a group in advance, when goal-setting takes place. Formative evaluation techniques—such as weekly logs or checklists—allow incremental measurement of progress over time. Summative evaluation—pre- and posttesting for knowledge or behavioral change—provides an indication of how well the content was absorbed and applied by the group members. Satisfaction data allows group members to provide feedback to the facilitator that can be used for program and process improvement.

SELECTING THE RIGHT INTERVENTION

Behavior management is a complex, interactive process that involves the teacher, the student, and a multitude of environmental and instructional variables. The prerequisites for a successful individualized intervention are: (1) schoolwide behavioral supports to encourage prosocial behavior and discourage inappropriate behaviors; (2) a structure and culture of the classroom community that supports students academically, behaviorally, and socially; and (3) a thorough individualized assessment that provides sufficient information to develop efficient, targeted intervention plans. Figure 6–10 provides a decision tree summarizing this process.

KNOWING WHEN TO REFER

Many teachers are comfortable dealing with the day-to-day problems of students with EBD, including resistance, social-skill deficits, aggression, and some fairly bizarre behavior. However, it is unrealistic to believe that even the most accomplished individual will be able to manage every situation that occurs with difficult-to-manage students. Threats to harm self or others, disclosure of abuse, and situations that pose a danger to individuals in the classroom often require specialized skills. Therefore, each building or special education program should develop clear guidelines regarding (a) the types of behaviors and issues teachers are expected to handle themselves, (b) the resources available in case of a crisis situation requiring external resources, and (c) the procedures for making referrals or requesting assistance. Chapter 13 will discuss making referrals to and forming alliances with community mental health providers and agencies. Further information on planning for and dealing with crisis situations is contained in Chapter 14.

CHAPTER SUMMARY

* Prevention of misbehavior in schools may be addressed at three levels: schoolwide strategies, classroom strategies, and individual strategies. This chapter focused on strategies for students who may not respond to schoolwide and classroom strategies, and who require additional, specialized interventions delivered individually or in small groups. Techniques for encouraging appropriate behavior and discouraging inappropriate behavior were presented, with guidelines for use. A variety of therapeutic expressive activities are appropriate for use with students with EBD. Many will also benefit from participation in psychoeducational groups, following the format provided.

CHECK YOUR UNDERSTANDING

1. *True or False.* Candy always works as a reinforcer.
2. You know that a reinforcer is working when the target behavior _____.
3. Define and provide an example for each of the following terms: modeling, shaping, chaining.
4. Telling students that if they finish their assignment with at least 90% they will get an extra 10 minutes of recess is an informal _____.
5. Define and provide examples of the following: bibliotherapy, journaling, pet therapy.
6. Define and provide an example for each of the following terms: extinction, overcorrection, response cost.
7. When Marta etched her name in the top of her desk, she was required to use sandpaper to repair the damage. This is an example of _____.
8. An appropriate stay in the time-out chair for a 6-year-old will be approximately _____ minutes.
9. Angela often tears up her spelling tests when she receives them back with grades lower than an A. Operationally define a replacement behavior you would like Angela to try instead; identify a technique to use that you believe would be successful.

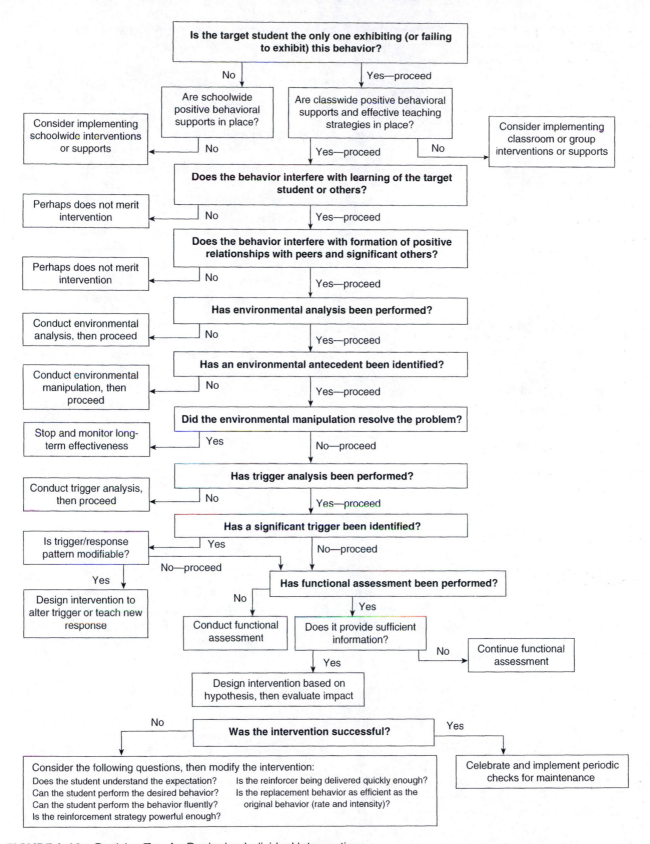

FIGURE 6–10 Decision Tree for Designing Individual Interventions

10. Bart is frequently tardy to his sixth-hour class. After observation and a discussion with Bart and his teacher, your hypothesis is that he is avoiding his English class. Design a contingency contract that addresses the following points: an incentive for punctuality, the function Bart's behavior is serving, and the consequences of continued tardiness.

APPLICATION ACTIVITIES

1. In Chapter 5, you designed an ideal resource room for students with EBD. Complete your classroom management plan by describing the techniques you will use to encourage appropriate behavior and discourage inappropriate behavior.

2. For *each* of the mini case studies below, answer the following set of questions:

   a. What do you believe the function of this student's behavior is? Why?

   b. What appropriate or replacement behavior would you select to increase? Why?

   c. What inappropriate behavior would you select to decrease? Why?

   d. What technique or techniques would you use to address the behaviors you selected in (b) and (c)?

   e. How would you collect data to evaluate the success of your intervention?

   Jerry is a sixth grader diagnosed as ADHD and LD. He receives 55 minutes per day of resource-room time. Jerry's sixth grade classroom teacher describes him as easily distracted by other children's questions and conversations. She says he rarely stays in his seat for an entire class period and has turned in fewer than 50% of his assignments. When verbally redirected, he complies and gets back on task for a minute or two. Lately, Jerry has begun acting angry during math class—tearing up his paper and being verbally negative (e.g.,"This is stupid. I hate math. I'm never going to get this done."

   Marquita is a high school junior who frequently arrives late for class. In the past two weeks, she has stopped participating in class discussion and complains that she does not feel well when directly questioned. You have noticed that she is spending less time with her usual friends and often walks down the hall alone, with eyes on the floor or her feet.

   Elena is a 5-year-old in your kindergarten class. She appears to be angry all of the time, and frequently is physically aggressive with her peers. When questioned about her behavior, Elena lies and denies having done anything wrong, then begins crying. She looks and sounds sincere, but you have seen her pinching and kicking other students when she thinks you are not looking at her. You have spoken to her mom, who says that Elena is the same way with her cousins at home. Mom says she uses spanking and time-out with Elena, but reports that neither has been effective at stopping the behavior. In fact, it seems to make her madder and sometimes more aggressive after the intervention.

   JD is a 14-year-old seventh grader. He is bigger than many of his classmates and reportedly bullies them. Other students have reported him for taking their lunch money, verbally threatening and shoving them in the bathroom, and coercing them into letting him copy their homework assignments. Recently, someone entered the art room during your lunch hour and splattered paint on all the posters hung around the room for parent night later this week. You have a feeling that JD is responsible; two students have reported seeing him hanging around your room during lunch.

3. Select a case study from Appendix A. Using Figure 6–10, identify those questions that you can answer and those you cannot. Assuming that schoolwide and classwide supports were in place, determine what individual behaviors you would target for intervention. Design a management plan that includes strategies for increasing positive behaviors and decreasing negative behaviors. Would you recommend that this student participate in a psychoeducational group? If so, describe the structure and format of such a group.

4. In teams of three or four students, design a psychoeducational group for students with anger-management problems. Determine how students will be identified for your group. Research available published curricula on this topic. Identify the topics and activities you will address, and write a plan for six weekly sessions, using the lesson planning form from Chapter 5.

PART 3

INTERVENTIONS FOR SPECIFIC POPULATIONS

CHAPTER 7 DISORDERS OF ATTENTION

CHAPTER PREVIEW

NOTE: *In educational literature, the abbreviations ADD and ADHD or AD/HD are used almost interchangeably, generally without reference to specific subtypes described in DSM-IV. To avoid confusion, in this chapter the abbreviation ADHD is used throughout unless the content refers specifically to students who do not exhibit hyperactive behaviors.*

CONNECTING TO THE CLASSROOM: *A Vignette*

As he grew up, Gerald was constantly labeled by his teachers and other adults. As a preschooler, he was "hyper" to his babysitter, "a holy terror" at his grandmother's house, and "a real handful" at home. Gerald never seemed to sit still for more than a few minutes at a time, and was constantly getting into trouble or getting hurt for acting on his impulses. His mother asked his pediatrician about Gerald's frequent accidents and falls; the pediatrician was not concerned. Gerald's high energy level continued through kindergarten and first grade, with his teachers frequently consulting with his parents to discuss his erratic behavior and academic progress. Gerald's new labels included "lazy," "unmotivated," and "slow learner." When his second-grade teacher suggested retaining him at the end of the year, Gerald's mother took him to the local mental health clinic where he was evaluated by a child psychologist. Gerald was diagnosed with ADHD, and prescribed a low dose of stimulant medication. He entered third grade a much calmer and more attentive student; however, it quickly became apparent that he was still having difficulty in reading and math, perhaps because of missed instruction during his first years of school. Gerald was assigned to a remedial reading group and tutored in math during the third and fourth grades. Although teachers still occasionally referred to him as a "space cadet" for not paying attention, his skills improved. In fifth grade, Gerald's standardized test scores were within the average range for his age, so the extra help was discontinued.

Gerald's grades through middle school were mostly Bs and Cs, with the occasional D in science—which he said was boring—and PE—where he tended to get into arguments with the coach about how to run the class. In junior high, Gerald displayed a knack for drawing and calligraphy, and he took every art class that was offered through the end of high school. He also was quite a wiz with computer graphics, which he used to work on the school newspaper and help redesign the school's Web site. Gerald displayed little enthusiasm for his academic subjects, but learned to take notes and study for tests. His grade point average slowly approached 3.0 and Gerald graduated from high school with his class. Gerald expressed interest in going into architecture, engineering, or drafting after high school, but had great difficulty with the college-preparatory math curriculum. He is currently attending a junior college, studying with a tutor to try to improve his math skills, and working part time in the copy center of a local office-supply store.

ATTENTION-DEFICIT/HYPERACTIVITY DISORDER (ADHD)

Attention-deficit/hyperactivity disorder (ADHD) is one of the most commonly diagnosed behavior disorder of childhood, estimated to be present in approximately 3% to 5% of school-age children (National Institutes of Health, 2003). Boys are identified with ADHD three times more often than girls (Barkley, 1991).

Description and Major Features

Treatment of ADHD has become a costly major public health program, with estimated public school costs alone in excess of $3 billion in 1995 (National Institutes of Health, 1998). While ADHD is not a federally funded category of special education under IDEA, children with this medical diagnosis account for more than 40% of all students in emotional/behavioral disorders (EBD) placements and 25% of those in programs for learning disabilities (LD) (Forness & Kavale, 2001).

In a survey of school psychologists, Smith (2000) reported that the other categorical designation commonly used for students with ADHD was Other Health Impaired (OHI). The study further indicated that only 14% of students not found eligible for special education services under IDEA were considered for Section 504 accommodations. Therefore, students with ADHD are a population that may be served: (1) in general or special education settings; (2) through accommodations and modifications, special education, related services, or none of these; and (3) under the auspices of IDEA or Section 504 of the Rehabilitation Act, or neither. See Figure 7-1 for an illustration of the varied diagnostic, educational, and service options for students with ADHD.

Children with ADHD may also have pronounced impairments in academic performance, vocational success, and social-emotional development, including frustration and low self-esteem (NIH, 1998). In addition, students with ADHD are at high risk for school failure, and more likely to be in special education, to be

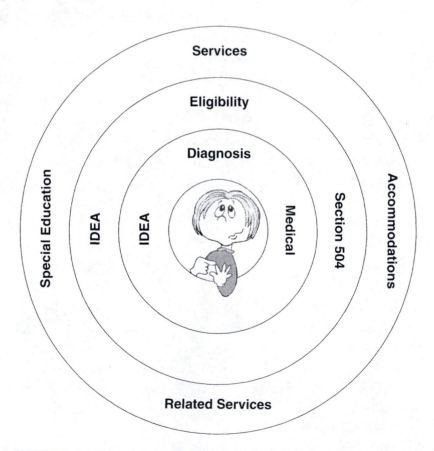

FIGURE 7–1 Diagnostic and Service Delivery Options for Students with ADHD

expelled or suspended, or to repeat a grade (LeFever, Villers, Morrow, & Vaughn, 2002).

Because ADHD is a medical diagnosis, students with the condition have been assessed and labeled by a physician or licensed mental health practitioner. The diagnosis is determined by whether the child meets the criteria for ADHD established in the American Psychiatric Association's *Diagnostic and Statistical Manual of Mental Disorders, Fourth Edition, Text Revision (DSM-IV-TR)*. (See Figure 7–2.) However, community practices vary widely regarding diagnosis and treatment, often based in part on the type of professional conducting the evaluation. In a University of Florida study (Bussing, Zima, & Belin, 1998), nearly 75% of the children with ADHD were served by primary care physicians, and 68% of these had no contact with a mental health provider. The study found that these children were diagnosed with fewer coexisting conditions, and had fewer treatment sessions, less treatment time, and less use of multimodal therapies than children served by mental health specialists. "Family practitioners were more likely than either pediatricians or psychiatrists to prescribe stimulants and less likely to use diagnostic services, provide mental health counseling, or recommend follow-up care" (Hoagwood, Kelleher,

---

A. Either (1) or (2):

(1) six (or more) of the following symptoms of **inattention** have persisted for at least 6 months to a degree that is maladaptive and inconsistent with developmental level:

Inattention

(a) often fails to give close attention to details or makes careless mistakes in schoolwork, work, or other activities
(b) often has difficulty sustaining attention in tasks or play activities
(c) often does not seem to listen when spoken to directly
(d) often does not follow through on instructions and fails to finish schoolwork, chores, or duties in the workplace (not due to oppositional behavior or failure to understand instructions)
(e) often has difficulty organizing tasks and activities
(f) often avoids, dislikes, or is reluctant to engage in tasks that require sustained mental effort (such as schoolwork or homework)
(g) often loses things necessary for tasks or activities (e.g., toys, school assignments, pencils, books, or tools)
(h) is often easily distracted by extraneous stimuli
(i) is often forgetful in daily activities

(2) six (or more) of the following symptoms of hyperactivity-impulsivity have persisted for at least 6 months to a degree that is maladaptive and inconsistent with developmental level

Hyperactivity

(a) often fidgets with hands or feet or squirms in seat
(b) often leaves seat in classroom or in other situations in which remaining seated is expected
(c) often runs about or climbs excessively in situations in which it is inappropriate (in adolescents or adults, may be limited to subjective feelings of restlessness)
(d) often has difficulty playing or engaging in leisure activities
(e) is often "on the go" or often acts as if "driven by a motor"
(f) often talks excessively

Impulsivity

(g) often blurts out answers before questions have been completed
(h) often has difficulty awaiting turn
(i) often interrupts or intrudes on others (e.g., butts into conversations or games)

B. Some hyperactive-impulsive or inattentive symptoms that caused impairment were present before age 7 years.

C. Some impairment from the symptoms is present in two or more settings (e.g., at school [or work] and at home).

D. There must be clear evidence of clinically significant impairment in social, academic, or occupational functioning.

E. The symptoms do not occur exclusively during the course of a Pervasive Developmental Disorder, Schizophrenia, or other Psychotic Disorder and are not better accounted for by another mental disorder (e.g., Mood Disorder, Anxiety Disorder, Dissociative Disorder, or a Personality Disorder).

FIGURE 7–2 Diagnostic Criteria for Attention-Deficit/Hyperactivity Disorder

Source: American Psychiatric Association. (2000). *Diagnostic and statistical manual of mental disorders* (4th ed., text revision). Washington, DC: American Psychiatric Association. Reprinted with permission from the *Diagnostic and Statistical Manual of Mental Disorders,* Copyright 2000. American Psychiatric Association.

Feil, & Comer, 2000, p. 198). As a result of the disparities among ADHD treatment providers, it is particularly important that schools conduct their own thorough, individualized evaluation of students referred for concerns in the area of attention.

Etiology

Like most other emotional and behavioral disorder diagnoses, ADHD has no single conclusive cause. Researchers believe that the condition results from the interaction of personal/biological factors with environmental factors. Emerging genetic research appears to point to an association with the neurotransmitter dopamine, and specifically with the D4 dopamine receptor gene (Faraone, 2000). In an interview with *The Brown University Child and Adolescent Behavior Letter* ("Review," 2000), three prominent genetic researchers agreed that genes alone cannot explain the presence of ADHD in a specific individual. They cited combined genetic and environmental factors, including social adversity, obstetric complications, fetal exposure to nicotine, brain injuries, and trauma.

Assessment

No single, independent diagnostic test can definitively identify students with ADHD. In addition to the general problems encountered in assessing emotional and behavioral traits covered in Chapter 2, differential identification of ADHD is particularly difficult for the following reasons:

* ADHD frequently presents with coexisting conditions.
* Behaviors resulting from other conditions may closely resemble those of children with ADHD.
* DSM-IV formal diagnostic criteria are designed for young children; there is no professional consensus on how to adjust them for adolescents and adults.
* All of the behaviors associated with ADHD occur at some point in nearly all typically developing children.

The National Institutes of Health's (1998) Consensus Statement on ADHD describes optimal assessment procedures as including: structured parent questionnaires, rating scales, input from parents and school, review of developmental (school-based) assessments, communication assessment, and monitoring at school. Figure 7-3 provides a selected overview of the published instruments commonly used to screen and diagnose ADHD.

Although ADHD is considered a clinical diagnosis, schools frequently conduct their own assessments of students referred for attention problems. According to a national survey of school psychologists (Smith, 2000), the most frequently used standardized tests for ADHD referrals are questionnaires and checklists. Some believe that analyzing subtest scores of the Wechsler Intelligence Scale for Children (WISC) (Wechsler, 1991) may provide information about attention problems, specifically: low scores in digit span, arithmetic, and coding, or a wide gap between verbal and performance scores (Hallowell & Ratey, 1995).

Some researchers have raised concerns regarding the diagnostic efficiency of commonly used measures. A recent study compared scores on two rating scale measures with information gathered through clinical diagnostic interviews with parents (Bussing, Schuhmann, Belin, Widawski, & Perwien, 1998). The rating scales yielded substantial numbers of false positives and false negatives. These results underline the importance of using multiple measures and multiple informants when assessing students with social, emotional, or behavioral problems.

Researchers have also raised concerns about over- and underidentification based on gender. Research has suggested males are four to nine times more likely than females to be referred by teachers and diagnosed with ADHD using current methods (Reid et al., 2000).

Classroom Organization: Providing Support with Structure

> Tommy was sighing and making loud noises throughout lessons. He crawled on the floor during transitions and sometimes even during class. As he laughed and shoved his way through the class to line up, he injured other children. He was playful and destructive at the same time. Instead of picking up the blocks when it was time to clean up, he would scatter them wildly with flailing arms and a big grin. Just when a bucket was filled with blocks, Tommy would dump it. (Fachin, 1996, p. 438)

As this example from a second-grade teacher demonstrates, children and youth with ADHD can challenge the behavior management skills and resources of even the most experienced educator. Interventions for this group of students should be based on the same proactive, self-esteem–building philosophy that guides behavior management in general. However, students with ADHD require extra planning and multifaceted interventions in the areas directly related to their classroom difficulties: focusing and sustaining attention,

Test Name	Characteristics	Population
AD/HD: Comprehensive Teacher's Rating Scale (ACTeRS)	Items designed to identify students with ADD and ADHD based on four factors: attention, hyperactivity, social skills, and oppositional behavior.	Ages 6 to adult
ADHD Rating Scale-IV	Rating scale directly linked to DSM-IV diagnostic criteria. Includes parent version in English and Spanish, and teacher version.	Ages 5 to 18
ADHD Symptom Checklist-4 (ADHD-SC4)	Rating scale used for screening and to monitor treatment response in children with ADHD and ODD.	Ages 3 to 18
ADHD Symptoms Rating Scale (ADHD-SRS)	Aids in symptom identification, diagnosis, treatment planning, and monitoring of treatment progress.	Ages 5 to 18
Adult Attention Deficit Disorders Evaluation Scale (A-ADDES)	Designed as a measure of ADHD in adults in the home and work environment.	Adults
Attention Deficit Disorders Evaluation Scales (ADDES-3)	Designed to provide a measure of each of the DSM-IV characteristics of ADHD. Available in school and home versions, in English and Spanish. Intervention manual available.	Ages 3 to 20
Attention Deficit Disorders Evaluation Scale: Secondary-Age Student (ADDES-S)	Measures characteristics of ADHD in adolescents; aligned with DSM-IV criteria and two most common subtypes: inattentive and hyperactive.	Ages 11.5 to 18
Attention-Deficit Hyperactivity Disorder Test (ADHDT)	Identifies ADHD in young children and adolescents using 3 subtests in areas of hyperactivity, impulsivity, and inattention.	Ages 3 to 23
BASC Monitor	Norm referenced, 47-item rating scale that evaluates ADHD characteristics. Subscales include: attention problems, internalizing problems, hyperactivity, and adaptive skills.	Ages 4 to 18
Brown ADD Diagnostic Form	Comprehensive evaluation for ADHD.	Adolescents & Adults
Brown Attention-Deficit Disorder Scales	Preliminary screening tool for ADHD.	Adolescents & Adults
Child Behavior Checklist (CBCL)	Thorough assessment of behavior problems, emotional disturbance, and psychopathology.	Ages 4 to 18
Conners' ADHD/DSM-IV Scales (CADS)	Includes the Conners' ADHD index and DSM-IV symptom scales that use DSM-IV criteria for ADHD.	Ages 5 to 18
Conners' Ratings Scales— Revised (CRS—R)	Diagnosis of ADHD using the Conners' ADHD index.	Ages 3 to 17; self-report 12 to 17
Conners' Adult ADHD Rating Scales (CAARS)	Measures ADHD symptoms in adult populations.	Adults
Spadafore ADHD rating scale (S-ADHD-RS)	Provides a quick examination of ADHD behaviors, and the severity of the problem behaviors.	Ages 5 to 19
Test of Variables of Attention (TOVA)	Computer-based assessment for ADHD diagnosis and for medication titration.	Ages 4 to adult

FIGURE 7–3 Sample Assessment Measures for ADHD

Note: Publisher information for these measures is included in Appendix B, and was compiled from publisher Web sites and the Mental Measurements Yearbook database.

gaining impulse control, and internalizing organizational skills. Because many students with ADHD have experienced repeated frustration and failure, they may also need additional training support in social, emotional, and behavioral areas. For most students with ADHD, long-term behavioral change may require use of powerful contingencies and multiple intervention strategies (Barkley, 1990).

In Tommy's case, the necessary interventions and supports included a personalized token economy implemented both at school and at home, fast-paced small-group tutoring using a game format, resource-room support in language arts, a classroom aide to assist with reinforcement and redirection, training in relaxation techniques, peer tutoring and cooperative learning, and close collaboration between school and home. The last month of his second-grade year, Tommy's pediatrician placed him on Ritalin, which significantly improved his ability to be successful in the classroom (Fachin, 1996).

Classroom Intervention Strategies

Because the population of students with ADHD is heterogeneous, it is important to structure interventions based on an individual functional assessment of behaviors. Teachers cannot assume that a single technique or class of interventions will be effective with all students who have ADHD (DuPaul, Eckert, & McGoey, 1997).

Before selecting individualized interventions for students with ADHD, spend time preparing the classroom. Organizing and arranging the classroom to effectively teach and manage a range of diverse pupils (as described in Chapter 5) may lessen the impact of ADHD characteristics. Consider environmental interventions first. If the student has trouble staying in his seat, negotiate acceptable alternatives to remaining seated. For example, if the desk is uncomfortable, have the student try using a table and chair or a beanbag, writing on a window ledge, standing at the desk, or draw a zone around the chair where he can stand or wander without being "out of bounds." Remember that careful planning and use of precorrection strategies will save instructional time in the long run. Pay particular attention to planning:

* Physical layout of the room, including seating, location of instructional materials, and traffic patterns
* Classroom rules, routines, schedules, and expectations (Barkley, 1990)

* Behavior management, including contingency management, point/token systems, consequences and response cost options, crisis management procedures

The following section provides general strategies and suggestions to address problems of attention, impulse control, and organization. The subsequent section describes techniques focused on social and emotional growth.

Attention Strategies. Students with ADHD may experience difficulty with all aspects of paying attention. It may be hard to gain their attention in the first place, or to keep it during instruction. They may be easily distracted or sidetracked by environmental stimuli, specific aspects of the tasks, or intrusive random thoughts.

For students with ADHD, problems in attention focus can be underselective or overselective in nature. For example, when given a worksheet of math problems with festive Halloween pumpkins as a banner, the underselective student will connect with varied stimuli on the page, such as the pumpkin, a specific math problem, or even a small stain or spot on the paper. Conversely, the overselective student may zero in on the pumpkin in the upper right-hand corner and notice nothing else on the paper. Both students may become stalled in completing the worksheet; however, redirection and intervention for each type of attention problem will differ.

Difficulties in attention often result in failure to complete assignments accurately and on time. Some students with ADHD will be easily frustrated, and lack perseverance. They may give up easily or become angry and agitated.

A number of general strategies may be used to assist students with ADHD in focusing and sustaining attention to task (Downing & Smith, 1999):

* Use verbal and nonverbal cues and prompts before giving important information or asking a question.
* Use proximity and eye contact to maintain attention.
* Keep instructions (both oral and written) short and explicit.
* Focus instruction on key points; use outlines or graphic organizers.
* Increase pacing of oral presentation and task sequencing.
* Use color, highlighting, and visual prompts.
* Use techniques that encourage active responding, immediate feedback, and reinforcement.

- Divide large assignments into shorter tasks with finite time limits (using a visual schedule and timer).
- Make assignments more interesting, using computers, game formats, and alternating preferred with nonpreferred activities.
- Give the student choices about how to complete assignments.
- Provide a peer buddy for students who need help getting started or need more frequent encouragement than the teacher can provide.
- Develop contingency contracts providing specific reinforcers for completed assignments.
- Decrease environmental distractions.
- Provide preferential seating in the least distracting location, away from windows, doors, and high-traffic areas.

Impulse-Control Strategies. Acting without thinking is one of the primary characteristics of students with ADHD. Impulsive students blurt out answers without being called on—and sometimes before the question has been completed. They rush through seatwork to get finished or to get on to a more desirable task. Waiting for the teacher to get around to them becomes intolerable and may lead to passive-aggressive or acting-out behaviors.

A general strategy for impulse control is to teach students to recognize their common triggers and redirect their energy into an acceptable replacement behavior. Develop strategies and routines for commonly occurring situations, such as raising hands before speaking, turn-taking in conversations or groups, or getting the teacher's attention to ask for assistance. These skills can be taught, monitored, and reinforced on a classwide basis or in a small-group social-skills environment, reducing the need for individual redirection (Posavac, Sheridan, & Posavac, 1999). Another strategy is to give students something to do while waiting or during inactive periods of instruction. The waiting behavior may be academic (e.g., "Go on to the questions you know while you wait for me to get to you"), or nonacademic (e.g., "Make doodles in the margin of the paper that remind you of what is happening in the film").

Teachers should not assume that a student who appears distracted is not paying attention. Sometimes students with ADHD can be doing something with their hands that appears totally unrelated, but have their mind focused on instruction.

Teaching stress-reduction techniques may also be useful for redirecting impulses (e.g., "Take a deep breath and imagine your favorite calm place").

Organizational Skills and Structure Strategies. To be successful with students who have ADHD, teachers must provide a high degree of external structure. Post and teach classroom rules, routines, and schedules and review and refer to them repeatedly. Keep unstructured time to a minimum. Give students a limited range of acceptable activity choices for free time. Avoid surprises by warning students of changes in schedules or imminent transitions. For example, use a bell as a 5-minute warning signaling the end of independent seatwork and providing students extra time to prepare for and make transitions.

If content acquisition is a concern, teachers can provide graphic organizers or lecture outlines to assist students in focusing attention and organizing information in meaningful ways. Materials developed at the University of Kansas Center for Research on Learning provide structured, step-by-step techniques to teach students important skills related to specific content areas (e.g., reading, math), as well as strategies directed at storing and remembering information, expressing information, and social competence (University of Kansas, 2004).

Completing and submitting independent seatwork and homework can present a real challenge for students with ADHD. Many students with ADHD turn in incomplete or poor-quality work, while others complete the work but fail to turn it in to be graded. Teachers can provide external structure in the form of in- and out-boxes for assignments; assignment notebooks or logs; checklists on posters; and cue cards outlining specific procedures to follow. Cooperative learning activities and peer helpers may also increase the likelihood of assignment completion (Rief, 1993). Students with ADHD may function better with a well-organized backpack and class folders than with a locker. That is, students with ADHD are more likely to have assignments, textbooks, and supplies with them in the classroom and at home for homework completion if they are organized in a backpack rather than buried somewhere in their locker.

Robin (1993) suggests additional accommodations designed to meet the challenges adolescents encounter in secondary settings. Arrange schedules to balance frustration and energy levels and minimize travel time. Schedule study hall as the last period of the day to provide a time to review daily assignment sheets and planners, and to organize for completing homework. Adjust evaluation procedures used in some secondary classes; for example, allow oral or untimed exams. Issue home and school progress reports, making desired privileges contingent on assignment completion and positive ratings.

Secondary students with ADHD also may feel overwhelmed by large-scale tasks that require planning and time management. For these students, it is helpful to teach goal setting and demonstrate how to break up large assignments into a series of small tasks that can be scheduled realistically. Young, West, Smith, and Morgan (1991) developed the WATCH strategy specifically to assist students in managing larger projects:

- **W**—Write down the assignment, the due date, and any special requirements for the assignment.
- **A**—Ask yourself if you understand the assignment and ask for clarification or help if necessary.
- **T**—Task analyze the assignment and schedule the tasks over the days available to complete the assignment.
- **CH**—Check each task as you do it for completeness, accuracy, and neatness (C/A/N).

Enhancing Social, Emotional, and Behavioral Growth

Empirical studies conducted using behavior-change techniques with students with ADHD have had mixed results. Although more studies have been conducted on the effects of medication than on behavioral interventions, studies combining medication with behavioral interventions (called multimodal treatment) have been the most efficacious ("Mental Health," 1999). A major review of research conducted by Pelham, Wheeler, and Chronis (1998) supported the use of parent training and behavioral interventions but *not* cognitive interventions. Their findings indicated that behavioral treatments did not make students with ADHD "normal," that the effects tended to decrease after the intervention was withdrawn, and that many children failed to demonstrate any improvement. However, the authors did express concern about adult follow-through, unsure whether parents and teachers implemented the interventions consistently. Also, most behavioral interventions were short-term, applied in clinical settings, and lacked maintenance and generalization procedures.

Trout, Reid, and Schartz (2002) found very different results in another review of 19 experimental and quasi-experimental studies conducted at the University of Nebraska-Lincoln. This analysis found that application of self-regulation techniques with students diagnosed as ADHD resulted in improvement in attention, on-task time, academic productivity and accuracy, and a decrease in maladaptive behaviors. Techniques used included self-reinforcement, self-recording, and self-evaluation. Approximately half of the studies involved students receiving medication. General classroom interventions appeared more effective than those in clinical settings, and three studies that conducted follow-up assessments found maintenance of effects several months later.

Despite conflicting data concerning outcomes of behavioral interventions with students who have ADHD, parents and teachers reported higher levels of satisfaction following participation (NIH, 1998). Teachers who choose to implement these interventions should do so based on individual student characteristics and functional behavior assessment data.

Cognitive Behavioral Interventions. **Cognitive behavioral interventions** attempt to address the student's thinking process, as well as behavior, with the eventual goal of self-management. A variety of techniques are included in this category, including self-talk or instruction, self-monitoring and recording, self-evaluation, self-reinforcement, and problem solving (Yell, Robinson, & Drasgow, 2001). These techniques may be taught individually or in groups, in isolation or as part of a sequential process. During the instructional process, teachers use shaping and fading procedures to move from teacher control to student control and from overt to covert cues.

Self-Talk or Instruction. When using the technique of self-talk, the teacher helps students develop a series of specific statements to make, or questions to ask, in a given situation. For example, to reduce somatic symptoms before spelling tests, Sally might learn to make statements about being calm, focused, and confident. Self-instruction may also be used to rehearse a strategy or set of skill steps to use in working through a problem. For example, while taking her spelling test, Sally can mentally review the steps she plans to follow: (1) Write my name and date in the upper right-hand corner of the page. (2) Number the paper from 1 to 20, skipping every other line. (3) Visualize the word as the teacher pronounces it. (4) Write the word, spelling it in my head as I write each letter. (5) Review the test for errors before handing it in.

Self-Monitoring or Recording. To use self-monitoring, teachers work with students to devise a format for collecting data on the target behavior, most often using frequency count or time-sampling techniques. Recording should be simple and easily learned by students with ADHD (e.g., a checklist, a grid with plus and minus signs, or a 5-point rating scale). For example, Andrew frequently leaves his seat without permission during independent seatwork and distracts his classmates. His teacher does not think Andrew is aware of how much study time he loses wandering around the room and has provided him with a card to track his behavior. Each time he leaves his seat, Andrew records the time he got up, the reason for his excursion, and the time he returned to his seat. The teacher keeps a similar card. Andrew and his teacher review their cards at the end of class to compare notes and discuss strategies for reducing Andrew's out-of-seat time.

Self-Evaluation. Teachers assist students in reviewing their performance and provide corrective feedback. The process of self-evaluation also allows the teacher to establish the reliability of student perceptions and recording. Melody frequently loses points on her written assignments for misspellings and errors in punctuation and capitalization. Her teacher has taught her to check her work prior to turning it in using a checklist: (1) Check spelling. Look up any words that I'm not sure about. (2) Make sure every sentence ends with a punctuation mark. (3) Capitalize the first letter of every sentence and all proper nouns. Melody circles and corrects every error she finds before turning the paper in to the teacher for grading.

Self-Reinforcement. When using self-reinforcement, teachers initially reinforce effort, recording accuracy and goal attainment. As students demonstrate a firm grasp of the skill required to self-instruct, monitor, and evaluate, responsibility for reinforcement shifts to the student.

For example, when Melody began using her proof-reading strategy, her teacher put a gold star on each paper that had been self-evaluated and corrected. Melody could use those stars as bonus points for the classroom token economy. After two weeks, when Melody was consistently turning in accurate work, her teacher gave Melody the stars and told her to reward herself by putting them on each paper she had proof-read carefully before handing it in.

Problem Solving. There are many published problem-solving systems designed for a variety of situations and student types. The SOCCSS strategy (Roosa, 1995) can be easily adapted to most academic and nonacademic problems encountered by students with ADHD or other emotional and behavioral challenges.

- **S**ituation—Define the problem in context (the antecedent).
- **O**ptions—Brainstorm all of the possible behaviors students could have chosen in that situation.

- **C**onsequences—Identify the outcome most likely to occur as a result of each choice/option.
- **C**hoices—Choose an option to try the next time this situation occurs that might have a better outcome.
- **S**trategies—Verbalize a plan for carrying out the choice in the future.
- **S**imulations—Formalize, rehearse, or role-play the desired substitute behavior.

Coaching. A trained adult or peer acting as a coach and mentor can provide additional support for students with ADHD. A peer who models good organizational skills might assist a student with ADHD in completing his homework/assignment log and assembling required materials prior to going home each day. The student with ADHD might check in with the school counselor at the beginning and/or end of the day to set goals and check progress. This process is sometimes referred to as educational triage. Coaching has also been successful in clinical settings, using either telephone or brief face-to-face conversations.

When coaching, Hallowell and Ratey (1995) suggest brief daily check-ins at first, using the following guided interview format:

- **H**elp—Ask the person you are coaching, what kind of help do you need?
- **O**bligations—Ask specifically what obligations are upcoming and what the person is doing to prepare for them.
- **P**lans—Ask about ongoing plans.
- **E**ncouragement—The most fun part of the coach's job ...don't be daunted by cynicism. It takes a while to overcome a lifetime of negativity. (p. 227)

Social Awareness and Skills. Many students with ADHD have associated deficits in social perception and skills. They may not pick up on verbal or nonverbal cues, or may ignore group norms to get their own needs met. Social interventions have been designed to meet a variety of student needs, including:

- Increasing feelings of self-determination, competence, and expectations of success
- Developing interpersonal relatedness
- Exploring and developing a range of interests and satisfactions related to learning
- Building awareness of personal motives and true capabilities
- Setting appropriate goals

- Learning to value and accept responsibility for choices
- Making more appropriate choices (Center for Mental Health, 2002, p. 7)

Another goal of social interventions might be to develop the goal-directed persistence that students with ADHD typically lack. This lack of goal directedness results in students with ADHD preferring a small immediate reward to a larger long-term payoff, or the avoidance of a future negative consequence (Barkley, 1995). Students with ADHD may do better in noncompetitive, nonteam sports activities that allow them to develop their own skills and work to improve their own performance, rather than focus on winning or beating the competition.

Because of the social competence problems of students with ADHD, many benefit from systematic skills training, such as the structured learning approach used in *Skillstreaming the Adolescent* (Goldstein, Sprafkin, Gershaw, & Klein, 1980) or from other psychoeducational techniques discussed in Chapters 5 and 6.

Stress Management Techniques. For students with ADHD who experience high levels of stress and anxiety, various techniques designed to help students relax, control breathing, and reduce anxiety may prove helpful. Rief (1993) provides guidelines for conducting stress management activities, including: fun and laughter, breathing techniques, yoga and slow movement exercises, walking meditations, visualization and guided imagery, and using music for relaxation, energy, and transitions.

Parent Training. Anna M. Thompson (1996), the parent of a child with ADHD, cites the need for understanding and regular open communication with educators, including scheduled conferences, informal school visits, telephone calls, logs, notes, newsletters, and report cards. Many schools also offer parents training in behavior management, particularly setting and enforcing appropriate expectations and limits. Many parents seek support and information from other parents or advocacy organizations such as Children and Adults with Attention Deficit Disorder (CHADD).

ADHD CHARACTERISTICS ACROSS THE LIFESPAN

Like other emotional and behavioral problems, ADHD may look very different in young children than it does in adolescents or adults. Figure 7–4 provides an overview of the developmental shifts across the lifespan. In the majority of individuals with ADHD, behaviors consistent with DSM-IV diagnostic criteria tend to decrease with age. As a result, only one-third of those diagnosed with ADHD as children continue to meet the full criteria at age 18. For many, the symptoms continue to diminish into the 20s, and their clinical diagnosis becomes ADHD in "partial remission" (Trollor, 1999). However, the long-term prognosis for another subgroup of children diagnosed with ADHD is quite grim. According to Barkley (1991): "Between 35 and 60% of ADHD individuals will have problems with aggressiveness, conduct, and violation of legal or social norms during adolescence, and 25% are likely to become antisocial in adulthood" (p. 2).

CONCERNS ABOUT UNDERIDENTIFICATION OF ADHD BY GENDER AND TYPE

The DSM-IV-TR diagnostic criteria for ADHD in Figure 7–2 were divided into three subsections—inattention, hyperactivity, and impulsivity. Approximately 85% of those identified with ADHD have the combined subtype (Barkley, 1998), displaying some characteristics in each of the three areas. However, a smaller group of students display primarily the inattentive symptoms of ADD, without the behaviors related to hyperactivity. The primarily inattentive ADD child may exhibit more internalizing symptoms (e.g., anxiety, withdrawal) and initiate fewer social interactions, but be less aggressive and have a generally better prognosis (Barkley, 1998; Bauermeister et al., 2005). However, because they do not attract as much negative adult attention as their hyperactive peers, it is conceivable that students with ADD are judged by their parents and teachers to be lazy or unmotivated. Therefore, they may be less likely to be recognized as having a diagnosable disorder, and less likely to be referred for special education evaluation.

Similar concerns have been raised regarding the marked difference between the rate of males and females identified with ADHD. A recent study found that, regardless of symptom type, teachers were more likely to refer for evaluation male students than female students (Sciutto, Nolfi, & Bluhm, 2004). This result appeared to relate, in part, to the teachers' perceptions about the level of disruption the behaviors caused in the classroom. Therefore, additional research is needed to determine whether female students and males without disruptive, hyperactive behaviors are being referred and treated in appropriate numbers.

Early Childhood

- Has unusually high rate of activity compared to same-age and same-gender peers
- Does not understand, remember, or follow instructions or rules
- Uses expressive language most often to get personal needs met
- Receptive language comprehension is very literal and concrete
- Becomes frustrated or gives up easily when the task is novel or perceived to be difficult
- Expects needs to be met instantly, unable to wait for reinforcement or for an answer
- Has difficulty focusing on what is important, often easily distracted or led astray by extraneous details
- Has difficulty making and keeping friends
- Does not self-monitor or realize how behavior affects others
- Does not problem solve or consider consequences of behavior

Elementary Grades

- Continues to have high level of motor activity compared to peers
- Continues to have difficulty with instructions and rules, needs them to be short, simple, and explicit
- Continues to exhibit low frustration tolerance
- Has difficulty profiting from instruction due to problems with focused attention and memory, often off task
- Completes assignments quickly, or inaccurately, or does not complete them at all
- Continues to have difficulty maintaining reciprocal friendships
- Works best with high levels of external structure and minimal unstructured time
- Continues to have difficulty with self-monitoring and problem solving

Adolescence

- Continues to have a higher activity rate than peers, but may have developed coping strategies to minimize impact
- May have developed strategies for focusing attention and memory, but continues to forget or avoid tasks that are difficult or not perceived relevant
- Needs direct instruction in study skills related to content acquisition and high-stakes testing
- May continue to have difficulty completing assignments, particularly in classes where the instructional style or content is not a good match for his needs and interests
- Has developed age-appropriate conversational skills, with an emphasis on gaining acceptance from peers
- May question or challenge authority figures (more than peers) concerning rules, routines, structure, assignments

Adulthood

- Continues to be easily frustrated by tasks/jobs that are tedious, uninteresting, or consistently difficult
- Chooses short-term, easily accomplished tasks that occur at the last minute, postponing more complex, difficult, or high-priority assignments
- Feels restless, and does better in a job that allows a high degree of physical movement or lends itself to being broken into smaller chunks that provide variety
- Accepts consequences of behavior, but may have difficulty accepting corrective feedback
- Misses nonverbal social cues and has a higher rate of interpersonal conflicts
- If interested in the task, shows ability to sustain attention for long periods of time
- Understands language, but may exhibit "selective memory" if not interested (unless taking notes)
- Tends to interpret events in terms of his own feelings, needs, and preferences
- Able to problem solve, but may need structured workspace, time to plan and prioritize
- Often does best with work that is fairly autonomous, self-paced, and allows time alone
- Needs to learn to identify frustration triggers and develop coping skills for reducing stress and avoiding conflict

FIGURE 7–4   Common Characteristics of Students with ADHD Across the Lifespan

CO-OCCURRING DISORDERS AND ADHD

One of the most confusing aspects of ADHD is that the symptoms are similar to—and can occur with or result from—many other conditions, including: anxiety, bipolar disorder, child abuse or neglect, chronic fatigue, conduct disorder, depression, fetal alcohol syndrome, hyperthyroidism or hypothyroidism, lead poisoning, learning disabilities, medication reactions, obsessive compulsive disorder, oppositional defiant disorder, personality disorders, posttraumatic stress disorder, schizophrenia, seizure disorder, situational stressors, sleep disorders, substance abuse, and Tourette's syndrome (Faraone, 2000; Faraone, Biederman, & Monteaux, 2000; Hallowell & Ratey, 1995). Students with ADHD also share characteristics with students who are gifted (Webb & Latimer, 1993). The most common cooccurring disorders appear to be learning disabilities (Barkley, 1991), depression, bipolar disorder, anxiety disorder, and tics or Tourette's (Children and Adults with Attention-Deficit/Hyperactivity Disorder, 2000).

THE ROLE OF MEDICATION IN THE TREATMENT OF ATTENTION DEFICIT DISORDER

Both the NIH consensus statement on ADHD (1998) and the Surgeon General's report on mental health and children (Mental Health, 1999) concluded that empirical studies, including randomized clinical trials, have established the efficacy of stimulants in treating the symptoms of ADHD. However, improvement in the core symptoms of ADHD—problems with attention, impulsivity, and hyperactivity—did not necessarily lead to improvement in academic or social functioning. Although most studies have involved the use of stimulants, antidepressants and antihypertensive medications have also been used with some success.

Prescription medication usage among students who have ADHD and other disorders has become much more commonplace in the past two decades, and school professionals have played an important role in medication monitoring (Gureasko-Moore, DuPaul, & Power, 2005). However, as a result of public concerns, CHADD reported in 2001 that about half the states had introduced legislation that restricted access to use of stimulant medications with school-age children (Ross, 2001).

On the other hand, some schools reportedly suggested to parents that their children would benefit from medication or required that the student be taking medication as a condition for evaluation, receiving services, or returning from suspension. As a result of these concerns, the 2004 IDEA Amendments included language prohibiting schools from requiring students to obtain prescription medications as a condition of receiving services. (See Sidebar 7-1.)

The American Academy of Child and Adolescent Psychiatry and the American Academy of Pediatrics have issued guidelines for their members on the assessment and treatment of children and adolescents with ADHD, including the appropriate use of medication with this population. The National Institutes of Health (1998) listed five concerns that remain to be addressed by empirical research:

> First, it cannot be determined if the combination of stimulants and psychosocial treatments can improve functioning with reduced dose of stimulants. Second, there are no data on the treatment of ADHD, Inattentive type, which might include a high percentage of girls. Third, there are no conclusive data on treatment in adolescents and adults with ADHD. Fourth, there is no information on the effects of long-term treatment (treatment lasting more than 1 year), which is indicated in this persistent disorder. Finally, given the evidence about the cognitive problems associated with ADHD, such as deficiencies in working memory and language processing deficits, and the demonstrated ineffectiveness of current treatments in enhancing academic achievement, there is a need for application and development of methods targeted to these weaknesses. (p. 12)

THERAPIES NOT SUPPORTED BY EMPIRICAL RESEARCH

As the diagnosis of ADHD has become more common, some researchers have proposed alternatives to the use of psychotropic medications for school-age children.

SIDEBAR 7-1

IDEA 2004 Prohibits Mandatory Medication

The 2004 reauthorization of IDEA includes language prohibiting state and local school personnel from requiring a child to obtain a prescription "as a condition of attending school, receiving an evaluation . . . or receiving services" (20 U.S.C. § 1412 [25] [a]).

Despite limited scientific data, some of these treatments have received widespread media attention. These alternative methods have been based on divergent views concerning the origin and causes of ADHD. A careful examination of the claims has shown that most of the evidence in support of these alternative treatments consists of individual case histories or testimonials. Studies generally lacked the rigor of large-scale clinical trials or experimental studies using control groups.

Dietary Interventions

One highly publicized diet promoted feeding children with ADHD food free from chemical additives, preservatives, and coloring. This diet has not been supported by well-controlled studies. At best, it may be said to be a healthier diet than that eaten by many American children. While the diet appears to have been helpful for a small number of children with specific sensitivity or allergies, no studies have demonstrated a significant impact on children's learning and attention problems. The same has been the case for high doses of vitamins and minerals, allergy elimination diets, and diets designed to control candida yeast and sugar intake.

Biofeedback

Recent advances in electronic imaging and EEG technology have produced new information about the differences between the brain activity patterns of individuals with and without ADHD. Based on this research, techniques involving biofeedback or neurofeedback have been developed to train children and adolescents with ADHD to regulate their own brain activity to more closely resemble the patterns seen in those without ADHD symptoms. The process involves attaching electrodes to the head using a computer that converts EEG patterns into images and sounds on a video display. The changes in brain waves are translated into changes in the display. Technicians then use a video-game–type format and operant conditioning techniques to train students to regulate their brain activity (Sterman, 2000). Although initial results were positive, few large-scale, systematic studies have been conducted using these techniques.

Critics of biofeedback have pointed to the time and expense of this individualized clinical intervention relative to other treatments for ADHD. However, Barabasz and Barabasz (2000) found that the 40 to 80 sessions typically required to achieve lasting effects could be reduced by half when combined with a technique called instant alert hypnosis.

Other Techniques

Researchers have made a number of claims regarding the use of perceptual stimulation/integration training and chiropractic manipulation with ADHD. However, there is no empirical evidence that these techniques have any impact on the core symptoms of the disorder (Barkley, 1991).

CHAPTER SUMMARY

- Students with ADHD have significant, long-term problems in the areas of attention, impulsivity/hyperactivity, or both. It appears that ADHD results from a combination of individual (genetic, biological) and environmental factors. While students with attention problems are frequently referred for special education evaluation, the diagnosis of ADHD requires a medical diagnosis that can rule out all of the various other conditions that resemble or coexist with ADHD.
- Classroom teachers need to provide external structure for these students by implementing a powerful combination of effective instructional strategies, behavior management techniques, and environmental modifications. In addition, cognitive behavioral interventions and social-skills instruction may be required to help children and adolescents with ADHD recognize and respond to social cues.
- While some children with ADHD will grow out of it as they enter adulthood, others will continue to display symptoms.
- Research has clearly demonstrated the effectiveness of stimulant medications at treating the core symptoms of ADHD; however, intensive interventions are also required at school and home to address academic, behavioral, and social deficits.

CHECK YOUR UNDERSTANDING

1. *True or False.* Girls are identified with ADHD two times as often as boys.
2. *True or False.* A process in which teachers assist students in reviewing their performance and providing effective feedback is called self-monitoring.
3. *True or False.* The formal diagnostic criteria in the DSM-IV are designed for adolescents and adults, with no professional consensus on how to adjust them for young children.

4. Which of the following methods is recommended for helping students with ADHD reduce the symptoms related to high levels of stress and/or anxiety? (a) breathing techniques, (b) running, (c) using a punching bag, or (d) none of the above

5. Which of the following is *not* a strategy suggested to assist students with ADHD in focusing and sustaining attention? (a) proximity, (b) eye contact, (c) increasing the pace of oral presentation, or (d) asking frequent questions about material

6. A study by the University of Nebraska-Lincoln (Trout et al., 2002) showed that the application of what kind of techniques resulted in improvement in attention, on-task time, and academic productivity, and a decrease in maladaptive behaviors for students with ADHD? (a) self-regulation, (b) behavioral interventions, (c) antecedent manipulation, or (d) punishment

7. List three controversial therapy techniques sometimes used with students with ADHD.

8. *True or False*. A high degree of external structure must be in place for students with ADHD to be successful in a classroom setting.

9. What are the steps in the WATCH strategy for use with adolescents with ADHD for managing large-scale projects?

10. Describe three of the deficits that students with ADHD may exhibit in the area of social perception.

APPLICATION ACTIVITIES

1. Select a grade level and design a classroom layout that would minimize problems for a student with ADHD. Diagram the classroom and list the critical features you included in your design.

2. Divide into small groups and role-play the following scenario: Your school uses interdisciplinary team teaching, and each member is an expert in a content area (language arts, math, social studies, science, etc.). Your principal just informed you that Julia, a transfer student, has been assigned to your team. Julia's mother reports that she has just been diagnosed with ADHD and the principal wants to know how your team plans to prepare for her arrival. Develop a list of potential environmental modifications and positive behavioral supports for Julia.

3. Using case study #4 in Appendix A, complete the following activities individually or in small groups:

   a. Review the case study and identify student characteristics that are consistent with a diagnosis of ADHD, as well as those that do not appear to be ADHD-related. Identify, operationally define, and prioritize three to five target behaviors.

   b. Based on information provided about this student, generate a functional hypothesis for each behavior. Use the format in Figure 3.10.

   c. Decide on a system of positive behavioral supports and environmental modifications to implement for this student.

   d. Write behavioral objectives that would be appropriate for an IEP or BIP for this student, using the format in Figure 3.11.

4. Using case study #4 in Appendix A or a child you have observed in a classroom setting, identify an academic or social behavior that could appropriately be addressed using one of the strategies introduced in this chapter (WATCH, SOCCSS, or HOPE). Develop a lesson plan or script for implementing the strategy with your student.

CHAPTER 8

DISRUPTIVE BEHAVIOR DISORDERS

CHAPTER PREVIEW

CONNECTING TO THE CLASSROOM: *A Vignette*

Miranda's mother describes her as a "cranky" infant. She fussed constantly, even when she had a full belly, a dry diaper, and somebody was rocking her. Miranda extended the tantrums and oppositional behavior of the "terrible twos" well into her kindergarten year. Her preschool and kindergarten teachers had concerns about her lack of emotional maturity and poor social skills with peers. Reportedly, Miranda insisted on having everything her own way, and would snatch toys and throw a screaming fit when she was thwarted by peers or told "no" by adults.

Toward the end of first grade, Miranda's teacher referred her for a special education evaluation because of her disruptive behavior and emerging academic problems in reading and receptive language. Miranda's mother attributed Miranda's behavior to her parents' recent divorce, and declined evaluation. Throughout elementary school, Miranda continued to struggle academically, falling a little further behind her peers each year, but getting Bs and Cs in most subjects. Her disruptive behavior had virtually disappeared, and although she sometimes appeared sullen and isolated, Miranda no longer objected when things did not go her way or when she was corrected by an adult.

At the age of 13, Miranda's grades abruptly plummeted, and she drastically changed both her appearance and her behavior. She was suspected of stealing small amounts of money from other students' gym lockers, but denied it and nothing was ever proven. Miranda became even more socially isolated, still attending class regularly but rarely interacting with peers and speaking to teachers only when they initiated the contact. Miranda's mother contacted the school counselor and expressed her concern that, when she returned home from her second-shift job at midnight, Miranda was often just arriving home and refused to say where she had been. Miranda's mother asked the counselor to talk to Miranda to find out where she was going and what she was doing. Before the counselor had a chance to meet with Miranda, she was picked up by the local police at a party and held in detention for curfew violation and possession of drug paraphernalia. The detention intake interview revealed that Miranda was a regular user of alcohol and marijuana, had been shoplifting and trading sex to obtain drugs, had numerous scars from self-inflicted burns and cuts, and had made at least one suicide attempt during the previous 30 days.

A CAVEAT REGARDING STUDENTS WITH DISRUPTIVE BEHAVIORS

As was mentioned in the preface to this text, well-intentioned educators disagree about whether students with disruptive behaviors should be considered eligible for special education in the category of emotional and behavioral disorders (EBD), or whether they should be managed administratively through discipline and alternative placement options. Some believe these students are willful rule breakers and potential sociopaths who waste precious (and scarce) special education resources. However, a wealth of evidence from a variety of professional fields—summarized in this chapter—demonstrates the complex array of individual, familial, school, community, and societal factors that, in combination, produce these most challenging students. Eleanor Guetzloe has stated three assumptions we believe are consistent with both the research evidence concerning disruptive behavior disorders and the philosophy of this text:

1. Violence and aggression are complicated problems, for which there are no simple solutions.
2. Aggressive and violent children and youth (whatever we may call them) should receive special education services, whether these are delivered in the same setting with nonaggressive and nonviolent students or in a separate setting.
3. The educational environment, behavior management system, and curriculum implemented in the classroom or any other setting should be appropriate for the most difficult, most disruptive, most destructive, and most violent students housed in that setting. (Guetzloe, 1992, Intro para. 3–5)

As Hall, Williams, and Hall (2000) point out regarding young people with oppositional defiant disorder (ODD), "Children with ODD have a biologically driven disorder. They did not choose to be born with this disorder. If they could crawl out of their temperament and grow a new one, they would. When the problem is cast in this light, compassion and understanding seem warranted. Most important, this approach sets the stage for comforting, not confrontation; for support, not shaming; and for bonding, not belittling" (p. 225).

OVERVIEW OF DISRUPTIVE BEHAVIOR PROBLEMS

Students with disruptive behaviors are a heterogeneous group. Most are boys; however, conduct problems are not uncommon among adolescent girls. Many youngsters exhibit individual traits and behaviors in early childhood that foreshadow a developmental path leading to more destructive and aggressive behaviors as adolescents and adults; others experience episodes of disruptive behavior that lasts only a year or two. One of the difficulties in identifying these disorders is that a certain amount of rowdy play and aggression may be viewed as developmentally appropriate, especially when the child is a toddler or adolescent. In both of these developmental stages, asserting one's independence and individual identity is an important part of growing up.

Unfortunately, schools and communities find themselves ill-equipped to address the complex, multifaceted needs of the increasing numbers of disruptive students. Walker and Golly (1999) suggest that schools are reporting more serious acts of deviance, including teacher assault, bullying, physical aggression, and inappropriate sexual behavior because of the increasing number of societal risk factors affecting young children. "Collectively these risk factors are producing children and youth who (a) see violence as a viable means of solving problems, (b) don't respect the rights of others, (c) are not socially responsible, (d) have not been taught basic manners and social conventions, and (e) don't value human life as they should" (p. 105). Brendtro and Long (1995) provide a similar description of these difficult-to-reach students: "Sources of stress abound: normal adolescent development, family conflict, poverty, the mean streets of dangerous neighborhoods. When stress is severe and prolonged, children adopt ingrained styles of defensive behavior. They may have a hostile bias toward all adults, carry a menacing interpersonal demeanor to school, and believe that respect can be gained only through intimidation" (p. 53).

Risk Factors and Predictors of Disruptive Behaviors

In the research base and recent reviews of literature, we can clearly identify the individual, family, school, and community characteristics associated with increased risk for disruptive behaviors. See Figure 8-1 for a list and citations.

Individual factors that predispose a child to disruptive behaviors include a difficult temperament, cognitive or learning impairments, neurophysiological problems, and mental illness. Family predictors, which may include both genetic and environmental components, are primarily harsh and ineffective parenting, or parental antisocial and pathological characteristics. Moss, Baron,

Individual/ Biological Factors	• Difficult temperament and inflexibility in early years[3,4,10] • Attitudes and beliefs[10] • Mental illness, may be caused by neurological trauma, disease, chemical imbalances[2,5] • Neurophysiological problems[5] • Cognitive problems[5]
Familial Factors	• Ineffective parenting (e.g., poor monitoring, coercive interactions)[1,5,6,7,11] • Parental indifference, detachment and rejection, emotional deprivation[5,6,11] • Child abuse or neglect[6,11] • Exposure to domestic violence[6] • Disruptions in family functioning (e.g., separation, divorce, unemployment, substance abuse)[1,2,4,7,11] • Parent criminality or antisocial acts[5,7] • Aggressive siblings[7]
School Factors	• Autocratic/punitive school climate[2,10] • Poorly trained teachers, ineffectual teaching practices[5,10] • Differential treatment of at-risk students (less instruction and praise, greater rejection)[10] • Feelings of stress, frustration, and alienation[2,6] • History of academic failure[6,11] • Academic learning problems[4,11] • Victimization by aggressive peers (e.g., bullying, sexual harassment)[7,11] • Competition for status among peers[6] • Unequal access to social recognition[11] • Placement outside the mainstream[11] • High rates of suspension, expulsion, and dropouts[11]
Community Factors	• Poverty[2,6,10] • Deteriorating neighborhoods[10] • High crime rate[11] • Lack of social cohesion[11] • Fragmented and ineffective social services[10] • Discrimination and racial conflict[5,6] • Limited opportunity for successful education/employment[6] • Limited recreational and after-school activities[11] • Values/expectations condone aggression, alcohol, and drug use[5,10]
Societal Factors	• Availability of illicit drugs/substance abuse[2,5] • Criminal acts related to acquiring or selling drugs[6] • "Unintentional" violent or criminal acts (e.g., causing an accident while driving drunk)[6] • Decreased inhibition, and acts committed while high (e.g., date rape)[9] • Acceptance of violence as a problem-solving tool[8] • Desensitization to violence through exposure to media coverage of the news, sports, politics, music[2,5,8]

[1] Adams, n.d.
[2] Brendtro & Long, 1995
[3] Center & Kemp, 2003
[4] Centre for Community Child Health, n.d.
[5] Guetzloe, 1999
[6] Hamburg, 1998
[7] Loeber & Stouthamer-Loeber, 1998
[8] Lowry, Sleet, Duncan, Powell, & Kolbe, 1995
[9] Marwick, 1992
[10] Van Acker & Wehby, 2000
[11] Walker & Golly, 1999

FIGURE 8–1   Risk Factors and Mediators Associated with Disruptive Behaviors

Hardie, and Vanyukov (2001) found that preadolescent children of fathers with alcohol or other drug dependence and antisocial personality disorder were at increased risk for both internalizing and externalizing disorders, including major depression, conduct disorder (CD), attention-deficit/hyperactivity disorder (ADHD), oppositional defiant disorder (ODD), and separation anxiety disorder (SAD). Children who have experienced interrupted parenting are also at increased risk of developing aggressive or disruptive behaviors. Simmel, Brooks, Barth, and Hinshaw (2001) studied a statewide sample of adopted youth ages 4–18 and found that 21% met criteria for ADHD, while 20% met criteria of ODD. The clearest associations for problem behaviors were a history of abuse or neglect, later adoption age, prenatal drug exposure, and multiple foster placements prior to adoption. The same study cited low birth weight and teen mothers as additional risk factors for disruptive behaviors.

School factors (which will be discussed at greater length in Chapter 14) include a history of academic failure, negative relationships with peers and adults, and a punitive school environment.

Community factors include access to drugs and alcohol, exposure to violence, lack of educational and employment opportunity, and acceptance of aggression as a problem-solving strategy.

Unfortunately, the research base concerning effective evaluation and treatment is much less complete than the available data identifying risk factors. Most studies have been conducted in clinical settings, with male subjects, and provide limited information concerning ethnicity and socioeconomic status (SES). Results of treatment interventions in residential settings have not transferred to natural settings, including the home or school (Abikoff & Klein, 1992). Most studies use single-subject methodology, which makes it more difficult to predict how effective the intervention will be with a group or classroom of children.

School-based group intervention studies with this population have been few in number, and the limited findings have shown disruptive students to be very resistant to treatment. "CD has long been regarded as relatively intractable and resistant to treatment interventions. Findings from the past 10 years suggest no giant leaps in treatment of CD but, instead, a number of small steps, such as new strategies in service delivery" (Burke, Loeber, & Birmaher, 2002, p. 1284).

The National Institute of Mental Health (NIMH) *Blueprint for Change* (National Advisory, 2001) identified critical gaps in the professional knowledge base concerning psychosocial treatment efficacy, including our understanding about comorbidity of disorders, potentially life-threatening conditions, and "gateway conditions" that may predict or lead to more serious disorders. Loeber and Stouthamer-Loeber (1998) have identified three distinct developmental pathways that result in problem behaviors, including disruptive behavior disorders, antisocial behaviors, and delinquency. Those pathways include an overt path, a covert path, and a defiant/disobedient path (see Figure 8–2). Recent research efforts (e.g., Loeber, Burke, Lahey, Winters, & Zera, 2000) have focused on defining predictive subtypes that will allow for differential diagnosis and programming for the heterogeneous group of children with disruptive behaviors.

The *Diagnostic and Statistical Manual of Mental Disorders,* Fourth Edition (American Psychiatric Association, 2000) lists four discrete clinical diagnoses that may be appropriate for students with specific patterns of disruptive behaviors: (1) oppositional defiant disorder (ODD), (2) conduct disorder (CD), (3) disruptive behavior disorder—not otherwise specified (DBD-NOS), and (4) intermittent explosive disorder (IED). (See Figures 8–3 through 8–6 for diagnostic criteria.) This chapter will address the DMS-IV diagnostic criteria for each disorder individually, but will then discuss risk factors, assessment considerations, and interventions that appear to be relevant across the continuum of disruptive behavior disorders found in school-aged children and youth.

OPPOSITIONAL DEFIANT DISORDER (ODD)

DSM-IV (American Psychiatric Association, 2000) describes oppositional defiant disorder as "a recurrent pattern of negativistic, defiant, disobedient, and hostile behavior toward authority figures that persists for at least 6 months" (p. 100). The entire set of criteria, contained in Figure 8–3, requires frequent evidence of at least four specific behaviors that include: losing temper; arguing with adults; defiance/noncompliance with adult requests; deliberately annoying others; blaming others; or being easily annoyed, angry/resentful, or spiteful/vindictive. These children actively defy rules while denying responsibility for their behavior. They are often keen social observers, and use this data to exploit others, while having a very limited perception of their own negative impact on other people. Students with ODD seem to thrive on conflict, anger, and negativity from others, and are often most difficult with the

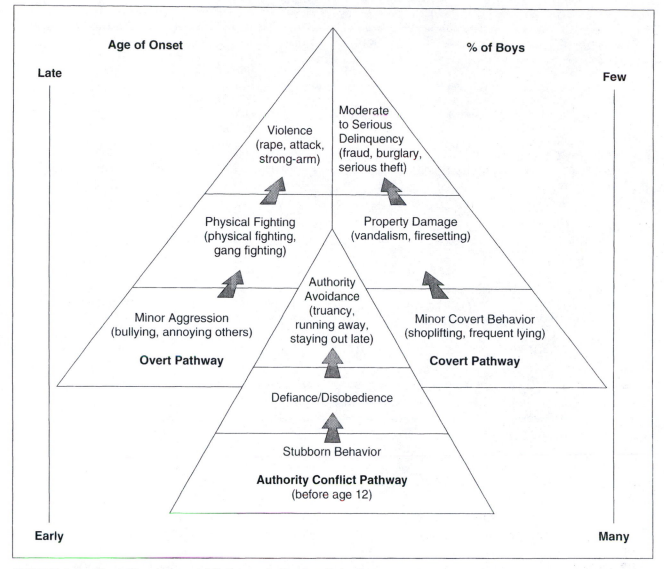

FIGURE 8–2 Three Developmental Pathways in Problem Behaviors

Source: Loeber, R., & Stouthamer-Loeber, M. (1998). Juvenile aggression at home and at school. In D. S. Elliott, B. A. Hamburg, & K. R. Williams (Eds.), *Violence in American schools* (p. 103, Figure 4.2). Cambridge, UK: Cambridge University Press. Reprinted with the permission of Cambridge University Press.

people they know well (Adams, n.d.; Centre for Community Child Health & Ambulatory Paediatrics, n.d.).

According to the Surgeon General's 1999 report, the prevalence of ODD is between 1% and 6% ("Mental Health"). DSM-IV (APA, 2000) reports prevalence of ODD as between 2% and 16%, depending on the population sampled and how the diagnosis was determined. ODD appears more often in males who were temperamental or hyperactive preschoolers, according to the DSM-IV (APA, 2000). Although the diagnosis of ODD is applied predominantly to males in the elementary

years, the prevalence of ODD following puberty appears to be relatively equal by gender. ODD is usually observed before the age of 8, but may emerge through late adolescence.

ODD often occurs with ADHD, which complicates diagnosis, treatment, and prognosis. Many in this comorbid group are more likely to ascribe hostile intent to the actions of others in ambiguous situations, and consequently respond with hostility (Coy, Speltz, DeKlyen, & Jones, 2001). Others with both ODD and ADHD demonstrate a different pattern; they have difficulty encoding

A. A pattern of negativistic, hostile, and defiant behavior lasting at least 6 months, during which four (or more) of the following are present:

(1) often loses temper
(2) often argues with adults
(3) often actively defies or refuses to comply with adults' requests or rules
(4) often deliberately annoys people
(5) often blames others for his or her mistakes or misbehavior
(6) is often touchy or easily annoyed by others
(7) is often angry and resentful
(8) is often spiteful or vindictive

Note: Consider a criterion met only if the behavior occurs more frequently than is typically observed in individuals of comparable age and developmental level.

B. The disturbance in behavior causes clinically significant impairment in social, academic, or occupational functioning.

C. The behaviors do not occur exclusively during the course of a Psychotic or Mood Disorder.

D. Criteria are not met for Conduct Disorder, and, if the individual is age 18 years or older, criteria are not met for Antisocial Personality Disorder.

FIGURE 8–3   DSM-IV Diagnostic Criteria for Oppositional Defiant Disorder

Source: American Psychiatric Association. (2000). *Diagnostic and statistical manual of mental disorders* (4th ed., text revision). Washington, DC: American Psychiatric Association. Reprinted with permission from the *Diagnostic and Statistical Manual of Mental Disorders,* Copyright 2000. American Psychiatric Association.

and recalling socially relevant information and may be perceived more as socially inept or not responsive to cues, rather than aggressive or hostile (Moore, Hughes, & Robinson, 1992). Clark, Prior, and Kinsella (2000) found that adolescents with ADHD plus ODD/CD had more difficulty generating solutions to problems and monitoring their own behavior than those with ODD/CD only.

Experts have described ODD as a developmental antecedent to CD for a significant number of children. However, if a child meets the diagnostic criteria for CD, then the CD diagnosis should be used instead of ODD. DSM-IV cautions that "a diagnosis of Oppositional Defiant Disorder should be considered only if the behaviors occur more frequently and have more serious consequences than is typically observed in other individuals of comparable developmental stage and lead to significant impairment on social, academic, or occupational functioning" (APA, 2000, p. 102).

CONDUCT DISORDER (CD)

The DSM-IV (APA, 2000) identifies CD as "a repetitive and persistent pattern of behavior in which the basic rights of others or major age-appropriate societal norms or rules are violated" (p. 93). They describe these behaviors as fitting into four groups: aggression toward

people and animals, harm to property, deceitfulness or theft, and serious rule violations. (See Figure 8–4 for a complete list of CD criterion behaviors.)

In the past, CD generally has been divided into two subtypes: overt and covert (also called socialized and unsocialized, or aggressive and nonaggressive). However, the task force charged with revising the CD definition for the DSM-IV chose instead to focus on the developmental course of the disorder and distinguish between subgroups based on age of onset (i.e., Childhood or Adolescent Onset Type). This decision was based, in part, on research that established a steep decline in aggression occurring around an age of onset of 10 years (Stahl & Clarizio, 1999). The diagnosis of CD is further defined by a description of severity as mild, moderate, or severe (see Figure 8–4). DSM-IV (APA, 2000) describes a number of associated features and mental disorders that may occur with CD, as follows:

- Little empathy or concern for the rights and feelings of others
- Frequent misperceptions of others' intentions as hostile or threatening, and responding with aggression
- Callous, lack of feelings of guilt or remorse
- Low or overly inflated self-esteem
- Early onset of risk-taking behavior, including sex, drinking, smoking, using drugs

A. A repetitive and persistent pattern of behavior in which the basic rights of others or major age-appropriate societal norms or rules are violated, as manifested by the presence of three (or more) of the following criteria in the past 12 months, with at least one criterion present in the past 6 months:

Aggression to people and animals

(1) often bullies, threatens, or intimidates others
(2) often initiates physical fights
(3) has used a weapon that can cause serious physical harm to others (e.g., a bat, brick, broken bottle, knife, gun)
(4) has been physically cruel to people
(5) has been physically cruel to animals
(6) has stolen while confronting a victim (e.g., mugging, purse snatching, extortion, armed robbery)
(7) has forced someone into sexual activity

Destruction of property

(8) has deliberately engaged in fire setting with the intention of causing serious damage
(9) has deliberately destroyed others' property (other than by fire setting)

Deceitfulness or theft

(10) has broken into someone else's house, building, or car
(11) often lies to obtain goods or favors or to avoid obligations (i.e., "cons" others)
(12) has stolen items of nontrivial value without confronting a victim (e.g., shoplifting, but without breaking and entering; forgery)

Serious violations of rules

(13) often stays out at night despite parental prohibitions, beginning before age 13 years
(14) has run away from home overnight at least twice while living in parental or parental surrogate home (or once without returning for a lengthy period)
(15) is often truant from school, beginning before age 13 years

B. The disturbance in behavior causes clinically significant impairment in social, academic, or occupational functioning.

C. If the individual is 18 years or older, criteria are not met for Antisocial Personality Disorder.

Code based on age at onset:

312.81 Conduct Disorder, Childhood-Onset Type: onset of at least one criterion characteristic of Conduct Disorder prior to age 10 years

312.82 Conduct Disorder, Adolescent-Onset Type: absence of any criterion characteristic of Conduct Disorder prior to age 10 years

312.89 Conduct Disorder, Unspecified Onset: age at onset is not known

Specify *severity*:

Mild: few if any conduct problems in excess of those required to make the diagnosis **and** conduct problems cause only minor harm to others

Moderate: number of conduct problems and effect on others intermediate between "mild" and "severe"

Severe: many conduct problems exist in excess of those required to make the diagnosis or conduct problems cause considerable harm to others

FIGURE 8–4 DSM-IV Diagnostic Criteria for Conduct Disorder

Source: American Psychiatric Association. (2000). *Diagnostic and statistical manual of mental disorders* (4th ed., text revision). Washington, DC: American Psychiatric Association. Reprinted with permission from the *Diagnostic and Statistical Manual of Mental Disorders,* Copyright 2000. American Psychiatric Association.

- High rates of suicidal ideation
- Lower-than-average cognitive ability, especially Verbal IQ
- Co-occurrence with Learning Disorders, Anxiety Disorders, Mood Disorder, and Substance-Related Disorders

As you might imagine from the characteristics of this disorder, the long-term prognosis for students with CD is grim. "Children with CD are at higher risk of developing mental health problems (such as anti-social personality disorder) in the future. It is one of the strongest predictors of late adolescent and early adult personality problems" (Centre for Community Child Health, n.d., Long-Term Outcomes section, para. 2). The behaviors of individuals with CD interfere with their ability to succeed in school or maintain gainful employment, so many do not function at the level predicted by their IQ. They have problems developing and maintaining relationships with adults and peers, have higher injury rates, higher school expulsion rates, and more frequent contact with juvenile authorities (Shaffer et al., 1996). Girls with a conduct disorder are more likely to run away from home, and become involved in drugs and prostitution.

According to the Surgeon General's Report ("Mental Health," 1999), prevalence estimates for CD are between 1% and 4% depending on how it is diagnosed and by whom. The report indicates that childhood onset type CD has a more negative prognosis, with between one-fourth and one-half of all antisocial children going on to become antisocial adults. The DSM-IV describes CD prevalence as increasing over the past decades, with a range of 1% to 10% of the population (APA, 2000). CD rates reportedly are higher in urban communities than in rural settings, and higher for males than females (APA, 2000).

Distinctions Between Childhood and Adolescent Onset CD

The DSM-IV (APA, 2000) indicates that CD may be evident as early as preschool, but most significant symptoms emerge from middle childhood through middle adolescent. Childhood-onset type CD is most common in males, and is frequently preceded by a diagnosis of ODD. Early onset is associated with a more negative prognosis.

McCabe, Hough, Wood, and Yeh (2001) found that childhood onset was primarily predicted by individual and familial factors, and that young children who exhibited CD behaviors were more likely to bully or threaten others than those diagnosed as CD in adolescence. The study found that adolescent onset was more likely to be associated with the influence of a deviant peer group and societal factors. Lahey and colleagues (1998) found that students whose behavior met criteria for CD before the age of 10 were 8.7 times more likely to exhibit at least one of the overt, aggressive behavior criteria for CD than young people with a later age of onset. DMS-IV indicates that individuals with adolescent onset CD, as well as those with milder symptoms, may have a better chance of adequate social and occupational adjustment as adults (APA, 2000).

The age of symptom onset has implications both for prognosis and for the type of intervention strategies likely to be most successful:

Early starters are likely to experience antisocial behavior and its toxic effects throughout their lives. Late starters have a far more positive long-term outcome because they are socialized to this behavior pattern by peers rather than by their family ecology. Early starters generally require comprehensive interventions involving caregivers, teachers, and peers while late starters often respond positively to school-based intervention programs. (Sprague & Walker, 2000, p. 370)

Co-occurring Conditions and Conduct Disorder

One of the challenges of diagnosing and treating CD is the high frequency of co-occurring (i.e., comorbid) conditions. The most frequent co-occurring disorder is ADHD, and this combination seems to be associated with the worst prognosis; some consider CD + ADHD a specific subgroup (Gresham, Lane, & Lambros, 2000). Loeber, Burke, and colleagues (2000) reviewed literature indicating children and youth with CD to be at increased risk of antisocial personality disorder, substance abuse, mania, schizophrenia, obsessive-compulsive disorder, anxiety disorders, mood disorders, and depression. Girls may be particularly at risk of more serious and potentially life-threatening outcomes, including pregnancy, substance abuse, or suicide (Loeber, Burke, et al., 2000). Shaffer and colleagues (1996) found that rates of depression, suicidal thoughts, suicide attempts, and suicide itself all occurred in higher-than-expected rates in young people with CD.

DISRUPTIVE BEHAVIOR DISORDER NOT OTHERWISE SPECIFIED (DBD-NOS)

DBD-NOS is used by DSM-IV to classify children and youth whose behavior is oppositional/defiant or conduct disordered, but does not meet all of the required criteria for either ODD or CD. The disruptive behaviors must still be considered clinically significant in terms of the individual's impairment level (see Figure 8–5).

This category is for disorders characterized by conduct or oppositional defiant behaviors that do not meet the criteria for Conduct Disorder or Oppositional Defiant Disorder. For example, include clinical presentations that do not meet full criteria either for Oppositional Defiant Disorder or Conduct Disorder, but in which there is clinically significant impairment.

FIGURE 8–5 Disruptive Behavior Not Otherwise Specified

Source: American Psychiatric Association. (2000). *Diagnostic and statistical manual of mental disorders* (4th ed., text revision). Washington, DC: American Psychiatric Association. Reprinted with permission from the *Diagnostic and Statistical Manual of Mental Disorders*, Copyright 2000. American Psychiatric Association.

A. Several discrete episodes of failure to resist aggressive impulses that result in serious assaultive acts or destruction of property.

B. The degree of aggressiveness expressed during the episodes is grossly out of proportion to any precipitating psychosocial stressors.

C. The aggressive episodes are not better accounted for by another mental disorder (e.g., Antisocial Personality Disorder, Borderline Personality Disorder, a Psychotic Disorder, a Manic Episode, Conduct Disorder, or Attention-Deficit/Hyperactivity Disorder) and are not due to the direct physiological effects of a substance (e.g., a drug of abuse, a medication) or a general medical condition (e.g., head trauma, Alzheimer's disease).

FIGURE 8–6 DSM-IV Diagnostic Criteria for Intermittent Explosive Disorder

Source: American Psychiatric Association. (2000). *Diagnostic and statistical manual of mental disorders* (4th ed., text revision). Washington, DC: American Psychiatric Association. Reprinted with permission from the *Diagnostic and Statistical Manual of Mental Disorders*, Copyright 2000. American Psychiatric Association.

INTERMITTENT EXPLOSIVE DISORDER (IED)

While the DSM-IV (APA, 2000) does not classify intermittent explosive disorder (IED) as a disorder often diagnosed in childhood or adolescence, it is a diagnosis some students bring with them to school. It is characterized by infrequent, unexpected outbursts of disruptive behavior that result in significant harm to people and/or property. The diagnosis of IED requires a careful differential clinical assessment, to rule out the possibility that the explosive episodes are the result of other disorders or conditions. See Figure 8–6 for complete diagnostic criteria.

CHARACTERISTICS ACROSS THE LIFESPAN: THE IMPORTANCE OF EARLY INTERVENTION

There is general agreement in the field that professionals can identify very young children who have disruptive behaviors, many of whom can be reliably predicted to move on to more serious behaviors without early intervention (e.g., APA, 2000; Atkins, McKay, Talbot, & Arvanitis, 1996; "Mental Health," 1999). According to Sprague and Walker (2000), "We have the necessary tools and assessment technology to accomplish early identification of many youth who are at an elevated risk for committing violence later in their lives" (p. 369). Marks and colleagues (2000) found that parent and teacher ratings of early verbal aggression, such as teasing, cursing, and threatening, were predictive of physical aggression that emerged one to two years later: "These data suggest that verbal aggression represents a stable, temperamental characteristic that may be of greater value than early physical aggression for predicting later physically aggressive acts" (p. 52).

A number of studies have described the stability of aggressive and disruptive behaviors throughout the lifespan. The Centre for Community Child Health & Ambulatory Paediatrics (n.d.) calls aggression one of the most persistent childhood traits, and suggests that "marked aggression in pre-school and early years should be taken seriously and intervention offered promptly. The greater the number of symptoms and the earlier the onset, the worse the outcome for the child" (Long-Term Outcomes section, para. 2). One study found that preschoolers with ODD are likely to continue to exhibit the disorder, with increasing likelihood of comorbidity with other conditions, including ADHD, anxiety, or mood disorders (Lavigne et al., 2001). In a group of 177 clinic-referred boys ages 7 to 12, Loeber, Green, Lahey, and Kalb (2000) found that approximately 90% of the boys who were described as fighters in the first year of the study continued to fight for at least one more year, and that about one-third of the students were persistent fighters. Kazdin (1985) has suggested that aggressive behavior, when it persists beyond age 8, should be regarded as a chronic condition, and treated as such.

Strain and Timm (2001) found that long-term results of intervention were related to the child's age at enrollment in the program; children who began at the earliest age experienced the most positive outcome from treatment. Thus, it appears clear that early intervention for disruptive and aggressive behaviors plays an important role in preventing or managing more serious behaviors as the child develops.

SOCIAL IMPLICATIONS AND THE ROLE OF PARENT TRAINING

The American Psychiatric Association (APA) Task Force charged with establishing criteria for effective interventions conducted a comprehensive review of literature. They found only two treatments for disruptive behavior disorders that qualified as "well-established" interventions; both programs focused on training parents to more effectively manage the behavior of their child. The task force identified ten additional interventions as "probably efficacious," including multisystemic therapy (MST) and rational-emotive therapy (Center & Kemp, 2003; National Advisory, 2001). The *Blueprint for Change* reported that, "multiple trials have indicated beneficial effects of MST for youth with conduct problems. Positive outcomes include decreasing externalizing symptoms and improving family functioning and school attendance" (National Advisory, 2001, Executive Summary, p. 3). Another multifaceted parent training program, called parent-child interaction therapy (PCIT) (Bahl, Spaulding, & McNeil, 1999), involves setting specific therapy goals, collecting parent and teacher reports, making observations in a clinical setting, and parental monitoring of daily practice sessions at home. The PCIT goals are to improve the relationship between parent and child by providing parents with more effective behavior management skills (e.g., praise and selective ignoring without criticism). Multifaceted problems with strong familial risk factors respond best to multifaceted programs that address the family system as well as the target child's disruptive behaviors. Kumpfer (1996) indicates that programs designed to strengthen protective factors and improve family functioning were more effective than interventions that targeted only the problem child or youth. "Family systems counseling is a treatment option that seems logical in the case of disruptive behavior disorders because not only the child is affected by his or her behaviors but also the family members and peers are affected" (Kann & Hanna, 2000, p. 78).

Among treatment methods aimed more directly at the offending child, the cognitive behavioral approach has support from research. For example, in a study of 250 children ages 2 to 14 referred for oppositional, aggressive, and antisocial behaviors, Kazdin and Wassell (2000) found that cognitive-behaviorally based treatment resulted in positive outcomes for the child, the parents, and the entire family unit. The children demonstrated reduced antisocial behavior, fewer behavior problems at home, and fewer disruptive symptoms overall. Parents experienced less stress and depression, and reported improvement in family functioning, relationships, and social support. These interventions may be particularly useful for adolescents, whose developmental needs for independence and peer alliances make parent training a less appropriate or effective option (Elliott, Hamburg, & Williams, 1998).

ASSESSMENT OF DISRUPTIVE DISORDERS

As was mentioned in Chapter 2, rating scales and checklists are commonly used in screening students for eligibility for EBD. However, although they are relatively quick and easy to administer and score, rating scales have a number of disadvantages that make them less useful in identifying disruptive behavior disorders. Many of the broad measures (e.g., child behavior checklist) have only a few items related to each diagnostic area or symptom cluster. Because the field has not reached consensus about what specific disruptive behaviors are the most important for diagnostic purposes, there is a scarcity of well-established scales that assess externalizing behaviors (Collett, Ohan, & Myers, 2003). Some rating scales have focused purely on opposition, or disruption, or aggression. More recent research measures have been based directly on the IDEA definition of emotional disturbance or the DSM-IV criteria for ODD or CD. However, Atkins and colleagues (1996) report that interrater and test-retest reliability of ODD and CD diagnoses are moderately low by psychometric standards. See Figure 8-7 for a list of assessment measures commonly used by school professionals, or that have appeared in research studies focused on aggression and disruptive behaviors.

Collett and colleagues (2003) point out additional concerns related to assessment of aggressive and disruptive behaviors:

1. It can be difficult to measure serious but infrequent behaviors using the same measurement system as frequent, but less serious ones (e.g., injuring a peer vs. arguing with adults).

2. It is difficult to assess infrequent behaviors (e.g., temper tantrums that occur only once or twice a month).

3. Covert behaviors (e.g., lying or stealing) are difficult to measure except by self-reports, which are likely to be unreliable.

Gresham and colleagues (2000) raise an additional confounding issue: the early symptoms of antisocial behavior have relatively high base rates in the general population. They cited a 1971 study by Werry and Quay

Test Name	Purpose	Population
Achenbach System of Empirically Based Assessment (ASEBA)	Integrated multi-informant system including parent, teacher, and self-report forms yielding internalizing, externalizing, and total problem scales; referenced to DSM-IV; school-age module includes Child Behavior Checklist (6-18), Teacher Report form (6-18), Youth Self-Report (11-18), Direct Observation Form (5-14), and Semi-Structured Clinical Interview for Children and Adolescents.	Ages 1.5 to 59, in 3 modules
Behavior Dimensions Rating Scale	Rating scale with bimodal choices (e.g., agreeable/quarrelsome) that can be completed by teachers, parents, or counselors; yields four subscale scores: aggressive/acting out, irresponsible/inattentive, socially withdrawn, and fearful/anxious.	Ages 5 to adult
Children's Aggression Scale—Parent Version (CAS—P)	Designed to assess the severity of aggression in five domains: verbal aggression, aggression against objects and animals, provoked physical aggression, unprovoked physical aggression, and use of weapons.	Kindergarten through grade 5
Children's Aggression Scale—Teacher Version (CAS—T)	Teacher version of the CAS—P with same domains designed to assess severity and frequency of aggressive acts in the school setting.	Kindergarten through grade 5
Eyberg Child Behavior Inventory	Parent checklist for disruptive behavior.	Ages 2 to 16
Scales of Independent Behavior—Revised (SIB—R)	Ratings scales linked to Woodcock-Johnson assessments; yields adaptive behavior scores in 14 cluster areas.	Infant to adult
Sutter-Eyberg Student Behavior Inventory Revised	Teacher checklist of disruptive behaviors.	Ages 2 to 16

Note: Publisher information for these measures is included in Appendix B, and was compiled from publisher Web sites and the *Mental Measurements Yearbook* database.

FIGURE 8–7 Assessment Measures for Disruptive Disorders

that found the following behaviors among nonreferred boys in kindergarten through grade 2: restlessness (50%), attention seeking (37%), disruptiveness (46%), boisterousness (34%), fighting (31%), disobedience (26%), and hyperactivity (30%). These high base rates make the decision "How much disruptive behavior is too much?" very subjective, and difficult for teachers and IEP teams to determine.

Walker and Severson (1990) designed the Systematic Screening for Behavior Disorders (SSBD) to address many of these concerns, and to minimize the potential impact of error and bias in identifying students who are likely to qualify for special education in the category of EBD. The test uses a multiple gating process to screen and then identify the students at highest risk. The gates consist of: (1) teacher nominations or rankings on externalizing and internalizing behavior patterns, (2) teacher rating scales and completion of a critical event index checklist, and (3) direct observation of behavior in both the classroom and the playground by trained observers who measure academic engaged time and peer social behavior. Students who pass all three gates would then be referred for a comprehensive evaluation.

In addition to a thorough, multifaceted assessment, Guetzloe and Rockwell (1998) suggest supplementing the usual functional behavioral assessment (FBA, described at length in Chapter 3) with the following questions to aid in developing targeted, effective interventions for aggressive and disruptive behaviors:

* Is the violent behavior related to physiological factors?
* Has the violent behavior been learned?
* Who or what in the environment is reinforcing the behaviors?
* Does the behavior reflect a need for attention, touch, or excitement?
* Is the environment safe, well organized, and predictable?
* What interventions have worked in the past? (pp. 155–157)

IEP teams and school psychologists may find that they are in conflict over their use of different diagnostic systems. It can be difficult to explain to other professionals, let alone to parents, that a child with one or more DSM-IV diagnoses may not qualify for special education services under the IDEA category of EBD. As Stahl and Clarizio (1999) point out, "Whereas DSM promotes the existence and identification of comorbidity, federal legislation such as IDEA precludes the notion of comorbidity. Yet, IDEA simultaneously calls for a comprehensive evaluation, creating a difficult position for those involved in the diagnosis of childhood and adolescent disorders" (p. 48). Therefore, assessment must be particularly thorough for students with disruptive behavior problems, using multiple instruments, observations, and informants to determine eligibility for services. While the IDEA definition includes students who are schizophrenic and excludes students who are socially maladjusted (unless they are also emotionally disturbed), the IDEA is silent concerning other specific mental disorders, including ODD and CD. Therefore, it is up to the IEP team to determine, on a case-by-case basis, whether each individual child meets the criteria set forth in federal and state regulations.

Impact of Gender, Ethnicity, and Socioeconomic Status on Referral for and Assessment of Disruptive Behavior

Although girls are diagnosed with disruptive behavior disorders—mostly in adolescence—they tend to have problems that are less severe than boys in both the childhood and adolescent onset groups. Because girls with disruptive behavior disorders (DBD) are less prevalent and their initial behaviors tend to be more covert, girls are perhaps more likely to be overlooked (and potentially underreferred) by teachers and others (Atkins et al., 1996). According to Gresham and colleagues (2000), these delayed-onset girls differ in the onset of their disruptive symptoms, but have risk factors similar to their male peers. They are also similar to the childhood-onset boys in terms of their cognitive problems and potential for more negative outcomes.

Although the field has recognized that girls with disruptive behaviors follow a different pathway than boys, it is difficult to determine whether the commonly used assessment and intervention techniques will work with girls in the same way they work with boys (Webster-Stratton, 1996). One of the difficulties is the scarcity of research in which female students with EBD were proportionately represented—if girls were included in the studies at all (Burke et al., 2002). In 2003, Mooney, Epstein, Reid, and Nelson reviewed 55 experimental studies on aggression or disruptive behavior disorders published between 1975 and 2002. They found that 44% of the studies were conducted with only male subjects; 40% were conducted with both males and females; and 16% did not report the participants' gender. None of the 55 studies were conducted with female-only samples.

As a result of these concerns, some researchers have questioned whether the DSM diagnostic criteria for ADHD, ODD, and CD should be adjusted to more proportionately include females with disruptive behaviors.

Researchers have expressed similar concerns regarding the overrepresentation of African-American youth in special education, and in the category of EBD. The 2003 meta-analysis by Mooney and colleagues also found that race/ethnicity was reported in only 13% of the 55 studies and socioeconomic status was reported in only 9% of the studies. CD appears to be more prevalent among African-American youth (Atkins et al., 1996), and Loeber, Burke, and colleagues (2000) speculated that prevalence rates of CD are highest in poor, urban communities. However, the available data makes it difficult to do more than speculate about the impact of ethnicity or SES on prevalence rates. It may be that the effects of discrimination and poverty combine to produce higher rates of aggression and disruptive behaviors, but it also may be possible that the assessment measures and methods commonly used to identify these disorders contain error or bias that results in the disproportionate representation of African-American youth from poor, urban environments.

Little research has examined the degree to which commonly used behavior rating scales have been constructed and normed to yield similar results across gender and ethnic differences. One such study used the IOWA Conners Rating Scale to examine teacher ratings of nearly 4,000 elementary-aged students (Reid, Casat, Norton, Anastopoulos, & Temple, 2001). They found that African-American students were more likely than European-American students to be rated more than two standard deviations above the mean (i.e., significantly deviant). The likelihood of receiving a significantly high score was 2.48 to 3.51 times greater for African-American males, and 3.60 to 5.27 times greater for African-American females. The study also found an interaction between the ethnicity of the rater and the score of the student being rated. Specifically, African-American teachers rated all children more similarly, while European-American teachers tended to rate African-American students as more inattentive/overactive and aggressive than their European-American peers. Reid and colleagues (2001) suggest three possible explanations for the results of this study, and others like it:

1. **Rater effects**—This type of bias may occur if raters from different cultural or ethnic groups perceive behaviors differently, or when the rater is making judgments about a student from a different ethnic group than their own.

2. **Differences in socioeconomic status**—This may be the result if raters tend to rate students differently based on their socioeconomic status, rather than strictly on their observed behavior.

3. **Halo effects**—This effect may occur when the student possesses some behaviors (e.g., oppositional or aggressive) and the rater tends to select all of the same class of behaviors, even when they have not actually observed them.

GENERAL STRATEGIES FOR MANAGING STUDENTS WITH DISRUPTIVE BEHAVIOR PROBLEMS

Research concerning interventions with disruptive students provides limited guidance for school-based interventions. Sprague and Walker (2000) provide some very basic research-based guidelines:

* Intervene as early as possible.
* Address both behavioral risks and strengths.
* Involve families as partners in the intervention.
* Match the strength of the intervention to the antisocial behavior. (p. 374)

The causes of aggressive and disruptive behaviors are varied and include complex social/environmental factors. Therefore, the needs of disruptive students will best be met by treatments that address their multiple individual risk factors and needs, including any comorbid conditions. "Frequently, successful prevention programs included a parent-directed component; other aspects of successful prevention included social-cognitive skills training (when combined with other interventions), academic skills training, proactive classroom management and teacher training, and group therapy (Burke et al., 2002, p. 1285). While it makes sense to plan treatment to include parents, Abikoff and Klein (1992) point out the paradox inherent in offering treatment to dysfunctional families: "The very targets of treatment, including defiance and hostility toward adults, inattention to detail, and family discord and disorganization, can interfere with the delivery of treatment. When parental psychopathology is also present, particularly antisocial behavior and ADHD, the risk of treatment failure is heightened" (Abikoff & Klein, 1992, p. 888).

This section will focus on 11 general strategies for preventing or minimizing oppositional and disruptive behavior in the classroom on a day-to-day basis (see Figure 8-8). The strategies are arranged from primary prevention and least intrusive, to tertiary prevention and most involved. Tertiary prevention programs, including parent support and mental health services, are included here, but will be discussed at greater length in Chapters 12 and 13. Crisis intervention planning and implementation for student behavior that presents an imminent danger to self or others will be addressed in Chapter 14.

Provide Developmentally Appropriate Programming

Chapter 5 stressed the importance of effective instruction and classroom-management skills. Programs for students with disruptive behavior problems must reflect all of those best practices, and more. The checklist in Figure 8-9 can be used to quickly assess potential areas for improvement.

Many students with disruptive behaviors also have cognitive and academic problems as well, requiring thorough evaluation and remediation of learning problems as a critical component of their IEP. As Van Acker and Wehby (2000) point out: "Students who possess the knowledge and skills necessary to be successful in school and who enjoy the assigned academic and social activities have little impetus to engage in disruptive behavior" (p. 94).

Once an effective, individualized academic program is in place, the teacher can focus on meeting the developmental needs of students. Brendtro and Long (1995)

provide a reminder of the basic needs all of our students, even the most challenging ones, bring with them to the classroom.

- **Attachment**—Positive social bonds are prerequisites to prosocial behavior.
- **Achievement**—Setting high expectations means refusing to accept failure.
- **Autonomy**—True discipline lies in demanding responsibility rather than obedience.
- **Altruism**—Through helping others, young people find proof of their self worth. (p. 56)

Students with EBD also need opportunities for appropriate socializing experiences and vigorous exercise (Guetzloe, 1992). Avoid taking away recess and nonacademic activities as a punishment for noncompliance or failure to complete work.

Build Therapeutic Relationships with Students

Developing rapport with the most hostile students in the school is a long-term process that requires patience, a calm demeanor, a sense of humor, more patience, forgiveness, commitment, and even more patience. Effective teachers of students with disruptive behaviors have learned to: avoid reacting to minor irritating behaviors; appear and sound unruffled when provoked; laugh at themselves and not take things personally; let students begin every day with a clean slate—even after a particularly unpleasant incident; and believe that every student can be successful long after everyone else has

---

Primary Prevention—for entire class

- Provide developmentally appropriate programming
- Build therapeutic relationships with students
- Adjust the classroom management system
- Avoid power struggles

Secondary Prevention—for targeted high-risk individuals/groups

- Revisit FBA and trigger analysis
- Use cognitive behavior management techniques to teach conflict resolution and anger-management skills
- Implement a bullying reduction program

Tertiary Prevention—for students with chronic DBD

- Provide mentors for individual students
- Provide parent training and support
- Debrief after a disruptive incident
- Provide therapy

FIGURE 8–8 General Strategies for Managing Students with Disruptive Behavior Problems

(Teacher rating scale: Circle yes or no for each item.)

Rules and Policies of Deportment (Clarity)

Y	N	A written schoolwide discipline policy exists
Y	N	I have written classroom rules or standards for classroom discipline
Y	N	The emphasis of schoolwide policies and rules is on how to behave
Y	N	The emphasis of my classroom rules is on how to behave
Y	N	Reinforcement is provided for adherence to the rules in my class
Y	N	Students have been involved in the development of the classroom rules
Y	N	The classroom rule list is kept short (5 to 7 rules)
Y	N	There is clear communication of classroom rules as evidenced by their being reviewed periodically with students and shared with parents at least yearly

Support for Staff and Policies

Y	N	Strong administrative support for staff exists (e.g., good teaching is recognized, faculty requests are acted on promptly)
Y	N	Strong staff support for one another exists (e.g., staff confer with one another regarding instructional and discipline methods)
Y	N	Strong teacher support and agreement with the school discipline policy exists

Allowances Made for Individual Differences Among Students

Y	N	Academic assignments are adjusted to students' functional level to assure frequent success
Y	N	The school assumes the responsibility for student learning
Y	N	Social skills necessary to relate positively to peers and do well academically are identified and taught
Y	N	Appropriate consequences for individual students are provided (the emphasis is on reinforcement and the same consequences are NOT provided to all students)
Y	N	Student involvement/participation in academic activities is high
Y	N	Students and staff understand, value, and respect ethnic/cultural differences
Y	N	Student involvement/participation in after-school activities is encouraged

FIGURE 8–9 School Contextual Factors Contributing to Antisocial Behavior

Source: Based on Mayer, G.R. (2001). Antisocial behavior: Its causes and prevention within our schools. *Education and Treatment of Children, 24*(4), 412–429, Table 1. Reprinted with permission from the publisher.

given up. Kann and Hanna (2000) suggest that building a therapeutic relationship based on empathy and respect may be especially important for female students who are unlikely to disclose information unless they feel understood.

Adjust the Classroom Management System

Students with oppositional and disruptive behavior may not respond to reinforcement and other management techniques in predictable ways. In fact, for some students, both reinforcement and mild aversive techniques (e.g., verbal reprimands) can provoke hostile behavioral outbursts. For others, praise actually may be a predictable antecedent for noncompliant behavior (Hall et al., 2000). Applying increasingly punitive behavior modification may seem appealing, but may tend to escalate the level of misbehavior because of the impulsivity and temperamental nature of students with ODD. Therefore, encouraging compliance and delivering mild

aversives may require the teacher to modify her usual behavior to achieve success with oppositional students. Praise should be delivered privately (e.g., a note, a whispered comment, or a restrained pat on the shoulder) rather than in front of peers (Woolsey-Terrazas & Chavez, 2002). Matter-of-fact descriptions of compliant behavior may be better received than enthusiastic praise (Filcheck, McNeil, & Herschell, 2001).

Set realistic expectations for student compliance, based on the present level of individual performance. Eyberg and Robinson (1983) point out that average children may only be compliant between 51% and 62% of the time. This suggests that teachers should use shaping and chaining techniques, accepting successive approximations of the desired behavior. Again, depending on the student's present level of misbehavior, this may mean ignoring or accepting minor disruptive behaviors while focusing on reduction of potentially dangerous ones. (**Note:** This may require an explanation to other teachers, building administrators, or parents.)

For the child who frequently reacts violently, scream-ing (even if it includes profanity) might be preferable to hitting, kicking, and biting. If teachers decide to accept profanity as a step in the process of learning alternatives to violent behaviors, they must reward profanity (in lieu of physical aggression), even when they themselves are the targets of the unkind remarks. The profanity could result in a mild aversive conse-quence (e.g., a verbal reprimand), but its extinction should not be considered as important as the reduc-tion of physical aggression. (Guetzloe & Rockwell, 1998, p. 158).

Establish rules, routines, and structure in advance, and implement them with monotonous consistency. Con-stant supervision is critical with this population. Focus on antecedent manipulation to increase compliance, and to prevent, reduce, or eliminate the need for puni-tive consequences and procedures (Kern, Choutka, & Sokol, 2002). Behavioral momentum (e.g., alternating difficult with easier tasks), contingency contracts, token economies, and level systems may be particularly useful with this group of students.

Filcheck and colleagues (2001) have reported that some studies indicate increasing compliance will require use of mild aversives for some disruptive stu-dents. When necessary, negative consequences should be delivered consistently, in a matter-of-fact, nonthreat-ening tone of voice, and should be proportionate to the misbehavior.

Avoid Power Struggles

Many students with disruptive behaviors need to estab-lish power and control. Their goal is to identify the teacher's "hot buttons" and use that information to pro-voke them. For the teacher, then, the goal is to avoid the provocation unless the stakes are too high to ignore (i.e., danger to self and others, major property damage, total disruption of teaching environment). Maag (2000) suggests that teachers shift their focus from viewing resistance as the child's behavior to viewing resistance as the result of the adult's behavior. Intervention strate-gies then should be focused on determining the func-tion of resistance and changing the adult behavior until the student responds with compliance. Use communi-cation techniques to prevent, deflect, or interrupt a power struggle at the earliest point possible. For example, whenever possible, ask the student what they need to do instead of telling them (Hewitt, 1999). Pro-vide options and choices in advance, especially when you anticipate student resistance. Keep in mind that both options need to be equally acceptable to the teacher. The goal is to sidetrack the student's energy from resistance into decision making. For example, if a student often becomes verbally agitated about doing math seatwork, provide as many age-appropriate options as seems reasonable (with a nod to Dr. Seuss and *Green Eggs and Ham*):

* Would you rather do the odd or even problems?
* Would you rather work individually or with a partner?
* Would you prefer to work with pencil and paper or on the dry-erase board?
* Would you rather work at your desk or at the table by the window?
* Would you rather use a calculator or the computer to check your work?
* Do you prefer wide-line or narrow-line paper?
* Would you rather finish the paper before turning it in or would you like me to check the first few before you proceed?
* Would you rather do it between 8:00 and 8:30 or between 8:30 and 9:00?

When it is necessary to issue a directive or request for compliance, Walker and Sylwester (1998) suggest using positively worded (i.e., alpha) rather than nega-tively worded (beta) statements:

Alpha commands involve a clear, direct, and specific directive, without additional verbalizations, that allow a reasonable time for a response. In contrast, beta com-mands involve vague or multiple directives, given simultaneously and accompanied by excess verbaliza-tion, and without a clear criterion or adequate oppor-tunity for compliance. (p. 54)

Initially, some students may test the limits by com-plying with exaggerated slowness or with some verbal resistance (e.g., mumbling about how stupid the assignment is while getting their book out in slow motion). Remember that the intent is probably to power struggle or to save face in front of peers; ignore this behavior if possible, even if it means that the stu-dent gets the last word.

In Jim Fay's *Parenting with Love and Logic*, he sug-gests that parents and teachers avoid saying "no" to chil-drens' reasonable requests whenever feasible. For example, rather than saying "No, you may not work on the computer until you have finished your assignment," the teacher could say, "I would love for you to work on the computer, and I will make sure you get a turn just as soon as your assignment is finished." A variation of this technique is also effective for delivering negative consequences with empathy: "I wish you could work on the computer, but unfortunately it is off limits for 24 hours as a result of your argument over sharing it with Melanie this morning. You may use the computer again at 10:00 tomorrow morning, if your work is done."

Some students use their verbal skills in a more covert effort to avoid complying with teacher requests or to establish power and control. Hewitt (1999) describes three of these tactics and the appropriate teacher responses as follows:

1. *Tactic:* The student finds unanticipated "loopholes" in the rules or in the teacher's directives.
   Response: Briefly discuss conforming to the spirit of the law rather than the letter of the law; give examples and nonexamples.
2. *Tactic:* Student incessantly asks "why" questions.
   Response: Say that you would be happy to answer all of their questions, but on their time, not during instructional time.
3. *Tactic:* The student blames others in an attempt to avoid responsibility or play staff and students off against each other (i.e., splitting or triangulating).
   Response: Maintain focus on the original topic and don't allow them to sidetrack or waste time arguing.

Use paradoxical directives that instruct the child to continue to engage in an undesirable behavior (Maag, 2000). If they comply, they aren't resisting; if they don't comply, they are no longer engaged in the problem behavior. For example, if a student is humming monotonously, the teacher might say, "I love music. Please keep humming until the end of the hour." The worst that could happen is that the student will continue humming—which is annoying and distracting. It is more likely that they will stop humming while thinking about your strange request, or that they will become bored with humming and stop on their own.

Revisit FBA and Trigger Analysis

Students with externalizing, disruptive behaviors may have slightly different motives than students with other, more garden-variety behavior problems. Once a student has been identified with a disruptive behavior disorder, it may be appropriate to further refine the functional behavioral assessment, paying particular attention to triggers and what the student appears to be getting from the behavior. A well-conducted FBA can help teachers avoid potential triggers (e.g., beta commands,

changes in routine, adult disapproval), and develop more successful interventions.

Collett and colleagues (2003) suggest a series of additional questions that could be used in conjunction with the FBA to identify patterns of aggressive behavior (e.g., fighting) and help develop targeted intervention strategies. Is the student's behavior:

- *Proactive or reactive*—Does the student initiate the aggression, or respond to another's aggressive act?
- *Affective or predatory*—Did she act under the influence of strong emotion (e.g., anger) or was the act coldly calculated in advance?
- *Hostile or instrumental*—Was the intent of the act to cause emotional or physical damage vs. to obtain something she wanted?
- *Direct or indirect*—Was the aggressive act an open attack on the victim or delivered by indirect means (e.g., convincing another student to vandalize the gym, spreading rumors that result in a student being ostracized by peers)?
- *Overt or covert*—Was the aggressive act observable (e.g., fighting in front of the teacher) or secretive (e.g., lying about stealing money from a purse)?

Use Cognitive Behavior Management Techniques to Teach Conflict Resolution and Anger Management Skills

Social-skills training is often recommended to address the deficits common in students with disruptive behaviors. Students may possess distorted perception of others' hostile intent and an impulsive responding style (Abikoff & Klein, 1992), aggressive styles of problem solving and conflict resolution (Brendtro & Long, 1995), and lack anger management skills (Centre for Community Child Health, n.d.; Hall et al., 2000; Kann & Hanna, 2000). However, as was discussed in Chapter 5, intervention research in this area has had mixed outcomes. A particular concern with grouping aggressive students (e.g., for anger management training) is that there is some evidence that concentrating these students in small groups actually maintains the antisocial behavior (Burke et al., 2002; Van Acker & Wehby, 2000). On the other hand, more generic community-based interventions generally have not resulted in behavioral change that translated into classrooms or other natural environments. A solution would be to "reverse mainstream" a few high-functioning, socially acceptable peer models into the training group with the targeted high-risk students. Then, as new skills were acquired, the positive peers and others in the general education environment could be trained to cue prosocial behaviors and provide feedback during generalization to other settings.

Researchers have found cognitive behavioral strategies to be effective in addressing the social-perception and social-skill deficits of students with impulsive and disruptive behaviors (Burke et al., 2002; Centre for Community Child Health, n.d.; Hoff & DuPaul, 1998; Kazdin & Wassell, 2000). (See Chapter 7 to review self-talk and instruction, self-monitoring and recording, self-evaluation, self-reinforcement, and problem solving.) Because cognitive-behavioral strategies quickly shift responsibility from the teacher to the student, they may be less likely to provoke oppositional/noncompliant behavioral responses than more teacher-directed approaches to social-skill instruction. Design interventions to address students' cognitive distortions, as well as their skill and performance deficits.

Implement a Bullying Reduction Program

Bullying is defined as a negative behavior that involves (1) a pattern of repeated aggression; (2) deliberate intent to harm or disturb a victim despite apparent victim distress; and (3) a real or perceived imbalance of power (e.g., due to age, strength, size), with the more powerful child or group attacking a physically or psychologically vulnerable victim. Bullies represent about 7% to 15% of sampled school-age populations; victims represent about 10%. Two percent to 10% of students are both bullies and victims. (AMA, 2002, data synthesis, para. 1).

Bullying is a serious and pervasive problem in American schools, as well as in other countries. It affects about 15% of students, with peak rates during the middle school years. As with other types of aggression, male and female students tend to bully others differently. Boys are more likely to use direct or physical force, while girls are more likely to tease, spread rumors, and socially isolate their peers (Quinn, Barone, Kearns, Stackhouse, & Zimmerman, 2003).

Students with disabilities may be at increased risk of victimization by bullies (Heinrich, 2003; Mishna, 2003), perhaps because of their low social status within the school, the stigma related to labeling, and frequent problems with peer relationships and rejection. Researchers have found that victims of bullies are at higher risk for depression and suicidal ideation (van der Wal, de Wit, &

Hirasing, 2003), especially if the bullying was accomplished through indirect, rather than direct, means. Approximately 10% to 20% of victims are bullies as well (Olweus, 2001). Bullying is a marker for more serious outcomes for the perpetrator, including later aggression (Nansel, 2003) and delinquent behavior (Olweus, 2001).

Heinrich (2003) identified four discrete groups of concern for educators and parents in schools where bullying is a problem:

1. *The passive target*, who does nothing to provoke the attack and may lack the skills needed to resist
2. *The provocative target*, who often seems to bring the attack on herself (e.g., by teasing or name calling)
3. *The bully*, who actually commits the acts of aggression or intimidation
4. *The bystander*, who observes the bullying and does not actively intervene or respond to protect the victim.

Educators should implement bullying interventions with a systematic approach, not just focusing on individual students but on the ecology of the behavior that supports the pattern of behavior at the school, class, and individual level. See Figure 8–10 for an annotated list of bullying prevention resources, and Figure 8–11 for the three-tiered approach to the problem of bullying developed by Dan Olweus (1993) and recognized as an exemplary Blueprints Model Program by the University of Colorado's Center for the Study and Prevention of Violence (Olweus, Limber, & Mihalic, 1999).

Provide Mentors for Individual Students

Mentoring is an intervention that holds promise for at-risk students, including those with disruptive behavior disorders (Brendtro & Long, 1995; Guetzloe, 1997). To use mentoring, pair high-risk students with a positive role model who is either an adult or an older student. That individual meets with the student on a regular basis to provide a sounding board, and to attempt to positively influence student problem solving and choice making.

Provide Parent Training and Support

The most effective interventions for children and youth with disruptive behavior disorders are multimodal, multifaceted interventions that address family functioning via parent training (Brendtro & Long, 1995; Burke et al.,

The Hamilton Fish Institute in Washington, DC, compiled a list of assessment measures related to the prevention of school violence. Their search feature allows Web site visitors to locate survey instruments by title, author, survey type, respondents, construct measured, cost of the instrument, and the reliability and validity. Available at http://www.hamfish.org/measures/b/search.php

Hoover, J.H., & Olsen, G.W. (2001). *Teasing and harassment: The frames and scripts approach for teachers and parents.* Bloomington, IN: National Education Service. This book suggests teaching students to interpret humor and teasing, and consider variables such as language and social development; sense of humor; racial, cultural, and gender-based issues that may lead to increased misunderstanding and hurt feelings.

The Institute on Violence and Destructive Behavior, University of Oregon, provides info on the First Step to Success program designed to reduce antisocial behaviors among high-risk kindergartners. http://www.uoregon.edu/~ivdb

Olweus, D., Limber, S., & Mihalic, S.F. (1999). *Blueprints for violence prevention: Bullying prevention program, book nine.* Boulder, CO: Center for the Study and Prevention of Violence. The University of Colorado's Center for the Study and Prevention of Violence chose the Bullying Prevention Program as an exemplary Blueprints Model Program. For information: http://www.colorado.edu/cspv/blueprints/model/programs/BPP.html

Quinn, K.B., Barone, B., Kearns, J., Stackhouse, S.A., & Zimmerman, M.E. (2003). Using a novel unit to help understand and prevent bullying in schools. *Journal of Adolescent & Adult Literacy, 47*(7), 582–591. This article includes detailed information on conducting a bullying bibliotherapy unit for middle school students (readability level = grade 4.5).

Teaching Tolerance magazine, published by the Southern Poverty Law Center. This publication and other resources are available free to teachers at http://www.tolerance.org/

Vancouver, British Columbia Public Library. This library provides an extensive bibliography of resources for children, adolescents, and adults. The Braving Bullies bibliography is available at http://www.vpl.ca/branches/LibrarySquare/chi/booklists/BravingBullies.html

FIGURE 8–10 Bullying Prevention Resources

General Prerequisites
* Awareness and involvement

Measures at the School Level
* Questionnaire survey
* School conference day on bully/victim problems
* Better supervision during recess and lunch time
* More attractive school playground
* Contact telephone
* Meeting staff—parents
* Teacher groups for the development of the social milieu of the school
* Parent circles

Measures at the Class Level
* Class rules against bullying: clarification, praise, sanctions
* Regular class meetings
* Role playing, literature
* Cooperative learning
* Common positive class activities
* Class meeting teacher—parents/children

Measures at the Individual Level
* Serious talks with bullies and victims
* Serious talks with parents of involved students
* Teacher and parent use of imagination
* Help from "neutral" students
* Help and support for parents
* Discussion groups for parents of bullies and victims
* Change of class or school

FIGURE 8–11 Overview of Olweus Bullying Intervention Program

Source: Olweus, D. (1993). Bullying at school: What we know and what we can do. Oxford, UK: Blackwell Publishing Ltd. Reprinted with permission.

2002; Center & Kemp, 2003). Activities may include training in behavior management, effective communication, and problem solving for both the target child and her parents. For more information concerning collaborating with families, see Chapter 12.

Debrief After a Disruptive Incident

All teachers who work with aggressive and disruptive students need to be well versed in behavior management. However, Guetzloe (1992) suggests that they also require specialized "training in conflict resolution, verbal de-escalation, and aggression control (including safe techniques for physical restraint)" (p. 6). This section will address the many disruptive incidents that can be handled within the confines of the classroom with verbal or physical redirection, and with use of voluntary time-outs or cooling-off places.

Often, the hierarchy of interventions for outbursts moves from the classroom to another classroom (sometimes called a "buddy room," "recovery room," or "safe space"), or to the office. Regardless of the location where de-escalation takes place, the purposes are to: provide the student with a chance to regain self-control, implement their relaxation and problem-solving skills, and engage in problem solving (Quinn et al., 2000). The debriefer's job is to show interest, empathy, and respect as the student is de-escalating, and to facilitate the problem-solving process. Depending on the student's age, as well as her cognitive and developmental level, this may involve processing verbally or asking the student to complete a "think sheet" (an example is included in Chapter 14, along with more information concerning developing and implementing a crisis intervention plan).

Provide Therapy

Although there is some evidence that individual therapy may not be the most effective intervention for ODD and CD (Burke et al., 2002), it may be useful as part of a multifaceted treatment plan that addresses coexisting conditions that do respond to clinical interventions. "Because comorbidity often involves the combination of internalizing and externalizing problems, it can complicate intervention (e.g., choice of treatment methods)" (Stahl & Clarizio, 1999, p. 48). Nonetheless, both multisystemic therapy (MST) and rational-emotive therapy are "probably efficacious" for this population (Center & Kemp, 2003; National Advisory, 2001) and should be considered as part of the IEP

and/or treatment plan, perhaps in conjunction with community mental health providers. See Chapter 13 for more information concerning school partnerships with other agencies.

CO-OCCURRENCE OF DISRUPTIVE PROBLEMS IN SCHOOL WITH DRUG USE AND JUVENILE DELINQUENCY

Sprague and Walker (2000) point out that "at-risk children and youth who are chronic discipline problems in school appear to substantially overlap with those who offend outside school" (p. 369). A substantial number of young people with disruptive behaviors appear to become involved in early, ongoing use of alcohol, tobacco, and other drugs. A substantial number of youth who become involved with the juvenile authorities for crimes against people or property also have histories of substance abuse. Brook, Whiteman, and Finch (1992) speculate about the possible connections between impulsivity, drug use, and delinquency: "Drug use might make an individual more impulsive, and, thus, less concerned with the immediate risks as well as the more remote consequences of delinquent acts. At the same time the drug user may be more attracted to the drug's immediate effects and, as a result, perform acts that she would not otherwise. A more indirect mechanism is exemplified by a drug user who commits crimes to obtain money to purchase a drug" (p. 370). A longitudinal study was conducted by the Office of Juvenile Justice and Delinquency Prevention on the co-occurrence of delinquency with drug use, problems in school, and mental health problems among 4,000 inner-city youth who were ages 7–15 in the first year of the study. They found that most youth in the study exhibited a problem behavior for only one year, so they focused their attention on those young people with problems lasting two or more years. Of the students with ongoing problems, "Twenty to thirty percent of males were serious delinquents; 14–17 percent were drug users; 7–22 percent had school problems; and 7–14 percent had mental health problems" (Huizinga, Loeber, Thornberry, & Cothern, 2000, p. 2). "Among females . . . 5 percent were serious delinquents, 11–12 percent were drug users, 10–21 percent had school problems, and 6–11 percent had mental health problems" (p. 3). The study's findings supported a statistically significant relationship between drug use and delinquency among both males and females, as follows: Among male delinquents, 34–44% used drugs, while

BOX 8–1   Guetzloe Perspective

PERSPECTIVE: ELEANOR GUETZLOE What We Know About Working with Students with Conduct Disorders

In the recent past, several stories about assaultive behavior by young children have made the national news. First, a kindergarten-age female with a history of tearing up her classroom and assaulting her teacher was shown in a videotape being handcuffed by local police in St. Petersburg, Florida. The ensuing public outcry attracted the attention of such notables as Al Sharpton and Jesse Jackson. After the police involved were not charged with a criminal act, the child's mother filed a civil lawsuit.

In New York City, a 9-year-old girl was playing with one of her closest friends when the two began to argue over a ball. According to police, the 9-year-old stabbed her 11-year-old friend in the chest with a steak knife, killing her.

Finally, in Tampa, Florida, a 7-year-old male beat, kicked, and bludgeoned his baby half-sister to death while he was an overnight visitor in his father's home. His stated reason was to "stop her from crying," but others close to the family said that he was angry because the baby was receiving "more attention" than he. The police are perplexed because the boy shows no remorse, and they simply do not know whether to charge him with murder, get psychiatric treatment for him, or pursue some other course of action.

In response to these horrifying acts, several authorities on child development have appeared on television news programs, explaining what is currently known about the origins of aggression and violence in children. Their explanations have focused primarily on (a) the outcomes of child abuse and neglect, and (b) the lack of understanding by young children that physical assaults can result in death and that death is permanent.

All of these authorities have agreed that intervention is necessary, but they do not agree on the specific path. Even when there have been opportunities for the listeners to respond (e.g., a "call-in" television program), I have carefully resisted the urge to scream my response. It is my contention that we *do* have interventions that work, and that carefully planned special education programs, including parent education, are among those that are both necessary and effective. Therapeutic and educational programs must focus on teaching appropriate responses to feelings of anger and frustration. Nonviolent responses can be learned, and they must be taught and reinforced every waking moment of the child's life, sometimes for a very long period of time.

It should be noted that, in each of these cases, the perpetrator already had a history of exhibiting anger, destructive behavior, or violent responses in normal situations. In the first case, the child's behavior was unmanageable in the regular kindergarten, and police had several times previously been called to the school. In the second case, the killer, while bright and inventive, often showed flashes of nasty, violent anger when she did not get her way. A neighbor commented, "When the tides were in favor of other children, she'd hit, kick, scratch, scream, and spit. She'd hit anyone on the head with a bottle if she was fighting. She'd beat them any way she could." In the third case, the boy had a history of acting aggressively and beating up other children. It should also be noted that in none of these cases was there any history of specific interventions aimed at changing the child's violent behavior.

What should be done with such violent youngsters? Effective strategies must include (in addition to an appropriate instructional program) carefully planned interventions in both home and school, including the following:

1. **A positive classroom climate, in which the norms and rules are functional for the group**. Very often, this will mean that the rules will be different for this group than for the rest of the school. It has been my experience that such a program is most easily delivered in a special setting—rather than the regular classroom. The classroom itself must be carefully structured to meet the needs of youngsters who lack

(continued)

self-control. There must be constant supervision of all activities, including play. These children must never be left unsupervised. The basic focus of the curriculum is upon extinguishing violent behavior and teaching acceptable social skills. Every "teachable moment" is used to advantage—to modify the students' cognitive strategies, stressing empathy, caring, and compassion. Competition among the students is reduced to the extent possible, being replaced with cooperative activities and service to others.

2. **An individualized program of behavior management for each student.** This must include a highly structured system of rewards for appropriate behavior and nonaggressive aversive consequences for inappropriate behavior. At the beginning of the program, it will probably be necessary to use concrete rewards, especially for young children. Consistent application of this program will require the services of a knowledgeable and highly skilled educator, who will not respond aggressively to a child's noncompliant or hostile behavior.

3. **Education of parents in appropriate behavior management techniques.** Violence must be disallowed at home to the same extent that it is at school. Television must be replaced with prosocial activity, such as helping others. Parents need to learn to apply a system of nonaggressive but aversive consequences for inappropriate behavior and rewards for appropriate behavior.

In summary, aggressive and violent children have become a serious concern to parents, educators, mental health professionals, government officials, and the community at large. Such behavior can be changed. The school and the family must cooperate to get the job done.

Eleanor Guetzloe is Professor Emerita in Education at the University of South Florida, and past president of both the International Council for Children with Behavioral Disorders (CCBD) and Teacher Educators for Children with Behavioral Disorders (TECBD). Dr. Guetzloe is a well-known trainer and presenter at national and international conferences, and has authored many publications in EBD.

46–48% of female offenders were drug users. Persistent mental health problems and serious delinquency were significant for males, but not for females. Of the youth with mental health problems, between one-third and one-half were also delinquents, while 25% of delinquent youth exhibited mental health problems. "These findings emphasize the importance of identifying and addressing the unique needs of individual youth, rather than proceeding under the assumption that all offenders require similar treatment, to most effectively prevent and reduce serious, chronic delinquency" (Huizinga et al., 2000, p. 1). These findings are consistent with the research cited earlier in this chapter indicating that children who are antisocial early in life are likely to continue those behaviors, and many will graduate into more serious risk-taking behaviors as adolescents.

THE ROLE OF MEDICATION IN THE TREATMENT OF DISRUPTIVE BEHAVIORS

In the longitudinal study conducted by the National Institute of Mental Health, Jensen and colleagues (2001) found that children with ODD/CD plus ADHD responded best to medication recommendations, with or without behavioral treatments, while youth with multiple comorbid disorders (anxiety and ODD/CD) responded best to combined medication and behavioral treatments. However, no drugs have been demonstrated to be consistently effective in treating CD or ODD.

Reports and clinical experience suggest that mood stabilizers, lithium, typical and atypical antipsychotics, clonodine, and stimulants may help with symptoms of CD. Abikoff and Klein (1992) see potential in the use of neuroleptics and lithium, particularly with the very explosive aggressive cases of CD, or for individuals whose disorder is more genetically defined.

Burke and colleagues (2002) caution that there have been relatively few randomized clinical trials of medications with this population. Lithium and methylphenidate have been found (in one double-blind placebo trial each) to reduce aggressiveness effectively in children with conduct disorder (Campbell et al., 1995; Klein et al., 1997). However, a third study with a similar design but shorter treatment duration did not have positive findings (Rifkin et al., 1997). In the 1997 Klein study, methylphenidate was superior to lithium and placebo. A third drug, carbamazepine, was found in a pilot study to be effective, but multiple side effects were also reported (Kafantaris et al., 1992). Clonidine was explored in an open trial, in which 15 of 17 patients showed a significant decrease in aggressive behavior, but there were also significant side effects that would require monitoring of cardiovascular and blood pressure parameters (Kempf, DeVane, Levin, Jarecke, & Miller, 1993). To further compound the conflicting efficacy results and side effect problems, the use of medication with this population raises additional questions concerning substance abuse and compliance with medication (i.e., taking it as prescribed).

CONTROVERSIAL TREATMENT INTERVENTIONS FOR DISRUPTIVE BEHAVIORS

The response of many elected officials to public concerns about increasing levels of student violence has tended to be both reactive and punitive—increased security, zero tolerance policies, suspension and expulsion, and referral to the juvenile justice system. However, as will be discussed further in Chapter 14, most of these approaches have failed to address the root causes of disruptive behavior and, therefore, have had a minimal impact on school violence. In addition to identifying potentially efficacious treatments, the *Blueprint for Change* also indicated that:

> Research has also identified treatments that are potentially ineffective or, worse yet, harmful. Some forms of institutional care do not lead to lasting improvements after the child is returned to the community. Some services provided to delinquent juveniles are also ineffective (e.g., boot camps and residential programs); peer-group-based interventions have been found to actually increase behavior problems among high-risk adolescents. (National Advisory, 2001, p. 3)

Thus, it appears that segregating disruptive, aggressive, and potentially violent children and youth with others who have the same behaviors results in perpetuation of the very behaviors for which the students were referred in the first place. (see also Box 8-1 on p.159)

CHAPTER SUMMARY

* Students with disruptive behavior disorders are a heterogeneous group who follow three pathways to serious behaviors: overt, covert, and oppositional. Researchers have identified an array of individual, familial, school, and community risk factors that predict the development of disruptive behavior

disorders. The DSM-IV has four diagnoses that may apply to students in this population: oppositional defiant disorder (ODD), conduct disorder (CD), disruptive behavior disorder—not otherwise specified (DBD-NOS), and intermittent explosive disorder (IED).

* An accurate, nonbiased assessment of DBD requires multiple measures and observers; this is particularly important given the potential underreferral of females and overidentification of African-American youth from poor, urban communities. Researchers have identified a number of potentially useful intervention strategies to minimize oppositional and disruptive behavior in the classroom; however, the research base has significant gaps in terms of data concerning group interventions, female students, and minority students. The interventions with the most persuasive data are multifaceted treatment approaches that address the family system and parenting skills, as well as individual student behaviors. Although medications may be effective in managing the symptoms of co-occurring disorders, none have been proven effective with the core symptoms of ODD or CD.

CHECK YOUR UNDERSTANDING

1. List one risk factor for each of the following: individual, familial, school, and community characteristics.
2. Describe the three pathways children and youth may follow in the development of disruptive and aggressive behaviors.
3. Compare and contrast the DSM-IV criteria for ODD and CD.
4. Describe the drawbacks of using rating scales to assess disruptive behaviors.

Briefly describe each of the following intervention strategies for increasing compliance and minimizing disruptive behavior, and provide a concrete example of how the strategy would be implemented in the classroom.

5. Providing developmentally appropriate programming
6. Establishing a therapeutic relationship
7. Adapting the classroom management system
8. Avoiding power struggles
9. Using cognitive behavioral techniques to teach conflict resolution
10. Implementing a bullying reduction program

APPLICATION ACTIVITIES

1. Review the vignette presented at the beginning of this chapter. Compare Miranda's characteristics to the IDEA criteria for ED. Does she qualify for special education or not? Defend your answer.

2. Examine the technical manuals for three of the behavior rating scales commonly used by school districts in your area. Compare the publisher's information concerning reliability, validity, and how the measure was normed.

3. Locate at least one of the bullying resources listed in Figure 8–10, using the Internet or your school library. Design an informational brochure for parents providing general information about bullying prevention.

4. Using case study 4 in Appendix A, complete a functional behavioral assessment using the format in Figure 3–10. Describe a minimum of two intervention strategies from this chapter that you would recommend be used for this student and explain why you selected those strategies.

CHAPTER 9

PERVASIVE DEVELOPMENT DISORDERS

Theresa L. Earles-Vollrath, Katherine Tapscott Cook, and Jennifer B. Ganz

CONNECTING TO THE CLASSROOM: *A Vignette*

Cannon is an 8-year-old student with autism spectrum disorder.[1] He is educated in the general education classroom for approximately 60% of the day. He receives special education services in the areas of math, reading, and written language in a resource room, and related services from a speech/language pathologist, an occupational therapist, and a physical therapist. Cannon currently uses one-word utterances to communicate; however, many of his communicative attempts are difficult to understand.

Cannon's individualized education program (IEP) contains primarily academic goals, with one behavioral goal focusing on decreasing his aggressive behavior. A functional behavioral assessment (FBA) has not been completed and he does not have a documented behavior intervention plan (BIP).

Cannon has demonstrated numerous behavioral difficulties throughout his educational career; however, this year his behavioral problems have become more intense. He drops to the floor and screams during transitions and will exhibit full-blown tantrums (dropping to the floor, screaming, crying, hitting and kicking others) when there are changes in his typical day. Recess, physical education, and lunch are also difficult. His teacher reports that while in recess, physical education, and lunch settings, Cannon initially seems to be just fine but then he will "lose it" and attack a peer. Cannon loves recess but his teacher reports that he primarily plays with female students and his play is limited to chase games. He also hangs on his peers and sometimes falls to the ground and attempts to wrestle with them. In one lunch-time incident, Cannon, who was returning his lunch tray to the rack, threw his tray to the floor and screamed. When his teacher attempted to get him to pick up his tray and food, Cannon began hitting the teacher and was then physically escorted to a time-out.

---

[1] There is currently a trend in the field to refer to autistic disorder, Asperger's disorder, and pervasive developmental disorders not otherwise specified as autism spectrum disorders (ASD). Rett's syndrome and childhood disintegrative disorder are also included on this continuum.

POPULATION DESCRIPTION AND MAJOR FEATURES OF PERVASIVE DEVELOPMENTAL DISORDERS (PDD)

Pervasive developmental disorders (PDD) is a general term used in the *Diagnostic and Statistical Manual of Mental Disorders* (4th edition, text revision; DSM-IV-TR) to describe a class of disorders characterized by impairments in reciprocal social interaction skills, impairments in communication skills, and the presence of restricted repetitive and stereotyped patterns of behaviors, interests, and activities (American Psychiatric Association, 2000). The five disorders under this category include autistic disorder, Rett's disorder, childhood disintegrative disorder, Asperger's disorder, and pervasive developmental disorders not otherwise specified (PDD-NOS). (See Figure 9-1.) According to the National Dissemination Center for Children with Disabilities, these neurological disorders share, to some extent, similar characteristics that are usually evident by 3 years of age (Tsai, 2003). While some physicians may diagnose children with ASD, this term refers to a category of disorders and is typically not used as a specific diagnostic label.

As discussed in earlier chapters, a DSM-IV diagnosis does not necessarily equate directly to a categorical special education label under IDEA, or predict special education placement or services. Although IDEA has included autism as a category of special education since the 1990 amendments, district teams may identify students with PDD diagnoses as eligible under the category of autism or under another category, such as emotional disturbance or other health impaired. Special educators trained in emotional disturbance, learning disabilities, mental retardation, or crosscategorical special education often provide services for students with ASD.

AUTISTIC DISORDER

Autistic disorder was first described by Leo Kanner in 1943. As a psychiatrist, he recorded anecdotal notes regarding a group of 11 children who shared similar characteristics but were different from children with any other syndrome. Kanner's seminal article, *Autistic Disturbances of Affective Contact* (1943), described what is currently referred to as autism or autistic disorder.

Autistic disorder—sometimes referred to as classical autism, early infantile autism, or Kanner's autism—is a neurological disorder characterized by impairments in social interactions, communication, and a restricted repertoire of activities and interests (APA, 2000). According to epidemiological studies, autistic disorder affects 5 in 10,000 individuals (APA, 2000); however, prevalence rates range as high 6 in 1,000 individuals (Centers for Disease Control and Prevention, 2001). Autism is four to five times more prevalent in boys than girls, and females diagnosed with this disorder are more likely to exhibit more severe mental retardation (APA, 2000).

According to DSM-IV-TR (APA, 2000), an essential characteristic of autistic disorder is the impairment of social-interaction skills. While the manifestation of this impairment varies across individuals, several commonalities exist. Individuals may demonstrate difficulties in using and understanding multiple nonverbal behaviors, such as eye-to-eye gaze, facial expressions, body language, and gestures. They may have difficulty developing peer relationships appropriate to their developmental level. Some children with autistic disorder, especially young children, may not seek out others for friendships. Older individuals may demonstrate an interest in developing friendships but may lack the skills necessary to do so. Children with autistic disorder may not spontaneously seek out others to share enjoyment, or to show, bring, or point out objects of interests. Additionally, students may not participate in simple social games (e.g., peekaboo, patty cake), may prefer to play alone, and may also "lack varied, spontaneous make-believe play or social imitative play" (APA, 2000, p. 70).

Deficits in communication skills are another feature of children with autism. Impairments in this area affect both nonverbal and verbal abilities. Not only do individuals with autism frequently not understand the nonverbal behaviors of others, they also may not use nonverbal

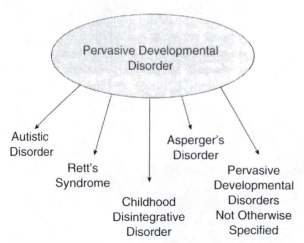

FIGURE 9–1 Pervasive Developmental Disorder

behaviors (e.g., eye gaze, gestures, facial expressions) to enhance their communicative message. In addition to delays in nonverbal communication, there may also be "a delay in, or total lack of, the development of spoken language" (APA, 2000, p. 70). Approximately 50% of children with autism are nonverbal; they do not develop speech. If they do develop spoken language, they may demonstrate difficulties in initiating and sustaining conversations, and may use repetitive or idiosyncratic language. An example of idiosyncratic language is the use of echolalia. **Echolalia** is the repetition of words or phrases previously heard. Echolalia can be broken down into three broad categories: immediate, delayed, and mitigated. **Immediate echolalia** is repeating words without delay following the original utterance (e.g., an adult says "Hi Johnny" and the child immediately says "Hi Johnny"). Prizant and Rydell (1984) define **delayed echolalia** as an utterance repeated at a significantly later period of time (e.g., repeating TV commercials verbatim hours, days, or weeks after hearing them). **Mitigated echolalia** reflects a progression toward more functional communication. For example, Billy comes up to the teacher and says, "Say Mommy, tie my shoe please." After teacher modeling, he says the more appropriate "Tie my shoe please," omitting the nonfunctional words. Mitigated echolalia is typically a positive step for students, as it demonstrates increased ability to recognize and use language in a more meaningful fashion. For some students who develop spoken language abilities, their first utterances may be echolalic phrases.

Pronoun reversals are another characteristic of some children with autism. For example, rather than requesting a drink of water by saying, "May I have a drink of water?" students with autism may say, "You want a drink of water." The use of pronoun reversals may be a by-product of delayed echolalia related to the student's gestalt style of cognitive processing (Prizant, 1983).

Individuals who develop verbal language may also demonstrate abnormalities in the rate, the tone, or the pitch of their speech.

The final group of characteristics essential to the diagnosis of autistic disorder is related to restricted repetitive and stereotyped patterns of interests and activities (APA, 2000). Individuals with autism can exhibit a variety of behavioral symptoms. Individuals may seem to be inflexible, demonstrating anxiety or aberrant behaviors due to changes in their internal routines (e.g., the need to turn around two times prior to sitting down, the need to walk around the perimeter of the playground prior to playing on equipment), or to external routines, such as classroom schedules or the route for driving from school to home.

The purposes of these routines and schedules are numerous and depend on the individual; however, for many students, routines provide structure and predictability, in a world that may seem very unpredictable and confusing. In addition, routines correspond with their gestalt style of cognitive processing.

Individuals with autism may exhibit stereotyped and repetitive motor movements (e.g., hand flapping, finger flicking, light filtering, rocking) and may demonstrate unusual reactions to sensory stimuli (e.g., undersensitive or oversensitive to pain, sensitivity to noise). Students with autism may also exhibit self-injurious behaviors, aggression toward others, impulsivity, and noncompliance to directions or adult-imposed routines.

Autism is sometimes referred to as a spectrum disorder as children with this diagnosis vary in severity of symptoms, age of onset, and associations with other disorders (National Research Council, 2001). The severity of symptoms can include a variety of characteristics such as one's cognitive and communication abilities. In many cases, individuals with autism also may have a diagnosis of mental retardation, which can range along a continuum from mild to profound. Although some individuals develop verbal abilities, approximately 50% of individuals lack verbal language.

Age of onset can also differ. By definition, characteristics of autism must be evident by 3 years of age. In most cases, children do not have a period of unequivocal normal development and therefore their symptoms are evident prior to age 3. In 20% of cases, however, parents report relatively typical development for the first one to two years (APA, 2000) and then a dramatic change in behavior and communicative abilities. According to the DSM-IV-TR (APA, 2000), individuals with autism can also be diagnosed with other disorders such as fragile X syndrome, tuberous sclerosis, and obsessive-compulsive disorder. In addition, approximately 25% of adolescents with autism develop seizures. See Figure 9–2 for DSM-IV-TR criteria for autistic disorder.

RETT'S DISORDER

Rett's disorder is a progressive, neurological disorder characterized by a loss of previously acquired skills after apparent normal development (APA, 2000; Cohen & Volkmar, 1997). While the full onset of this disorder occurs by 4 years of age, it usually is apparent in the first or second year of life and is a lifelong disability (APA, 2000). Historically, Rett's disorder has only been reported in females. Girls diagnosed with Rett's disorder exhibit a unique course of development. The prenatal

A. Qualitative impairment in social interaction, as manifested by at least two of the following:
   * Marked impairment in the use of multiple nonverbal behaviors such as eye-to-eye gaze, facial expression, body postures, and gestures to regulate social interaction
   * Failure to develop peer relationships appropriate to developmental level
   * Lack of spontaneous seeking to share enjoyment, interests, or achievements of other people (e.g., by lack of showing, bringing, or pointing out objects of interest)
   * Lack of social or emotional reciprocity

B. Qualitative impairments in communication as manifested by at least one of the following:
   * Delay in or total lack of the development of spoken language (not accompanied by an attempt to compensate through alternative modes of communication, such as gesture or mime)
   * In individuals with adequate speech, marked impairment in the ability to initiate or sustain a conversation with others
   * Stereotyped and repetitive use of language or idiosyncratic language
   * Lack of varied, spontaneous make-believe or social imitative play appropriate to developmental level

C. Restricted repetitive and stereotyped patterns of behavior, interests, and activities, as manifested by at least one of the following:
   * Encompassing preoccupation with one or more stereotyped/restricted patterns of interest, abnormal either in intensity or focus
   * Apparently inflexible adherence to specific, nonfunctional routines or rituals
   * Stereotyped and repetitive motor mannerisms (e.g., hand or finger flapping, or twisting, or complex whole-body movements)
   * Persistent preoccupation with objects

D. Delays or abnormal functioning in at least one of the following areas, with onset prior to age 3 years:
   * Social interaction
   * Language as used in social communication or
   * Symbolic or imaginative play

E. The disturbance is not better accounted for by Rett's Disorder or Childhood Disintegrative Disorder

FIGURE 9–2 DSM-IV-TR Diagnostic Criteria for Autistic Disorder

Source: American Psychiatric Association. (2000). *Diagnostic and statistical manual of mental disorders* (4th ed., text revision). Washington, DC: American Psychiatric Association. Reprinted with permission from the *Diagnostic and Statistical Manual of Mental Disorders*, Copyright 2000. American Psychiatric Association.

and perinatal periods of development up to 5 months of age seem apparently normal; however, once it is diagnosed, a review of the developmental history reveals that approximately 80% of girls with Rett's Disorder exhibited less obvious developmental abnormalities such as hypotonia (weak muscle tone), tremulous neck movements, abnormal hand use, and impaired social and language skills (Cohen & Volkmar, 1997).

The fundamental characteristic associated with the diagnosis of Rett's Disorder is the loss of previously acquired functional hand use. Purposeful hand use is replaced by continuous stereotypical hand wringing/hand washing, or hand-to-mouth movements. The loss of functional hand use remains permanent throughout the life of the individual with Rett's Disorder.

Other prominent characteristics associated with Rett's Disorder include irregular breathing patterns, teeth grinding, decreased head growth, and severe to profound mental retardation (Cohen & Volkmar, 1997).

Hagberg and Witt-Engerstrom (1986) identified four stages of Rett's Disorder, which were developed to facili-

tate identification and classification of the progression of this disorder. The four identified stages include: (1) early onset stagnation phase, (2) rapid destructive stage, (3) pseudostationary stage, and (4) late motor degeneration stage. See Figure 9-3 for a description of the stages of Rett's Disorder and Figure 9-4 for DSM-IV-TR criteria for Rett's Disorder.

CHILDHOOD DISINTEGRATIVE DISORDER

According to DSM-IV-TR (APA, 2000) diagnostic standards, children identified with **childhood disintegrative disorder (CDD)** demonstrate behavior patterns similar to those of children with autistic disorder. They typically display the same qualitative social interaction, communication, behavior, and interest impairments as children with autism. The distinction relates to the age of onset of the disability. That is, children diagnosed with autistic disorder display symptoms of pervasive developmental disorder prior to 3 years of age. In contrast, children with CDD have a period of normal growth and

Stage	Profile
1. Early Onset Stagnation Phase (6–18 months)	• Decreased rate of motor development or a degeneration of motor development • Low muscle tone may be apparent • Deviation from normal developmental sequence may be noted
2. Rapid Destructive Stage (1–3 years)	• Previously acquired abilities deteriorate or are lost: ○ Functional hand use ○ Cognitive abilities ○ Social interactions ○ Speech use ○ Gait (stiff legs with side-to-side swaying) • Development of stereotyped hand movements or hand wringing/handwashing • Development of abnormal patterns of breathing including breath holding and hyperventilation • Increased agitation • Abnormal sleep patterns • Seizure activity in one-quarter of those identified
3. Pseudostationary Stage (2–10 years)	• Improved social interactions • Appear to be aware of their surroundings • Improved communication skills: ○ Use of eye gaze to communicate ○ Increased babbling ○ Use of word pieces to communicate • Seizures in up to 80% of those identified • Rigid muscle tone with jerky movements • Scoliosis
4. Late Motor Degeneration Stage (10+ years)	• Decreased mobility • Cognitive functioning remains stable following within the severe mental retardation range • Improved eye contact • Seizure activity may decrease • Receptive and expressive language skills are absent

FIGURE 9–3   Rett's Disorder Classification Stages

Source: Adapted from Hagberg & Will-Engerstrom (1986).

development prior to manifesting social interaction, communication, and behavioral impairments. Thus, following at least two years of apparently normal development (but before 10 years of age), children diagnosed as having childhood disintegrative disorder display "a clinically significant loss of previously acquired skills in at least two of the following areas: expressive or receptive language, social skills or adaptive behavior, bowel or bladder control, play or motor skills" (APA, 2000, p. 77). Childhood disintegrative disorder is extremely rare, and is reported to affect males at a higher prevalence rate.

There are varying patterns in the onset of CDD, including abrupt loss of skills (days to weeks) or, more frequently, the onset takes place over a period of weeks to months. Prior to the deterioration of skills associated with the onset of CDD, children experience periods of agitation, anxiety, and depressed mood (Volkmar, Klin, Marans, & Cohen, 1997).

Although CDD is identified with a period of marked regression of previously acquired skills, this regression takes one of three routes. Researchers have reported that in approximately 75% of CDD cases, the child's behavior and development regresses to a much lower level, where it remains. A second group of children with CDD go through a period of regression, followed by a period of partial recovery of lost skills and behaviors. However, it must be noted that although some children regain previously lost skills, often they do not return to the level of skills exhibited prior to the onset of the disorder

A. All of the following:

- Apparently normal prenatal and perinatal development
- Apparently normal psychomotor development through the first 5 months after birth
- Normal head circumference at birth

B. Onset of all of the following after the period of normal development:

- Deceleration of head growth between ages 5 and 48 months
- Loss of previously acquired purposeful hand skills between ages 5 and 30 months with the subsequent development of stereotyped hand movements (e.g., hand wringing or hand washing)
- Loss of social engagement early in the course (although often social interaction develops later)
- Appearance of poorly coordinated gait or trunk movements
- Severely impaired expressive and receptive language development with severe psychomotor retardation

FIGURE 9–4 DSM-IV-TR Diagnostic Criteria for Rett's Disorder

Source: American Psychiatric Association. (2000). *Diagnostic and statistical manual of mental disorders* (4th ed., text revision). Washington, DC: American Psychiatric Association. Reprinted with permission from the *Diagnostic and Statistical Manual of Mental Disorders*, Copyright 2000. American Psychiatric Association.

A. Apparently normal development for at least the first 2 years after birth as manifested by the presence of age-appropriate verbal and nonverbal communication, social relationships, play, and adaptive behavior.

B. Clinically significant loss of previously acquired skills (before age of 10 years) in at least two of the following areas:

- Expressive or receptive language
- Social skills or adaptive behavior
- Bowel or bladder control
- Play
- Motor skills

C. Abnormalities of functioning in at least two of the following areas:

- Qualitative impairment in social interaction (e.g., impairment in nonverbal behaviors, failure to develop peer relationships, lack of social or emotional reciprocity)
- Qualitative impairments in communication (e.g., delay or lack of spoken language, inability to initiate or sustain a conversation, stereotyped and repetitive use of language, lack of varied make-believe play)
- Restricted, repetitive, and stereotyped patterns of behavior, interests, and activities, including motor stereotypes and mannerisms

D. The disturbance is not better accounted for by another specific Pervasive Developmental Disorder or by Schizophrenia.

FIGURE 9–5 DSM-IV-TR Diagnostic Criteria for Childhood Disintegrative Disorder

Source: American Psychiatric Association. (2000). *Diagnostic and statistical manual of mental disorders* (4th ed., text revision). Washington, DC: American Psychiatric Association. Reprinted with permission from the *Diagnostic and Statistical Manual of Mental Disorders*, Copyright 2000. American Psychiatric Association.

(Volkmar & Cohen, 1989). The third group of individuals diagnosed with CDD appears to go through a period of regression, which does not stabilize and often concludes with death (Corbett, 1987). See Figure 9–5 for DSM-IV-TR criteria for childhood disintegrative disorder.

ASPERGER'S DISORDER

Asperger's disorder, also referred to as Asperger syndrome, is a developmental disorder characterized by qualitative impairments in social interactions and restricted and unusual patterns of interest and behavior. A clinical diagnosis currently cannot be made with confidence prior to age 5 (Gillberg, 2002). In 1944, not long after Leo Kanner published his article on autism, Hans Asperger, a Viennese pediatrician, documented information concerning a group of boys with autistic-like characteristics but who exhibited normal intelligence and language development. The work of Asperger was not widely acknowledged in the United States until the late 1980s and early 1990s, beginning with the writings of Lorna Wing in 1981. Her work increased recognition of Asperger's disorder and facilitated a debate in the field.

A. Qualitative social interaction impairment as manifested by at least two of the following:
   * Marked impairment in the use of nonverbal behaviors, including eye-to-eye contact, facial expressions, body postures, and gestures to regulate social interaction
   * Failure to develop relationships appropriate to developmental level
   * A lack of spontaneous seeking to share enjoyment, interests, or achievements with other people (e.g., by a lack of showing, bringing, or pointing out objects of interest to other people)
   * Lack of social or emotional reciprocity
B. Restricted repetitive and stereotyped patterns of behavior, interests, and activities as manifested by at least one of the following:
   * Encompassing preoccupation with one or more stereotyped and restricted patterns of interest that is abnormal either in focus or intensity
   * Apparently inflexible adherence to specific nonfunctional routines or rituals
   * Stereotyped and repetitive motor movements (e.g., hand or finger flapping or twisting, or complex whole-body movements)
   * Persistent preoccupation with parts of objects
C. The disturbance causes clinically significant impairment in social, occupational, or other important areas of functioning.
D. There is not clinically significant general delay in language (e.g., single words used by age 2 years, communicative phrases used by age 3 years).
E. There is not clinically significant delay in cognitive development or in the development of age-appropriate self-help skills, adaptive behavior (other than in social interaction), and curiosity about the environment in childhood.
F. Criteria are not met for another specific Pervasive Developmental Disorder or Schizophrenia.

FIGURE 9–6 DSM-IV-TR Diagnostic Criteria for Asperger's Disorder

Source: American Psychiatric Association. (2000). *Diagnostic and statistical manual of mental disorders* (4th ed., text revision). Washington, DC: American Psychiatric Association. Reprinted with permission from the *Diagnostic and Statistical Manual of Mental Disorders,* Copyright 2000. American Psychiatric Association.

Asperger's disorder, and pervasive developmental disorders not otherwise specified demonstrate sensory impairments. Sensory impairments are often observed as terrified, shocked, or painful reactions to certain sensory experiences or sensory stimuli; additionally, these students often display emotional difficulties that are directly related to their sensory-processing problems. Greenspan and Weider (1998) found that in a study of 200 children with PDD, 94% exhibited sensory dysfunction. Additionally, when looking at the sensory characteristics of this population, Kientz and Dunn (1997) reported that a child with PDD is more likely to engage in the following behaviors or responses (related to their difficulty appropriately responding and reacting to sensory stimuli) than their neurotypical peers or students with attention-deficit/hyperactivity disorder:

* Seeks movement that interferes with daily activities
* Exhibits emotional outbursts when unsuccessful with tasks
* Displays difficulty with changes in routine
* Demonstrates stubborn or uncooperative behavior
* Demonstrates difficulty making friends
* Displays evidence of weak muscles
* Demonstrates a weak grasp
* Exhibits difficulty lifting heavy objects
* Shows self-imposed limitations to particular food textures or temperatures

* Demonstrates difficulty paying attention
* Exhibits difficulty expressing emotions
* Looks away from tasks to notice all actions in the room
* Writes illegibly
* Looks carefully or intensely at objects/people
* Stares intensely at objects/people
* Avoids eye contact
* Walks on toes
* Expresses distress during grooming
* Has fears that interfere with daily routines
* Avoids getting messy
* Displays unusual need for touching things
* Demonstrates difficulty perceiving body language or facial expressions

There is a current trend in the field to use the term Autism Spectrum Disorders (ASD) to refer to a more broad definition of autism which includes the classical form of this disability with other disabilities that share many of the core characteristics (i.e., Asperger Syndrome, Pervasive Developmental Disorders Not-Otherwise Specified). Rett's Disorder and Childhood Disintegrative Disorder can also be included in the use of this term. To adhere to the current trend, the remainder of this chapter will use the term ASD to refer to interventions designed for students with these disabilities.

CLASSROOM INTERVENTION STRATEGIES

Researchers have found a variety of effective interventions for students with ASD (APA, 2000). However, it is imperative that professionals understand that no one intervention or approach will be successful for every student. Interventions and curriculums should be individualized to meet the unique needs of each student. For example, many children with ASD will benefit from a visual schedule to understand and predict daily events. However, a student with autism and limited reading abilities may require a visual schedule that utilizes pictures to represent the day's events, while a child with Asperger's disorder and strong reading abilities may be able to use a visual schedule with words or phrases that detail the day's activities. Many of the interventions presented can be modified for students along the ASD continuum.

Developing Academic Skills

Students with ASD require differing levels of classroom support in academic instruction ranging from intensive, specially designed individualized programs to less intensive modifications and accommodations. This section will provide information on discrete trial instruction, priming, assignment modifications, graphic organizers, and homework completion strategies.

Discrete Trial Instruction.   While there are a variety of methods for teaching students with ASD to acquire new skills, many of the preferred strategies utilize the principles of applied behavior analysis (ABA) (Heflin & Simpson, 1998). One strategy based upon the ABA model that is often recommended for children with autism is discrete trial instruction (DTI) or discrete trial teaching (DTT). The term DTI is sometimes used interchangeably with the term ABA; however, these two terms are not synonymous. **Applied behavior analysis (ABA)** is a science that focuses on the search for the relationships between a behavior and its causes. ABA is based on observable, measurable actions of an individual, assumes that behavior is under the control of the environment, and states that behavior is learned and that this learning occurs as a result of consequences that follow the behavior (Alberto & Troutman, 2003). **Discrete trial instruction**, conversely, is a vehicle for applying the principles of ABA when providing instruction to children with autism but only represents one of many teaching strategies within the field of ABA.

While many of the principles of ABA can be dated back to the early nineteenth century, the terms ABA and DTI are often associated with a well-known researcher, Ivar Lovaas. Dr. Lovaas advanced the field through the publication of numerous studies and other works such as *Teaching Developmentally Disabled Children: The Me Book* (1981) in which he described the application of the principles of ABA in teaching children and youth with autism and other developmental disabilities.

DTI is generally implemented in—but not limited to—a 1:1 student/teacher situation, and relies on highly structured teaching sessions that break tasks into smaller increments known as trials. Each discrete trial is composed of four distinct parts: (1) the discriminative stimulus (S^D); (2) the child's response (R); (3) the consequence (C); and (4) the intertrial interval (ITI). These four components are presented in this exact order. When initially teaching a skill, the trial will also contain a fifth component, the prompt.

The first component of the trial, the **discriminative stimulus (S^D)**, is an antecedent that serves as a cue for the target behavior to occur and therefore result in reinforcement (Alberto & Troutman, 2003). The S^D is a brief, clear instruction or question that is relevant and appropriate to the task. Examples of an S^D may include: "Do this" for a motor imitation task, "Point to" for a receptive identification task, "What is this?" for an expressive labeling task, or "Read" for a reading task.

The second component of the trial, the **student response (R)**, is the behavior the child performs in response to the S^D. This component could be a correct response, an incorrect response, or the failure to respond (i.e., no response).

The **consequence (C)** is the third component of the trial. A consequence is a stimulus that occurs after a response that either increases or decreases the likelihood that the behavior will occur again. If the response is correct, it should be reinforced. If the student gives an incorrect response, reinforcement should be withheld and a variety of consequences can be implemented. Examples of consequences for incorrect responses include saying "No" and briefly turning the head or removing materials from the teaching area and implementing an error-correction procedure. An **error-correction procedure** is the process of assisting the student in responding correctly following no response or an incorrect response (Westling & Fox, 2004).

The fourth component of the trial is the **intertrial interval (ITI)**. The intertrial interval is a 3- to 5-second pause that occurs after the consequence and before the S^D for the next trial is presented. This brief period of time signals to the child the end of one trial and the upcoming beginning of another trial. During the intertrial

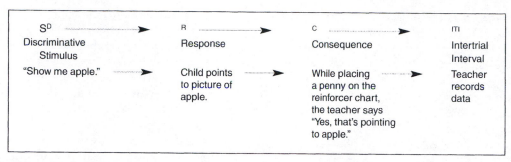

FIGURE 9–7 Example of a Discrete Trial

interval, the child can be involved with the reinforcer and the teacher can record data and prepare for the next trial. See Figure 9–7 for an example of a discrete trial.

Some trials, especially during the initial teaching of a skill or target behavior, may include a fifth component, a prompt. A **prompt** is an instructional technique that "is added to a situation in which the naturally occurring stimuli does not yet control the target response" (Maurice, Green, & Fox, 2001, p. 37). Prompts are implemented to ensure that students respond correctly and therefore learn the connection between the naturally occurring stimuli and the target behavior. There are a variety of prompts that can be used in teaching new skills. The following is a list of some of the most common categories of prompts, from least intrusive to most intrusive:

- **Verbal prompts** are statements that assist the student in knowing what to do and how to do it (Westling & Fox, 2004). A verbal prompt may take the form of a complete instruction, a question, a word, part of a word, or other verbal assistance. For example, the teacher holds up a card on which the word "dog" is printed and then says "dog." By saying "dog," the teacher is verbally prompting the student to make the correct response. Using the verbal prompt teaches the student to respond to naturally occurring stimuli (S^D)—saying "dog" when the student sees the dog (S^D). Use verbal prompts in conjunction with other types of prompts. If possible, limit the use of verbal prompts, as they are one of the most difficult types of prompts to fade.
- **Gestural prompts** are any physical movements or gestures made by another individual that lead the student to engage in the correct behavior in the presence of the S^D (Miltenberger, 2004). Gestural prompts may include a nod of the head, pointing, performing the motion of an activity, and so on. For example, if a student is learning to discriminate a

penny from a nickel, the teacher may give the S^D "Point to penny" and then immediately point to the penny to indicate the correct response.
- **Modeling prompts** are demonstrations of the target behavior by another person that make it more likely that the correct behavior will occur upon subsequent presentations of the S^D. For example, when teaching a student to play basketball, the teacher may say, "bounce ball" and then proceed to bounce the ball. In order for modeling to be a useful prompting procedure, a student must be able to imitate others (Miltenberger, 2004).
- **Physical prompts** involve someone, usually an adult, using some form of physical contact to help a child perform the target behavior at the correct time (i.e., in response to the S^D). A physical prompt may range from a slight touch of the hand to complete hand-over-hand guidance. For example, a teacher could say, "write your name" and then place her hand on the student's hand to physically guide the student in writing his name.

While prompts are beneficial and many times are a necessary strategy for teaching students with ASD, if not implemented correctly, they can also interfere with the learning process. A common mistake is to utilize prompts longer then necessary. When prompts are not faded correctly, students may become dependent on the prompt. While some experts believe that prompt dependency is a learning characteristic inherent in students with ASD, it is actually a result of improper prompt-fading in which the control is not transferred from the prompt to the naturally occurring stimuli. To prevent students from becoming prompt dependent, establish a prompt-fading strategy and appropriate success criteria *prior* to implementing the prompts. In addition, use the least intrusive prompt necessary to guarantee a correct response and resort to more intrusive types of prompts only when they are necessary (Miltenberger, 2004).

Priming. **Priming** is a strategy that focuses on the introduction of information, assignments, or activities prior to their use. The primary purpose of this strategy is to increase a child's competence and comfort with a given situation in the hopes that this predictability will then decrease the likelihood that problems will occur (Wilde, Koegel, & Koegel, 1992).

Priming can occur any time before the new material is to be presented in class. Wilde and colleagues (1992) recommend that the activity or information be presented in the same manner in which it will be presented in the classroom and, if possible, utilizing the same materials. Examples of priming activities could include reviewing a set of questions about a book or passage being read in class, or reviewing a schedule change prior to the change occurring. Moore (2002) reports that her son's teachers sent home tests to be reviewed the night before so her son would better understand the expectations and therefore decrease his anxiety.

In some instances, priming may occur immediately prior to a given activity. For example, prior to the introduction of a cooperative group activity, an adult may review the expectations, rules, topic, and the student's role in the activity (Myles & Adreon, 2001). Educators and parents should remember that the purpose of priming is to familiarize the student with the information, activity, or expectations of a given situation and not to teach new material to mastery or to play "catch up" (Wilde et al., 1992).

Assignment Modifications. Some students with ASD may need modified assignments to ensure academic success. While some children with ASD, especially children diagnosed with Asperger's disorder, demonstrate average to above-average intelligence, they may require additional time to process the expectations of the assignment and may become easily overwhelmed by a large number of problems, thinking that the assignment will never end. Assignment modifications can be categorized into three main categories: (1) length of assignments, (2) response modes, and (3) assignment format.

Length of Assignments. Some students may be overwhelmed by a worksheet containing numerous problems or questions because they cannot conceptualize how long it may take to complete the task and therefore believe that the task is never-ending. In addition, many students with Asperger's disorder have poor fine-motor abilities and may write very slowly or refuse to write at all. If the students attempt to complete the assignment they may do so at a much slower rate than their peers. Therefore: "It is often in the best interest of the student and the teacher to match the number that should be completed to the time available and the student's rate" (Myles & Simpson, 2003, p. 66).

Some students with ASD may be able to show competence in the target skill with a fewer number of trials. If the entire assignment must be completed, rather than giving the entire assignment at once, break it down into several smaller, more manageable pieces.

Response Modes. Give students choices about whether they would like to give oral responses, type their responses, or write their responses.

Assignment Format. Instead of an essay exam, allow the student to take a multiple-choice exam (Myles & Simpson, 2003). If writing is a necessary component, allow students to write in an outline form, rather than paragraph form.

Implement other creative format ideas. For example, allow students to develop PowerPoint™ presentations, role-play scenarios, or develop a physical representation of an idea.

Graphic Organizers. **Graphic organizers**, also known as concept maps, mind maps, or entity relationship maps, are a pictorial way of organizing seemingly disjointed facts and information into a structured, simple-to-read, visual display. Graphic organizers utilize the visual strengths of students with ASD and therefore can be very effective when developing instruction. Graphic organizers visually and concretely depict relationships between key terms within a given topic area and are useful when teaching content area material (Myles & Simpson, 2003).

Homework Completion Strategies. For a variety of reasons, some students with ASD may have difficulty completing homework assignments. The teacher and the parents should work together to determine if homework is a necessary component of the student's educational experience and, if so, how much homework is necessary for the student to demonstrate mastery (Myles & Simpson, 2003). If you determine that homework will be assigned, you can implement a variety of strategies to ensure student success:

- Communicate expectations to the child and the parent using an assignment sheet, a school planner, or an assignment notebook.
- If you require students to write the assignment into their planner or assignment notebooks, review the

planner or notebook to ensure that the information was recorded correctly.

- When using an assignment sheet, planner, or assignment notebook, set up a system to ensure that they reach their destination. Because some students with ASD have difficulties with organization, the materials may get lost, left in a locker, or buried at the bottom of a backpack (Myles & Simpson, 2003).
- Ask a peer to volunteer to serve as a back-up to the use of a planner or assignment notebook. Should a student arrive home and not be able to complete the homework, he could call a peer to get clarification.
- Some schools have established a homework line that parents can access to gain information regarding homework assignments (Myles & Simpson, 2003).
- If you use assignment sheets, place them on the class Web site or e-mail the information to selected parents using group e-mail.
- For long-term projects such as term papers, develop detailed time lines to assist the student in completing the assignment in a timely fashion. Some students with ASD have difficulty understanding the concept of time and cannot look at an assignment and estimate how long it will take to complete. This difficulty may cause students to wait until the day before an assignment is due and then expect to complete the entire assignment in this short period of time. When a long-term assignment is given, the teacher and/or a parent can review the requirements of the assignment, assist the student in breaking down the assignment into smaller tasks, and then, using the planner or a calendar, lay out due dates for each of the smaller tasks. See Chapter 7 for more information regarding the WATCH strategy.

Curriculum Enhancement and Interest Areas

It is important to consider motivation when working with students with ASD. Many students with ASD will not complete an assignment just because it is the "right" thing to do, or because incomplete work will affect their grades.

One means of motivating students is to utilize obsessions or areas of interest. Many students with ASD have an obsession or area of interest that preoccupies their thoughts and their leisure time. For example, a student may be interested in the presidents of the United States. If allowed, they will talk about the presidents during conversations, will read books about the presidents,

will conduct research on the Internet about the presidents, and may draw pictures of the presidents. While these obsessions can interfere with daily activities and with the development of appropriate social interactions, many times they serve a purpose for the student. For example, some students may resort to talking about areas of interest during times of high anxiety. Discussing these preferred topics can increase the individual's sense of control by providing routine and predictability in unfamiliar or anxiety-provoking situations. Areas of obsession or interest can also provide students with a familiar way of initiating a conversation and demonstrating their level of intelligence during times that they feel uncertain (Attwood, 1998).

Having an obsession or areas of interest can be seen as a strength and can usually be used as a means of facilitating motivation. For some students with ASD, however, using areas of interest or obsessions can actually interfere with the educational process as students may become so involved in the target interest that they cannot complete the assignment in the designated format. Therefore, remember that the selection of interventions should be based on the unique and individual needs of each student.

Facilitating Behavioral Growth

Teachers can implement a variety of interventions to address the behaviors exhibited by students with ASD. Recommended strategies include: providing a highly structured learning environment that uses classroom organization and visual supports, providing choice-making opportunities, teaching tolerance for change and flexibility, and using behavior cue cards. The next section will address these and other strategies.

THE HIGHLY STRUCTURED EDUCATIONAL ENVIRONMENT

One method of addressing behaviors that may be exhibited by students with ASD is to provide a highly structured and predictable learning environment. Organizing the classroom, using visual supports, and using other tactics that establish routines can provide this structure.

Organization of the Classroom

Room set-up can be a very crucial element for ensuring success for some individuals with autism. Using techniques that provide structure and predictability facilitates the individual's ability to understand the environment, therefore decreasing the likelihood of worry and agitation (Earles-Vollrath, Cook, Robbins, Ben-Arieh, 2006). These strategies can also increase independence and stimulate language development.

One way to provide organization to the classroom is to label the environment. Labeling the furniture and the objects in the room can have numerous benefits. The labels provide visual clues that help students with autism organize their space. For example, use labels to delineate specific areas of the room by hanging enlarged symbols representing snack area, art area, reading table, and math area above, or taped to, the specified area.

If the labels used to delineate objects and furniture in the classroom are correlated with the students' communication level, the strategy can be utilized to facilitate language development. For example, labeling furniture provides students with a visual cue to pair with the verbal cue of the teacher when given directives, such as "Sit in the chair," or "Stand by the door." (Earles-Vollrath, Cook, Robbins, et al., 2006).

Another strategy is to mark tubs and containers with a visual representation, such as a miniature object, icon, and/or written label that corresponds with the object in the bin. The shelf that houses the bin should also be marked with the same label. You can then teach the student to match the labels on the container to the labels on the shelf when he is asked to retrieve or return an activity to its appropriate place in the classroom.

A second method of providing structure and organization to the classroom is to utilize boundaries. Using boundary markings to establish areas for play, for reading, for cooking, for leisure activities, and so on will help students with autism learn what is expected from them. You can accomplish this by sectioning off the floor with colored tape, rugs, and remnants of carpet or other materials that indicate to the student where he or she should remain during a given activity (Dalrymple, 1993).

If two or more activities must be completed in the same area or at the same table, adding a tablecloth to the table for the second subject or task will distinguish it from the first activity. For example, if reading and snack are both completed at the same table, reading can take place at the table. When it is time for snack, a checkered tablecloth can be used to cover the table (Earles-Vollrath, Cook, Robbins, et al., 2006).

Visual Supports

Visual supports is a broad term used to describe strategies that organize the environment and facilitate the students' ability to make sense of their surroundings,

predict events and activities, anticipate change, and understand expectations. Visual supports include visual schedules, minischedules, and task organizers.

Visual Schedules. Visual schedules provide students with a general overview of the day's activities. Visual schedules can benefit students with autism in a variety of ways. Schedules allow individuals to anticipate upcoming events and activities, develop an understanding of time frames, and facilitate the ability to predict change (Brown, 1991; Twachtman, 1995). In addition, you can use schedules to stimulate communicative exchanges through the discussion of past, present, and future events (Twachtman, 1995) and to teach new skills such as cooking skills and self-care and grooming skills. Schedules can be used to increase students' ability to independently transition from one activity to another (MacDuff, Krantz, 1993). Another benefit of visual schedules is that this technique capitalizes on the visual strength of many individuals with ASD.

Because visual schedules can be designed in a variety of ways, when constructing schedules teachers must make numerous decisions based upon the strengths and the needs of the targeted students. These decisions include determining the level of visual representation, the format, the arrangement, the placement, and the means of indicating that an activity is finished.

Level of Visual Representation. You can construct visual schedules according to a hierarchy of levels of visual representation ranging from concrete to abstract. As would be expected, the more abstract the visual schedule, the higher the level of representation. For students who require concrete visual cues to understand upcoming events, design an object schedule, which utilizes the actual materials from each of the scheduled activities. For example, if the leisure activity requires the use of Play-Doh™ and cookie cutters, then use a jar of Play-Doh™ to represent leisure. Or, if after lunch, the student will be asked to brush his teeth, place a toothbrush on the schedule to indicate to the student that it is time to brush his teeth. Other students may benefit from schedules that use photographs of them completing the targeted activities, from black and white icons that define the target activities, from written words, or from sentences.

Format. Develop schedules utilizing a variety of formats, such as in a photo album or three-ring binder, arranged across the wall using Velcro,™ or written on a wipe-off board. For children with reading abilities, visual schedules can take the form of a list. As the student completes each activity designated on the list, he places a check mark next to the corresponding activity, or draws a line through the word. Type the list on an index-sized card or an 8½ × 11 piece of paper.

Arrangements. Arrange schedules either in a left-to-right manner or in a top-to-bottom manner. The left-to-right arrangement facilitates the behavior required for reading.

Placement. Schedules can be placed in a variety of locations in the classroom, such as on a wall, at the student's desk, at a workstation, on the chalkboard, or on a shelf next to the student's desk. In addition, students may want to carry the schedule on a belt hoop, in an organizer or assignment book, or in their pocket.

Activity Completion. An integral part of constructing a visual schedule is determining how a student will indicate and therefore understand that an activity is completed. For example, hang finished pockets near the schedule so that when the student completes an activity, he then removes the representative object, photograph, or icon and places it into the finished pocket. During this time, the teacher or paraprofessional could say and/or sign the following phrase: "Reading is finished, it's time for lunch." Other methods of indicating that an activity is complete may include the following:

* Turning a card around so that it is facing backward
* Placing an object in a finished box
* Crossing out a word or phrase written on a chalkboard or piece of paper
* Wiping off a word or sentences written on a wipe-off board
* Setting timers for the specified period of time

See Figure 9–8 for an example of a visual schedule using icons and Figure 9–9 for an example of a visual schedule using a list format.

Mini schedules. While visual schedules provide students with a general overview of their day, if needed, students can use minischedules to provide even more detailed information. **A mini schedule** breaks down the general activities depicted on the visual schedule by specifying the exact tasks that will occur. For example, if "reading" is listed as the next activity on the visual schedule, the student would then go to the reading area and locate the corresponding mini schedule. The mini schedule for "reading" would then detail the activities that should take place during this time (e.g., read vocabulary words, make sentences, read sentences, complete comprehension worksheet). See Figure 9–10 for an example of a minischedule for gym class.

Task Organizers. Task organizers are yet another type of visual support that can be combined with visual schedules and minischedules to provide even more information, as needed by students. A **task organizer** lists the exact step-by-step process a student follows to complete a task listed in the minischedule (Hodgdon, 1995). For example, in the "reading" minischedule is an activity labeled "comprehension worksheet." You can develop a task organizer to list the exact steps required for completing the comprehension worksheet (e.g., get the worksheet out of my reading folder; get a pencil out of my pencil box; put my name at the top of the paper; read the story; answer questions 1, 2, 3, 4, and 5; reread the story and check my answers; put the worksheet in the finished tray). Task organizers can also be developed to facilitate the learning of multiple-step routines (e.g., getting ready to go home) and activities of daily living (e.g., making popcorn, brushing teeth, making the bed).

Activity-Completion Signals

Activity-completion signals provide students with information regarding how much longer an activity may last or when it is necessary to stop one activity and begin another. As discussed previously, a finished pocket, a finished box, turning a visual schedule card around so that it is facing backward, or crossing out a word or phrase written on a list schedule are all forms of activity-completion signals and can provide support for transitions. Other types of activity-completion signals may include setting timers for a specified period of time or using colored disks to indicate the passing of time. For example, set a timer at the beginning of an activity. As time passes, give verbal signals such as, "five more minutes, then recess will be finished." Prior to the timer sounding, provide a verbal reminder such as, "snack is almost finished, it will be time for math next" to prepare the student for the transition.

For some students, using a visual cue in addition to a timer is more beneficial than is a purely auditory strategy because it makes the concept of time a little more concrete. When you first set the timer, place a green circle on the work surface. With 5 minutes left, place a yellow circle on top of the green circle. Just prior to the timer sounding, place a red circle on the yellow circle.

As with visual schedules, consider the student's functional level when determining the level of abstraction for a completion signal.

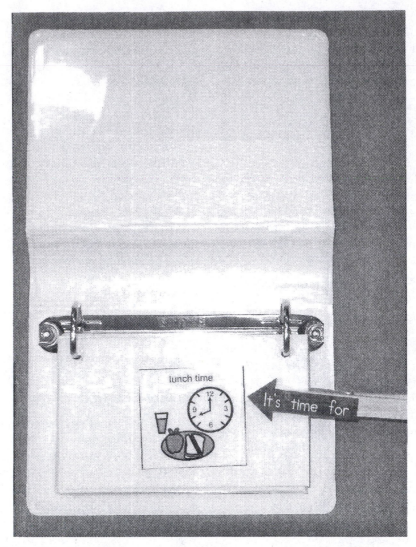

FIGURE 9–8 Sample of a Visual Schedule

Note. Schedules and other visual supports made with the Boardmaker™ and Picture Communication Symbols. © 1981–2005 by Mayer-Johnson LLC, PO Box 1579, Solana Beach, CA 92075, 858/550-0084, fax 858/550-0449, e-mail: mayerj@mayer-johnson.com.

Waiting Supports

Waiting is a difficult skill for many children to learn, whether it is waiting in line, waiting for their turn at a preferred activity, or waiting for teacher assistance. For students with ASD, waiting frequently presents problems because they have limited ability to delay gratification and often do not understand the concept of time. Therefore, these students will most likely require specific instruction to develop appropriate waiting behavior. First, provide role-playing or practice sessions using direct instruction to ensure that students possess the prerequisite skills necessary to engage in waiting behavior. These simulated activities should be authentic and take place in natural settings.

Waiting skills should be taught across a variety of settings to increase the likelihood of generalization. For example, providing a peer model or peer buddy during waiting times can offer visual support for the desired behavior. Specific physical supports such as placing chairs near the waiting area, setting a timer, holding a picture representing "wait," or teaching a hand signal that means wait may also enhance the learning of this concept.

Introducing Change and Building Flexibility

As discussed previously, one benefit of using visual schedules is that they provide students with the ability to predict change (Brown, 1991; Twachtman, 1995).

1.	Bell work	☑
2.	Reading	☑
3.	Math	☑
4.	P.E.	☐
5.	Bathroom	☐
6.	Lunch	☐
7.	Recess	☐
8.	Science	☐
9.	Group Work	☐
10.	Complete Planner	☐
11.	Go Home	☐

FIGURE 9–9 Example of a List Schedule. A list schedule can be taped to a desk; the student checks off the items as they are completed.

Because many students with ASD appear to find comfort in routines, understanding and accepting change can be difficult. The concept of change can be introduced through the use of schedules. For example, a change symbol, such as the word "change" or a pictorial representation of change, can replace the symbol for the

FIGURE 9–10 Sample Minischedule for Gym Class
Source: Schedules and other visual supports made with the Boardmaker™ and Picture Communication Symbols.© 1981-2005 by Mayer-Johnson LLC, PO Box 1579, Solana Beach, CA 92075, 858/550-0084, fax 858/550-0449, e-mail: mayerj@mayer-johnson.com.

expected activity (Earles-Vollrath, Cook, & Ganz, 2006; Earles-Vollrath, Cook, Robbins, & Ben-Arieh, 2006). It is important to involve the student in replacing the symbol of the expected activity with the change symbol and to discuss what will happen instead of the scheduled activity. For example, if it is raining and the students cannot go outside for recess, but will be going to the multipurpose room instead, place the change symbol in the time slot usually slated for recess. It also may be necessary for students to visit the multipurpose room while carrying the change symbol.

Posting a phrase such as "we usually have . . ." at the top of a schedule can help the student understand that change is an expected variation in the routine (Gray, 1995).

Moore (2002) suggests using a Change in Routine card. An example of a Change in Routine card is provided in Figure 9-11. It is important that when it is determined that a change in routine is going to take place, that the change be reviewed with the student, that the student's visual schedule be referenced, and that the change be depicted in a visual format (i.e., change symbol, Change in Routine card, etc.).

Providing Choice-Making Opportunities

The opportunity to make choices is an integral part of the education of all students with ASD. Choice making provides students control over their environment, promotes independence, increases motivation to learn, and allows the teacher an opportunity to provide instruction within the context of the natural environment (Bambara & Koger, 1996; Brown, Belz, Corsi, & Wenig, 1993). Opportunities for choice making also facilitate, "personal satisfaction and quality of life" (Bambara & Koger, 1996, p. 3).

There are a variety of ways of incorporating choices into a student's educational experience. Allow students to select the reinforcer for which they want to work, decide whether they want to write or type their spelling words, choose who they want to sit by during circle time, or decide the order in which they want to complete their bell work.

Student's choice selections can be organized and visually represented in a variety of ways. Place a choice board displaying objects, pictures, icons, or words that represent a menu of activities or reinforcers next to a student's daily schedule. When a designated choice time or break time arrives, the student can select a preferred activity from the board. Additionally, place choice boards displaying preferred activities near the free-time or break area of the room, providing a stimulus for independent selection of an activity.

To address the issues of portability and wall space, choose pictures, icons, or words that represent available choices. Then, place them inside a three-ring binder, write them on a dry-erase board, type them on an index card, or place them on an "O" ring.

Behavior Cue Cards

Behavior cue cards are a visual means of teaching target behaviors and/or reminding students of the behaviors that should occur under specific situations. The behavior cue card visually depicts, either with a drawing or in writing, the target behavior or the steps the student should follow within a given situation. Figures 9-12, 9-13, and 9-14 provide examples of behavior cue cards.

Power Cards

Power cards are developed and utilized with the premise that by providing the student with ASD a

---

Change in Routine

NOTICE: _____ will be changed

on _____ because _____

_____

The new _____

is _____

FIGURE 9-11 Example of a Change in Routine Card

Source: Moore, S.T. (2002). Asperger syndrome and the elementary school experience: Practical solutions for academic and social difficulties. Shawnee Mission, KS: Autism Asperger Publishing Company. Reprinted with permission.

visual support that incorporates their unique special interest, they in turn will be more motivated to practice a specific skill or perform a desired task (Gagnon, 2001). The power card, approximately the size of a business card, is carried by the individual with ASD and used as a visual reminder for desired behavioral outcomes. To use power cards as an intervention, write a script describing the desired behavior and how the individual's special interest has addressed the targeted area or skill. When developing the power card script, compose only two or three sentences, written at the student's communication level. See Figure 9–15 for a sample power card.

Home Base

Many students with ASD find the school environment very stressful. Because many students with ASD already possess a heightened level of anxiety, the management plan should allow the student to go to a safe and predictable comfort zone—or **home base**—when needed. Home base options may be a corner of the classroom with a beanbag chair, a buddy room, or a visit with the principal, counselor, or another comforting adult within the school environment. Home base is a place where the student is allowed to go when they are under stress to de-escalate and prevent behavioral outbursts that separate them from their peers and inhibit their ability to successfully complete or learn from academic tasks. Home base should not be a place to escape or avoid an activity, but rather a safe place where the child can regroup, refocus, and calm down. After de-escalation, the student can return to the academic task ready to learn.

Home base can also be used proactively, as a place for the student to start and end their school day. This

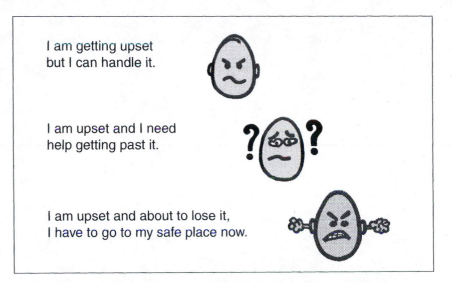

FIGURE 9–12 Example of a Behavior Cue Card

Source: Schedules and other visual supports made with the Boardmaker™ and Picture Communication Symbols. © 1981–2005 by Mayer-Johnson LLC, PO Box 1579, Solana Beach, CA 92075, 858/550-0084, fax 858/550-0449, e-mail: mayerj@mayer-johnson.com.

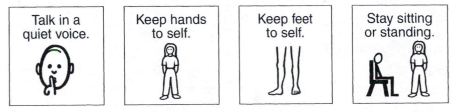

FIGURE 9–13 Example of a Behavior Cue Card

Source: Schedules and other visual supports made with the Boardmaker™ and Picture Communication Symbols. © 1981–2005 by Mayer-Johnson LLC, PO Box 1579, Solana Beach, CA 92075, 858/550-0084, fax 858/550-0449, e-mail: mayerj@mayer-johnson.com.

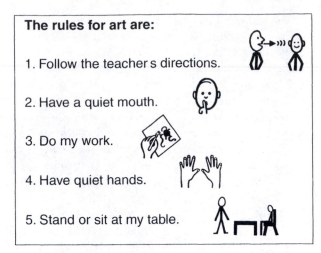

The rules for art are:

1. Follow the teacher's directions.

2. Have a quiet mouth.

3. Do my work.

4. Have quiet hands.

5. Stand or sit at my table.

FIGURE 9–14 Example of a Behavior Cue Card

Source: Schedules and other visual supports made with the Boardmaker™ and Picture Communication Symbols. © 1981–2005 by Mayer-Johnson LLC, PO Box 1579, Solana Beach, CA 92075, 858/550-0084, fax 858/550-0449, e-mail: mayerj@mayer-johnson.com.

Slammin' Sam likes to wrestle, just like you like to wrestle. However, Sam only wrestles during wrestling practice and matches. Sam also wants you to have fun at school, so he wants you to remember:

At school:
1. Keep my hands to myself.
2. Do not bump into my friends.
3. Do not tackle my friends on the playground.

Sam is very proud of you when you remember to do these 3 things. And Slammin' Sam says, "Have fun wrestling at wrestling practice."

FIGURE 9–15 Example of a Power Card

process, sometimes called triage, starts the day off in a predictable manner and ends the day with an opportunity to evaluate and summarize the day's activities.

ENHANCING COMMUNICATION AND SOCIAL/EMOTIONAL GROWTH

In addition to specialized academic instruction, students with ASD will benefit from additional supports in the areas of communication and social competence. This section will provide information on the Picture

Exchange Communication System, which will benefit students with expressive language deficits or delays. We will also describe several strategies for enhancing social and emotional growth, as well as addressing hidden curriculum and problem-solving skills.

Picture Exchange Communication System (PECS)

The **picture exchange communication system (PECS)** is an icon-based augmentative communication system commonly utilized with individuals with autism

(Frost & Bondy, 1994). Speech deficits are a common characteristic of individuals identified as having autism; 50% of this population is nonverbal. Thus, it is essential that communication be a principal goal for educators as they develop individualized education programs. Within this framework, PECS is one augmentative communication system that builds upon the visual strength of students with ASD while simultaneously teaching them to initiate communication, often a communicative deficit.

The PECS system utilizes a six-phase program that facilitates the communication process within a social context. PECS is based upon the principles of applied behavioral analysis, utilizing the principles of backward chaining, prompting, shaping, and reinforcement. PECS requires no communicative or behavioral prerequisites prior to implementation, making this system appropriate for all students regardless of age or severity of their disability. Additional benefits of PECS are the use of items and activities reinforcing to the child during the initial phases, therefore increasing the child's motivation to communicate, and the system can be implemented in any environment.

Within the teaching structure of PECS, the student is taught to choose a picture representing a desired object and hand the pictorial representation to a communicative partner. At that point, they receive the actual item requested. For example, the teacher places a picture of M&Ms on the table and holds an M&M in one of her hands. The student is then taught to pick up the picture and hand it to the teacher, at which time the teacher gives the student the M&M.

In addition, follow a formula that contains four types of sentences, with zero-to-one directive and/or control statements for every two-to-five descriptive and perspective sentences (Gray, 1994). Directive sentences describe or tell the student what they need to do in the given situation. Descriptive sentences tell where a situation occurs, who is involved, what they are doing, and/or why. Perspective sentences describe reactions and emotions of the student, or the emotional responses/states of others. Control sentences, which are optional, assist the student in remembering taught social responses to specific situations.

Although the goal of this system is to teach the initiation of communication, speech is never required of the individual. However, speech has been noted to develop in a large number of students, primarily following the implementation of the fourth phase of PECS (Ganz & Simpson, 2004). By this phase students have learned to initiate the communicative exchange by exchanging a picture for a preferred item, travel to the communica-

tive partner, travel to the communication notebook, discriminate between pictures, and use a sentence strip containing the phrase "I want."

Social Interventions

Impairments in social interactions are a major concern for students with ASD. As a result, direct instruction in the area of social skills should be a primary component of any intervention program. Educators can implement a variety of interventions to teach and reinforce social skills while addressing the particular communication and behavioral challenges of students with ASD. These include social stories, comic-strip conversations, circle of friends, social autopsies, and the direct instruction of social skills.

Social Stories. Carol Gray first developed **social stories** in 1994 as short narratives that describe social situations in terms of pertinent social cues, while simultaneously providing the student with appropriate social responses. Social stories facilitate appropriate responses, while minimizing the level of adult-provided prompts that are often necessary in social-skill instruction. Additionally, an essential feature of a social story is the possible inclusion of visual cues or pictures that illustrate a specific situation; therefore, building upon the visual strength of many individuals with ASD.

Social stories are based on situations that are difficult for students and they prepare students for a new situation that may be challenging. The purpose of a social story may be to describe a specific social situation, correct a student's response to a social situation, teach routines, or address behaviors including aggression, fear, or obsessions (Gray, 1994).

To develop a social story, first observe the student's responses to social situations. This valuable information will help you identify where the student's social skills break down or determine what social skills or social perceptions are misunderstood. From this information, compose the social story, possibly with the assistance of the student. It is essential to write social stories in the first person, as if to simulate the actions of the target student. Gray (2000) outlined several types of sentences that are used in writing effective social stories. In addition, she emphasized the need to follow a formula of zero-to-one directive or control sentences for every two-to-five descriptive, perspective, affirmative and/or cooperative sentences. The purpose of this formula is to ensure that the social story provides the student with information as done in the use of descriptive, perspective and affirmative sentences rather than merely informing the student of how he should behave as done in a directive sentence.

Basic social stories include the following sentences:

- Directive sentences describe or tell the student what they should do in a given situation
- Descriptive sentences tell where a tell where a situation occurs, who is involved, what they are doing, and/or why
- Perspective sentences describe reactions and emotions of the student or the emotional responses/states of others
- Affirmative sentences often enhance the meaning of previously stated sentences by reflecting general, commonly-held values or opinions
- Partial sentences are similar to fill-in-the-blank statements. These sentences require students to predict the next step in a sequence, guess the response of another person, predict the student's own behavior and/or demonstrate the understanding of a new skill or concept. Directive, descriptive, perspective, or affirmative sentences can be written as a partial sentence.

Complete social stories include the basic sentences and the sentences listed below:

- Control sentences, which are optional, are student generated statements that assist the student in recalling the information and skills detailed in the social stories
- Cooperative sentences describe how others will support the student as he learns the new skill

For this strategy to be effective, it is not enough to simply compose the story based on the social needs of the student. The story also must be read, modeled for the student, and practiced by the student. The most appropriate time to read a social story is immediately prior to the relevant situation, to prime the student for their desired behavior and behavioral response.

Comic-Strip Conversations. Comic-strip conversations, also developed by Carol Gray (1994), are a visual strategy that assists students in comprehending communication, behavior, and social situations. Comic-strip conversations facilitate a greater understanding of social situations by visually representing what has occurred in that social situation and why. Within this framework, a **comic-strip conversation** is a simple drawing illustrating a conversation between two or more people.

One of the many benefits to using comic-strip conversations is that not only do they assist the student by providing a greater understanding of what people may be thinking or feeling, they also provide parents and professionals with a greater understanding of the perspective of the student (Gray, 1995). Another benefit is that the process of writing a comic-strip conversation should only occur during a conversation between the student and an adult while simultaneously illustrating the social situation. This teacher-student interaction reinforces the social skills targeted by this intervention.

Carol Gray (1994) recommends a specific framework for the development of comic-strip conversations utilizing two sets of symbols: the conversation symbols dictionary and the personal symbols dictionary. The conversation symbols dictionary is a set of eight symbols that identify conversation concepts such as listening, interrupting, talking, thoughts, and loud/quiet words. Personal symbols are specific pictures or symbols—identified by the student—that are relevant to them. The personal symbols dictionary continues to evolve as the student becomes more comfortable with writing comic-strip conversations.

The third element involved in developing comic-strip conversations is the representation of feelings. Emotions are represented within the comic-strip conversation through the use of specific colors. For example, yellow represents frightened, purple represents proud, and blue represents sad or uncomfortable.

Circle of Friends. The Circle of Friends strategy was initially developed to support inclusion of individuals with disabilities (who previously had been living in institutions) into their local communities, and to integrate students previously educated in separate schools into mainstream schools (Forest & Lusthaus, 1989; Frederickson & Turner, 2003). This procedure has also been adapted to support children experiencing emotional, behavioral, and social difficulties in the school setting (Frederickson & Turner, 2003; Taylor, 1997).

A **Circle of Friends** is a group of students who have volunteered or who have been selected by the teacher. The purpose of this group is to provide support to the student with disabilities in achieving his or her target goals and to facilitate the inclusion of the focus student into typical, day-to-day school-related activities. Once students have been selected to participate in Circle of Friends, facilitators provide training to ensure the peers understand the target student's disability and the guidelines that will be followed during the Circle of Friends meetings and activities. Facilitators also assist the target student in selecting goals or skills that he would like to learn and focus on during the organized activities. Typically, Circle of Friends meetings occur on a consistent basis (e.g., once a week).

Social Autopsies. Social autopsies, first developed by Lavoie (Bieber, 1994), are a means for assisting individuals in understanding their social errors. Because inability to understand and interpret social situations correctly is a common trait among individuals with ASD, this strategy provides a supportive and solution-oriented framework.

Immediately following a social error, an adult guides the student through specific steps in an effort to gain a clear understanding of where, why, and how the social error occurred. The four main steps of the dissection of the social error are: (1) identify the social error, (2) identify if anyone—and if so, who—was harmed by the social error, (3) plan a means for correcting the social error, and (4) create a social plan to ensure that the social error does not occur again (Myles & Adreon, 2001). Figure 9–16 is a sample worksheet that can be used when completing social autopsies.

Direct Instruction of Social Skills. Autism spectrum disorders impair the ability to innately learn the rules that govern social interactions. Therefore, individuals with ASD must be explicitly taught the specific skills needed for social interactions. Myles and Southwick (1999) offer the following six steps as essential components to direct social skill instruction: (1) rationale, (2) presentation, (3) modeling, (4) verification, (5) evaluation, and (6) generalization. Figure 9–17 details these steps.

Hidden Curriculum

Almost every school has two curricula. The first curriculum is referred to as the **explicit curriculum**, the one of which students are aware and with which they are familiar. The explicit curriculum can be derived from the school's code of conduct, from instructional material, and from other printed resources. The second curriculum, the **hidden curriculum**, outlines the unspoken, unwritten rules of conduct that most students automatically understand and do not have to be directly taught (Bieber, 1994). While most students may be aware of the hidden curriculum, many students with ASD usually are not and therefore frequently and unknowingly violate these rules. The hidden curriculum includes a variety of subtle issues such as how to dress, how to act, whom to talk to, whom to ignore, what to say and when, and so on (Myles & Adreon,

2001). For example, most students figure out in a matter of days which teachers will tolerate a student being late to class and which teachers will not, which teachers can be led off subject by a student who brings up a favorite topic and those who would immediately redirect discussion back to the topic at hand. In addition, a student must understand to whom jokes can be told. For example, a student can tell a dirty joke to a peer but not to the principal. To be more specific, telling a dirty joke to a peer who is considered to be a good friend or of the same gender may be acceptable, but telling the same joke to another peer may be offensive due to the social implications, the setting, the timing, and so on.

The student with ASD typically does not intuitively pick up these unspoken rules and needs to be taught them directly. Myles and Simpson (2003) list several items that students with ASD should be taught as part of the hidden curriculum: (a) teacher expectations, (b) teacher-pleasing behaviors, (c) which students to interact with and which to avoid, and (d) what behaviors attract both positive attention and negative attention. Students must also be taught that the hidden curriculum varies across settings, people, age, situations, and cultures (Myles & Simpson, 2003). For example, the hidden curriculum for behavior at a church is certainly very different than the hidden curriculum for behavior at a high school football game.

Problem-Solving Strategies: SOCCSS

Some students with ASD demonstrate difficulty solving problems and being able to predict the consequences of their behavior. One method of assisting students in this area is a strategy referred to as SOCCSS (Roosa, 1995). The SOCCSS strategy provides a map of a situation and then allows students to visually examine their options and the consequences for each of these options. SOCCSS is a mnemonic device that stands for Situation, Options, Choices, Consequences, Strategies, and Simulations. The steps of the strategy are described in more detail in Chapter 7 of this text. See Figure 9–18 for a sample SOCCSS worksheet.

PLANNING FOR TRANSITION AND COMMUNITY LIVING

Outcomes for students with ASD vary depending on the severity of the disability, the strength of previous educational experiences, and the level of support

Social Autopsies Worksheet

What happened? _____

_____

_____

_____

What was the social error?	Who was hurt by the social error?

What should be done to correct the error? _____

_____

_____

_____

What could be done next time? _____

_____

_____

_____

_____

_____

FIGURE 9–16   Example of Social Autopsies Worksheet

Source: Myles, B. S., & Adreon, D. (2001). *Asperger syndrome and adolescence: Practical solutions for school success.* Shawnee Mission, KS: Autism Asperger Publishing Company. Reprinted with permission.

- **Rationale**—providing students with the how and why information is relevant.
- **Presentation**—small incremental steps are taught using visual and auditory modalities.
- **Modeling**—student's attention is gained and each social step is modeled and taught in a variety of appropriate settings. The student is shown and taught what to do instead of what *not* to do.
- **Verification**—monitor the student's emotional state.
- **Evaluation**—assess the student's correct use and understanding of the targeted social skill.
- **Generalization**—program for generalization to ensure skill acquisition, especially in less-structured environments.

FIGURE 9–17 Direct Skill Instruction Steps

Source: Based on Myles, B. S., & Southwick, J. (1991). *Asperger syndrome and difficult moments: Practical solutions for tantrums, rage, and meltdowns.* Shawnee Mission, KS: Autism Asperger Publishing Company. Reprinted with permission.

received during the transition from school-based services to postschool life. Research regarding students with autistic disorder indicates generally poor adult outcomes. In a review of studies from the mid 1950s to the late 1980s, researchers determined that fewer than 10% of the study participants had a good outcome, which was defined as the person demonstrating the ability to hold a job, and in some cases have a family. Approximately 60% of the study participants had a poor outcome due to their dependence on other adults for assistance in all aspects of life (Earles, 1998).

Outcomes for Students with High-Functioning Autism

Although a growing number of students with high-functioning autism are attending college, a study conducted by Lord and Venter (1991) indicated that only 1 of 18 study participants graduated with a college diploma. Indicating more promising outcomes, a study conducted by Szatmari, Bartolucci, and Bremner (1989) found that 7 of 16 study participants with high-functioning autism were college graduates.

Outcomes for Students with Asperger Syndrome

The postschool outcomes for students with Asperger's disorder are unclear as preliminary research is currently being conducted. Employment options for individuals with Asperger's disorder are as numerous and varied as for individuals without disabilities. Some students with Asperger's disorder possess the skills necessary to compete in the workforce, while other students require more extensive supports, such as those provided in supported employment. **Supported employment** is placement in community-based jobs with support from a job coach or other trained professionals who identify and develop the supports required for the individual to

perform the duties of the job and to participate in workplace activities (Sitlington, Clark, & Kolstoe, 2006).

Frequently, adults with Asperger's disorder will gravitate to a job or profession that relates to their areas of special interest and they may become very proficient at this job. Self-employment is a promising employment option for some individuals with Asperger's disorder because it allows the individual to follow his own routine, focus on his primary areas of interest, requires fewer social interactions, and provides freedom from the typical rules—both open and hidden—that govern most work environments.

While many students with Asperger's disorder have the cognitive ability to be academically successful, anecdotal evidence suggests that these students are underrepresented in college and vocational schools (Bolick, 2001). This lack of representation may be due to several factors. First, possibly the most difficult aspect for students with Asperger's disorder to navigate in postsecondary institutions is the social requirements. Students may demonstrate difficulty getting along with their roommates, working on group projects, and dealing with issues such as dating, alcohol, and drugs. A second problematic element of the postsecondary environment is the structure, or lack thereof. Many students with Asperger's disorder demonstrate difficulties with organization, time management, and self-management. "In middle school and high school, structure, predictability, parental support, and (often) special education services compensated for the student's relative weakness in these executive functions" (Bolick, 2001, p. 176). However, many postsecondary institutions do not provide this type of support.

Transition Planning

The beginning step in addressing the transition needs of students with ASD is to view the process as continuous and ongoing, beginning at birth and continuing

SOCCSS WORKSHEET

Situation	
Who	What
When	Why

Options	Consequences	Choices

Strategies

Simulation Type	Simulation Outcomes

Follow-up

FIGURE 9–18 Example of SOCCSS Worksheet

Source: Myles, B. S., & Simpson, R. L. (2003). *Asperger syndrome: A guide for educators and parents* (2nd ed.). Austin, TX: Pro-Ed. Copyright 2003 by Pro-Ed Inc. Adapted with permission.

throughout the lifespan. The transition plan will change as student interests, skills, and aspirations develop (Sitlington, Clark, & Kolstoe, 2006). While it is sometimes difficult for parents and other IEP team members to focus on adult outcomes when students are young, it may be easier to analyze the numerous transitions that individuals make during their life (i.e., transition from early intervention services to early childhood special education, from home to preschool, from elementary school to middle school, and so on) and determine the skills necessary for the student to succeed in each of the current or immediately upcoming transitions. Providing students with skills necessary to be successful in early transitions will increase their likelihood of success during later transitions (Sitlington et al., 2000).

One challenge that students and their families face during transition planning is what to disclose about their disability, and to whom. While businesses and postsecondary institutions cannot ask if a prospective employee or student has a disability, they also cannot make the reasonable modifications that may lead to a successful college or on-the-job experience without this information. It is important for the individual with the disability to weigh the pros and the cons of disclosing such information. For the student entering the workforce, he and his guardians may want to consult with their local vocation counselor or job coach regarding disclosing his disability on job applications (Bolick, 2001). For the adolescent who is transitioning into a postsecondary institution, Bolick details several factors to consider:

- Will the student benefit from access to a "Learning Skills Center" or a similar service at college?
- Will modifications to course assignments, exams, and projects be necessary?
- Will the student require additional support (e.g., note taker, copies of professor's lecture notes, tape record lecture)?
- Will the student benefit from a specialized mentor or advisor, rather than a general academic advisor?
- Will the student benefit from a single room or housing in the "quiet dorm" as a means of addressing sensory or social challenges? (pp. 166–167)

Planning for the transition from school to adult life is extremely important for students with ASD. The transition process is particularly important for students with disabilities because of increased high school drop-out rates, high rates of unemployment and underemployment, and poor wages. In addition, students with ASD

demonstrate cognitive, social, communication, and behavioral characteristics that span the entire functional continuum. Therefore, the extent of planning, types of interagency linkages, and adult service options should be determined based upon the individual needs and interests of the student. Some students with ASD will have the interest and skills necessary to attend a postsecondary institution while another student may go straight into the workforce with the use of a job coach. The ultimate goal of the IEP team and the transition planning process should be a better quality of life for the student.

USE OF ALTERNATIVE THERAPIES FOR STUDENTS WITH AUTISM SPECTRUM DISORDERS

Many alternative therapies for ASD are unsupported by empirical research. Due to the severity and impact of the ASD diagnosis on the individual and their family, primary stakeholders may be willing to try unproven interventions that promise a cure. Despite their appeal and popularity with some parents and practitioners, sometimes research proves these interventions to be totally without merit and a waste of time and money.

Alternative therapies are sometimes called controversial therapies. However, the use of the term **controversial therapies** as applied to interventions for individuals with ASD does not necessarily mean that the intervention has shown limited success or may cause harm to the individual. The technique might also be termed controversial because it is relatively new and lacks an empirical research base. Further research will determine whether these controversial therapies are effective or not for children and youth with ASD. See Figure 9–19 for an abbreviated list of controversial therapies for individuals with ASD. Also see Box 9-1.

THE ROLE OF MEDICATION IN THE TREATMENT OF PERVASIVE DEVELOPMENTAL DISORDERS

There are no cures for autism, Asperger's disorder, or any of the other disorders discussed in this chapter. However, while prescription medications cannot cure ASD or alter the core social and communication characteristics of individuals with ASD, they are often prescribed to reduce the frequency and intensity of

BOX 9-1   Simpson Perspective

PERSPECTIVE: RICHARD L. SIMPSON Effective and Scientifically Supported Methods for Students with Pervasive Developmental Disorders

In spite of significant advancements in educating, treating, and understanding children and youth with pervasive developmental disorders (PDD) the disability remains an enigma. Indeed, individuals with autism-related disorders remain a significant mystery. The highly unique characteristics and multiple disabilities among individuals with PDD have also created significant debates related to causes of the disability and choices for intervention and educational strategies.

PDD is generally thought to be such a unique disability that persons diagnosed with the disorder require specialized intervention methods, curricula, and programs. There has been no shortage of novel specialized methods for students with PDD that purportedly provide benefit and there is a strong legacy of controversial and unproven methods used to educate, treat, and otherwise intervene with students with PDD. Controversial, in this context, is a reference to a method being untested. That is, calling a strategy or intervention approach "controversial" may be nothing more than a caveat for noting that it lacks scientific validation. Thus, alleged controversial methods may prove to be useful, or they may be found to lack utility.

The plethora of innovative and novel interventions and educational methods designed for persons with PDD has had both a positive and negative influence. On the one hand, novel interventions and treatments have effectively challenged and changed incorrect and unproductive notions and practices. In the 1960s and 1970s so-called controversial behavioral methods that challenged assumptions about basing programs for students with PDD on psychodynamic methods that highlighted interpersonal relationships believed to be caused by an absence of maternal warmth and caring clearly had a beneficial effect on the field and on countless students. In contrast, methods such as facilitated communication have had a detrimental effect on many persons with PDD.

Presently, there is a significant and strident debate over what constitutes an appropriate program for students with PDD. This debate is complicated by the fact that the PDD field is well known for its liberal tolerance toward unproven and controversial interventions and treatments. That a number of these purportedly effective methods have been determined to have neither empirical nor logical foundation is troubling. Moreover, many interventions and treatments commonly used with children and youth with PDD have not been thoroughly evaluated; and, even scientifically supported strategies such as applied behavior analysis are being investigated in relation to expected outcomes and methodological matters such as extensive and exclusive use.

That the list of interventions and treatments for students with PDD is rapidly increasing has further intensified the problem of professionals' and parents' ability to agree upon effective strategies. The juxtaposition of a highly diverse and misunderstood disability in combination with an ever-increasing number of well-hyped interventions that have not been tested or validated explains the treatment and intervention controversy in the PDD field.

The need for new and improved approaches that better serve children and youth with PDD is evident. Equally evident is the need for ongoing evaluation of purported interventions and treatments. This evaluation process is particularly important related to interventions, strategies, and programs that supposedly restore an individual with PDD to normalcy, or that significantly advance the development of skills, knowledge, and overall progress beyond that typically found with established effective practice methods.

Richard L. Simpson is professor of Special Education at the University of Kansas. He has authored numerous books, book chapters, and articles on EBD and autism, and serves as senior editor of the quarterly professional journal Focus on Autism and Other Developmental Disabilities.

Intervention	Rating of Intervention	Definition of Intervention	Appropriate Ages for Intervention	Suggested Cognitive Ability Level
Gentle Teaching (McGee, 1985)	Limited supporting information for practice	A philosophical approach that focuses on environmental and interpersonal factors to create bonded relationships	Any age	Severe cognitive impairment to average intelligence
Option Method (Son-Rise Program) (Kaufman, 1976)	Limited supporting information for practice	Utilizes behaviors of the child with PDD to establish a mutual connection and relationship	Any age	Severe cognitive impairment to average intelligence
FastForWord (Tallal & Merzenich, 1997)	Limited supporting information for practice	Computer program designed to remediate auditory problems by assisting in the development of fundamental auditory skills needed for language and reading success	School-age	Mild to average intelligence
Auditory Integration Training (Edelson, 1995)	Limited supporting information for practice	An intensive 30-day training protocol designed to remediate deficits in sound sensitivity and auditory-processing deficits	Preschool– adulthood	Severe cognitive impairment to average intelligence
Glutein Casien Intolerance (Reichelt et al., 1990)	Limited supporting information for practice	The removal of glutein (wheat products, among many others) and casein (a protein found in cow's milk) from diet	All ages	Severe cognitive impairment to average intelligence

(continued)

FIGURE 9–19   Examples of Alternative Therapies

Megavitamin Therapy (Rimland, Callaway, Dreyfus, 1978)	Limited supporting information for practice	Based on the premise that PDD may be related to biochemical errors; thus, megavitamin supplements are given to prevent nutritional deficiencies that may impact perception, information processing, and sensory integration	All ages	All intellectual abilities
Holding Therapy (Welch, 1988)	Not recommended	Based on the premise that intense physical and emotional contact will repair the broken caregiver bond needed for normal development	Birth to age 10	Average to above-average intelligence
Facilitated Communication (Biklen, 1990)	Not recommended	Developed as an augmentative communication method where nonverbal individuals are provided light physical support to type their verbal communication	All ages	Severe cognitive impairment to average intelligence

Source: Adapted from Simpson, R. L., deBoer-Ott, S., Griswold, D., Myles, B. S., Byrd, S. et al. (2005). *Autism Spectrum disorders: Interventions and treatments for children and youth.* Thousand Oaks, CA: Corwin Press.

FIGURE 9–19   Examples of Alternative Therapies (continued)

symptoms associated with the disorder (Simpson & Zionts, 2000; Tsai, 2001). According to Tsai (2001), examples of associated affective and behavioral symptoms of ASD for which psychotherapeutic medications may be prescribed include agitation, anxiety, mood instability, hyperactivity, impulsiveness, aggression, self-injury, and repetitive, stereotypic, and compulsive behaviors.

Medications may also be used to address other disorders that may co-occur with ASD. As mentioned previously, approximately 25% of adolescents with ASD, particularly autistic disorder, experience seizures (APA, 2000). Because of this vulnerability, doctors often prescribe anticonvulsants and antiepileptic drugs.

Psychotherapeutic medications can have a great impact on health and behavior and therefore must be considered as a viable treatment option for students with

ASD. It is imperative, however, to understand that there are no cures for ASD and therefore medication therapy should be used to support many other interventions (Simpson & Zionts, 2000) that were discussed previously in this chapter.

CHAPTER SUMMARY

- This chapter provided an overview of the five disorders that fall under the category of pervasive developmental disorders in the DSM-IV-TR. Autistic disorder—or autism—is a neurological disorder with onset before age 3. Autism is characterized by deficits in social interaction and communication skills, as well as restricted, repetitive, or stereotypical activities and interests. While symptoms may fall on a spectrum from mild to severe, approximately half of the students with autism have significant cognitive impairments and do not develop spoken language. Rett's Disorder is a progressive neurological disorder in girls that causes loss of previously gained skills, particularly purposeful hand movements. Childhood disintegrative disorder is similar in appearance to autism; however, CDD occurs after at least two years of normal development, but prior to age 10. Regression of skills may follow several different patterns. Asperger's disorder—or Asperger syndrome—is a developmental disorder with qualitative impairments in social interactions and unusual or restricted interests and activity patterns. Some consider it to be a mild or high-functioning form of autism. Students with Asperger's disorder typically do not experience significant delays in communication or cognition. Pervasive developmental disorders not otherwise specified (ASD-NOS) includes children with atypical autism or those who meet some, but not all, of the criteria for autism.

- Many students with pervasive developmental disorders also experience sensory impairments or unusual responses to sensory stimuli.

- Classroom interventions for students with ASD must be individualized for each child; however, some strategies have been found successful with these students. Academic strategies include discrete trial instruction, priming, assignment modifications, and graphic organizers. Students with ASD benefit from a highly structured and predictable classroom environment. Strategies include classroom organization, visual supports, activity-completion signals, waiting supports, choice-making opportunities, cue cards, and home base. Alternative communication systems and social interventions are also necessary for many students with ASD.

CHECK YOUR UNDERSTANDING

1. Why is autism referred to as a spectrum disorder?
2. *True or False*. Historically, Rett's disorder has only been reported in females.
3. What is the fundamental characteristic associated with Rett's Disorder?
4. What is the main difference between autistic disorder and childhood disintegrative disorder?

5. What are two main ways of differentiating autistic disorder and Asperger's disorder?
6. *True or False*. Applied behavior analysis and discrete trial instruction are the same; therefore, the terms can be used interchangeably.
7. List the five components of a discrete trial.
8. What are the benefits of using a visual schedule for a student with ASD?
9. Define theory of mind and describe its impact on students with pervasive developmental disorders.
10. List five controversial therapies and a definition for each.

APPLICATION ACTIVITIES

1. Use the vignette at the beginning of this chapter to answer the following questions:

   a. Cannon is trying to communicate a variety of messages through his behavior. What are they?

   b. What strategies could be put in place to assist Cannon in being successful in his current educational setting?

2. Using case study #3 in Appendix A, complete the following activities individually or in small groups:

   a. Review the case study and identify student characteristics that are consistent with a diagnosis of Asperger's disorder. Identify and operationally define a target behavior that is interfering with his academic success.

   b. Decide on a system of positive behavioral supports and environmental modifications to implement for this student.

3. Using case study #3 in Appendix A, or a child you have observed in a classroom setting, identify a social behavior that could appropriately be addressed using one of the strategies introduced in this chapter (SOCCSS, social stories, social autopsies). Develop a lesson plan or script for implementing the strategy with your student.

4. Using case study #3 in Appendix A, develop a list of accommodations that can used to address the student's difficulties in completing written tasks and his problems with work completion.

10

ANXIETY AND MOOD DISORDERS

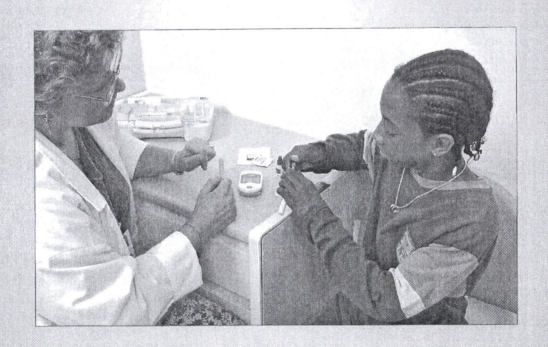

CHAPTER PREVIEW

CONNECTING TO THE CLASSROOM: *A Vignette*

Renee is a quiet 10-year-old in fifth grade, referred to the school-based team by Ms. Andrews, the middle school nurse. Renee initially appeared in the nurse's office complaining of a recurrent rash on her face, neck, and arms. The rash did not appear to be measles or chicken pox. Renee did not have a fever or other symptoms of illness, and reported that she did not feel sick, just itchy. After reviewing Renee's health files and finding she had no known allergies, Ms. Andrews contacted Renee's mother, who agreed to take her to the pediatric walk-in clinic at the local mall. Renee's pediatrician examined her, ruled out infectious illness, and determined the rash was not serious. The doctor suggested a topical over-the-counter gel to reduce itching and asked Renee's mother to keep a log of her daughter's activities, including what she ate, and when the rash appeared.

Over the next two weeks, Renee continued to attend school, and continued to have the rash intermittently. Ms. Smith, Renee's teacher, noticed that the rash appeared to become more evident during times of stress, such as before a test or when Renee was asked to read aloud. Renee also appeared increasingly distracted and unfocused in the classroom; her grades began to reflect her difficulty staying on task or completing assigned independent work in a reasonable amount of time. Ms. Smith again sent Renee to Ms. Andrews, who conducted a more extensive interview and found that Renee had other physical complaints as well, including a tight chest, lightheadedness, trouble concentrating, and difficulty falling asleep. When Ms. Andrews asked if Renee ever felt really worried about anything, Renee disclosed that her father was a laborer who often was out of work. She also reported that her parents argued constantly about money. Renee was convinced that they were going to get divorced, that she was going to have to move back to her mother's hometown, change schools, and lose all her friends. Now, because she had this unexplained rash and her grades were dropping, Renee's parents were also arguing about her. Renee was convinced that if they did split up, it would be her fault. She said she couldn't stop worrying about it, even when she tried.

Ms. Andrews again spoke with the school team concerning Renee. The student-assistance team asked Ms. Andrews and the school counselor to speak with Renee's parents, and to share educational fact sheets concerning anxiety and stress management. The counselor also planned to ask Renee's parents to sign an informed consent for her to speak with Renee's pediatrician. The team suggested that Renee join a weekly peer support group after school, with parent permission. They also agreed that, if the symptoms persisted for another 30 days, they would refer Renee for special education evaluation.

OVERVIEW OF ANXIETY AND MOOD DISORDERS

While it is not uncommon for children and youth to experience anxiety and to feel sad or unhappy occasionally, those who experience these feelings in an intense or chronic fashion may suffer from a treatable anxiety or mood disorder. The National Institute of Mental Health (2001a) found that **anxiety disorders** are the most common mental illnesses in America, and estimate that more than 19 million Americans are affected by anxiety disorders each year. (See Figure 10–1.) Although most studies have involved only adults, the U.S. Department of Health and Human Services' *Mental Health: A Report of the Surgeon General* (1999) estimates that 13% of all children and adolescents also experience these anxiety disorders. **Mood disorders** (sometimes called affective disorders) are also fairly common in school-aged children and youth, although young people with depression and bipolar disorder may experience different symptoms than adults with the same diagnoses.

Anxiety and mood disorders have both short- and long-term negative impacts on work or school, social life, and family functioning (Kennedy & Schwab, 2002). Children with these disorders may not be the most obvious referrals for special education because their behaviors tend to be internalizing or self-directed, rather than disruptive. However, students with anxiety and mood disorders may be reluctant to attend school,

be so consumed with worrying or compulsive thoughts that they cannot concentrate, or have difficulty developing satisfactory peer relationships. Students with untreated anxiety disorders also may have repeated school absences or may drop out, experience low self-esteem, experiment with drugs and alcohol, and continue to suffer from anxiety disorder in adulthood (Substance Abuse and Mental Health Services Administration, 2003b). Students with untreated mood disorders are at higher risk for school and social problems, and have an increased risk of suicide.

This chapter will describe the anxiety and mood disorders most common in children, as well as other mental health disorders occurring in young people that respond to similar intervention strategies. The diagnostic labels used in this chapter are those used in the American Psychiatric Association's *Diagnostic and Statistical Manual of Mental Disorders, Fourth Edition, Text Revision* (2000), hereafter referred to as DSM-IV-TR. (See Figure 10–2 for a list of anxiety-related diagnostic categories with brief descriptions and Figure 10–3 for a visual overview of the anxiety-related disorders covered in this chapter.) These diagnoses require a clinical assessment performed by a mental health professional, most often a child psychiatrist. While DSM-IV-TR labels are useful for discussing common behaviors and characteristics that students in the special education classroom may exhibit, they do not directly correspond to any of the categories of special education provided in the Individuals with Disabilities Education Act (IDEA, 1997). That is, having one (or more) DSM-IV-TR diagnosis does not guarantee that a student will be eligible for special education and related services under IDEA. As described in Chapter 2, districts may consider independent or external clinical evaluations and diagnoses as part of the decision-making process, but must make a separate determination of the child's eligibility and need for special education services based on IDEA criteria. Students with mental health diagnoses may qualify for IDEA special education services under the categories of emotional/behavioral disorders, learning disabilities, or other health impaired; alternatively, they may need general education accommodations and modifications under Section 504 of the Rehabilitation Act. Others whose symptoms are in remission or manageable with treatment and medication will be able to function in the classroom with monitoring.

This chapter will discuss criteria and characteristics of common anxiety and mood disorders, then provide strategies for addressing affective issues in school settings.

	Percent	Population Estimate* (Millions)
Any Anxiety Disorder	13.3	19.1
Panic Disorder	1.7	2.4
Obsessive-Compulsive Disorder	2.3	3.3
Post-Traumatic Stress Disorder	3.6	5.2
Any Phobia	8.0	11.5
Generalized Anxiety Disorder	2.8	4.0

*Based on 7/1/98 U.S. Census resident population estimate of 143.3 million age 18–54.

FIGURE 10–1   Anxiety Disorders One-Year Prevalence (Adults)

Source: National Institute of Mental Health. (2001a). *Facts about anxiety disorders.* Bethesda, MD: Author.

Acute Stress Disorder is characterized by symptoms similar to those of Posttraumatic Stress Disorder that occur immediately in the aftermath of an extremely traumatic event.

Agoraphobia is anxiety about, or avoidance of, places or situations from which escape might be difficult (or embarrassing) or in which help may not be available in the event of having a Panic Attack or panic-like symptoms.

Agoraphobia Without History of Panic Disorder is characterized by the presence of Agoraphobia and panic-linked symptoms without a history of unexpected Panic Attacks.

Anxiety Disorder Due to a General Medical Condition is characterized by prominent symptoms of anxiety that are judged to be a direct physiological consequence of a general medical condition.

Anxiety Disorder Not Otherwise Specified is included for coding disorders with prominent anxiety or phobic avoidance that do not meet criteria for any of the specific Anxiety Disorders defined in this section (or for anxiety symptoms about which there is inadequate or contradictory information).

Generalized Anxiety Disorder is characterized by at least 6 months of persistent and excessive anxiety and worry.

Obsessive-Compulsive Disorder is characterized by obsessions (which cause marked anxiety or distress) and/or by compulsions (which serve to neutralize anxiety).

Panic Attack is a discrete period in which there is the sudden onset of intense apprehension, fearfulness, or terror, often associated with feelings of impending doom. During these attacks, symptoms such as shortness of breath, palpitations, chest pain or discomfort, choking or smothering sensations, and fear of "going crazy" or losing control are present.

Panic Disorder Without Agoraphobia is characterized by recurrent unexpected Panic Attacks about which there is persistent concern. **Panic Disorder With Agoraphobia** is characterized by both recurrent unexpected Panic Attacks and Agoraphobia.

Posttraumatic Stress Disorder is characterized by the reexperiencing of an extremely traumatic event accompanied by symptoms of increased arousal and by avoidance of stimuli associated with the trauma.

Reactive Attachment Disorder of Infancy or Early Childhood* is markedly disturbed and developmentally inappropriate social relatedness in most contexts that begins before age 5 years old and is associated with grossly pathological care.

Selective Mutism* is the persistent failure to speak in specific social situations (e.g., school, with playmates) where speaking is expected, despite speaking in other situations.

Separation Anxiety* is excessive anxiety concerning separation from the home or from those to whom the person is attached.

Social Phobia is characterized by clinically significant anxiety provoked by exposure to certain types of social or performance situations, often leading to avoidance behavior.

Specific Phobia is characterized by clinically significant anxiety provoked by exposure to a specific feared object or situation, often leading to avoidance behavior.

Substance-Induced Anxiety Disorder is characterized by prominent symptoms of anxiety that are judged to be a direct physiological consequence of a drug of abuse, a medication, or toxin exposure.

---

*Categorized by APA under "Disorders Usually First Diagnosed in Infancy, Childhood, or Adolescence."

FIGURE 10–2 Anxiety-Related Disorders

Source: American Psychiatric Association. (2000). *Diagnostic and statistical manual of mental disorders* (4th ed., text revision). Washington, DC: American Psychiatric Association. Reprinted with permission from the *Diagnostic and Statistical Manual of Mental Disorders,* Copyright 2000. American Psychiatric Association.

ANXIETY DISORDERS

As Figures 10-2 and 10-3 illustrate, the term *anxiety disorders* includes a number of diagnostic categories with distinct characteristics. This section will describe those conditions most often observed in school-age children: generalized anxiety disorder, obsessive-compulsive disorder, post-traumatic stress disorder, reactive attachment disorder, separation anxiety disorder, social phobia, and selective mutism.

Generalized Anxiety Disorder (GAD)

While a certain amount of anxiety is a normal part of living and may be developmentally appropriate or even useful at certain times, anxiety or fears that are persistent

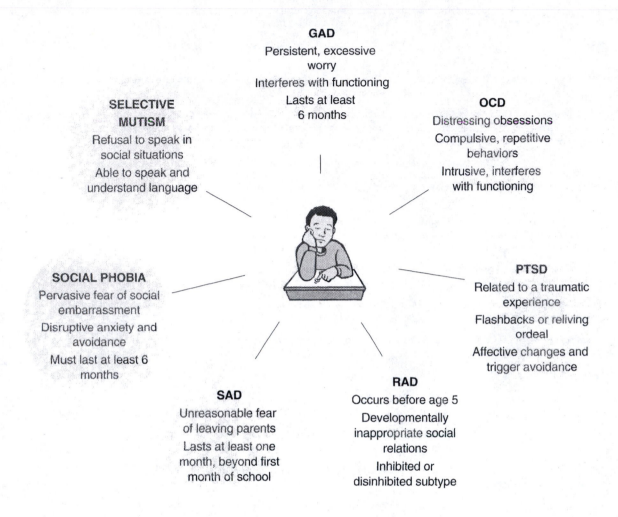

GAD
Persistent, excessive worry
Interferes with functioning
Lasts at least 6 months

SELECTIVE MUTISM
Refusal to speak in social situations
Able to speak and understand language

OCD
Distressing obsessions
Compulsive, repetitive behaviors
Intrusive, interferes with functioning

SOCIAL PHOBIA
Pervasive fear of social embarrassment
Disruptive anxiety and avoidance
Must last at least 6 months

PTSD
Related to a traumatic experience
Flashbacks or reliving ordeal
Affective changes and trigger avoidance

SAD
Unreasonable fear of leaving parents
Lasts at least one month, beyond first month of school

RAD
Occurs before age 5
Developmentally inappropriate social relations
Inhibited or disinhibited subtype

FIGURE 10–3   Anxiety Disorders Overview

and interfere with an individual's ability to function may be signs of an anxiety disorder. For example, being concerned about a big test tomorrow may influence Adrienne to stay home tonight and study harder; as a result she might end up with a higher grade. However, being so worried about the test that she cannot concentrate or remember what she has read, cannot sleep the night before, and throws up right before taking the test is probably not helpful. **Generalized anxiety disorder (GAD)**, according to DSM-IV-TR (APA, 2000), is characterized by excessive anxiety or worry about several things, often everyday occurrences, over a period of at least 6 months. Additional symptoms (one of which is required

for a diagnosis of GAD in children) are: restlessness, continual fatigue, difficulty concentrating, irritability, muscle tension, and disturbed sleep. Although individuals with GAD, especially children, may not recognize their anxiety as being "excessive," they usually will describe some level of concern about being unable to control their worrying, or about the resulting impact on their schoolwork or functioning level. Children and adolescents with anxiety tend to be preoccupied with the quality of their schoolwork, their performance in sports, or their friendships (American Academy of Child and Adolescent Psychiatry, 2000; APA, 2000). They may be pessimistic and exhibit somatic complaints: "Children and adolescents with this disorder usually anticipate the worst and often complain of fatigue, tension, headaches, and nausea" (National Alliance for the Mentally Ill, 2006a, p. 1). Anxious students also may be concerned with the teacher's opinion of them, seeking constant reassurance, or be very compliant and eager to please (AACAP, 2000).

Prevalence. The National Institute of Mental Health (2000b) estimates the one-year prevalence of GAD in the United States at 4 million. According to the U.S. Department of Health and Human Services (NIMH, 1999a), that means that 3.5% to 4.0% of the general population meet the criteria for GAD in any one year, making it one of the most frequent diagnoses in primary care. Experts estimate that prevalence rates for children and adolescents are similar to those for adults (Schlozman, 2002b).

Etiology and Risk Factors. While the etiology—or specific cause—of anxiety disorders is unknown, like most other mental health disorders, GAD is presumed to be a combination of individual biological characteristics and environmental stressors (NAMI, 2006a). A number of studies currently underway are exploring various potential biological causes of GAD. Research sponsored by the National Institute of Mental Health concerning biological factors and anxiety is focused on finding ways to increase the control of the cerebral cortex (the thinking part of the brain) over the amygdala (the part that manages the body's unconscious protective physiological response to fear) (NIMH, 1999a). Researchers have designed further studies to compare the effectiveness of pharmacological and cognitive behavioral therapies on anxiety disorder symptoms. Additional research is being conducted into the role of neurotransmitters and other brain chemicals, and of the body's various hormone levels on anxiety.

Although this extensive research effort appears promising, no direct causal link has been found that explains anxiety disorders; however, considerably more is known concerning biological and environmental factors that predict development of anxiety disorders. The National Epidemiology Study (Eaton et al., 2004) reviewed a number of published studies and found the most significant risk factors for GAD included being female, having poor educational attainment, and parental alcohol abuse, with an increased odds ratio (OR) of approximately 2.0 to 2.7. This means that an individual with one or more of these risk factors would have a 2.0 to 2.7 times greater chance of being diagnosed with GAD than someone without these characteristics.

In the same meta-analysis, cigarette smoking was also identified as a significant predictor for GAD (OR = 5.53). However, although cigarette smoking has been *associated* with anxiety disorders, and a higher proportion of individuals with anxiety disorders are smokers, a *cause-effect* relationship has not been established. In fact, it appears that there may be a chicken-and-egg process at work. That is, adolescents with emerging symptoms of anxiety disorders may use cigarette smoking, drinking, or other forms of self-medication as a coping mec hanism to take the edge off their anxiety or to manage their feelings.

Obsessive-Compulsive Disorder (OCD)

Careful organization and scrupulous attention to detail are skills that we teach young people to help them learn to organize the growing complexity of their lives. We should not confuse [OCD] with normal levels of obsessive behavior that characterize specific developmental stages or with the behavior of a particularly scrupulous and compulsive—yet relatively happy—individual. (Schlozman, 2002c, p. 96)

Students with **obsessive-compulsive disorder (OCD)** experience persistent and intrusive thoughts and feel driven to perform ritualistic, often purposeless tasks. One of the challenges in the diagnosis of OCD is to differentiate between clinically significant symptoms and developmental or personal characteristics that may actually be functional, such as attention to detail, desire for order, or intense focus on an area of interest or study. Many young people are particularly concerned about the way their room is organized, or the way their hair looks. Others may have a hobby (e.g., collecting baseball cards) that friends and family members regard as an obsession. However, for a student to be diagnosed with OCD, she must have obsessions or compulsions that are excessive or unreasonable, that consume at least an hour a day, and that interfere with her ability to function in everyday academic or social situations.

The DSM-IV-TR (APA, 2000) defines obsessions and compulsions as follows: "**Obsessions** are persistent ideas, thoughts, impulses, or images that are experienced as intrusive and inappropriate and that cause marked anxiety or distress" (p. 457). The most common obsessive patterns concern ordering things, worrying about cleanliness, having self-doubts, experiencing recurring aggressive or horrific thoughts, or visualizing sexual images. "**Compulsions** are repetitive behaviors (e.g., hand washing, ordering, checking) or mental acts (e.g., praying, counting, repeating words silently) the goal of which is to prevent or reduce anxiety or distress, not to provide pleasure or gratification" (p. 457). The person with OCD feels driven to perform compulsive behaviors or rituals to reduce anxiety related to an obsession, or to prevent some feared event. "However, they are either not connected in a realistic way with what they are intended to prevent or neutralize, or are clearly excessive" (Eaton et al., 2004, OCD section, para. 1).

While adults with OCD generally realize their obsessions are unwarranted or unreasonable, young people with the disorder may lack the maturity and cognitive ability to recognize this. Figure 10–4 provides classroom vignettes illustrating obsessive-compulsive patterns.

Like other anxiety-related disorders, OCD can interfere with both the academic and social aspects of school. Obsessive thoughts and compulsive behaviors are very intrusive and time-consuming; therefore, they can significantly hamper learning by interfering with concentration and persistence. Schoolwork often is affected negatively as the student becomes an increasing perfectionist about assignments, or so distracted by the obsessive thoughts and time-consuming compulsive behaviors that she literally doesn't have time to complete her schoolwork. Avoidance of objects or situations that trigger OCD behavior can also restrict the child's ability to function in school or in community activities (e.g., scouting, church, sports).

Because children with OCD may not understand the reasons for their obsessions and compulsions, they often feel embarrassed, different from their peers, and may believe that they are "going crazy" (NAMI, 2006b, para. 6).

Children and adolescents are more likely to involve parents and others in their compulsive rituals than

Joan's obsession is ordering. Her compulsion is to rearrange or count objects, often repeatedly. When she first enters the classroom in the morning, she walks around the perimeter straightening things. Joan's desk has to be in precisely the same position every day, with the legs on a specific place on the tiled floor. Joan cannot begin classwork until she has inspected and arranged her materials on the desk. Pencils must be sharpened to a perfect point. She throws them away when the eraser starts wearing down. Her paper must be clean and free of spots or wrinkles; Joan refuses to use spiral-bound paper because she cannot tolerate the ragged edge. She often spends so much time getting everything set up that she does not have time to do the assignment.

Bobby's obsession is cleanliness, and his compulsion involves hand washing and cleaning things. He fears that he will contract cancer and die from being contaminated by germs on things other people have touched. Even though several people have explained to him that you do not get cancer from germs, he needs to wash his hands every time he touches something another person has handled (e.g., every time papers are passed out). Bobby wants to wear gloves at recess, even in good weather, to protect him from germs on the ball or on the swings. Before using the computer in the classroom, he has to clean the keyboard and mouse off with a disposable sanitary wipe. Bobby's hands are often chapped and raw from frequent use of soap and water, but if he is not allowed to wash them, he becomes increasingly agitated and eventually throws a tantrum.

Graciella is an anxious perfectionist whose obsession relates to self-doubts. Her compulsions are to request or demand reassurance from adults, perform frequent and repeated self-checks, and to demand that her classwork be 100% accurate. During independent seatwork, Graciella wants the teacher to check her work after every problem. When the teacher is busy, she may wait for a minute or two, but Graciella becomes increasingly agitated, fidgets with her materials, and begins twisting her hair. Her mother says she sees the same pattern at home, and has to stay with Graciella providing constant feedback if she wants her to complete her homework. If Graciella makes an error on a paper, she either erases the mistake so violently that the paper rips, or wads it up and starts over. She refuses to hand in a paper that is not perfect, and consequently rarely hands anything in. Although Graciella's IEP provides for accommodations during standardized testing, including individualized administration and frequent breaks, she often becomes ill the day of the test and performs significantly below her observed ability level, partly because she refuses to guess on items she does not know.

Victor has recurrent horrific thoughts about his parents dying violently. He copes by avoiding triggers (e.g., watching the television or reading the newspaper) and performing ritualistic acts that he believes will prevent his parents from coming to harm. After seeing the September 11th news coverage of the terrorist attacks, he became convinced that his parents would be killed by terrorists at work. Victor's protective ritual includes saying "I love you" to both parents before leaving the house each morning, and walking precisely the same route to school each day. On his way to school, he avoids stepping on the cracks in the sidewalk, taking exactly two steps per square (left foot, then right), and counting each step he takes. If something distracts him or he loses count, he has to go home and start over. During the school day, when his negative thoughts frequently intrude, Victor closes his eyes and says a protective prayer.

FIGURE 10–4 Classroom OCD Vignettes

adults with OCD: "They may insist that their laundry be washed multiple times, demand that parents check their homework repeatedly, or become outraged if household items are in disarray" (NAMI, 2006b, para. 10). Parents may feel guilty and responsible for the child's OCD, if there is a familial pattern of the disorder. On the other hand, if they are unfamiliar with OCD or anxiety disorders, parents may feel embarrassed, confused, frustrated, or angered by their child's bizarre behavior. Some adults minimize the symptoms of OCD as a "phase" the child is going through. If the OCD symptoms appear early (e.g., at age 3 or 4), they are particularly likely to be overlooked by parents and caregivers.

Prevalence. According to the National Institute of Mental Health (2001c), OCD is the fourth most common mental disorder, with a one-year prevalence of approximately 2.3% of the U.S. population ages 18 to 54. The National Alliance for the Mentally Ill estimates that 1 million children and adolescents in the United States have OCD: "This can mean three to five youngsters with OCD per average-sized elementary school and about 20 teenagers in a large high school" (2006b, para. 2). Some variation in the prevalence rate is due to underreporting of symptoms; being secretive is part of the disorder. Additionally, many other disorders have similar characteristics (e.g., anxiety and PTSD) and behaviors (e.g., compulsive gambling and anorexia), making the initial diagnosis of OCD difficult.

OCD can be comorbid with depression, panic disorder, and substance abuse (sometimes as self-medication to numb anxiety). Individuals with OCD may have co-occurring personality disorders as well. A fairly high percentage (35% to 50%) of individuals with Tourette's disorder also have a diagnosis of OCD. Conversely, only 5% to 7% of those with OCD have full-blown Tourette's, although as many as 20% to 30% have a history of tics (APA, 2000; Spengler & Jacobi, 1998). (See Chapter 11 for a more extensive description of Tourette's disorder.)

In childhood, OCD is more common in boys; however, in adulthood, the rates among males and females are relatively even. OCD symptoms typically begin in childhood or adolescence. Rapoport (1990) indicates that 30% to 50% of adults with OCD reported childhood onset. The National Institute for Mental Health (1999b) estimates that OCD costs the United States $8.4 billion per year in social and economic losses.

Etiology and Risk Factors. OCD appears to have a genetic component, since prevalence rates are higher in first-degree relatives (i.e., parents and their biological offspring) than in the general population. The biological etiology of OCD is becoming more clear, as neuro-imaging studies (e.g., PET scans) have revealed abnormalities in specific parts of the brain of individuals with OCD, including the frontal lobes of the cerebral cortex, the basal ganglia, the striatum, and the circuits connecting those regions of the brain (NIMH, 1999b; NIMH, 2001c; U.S. Department of Health and Human Services, 1999).

There may be an autoimmune disorder connection for a small group of children who experience sudden onset of OCD symptoms or tics immediately after having streptococcal infections (e.g., scarlet fever or strep throat). These symptoms are called PANDAS (pediatric autoimmune neuropsychiatric disorders associated with streptococcal infections). Arnold and Richter (2001) suggest the PANDAS immune response may interact with an underlying genetic predisposition to trigger OCD.

The National Epidemiology Study (Eaton et al., 2004) examined five longitudinal community-based studies to identify risk factors for OCD. Significant risk factors included cocaine and marijuana use, being female, not working for pay, prior history of psychiatric disorders, and history of depression or substance abuse. Some risk factors appeared related to age of onset: "Childhood conduct disturbances predicted OCD symptoms in early adolescence, childhood tics and early adolescent separation anxiety predicted the development of OCD symptoms in late adolescence, and tics and ADHD in late adolescence predicted more OCD symptoms in adulthood" (OCD section, para. 4). Race, age, stressors, and socioeconomic status also predicted OCD in one study conducted in the southeastern United States (Valleni-Basile et al., 1996). Masellis, Rector, and Richter (2003) found that comorbid depression was the greatest predictor of poor quality of life in individuals with OCD, with the second factor being severity of the persons' obsessions.

Post-Traumatic Stress Disorder (PTSD)

Post-traumatic stress disorder (PTSD) is a specific type of anxiety disorder that can develop after an individual is exposed to a terrifying event in which serious physical harm occurred or was threatened (APA, 2000; NIMH 2002). "Many people with PTSD repeatedly re-experience the ordeal in the form of flashback episodes, memories, nightmares, or frightening thoughts, especially when they are exposed to events or objects reminiscent of the trauma" (NIMH, 2002, Symptoms, para. 1). Children with PTSD may re-enact the trauma through their artwork or play (APA, 2000). Children may also have vague nightmares about the traumatic experience, without being able to recall or recount what frightened them. Some individuals with PTSD experience emotional numbing, feelings of detachment, or dissociation. Others may appear depressed, anxious, or irritable. Angry outbursts and feelings of intense guilt are also common among people with PTSD (NIMH, 2001b).

Individuals with PTSD will go to great lengths to avoid physical or sensory reminders that trigger their traumatic memories. This avoidance may result in a change in normal routines and activities, as well as distancing from specific people or situations.

In the classroom, children with PTSD may appear distracted or unable to concentrate. They may also exhibit hypervigilance (or extreme wariness) and an exaggerated startle response (APA, 2000).

Typically, signs of PTSD emerge within 3 months of the significant traumatic event, although some individuals may not experience them until years later.

Prevalence. The National Institute of Mental Health (2000c, 2001b, 2002) estimates that 5.2 million Americans experience PTSD in any given year, or about 3.6% of the population ages 18 to 54. More than twice as many women experience PTSD after experiencing trauma, compared to men who have similar experiences.

Etiology and Risk Factors. As with most DSM-IV-TR (APA, 2000) diagnostic conditions, PTSD seems to be caused by a combination of individual biological factors and environmental stressors. The biological basis of PTSD is an apparent malfunction in the body's own self-protective mechanism for dealing with potentially dangerous situations:

> Fear, an emotion that evolved to deal with danger, causes an automatic, rapid protective response in many systems of the body. It has been found that the fear response is coordinated by a small structure deep inside the brain, called the amygdala. The amygdala, although relatively small, is a very complicated structure, and recent research suggests that different anxiety disorders may be associated with abnormal activation of the amygdala. (NIMH, 2001b, p. 2)

Researchers are also looking at another part of the brain—the hippocampus—that appears to be different in some individuals with PTSD and may be responsible for short-term memory problems, intrusive memories, and flashbacks (NIMH, 2002).

In addition to activating specific parts of the brain, the body's automatic defenses produce natural chemicals to increase strength and stamina and to mask pain during times of extreme stress and physical danger. It appears that individuals with PTSD may continue to produce high levels of these natural chemicals even after the immediate danger has passed (NIMH, 2002).

Other hormones may be affected by high levels of stress as well. NIMH-sponsored biomedical research has found lower cortisol levels and higher levels of epinephrine and norepinephrine that may be responsible for the vivid and intense emotional memory storage in individuals with PTSD (NIMH, 2002).

The environmental predictors of PTSD include violent personal assaults including child abuse or mugging, natural or human-caused disasters, accidents, or military combat.

> Among those who may experience PTSD are military troops who served in the Vietnam and Gulf Wars; rescue workers involved in the aftermath of disasters like the terrorist attacks on New York City and Washington, DC; survivors of the Oklahoma City bombing; survivors of accidents, rape, physical and sexual abuse, and other crimes; immigrants fleeing violence in their countries; survivors of the 1994 California earthquake, the 1997 North and South Dakota floods, and hurricanes Hugo and Andrew; and people who witness traumatic events. (NIMH, 2001b, p. 1)

Not everyone who experiences a trauma, either as a victim or a witness, will develop PTSD. However, specific traumatic experiences greatly increase the likelihood of an individual developing PTSD. The National Epidemiology Study (Eaton et al., 2004) examined research assessing risk factors before and after a specific traumatic event, and predicting the risk of developing PTSD after exposure. The study found that the odds of developing PTSD are significantly increased for individuals with prior childhood abuse and neglect, with the average odds ratio (OR) ranging from 1.63 to 16.5 across various studies. That is, a victim of child abuse or neglect is between 1.63 and 16.5 times more likely to develop PTSD than someone without a history of abuse. The study also found that additional significant predictive factors for PTSD are prior anger problems, the injury or death of a close relative or friend in the event, the severity of injury, combat exposure, parental distress, and depressive symptoms immediately following trauma. Eaton and colleagues (2004) also found that certain kinds of thoughts and feelings immediately following trauma predict higher rates of PTSD, including avoidance, intrusive thoughts, emotional distress, anxiety, depression, dissociation, guilt, numbness, and disbelief or confusion.

Previous mental health diagnoses are also significant predictors of PTSD. A prior PTSD diagnosis increases the odds of another episode by a factor of 12.99, prior psychopathology by 7.86, and prior substance abuse or dependence by 1.7. Having survived sexual assault or a serious threat to life also increases the odds for PTSD.

For rescue workers, those who worked with burn victims, those who worked at the actual site of disaster, or those who were exposed to bodies at the site were more likely to develop PTSD. The educational level of the rescue worker appeared to mediate the risk, with a higher amount of education reducing the odds for PTSD.

Two studies found females more likely than males to develop PTSD in similar traumatic circumstances (OR = 4.8 in Daviss et al., 2000; OR = 3.64 in Frommberger et al., 1998). It appears that counseling or treatment immediately following the trauma improves the outcomes for individuals with PTSD (NIMH, 2002).

PTSD may co-occur with other anxiety disorders, depression, alcohol or drug abuse, sleep disturbances, and physical symptoms. In fact, NIMH (2001b) reports that doctors often treat individuals suffering from PTSD for their physical symptoms without realizing that an anxiety disorder is causing their illness. See Box 10-1 for more information.

Reactive Attachment Disorder (RAD)

Description and Major Features. The DSM-IV-TR (APA, 2000) describes **reactive attachment disorder (RAD)** as markedly disturbed and developmentally inappropriate social relatedness before the age of 5. RAD generally fits into two clinical patterns: (1) the inhibited subtype, in which attachment is absent, resulting in the child being withdrawn and unattached to caregivers; and (2) the disinhibited subtype, in which attachment is indiscriminate, resulting in the child being friendly and attaching to anyone, including strangers. Some children display a disorganized or ambivalent pattern of attachment, exhibiting a mixture of approach and avoidance behaviors. Regardless of the pattern, researchers have associated RAD symptoms with "grossly pathological care" (APA, 2000, p. 127) and have found symptoms in children who have been abused and neglected, as well as

BOX 10–1   Smith Perspective

PERSPECTIVE: AVIS SMITH, ACSW, LSCSW, LCSW
Guidelines for Educators Who Work with Children Who Have Histories of Abuse or Trauma

Students who have experienced abuse or trauma have difficulty with trust and boundaries. Children whose trust has been severely violated may act out aggressively by pushing, shoving, fighting, stealing, etc. At times they may re-enact the trauma or abuse through play or behavior with others. To encourage trust and good boundaries, use these strategies:

* Set clear, simple rules for classroom behavior based on respecting each other. (Involve students in rule setting.)
* Remind students of rules in a calm manner; include the reason for the rule (e.g., We don't hit because that hurts others).
* Keep your cool when these students act out. They will constantly test limits because they come from situations where the limits always change. It will take time and patience for them to trust that you *say what you mean and mean what you say*, and are not angry with them or going to hurt them.
* Talk with students who have broken rules privately. Do not embarrass them in front of peers. Have preset consequences for misbehavior that are appropriate but not harsh.
* Do not debate or argue with students. Later, when they are calm, provide choices for how they can repair relationships and/or property.

Children with histories of trauma and abuse often appear moody, depressed, anxious, aggressive, and preoccupied with control; their behavior looks manipulative. Remember that the students' inappropriate behavior was (and still may be) necessary for survival outside of the classroom. Help these students understand and label their feelings. Often, the only feeling they are aware of is *anger*. Help them understand that other feelings (hurt, sadness, fear) usually are underneath anger. Getting in touch with these feelings can aid students in taking responsibility for their behavior. The following strategies will provide a safe environment where students can learn to cope with and identify their feelings:

* Reflect feelings back to students; name the feeling and provide options for dealing with it. Drawing, hitting a pillow, crushing newspaper, journaling, writing, creating expressive art, or becoming involved in exercise or sports are positive options for dealing with overwhelming feelings.
* Provide a safe, predetermined place for students to go that will not result in punishment when they are overwhelmed with feelings.

Like children with attachment difficulties, some children with histories of trauma and abuse are so emotionally needy that they will follow anyone who is kind to them. Assist emotionally needy students by using the following strategies:

* Teach students appropriate boundaries in regard to their own physical space, their bodies, their belongings, and their feelings.
* Teach *assertive* social skills that provide a sense of safety and mastery.
* Help them learn that people will like them for who they are even if they say "no" to someone, or do not perform perfectly.

Children with histories of trauma often have shortened concentration and difficulty focusing; they may be diagnosed with attention deficit disorder (ADD or ADHD). Often, these children are preoccupied with a constant sense of danger, or are worrying about what is happening at home, etc. The following strategies will lessen anxiety and build student confidence and concentration:

* Give clear, simple, one-step directions. If you notice that children are off task, walk to their desk and speak quietly.
* Traumatized children often startle easily. Do not startle a child on purpose or allow other children to do so.
* Provide a "reduced stimulus area" in the classroom and allow *all children* access to it when needed.
* Post schedule changes and go over them with students. Change is difficult for many of these students.

Children with a history of trauma and abuse are often keenly aware of the needs of others but unaware of their own needs. They may be the straight-A students in your class. They may focus on helping others to their own detriment as a way of avoiding their own feelings. They may also try to be perfect so no one will suspect that anything is wrong. Be alert to those students who are involved in so many activities that they do not have time to rest or have fun.

Traumatized children/youth may avoid thinking about or remembering what happened by drinking or using drugs. Using substances can also be an attempt to reduce tension. These youth may exhibit other obsessive-compulsive behaviors, such as eating disorders, addiction to exercise, compulsive sexual behavior, etc. Remember that these behaviors are *symptoms* of the problem, not the problem itself.

Children with histories of trauma and abuse may experience disturbances in identity, memory, or consciousness: spacing out, becoming numb, having amnesia for certain events (sometimes seen as lying), or witnessing events as happening outside their bodies (depersonalization). Calmly orient these students to what has happened and aid them in taking responsibility for their actions. Children with these symptoms are candidates for mental health treatment.

Traumatized children sometimes engage in risk-taking behaviors, or show signs of self-harm or suicide. Always take signs of these behaviors seriously and seek outside supports.

Avis Smith is manager of prevention programs at Crittenton Behavioral Health in Kansas City, Missouri, and teaches in the graduate social work program at the University of Kansas.

in institutionalized children (e.g., those in foreign orphanages). Deprived of a nurturing or caring environment in the early years, these children often lack the basic nutrition and interactive social stimulation necessary for normal physical and mental development. According to the National Clearinghouse on Child Abuse and Neglect Information (2001):

> Each one of these children already may have suffered damage to their growing brains. Their brains may be locked into perceiving the world as a cold or dangerous place. They may have great difficulties responding to the caring concern of others. Because their brains' energies have been focused on survival, on meeting their own needs, these children may not have developed the physical, cognitive, social, and emotional capabilities one would expect of them. (p. 11)

Reber (1996) indicates that children with RAD may lack empathy, use limited eye contact, be cruel to siblings or animals, have poor impulse control, lack cause-effect thinking and conscience, develop abnormal speech patterns, or be inappropriately affectionate with strangers. In a study by Hall and Geher (2003), "children with RAD were rated significantly higher than non-RAD children on the dimensions of general behavior problems, social problems, withdrawal, somatic complaints, anxiety/ depression, thought problems, attention problems, delinquent behavior, and aggressive behavior" (p. 157). Hall and Geher round that children with RAD scored lower on empathy but higher on self-monitoring that non-RAD children, and suggest that children with RAD may be adjusting their behavior to present themselves in a more socially acceptable light to others.

Attachment problems, if not resolved, usually persist into adulthood and may result in ineffective coping styles. In a group of nonclinical female college students, Calamari and Pini (2003) found a coherent pattern among girls without secure attachments: "Self-reported anger is higher in insecure females, who are likely to develop a tendency to use dissociation as a coping style" (p. 298). These findings underscore the importance of early mental health and counseling interventions for children with attachment problems to prevent more serious adjustment problems later in life. See Figure 10–5

Social/Emotional	• Is superficially charming and engaging[3] • Expansive mood may mask low self-esteem or guilt[1] • Does not make eye contact[3] • Has poor peer relations[1,3] • Engages in persistent questions or incessant chatter[3] • Controlling (usually for self-gain)[1,3] • Is indiscriminately sociable or affectionate with strangers[2,3] • Is not appropriately affectionate with parents or caregivers[2,3] • Is hypervigilant or watchful[1,2] • Is inappropriately demanding or clingy[3]
Behavioral	• Engages in persistent lying, stealing, and other covert behaviors[1,3] • Is destructive to self, others, or objects[1,3] • Is cruel to animals or siblings[3] • Lacks impulse control[3] • Is distractible with shortened attention span under stress[1] • Hoards food or stuffs themselves[3] • Is preoccupied with fire, gore, or blood[3]
Developmental	• May experience developmental lags[3] • May have abnormal speech patterns[3] • Blames others, denies responsibility[1] • Sees self as victim, rationalizes hurtful behavior[1] • Lacks cause-and-effect thinking[3] • Lacks a conscience[3]

[1] Alston, n.d.
[2] APA, 2000
[3] Reber, 1996

FIGURE 10–5　Characteristics of Children with RAD

for a more exhaustive list of common social/emotional, behavioral, and developmental characteristics of RAD.

Prevalence. The DSM-IV-TR (APA, 2000) states: "Epidemiological data are limited, but reactive attachment disorder appears to be very uncommon" (p. 129). Not everyone in the fields of psychiatry and social welfare agrees with this assessment, citing a number of factors that might lead to underreporting of RAD, including: (a) large numbers of children with RAD symptoms in known high-risk groups; (b) possible caretaker bias; (c) relatively new and overly restrictive DSM-IV definition and classification criteria; and (d) lack of epidemiological research on RAD.

The National Adoption Center (cited in Reber, 1996) estimates that approximately one-half of adoptable children may have RAD symptoms, and studies of young children in institutional care reveal similarly high rates of attachment problems. For example, in a study examining the attachment behaviors of 61 young children in a Romanian orphanage, Zeanah, Smyke, and Dumitrescu (2002) compared toddlers in a "traditional" orphanage unit staffed by 20 individuals on rotating 8-hour shifts to those where four staff members were assigned to a group of 10 to 13 toddlers. They found that a majority (69%) of children on the traditional unit exhibited high levels of indiscriminate attachment behavior, while only 34% of the children in the "family-style" unit did. Behaviors identified as indiscriminate included failure to identify a preferred attachment figure, wandering off without checking back, lack of reticence with unfamiliar adults, and willingness to go off with a stranger. In a second study, Smyke, Dumitrescu, and Zeanah (2002) interviewed caregivers in the same Romanian orphanage, as well as parents of young children who had never been institutionalized in the same community. They again found many children with more serious attachment problems in the traditional orphanage unit than in the "family-style" unit or among toddlers living at home. Children in the traditional unit also had higher incidence of stereotypical behaviors (e.g., rocking back and forth), which was also associated with delays in communication.

Some researchers, including McKay (2003), have expressed concerns regarding caretaker or informant bias in diagnosing young children with RAD. That bias could lead caretakers to overreport or underreport symptoms based on factors not related to the child's actual behavior. Parents and foster parents may have limited experience with children of specific ages, not know what behaviors are developmentally appropriate, or simply not be concerned about clinically significant behaviors.

Teachers, on the other hand, have plenty of day-to-day experience with children, but only in the classroom setting, where they may not have observed the child's most significant attachment-related problems. Zeanah and Smyke (2003) suggest reducing biased evaluations by comparing information from several informants and using a combination of methods including questionnaires, semistructured interviews, and structured and unstructured observations. "Foster parents, like many caregivers, sometimes hesitate to identify child behavioral challenges because they do not want to be perceived as incompetent. Other foster parents may be preoccupied by the child's behavior and make attributions regarding behavior that do not derive exclusively from child characteristics" (Zeanah & Smyke, 2003, p. 1268).

The diagnosis of RAD is relatively new, and was first introduced to the American mental health classification system in the DSM-III published in 1980 (Boris & Zeanah, 1999). In the intervening 25 years, little research has been conducted to validate the definition and criteria of either the original DSM-III or the revised version introduced in DSM-IV. "We are far from a comprehensive understanding of attachment disorders—their behavioral manifestations, diagnoses, and treatments" (Wilson, 2001, p. 37). Some RAD researchers consider DSM-IV-TR criteria too restrictive and dispute the notion that children with RAD must conform to one of two diametrically opposed patterns that result from abuse and neglect. They have proposed an alternative definition that recognizes attachment problems that occur across a spectrum or continuum, without requiring demonstration of pathogenic care, which can be difficult to establish (Boris et al., 2004). Even within populations that are at high risk for RAD (e.g., children in state-ordered foster care), often it is difficult to prove the causal factor of neglect or abuse that is currently necessary for the diagnosis of RAD. Additionally, some RAD researchers feel the DSM-IV-TR (APA, 2000) criteria for RAD are overly restrictive because they do not reflect the past 25 years of research in the areas of child development and attachment theory: "If attachment disorders are defined by criteria derived from findings in attachment research, they become applicable to a broader range of children in severely disturbed relationships with their primary caregivers, rather than only to some children who have been physically abused or extremely deprived" (Zeanah, 1996, p. 43).

Etiology and Risk Factors. The DSM-IV-TR (APA, 2000) attributes RAD to pathological care during early childhood (i.e., abuse and neglect). In normal infant development, a mutually reinforcing pattern of behavior results in bonding or attachment between the child and its caregivers. When the infant's needs are not met because of abuse, neglect, separation from the parent, or inconsistent care, the development of trust needed to form a lasting attachment or bond is often missing (Wilson, 2001, p. 41). As a consequence, many of these children develop attachment problems, and some develop a clinically significant attachment disorder.

Separation Anxiety Disorder (SAD)

Description and Major Features. While most young children are excited about the prospect of going to school, some children are resistant (e.g., getting dressed slowly, missing the bus, complaining of vague physical illness that passes by midmorning) or refuse to go to school (e.g., won't get up or get dressed, scream and cry). Students who experience extreme or prolonged difficulty separating from parents may have **separation anxiety disorder (SAD)**. (See Figure 10-6.) The American Academy of Child and Adolescent Psychiatry (1998) points out that not wanting to go to school is most common in children ages 5 to 7 and 11 to 14, or at times of transition into a new situation or returning from a break (e.g., summer vacation). SAD may also be more common, and potentially overdiagnosed, in dangerous neighborhoods where there may be good

reasons to be concerned about waiting for the bus or walking to school (U.S. Department of Health and Human Services [HHS], 1999).

Children with SAD have an unreasonable fear of leaving their parents or going to school, and may:

* Feel unsafe staying in a room by themselves
* Display clinging behavior
* Display excessive worry and fear about parents or about harm to themselves
* Shadow the mother or father around the house
* Have difficulty going to sleep
* Have nightmares
* Have exaggerated, unrealistic fears of animals, monsters, burglars
* Fear being alone in the dark, or
* Have severe tantrums when forced to go to school (HHS, 1999, p. 1)

Children with SAD may fear for their parents' safety, experience headaches and stomachaches when forced to separate from them, and often want to sleep with their parents. Some students are fine once they get to school, because their anxiety is about leaving home or leaving the parent. Others continue to worry about their parents long after they are out of sight. To be clinically significant, SAD symptoms must persist for at least 1 month and extend beyond the first month of school,

---

A. Developmentally inappropriate and excessive anxiety concerning separation from home or from those to whom the individual is attached, as evidenced by three (or more) of the following:
  (1) recurrent excessive distress when separation from home or major attachment figures occurs or is anticipated
  (2) persistent and excessive worry about losing, or about possible harm befalling, major attachment figures
  (3) persistent and excessive worry that an untoward event will lead to separation from a major attachment figure (e.g., getting lost or being kidnapped)
  (4) persistent reluctance or refusal to go to school or elsewhere because of fear of separation
  (5) persistently and excessively fearful or reluctant to be alone or without major attachment figures at home or without significant adults in other settings
  (6) persistent reluctance or refusal to go to sleep without being near a major attachment figure or to sleep away from home
  (7) repeated nightmares involving the theme of separation
  (8) repeated complaints of physical symptoms (such as headaches, stomachaches, nausea, or vomiting) when separation from major attachment figures occurs or is anticipated
B. The duration of the disturbance is at least 4 weeks.
C. The onset is before age 18 years.
D. The disturbance causes clinically significant distress or impairment in social, academic (occupational), or other important areas of functioning.
E. The disturbance does not occur exclusively during the course of a Pervasive Developmental Disorder, Schizophrenia, or other Psychotic Disorder and, in adolescents and adults, is not better accounted for by Panic Disorder With Agoraphobia.

FIGURE 10–6 Diagnostic Criteria for Separation Anxiety Disorder

Source: American Psychiatric Association. (2000). *Diagnostic and statistical manual of mental disorders* (4th ed., text revision). Washington, DC: American Psychiatric Association. Reprinted with permission from the *Diagnostic and Statistical Manual of Mental Disorders,* Copyright 2000. American Psychiatric Association.

when many young children experience separation anxiety symptoms (APA, 2000).

The short-term negative effects of SAD are poor school attendance and performance, as well as social problems and impaired peer relationships if students are absent for a long period of time. Long-term effects of SAD may include development of anxiety and panic disorders in adulthood (AACAP, 1998). SAD also has a potentially negative effect on the parents' functioning if they are extremely worried about their child, or cannot pursue their own activities (Flood & Wilder, 2004).

The DSM-IV-TR (APA, 2000) indicates that depressed mood is common among children with SAD, as well as other coexisting anxiety disorders. A study examining the comorbidity of anxiety disorders in children 8 to 13 found that those with SAD as a primary diagnosis also had an increased number of specific phobias and functional enuresis (Verduin & Kendall, 2003).

Prevalence. Roughly 4% of children and adolescents have SAD (Schlozman, 2002b), with the numbers decreasing as the child matures (APA, 2000). Some variation in the reported prevalence may be related to lack of agreement between parents, or between parents and children, in reporting symptoms of SAD. A study conducted by Foley and colleagues (2004) found the agreement of mothers and children in separate interviews was poor, and between other informants was not better than chance, even when clinically significant SAD symptoms and impairment were present. The authors suggest that parent ratings of SAD may be inflated due to interactions between the child's characteristics (e.g., oppositional, temperamental) and their own issues (e.g., marital conflict). Therefore, evaluation of SAD must include data and reports from a variety of sources, not just subjective information gathered from parents.

Etiology and Risk Factors. There appears to be a familial pattern of SAD, as the disorder is more common among first-degree relatives than in the general population. SAD appears to be more prevalent in extremely close-knit families (APA, 2000; HHS, 1999), and may vary from culture to culture depending on the value the family places on interdependence (APA, 2000).

Social Phobia (Social Anxiety Disorder)

People with **social phobia** have a significant and persistent fear of embarrassment in situations involving social interactions or performance. The individual with social phobia exhibits anxious behaviors, which may take the form of a panic attack or avoidance. The fear, anxiety, and avoidance behaviors cause a significant disruption in the individual's routine, including school attendance, academic functioning, and peer relationships. The phobia may be generalized (i.e., fear of all social or performance situations) or restricted to a specific type of situation (e.g., formal public speaking in front of large groups).

Children under 18 must have symptoms for at least 6 months to be diagnosed with social phobia. According to DSM-IV-TR (APA, 2000), individuals with social phobia may also have the following associated features: "Hypersensitivity to criticism, negative evaluation or rejection; difficulty being assertive; and low self-esteem or feelings of inferiority" (p. 452). Students with social phobia may have poor social skills and be underachievers who have marked difficulty with test taking or classroom participation.

To some degree, the level of functional impairment may be related to the ability of the individual with social phobia to control her environment and avoid triggering situations. For example, school-aged children often are unable to escape the demands to perform since most classroom routines include reading aloud, answering questions in front of peers, participating in discussions, and taking tests. Therefore, a child or adolescent with social phobia might display more symptoms of the disorder than an adult whose job did not include performance demands that triggered anxiety.

Prevalence. DSM-IV-TR (APA, 2000) places the lifetime prevalence of social phobia in the 3% to 13% range. There is considerable variation in prevalence rates based on whether studies included individuals with generalized versus specific fears. It appears that between 10% and 20% of those in outpatient treatment for anxiety disorders have some degree of social phobia.

Etiology and Risk Factors. Like other anxiety disorders, there appears to be a genetic component in social phobia, particularly the generalized subtype, because it is more commonly observed in first-degree biological relatives than in the population at large (APA, 2000).

Selective Mutism

Selective mutism (formerly elective mutism) is the refusal to speak in social situations despite the ability to comprehend and produce language. It interferes with the student's ability to function both academically and socially. To meet the criteria for the DSM-IV-TR (APA, 2000) diagnosis of selective mutism, the disturbance must last for at least 1 month, and must persist beyond the first month of school, during which many students are shy and quiet. Often, children with selective mutism will speak at home with family members, but not at school with peers or teachers. Rather than talking, the student may use gestures to communicate her needs or to respond to questions (e.g., nodding or shaking her head, pointing, pushing, pulling). Some children will use limited speech, either speaking in an altered voice (e.g., whisper or monotone), or responding in monosyllables (e.g., yes, no, uh-huh, okay) (APA, 2000). In many students, selective mutism will dissipate after a few months; however, others may continue to exhibit the disorder for years, even into adulthood.

Selective mutism may co-occur with a communication disorder or mental retardation. Children with selective mutism also generally are diagnosed with another anxiety disorder, particularly social phobia (APA, 2000).

Prevalence. Selective mutism is a relatively rare condition that is often first identified in the school setting (Giddan, Ross, & Sechler, 1997). The APA (2000) estimates that it is found in fewer than 1% of individuals seen by mental health professionals and is slightly more common in females than in males. A recent Swedish study found selective mutism had a prevalence rate of 18 in 10,000 school children aged 7 to 15 years old (Kopp & Gillberg, 1997).

Etiology and Risk Factors. Selective mutism is an anxiety disorder, generally associated with excessive shyness. Research has not yet established a specific causal pattern for the disorder, although some children exhibit selective mutism after hospitalization or extreme psychosocial stressors (APA, 2000).

CHILD AND ADOLESCENT DEPRESSION

The Surgeon General's report on mental health (HHS, 1999) identifies reactive depression—or adjustment disorder with depressed mood—as the most common mood problem for children and adolescents. Adolescents frequently exhibit **reactive depression** in response to an unpleasant experience (e.g., a disappointment or loss, breaking up with a boyfriend). These sad feelings are transient and temporary, often lasting only a few hours or days. A change of activity may result in a rapid change from a depressed mood back to a normal affect. However, other school-aged children and youth may exhibit more severe or long-term symptoms consistent with mood disorders.

The most common clinically significant mood disorders experienced by children and youth are depression and bipolar disorder. The Surgeon General's report on mental health (HHS, 1999) cautions that "despite some similarities, childhood depression differs in important ways from adult depression" (p. 150).

As you can see in Figure 10–7, the DSM-IV-TR (APA, 2000) provides criteria for a number of mood disorders. Because of the clinical complexity of the diagnostic criteria, and their lack of relevance to most EBD classrooms, we will limit this section to a general discussion of depression and bipolar disorders, as they are manifested in school-aged children and adolescents. (See Figure 10–8 for a diagram representing the disorders discussed in this chapter. For specific diagnostic criteria for all of the mood disorders, see the DSM-IV-TR [APA, 2000, pp. 345–426].)

Depression

Children and adolescents with unipolar mood problems may be diagnosed either with dysthymic disorder (also called dysthymia) or major depressive disorder (generally called depression). This section will briefly describe the features of both conditions.

Dysthymic disorder is a mood disorder that is more persistent than the diagnosis of major depression, but with fewer symptoms. However, because dysthymia tends to be more chronic, it may interfere with the individual's long-term functioning and adjustment. The child with dysthymia may be sad most of the time for a period of years, sometimes for so long that she doesn't even recognize her mood as being depressed (HHS, 1999). Children with dysthymia may also have changes in their eating or sleeping habits, be tired, have low self-esteem, have difficulty concentrating or making decisions, and feel hopeless (APA, 1999). Approximately 10% of individuals initially diagnosed with dysthymia will go on to have at least one major depressive episode (APA, 2000).

Major Depressive Disorder The DSM-IV-TR (APA, 2000) criteria for **major depressive disorder** require that the mood disturbance be unipolar (i.e., not include manic, hypomanic, or mixed episodes). The symptoms of depression in children and adolescents include:

* Irritability, depressed mood, persistent sadness, frequent crying

Major Depressive Disorder is characterized by one or more Major Depressive Episodes (i.e., at least 2 weeks of depressed mood or loss of interest accompanied by at least four additional symptoms of depression).

Dysthymic Disorder is characterized by at least 2 years of depressed mood for more days than not, accompanied by additional depressive symptoms that do not meet criteria for a Major Depressive Episode.

Depressive Disorder Not Otherwise Specified is included for coding disorders with depressive features that do not meet criteria for Major Depressive Disorder, Dysthymic Disorder, Adjustment Disorder With Depressed Mood, or Adjustment Disorder With Mixed Anxiety and Depressed Mood (or depressive symptoms about which there is inadequate or contradictory information).

Bipolar I Disorder is characterized by one or more Manic or Mixed Episodes, usually accompanied by Major Depressive Episodes.

Bipolar II Disorder is characterized by one or more Major Depressive Episodes accompanied by at least one Hypomanic Episode.

Cyclothymic Disorder is characterized by at least 2 years of numerous periods of hypomanic symptoms that do not meet criteria for a Manic Episode and numerous periods of depressive symptoms that do not meet criteria for a Major Depressive Episode.

Bipolar Disorder Not Otherwise Specified is included for coding disorders with bipolar features that do not meet criteria for any of the specific Bipolar Disorders . . . (or bipolar symptoms about which there is inadequate or contradictory information).

Substance-Induced Mood Disorder is characterized by a prominent and persistent disturbance in mood that is judged to be a direct physiological consequence of a drug of abuse, a medication, another somatic treatment for depression, or toxin exposure.

Mood Disorder Not Otherwise Specified is included for coding disorders with mood symptoms that do not meet the criteria for any specific Mood Disorders and in which it is difficult to choose between Depressive Disorder Not Otherwise Specified and Bipolar Disorder Not Otherwise Specified (e.g., acute agitation).

FIGURE 10–7 Mood Disorders

Source: American Psychiatric Association. (2000). *Diagnostic and statistical manual of mental disorders* (4th ed., text revision). Washington, DC: American Psychiatric Association. Reprinted with permission from the *Diagnostic and Statistical Manual of Mental Disorders,* Copyright 2000. American Psychiatric Association.

* Thoughts of death or suicide
* Loss of enjoyment in favorite activities
* Frequent complaints of physical illnesses such as headaches or stomach aches
* Low energy level, fatigue, poor concentration, complaints of boredom
* Major changes in eating or sleeping patterns, such as oversleeping or overeating (AACAP, 2002a, p. 1)

In a series of recent studies, depressed high school students reported being less popular and having fewer friends, and described their peer relationships as being less than ideal. They spent less time exercising or working on homework than their nondepressed peers, and consequently had lower grade point averages (GPA). Conversely, students who exercised more had better parental relationships, were less depressed, used fewer drugs, and had higher GPAs (Field, Diego, & Sanders, 2001b). Students with depression also reported higher marijuana and cocaine use, but similar alcohol and tobacco use, when compared to their peers (Field, Diego, & Sanders, 2001a; 2002).

Prevalence. The National Epidemiology Study reported the 1-year prevalence of depression at about 5% for ages 18 and older, and estimated that the prevalence among young people may be two to three times as high: "At any one point in time, between 10 and 15 percent of the child and adolescent population have some symptoms of depression" (Eaton et al., 2004, Major depression section, para. 1). According to the World Health Organization (2006), depression is the leading cause of disability worldwide.

Etiology and Risk Factors. Depression is more common in boys prior to adolescence; however, girls overtake them during teenage years and have a higher depression rate through their twenties. The reason for this shift is unclear, and may vary somewhat across cultures. It has been suggested that "changes in social development, social role expectations, and/or biology may play significant roles, but research concerning these factors is scarce and inconsistent" (Hazler & Mellin, 2004, p. 18).

Dysthymia
Persistent but fewer symptoms than major depression
Chronic sadness

Bipolar Disorder
Alternating episodes of depression and elevated mood
Presents differently in children than in adults

Major Depression
Unipolar, persistent sadness or irritability
Thoughts of death or suicide
Somatic symptoms
Changes in activity

FIGURE 10–8 Mood Disorders Overview

A European study showed that gender differences in depressed teenagers were related to the impact of developmental issues around the time of transition to high school (Marcotte, Fortin, Potvin, & Papillon, 2002). Specifically, girls were less satisfied with their bodies, had lower self-esteem, and reported more negative stressful life events than boys at the same age.

A number of studies have related depression, especially among teenage girls, to the quality of their interpersonal relationships with parents, peers, and teachers. An Australian study found that depression in adolescent girls was predicted by interpersonal concerns, self-critical concerns, and the quality of parent and peer

attachment (Milne & Lancaster, 2001): "Adolescent females are more vulnerable to symptoms of depression when they perceive low levels of maternal care, experience feelings of dependency, experience self-criticism, experience feelings of guilt, have poor attachment to parents, or have poor attachment to peers" (p. 218). A study of middle-class, urban Mexican female adolescents examined depressive attitudes in the context of a family-centered culture (Gil-Rivas, Greenberger, Chen, & Montero y López-Lena, 2003). The researchers found that high levels of parental warmth, acceptance, and monitoring were correlated with lower levels of depression, while higher levels of parent-adolescent conflict were related to higher rates of depression in teenage girls. Girls also exhibited a more ruminative coping style than boys, characterized by inactivity and focusing large amounts of time and attention on thinking about their depressed mood and personal deficiencies. Videon (2002) examined data from the National Longitudinal Study of Adolescent Health to determine the impact of parental separation on adolescent depression. She found that the quality of the parental relationship prior to the separation moderated the effects, and that the relationship with the opposite-gender parent had a significant influence on adolescent depression. That is, the more positive the relationship between girls and their fathers (or between boys and their mothers), the less likely they were to exhibit depressive symptoms. Field, Diego, and Sanders (2002) also found that students who report high-quality parental relationships also demonstrate higher grade point averages, less drug use, and fewer depressive symptoms.

A South African study interviewed girls ages 11 to 14, identified by someone close to them as having non-clinical levels of depression (Snyman, Poggenpoel, & Myburgh, 2003). A number of common themes emerged; one is of particular interest to educators: "Dysfunctional relationships with teachers range from experiences of favoritism and victimization to feelings of mistrust and betrayal. These encounters inevitably have a negative impact on the mental well being of the young adolescent girls and tend to promote or maintain depression" (p. 281).

High-quality peer relationships have been correlated with higher grade point averages, fewer depressive symptoms, and lower rates of drug use (Field, Diego, & Sanders, 2002). Social isolation contributes to depression and feelings of hopelessness, often as a result of abuse or bullying (Hazler & Denham, 2002). As reported in Chapter 9, both bullies and their victims have higher rates of depression and suicidal ideation than their peers not involved in bullying. A study of more than 2,000 eighth graders found depression and suicidal ideation to be significantly higher for girls than for boys in both groups—bullies and victims (Roland, 2002). Two studies measuring students' sense of belonging within a school community were conducted as part of the Adolescent Health Project (Anderman, 2002). The studies found that feelings of belonging were lower in large, urban schools and in schools that used busing. The data also revealed that student perceptions of belonging were inversely related to depression, social rejection, and school problems.

Bipolar Disorder

Bipolar disorder in children and adolescents has been difficult to recognize and diagnose because it does not fit precisely the symptom criteria established for adults, and because its symptoms can resemble or co-occur with ADHD and CD. In addition, symptoms of bipolar disorder may be initially mistaken for normal emotions and behaviors of children and adolescents. However, unlike normal mood changes, bipolar disorder significantly impairs functioning in school, with peers, and at home with family (NIMH, 2000a).

Bipolar disorder is characterized by alternation of episodes of depression with episodes of elevated mood or mania:

> Adolescents with mania or hypomania feel energetic, confident, and special; they usually have difficulty sleeping but do not tire; and they talk a great deal, often speaking very rapidly or loudly. They may complain that their thoughts are racing. They may do schoolwork quickly and creatively but in a disorganized, chaotic fashion. When manic, adolescents may have exaggerated or even delusional ideas about their capabilities and importance, may become overconfident, and may be "fresh" and uninhibited with others; they start numerous projects that they do not finish and may engage in reckless or risky behavior, such as fast driving or unsafe sex. Sexual preoccupations are increased and may be associated with promiscuous behavior. (U.S. Department of Health and Human Services, 1999, p. 151)

According to the AACAP (2002a), students in a manic phase will experience more drastic changes in mood compared to their peers. They can appear happy or silly on the one hand—or very irritable, angry, agitated, or aggressive on the other—during a manic episode. They may feel extremely energetic and go for days with little or no sleep and not feel tired. They can be unusually talkative or distractible, switching topics without regard for their audience. It is not uncommon for students with bipolar disorder to tell the teacher how to run the class (Geller & Luby, 1997) or to engage in extreme risk-taking behaviors. They believe normal rules and logical reasons do not apply to them; they believe they are smarter than the adults and can "beat the system."

Some researchers believe that early-onset bipolar disorder may be a different, more serious form of the disorder (Geller & Luby, 1997). Juvenile bipolar disorder has more mixed symptoms, with depressed and manic behaviors occurring simultaneously or cycling back and forth more rapidly than is usual in adults (Schlozman, 2002a). This rapid cycling has been associated with poorer outcomes. The National Institute of Mental Health (2000a) described the differences as follows:

> When the illness begins before or soon after puberty, it is often characterized by a continuous, rapid-cycling, irritable, and mixed symptom state that may co-occur with disruptive behavior disorders, particularly attention deficit hyperactivity disorder (ADHD) or conduct disorder (CD), or may have features of these disorders as initial symptoms. In contrast, later adolescent- or adult-onset bipolar disorder tends to begin suddenly, often with a classic manic episode, and to have a more episodic pattern with relatively stable periods between episodes. There is also less co-occurring ADHD or CD among those with later onset illness. (p. 10)

According to the National Alliance for the Mentally Ill (2006c), many parents report that their children with bipolar disorder were difficult as infants, displaying an increasingly disturbing array of symptoms during later development. These problems may include hyperactivity, resistance to change, separation anxiety, low frustration tolerance, lack of anger control, impulsivity, and impatience. Many young children with bipolar disorder have intensely angry responses to frustration, including violent temper tantrums with minimal warning. Students with bipolar disorder may be particularly disruptive in the classroom because their behavior "derails development, strains friendships, and stifles learning" (Schlozman, 2002a, p. 90). In adolescents as well, the manic phase may not manifest as elevated mood; instead, they may have increased irritability and rages in response to adult demands or restrictions. Oppositional or defiant behavior is not uncommon during the manic phase. Some children and adolescents with bipolar disorder may exhibit an unusual sensitivity to sensory stimuli, including temperature, odors, the way their clothing feels, and so on (Wilkinson, Taylor, & Holt, 2002).

Bipolar disorder has potentially devastating outcomes, if not treated effectively. Between 10% and 15% of individuals with bipolar disorder commit suicide, mostly when in the depressed state. Manic episodes have been associated with perpetration of child abuse, spousal abuse, and other violent behaviors. Other problems associated with bipolar disorder may include alcohol or substance abuse, school truancy, school failure, and episodic antisocial behavior. Bipolar disorder may co-occur with eating disorders, ADHD, panic disorder, and social phobia.

Some physicians have a tendency to diagnose schizophrenia rather than bipolar disorder in young people. The AACAP (2002a) estimates that about one-third of the 3.4 million children and adolescents diagnosed with depression may actually be experiencing the onset of bipolar disorder (i.e., a major depressive episode that will be followed by one or more manic episodes). Approximately one-third of the school-aged children diagnosed with ADHD may have bipolar disorder.

The problematic, and often conflicting, symptoms make bipolar disorder particularly difficult to diagnose early in children and adolescents. However, early intervention is critical to reduce the rates of truancy, drug use, suicide, and other negative outcomes for young people with bipolar disorder. (Wilkinson, Taylor, & Holt, 2002).

Prevalence. The National Institute of Mental Health (2000a) estimates the one-year prevalence of bipolar disorder at about 1% of the U.S. population, or 2.3 million Americans. Bipolar disorder also occurs in children and adolescents, and 20% to 40% of adults with bipolar disorder report that their symptoms started before the age of 18 (Geller & Luby, 1997). While no major studies have been conducted to date concerning the epidemiology of early-onset bipolar disorder, it appears that the prevalence is at least the rate reported in the adult literature, and the diagnosis has been used with increasing frequency over the past decade (Geller & Luby, 1997).

Etiology and Risk Factors. The current consensus of NIMH-sponsored research is that, for most individuals, bipolar disorder results from a complex combination of multiple genes and nongenetic factors (NIMH, 2000a). Family, twin, and adoption studies have demonstrated repeatedly the heritable, or genetic, aspect of bipolar disorder (AACAP, 2002a; NIMH, 2000a; Schlozman, 2002a). The chances of developing bipolar disorder are demonstrably greater if one or both parents have it.

Researchers tracing potential biophysical causes of bipolar disorder have used magnetic resonance imaging (MRI) to look at brain structures; they have identified specific abnormalities that occur in the brains of some individuals with bipolar disorder. Other researchers are using modified versions of MRI and PET scans to study changes in how the brain actually functions under different conditions, tracking the changes in brain chemistry and activity (NIMH, 2000a).

For teenagers, a family history of drug or alcohol abuse also may be predictive of bipolar disorder (AACAP, 2002a). For some, early-onset bipolar disorder appears to be triggered by puberty, a significant loss, or a trauma (Wilkinson, Taylor, & Holt, 2002).

SELECTED INTERVENTIONS FOR STUDENTS WITH ANXIETY AND MOOD DISORDERS

The effective treatment of students with anxiety and mood disorders is a multidisciplinary process that involves medical and mental health professionals, the child and her family, school personnel, and representatives of other community agencies working with that child. Ongoing treatment of anxiety and mood disorders proceeds through two major phases, depending on the acuity of the illness. Because of the cyclical or episodic nature of many of these disorders, relapse is not uncommon. Therefore, students may move back and forth between acute and community-based care a number of times during treatment.

The acute phase of an illness is generally the province of the medical and mental health professionals. The initial differential diagnostic process will result in a multidisciplinary treatment plan generally consisting of psychopharmacological or biomedical treatment—along with behavioral, cognitive, or psychotherapy—to stabilize acute symptoms.

During the acute phase of anxiety and mood disorders, some patients may require psychiatric hospitalization, residential treatment, or intensive outpatient treatment (sometimes called partial hospital or day treatment). Some may move to therapeutic foster homes operated by individuals trained to parent students with serious emotional or behavioral problems. Others will continue to live at home and attend school, on at least a part-time basis.

During the acute phase of a mental illness, the focus is stabilization of acute symptoms, and educational issues are likely to be secondary to biopsychosocial treatment. Psychoeducational programs are often introduced during the initial or acute phase of treatment, and continued after the child's symptoms are more stable. These programs educate children and families about the nature of the disorder, symptoms and warning signs of relapse, and medication and treatment options. Transition planning to reintegrate the child into her natural environments begins early in the first phase, and educational accommodations and modifications may be an important part of the transition plan.

The second phase of treatment focuses on relapse prevention. During this phase, school personnel often become more involved in implementing the treatment plan as interventions typically occur in community settings. Most students with anxiety and mood disorders will continue to participate in outpatient treatment, counseling, and medication management during the relapse-prevention phase. Parents may be involved in ongoing parent education classes, support groups, or family therapy. Teachers, counselors, and school nurses may assist in monitoring the efficacy of medication, teaching students stress reduction and problem-solving skills, and training social skills designed to improve interpersonal relationships. Related service personnel also may need to be involved in working with students with anxiety and mood disorders or consulting with teachers. For example, the speech pathologist should have input into an appropriate school program for a student with selective mutism.

Evans and Frank (2004) point out that psychiatric comorbidity is the rule, rather than the exception, for children and adolescents. That is, students with one DSM-IV-TR (APA, 2000) diagnosis usually have other significant problems as well. To prevent relapse, it is also necessary to address the underlying and potentially additive components that exacerbate anxiety and mood disorders (e.g., attention problems, learning problems, interpersonal conflicts, externalizing behaviors, depression, alcohol abuse).

Ideally, each student with an anxiety or mood disorder would have a case manager, who could obtain informed consent for information sharing among all parties and coordinate all activities related to ongoing treatment. (See Chapter 13 for a more thorough discussion of the issues involved in consultation between the schools and community mental health professionals.) Alternatively, the parent may choose to be the conduit for information concerning their child.

There has been little research to date on the school-based treatment of students with anxiety and mood disorders. Much of the existing research is based on interventions conducted in clinical settings, or with an intervention tested on an adult population and later adapted for adolescents (Hazler & Mellin, 2004). Therefore, the intervention strategies that follow are based on the existing empirical literature, as well as on published professional experiences with children and adolescents with anxiety and mood disorders (e.g., case studies). School-based activities should be congruent with the goals of the treatment plan, and focused on the long-term academic and social-emotional growth of the student. As with any other intervention, if the student's affect or behavior appears to become worse, stop the intervention.

Cognitive Behavioral Therapy

Introduced in Chapter 7, cognitive behavioral techniques are a blending of two approaches: (1) *behavioral*, which focuses on using reinforcement, extinction, and other techniques to teach, maintain, increase, and decrease student behaviors; and (2) *cognitive*, which focuses on identifying and changing faulty thinking patterns that result in self-defeating feelings and behaviors. With cognitive behavioral strategies, teachers and counselors can help students develop new and more effective responses to potentially difficult or stressful situations.

A number of clinical studies have validated the use of cognitive behavioral therapy (CBT) with adults and adolescents who have all types of anxiety and mood disorders (e.g., Ginsburg & Drake, 2002; Layne, Bernstein, & Egan, 2003; Nauta, Scholing, & Emmelcamp, 2003). Recent applied studies have demonstrated that CBT can be effective in school settings and with diverse populations as well. CBT also can be applied at all three levels of prevention, in conjunction with the school guidance program or in the special education continuum of services, as follows:

1. **Primary prevention**. Provide the entire student body or class with information about normal adolescent growth and developmental issues, including anxiety and depression. Address the importance of making healthy lifestyle choices (e.g., eating balanced meals; getting enough sleep and exercise; avoiding cigarettes, alcohol, and drugs). Teach stress management, problem solving, and interpersonal conflict-resolution techniques.

2. **Secondary prevention**. Offer small-group education and support, based on risk factors, and help students process their actual experiences from the week. Introduce specific CBT strategies, such as thought testing (questioning and countering students' automatic or negative internal messages) and cognitive restructuring or reframing. (See Figure 10–9 for examples.) The teacher or counselor can ask questions, assist with reframing, and provide a safe environment in which to role-play new coping strategies for difficult situations.

3. **Tertiary prevention**. Provide individual or small-group counseling and support for students with anxiety and mood disorders. The purpose of these sessions should be aimed at achieving/maintaining stability, minimizing the impact of anxiety or depression on day-to-day functioning, and performing crisis intervention as needed. Adjust the student's schedule to incorporate daily relaxation opportunities and to include activities the student has mastered and enjoys.

In addition to in-group activities, give students "homework" between sessions, using contingency contracts

Distorted Thinking	Reality Testing	Reframing
There is no way I will ever pass this algebra test.	Not under any conditions? Not if you live to be 100? What if you had a study partner? What if you had more time? What if we did a review session? What if you studied for 30 minutes every night with your mom?	I won't pass this algebra test unless I really focus and study harder between now and Friday.
Nobody likes me. Everybody hates me.	Nobody likes you? What about . . . ? [Name friends and why they like her.] I like you because . . . Your family members like you because . . . Hate is a strong emotion. Out of the 450 students in this school, who do you think hates you? [Calculate percentage.]	I'm having a hard time getting along with my parents right now. Recently, I've also turned my friends down every time they asked me to do something, or backed out at the last minute. I need to make plans to do something fun with one of my friends and carry through on it.

FIGURE 10–9 Examples of CBT Conversations

and a system of reinforcement to encourage completion. Ask students involved in CBT to monitor their mood, thinking, and behaviors on a daily basis and record that information in a journal or log (i.e., self-monitoring). Then use these records in individual CBT sessions to thought-test and reframe faulty thinking patterns. Students learning new coping skills in group may be asked to try out those skills in the real world—at home or in the classroom. This generalization beyond the group is particularly important for students who have been socially withdrawn or isolated (Hazler & Mellin, 2004).

Maag (2002) suggests manipulating the context of depressive behaviors to help students understand that their behaviors are controllable. The teacher directs the student to engage in the problem behavior, but changes the rate, time, location, or topography of the behavior:

1. A student can engage in more of the behavior. For example, a student whose main expression of helplessness is passivity can be instructed to wait for people to open doors for her.
2. A student can engage in the behavior at a different time. For example, she may be instructed to feel depressed from 2:30 to 3:15 p.m.
3. A student can engage in the behavior at a different location. For example, she may be instructed to stand by the classroom window when feeling most depressed.
4. A student can engage in the behavior using a different topography (i.e., appearance). For example, she may be instructed to cross her arms when feeling the most depressed. (p. 151)

NOTE: Because these techniques are designed to manage, not stop, the depressed behavior, they are not appropriate for dangerous or self-damaging depressed behaviors.

Creating Environmental Supports

Teachers can provide classroom support for students with anxiety and mood disorders by being empathetic, providing preferential scheduling, offering choices, and respecting the coping mechanisms students have developed to deal with their feelings. Classroom accommodations must be individualized, based on each child's triggers and preferences.

Preferential scheduling of classroom activities may be necessary for some students with anxiety and mood disorders. Students with bipolar disorder benefit from a very structured routine; the predictable rhythm of the day seems to decrease their rapid cycling and lessen the frequency of manic episodes (NIMH, 2000a). Students with separation anxiety disorder also benefit from a structured routine that includes a good-bye ritual with parents; however, the amount of time with parents should be faded as the child adapts (Flood & Wilder, 2004). Generally, difficult and more pleasant activities should be alternated during the school day, providing anxious or depressed students with opportunities to relax and to feel competent.

Allowing students to help design their daily schedule will increase their feelings of control and decrease anxiety. For example, students with test anxiety may perform better if any tests are taken first thing in the morning, to "get it over with" (Schlozman, 2002b). Students with a hand-washing compulsion may be reassured by knowing that they will get to wash their hands at specific times during the day (e.g., after recess, before and after lunch, after art).

In addition to deciding *when* to do work, another type of classroom accommodation allows students to make choices about *how* to accomplish certain tasks they find particularly stressful. For example, a student whose anxiety is triggered by making oral book reports could be given several alternatives: (a) prepare a written book report, (b) tape-record the report at home the night before, or (c) present the report privately to the teacher or paraprofessional.

To the extent that it is practical, establish a home base or safe zone in or near the classroom (see Chapter 9). In the home base area, provide materials that students can use to decrease stress and regroup. Make these materials available to all students (e.g., a rocking chair) or tailored to a specific student's stress management strategy (e.g., a personal CD player with a specific relaxation CD).

Stress-Reduction Techniques

Adolescence is a stressful time, and is made even more difficult by anxiety and mood disturbances. Students' everyday experiences include a variety of potential stressors or triggers. The American Academy of Child and Adolescent Psychiatry (2002b) provides a list of common sources of student stress:

* School demands and frustrations
* Negative thoughts and feelings about themselves
* Changes in their bodies
* Problems with friends and/or peers at school
* Unsafe living environment/neighborhood
* Separation or divorce of parents

- Chronic illness or severe problems in the family
- Death of a loved one
- Moving or changing schools
- Taking on too many activities or having too high expectations
- Family financial problems (p. 1)

A visit to any large bookstore's self-help section will provide a wealth of information on nutrition, exercise, mental health and wellness, stress management, and relaxation. Much of this information concerns a healthy lifestyle and may seem like common sense. The American Academy of Child and Adolescent Psychiatry (2002b) suggests the following stress-management strategies that can be useful for all children and adolescents:

- Exercise and eat regularly.
- Avoid excess caffeine intake, which can increase feelings of anxiety and agitation.
- Avoid illegal drugs, alcohol, and tobacco.
- Learn relaxation exercises (abdominal breathing and muscle relaxation).
- Develop assertiveness training skills. For example, state feelings in polite, firm and not overly aggressive or passive ways: "I feel angry when you yell at me," "Please stop yelling."
- Rehearse and practice situations that cause stress. One example is taking a speech class if talking in front of a class makes you anxious.
- Learn practical coping skills. For example, break a large task into smaller, more attainable tasks.
- Decrease negative self talk: challenge negative thoughts about yourself with alternative neutral or positive thoughts. "My life will never get better" can be transformed into "I may feel hopeless now, but my life will probably get better if I work at it and get some help."
- Learn to feel good about doing a competent or "good enough" job rather than demanding perfection from yourself and others.
- Take a break from stressful situations. Activities like listening to music, talking to a friend, drawing, writing, or spending time with a pet can reduce stress.
- Build a network of friends who help you cope in a positive way. (p. 2)

Students with anxiety and mood disorders generally need more than healthy-living strategies. They often need to learn a structured, systematic set of stress-reduction and coping skills. Relaxation and self-suggestion techniques can be introduced in the classroom, in a small group, or in individual sessions with students.

A general strategy for relaxation or meditation is to dim the lights, and have each student select a comfortable position. Some will prefer sitting; others will do better lying on the floor. Playing quiet classical or new-age music is optional, but for some students, using specific music can become a conditioned cue to relax. Once students are comfortable, have them close their eyes and focus on taking deep, diaphragmatic breaths. As they exhale, ask each student to silently think a positive or self-calming message with every expelled breath. Initially, the teacher may need to provide them with a model, for example: "I am feeling very calm," or "I can let my worries go." Some students will fall asleep, which is fine. Initially, relaxation techniques should be practiced for 15 to 20 minutes, daily if possible. Once students have mastered the technique, encourage them to practice at least once or twice a day on their own at significant times of stress.

Two specific types of relaxation training have been tested empirically and found to reduce anxiety symptoms. **Progressive muscle relaxation (PMR)** has been successful with high school students who had generalized anxiety, mild depression, agoraphobia and panic attacks, and specific phobias (Rasid & Parish, 1998). PMR involves systematically tensing, then releasing the major muscle groups in a specific sequence:

> The basic procedure consists of the following muscle groups being sequentially tensed and then relaxed: dominant hand and forearm; dominant biceps; non-dominant hand and forearm; non-dominant biceps; forehead, upper cheeks, and nose; lower cheeks and jaws; neck and throat; chest, shoulders, and upper back; abdominal or stomach region; dominant thigh; dominant calf; dominant foot; non-dominant thigh; non-dominant calf; and dominant foot. (Harris, 2003, p. 146)

Similar results have been achieved with **autogenic relaxation therapy (ART)** in Germany, which combines relaxation with autosuggestions (e.g., "I am completely calm and relaxed"). A study by Goldbeck and Schmid (2003) with 50 children between ages 8 and 15, found that eight 30-minute small-group sessions of ART resulted in reductions in behavior problems, stress, and somatic complaints.

Self-Monitoring Strategies

Students with anxiety and mood problems often have a distorted picture of their daily activities and interactions with others. Journaling can be a helpful device for tracking and reviewing their experiences with the teacher or counselor. For example, a student who thinks she is depressed all the time may find that she forgot about it during art, physical education, and the social-studies video on the Civil War. The journal provides her with a "reality check" and can provide clues to the types of activities that are distracting or reinforcing for the student. The journal can also provide insight into what situations produce the highest level of stress and act as triggers to anxious or depressed thinking and behavior. Once triggers have been identified, students can select a self-calming strategy to try whenever triggers occur. For young children, sitting in a rocker with a stuffed animal may work; for adolescents, a less juvenile coping strategy may be desirable. They may choose to squeeze a stress ball, take 10 deep breaths, or exercise. A self-monitoring strategy called Stop-Drop-Roll is based on the familiar fire-safety procedure:

> The students were instructed that when they physically felt the "fire" of anxiety and stress, they should "stop" (actually put down their pencils and place their hands on the table while concentrating on the coolness of the surface). Then they were to "drop" their heads forward, and "roll" them around gently while taking three deep breaths. (Cheek, Bradley, & Reynolds, 2002, p. 167)

Addressing Physical and Somatic Complaints

Many students with anxiety and mood disorders may also suffer from legitimate physical complaints, either as a result of chronic medical conditions, or as a side effect of prescription and over-the-counter medications. The fact that the student is physically ill can also exacerbate anxiety and mood concerns.

As Schlozman (2002d) points out, health-related anxieties change as the student moves through the normal developmental stages. For example, it is relatively common for preschool-aged children to believe they are responsible for their own illness, and that it is a result of past transgressions. Elementary-aged students may also believe that an injury to one part of their body will result in the loss of function of their entire body. Older elementary children find comfort in routines and treatment regimens, while teenagers typically rebel and become oppositional about complying with their treatment. Regardless of the student's age or illness, Schlozman suggests that teachers avoid assuming they know how students feel. Ask questions. With parents' permission, talk frankly with children about their illness and limitations.

It is necessary to follow the students' treatment plan and provide accommodations necessary to their comfort. For some students this might include more frequent rest breaks or a nap, a shortened or modified school schedule, adapted physical education and recreational activities, more frequent drinks or trips to the restroom, a special diet, or use of sunscreen before going outdoors. Consult the school nurse whenever a child reports repeated (or mysterious) physical ailments to rule out conditions that require treatment, or to monitor potentially problematic side effects of medication.

Diagnosis-Specific Strategies

The preceding section provided an overview of interventions commonly used with students who have anxiety or mood disorders. The interventions that follow are designed specifically to address behaviors related to the diagnostic categories of selective mutism, separation-anxiety disorder, obsessive-compulsive disorder, and reactive attachment disorder.

Selective Mutism. Treatment for selective mutism is generally administered by the speech-language pathologist, or by a multidisciplinary team, although behavioral interventions (e.g., mystery motivators, differential reinforcement) and cognitive-behavioral strategies (e.g., self-modeling, self-reinforcement) have also been effective (Amari, Slifer, Gerson, Schenck, & Kane, 1999; Kehle, Madaus, & Baratta, 1998). One successful behavioral strategy for selective mutism is shaping (e.g., pointing, whispering, uttering single words), with the ultimate goal of developmentally appropriate speech across settings (Amari et al., 1999). For persistent selective mutism, when other therapies are not successful, medication may be helpful, such as SSRI citalopram (Thomsen, Rasmussen, & Andersson, 1999).

Separation Anxiety Disorder. Severity of symptoms and medication status may predict student response to treatment in students with school phobia (Layne et al., 2003). Students with SAD can be more resistant to treatment than students with other anxiety disorders. A study with adolescents (Last, Hansen, & Franco, 1998) found an educational support group as effective as systematic desensitization. Always perform a functional behavioral assessment when children exhibit SAD to determine whether the child is being reinforced in some way by staying home or being clingy. For many young children with SAD, gradual integration or reintegration into the classroom is essential. Miller (2002) suggests the following strategies:

* Alter the child's schedule to gradually increase time in school.
* Encourage consistent departure rituals (e.g., parents say good-bye the same way each day, don't sneak out, and return when promised).
* Provide comfort stations with a comfortable chair or stuffed animal where the child can comfort herself.
* Ask parents to leave a concrete object as a reminder of their promise to return (e.g., a scarf, picture, etc.).

Obsessive-Compulsive Disorder. Treatment for OCD uses cognitive-behavioral techniques paired with progressive exposure to the triggering stimulus (similar to systematic desensitization) and response prevention (or delay). The goal of treatment is to extinguish the obsessive thinking and compulsive behaviors of OCD that interfere with normal functioning. To do this, ask the student to describe her obsessive fears, and rank them in hierarchical order from least to most problematic. The therapist then develops a plan to think about, discuss, and experience each feared situation, beginning with the least scary one. The student is then asked to suppress or delay the compulsive response while practicing relaxation techniques. To be successful, these techniques must be carried out daily, consistently, and incrementally. However, because recovery generally requires a long period of time, the teacher's role may be more related to accepting and accommodating the student's compulsions (e.g., maintaining a structured classroom routine, allowing the student to keep sanitary wipes in their desk or visit the restroom more frequently than others) (Schlozman, 2002c).

Reactive Attachment Disorder. Because of the nature of the disorder, RAD is extremely difficult to treat: "These children can be resistant to conventional therapies that are based on a reciprocal relationship of trust because children with RAD do not trust others" (Wilson, 2001, referring to Reber, 1996). Attachment therapies focus on developing self-control and self-identity, understanding natural consequences, and reinforcing reciprocity and nurturing. The focus is on the child as a component in the family system. Attachment therapy, as defined by some of its proponents, may also include the use of

holding therapy as one component. (See the Alternative Therapies section.)

Alternative Therapies

As with other mental health disorders, a variety of claims have been made regarding the efficacy of specific diets, chiropractic treatment, and so on in the treatment or cure of anxiety and mood disorders. While a healthy lifestyle is desirable and may result in better overall mental health, there is no empirical evidence to support these claims.

Biofeedback (introduced in Chapter 7) has been recommended to assist in training individuals with anxiety and depression in the areas of stress reduction and muscle relaxation (SAMHSA, 2003a; SAMHSA, 2003b). However, the expense of the equipment and the training and time involved make biofeedback impractical in most public school settings.

The most controversial therapy in the area of anxiety and mood disorders is the use of holding therapy or rebirthing techniques for children with RAD. These techniques generally involve physically restraining the child, often with the application of firm pressure using a blanket, sleeping bag, or pillows. Holding therapy lacks empirical support; the few published studies have evaluated residential programs for children with RAD that included holding therapy, not just the holding therapy component, and had small sample sizes. From these studies, some children with RAD had reduced aggression levels; however, there was no indication that treatment affected ability to form stable attachments (Wilson, 2001). At least two children have died of suffocation during administration of these interventions. Because of the risks involved, these techniques should never be used by school personnel. Parents who are involved in using holding therapy with their child should never be allowed to do so on school grounds.

THE ROLE OF MEDICATION IN THE TREATMENT OF ANXIETY AND MOOD DISORDERS

The *Journal of the American Academy of Child and Adolescent Psychiatry* dedicated a special section of its May 1999 issue to the topic of pediatric psychopharmacology. The summary article (Jensen et al., 1999) provided an overview of the problems related to the use of medications to treat mental health disorders in children. For one thing, there is simply not sufficient evidence of the effectiveness of these medications with young people. The most commonly used drugs have been developed, tested, and approved by the Federal Drug Administration (FDA) for use in treating adults with specific conditions. Their use with children is commonly called "off-label," which means that they are not being prescribed precisely as the FDA approved them (e.g., at a different dosage, for a different condition, or for younger children than specified). While there have been two national studies concerning the frequency with which certain classes of psychotropic drugs are prescribed for children and youth, there have been a limited number of smaller studies concerning the effectiveness of the medications for treatment of specific disorders in children and youth. The Jensen review of these studies "graded" the eight most common groups of psychotropic drugs based on long- and short-term effectiveness and safety as demonstrated by published research studies. They gave a grade of A to medication types that were supported by two or

more randomized controlled trials (RCT) with minimal adverse affects; those receiving a B were supported by at least one RCT with possible rare side effects; and those receiving C were those tested only with adults with minimal data on side effects. As Figure 10–10 demonstrates, stimulant medications are the only group about which there was good evidence of short-term effectiveness (i.e., a grade of A), and any assurance of long-term safety (i.e., a grade of B) in the pediatric population. Thus, as Jensen and his colleagues (1999) point out, there is a significant mismatch between the frequency with which these medications are prescribed for DSM-IV-TR conditions in children and youth and the existing evidence of efficacy.

Caution in the use of medication is warranted, particularly in the prescribing of antidepressants for children and youth. The use of selective serotonin reuptake inhibitors (SSRIs) became common in the 1990s for anxiety and depression. However, some evidence indicates these medications may have increased adverse side effects in adolescents, including increased irritability,

Category	Indication	Level of Supporting Data				Estimated Frequency of Use	
		Short-term efficacy	Long-term efficacy	Short-term safety	Long-term safety	Rank in descending order*	Rank in descending order**
Stimulants	ADHD	A	B	A	A	1	1
SSRIs	Major depression	B	C	A	C	2	2
	OCD	A	C	A	C		
	Anxiety disorders	C	C	C	C		
Central adrenergic agonists	Tourette's disorder	B	C	B	C	3	4
	ADHD	C	C	C	C		
Valproate and carbamazepine	Bipolar disorders	C	C	A	A	4	7
	Aggressive conduct	C	C	A	A		
TCAs	Major depression	C	C	B	B	5	3
	ADHD	B	C	B	B		
Benzodiazepines	Anxiety disorders	C	C	C	C	6	6
Antipsychotics	Childhood schizophrenia & psychoses	B	C	C	B	7	5
	Tourette's disorder	A	C	B	B		
Lithium	Bipolar disorders	B	C	B	C	8	8
	Aggressive conduct	B	C	C	C		

*Data from 1995 National Ambulatory Medical Care Survey
**Data from 1995 National Disease and Therapeutic Index

FIGURE 10–10 Efficacy of Psychotropic Drugs in Children

Source: P. S. Jensen et al. (1999). Psychoactive medication prescribing practices for U.S. children: Gaps between research and clinical practice. *Journal of the American Academy of Child and Adolescent Psychiatry, 38*, 557–565. Reprinted with permission.

aggression, and suicidality (Garland, 2004). In fact, on February 2, 2004, the U.S. Food and Drug Administration issued a warning that patients taking SSRIs should be monitored closely (FDA, 2004), while the British drug regulatory agency banned use of all SSRIs but Prozac in those under age 18 (Department of Health, 2003). The National Institute of Mental Health (2000a) issued this warning concerning medications for bipolar disorder:

Antidepressant medications have long been used to treat the depressive phase of bipolar disorder. However, research has shown that antidepressants, when taken without a mood-stabilizing medication, can increase the risk of switching into mania or hypomania, or of developing rapid cycling, in people with bipolar disorder. Therefore, *mood-stabilizing medications are generally required, alone or in combination with antidepressants, to protect patients with bipolar disorder from this switch.* (p. 6)

CHAPTER SUMMARY

- Children and adolescents may be diagnosed with a variety of anxiety and mood disorders, all of which may interfere with academic performance, peer relationships, and their ability to function in various environments. Generalized anxiety disorder results in excessive and unwarranted worrying about a variety of everyday occurrences. Obsessive-compulsive disorder is characterized by obsessions (persistent and intrusive ideas) and compulsions (feeling driven to perform ritualistic acts). Post-traumatic stress disorder consists of re-experiencing or re-enacting a dangerous or life-threatening experience. Reactive attachment disorder is caused by severe abuse or neglect, and results in the child having disturbed relationships with primary caregivers and others. Separation anxiety disorder is the unreasonable fear

---

American Academy of Child and Adolescent Psychiatry (AACAP). Facts for Families is a series of short educational materials appropriate for use in educating parents, teachers, and others about a variety of mental health issues. Available in English, Spanish, German, French, Polish, and Icelandic. Hard copies may be ordered from AACAP, or are available online: http://www.aacap.org/publications/factsfam

Child and Adolescent Bipolar Foundation. This organization provides free membership and support to families dealing with bipolar disorder. Resources include educational information, information concerning clinical trials, discussion boards, links to local support groups, and a professional referral service. They also offer parent advocacy classes online. Web site: http://www.bpkids.org

Depression and Bipolar Support Alliance (DBSA). This organization's Web site offers confidential online screening for depression and bipolar disorder, educational resources, and discussion groups. They maintain a list of local support groups and operate a speaker's bureau. Web site: http://www.dbsalliance.org/

The International Foundation for Research and Education on Depression (iFRED). iFRED was formed in 1983 to educate the public and professionals about affective disorders. They operate a referral service and encourage ongoing biomedical research. iFRED also publishes a series of informational articles called "iFacts News," available online. Web site: http://www.iFRED.org

National Alliance for the Mentally Ill (NAMI). Formed in 1979, NAMI is a national nonprofit policy and advocacy organization for individuals with mental illness. They publish a series of consumer-oriented fact sheets on various mental health and mental illness topics. NAMI's state and local affiliates focus on impacting public policy and programs in their own communities. Web site: http://www.nami.org/

National Institute of Mental Health (NIMH). NIMH publications cover a wide variety of topics related to the prevention and treatment of mental illness. Publications are designed for consumers, and written at a low level of readability. Some are available in both English and Spanish. Print copies may be ordered from NIMH, or are available online: http://www.nimh.nih.gov/publicat/index.cfm

National Mental Health Association (NMHA). Founded in 1909, NMHA's mission is to improve the mental health of all Americans, especially the 54 million people with mental disorders, through advocacy, education, research, and service. Their 340+ affiliates nationwide have been instrumental in furthering mental health reforms in the United States. The NMHA Web site includes mental-health–related news and educational information, as well as links to state and local organizations. Web site: http://www.nmha.org.

FIGURE 10–11 Educational Resources for Anxiety and Mood Disorders

of leaving one's parents (e.g., to go to school). Social phobia is an extreme fear of embarrassment in social performance situations. Selective (or elective) mutism is the refusal to talk in social situations, although the child is able to speak. Dysthymia is characterized by a chronic or persistently depressed mood. Depression results in persistent sadness, changes in activities and energy levels, and may lead to suicidal ideation. Bipolar disorder consists of cyclical episodes of depression and elevated or manic moods.

* Suggested strategies for teachers of students with anxiety and mood disorders include: making individualized classroom accommodations, teaching stress reduction and relaxation training, and using cognitive behavioral techniques. An annotated list of informational resources on anxiety and mood disorders is contained in Figure 10–11.

CHECK YOUR UNDERSTANDING

1. *True or False.* Children with generalized anxiety disorder may not be eligible for special education services under IDEA.

2. *True or False.* Students with selective mutism have something wrong with their vocal cords that makes it hard to talk.

3. *True or False.* Jimmy has OCD and wants to wash his hands constantly. The teacher should not let him use the restroom except when the entire class is scheduled to go.

4. *True or False.* Students with bipolar disorder are likely to engage in high rates of risk-taking behaviors when they are in an elevated or manic cycle.

5. *True or False.* Relaxation training should only be conducted by a trained hypnotherapist.

6. *True or False.* The prevalence rate for depression remains even for boys and girls across the lifespan.

7. *True or False.* Cognitive behavioral techniques are designed primarily to correct faulty thinking patterns.

8. *True or False.* Students with anxiety disorders may benefit from a classroom that provides structure and a regular schedule of activities.

9. List three ways a teacher might modify classroom expectations to accommodate students with anxiety and mood disorders.

10. Describe three strategies designed to help students with anxiety and mood disorders develop better coping skills.

APPLICATION ACTIVITIES

1. Using the lesson planning format included in Chapter 5, develop a lesson plan to introduce a relaxation and stress management technique to a group of students.

2. Using case study #4 in Appendix A, complete the following activities individually or in small groups:

   a. Review the case study and identify student characteristics that are consistent with a diagnosis of bipolar disorder, as well as those that do not appear to be related. Identify, operationally define, and prioritize three to five target behaviors to address with this student.

   b. Based on information provided about this student, develop a functional hypothesis for each target behavior using the format in Figure 3–10. Consider the degree to which Carlotta's DSM-IV-TR diagnosis influences your determination of what the student is "getting out of" her behavior?

   c. Decide on a system of positive behavioral supports and environmental modifications to implement for this student that specifically accommodate her mood disorder needs.

   d. Write behavioral objectives that would be appropriate for Carlotta's IEP or BIP, using the format in Figure 3–11.

3. Research your local community's resources for students who have anxiety and mood disorders to share with the class.

4. Research the organizational resources listed in Figure 10–11.

OTHER DISORDERS OF CHILDHOOD AND ADOLESCENCE

CHAPTER PREVIEW

CONNECTING TO THE CLASSROOM: *A Vignette*

Andrew is a bright 16-year-old who enjoys playing football with his cousins. He also plays trumpet in the school band. When he was 8 years old, his mother noticed that he constantly was sniffing and blinking his eyes. Thinking Andrew had an allergy or cold, she took him to the pediatrician, who diagnosed Andrew with Tourette's syndrome. The sniffing and blinking were identified as involuntary tics that occurred many times during the day, but were subtle enough that Andrew's peers and teachers just ignored them.

As Andrew entered junior high (and entered puberty), his tics became more pronounced and varied. In addition to sniffing, Andrew also frequently made a noise that sounded like a cross between barking and coughing. His eye blinking sometimes would spread to one entire side of his face, causing strange facial grimaces. The tics also started getting more unwanted attention from peers, and Andrew became more embarrassed and self-conscious. His junior high teachers reacted to Andrew's frequent vocal interruptions in a variety of ways. Most still ignored them, but one teacher thought he was trying to be funny and put him on a behavior contract for making noises during class. Predictably, Andrew's tics became worse in that class as he struggled to control them. He would become more and more anxious as he felt the tension building. Sometimes he managed to put them off until after class, when he could run into the bathroom or find a quiet corner and "let the tics out."

During ninth grade, Andrew became so frustrated that he started complaining of stomachaches and headaches to avoid going to school. Andrew's mother finally talked to the school counselor, who was familiar with Tourette's, but did not know that Andrew had the disorder. He agreed to visit with the ninth-grade team about Andrew's situation, and found that they hadn't realized the tics were involuntary. After that, the teachers were more sympathetic and it became a little less difficult to get Andrew to go to school. His favorite class was band; Andrew found that his tics stayed away while he was playing the trumpet.

LOW-INCIDENCE EMOTIONAL/ BEHAVIORAL DISORDERS

The first four chapters in this section of the book addressed the types of students most frequently found in special education programs under the EBD label: those with disorders of attention, disruptive behavior disorders, pervasive developmental disorders, and anxiety and mood disorders. This chapter will cover a variety of additional students who may qualify for special education under the IDEA rubric for ED. However, the problems these students exhibit occur relatively infrequently and often in combination with disorders discussed in prior chapters, or with symptoms that emerge in the later adolescent years. These students may, or may not, have been diagnosed with a DSM-IV-TR mental health disorder (American Psychiatric Association, 2000).

It is beyond the scope of this book to include every genetic syndrome that may result in behavior problems (e.g., Prader-Willi syndrome), or every possible combination of coexisting disorders (e.g., EBD and fetal alcohol effects). For information on those relatively unusual individual situations, please consult the Internet and your local library. This chapter will focus on tic disorders (including Tourette's syndrome), schizophrenia and psychotic disorders, eating disorders, self-damaging behavior, suicidal behavior, and adolescent issues.

Tourette's Disorder and Other Tic Disorders

Tic disorders result from a neurological condition, and are not considered mental illnesses; however, they are included in the DSM-IV-TR (APA, 2000) and often co-occur with anxiety disorders. The primary features of Tourette's and other tic disorders are involuntary motor and vocal behaviors called tics. The National Alliance for the Mentally Ill (NAMI) fact sheet on Tourette's syndrome (2004) describes "multiple tics that are sudden, rapid, recurrent, non-rhythmic, stereotypical, purposeless movements or vocalizations" (paragraph 1).

The most frequent tic disorder educators encounter is **Tourette's disorder** (also known as Tourette's syndrome), which is typically a chronic or lifelong condition, although symptoms may change over time, or disappear for periods of weeks to years. (See Figure 11-1 for DSM-IV-TR criteria for Tourette's disorder.) A student with Tourette's will exhibit multiple motor tics and at least one vocal tic, many times a day, over a period of at least 1 year. Individuals with Tourette's are never tic-free for more than 3 months at a time. Symptoms may begin with a single tic, most often eye blinking, and may involve any part of the body. Tics can be simple, rapid contractions of one muscle (e.g., a facial twitch), or complex contractions involving entire muscle groups (e.g., deep knee bends). Vocal tics may produce words and/or sounds, including "clicks, grunts, yelps, barks, sniffs, snorts, and coughs" (APA, 2000, p. 111). Less than 10% of the individuals with Tourette's disorder exhibit coprolalia, which is a complex tic that causes the person to utter obscenities.

The DSM-IV-TR (APA, 2000) lists obsessions and compulsions as the most common associated symptoms of Tourette's disorder. According to NAMI (2004), about half of those with Tourette's may also have ADHD; one-third may meet criteria for OCD or anxiety; and learning disabilities and developmental stuttering are common. Additionally, students with Tourette's may need assistance with fine motor tasks, such as buttoning, zipping, and handwriting. Students with Tourette's often are misunderstood by their peers and adults, and may suffer related problems with self-concept and social skills.

The onset of Tourette's occurs during childhood or early adolescence, and must be evident before the age of 18. While symptoms may occur as early as 2 years of age, the median age of onset is between 6 and 7 years (APA, 2000).

Prevalence. According to the American Academy of Child and Adolescent Psychiatry (AACAP), up to 10% of young children have occasional or "transient" tics that appear when the child is under stress, or when he is tired or taking medication (2000b). Tourette's disorder is the most common chronic condition involving tics. The prevalence of Tourette's is related to age, according to the DSM-IV-TR: "Many more children (5–30 per 10,000) are affected than adults (1–2 per 10,000)" (APA, 2000, p. 112). The disorder is at least twice as common in males as in females.

Etiology and Risk Factors. The cause of tic disorders has been linked to abnormal metabolism of the neurotransmitter dopamine, and possibly to other neurotransmitter substances as well (NAMI, 2004). It appears that Tourette's is a genetically inherited disorder, most likely carried in an autosomal dominant gene; however, family members may have different symptoms and types of tics (NAMI, 2004). As a result of the way the dominant gene is expressed, three times more boys than girls have Tourette's. As a result, 70% of girls who have the gene will exhibit symptoms, versus 99% of boys with the gene. The DSM-IV-TR (APA, 2000) acknowledges that for some individuals with Tourette's

A. Both multiple motor and one or more vocal tics have been present at some time during the illness, although not necessarily concurrently. (A tic is a sudden, rapid, recurrent, nonrhythmic, stereotyped motor movement or vocalization.)
B. The tics occur many times a day (usually in bouts) nearly every day or intermittently throughout a period of more than 1 year, and during this period there was never a tic-free period of more than 3 consecutive months.
C. The onset is before age 18 years.
D. The disturbance is not due to the direct physiological effects of a substance (e.g., stimulants) or a general medical condition (e.g., Huntington's disease or postviral encephalitis).

FIGURE 11–1   Diagnostic Criteria for Tourette's Disorder

Source: American Psychiatric Association. (2000). *Diagnostic and statistical manual of mental disorders* (4th ed., text revision). Washington, DC: American Psychiatric Association. Reprinted with permission from the *Diagnostic and Statistical Manual of Mental Disorders*, Copyright 2000. American Psychiatric Association.

disorder there is no evident family pattern and another more complex mode of transmission may be responsible.

Classroom Intervention Strategies.   Sometimes people with Tourette's disorder may blurt out obscene words, insult others, or make obscene gestures or movements. They cannot control these sounds and movements and should not be blamed for them. Punishment by parents, teasing by classmates, and scolding by teachers will not help the child to control the tics but will hurt the child's self-esteem (AACAP, 2000b, para. 5).

The most effective classroom intervention for tics may be to educate classmates and other school personnel, and then ignore the tics. Calling attention to students' involuntary behaviors often increases tension and may, in fact, result in higher rates of tics. Therefore, designing an applied behavior analysis program to decrease or extinguish tics is unlikely to have positive results. However, students with Tourette's and their teachers can adopt coping strategies that may help minimize the negative impact of involuntary tics in the classroom. Some students with tics may be able to identify when tics are likely to happen and move to their home base area to "let the tics out" in a safe, less public environment.

Students with symptoms of anxiety disorders or OCD may benefit from the stress reduction techniques discussed in Chapter 10; however, relaxation training has not been particularly helpful in reducing tics. Prestia (2003) suggests students with Tourette's be evaluated by an occupational or physical therapist to assist in developing classroom accommodations and teaching strategies, particularly related to performance of fine-motor tasks.

Medication and Medical Interventions.   Many students with tic disorders experience relatively mild symptoms. In these instances, the tics and associated behaviors cause minimal disruption to the student's ability to function and do not require medical intervention. For students with coexisting conditions—such as ADHD or OCD—or for more severe or disabling conditions, a doctor may prescribe medication to assist in managing those symptoms (Munson, 2005).

Early-Onset Schizophrenia and Psychotic Disorders

It is not uncommon for children to have imaginary playmates, talk to themselves, or imagine scary things under the bed. However, persistent delusions, or paranoid or bizarre beliefs, may be symptomatic of psychotic thinking.

Description and Major Features.   Schizophrenia is one of the most puzzling—and potentially devastating—mental disorders that may occur during the school-age years. It causes disordered thinking and behavior and can be hard to recognize in its early phases, especially because it may appear differently in children than in adults. In adults, the disorder frequently occurs suddenly; however, in early-onset schizophrenia, behaviors may change slowly over time, as children withdraw from friends and peer activities into their own world (AACAP, 2000a). Children may start articulating strange ideas, talking about unusual fears, believing people are plotting against them, or may simply make less sense than usual. In the classroom, these students may have difficulty with attention, concentration, memory, and reasoning. They may exhibit speech delays or affective disturbances similar to children with pervasive developmental disorders, including inappropriate or flattened expression, poor social skills, and depressed mood: "Such children may laugh at a sad event, make poor eye contact, and show little body language or facial expression" (National Institute of Mental Health, 2003a, p. 2). Children with schizophrenia often display little or no interest in friendships.

Schizophrenia is a disorder that lasts for at least 6 months and includes at least one month of active-phase symptoms (i.e., two [or more] of the following: delusions, hallucinations, disorganized speech, grossly disorganized or catatonic behavior, negative symptoms). Definitions for the Schizophrenia subtypes (Paranoid, Disorganized, Catatonic, Undifferentiated, and Residual) are also included in this section.

Schizophreniform Disorder is characterized by a symptomatic presentation that is equivalent to Schizophrenia except for its duration (i.e., the disturbance lasts from 1 to 6 months) and the absence of a requirement that there be a decline in functioning.

Schizoaffective Disorder is a disorder in which a mood episode and the active-phase symptoms of Schizophrenia occur together and were preceded or are followed by at least 2 weeks of delusions or hallucinations without prominent mood symptoms.

Delusional Disorder is characterized by at least 1 month of nonbizarre delusions without other active-phase symptoms of Schizophrenia.

Brief Psychotic Disorder is a disorder that lasts more than 1 day and remits by 1 month.

Shared Psychotic Disorder is characterized by the presence of a delusion in an individual who is influenced by someone else who has a longer-standing delusion with similar content.

In **Psychotic Disorder Due to a General Medical Condition**, the psychotic symptoms are judged to be a direct physiological consequence of a general medical condition.

In **Substance-Induced Psychotic Disorder**, the psychotic symptoms are judged to be a direct physiological consequence of a drug of abuse, a medication, or toxin exposure.

Psychotic Disorder Not Otherwise Specified is included for classifying psychotic presentations that do not meet the criteria for any of the specific Psychotic Disorders . . . or psychotic symptomatology about which there is inadequate or contradictory information.

FIGURE 11–2 Schizophrenia and Other Psychotic Disorders

Source: American Psychiatric Association. (2000). *Diagnostic and statistical manual of mental disorders* (4th ed., text revision). Washington, DC: American Psychiatric Association. Reprinted with permission from the *Diagnostic and Statistical Manual of Mental Disorders,* Copyright 2000. American Psychiatric Association.

* Seeing things and hearing voices which are not real (hallucinations)
* Odd and eccentric behavior, and/or speech
* Unusual or bizarre thoughts and ideas
* Confusing television and dreams with reality
* Confused thinking
* Extreme moodiness
* Ideas that people are "out to get them" or talking about them
* Behaving like a younger child
* Severe anxiety and fearfulness
* Difficulty relating to peers and keeping friends
* Withdrawn and increased isolation
* Decline in personal hygiene

FIGURE 11–3 Schizophrenia Warning Signs in Children
Source: AACAP, 2000a, p. 1.

Figure 11-2 provides brief categorical descriptors for schizophrenia and other psychotic disorders listed in the DSM-IV-TR (APA, 2000). Figure 11-3 lists potential early warning signs in children and adolescents with schizophrenia.

Differential diagnosis of schizophrenia is difficult because the symptoms overlap with depression, bipolar disorder, PTSD or dissociative disorder, substance abuse, and other DSM-IV-TR diagnoses. Historically, diagnosis of childhood-onset schizophrenia has resulted in a high rate of false positives. That is, many of those initially diagnosed with schizophrenia were later determined *not* to have the disorder after more extensive evaluation (NAMI, 2001a; NIMH, 2003a; Stayer et al., 2004).

A variety of factors make diagnosis of schizophrenia particularly difficult in children. A surprising number of children and adolescents report hallucinations; however, these may be transient psychotic episodes caused by extreme stress or by other disorders, such as PTSD. Children also are more vulnerable to leading questions (e.g., "Do you hear voices?") and may overreport for other reasons (e.g., trying to please the adult) (NAMI, 2001a). Children with pervasive developmental disorders (PDD) may have social difficulties and disordered language that appears similar to that of individuals with schizophrenia (NIMH, 2003a). Therefore, it is necessary to rule out other possible conditions to arrive at an accurate diagnosis of schizophrenia in children and adolescents. It is important that this differential diagnosis take place as soon as symptoms become evident because research suggests that early intervention may reduce the severity of long-term impairment associated with schizophrenia (NAMI, 2001a).

Prevalence. About 1% of the adult population worldwide has schizophrenia. A minority of individuals with this diagnosis have onset of symptoms during adolescence, and schizophrenia in children under 13 is "exceedingly rare" (NAMI, 2001b). The National Institute of Mental Health (2003a) estimates that schizophrenia affects about 1 in 40,000 school-age children (or less than 0.003%).

Etiology and Risk Factors. It appears that schizophrenia is caused by the convergence of several factors: "Evidence suggests that it is a neuro-developmental disease likely involving a genetic predisposition, a prenatal insult to the developing brain, and stressful life events" (NIMH, 2003a, p. 2). Research has demonstrated that the development of schizophrenia clearly has a genetic component. A student with one schizophrenic parent is 10 times more likely to develop schizophrenia than a student with no family history of the disorder (i.e., 1 in 10 vs. 1 in 100) (Substance Abuse and Mental Health Services Administration, 1998b). The risk of schizophrenia rises to 50% if the child's identical twin has the disorder (NIMH, 2003a).

Other factors that may cause schizophrenia are prenatal problems, abnormal brain structure or biochemistry, or environmental stressors. Potential prenatal factors that predict schizophrenia include viral infections, lack of oxygen during delivery, and untreated blood type incompatibility. Children and adults with schizophrenia also appear to have similar abnormalities in the structure and biochemical activity of the brain; however, in child-onset schizophrenia the differences are more pronounced (NIMH, 2003a). Environmental stressors may trigger the onset of symptoms: "Researchers tend to agree that environmental influences—such as a viral infection, a highly stressful situation in adulthood, or a combination of these—may be involved in the onset of schizophrenia" (SAMHSA, 1998b, p. 1).

Individuals with schizophrenia should be monitored for diabetes and impaired glucose tolerance (Subramaniam, Chong, & Pek, 2003). This complication may be related to poor overall health of many individuals with schizophrenia, including poor diet, minimal exercise, and smoking, as well as other biological causes. Certain psychotropic medications may exacerbate the condition (e.g., lithium, chlorpomazine).

Classroom Intervention Strategies. Students with schizophrenia are likely to be more successful in smaller classes, with teachers trained to work with students who have EBD (NAMI, 2001a). They may need adjusted schedules and work loads, or may require strategies to address problems with attention, concentration, and low frustration tolerance (see Chapter 7). Children and adolescents with schizophrenia often have difficulty with peer relationships, and may benefit from social-skills instruction. Some of the reality-checking strategies described in Chapter 10 may be useful (e.g., journaling and CBT).

Medication and Medical Interventions. Antipsychotic medications (also called neuroleptics) are often required to control biochemical imbalances and to reduce the intrusiveness of the psychotic symptoms (SAMHSA, 1998b). However, medication alone has not been as successful as it has been in combination with other types of treatment including individual and family therapy (NAMI, 2001a). Note that some of these medications cause troubling side effects, including weight gain, drowsiness, and neurological problems (e.g., involuntary jerky movements); therefore, ongoing medical management is essential. Many individuals with schizophrenia choose not to take their medication consistently, either because they think it is unnecessary, or because they do not like the side effects.

Eating Disorders

The DSM-IV-TR (APA, 2000) provides criteria for three categories of eating disorders: anorexia nervosa, bulimia nervosa, and eating disorders not otherwise specified (NOS). See Figures 11–4, 11–5, and 11–6 for diagnostic criteria.

Description and Major Features. Anorexia nervosa has been described as "an anxious avoidance of weight gain, obsession with weight and shape, and compulsion surrounding control of eating and weight" (Steiger, 2004, p. 21) while **bulimia** is driven by a cycle of compulsive diet and disinhibition. The common view of anorexia is that the individual is controlling intake to the point of starvation, while the individual with bulimia is bingeing and purging. However, the two disorders and their symptoms are not mutually exclusive. As a result, some researchers and clinicians are not entirely in agreement with the categorical approach that the DSM-IV-TR (APA, 2000) has taken in the area of eating disorders. Specifically, rather than dividing eating disorders into two major categories, some prefer to view them as existing along a continuum of eating behaviors that ranges from normal to problematic (Perosa & Perosa, 2004). The proponents of the continuum model believe it addresses the similarity between the anorexic and bulimic behaviors, as well as the relatively large number of individuals who are labeled as having eating disorders not otherwise specified. A continuum

A. Refusal to maintain body weight at or above a minimally normal weight for age and height (e.g., weight loss leading to maintenance of body weight less than 85% of that expected; or failure to make expected weight gain during period of growth, leading to body weight less than 85% of that expected).
B. Intense fear of gaining weight or becoming fat, even though underweight.
C. Disturbance in the way in which one's body weight or shape is experienced, undue influence of body weight or shape on self-evaluation, or denial of the seriousness of the current low body weight.
D. In postmenarcheal females, amenorrhea, i.e., the absence of at least three consecutive menstrual cycles. (A woman is considered to have amenorrhea if her periods occur only following hormone, e.g., estrogen, administration.)
Specify type:
Restricting Type: during the current episode of Anorexia Nervosa, the person has not regularly engaged in binge-eating or purging behavior (i.e., self-induced vomiting or the misuse of laxatives, diuretics, or enemas)
Binge-Eating/Purging Type: during the current episode of Anorexia Nervosa, the person has regularly engaged in binge-eating or purging behavior (i.e., self-induced vomiting or the misuse of laxatives, diuretics, or enemas)

FIGURE 11–4   Diagnostic Criteria for Anorexia Nervosa

Source: American Psychiatric Association. (2000). *Diagnostic and statistical manual of mental disorders* (4th ed., text revision). Washington, DC: American Psychiatric Association. Reprinted with permission from the *Diagnostic and Statistical Manual of Mental Disorders,* Copyright 2000. American Psychiatric Association.

A. Recurrent episodes of binge eating. An episode of binge eating is characterized by both of the following:
   (1) eating, in a discrete period of time (e.g., within any 2-hour period), an amount of food that is definitely larger than most people would eat during a similar period of time and under similar circumstances.
   (2) a sense of lack of control over eating during the episode (e.g., a feeling that one cannot stop eating or control what or how much one is eating).
B. Recurrent inappropriate compensatory behavior in order to prevent weight gain, such as self-induced vomiting; misuse of laxatives, diuretics, enemas, or other medications; fasting; or excessive exercise.
C. The binge eating and inappropriate compensatory behaviors both occur, on average, at least twice a week for 3 months.
D. Self-evaluation is unduly influenced by body shape and weight.
E. The disturbance does not occur exclusively during episodes of Anorexia Nervosa.
Specify type:
Purging Type: during the current episode of Bulimia Nervosa, the person has regularly engaged in self-induced vomiting or the misuse of laxatives, diuretics, or enemas
Nonpurging Type: during the current episode of Bulimia Nervosa, the person has used other inappropriate compensatory behaviors, such as fasting or excessive exercise, but has not regularly engaged in self-induced vomiting or the misuse of laxatives, diuretics, or enemas

FIGURE 11–5   Diagnostic Criteria for Bulimia Nervosa

Source: American Psychiatric Association. (2000). *Diagnostic and statistical manual of mental disorders* (4th ed., text revision). Washington, DC: American Psychiatric Association. Reprinted with permission from the *Diagnostic and Statistical Manual of Mental Disorders,* Copyright 2000. American Psychiatric Association.

The Eating Disorder Not Otherwise Specified category is for disorders of eating that do not meet the criteria for any specific Eating Disorder. Examples include:
1. For females, all of the criteria for Anorexia Nervosa are met except that the individual has regular menses.
2. All of the criteria for Anorexia Nervosa are met except that, despite significant weight loss, the individual's current weight is in the normal range.
3. All of the criteria for Bulimia Nervosa are met except that the binge eating and inappropriate compensatory mechanisms occur at a frequency of less than twice a week or for a duration of less than 3 months.
4. The regular use of inappropriate compensatory behavior by an individual of normal body weight after eating small amounts of food (e.g., self-induced vomiting after the consumption of two cookies).
5. Repeatedly chewing and spitting out, but not swallowing, large amounts of food.
6. Binge-eating disorder: recurrent episodes of binge eating in the absence of the regular use of inappropriate compensatory behaviors characteristic of Bulimia Nervosa.

FIGURE 11–6   Diagnostic Criteria for Eating Disorders Not Otherwise Specified

Source: American Psychiatric Association. (2000). *Diagnostic and statistical manual of mental disorders* (4th ed., text revision). Washington, DC: American Psychiatric Association. Reprinted with permission from the *Diagnostic and Statistical Manual of Mental Disorders,* Copyright 2000. American Psychiatric Association.

approach would also accommodate binge-eating disorder, which currently falls under eating disorders not otherwise specified, but has been suggested as a third category (NIMH, 2001).

Students with eating disorders may present with vague somatic complaints, including weakness, dizziness, or fatigue. They may try to disguise weight loss with baggy clothing, or by drinking large quantities of fluids, especially water, before weighing (Kaplan Seidenfelf, Sosin, & Rickert, 2004). Students with eating disorders are likely to be perfectionists who place a high value on control and competition (Schlozman, 2002a). The National Eating Disorders Association (2002) poses a set of questions that teenagers can use as a self-screening measure for risk of eating disorders:

* Do you avoid eating meals or snacks when you're around other people?
* Do you constantly calculate numbers of fat grams and calories?
* Do you weigh yourself often and find yourself obsessed with the number on the scale?
* Do you exercise because you feel like you have to, not because you want to?
* Are you afraid of gaining weight?
* Do you ever feel out of control when you are eating?
* Do your eating patterns include extreme dieting, preferences for certain foods, withdrawn or ritualized behavior at mealtime, or secretive bingeing?
* Has weight loss, dieting, and/or control of food become one of your major concerns?
* Do you feel ashamed, disgusted, or guilty after eating?
* Do you worry about the weight, shape, or size of your body?
* Do you feel like your identity and value is based on how you look or how much you weigh? (NEDA, 2002, p. 1)

Eating disorders are associated with life-threatening complications in both anorexia (e.g., heart irregularity, permanent loss of bone density) and bulimia (e.g., dental problems, esophageal and stomach damage). Anorexia leads to death in about 10% of cases (SAMHSA, 1998a).

Prevalence. Approximately 95% of those with eating disorders are female and between the ages of 12 and 25 (SAMHSA, 1998a). The prevalence of eating disorders in American teenage girls may be as high as 10 in 100 (AACAP, 1998b), with perhaps twice as many exhibiting subclinical symptoms related to poor eating habits and compulsive dieting. Eating disorders occur considerably less often in males and women over 40 (APA, 2000). While eating disorders used to occur predominantly in higher-income families in developed countries, the spread of popular culture via the Internet and mass media has resulted in an apparent demographic shift in the past decades (Schlozman, 2002a).

Etiology and Risk Factors. Research supports a multifactor biopsychosocial cause for eating disorders that Steiger (2004) calls a "collision" among:

* **Biologic factors**—heritable influences on appetite, mood, temperament, and impulse controls
* **Social pressures**—promoting body consciousness or generalized self-definition problems
* **Psychologic tendencies**—autonomy disturbances, perfectionism, preference for order and control, and
* **Developmental processes**—conducive to self-image or adjustment problems. (p. 21)

Little research has been conducted into factors that predict eating disorders in preteens. Tanofsky-Kraff and colleagues (2004) found that many children reported occasional overeating, but overweight children reported higher levels of uncontrolled binge eating. Conversely, children who reported high levels of binge eating had higher levels of body fat and were more likely to have eating-disordered cognitive patterns.

Preteens (ages 10–14) who diet are at high risk for eating disorders and report unhealthy eating habits and attitudes at early ages, suggesting that prevention should start earlier than high school (McVey, Tweed, & Blackmore, 2004). In adolescence, risk factors include an expressed desire to be thinner, fear of being overweight, dieting, bingeing, self-induced vomiting, and a higher body mass index (BMI). A survey of 496 adolescent girls used self-report and a psychiatric interview to examine the risk factors for body dissatisfaction (Stice & Whitenton, 2002). The researchers found that higher body mass (or weight gain), the perceived pressure to be thin, an idealized thin image, and low levels of social support were the most predictive risk factors for disordered eating habits. Body dissatisfaction, in turn, is related to a higher tendency to develop eating pathology and depression. This study did not support the hypotheses that early onset of puberty or weight-related teasing were predictive factors.

Intervention Strategies. Eating disorders are particularly resistant to treatment. Only half of individuals with full-blown eating disorders recover completely, another 30% make a partial recovery, and 20% never recover (Schlozman, 2002a). In about 10% of cases, weight loss and medical complications from eating disorders are fatal.

An eating disorder treatment program often consists of two phases, similar to the multidisciplinary treatment programs for anxiety and mood disorders described in Chapter 10 (NIMH, 2001). The acute phase consists of intensive treatment designed to restore weight and interrupt eating-disordered behavior patterns. This phase may take place in an inpatient setting if weight loss has been severe, or if the individual continues to lose weight or binge/purge during outpatient treatment. Psychosocial treatment begins during the acute phase and continues during relapse prevention. The focus of relapse prevention is to address underlying emotional and cognitive issues (e.g., distorted body image, low self-esteem, interpersonal conflicts, depression), and to achieve and maintain a healthy lifestyle.

Successful treatment of eating disorders requires a multidisciplinary team approach. For example, the primary care physician may conduct a complete physical history and perform blood tests to rule out potential medical causes for weight loss or other eating disturbances. A mental health professional or team provides psychosocial interventions designed to identify and address cognitive distortions and eating-disordered behaviors (e.g., fasting, bingeing, purging). The team generally includes a dietitian or nutritionist who provides education and nutritional counseling designed to restore the individual to health and to teach healthy eating habits. Ongoing medical monitoring is also necessary to achieve long-term remission and rehabilitation.

While education generally is not a priority concern during the initial intensive phase of eating disorder treatment, teachers can be an important part of the team in the ongoing recovery process. For example, students returning to school after an inpatient stay may be involved in ongoing daily monitoring of weight, daily food and liquid intake, and exercise. Students with a history of self-induced vomiting may be restricted from visiting the restroom for a period of time following meals.

The cognitive behavioral therapy model (CBT, described in Chapter 10) can be used in combination with journaling to track the thinking of students with bulimia before, during, and after binge eating. In conjunction with the team treatment plan, teachers can also use CBT to identify negative self-beliefs (e.g., "I am too fat"), and to assist with reframing or restructuring thinking (e.g., "I am at 85% of my ideal body weight and

I look and feel healthy") (A new cognitive model, 2004). Teachers can assist students with practicing their new, healthy eating and thinking skills. Teachers also can help counteract the negative effect of media influence by de-emphasizing the focus on weight or body image, and helping students redirect their energy toward long-term personal and professional goals. School staff should be sensitive to peer influences and enforce a zero tolerance policy for teasing based on appearance.

Medication and Medical Interventions. Researchers have found that an antiepileptic medication called topiramate is effective in addressing the symptoms of eating disorders, including binge/purge behaviors, and obsession with food and weight. Topiramate is also helpful in reducing anxiety and depression while increasing self-esteem in individuals with bulimia (Treating bulimia, 2004). Some selective serotonin reuptake inhibitors (SSRIs) assist individuals with anorexia in maintaining their weight and resolving anxiety and depression; however, these psychotropic medications should not be used until weight has stabilized at an acceptable level (NIMH, 2001).

Self-Damaging Behaviors

Description and Major Features. Self-damaging or **self-injurious behavior (SIB)** is distinguished from suicidal behavior by both the mechanism (i.e., method or means) and the intent. The means are generally less lethal, and the act is usually not meant to be life threatening. Nonsuicidal SIB generally is preceded by anxiety or distress, sometimes interpersonal and sometimes aimed at oneself (Gerson & Stanley, 2003).

SIB appears to serve different purposes for different individuals, including reducing tension and restoring emotional equilibrium, albeit temporarily. For some adolescents, self-damaging is an act of dissociation and they do not experience physical pain; for others, the physical pain serves to validate their psychological distress (Gerson & Stanley, 2003). Some students with anxiety and mood disorder identify self-damaging behavior as a coping mechanism. "Students who mutilate themselves report that cutting or scratching makes them feel better briefly, giving them a sense of control and a way to express bad feelings" (Bostic, Rustuccia, & Schlozman, 2001, p. 81). In some cases, students describe SIB as a nonlethal response to suicidal feelings. SIB has also been observed in some individuals with spinal cord injuries and appears to be related to **dysesthesia**—feeling pain in the absence of stimuli that would normally be considered painful (Vogel & Anderson, 2002).

Matthews and Wallis (2002) describe three general categories of self-damaging behaviors, as follows:

1. **Repetitive minor cuts and burns**—also hitting, keeping wounds from healing, hair pulling, and breaking bones. For these individuals, SIB is often intended to contain anxiety, depression, or suicidal feelings. The act usually helps for a while, then tension starts to build again. This type of SIB may also be symptomatic of Munchausen syndrome (i.e., the adolescent uses strange skin problems to get medical attention). Many individuals in this group are females with onset in adolescence through age 30, and a history that includes abuse, perfectionism, body dissatisfaction, parental substance abuse, or depression (Stone & Sias, 2003).
2. **Extreme and bizarre injuries**—may include injury to genitals, eyes, and even amputation of body parts. This type of SIB is very rare, mostly committed in a psychotic state, often under command hallucinations. It also occurs among individuals with severe cognitive impairments.
3. **Repetitive movements**—including head banging, self-biting, hair-pulling, picking at skin or scabs. This type of SIB is usually associated with pervasive developmental disorders. The physical damage is generally inversely related to IQ; that is, the lower the IQ, the greater the physical damage is likely to be. Trichotillomania is a compulsive form of SIB that involves pulling hair from the head or other body parts.

Prevalence. The prevalence of nonlethal self-damaging behavior is approximately 1,400 in 100,000 and increasing (Stone & Sias, 2003). This number would be larger if it included multiple piercings, tattoos, and body alterations. The prevalence rate of SIB differs by type and group, and is most often seen in individuals with anxiety disorders, eating disorders, and schizophrenia. SIB also may be found in individuals with mental retardation, Tourette's disorder, developmental disabilities, and borderline personality disorder (White Kress, 2003).

Etiology and Risk Factors. Self-injurious behaviors generally occur in association with another mental health diagnosis, as listed above. However, some behaviors considered self-damaging in one culture may be acceptable in another. In some cultures, body art or body modifications are a traditional rite of passage into adulthood or a badge of honor. For some American adolescents, self-mutilation also has a strong social and cultural component. Body piercing and tattoos have become increasingly popular among American teens over the past 20 years. For some adolescents, body modifications or body art may represent a nonlethal—but obvious—way of taking risks, rebelling, or rejecting their parents' values. For others, it may be a way of expressing their individuality or being accepted by their peers (AACAP, 1999). Carroll and Anderson (2002) found a significant correlation between anger, depression, and negative feelings about their bodies and number of piercings and tattoos among 79 at-risk high school girls. All 79 (i.e., 100%) of the girls reported that they had engaged in at least one body modification, or body art, procedure.

Peer pressure and contagion can contribute to self-harm (e.g., "playing chicken" with lit cigarettes or getting tattoos in a group).

Classroom Intervention Strategies. When addressing SIB, it is important to work with the individual *and* the family system in a way that is sensitive to the issue of cultural norms, especially regarding tattooing and piercing. Ask the student to keep a journal to identify patterns of thinking that prompt SIB, since self-damaging is usually done in secret (Stone & Sias, 2003). Provide support and allow the student to talk about his feelings without being judgmental. Use cognitive behavioral strategies to address cognitive distortions and to teach and maintain alternative coping strategies for stress. However, never try to take away a student's coping strategy without replacing it with a less injurious alternative that fills the same function. If the student is using SIB to deflect thoughts of suicide, contracting with him to avoid SIB behaviors could be dangerous. An alternative strategy is to focus on delaying or redirecting the self-damaging impulse to a behavior that is less injurious. The American Academy of Child and Adolescent Psychiatry (1999) provides the following examples of delaying or redirecting: "counting to ten, waiting 15 minutes, saying 'NO' or 'STOP!', practicing breathing exercises, journaling, drawing, thinking about positive images, using ice and rubber bands" (p. 2). Use relaxation strategies to help reduce tension and stress that precipitate SIB. Teach social skills and problem-solving strategies (e.g., SOCCSS) to students whose triggers relate to problems with interpersonal relationships. Always assess suicidal intent by determining method and intent. If the means or intent is lethal, implement your suicide prevention plan.

Strategies for students with cognitive impairments or pervasive developmental disorders must rely more on adult observation, redirection, and external controls. Functional assessment of SIB is particularly important to determine whether it represents attention, escape, communication, or sensory self-stimulation. Applied behavior analysis (ABA) has been very successful at managing SIB in individuals who have serious cognitive limitations. (See, for example, the work of Brian A. Iwata at the University of Florida.) Most studies have been conducted in well-controlled, clinical environments, usually in a one-on-one setting. Very little empirical evidence is available concerning use of ABA for SIB in natural settings, such as the classroom or the home, where variables are more difficult to control. Little has been written concerning ABA applications with higher-functioning students who exhibit SIB. However, despite the lack of pertinent research data, it is necessary to stop SIB to prevent serious tissue damage or permanent harm to the individual. Similar to the process used in selecting classroom interventions for more common behavior problems, teachers should perform a functional behavioral assessment and select the least intrusive approach that is effective at interrupting the SIB. Ideally, an intervention plan would be developed by the student's IEP team, perhaps with consultation from a community mental health provider. Because interventions for SIB may be intrusive or restrict students' freedom of movement, these interventions require informed parental consent and the same level of careful consideration given to interventions that involve punishment or aversive consequences. A sample hierarchy of intervention levels might be:

1. **Redirection/distraction**—Provide a verbal prompt in a calm tone of voice at the child's receptive language level (e.g., "stop biting") or suggest an alternative preferred activity (e.g., "Time for computer!"). Avoid unintentionally reinforcing the SIB by hovering, or by sounding alarmed or upset.
2. **Physical contact with redirection but no restraint**—Pair the verbal prompt or alternative suggestion with a physical touch on the arm, shoulder, hand, or affected body part. The touch can provide a gentle push in the right direction, but should not forcibly stop the SIB.
3. **Physical restraint**—Interrupt the SIB by holding the student in such a way that he cannot continue to self-damage. Use the minimum restraint

necessary to stop the SIB. For example, if the student is eye gouging with his thumbs, you just need to keep his arms away from his face.
4. **Assess the need for protective equipment**—If the student self-damages frequently, the team should discuss whether protective clothing or equipment is needed to deter ongoing, potentially serious SIB. Again, the intervention should be the minimum needed to provide safety. A child who bites his arm just needs something to protect the arm (e.g., padded sleeves, an arm guard, or a splint). Other adaptive equipment choices would include gloves to protect the hands, special shoes, snowsuits or padded clothing to protect the torso, plastic helmets for head banging with a face shield to protect the eyes if needed, retainers and tongue guards for students who grind teeth and bite tongues. For long-term reduction of SIB, pair the use of protective equipment with an ABA intervention, and fade the use of the equipment as soon as possible.

Medication and Medical Interventions. The role of medication in treating SIB has not been well researched. "Generally there has been very little integration between behavioral and pharmacological approaches, and the relationship between learned and biological determinants in self-injury remains poorly understood" (Davies, Howlin, Bernal, & Warren, 1998, p. 26). For individuals with spinal cord injuries, it appears that anticonvulsant medication may be helpful in suppressing both the dysesthesia and SIB symptoms (Vogel & Anderson, 2002).

Suicidal Behaviors

Many school-age children and adolescents deal with clinically significant levels of anxiety and depression on a daily basis. Adolescence is a stressful time for most children, as they begin establishing their individuality and dealing with the increased pressure and rejection of exploratory relationships. For some, those stresses seem intolerable and suicide seems like a viable option for stopping the pain.

Prevalence. Although total adolescent deaths by suicide have been on the decline during the past decade, the total rate has tripled since 1950 and is still unacceptably high. Suicide is the third leading cause of death for Americans ages 10 to 24 (Anderson &

By Age
- Suicide is the third leading cause of death among young people ages 10 to 14 (n=272), 15 to 19 (n=1,611), and 20 to 24 (n=2,360).[1,2]
- Unintentional injuries, homicide, and suicide combined account for 75% of all deaths for those 15 to 19 years of age, 72% of deaths for those 20 to 24 years of age, and 53% of deaths for those 25 to 34 years of age.[1]
- In 2002, suicide attempts or other self-harm incidents resulted in 124,409 visits to U.S. emergency rooms for persons ages 10 to 24 years.[2]

By Gender
- Of the total number of suicides among ages 15 to 24 in 2001, 86% (n=3,409) were male and 14% (n=562) were female.[1]
- Suicide is the eighth leading cause of death for males of all ages[1] and men are four times more likely to die from suicide than females.[2]

By Race/Ethnicity
- Suicide rate varies by race. It is the 8th cause of death for American Indians, Asians, and Pacific Islanders; 10th for Whites; 13th for Hispanics; and 16th for Blacks.[1]
- American Indian and Alaskan Natives, and Asian and Pacific Islanders have the highest rate of suicide in the teenage group, ranking second for those groups.[1]

By Method
- Although the overall suicide rate among young people has declined over the past decade, along with use of firearms, there has been an increase in suicide by suffocation in youth ages 10 to 19.[3]
- In 2001, 49% of youth suicides used firearms, followed by suffocation (mostly hanging) at 38%, and poisoning at 7%.[1,3]

[1]Anderson & Smith, 2003
[2]CDC, 2004a
[3]CDC, 2004b

FIGURE 11–7 Suicide Facts

Note: All data are drawn from the 2001 morbidity and mortality database, unless otherwise specified.

Smith, 2003; Centers for Disease Control, 2004a). See Figure 11-7 for additional data on suicide in the United States.

Etiology and Risk Factors. Although depression is a factor, research has not produced an accurate predictive model of suicidal behavior (Rogers, Lewis, & Subich, 2002). Therefore, researchers are trying to more accurately predict levels of risk. In a survey of 88 high school seniors, 18% (nearly 1 in 5) said they sometimes felt suicidal (Field, Diego, & Sanders, 2001). Multivariate analysis showed suicidal teens differed from their nonsuicidal peers in terms of quality of family relationship, family history of depression, peer relations, emotional well being, drug use, and grade point average. The researchers reported that "how happy the adolescent feels accounted for 46% of the variance, suggesting that extreme depression is not necessary for suicidal ideation" (p. 246). Additional risk factors include prior attempts, a history of substance abuse, family history of suicide, and presence of a suicide plan (especially if it is to take place within 48 hours) (Ruddell & Curwen, 2002). Figure 11-8 provides an overview of the most common factors associated with suicidal behavior.

Classroom Intervention Strategies. Teachers and parents should always take threats of suicide or lethal self-harm seriously. Treat suicide threats with the same level of concern as a medical emergency (Bostic, Rustuccia, & Schlozman, 2001). Don't call the bluff of someone making a suicide threat. Validate their feelings. Don't allow students to sidetrack you with personal questions about your experience with suicide, drugs, etc. (Bostic et al., 2001).

Every school should have a three-level crisis prevention plan in place that addresses suicide threats and gestures, with guidelines for teachers and other personnel. A sample plan is outlined in Figure 11-9. Several instruments are available for school counselors and other personnel to use in assessing suicide risk, including the Suicide Assessment Checklist (SAC). The SAC includes 21 items to be completed by a counselor, including history, intentionality, plan, availability of means, and ratings of client's clinical status for: sense of worthlessness, sense of hopelessness, social isolation, depression, impulsivity,

Individual/ Biological Factors	• Depression or other diagnosable mental disorder[1,5] • Feelings of hopelessness, worthlessness, or guilt[1,4,6] • Drug and alcohol abuse[2,5] • Previous suicide attempt[5] • Lower levels of neurotransmitters[5] • Impulsivity and difficulty concentrating[4,5] • Aggressive, destructive, defiant behavior (e.g., running away)[1,4] • Drastic change in personality or habits[1,4] • Hallucinations or bizarre thoughts[1,2,4]
Familial Factors	• Family history of suicide[2,5] • Parental psychopathology[2] • Loss[2] • Family dysfunction[2] • Family violence, including abuse and neglect[3,5] • Strict family[6] • High expectations and low levels of affection[6] • Access to firearms in the home[3,5] • Exposure to suicide (e.g., a friend or classmate)[5] • Impending legal or disciplinary action[3]
School Factors	• Problems with peer functioning (e.g., loneliness)[2] • Impending disciplinary action[3] • Poor school performance[2,4]
Community Factors	• Ethnic and cultural differences[2]
Societal Factors	• Media coverage of suicide[2]

[1]AACAP, 1998a
[2]Ayyash-Abdo, 2002
[3]Bostic et al., 2001
[4]NAMI, 2001b
[5]NIMH, 2003b
[6]Portes, Sandhu, & Longwell-Grice, 2002

FIGURE 11–8   Risk Factors and Symptoms Associated with Suicidal Behaviors

hostility, intent to die, environmental stress, and future time perspective (Rogers et al., 2002).

Recommended counseling methods include: (a) the solution-focused approach (leading the student to explore options other than suicide to resolve difficult issues); (b) cognitive therapy (contradicting the student's suicidal thoughts and providing arguments for living); and (c) rational emotive behavior therapy (assisting the student in objectively facing the situation and dealing with it more unemotionally/rationally) (Palmer, 2002).

ADOLESCENT ISSUES

This section will address two situations that are common enough among students with EBD that they warrant

discussion here—homosexuality and substance abuse. Please note that these are included because they are issues that adolescents with EBD may be struggling with and that may compound the effects of students' other mental health problems.

EBD and Homosexuality

A certain amount of rebellion and risk-taking behavior is to be expected during adolescence. Part of the natural development process during the teenage years is expression of the student's emerging sexuality. For many teenagers, it is an exciting but stressful time. For students who are homosexual, adolescence can be a time of increasing conflict, rejection, and frustration, often leading to an increased rate of clinical depression and suicide risk (AACAP, 2002). (See Figure 11–10.)

Primary Prevention
* Develop a school-specific policy and procedure that specifies how suicidal threats and gestures will be handled.
* Train school personnel in the risk factors for suicide, and define roles for teachers, nurses, counselors, and administrators in case of a suicidal threat or gesture.
* Include suicide prevention education in the school guidance or mental health program.
* Foster a spirit of community within your school that will reduce feelings of isolation and loneliness and prevent bullying, teasing, and other divisive behaviors.

Secondary Prevention
* Provide specialized training for staff in suicide risk assessment (e.g., counselors, special educators).
* Screen student body, particularly those in identified high-risk groups.
* Develop and implement group and individual counseling and support services for high-risk students.

Tertiary Prevention/Postvention
* Respond to a suicidal threat, gesture, or completed act immediately.
* Following the crisis plan, notify key staff of what has occurred and what needs to be done.
* Provide information to remaining staff, parents, students, and the public on an as-needed basis.
* Provide ongoing counseling services to the individual student in the event of a suicidal threat or gesture.
* Provide ongoing counseling services to other students and staff in the event of a completed suicide.
* Provide debriefing for the crisis team.

FIGURE 11–9 Designing a Three-Level Suicide Prevention Plan

Source: Adapted from King, K.A. (2001). Developing a comprehensive school suicide prevention program.

* Social stigmatization
* Social isolation
* Risk for discrimination
* School avoidance
* Risk for coercion to change
* Runaway phenomenon
* Possible prostitution
* Hypervigilance/self-monitoring
* Poorly developed dating skills
* Higher rate of indiscriminant sexual contacts
* Self-hatred
* Higher risk for alcohol/drug abuse
* Higher risk of STD/HIV/pregnancy
* Family nonrecognition/rejection
* Family harassment/violence
* Feelings of sinfulness
* Possible limited police protection
* Risk for violence/abuse
* Positive role model deprivation
* Throwaway phenomenon
* Impeded same-sex friendships
* Feelings of inferiority
* Lack of appropriate social network
* Increased depression and suicide risks
* Possible employment loss
* Possible male eating problems

FIGURE 11–10 Potential Problems of Homosexual Adolescents

Source: Harrison, T.W. (2003). Adolescent homosexuality and concerns regarding disclosure. *Journal of School Health*, 73(3), 107–112. Reprinted with permission. American School Health Association, Kent, Ohio.

Society continues to stigmatize and marginalize homosexuality. To avoid rejection and hostility, homosexual adolescents are pressured to hide their sexual identities. This fact compounds the anticipated normal developmental concerns of adolescence and can create unique problems for the homosexual adolescents. Homosexuality can place them at risk for social stigmatization, isolation, depression, suicide, abuse, and rejection by their families and friends. (Harrison, 2003, p. 107)

EBD and Substance Abuse

Most studies consistently demonstrate an association between substance abuse and other problems: medical complications directly related to prolonged or even single use of illegal drugs or alcohol, accidental deaths from impaired driving and behavior, and depression or even suicidal mood changes as drugs take effect or wear off. In addition, teenagers with other psychiatric diagnoses often "medicate" themselves with illicit substances, with the result that serious psychiatric problems—such as depression, anxiety, bipolar disorder, and attention deficit hyperactivity disorder (ADHD)—may go unrecognized and untreated. (Schlozman, 2002b, p. 87)

Experimentation with drugs and alcohol are fairly common during the teenage years. However, for students with anxiety and mood disorders, or with other risk factors, experimentation may lead quickly to substance abuse and dependence. Co-occurring disorders vary by gender. For girls, the diagnoses most often associated with substance abuse are depression and specific phobias. Boys who become substance abusers are more likely to have had symptoms consistent with conduct disorder, antisocial personality disorder, panic disorder, and other anxiety disorders (Schlozman, 2002b).

The warning signs vary by the substance of choice; however, teachers may see a combination of physical, emotional, and family factors that place students at increased risk or that are indicative of active substance use:

- **Physical indicators** may include fatigue, repeated health complaints, red and glazed eyes, and a lasting cough.
- **Emotional indicators** may include personality change, sudden mood changes, irritability, irresponsible behavior, low self-esteem, poor judgment, depression, and a general lack of interest.
- **Family indicators** may include starting arguments, breaking rules, or withdrawing from the family. (AACAP, 1998c, p. 1)

Some consider use of tobacco to be a significant risk factor, associated both with underlying mood disorders and serving as the gateway to alcohol and drug use. "The literature suggests that smokers are more likely to be depressed, while people who are depressed are more likely to smoke" (Vogel, Hurford, Smith, & Cole, 2003, p. 57). Vogel and colleagues (2003) found participants were also more likely to smoke if their parents smoked, or if they had feelings of helplessness, social isolation, or withdrawal. A study of high school seniors found that students with low GPAs, high popularity, and high depression were more likely to smoke cigarettes, drink alcohol, and smoke marijuana (Diego, Field, & Sanders, 2003). The progression of experimentation followed the notion that smoking and alcohol are gateway drugs, with both predicting marijuana use; marijuana use in turn predicted use of cocaine.

A three-level prevention model should be used to develop a plan for substance abuse prevention. All levels should involve parents and relevant community systems (e.g., juvenile court, public health). Often, adolescents are referred for substance abuse treatment without a thorough evaluation to identify other underlying problems that may precipitate the substance abuse. Co-occurring problems should be treated at the same time. Adults should balance tolerance and empathy with education and concern.

CHAPTER SUMMARY

- This chapter included some low-incidence conditions and behaviors that students with EBD might experience. This chapter focused on tic disorders (including Tourette's syndrome), schizophrenia and psychotic disorders, eating disorders, self-damaging behavior, suicidal behavior, and adolescent issues. Classroom approaches suited to each topic were provided.

CHECK YOUR UNDERSTANDING

1. *True or False.* Students with Tourette's disorder can be trained to stop their tics using ABA procedures.
2. *True or False.* Children with Tourette's are also more likely to have OCD or ADHD than other students in the classroom.
3. Describe possible classroom accommodations for students with Tourette's.
4. *True or False.* Schizophrenia has a strong genetic component.

5. *True or False.* Individuals with schizophrenia rarely need to take psychotropic medication.
6. Describe possible school-based interventions for a student with schizophrenia.
7. Briefly describe the characteristics of anorexia, bulimia, and eating disorders NOS.
8. *True or False.* The media image of feminine beauty (e.g., extremely thin models) has contributed to the spread of eating disorders around the world.
9. Briefly describe why homosexuality places students at higher risk for mood disorders and suicide.
10. Briefly describe the interaction between emotional disorders and substance abuse.

APPLICATION ACTIVITIES

1. Research your local community's resources for students who have disorders or behaviors described in this chapter.

2. Contact a local school district and request a copy of their suicide prevention and crisis intervention plan. Then, in a small group, compare the plans to the general outline provided in this chapter. Discuss possible improvements or design your own plan.

3. Research the organizational resources in your community for students or families needing resources for:

   - Tourette's disorder
   - Schizophrenia
   - Eating disorders
   - Suicide prevention
   - Homosexuality
   - Substance abuse

PART **4**

CONSULTATION AND COLLABORATION

CHAPTER

COMMUNICATION AND COLLABORATION SKILLS
Working with Parents and Other Professionals

CONNECTING TO THE CLASSROOM: *A Vignette*

TEACHER A

Miss Allison teaches elementary special education. Her classroom is in what used to be a storage area adjacent to the school gymnasium. It's a bit small, but she only has eight students. There aren't any windows, but she has brought in lamps, a rocking chair, and colorful posters to brighten up the room and make it seem more comfortable. The room is separated from the rest of the classrooms in the building, and because it is next to the gym, it is pretty noisy. However, it means her special students cause less of a disruption for the "normal" students.

Miss Allison's students are a variety of ages and possess widely varied academic, social, and behavioral skills. Each student's daily schedule and program are totally individualized, based on individualized education program (IEP) objectives.

Miss Allison teaches from an assortment of older textbooks that she had to beg, borrow, and steal from other teachers, as well as materials she has purchased using money out of her own pocket. She has only one-third the supply budget of a normal teacher, since she has just eight students. There is no computer in the classroom, but Miss Allison can use the one in the library before and after school, or during her planning time.

Miss Allison's students are "mainstreamed" with their age group to attend music, art, and physical education. However, the paraprofessional she shares with the kindergarten teacher has to go with them, and they are frequently sent back for misbehaving. Miss Allison has offered to work with the other teachers on positive behavioral supports and interventions that would help her students be more successful in their mainstream classes, but they have not been able to find time to schedule a training session. The principal has made it plain that he does not like having special education students in "his" building. He has made it clear that he expects teachers to handle their own discipline problems and has asked Miss Allison to keep "her" students out of sight when visitors are in the building.

TEACHER B

Miss Bateman is certified in K–12 crosscategorical special education and teaches at the elementary level. She shares a bright, cheerfully decorated classroom off the main hallway near the office with the English-as-a-second-language teacher, but she rarely is at her desk. First thing every morning, Miss Bateman and the school counselor "triage" all of the students with emotional or behavioral problems. Some are on IEPs and some are not. Some of the students on Miss Bateman's caseload talk to her; others choose to talk to the counselor. After a brief check-in and goal-setting conversation, all of the students are off to their general education classrooms.

During the morning, Miss Bateman rotates in and out of classrooms where students with IEPs are assigned. In the first grade class, Miss Bateman, the classroom teacher, and a paraeducator each work with a small reading group on a phonemic awareness activity. Next, Miss Bateman and the sixth-grade teacher coteach a series of writing strategy lessons. They take turns presenting and leading discussion, then both circulate and provide feedback during independent seatwork. In the fifth-grade science class, Miss Bateman reviews the major concepts of the last unit on geology with a group of students who are struggling to keep up, while the rest of the class completes an extension activity on volcanoes. Right before lunch, Miss Bateman conducts a social-skills group in her classroom with a group of students identified as EBD and several of their high-status, nondisabled peers who serve as models.

During the afternoon, Miss Bateman meets with teachers during their planning times, both individually and in grade-level teams, to discuss student progress toward curriculum and IEP goals, to collaborate on instructional modifications, and to schedule the next week's rotation. She loans the new fourth-grade teacher some materials on working with students who have oppositional behavior, and schedules a time to drop by, observe, and take scatterplot data on the child's disruptive behaviors. Miss Bateman has time to return a couple of parent phone calls and answer her e-mails before heading back down to the counselor's office to help her triage students check out. As she passes the principal's office, he comments on how rarely the special education students have appeared in his office since Miss Bateman and the behavioral support team conducted the inservice on positive behavioral supports and implemented the new reward system.

PUTTING COLLABORATION IN CONTEXT

Shifts in American demographics and values have resulted in a number of trends that affect the practice of special educators, including those who work with students who have emotional and behavioral disorders (EBD). This section will describe three such trends: ongoing educational reform efforts, the emergence of "systems of care" to address health and mental illness, and the evolving roles played by special educators.

Sidebar 12-1

According to Hernandez and Hodges (2003), a system of care for students with EBD is "an explicit organizational philosophy that emphasizes services that are family focused, individualized, provided in the least restrictive environment, coordinated among multiple agencies, and culturally competent" (p. 19).

Educational Reform

Educational reform is not a new phenomenon. Almost as soon as schools were established in the American colonies, someone was trying to reform them. However, partially as a result of increasing federal involvement in education during the past three decades (see Figure 1-1), recent reform efforts have resulted in more extensive changes in the way schools operate.

Turnbull and colleagues (1999, 2001) have identified three major phases of recent efforts to reform education in general: (1) **enhancing the curriculum**, which is focused on increasing academic performance for all students; (2) **restructuring school governance**, which is focused on providing state and local flexibility; and (3) **reshaping service delivery**—integrating educational, health, and mental health services into one **system of care**. Each of those phases has resulted in legislative action and shifts in professional practice that continue to change the way special educators meet the needs of students with EBD and other IDEA diagnoses. First, in the area of curriculum, there continues to be an emphasis on access to the general education curriculum for all students—including those with disabilities. States, school districts, individual schools, and in some cases individual teachers are being held increasingly accountable for student progress toward state-defined educational goals, as measured by standardized, high-stakes tests. Second, in the area of school governance, the federal government has offered more funding for nontraditional educational models and strategies, including charter schools, alternative schools, school vouchers, faith-based initiatives, and waivers. The third trend—emergence of the systems-of-care approach—has particular significance for special educators who work primarily with students who have EBD.

However, complex organizations—specifically school systems—do not change overnight as result of legislative mandates. The commitment of all stakeholders (i.e., parents, teachers, administrators, related services personnel, and community providers) is necessary if schools are to successfully incorporate and implement new legal directives. Walther-Thomas, Korinek, and McLaughlin (1999) identified the six key components of successful organizational change: shared leadership, a coherent vision, comprehensive planning, adequate resources, sustained implementation, and continuous evaluation for improvement. While this chapter focuses specifically on the increasingly collaborative role of special educators, a successful district or program will require that these other components be addressed effectively at the organizational level as well.

Developing Systems of Care

There appears to be an emerging consensus that schools do not exist solely to provide academic instruction, and that they cannot operate effectively in isolation from the rest of the community (Chesapeake Institute, 1994). Rather, schools must work collaboratively with other community agencies and stakeholders to provide services that "wrap around" the child with special needs and work as a cohesive system. The SED National Agenda (introduced in Chapter 4) identified seven target areas to address in developing a model for "enhancing the capacity of schools to foster the emotional adjustment of all students with emotional and behavioral problems" (Osher & Hanley, 2001, p. 374). Their national study on implementation of the research agenda identified common components of successful programs for students with EBD that includes: (a) building the capacity of the organization to extend supports into students' natural environments, providing wrap-around services and linkages that extend beyond the school; (b) a focus on culturally competent approaches that value diversity, encourage reflective assessment, and recognize intercultural dynamics; (c) collaboration with families that encourages active involvement in planning, implementation, and evaluation of programs for their children; and (d) building the capacity of the professional staff to engage in flexible collaborative service delivery to students with EBD. A study conducted in the state of Ohio found that successful interagency collaborative efforts were characterized by: organizational commitment, open lines of communication, strong leadership from key decision makers, an understanding of the cultures of each participating agency, adequate resources (time and money), effective strategies to minimize turf issues, and serious preplanning for collaboration (Johnson, Zorn, Tam, Lamontagne, & Johnson, 2003). However, within the general framework provided by the common goals, the details of each collaborative partnership will vary from school to school. That is, the membership and components of each wrap-around system must be determined by the stakeholders—children, families, teachers, and professionals from other agencies—based on unique community resources and needs.

For example, one such collaborative system of care in a southwestern U.S. suburb (Duckworth et al., 2001) resulted in formation of a behavioral support team that included university special education professors, undergraduate special education students serving as mentors, the special education teacher and teaching assistant, the school guidance counselor and principal, a child psychologist from the local mental health agency, the director of the local alternative school, and parents of students with EBD. The team selected and implemented the following program components: data-based behavioral instruction with a classroom observation booth available for parents or others; an alternative-to-suspension program to reduce out-of-school suspensions; cost-free, direct psychological services to students provided in their classrooms; off-site family counseling provided at the local mental health agency; a mentoring program; instruction in a research-based social skills curriculum; monthly parent meetings; and home visits, as needed. As a result of implementing this array or menu of services, the

TABLE 12–1 Key System-of-Care Values and Principles and Their Relative Impacts on Effectiveness, Efficiency, and Equity

Values/Guiding Principles	Effectiveness	Efficiency	Equity
Value			
Child-centered, family-focused services	High	Low	Medium
Community-based services	Low	Low	High
Cultural competency	High	Low	High
Principle			
Access to comprehensive array of services	Medium	Medium	High
Individualized services	High	Low	Medium
Least restrictive and normative environment	Medium	High	Low
Family participation	High	Low	Low
Integrated services	Low	High	Medium
Case management and service coordination	High	High	Low
Early identification and intervention	Medium	High	High
Smooth transitions to adult system	Medium	Medium	High
Protect and promote children's rights	Low	Low	High
Services delivered without regard to race, religion, national origin, gender, physical disability, and responsive to cultural differences and special needs	Medium	Low	High

Source: From "Deconstructing research on systems of care for youth with EBD: Frameworks for policy research" by A. Rosenblatt and M. W. Woodbridge, 2003, *Journal of Emotional and Behavioral Disorders, 11,* 27–37, Table 2. Copyright 2003 by PRO-Ed, Inc. Adapted with permission.

school experienced reductions in absences, office referrals, and suspensions while voluntary parent-teacher conferencing increased fourfold.

The research base for this model remains relatively new and, as yet, incomplete. The wrap-around or systems-of-care approach is based on a set of values and principles that address the goals of effectiveness, efficiency, and equity (Rosenblatt & Woodbridge, 2003). However, as illustrated in Table 12–1, the components do not affect the three goal areas in equal measure. It is also apparent from research and experience that interventions at the system level have not always resulted in the anticipated or hoped-for improvement in emotional/behavioral outcomes for individual students. Hernandez and Hodges (2003) pose two research questions related to the relationship between systems-level and child-level interventions: "Do systems of care moderate delivery of effective interventions? Do systems of care mediate delivery of effective interventions?" (p. 24). Researchers must study this relatively recent service-delivery model thoroughly, applying what is known about best practice in systems change and best practice in individual interventions to examine the relationship between the two.

Roles of the Special Educator

Thirty years ago, the common impression of a special educator's job might have been similar to the situation described at the beginning of the chapter in Vignette A. When schools identified students as eligible for special education, many of them were "pulled out" of the general education classroom and received the bulk of their academic instruction in a small classroom with other students with disabilities. While dedicated special education schools and classrooms still exist where they are

needed, the trend is toward inclusive programming. Therefore, many special educators now function more like Teacher B. This increasingly collaborative role has evolved over time, requiring special education teachers to possess greater flexibility and a more extensive and diverse set of skills. Increasingly, in practice, general education and special education share responsibility for the education of all students, regardless of ability or disability. The primary responsibilities of these "new" special educators fall in the areas of instruction, assessment, communication, leadership, and record keeping (Fisher, Frey, & Thousand, 2003; Lucas, 2004). These roles and responsibilities are often fluid, based on the needs of students in their caseload. The roles may change over time or even within the school day, from direct instruction to assessment to coteaching to collaborative consultation.

OVERVIEW OF COLLABORATIVE CONSULTATION

In the **collaborative consultation** process, group members agree to a set of common values about working together and with students. They share leadership, delegate responsibilities, and hold each other accountable for following through on their commitments (Idol, Nevin, & Paolucci-Whitcomb, 1995). Idol, Paolucci-Whitcomb, and Nevin (1995) identified four essential principles of the collaborative consultation model: "(1) team ownership of the problem, (2) recognition of individual differences in the developmental process, (3) application of reinforcement principles and practices results in improved skills, knowledge, and attitudes for all members of the team, and (4) making data-based decisions through a functional analysis of behaviors" (pp. 333–337). See Figure 12–1 for some helpful definitions.

Collaboration—"Style for direct interaction between at least two coequal parties voluntarily engaged in shared decision making as they work toward a common goal" (Friend, 2005, pp. G3–G4).

Consultation—"Voluntary process in which one professional assists another to address a problem concerning a third party; in schools, consultants are often psychologists or other specialists, consultees often are teachers, and clients usually are students" (Friend, 2005, p. G4).

Collaborative Consultation—"Interactive process that enables people with diverse expertise to generate creative solutions to mutually defined problems. The outcome is enhanced, altered, and produces solutions that are different from those that the individual team members would produce independently. The major outcome of collaborative consultation is to provide comprehensive and effective programs for students with special needs within the most appropriate context, thereby enabling them to achieve maximum constructive interaction with their nonhandicapped peers" (Idol, Paolucci-Whitcomb, & Nevin, 1995, p. 329).

FIGURE 12–1 Definitions

COLLABORATIVE CONSULTATION SKILLS AND COMPETENCIES

Turnbull and Turnbull (2001) describe a number of professional obligations for building reliable alliances with families. Those responsibilities include, among others: knowing yourself, knowing families, honoring cultural diversity, and practicing positive communication skills. While the Turnbulls discussed these obligations in the context of building empowering alliances specifically with parents of students with disabilities, the concepts apply equally well to working with other professionals in a collaborative fashion.

Knowing Yourself

Individuals interpret observations, perceptions, and experiences through the filters of their own prior experiences and values system. Before entering into a collaborative relationship with another professional or a parent, it is helpful to examine one's own preconceptions and comfort level about working with others. For example, working closely with other teachers may require a relatively high degree of comfort about sharing power and responsibility for classroom instruction (Keefe, Moore, & Duff, 2004). Collaboration requires the ability to compromise and be flexible about how tasks are accomplished. If your collaborative partner is from a different ethnic or cultural background, explore your own culture, heritage, beliefs, and values—as well as learning about your partner's experience (Santos & Reese, 1999; Shaw, 1997). The questions in Figure 12-2 may help identify issues to work on—or to be sensitive to—in developing alliances with potential collaborative partners.

Knowing Your Collaborative Partners

An essential component of collaborative problem solving is recognizing that each stakeholder brings to the table a unique set of concerns, based on her role and her relationship to the problem being addressed. Walther-Thomas and colleagues (1999) describe the varying perspectives and agendas that may be found among the types of individuals that might be present at an IEP meeting:

> Principals tend to focus on schoolwide issues such as achievement trends, financial implications, professional development, student placement, professional schedules, and community relations. Teachers and specialists typically are more interested in classroom issues such as individual and group performance, IEP planning, and

new demands on their roles and responsibilities. Added to this complex mix of concerns are the priorities of families, who care most about the potential impact of new initiatives on their children. (p. 2)

Like families, schools are made up of a complex network of interactions that shift and evolve over time. Both the family systems approach and organizational learning theory provide strategies for addressing collaboration. For example, Turnbull and Turnbull (2001) suggest that teachers who work most effectively with families make a concerted effort to learn about the family's characteristics, interactions, functions, and life cycle (or developmental) issues. Organizational development theory suggests that organizations, like families, are systems that develop their own culture and go through specific stages over time. Nevis, DiBella, and Gould (1994) describe the three stages of organizational development as follows:

1. **Knowledge acquisition**—The development or creation of skills, insights, relationships.
2. **Knowledge sharing**—The dissemination of what has been learned.
3. **Knowledge utilization**—The integration of learning so it is broadly available and can be generalized to new situations. (Introduction, para. 7)

An awareness of which developmental stage the collaboration is in allows team members to identify and focus on their mutual agenda, delegate responsibility appropriately, and use their time effectively.

One of the first tasks in any new relationship is getting to know the other person, exploring common interests and experiences, and identifying differences in approach or philosophy. Make time to develop rapport and trust among collaborative partners *before* tackling the problems to be solved. (Mattessich & Monsey, 1993).

One facet of getting to know your collaborative partners is working out how the team will share information and skills. In a collaborative effort, leadership tends to be situational rather than hierarchical; that is, the person assuming the role of meeting facilitator may be the individual with the most knowledge or skill related to the situation, rather than the highest-ranking person in the room. As are other roles in collaborative relationships, leadership may also be fluid, changing based on the team members, the situation, or the goal of the group.

Because the special educator is often the team member with the most information concerning the IDEA process, developing accommodations and modifications, and behavior management, frequently she is the logical person to assume the leadership role in a collaborative

Collaborating with Other Teachers

How comfortable are you thinking about . . .

- sharing your classroom with another teacher?
- going into another teacher's classroom to coteach?
- sharing instructional responsibilities (direct instruction, making assignments, leading discussions)?
- observing another teacher and providing feedback?
- having another teacher observe you and provide feedback?
- sharing responsibility for developing and administering curriculum-based assessments?
- sharing responsibility for assigning grades?
- sharing classroom management responsibilities?
- working with a teacher whose beliefs about students with disabilities is very different than your own?
- working with a teacher whose style or methods appear to be very different than your own?
- working with a teacher whose background appears to be very different than your own?

Do you have any preconceived notions about regular educators or subject area teachers that would make collaboration more difficult?

Collaborating with Parents

How comfortable are you thinking about . . .

- working with parents who are divorced, separated, or who were never married?
- working with nontraditional types of families (e.g., single parent, foster parent, adoptive parent, same-sex couples, extended families or kinship arrangements)?
- sharing information about your personal life, values, and experiences?
- asking questions about their personal life, values, and experiences?
- working with parents whose parenting style appears to be very different than your own?
- working with parents whose beliefs about their child are very different than your own?
- working with parents whose background appears to be very different than your own?

Do you have any preconceived notions about parents and families that would make collaboration more difficult?

Collaborating with Other Paraprofessionals

How comfortable are you thinking about . . .

- sharing your classroom with a paraprofessional?
- sharing or delegating responsibility for instruction and behavior management?
- supervising another adult and providing feedback?
- providing on-the-job training for a paraprofessional?
- working with a paraprofessional whose beliefs about students with disabilities is very different than your own?
- working with a paraprofessional whose background appears to be very different than your own?

If your immediate response to any of these questions is negative, it may signal an issue that will require further thought or study, or additional negotiation with your collaborative partner.

FIGURE 12–2   Finding Your Collaborative Comfort Zone

session or team meeting. Idol, Paolucci-Whitcomb, and Nevin (1995) suggest that the special educator/consultant who finds herself in a leadership position match her style to the skills and needs of the other participants (e.g., parent, regular teacher, paraprofessional, counselor) who will act as mediators in applying new skills with students. Idol and her colleagues provide examples of four different situational leadership styles applied to collaborative teacher interactions:

1. **Telling**—When the mediator is inexperienced or insecure and does not have the requisite skill or attitude, the consultant typically uses Leadership Style 1 (telling) by providing specific information (even to the point of modeling the task until it is demonstrated accurately by the mediator) and by closely supervising the mediator's performance.

2. **Selling**—When the mediator is inexperienced but has a positive attitude about the required process, the consultant should use Leadership Style 2 (selling) by providing the necessary information, providing an opportunity for clarification and accurate demonstration by the mediator, but requiring only intermittent supervision.

3. **Participating**—When the mediator has demonstrated the necessary skills but is insecure or has less than a positive attitude about being able to accomplish the required process successfully, Leadership Style 3 (participating) is utilized. Here, both the consultant and mediator share ideas and help facilitate progress.

4. **Delegating**—When the mediator has demonstrated all of the necessary skills and has a positive attitude about completing the required process effectively, efficiently, and affectively, the consultant should use Leadership Style 4 (delegating). Here, the consultant relies on the skills of the mediator and the mediator's positive attitude to complete the process successfully. If the mediator has already demonstrated the effective use of a variety of the suggested techniques, the consultant can move from the role of instructor to the role of support person. (pp. 339–340)

Successful collaborative relationships require mutual respect, understanding, and trust. However, like other relationships, they require some effort from all parties concerned. Four strategies that will encourage building of rapport among group members include: (1) presenting your own intentions and agendas honestly, (2) taking sufficient time to build a strong relationship, (3) taking sufficient time to understand the cultural context of the team (e.g., the individual members, the agency or school), and (4) exploring commonalities among the group members outside the collaborative relationship (Mattessich & Monsey, 1993).

Developing Cultural Competence

Because of the divergent ways that different cultures view childrearing, medicine, and disability, teachers' and parents' reactions to direct personal questions may vary drastically (Hanson & Lynch, 1990). Cultural viewpoints will also influence the degree to which families wish to share information or become active participants in educational decision making regarding their child. For example, a family whose culture treats disability as a shameful secret may feel very uncomfortable with the entire IDEA process, which involves frank discussions with a number of professional strangers talking about and labeling their child.

One of the challenges facing schools is working effectively with an increasingly diverse student population when the professional educational staff does not reflect the demographics—or the experience—of the students and their families. Shaw (1997) suggests that those teachers who grew up as part of the White, majority culture may bring little intercultural experience to the classroom. Accustomed to seeing their own culture and values reflected in educational and social institutions, they may have had relatively few opportunities to explore their cultural beliefs and values:

> Their education likely has been characterized by *tracking* (the process of assigning students to different groups, classes, or programs based on measures of intelligence, achievement, or aptitude), traditional instruction that appeals to a narrow range of learning styles, and curricula that exclude the contributions of women and people of diverse cultures. (Overview, para. 8)

Thus, teachers raised as part of the majority culture must consciously extend themselves, explore the various communities where they live, and participate in training experiences that go beyond surface-level tolerance activities (McConnell & Townsend, 1997). Santos and Reese (1999) suggest a series of questions to help teachers learn as much as they can about the cultural beliefs, values, and traditions of the parents they work with:

- Are there specific accomplishments the family or community is proud of?
- What do they believe are the most important things their children should learn?
- Who are the members of the family and what are their roles?
- How do they see their role as parents?
- Are there elements of their culture they guard from outside eyes? If so, why? How will this affect intervention?
- Do they have concerns about stereotyping, prejudice, and discrimination?
- What is their history with educational, health, and welfare institutions?
- How do their experiences with those services affect their willingness to access services? (p. 1)

These cross-cultural challenges are not unique to the field of education. They extend to many of the community agencies that might serve as collaborative partners for serving students with EBD. For example, Walker (2001) interviewed caregivers of 296 children involved in community counseling and found that approximately half of the parents felt mental health service providers had not demonstrated respect of their culture. A large proportion of the low-income caregivers also described service providers as insensitive to the additional stresses placed on their families by their limited incomes. Therefore, cultural competence activities

1. Develop a clearer sense of your own ethnic and cultural identity.
2. Examine your attitude toward other ethnocultural groups.
3. Learn about the dynamics of prejudice and racism and how to deal with them in the classroom.
4. Learn about the dynamics of privilege and economic oppression and about school practices that contribute to the reproduction of social inequalities.
5. Learn about the histories and contributions of various ethnocultural groups.
6. Learn about the characteristics and learning styles of various groups and individuals, as well as the limitations of this information.
7. Study sociocultural research about the relationships among language, culture, and learning.
8. Learn how to gain more information about the communities represented in your classroom.
9. Learn how to assess the relationships between classroom methods and the preferred learning and interaction styles in your students' homes and communities.
10. Use a variety of instructional strategies and assessment procedures sensitive to cultural and linguistic variations; adapt classroom instruction and assessment to accommodate the cultural resources that your students bring to school.
11. Study examples of successful instruction of ethnic- and language-minority students.
12. Implement new strategies with colleagues who can provide both intellectual challenge and social support.

FIGURE 12–3   Preparing to Work with Diverse Students and Families

Source: Adapted from *Educating Teachers for Diversity* by Carla Cooper Shaw, available online at http://www.ncrel.org/sdrs/areas/issues/educatrs/presrvce/pe300.htm. Copyright © 1997 by North Central Regional Educational Laboratory, a wholly owned subsidiary of Learning Point Associates. Adapted with permission from Zeichner, K.M. (1993, February). *Educating teachers for cultural diversity* (NCRTL special report). East Lansing, MI: National Center for Research on Teacher Learning. (ERIC Document Reproduction No. ED 359 167)

should be made available to all collaborative partners. Figure 12–3 outlines a sample cultural competence curriculum sequence for teachers preparing to work with a diverse student population.

Communicating Effectively

Effective collaborators must first be effective communicators. This section will provide an overview of essential communication skills for the EBD teacher, including being prepared, listening and responding, questioning and feedback techniques, and dealing with resistance.

Being Prepared.   Before a meeting with parents or other collaborative partners, engage in preplanning and preparation. Being unprepared gives others the impression that you do not value their time, or that the topic under discussion is not important to you. Have any necessary forms, data, and information gathered, copied, and prepared prior to meeting time. If there will be an agenda or handouts for the meeting, provide them to participants in advance so that they may also come prepared. If there is no formal agenda, develop a list of key points you want to cover in the meeting.

Also consider the meeting location and furnishings. Level the playing field by providing comfortable seating of equal height around a table; avoid meeting with someone across a desk. Consider meeting in the library or other neutral location rather than on your own turf.

Listening and Responding.   In his book *Seven Habits of Highly Effective People* (2004), Stephen Covey suggests that effective individuals seek first to understand others, then to make themselves understood. In a collaborative relationship, both listening and speaking can be equally important. Active listeners are not passive or mute. Rather, they use verbal and nonverbal cues to acknowledge and encourage their communicative partner. Making eye contact, nodding, and leaning toward the individual all give the speaker the impression of complete attention. Other nonverbal considerations include providing a comfortable amount of personal space, taking turns and leaving enough silence or wait time to be sure the speaker is finished, and keeping a pleasant and attentive facial expression. When listening to a collaborative partner, it is important to be nonjudgmental, and attend to the other person's feelings, not just the words (Aldinger, Warger, & Eavy, 1991). Your partners will also appreciate the appropriate use of humor, as well as use of a common vocabulary rather than professional jargon.

Questioning and Feedback Techniques.   Soliciting information from other people may involve a variety of question and feedback types, depending on the situation. If you are meeting with someone for the first time, you may want to ask easy questions first, and work your way up to more difficult topics as you develop rapport (Aldinger et al., 1991).

To draw out the other person or to obtain general, qualitative information, you may wish to ask **open-ended questions**. For example, "Tell me more about Janine's early school experiences."

Closed questions have a predetermined set of answers (e.g., yes/no, time of day). They are useful if you need specific, quantitative information. For example, "What was Janine's reading level on the last standardized test?"

Some types of questions are used to provide feedback to the speaker, as well as to verify information or to check understanding. **Paraphrasing** involves restating what the other person said, in your own words: "So Janine was reading on grade level until the end of second grade?" A **clarifying question** often is a follow-up, designed to get more information, "Help me understand why the team decided not to refer Janine to special education." **Reflecting** provides an opportunity to restate the content of the conversation, as well as the affect or underlying feeling you believe you are hearing. For example, "It sounds like the past year has been very frustrating in terms of Janine's reading problems." Irmsher (1996) suggests two additional types of feedback that may be appropriate in a collaborative setting: praise and "I" messages. Some parents and teachers, particularly those who are feeling discouraged or frustrated, may benefit from recognition of their efforts and accomplishments. **Praise** should not be insincere or "gushy" but should be an honest expression of appreciation. For example, "You have really hung in there with Janine and with the team while we tried to figure things out. I appreciate your patience." **"I" messages** acknowledge the needs of the speaker, or the way others' behavior affects the speaker, without casting blame. "When everyone is talking at the same time, I can't hear the speaker, and I'm beginning to feel frustrated." (As opposed to, "Would you be quiet so I can hear?")

Dealing with Resistance. Collaboration is usually initiated when there is a problem to solve, or as part of an organizational change process. Many parents, teachers, administrators, and other potential collaborative partners may be resistant to change. Their reasons may include a lack of skill, a lack of confidence in their own ability, a lack of motivation to change the way they do things, or a negative attitude toward the collaborative partnership (Aldinger et al., 1991). If you can identify the source of their resistance, you may be able to provide the information, encouragement, or positive model they need. According to Aldinger and colleagues, behaviors that signal resistance include: (1) stalling, wasting time, or using delaying tactics; (2) questioning the methods, techniques, or strategies proposed for implementation; (3) agreeing in the meeting but taking no action afterward; (4) justifying or intellectualizing the lack of interest or action; (5) continuing to search for solutions or do more research when everyone else is ready to act; and (6) blaming others or engaging in personal attacks. In each case, the consultant should remain calm and professional and use active listening and questioning techniques to try to move the group toward agreement on a mutual goal and the plan for reaching it.

CONSULTATION WITH OTHER PROFESSIONALS

Working with Teachers

When teachers collaborate with other teachers, they need to negotiate the parameters of their relationship. This section will discuss the importance of clarifying roles, as well as overview common coteaching models.

Clarifying Roles. As Keefe and Colleagues (2004) point out, to be a successful coteacher "you need to (a) know yourself, (b) know your partner, (c) know your students, and (d) know your 'stuff'" (p. 37). This is also true for EBD professional educators who are providing pull-out services, consulting with classroom teachers on individual student accommodations and modifications, serving on a student assistance team, or providing inservice training for colleagues on positive behavioral supports or functional behavioral assessment. For special educators whose job description includes all of those activities in the course of a week, clarifying roles is an important first step to planning and prioritizing the week's schedule of activities. Robinson (1989) stresses the importance of negotiating collaboration or coteaching roles based on the needs of specific students. Topics for discussion between regular and special educators typically include: (a) modifying materials or assignments, (b) monitoring problem behavior, (c) providing large-group instruction, (d) providing small-group instruction, (e) observing/charting behavior, (f) circulating to check work and provide brief reteaching, and (g) grading papers/assessing progress.

An important consideration in negotiating your role with another professional is the degree to which you are able to "give up" some of the responsibility that may have been yours in the past. Keefe and colleagues (2004) suggest that prospective collaborators ask themselves the following questions:

- How much am I willing to surrender to another teacher? Can I allow her to create a unit, a lesson, a modification, or even an assignment in an area that I feel is my bailiwick?
- How much am I willing to learn from a colleague? Will I resent or be intimidated by suggestions from someone not considered to be my superior? How will I react to new information, methods, or ideas that are not my own?
- How much am I willing to share the bond that I have developed with my students? Will the other teacher become the inspiration that I hoped I would be? Will they be asked the questions that I want to answer?
- How much am I willing to step in when I know that I can contribute to a plan, an activity, or a project that I haven't created? Will I be supportive and offer assistance graciously?
- How much am I willing to share control over classroom organization and management issues, particularly discipline and grades? (p. 38)

The final consideration when determining collaborative roles involves carving out sufficient time for both individual and joint planning and evaluation.

Coteaching, Team Teaching, and the Class-Within-a-Class Model. When the terms coteaching, team teaching, or class-within-a-class are used in the context of collaboration between special and general educators, they represent a variety of styles for sharing responsibility in inclusive settings. Cook and Friend (1996) suggest teachers become familiar with the various models of coteaching, and select the style that is most appropriate for a particular situation, or a particular subject. Friend and colleagues (Friend, 2005; Friend & Cook, 2003) have developed descriptive labels for six of the most common configurations:

1. **One teach, one observe**—Teacher A leads the group discussion while Teacher B observes and takes data.
2. **One teach, one assist**—Teacher A leads the lesson while Teacher B monitors the class and provides individual assistance, as needed.
3. **Parallel teaching**—Teacher A and Teacher B divide the class and each teach a small group at the same time.
4. **Station teaching**—Teacher A and Teacher B are located in different places in the room and provide a specified portion of the lesson as students rotate among stations.
5. **Alternative teaching**—Teacher A and Teacher B take turns leading classroom instruction.
6. **Teaming**—Teacher A and Teacher B direct instruction together.

Coteaching is not a new phenomenon; some schools implemented coteaching as part of the special education continuum of services in the early days of PL 94–142. An early study of the class-within-a-class (CWC) model interviewed teachers in one of the first training groups sponsored by the University of Kansas in the mid-1980s. The teachers identified the following aspects of CWC as being critical for successful implementation: (a) the philosophies and personalities of the two teachers should be compatible, (b) teachers had to be willing to compromise, (c) all students must be treated similarly/equally by both teachers, and (d) CWC assistance should be available to all students, not just those identified as eligible for special education (Dissinger, 1988).

Almost 15 years later, Arguelles, Hughes, and Schumm (2000) identified seven factors that influenced the effectiveness of coteaching: (1) common planning time, (2) flexibility, (3) risk taking, (4) defined roles and responsibilities, (5) compatibility, (6) communication skills, and (7) administrative support. Keefe and Moore (2004) conducted interviews with secondary coteachers and also found that compatibility and open communication were important factors in successful teaming. However, at the secondary level, the ability to teach the content or curriculum became more important; both general and special educators stressed the need for the secondary special educator to be competent to teach the course content.

Despite more than two decades of collaborative experiences, Weiss (2004) reviewed more than 700 articles and books on coteaching and found the research base to be incomplete. Many articles reflected the lack of clear definition of roles, a lack of a consensus on the definition of coteaching, and a lack of specific measurable student outcomes. In addition, Weiss found that the variable for success upon which there was most agreement appeared to be personality, which is difficult to define or quantify. Many studies identified lack of common planning time as the biggest barrier to collaboration (e.g., Keefe & Moore, 2004; Robinson, 1989). "When general and special educators collaborate, planning time becomes sacred" (Wunder & Lindsey, 2004, Plan Together section). This may require the assistance of administration and colleagues in adjusting schedules, instructional, and noninstructional responsibilities to assure a consistent time when collaborative teams can meet. Ideally, this would be a scheduled release period; however, creative scheduling of assemblies, homeroom or advising periods, extracurricular activities, and clubs also can provide an opportunity for teams to meet while students are supervised by other school personnel.

In an effort to address the time constraints of full-time coteaching, Walsh and Jones (2004) developed three variations called Collaborative Scheduling. In Option A, the special educator travels between two different classrooms during one class period. In Option B, the special educator is present for the entire period on alternate days, providing differentiated instruction. Option C uses one or more paraprofessionals as part of the general/special education team, to extend the support of the special education program to students in general education settings.

Working with Paraprofessionals

Friend (2005) defines paraeducators as follows: "Para-educators—also called **paraprofessionals**, teaching assistants, instructional assistants, one-to-one assistants, or aides (although this last term is no longer preferred)—are educators who work under the direction of a teacher or another school professional to help in the delivery of services for students with disabilities" (p. 50). (We will use the term paraprofessional in this discussion.) Paraprofessionals have been part of the special education system of service delivery since passage of PL 94–142; however, changing social conditions and educational priorities have led to a dramatic increase in the use of paraprofessionals in the past decade. During the 1994–1995 school year, 450,598 educational aides comprised 9.4% of the total elementary and secondary education workforce (National Center for Educational Statistics, 1995). In 2002–2003, 664,385 paraprofessionals made up 11.2% of the K–12 workforce, a 47% increase compared to an increase in the total student population of only 11% during the same period of time (National Center for Educational Statistics, 2005).

French (2003) identified five factors that appear to have contributed to the apparent shift toward use of less-trained service providers:

1. **Inclusion**—To provide greater attention and support for students with special needs being served in general education classrooms.
2. **High academic standards**—To assist students in making adequate yearly progress in the general education curriculum on assessments mandated by NCLB and IDEA.
3. **Legislative changes and litigation**—To assist in delivering special education services as part of a free, appropriate public education in accordance with IDEA 1997 and Title I as extended by NCLB.
4. **Related services**—To assist in providing nonmedical related services under the supervision of a trained supervisor (e.g., nurse, speech pathologist, occupational/physical therapist).
5. **Shortage of fully qualified professionals**—To augment the special education staff by performing day-to-day classroom activities under the supervision of a qualified educator.

In addition, paraprofessionals have provided some districts with an opportunity to diversify their instructional staff by employing individuals who live in the same community and share the same culture or language with their students and families (Bernal & Aragon, 2004; Chopra et al, 2004; French, 2004).

The No Child Left Behind Act of 2001 (NCLB) specified that paraprofessionals employed in Title I schools must have completed a minimum of two years of college to be considered qualified to work with high-risk students. IDEA 1997 specifically authorized the use of paraprofessionals to support students with disabilities; however, no minimum standards were established for their educational qualifications. Therefore, states have established varying criteria and policies regarding paraprofessionals, and the type of work paraprofessionals are allowed to do varies from state to state.

A study conducted with 737 school personnel and parents in the state of Vermont examined how special education paraprofessionals spent their time during the school day (Giangreco & Broer, 2005). Results indicated that, overall, paraprofessionals spent almost half of their time (47.34%) delivering instruction that had been planned by special educators, with the remainder divided between behavior support (19.05%), self-directed activities not planned by special educators (17.29%), supervising students (6.84%), clerical activities (4.40%), personal care (3.40%), and other (1.26%). However, there was considerable variation among paraprofessional activities depending on whether they were working with a group or with individual students. For some students, it appeared that the bulk of their instruction was provided by the paraprofessional, rather than by the general or special educator. Giangreco and Broer (2005) raise the concern that the least qualified personnel are in some cases responsible for working with the students with the most difficult learning characteristics: "Do we really want a model where if you are *not* disabled, you receive your instruction from a highly qualified teacher, and if you have a disability, especially if it is considered severe, you receive the bulk of your instruction from paraprofessionals, with no guarantee of their qualifications?" (p. 24).

Stakeholder perceptions of paraprofessionals, including those teachers, parents, and students with disabilities, have mostly been positive, however (e.g., Broer, Doyle. & Giangreco, 2005; Giangreco, 2003; Werts, Harris, Tillery, & Roark, 2004). Often, paraprofessionals provide a vital connection between the school and parents (Chopra et al., 2004). Many paraprofessionals get to know individual students and parents well, and become the principal channel of communication between home and school. They are often the person responsible for meeting the student at the door in the morning and sending home progress notes or other information at the end of the school day. If parents and teacher speak a different language, bilingual paraprofessionals can bridge the gap by providing services for students with limited proficiency in English, and by translating information for family members (Bernal & Aragon, 2004; Chopra et al., 2004; French, 2004). Because paraprofessionals may spend more time with students, they often gain valuable insights into their academic and social behaviors (Chopra & French, 2004).

Teachers of students with EBD can ensure the effectiveness of their paraprofessionals and their special education program in several ways. In any collaborative relationship, roles and responsibilities must be clearly defined, in this case based on the needs of the student(s) and the skills of the paraprofessional. Generally, the trained special or general educator is responsible for planning instruction, and the paraprofessional is responsible for implementing the activities as planned. While paraprofessionals may collect student data and grade papers, the teacher analyzes the results and translates the data into programming. Paraprofessionals may share information about daily activities, but information concerning academic and behavioral progress may best be addressed by the special educator responsible for implementing the IEP (Chopra & French, 2004). It is the responsibility of the teacher to work with the paraprofessional—and families—to establish and maintain these professional boundaries.

The supervisory relationship requires clear communication and regular feedback sessions during which the special educator provides constructive feedback and reinforcement to the paraprofessional. Giangreco (2003) suggests that the teacher should provide an orientation to the classroom and the students in it, and treat the paraprofessional as a respected, valuable member of the team. Many paraprofessionals will require training in pedagogical techniques and content-specific knowledge. French (2003) provides a list of common paraprofessional training needs based on a review of literature:

- Knowledge of specific disabilities (autism is most frequently mentioned)
- Understanding and following team plans for instruction
- Behavior management: supervision of large groups of children
- Communicating with children
- Social-emotional, physical, and communication development in children
- Learning styles, characteristics of human learning
- Instructional techniques for students with varying abilities
- Instructional techniques for students who are learning to speak English
- Rationale and current issues in inclusion
- Assistive technology
- Promoting social acceptance of children with disabilities
- Individual and small-group instruction
- Working with adults (communicating and conflict management)
- Special education process and laws
- Specific information about targeted students (p. 10)

While responsibility for formal training of paraprofessionals rests with the hiring district, a great deal of their training will occur informally and on the job. Therefore, the EBD teacher may provide both essential information and a positive model of the skills and dispositions desired in paraprofessionals. For districts interested in improving their use of paraprofessionals, *A Guide to Schoolwide Planning for Paraeducator Supports* (Giangreco, Edelman, & Broer, 2001/2002) provides a field-tested process for improving paraeducator supports and ultimately improving student outcomes (Giangreco, Edelman, & Broer, 2003).

CONSULTATION WITH FAMILIES

What is a family? There are many, and varied, definitions. For the purposes of this discussion, we will use the definition of a family proposed by Hanson and Lynch (1992):

A family is considered to be any unit that defines itself as a family including individuals who are related by blood or marriage as well as those who have made a commitment to share their lives. The definition includes the "traditional" nuclear family but also embraces life-styles that range from extended family and kinship networks to single parents and same-sex partners living together. The key elements are that the members of the unit see themselves as a family, are affiliated with one another, and are committed to caring for one another. (p. 284)

As described earlier in this chapter, Turnbull and Turnbull (2001) have identified a number of ways to build empowering collaborative relationships with families of children with disabilities. Several of those strategies—knowing yourself, knowing families, honoring cultural diversity, and practicing positive communication skills—were discussed as they might apply to all collaborative or consultative relationships with other adults. Figure 12-2 provided questions for self-reflection that will allow you to examine your own comfort level in working with parents. In Figure 12-3, Shaw suggested a number of strategies to prepare yourself to work with children and families whose culture and experience are different than your own. Teachers of students with EBD who wish to form reliable, empathetic alliances with families must demonstrate seven essential characteristics of effective allies:

- They know about families.
- They honor families' cultural diversity and mores.
- They affirm and build on families' strengths.
- They promote families' choices.
- They create great expectations for themselves and students.
- They practice positive interpersonal communication techniques.
- And, as a result of doing all of this, they warrant the trust and respect of one another. (Turnbull & Turnbull, 2001, p. 82)

COLLABORATING WITH OTHER AGENCIES IN THE COMMUNITY

Establishing linkages with community agencies that serve youth with EBD and their families is particularly important when planning for student transitions or when the needs of the student for mental health treatment or other services exceed the capacity of school personnel (Walther-Thomas et al., 1999). These agency relationships may be accessed informally, on an as-needed basis, or included in a carefully planned system of service delivery. Chapter 13 will specifically

address collaborative relationships with community mental health providers.

CHAPTER SUMMARY

- As society has changed, so too have the job descriptions of special educators. Increasingly, special education teachers work as consultants and in collaborative teams, rather than in self-contained classrooms. This shift in roles requires a more complex and varied set of skills, particularly effective communication skills for working both with parents and with other professionals. Successful collaboration requires individual teachers to extend themselves beyond their normal comfort zones and develop cultural competence that will allow them to address the needs of an increasingly diverse population of students in a variety of settings.

CHECK YOUR UNDERSTANDING

1. *True or False.* Teaching special education today is very much like it was 25 years ago.
2. Define consultation.
3. Define collaboration.
4. Define collaborative consultation.
5. *True or False.* There is a solid research base that supports coteaching.
6. Differentiate between open and closed questions.
7. Turn the following closed question into an open question: "Does Janine have a specific time and place to do her homework every night?"
8. Turn the following blaming statement into an "I" message: "Why can't you mind your own business and stop tattling?"
9. List and briefly describe the six models of coteaching described by Friend and colleagues.
10. Provide your own answer to the question, "What is a family?"

APPLICATION ACTIVITIES

1. Individually, answer the questions in Figure 12-2. Then, in a small group, discuss your answers and identify areas where you would need more information to engage in a thorough discussion with your collaborative partners.
2. Visit the North Central Regional Educational Laboratory (NCREL) Web site at

http://www.ncrel.org. Do a search for *Critical Issue: Educating Teachers for Diversity*. Scan through the topics and identify at least one that you will explore through further reading and study.

3. Download *A Guide to Schoolwide Planning for Paraeducator Supports* from http://www.uvm.edu/~cdci/parasupport/downloads/guide.pdf. Interview a teacher, administrator, or paraprofessional from an area school district concerning their use of paraprofessionals in special education, using the self-assessment instrument that begins on page 7 of the guide as the basis for your questions.

4. Select a case study from Appendix A. Based on what you know about this child, what do you know about the family's characteristics, interactions, functions, and life-cycle issues? Make a list of questions you would like to ask if you were this child's teacher and were scheduled to meet with the parent or parents tomorrow.

SCHOOL PARTNERSHIPS WITH MENTAL HEALTH AND MEDICAL PROFESSIONALS

Bill J. McHenry, Jr.

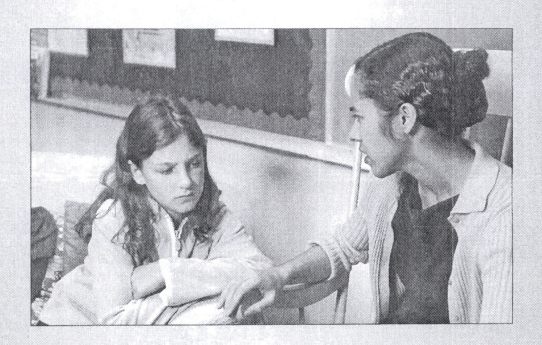

CHAPTER PREVIEW

CONNECTING TO THE CLASSROOM: *A Vignette*

Amy is a 14-year-old Caucasian girl who has typically shown great interest in school. Prior to the last few weeks, she was an energetic and active member of the junior choir, the marching band, and the varsity volleyball team. She was very outgoing and vibrant, but, over the last month, Amy has been far less engaged in her regular activities in the classroom and is not putting her typical amount of work into class projects. You have overheard some of her peers saying that she has stopped attending volleyball practice and has begun showing up late for band practice. Additionally, she missed the band competition last weekend. You have noticed that her affect appears to be blunted, and she seems to have very little energy. It is obvious to many, including you, that something significant has changed in Amy's life. You spoke with another of her teachers who noticed the same types of behavior and also added that Amy has reported that she is having trouble just getting going in the morning. Amy also told this teacher that she is trying to not let things bother her, but feels like her life has no meaning and she doesn't really want to do anything. Two weeks ago, Amy missed four days of school and on the one day she attended she appeared to be very lethargic and sad. Last week, she missed the entire week of school.

MENTAL HEALTH ISSUES

The number of students diagnosed with mental illnesses is on the rise (Baker & Gerler, 2004). Common mental health concerns addressed by teachers of students with EBD include eating disorders, anxiety disorders, depression (which may be Amy's diagnosis), attention-deficit disorder, substance abuse, self-injurious behavior, and conduct disorders. Because of the sharp rise in these and many other mental health concerns, school personnel must take on more diagnostic and evaluative roles in relation to mental illness and psychological imbalance. Therefore, *all* school personnel must be aware of the mental health needs of students and the various services provided by other school professionals. To maximize their effectiveness in this area, educators should get to know their school counselors, psychologists, social workers, and other related services and ancillary personnel on a professional level, learn how they define their roles in helping students, and find out what strategies and techniques they use to work with students. Teachers can collaborate and become more effective in helping students by finding out what information the helping professional needs in order to best work with students whom the educator has referred.

Students sometimes fall through the cracks not because school personnel are uncaring, inefficient, or inept, but simply because the students are not connected with the helping professionals available. Other times, their problems are not noticed. Through effective identification and referral of students who have emotional and behavioral problems—whether or not they are eligible for special education and related services for EBD—teachers and administrators can go a long way to avoiding that common error of omission.

This chapter addresses the need for school personnel to understand and effectively utilize resources both within and outside the school's walls to provide students with EBD the professional help they need to achieve their academic, social, emotional, and holistic potential. We pay special attention to collaborations among teachers and other professionals, and the significant relationships that must exist between schools and other agencies. We also provide an introduction to some of the mental health professionals and highlight major approaches and techniques used by these experts (individual and group counseling, group therapy, family counseling, play therapy, pharmacological interventions, etc.).

PERSONNEL WITHIN THE SCHOOL

In addition to teachers, a variety of professionals may work with students who have EBD. The two most common groups are school counselors and school psychologists.

School Counselors

One of the primary ways schools detect and address student mental health concerns is through the school counselor (Baker & Gerler, 2004). Positioned *within* the school, school counselors are usually the most accessible professional resource available to other school staff members. Active and engaged school counselors promote open discussions with students about their concerns or issues. The school counselor's office plays an important role in helping students with psychological concerns (Myrick, 2003).

While students often refer themselves to the counseling office for help, in other cases administrators, teachers, school nurses, social workers, parents, or other students refer the student (Thompson, 2002). Once the student arrives at the school counselor's office, the counselor will do a quick assessment to ascertain the source of the problem. The counselor may ask the student questions such as: "How long have you been having the problem?" or "Do you remember when the problem started?" Though many school counselors are neither trained nor competent to do a full psychological evaluation and provide a diagnosis, school counselors *are* trained to listen for threats of harm to self or others and explore possible individual or familial stressors. They are also able to provide short-term counseling services.

There are times, of course, where the school counselor may determine that neither individual nor group intervention within the school is adequate to deal with the issue(s) presented. Examples of issues that may demand specialized, long-term therapy from outside professionals include sexual abuse or trauma, suicidal ideation, homicidal ideation, eating disorders, or suspicion of severe mental illness such as schizophrenia. Note, however, that the school counselor may continue to work with the student and his or her family in an adjunct or supportive role, especially if the student is a minor. At times, the school counselor will also need to engage other school personnel such as administrators, school nurses, school social workers, and school psychologists in the decision concerning referral.

Who Pays for Related Services?

As discussed in Chapter 3, **related services**, including counseling, psychological, and social work services, may be a critical component of a free, appropriate public education (FAPE) for students with EBD. However, some school personnel may feel reluctant to refer students to professionals outside the building due to concerns about financial responsibility. Downing (2004) provided this summary of the funding options for counseling and other related services.

Who Pays for Related Services?

As the costs of providing related services have shifted to the schools, increasing attention has been concentrated on developing effective funding mechanisms, particularly for complex medical and health-related services (Katsiyannis, 1990; Maag & Katsiyannis, 1996; Rodman et al., 1999; Walsh, 1999). Several laws have specifically sanctioned pursuit of external public and private funding for related services by public schools. The 1986 reauthorization of IDEA referred to the need for external funding and interagency agreements and stipulated that states were not allowed to reduce Medicaid or other financial assistance to eligible clients. The Medicare Catastrophic Coverage Act of 1988 confirmed Medicaid agencies' responsibility for reimbursing eligible related services costs as part of their state benefits package.

A national survey of special education directors identified a number of barriers to efficient financing of related services (Rodman et al., 1999), including the high cost of services for assistive technology and communicative devices and difficulty accessing third party payers due to concerns about lifetime benefit limits. Related service costs accounted for about 20% of districts' special education funding, or about $1,000 per pupil additional expenditure. The same study pointed to a number of strategies that facilitated Medicaid financing of related services in schools, including developing interagency agreements defining the process for determining eligibility and reimbursement, clarifying the responsibility of each agency, and establishing lines of communication and data sharing. It is clear that the "free" requirement of FAPE means that parents cannot be required to pay for services needed for the student to benefit from special education. Thus, while IDEA allows districts to access public insurance programs like Medicaid, the following limitations have been placed on use of those funding sources:

- The public agency may not require parents to sign up or enroll in public insurance programs in order for their child to receive FAPE under Part B of IDEA.
- The public agency may not require parents to incur an out-of-pocket expense, such as the payment of a deductible or co-pay amount incurred in filing a claim for services. The public agency, however, may pay the cost that the parent would otherwise be required to pay.
- The public agency may not use a child's benefits under a public insurance program if that use would (a) decrease available lifetime coverage or any other insured benefit; (b) result in the family paying for services that would otherwise be covered by the public insurance program and that are required for the child outside of the time the child is in school; (c) increase premiums or lead to the discontinuation of insurance; or (d) risk loss of eligibility for home and community-based waivers, based on the sum total of health-related expenditures (NICHCY, 2001, p. 15). School districts may also access a parent's private insurance coverage by securing informed consent from the parent each time they wish to access the proceeds (§300.142(f) (1–2)).

As was mentioned in Chapter 12, many school counseling programs are moving to a more proactive and comprehensive system-of-care approach toward student development. The goal of such programs is to help students gain insights into their own identities as they grow and develop from children to young adults. Good comprehensive programs do this in a way that is systematic and developmental. These programs attempt to merge each part of the comprehensive school program with all others in order to best address student needs. There is a clear and conscious attempt to merge all school programs into a complete and effective whole which centers on the effective delivery of services to every student. One example of such a program is in operation in a school district in west-central Missouri. In this district, teachers and counselors have integrated preventative mental health topics into daily classroom activities using The Missouri Comprehensive Guidance Model (Missouri Department of Elementary and Secondary Education, 1998). The school uses the program in every grade. For example, in grades K–6, in a section on understanding self, students fill in age- and developmental-stage-appropriate forms that ask them to identify how they are feeling during certain activities. At each grade level, teachers and counselors assist students in identifying, categorizing, and coping with their feelings. In one introductory exercise at the elementary level, "How I feel when I eat my favorite food," the student identifies feelings by choosing from one of three faces presented: one smiling (happy), one frowning (not happy), and one neither smiling nor frowning (neutral) (Missouri Department of Elementary and Secondary Education, 1998). As the students age and develop, building upon elementary-level lessons and insights, students in grades 9–12 are asked to identify and rank their feelings about what activities and things make them most happy.

Using comprehensive models such as the one described above, schools enable students to gain greater awareness of self and others, and tangentially create opportunities for the school counselor and other school personnel to identify and address concerns students may be having.

School Psychologists

Another key professional who works with students with EBD and mental health concerns is the **school psychologist.** School psychologists are trained to assess students through formalized psychological tests and instruments. They are also trained to provide diagnoses and work with students with learning problems and disabilities. School psychologists may also provide significant consultation expertise working with both school staff members and parents/guardians of students. While fully fledged staff members in the school district, school psychologists often have assignments that require them to serve more than one school building or campus. In fact, in rural areas, one school psychologist may have responsibility for coverage of several area school districts.

PERSONNEL OUTSIDE THE SCHOOL

When students with EBD are working with mental health professionals outside the school building, information regarding the student must be shared among the professionals involved. The school personnel working with the student may be asked to provide follow-up documentation of behaviors, become engaged in a plan for wellness provided by the outside mental health provider, or in some cases discontinue services to the student (if, for example, a school employee has unwittingly fallen into an enabling relationship with the student and is actually supporting the undesirable behavior).

Although the work of professionals outside of the school overlaps in various ways, there are differences in their overall job description and scope of competence. What follows is a short list of professionals whom educators may contact and utilize in their comprehensive effort to better serve students with EBD. These experts—clinical social workers, psychiatric nurses, clinical psychologists, and psychiatrists—can provide assistance in ways that are beyond both the scope and the expertise of the day-in and day-out work of school personnel.

Clinical Social Workers

Clinical social workers hold a master's degree in social work augmented with either a certification or license to work with clients. These professionals usually focus on environmental issues that may be affecting the student's thoughts or behaviors (Nugent, 1994). Clinical social workers also receive specialized training in working with entire family systems as a means to helping the student. Clinical social workers can help the student overcome problems encountered in life, thereby facilitating a stronger sense of connection to society (Compton & Galaway, 1999).

Psychiatric Nurses

Psychiatric nurses are registered nurses (RNs) who have a specialized focus on issues such as terminal illness, aging, and problems that include both physical and mental dysfunctions (Nugent, 1994). Typically working in in-patient psychiatric hospitals and out-patient clinics, these medical professionals function as liaison between students and psychiatrists.

Clinical Psychologists

Clinical psychologists (usually possessing a Ph.D. or Psy.D.) are trained specifically to diagnose, evaluate, and treat individuals with mental illnesses. They receive substantial training in administering and interpreting psychological tests and assessments. They may also receive training to work with children with severe dysfunctions. Clinical psychologists usually either have a private practice in which they see clients, or work in community-agency mental health clinics.

Psychiatrists

Psychiatrists are medical doctors who have received specialized training in working with people with psychological impairments. Psychiatrists diagnose and treat mental illnesses, usually through a combination of talk therapy and medications. Psychiatrists may have a private practice or work within a psychiatric mental health hospital, or both. The primary role of the psychiatrist is to prescribe and monitor psychotropic medications.

APPROACHES

Because of differences in training, mental health professionals may use a variety of techniques and approaches in helping students overcome psychological issues. The two main intervention approaches are counseling and the use of medications.

Individual Counseling

Counselors, psychologists, psychiatrists, psychiatric nurses, and social workers provide individual counseling to students. (The term *counselor* is used to encompass those professionals who have received adequate and appropriate professional educational and professional experiences as mandated by their state to render counseling services.) Depending on the counselor's

FIGURE 13–1 Individual Counseling
Copyright © 2005 Lisa Walker

individual philosophies, beliefs, theoretical orientation, and personality, individual counseling may look very different from one counselor to another (Corey & Corey, 2003). Further, depending on the specific needs of the individual student, sessions with different students conducted by the same counselor may look somewhat different as well (Ivey & Ivey, 2003). Generally, however, counselors conducting individual counseling sessions use one of two mediums: talk therapy or play therapy.

In **talk therapy**, the client and counselor engage in a therapeutic verbal interaction regarding the issues or concerns the student is having (Young, 1998). The counselor may ask questions about the problem, may paraphrase what the student is saying, or may confront the student about mistaken goals or beliefs (Brammer, Abrego, & Shostrum, 1993). The following example is a brief look at what a typical individual counseling session may sound like.

Counselor: So what brought you here today?

Student: I'm not feeling like myself lately.

Counselor: You're feeling different than you normally feel.

Student: Yeah, I feel like everyone is mad at me lately.

Counselor: It sounds like you feel like the entire world is not happy with you.

Student: Yeah, I mean, it's like with my friend Mary, she yelled at me today because I was talking too much.

Counselor: So Mary yelled at you because she felt you were talking too much.

In the above example, the counselor asked a question and then paraphrased what she was hearing. In doing this, the counselor helped the student to continue to talk about the problem and become more specific with his concern. Most good individual counseling has three main components: the counselor is empathetic, the counselor has unconditional positive regard for the client, and the counselor is genuine (Rogers, 1951).

In **play therapy**, as the name implies, the counselor creates a therapeutic environment for the student to play through his issues (Webb, 1999). This is accomplished primarily by using toys and games as a means for the child to act out his concerns or problems (Axline, 1969). The counselor does not attempt to intervene through questions, but rather may simply provide a play-by-play description of what the child is doing (Landreth, 1991). In this way, the student has an opportunity to re-create his dilemma in the course of play, and find alternative solutions, again through play.

Group Counseling

Counselors often implement **group counseling** as a means of helping people with similar concerns (Myrick, 2003). Group topics may take the form and shape of open groups (ongoing throughout the school year, with students being added and removed during the life of the group), or closed groups (Capuzzi & Gross, 1992), starting with a number of students, usually between five and eight, that remain intact throughout the life of the group. The latter groups may run from 4 or 5 sessions to 12 to 15 sessions in duration. Group topics may focus on body image, grief and loss, coping with parents' divorce, or a myriad of others.

The goal of many groups is to encourage students to try new ways of coping with their problems and to understand how they relate to and are perceived by others (Yalom, 1995). Groups offer a place for students to feel supported by others, while at the same time students are confronted on their irrational or problematic behaviors (Yalom, 1995). The following excerpt illustrates a closed group that is in its sixth session.

FIGURE 13–2 Play Therapy
Copyright © 2005 Lisa Walker

FIGURE 13–3 Group Counseling
Copyright © 2005 Lisa Walker

Johnny: I am really tired of all of the negativity in this group, you people need to start looking at life for happy things.

Counselor (group facilitator): Johnny, I heard you say that to the entire group; I think that you probably have someone in mind as you say it. Was there someone specific that you wanted to say that directly to?

Johnny: Well . . . yeah . . . I guess, Steve.

In this example, the group facilitator has engineered a direct comment from one student to another that provided feedback to the second student (Steve). As a result of that exchange, Steve may be able to understand that Johnny and possibly others perceive him as being negative. By gaining insight into how others perceive them, group members may begin to effect positive behavioral changes and develop new ways of acting with others. The facilitator asked Johnny to be direct rather than indirect, while Johnny asked Steve to be more positive and less negative. Great care must be taken by the counselor in this instance not to provide too much feedback to the student before they are ready to hear it. For example, providing such feedback in the first session may be more problematic than helpful as the group is developing rapport and trust. However, by the sixth session, the counselor and group members have a better understanding of who they are and what they can share with each other in the group.

Family Therapy

Family therapy includes a number of subtheories within its boundaries, some of which are systemic therapy, Adlerian family therapy, structural therapy, and multigenerational family therapy (note that this is not an all-inclusive list). In general terms, **family therapy** takes place when more than one member of a family participates in counseling services simultaneously (Corey, 2001).

When a student is referred to a family therapist, members of the family are invited to join in the therapy process. The major underlying rationale is the belief that the student's problem is a manifestation of behaviors, rules, patterns, and thoughts held and supported (whether consciously or unconsciously) by the entire family system (or subsystems) (Corey, 2001). For example, some college students attend college because it is a family rule that everyone in the system must get a college education. This is certainly not a bad thing. However, sometimes family rules run counter to the rules of the dominant culture, causing strife in the lives of the family members. For example, if the family system does *not* value education—and in fact, older family members generally disliked attending school themselves—and the children act out the family rule by skipping school, school administrators may be at a loss as to what to do. It is difficult to convince a student of the benefits of school when the student is aware that showing any enjoyment or benefit from school will cause problems at home.

How do family therapists intervene in such troubling cycles? One approach is to find out from the family system if there are any acceptable exceptions to the general rules of the family. Taking the above example, a family therapist may be interested in whether anyone from either side of the extended family (going back several generations) has ever had anything useful come from school. Usually, with some coaxing, the family is able to agree that one or more people did, in fact, get something out of the experience of attending school. This then provides the student with an avenue to have a good experience within school without violating the norms of the family.

Another way that family therapists try to interrupt seemingly unproductive patterns is by changing the way in which family members associate with one another. Believing that each family member exerts an influence on every other family member, the counselor will try to recognize, examine, and change unhealthy family patterns and sequences of interactions. For example, in a family with a student who has been diagnosed as having depression, the family therapist may explore the effect this depressive state has on the rest of the family. The following is an example of a discussion between a family and their family counselor:

Counselor: So as I understand things, it appears that the onset of your depressive episodes has no real cause or defining moment. The depression comes when it wants and leaves when it wants. Right?

Student: Yeah. I have no idea that I am about to become depressed, and then it hits me.

Counselor: I have seen this before. I am wondering if anyone in the family notices anything different about Sam before the depression hits.

Father: It seems to me that right before he gets depressed, he and his mom have an argument over something.

Counselor: Oh really, what do these arguments look like?

Mom: They usually only take a few minutes. He tells me what he wants, usually a new piece of clothing or video game. I tell him that he can't have one. Money is tight right now, and then that's it.

Counselor: So the depression arrives after you two have an argument about something that is wanted but cannot be purchased by the family at that time. I'm wondering if there is a pattern to when the depression leaves.

Dad: I usually break down and buy what he wanted.

This example suggests how the student's behavior is both created and maintained by the family system. He has learned that he can move his father around by having a depressive episode that can then be blamed on his mother.

At this point the family and family counselor have a number of options available. They can work on changing the communication patterns among various family members, including those existing between Sam and his mother, and/or they can attempt to set clearer boundaries within the family system. One major goal might be to establish for everyone that "no" means no.

Family patterns of conflict can often be exacerbated by multicultural and intergenerational issues. Sometimes, for example, students may feel that they are more acculturated than their parents (Sue & Sue, 2003). When this occurs, both parental authority and family rules may be ignored, denounced, or violated by the student in his efforts to be more American in order to fit in with dominant cultural themes and trends deemed appropriate for child or adolescent behavior (Ruiz, 1990).

THEORETICAL ORIENTATIONS

Counselors often vary their counseling techniques and approaches to a client, depending on the individual's needs. Approaches may range from noninvasive psychoeducational approaches like comprehensive guidance, to invasive physician-prescribed psychotropic medications (e.g., Ritalin).

There are a number of distinct theoretical orientations specific to the field of counseling and psychotherapy. The broad categories of individual, group, and family therapy have previously been discussed. This portion of the chapter will focus on therapeutic approaches used in talk therapy that are anchored in a specific theoretical orientation.

Brief Therapy

Brief therapy is a short-term set of interventions used to help a student overcome current life issues. Some

examples of this counseling approach include solution-focused brief therapy (de Shazer, 1985), problem-solving therapy (Haley, 1986), narrative therapy (White & Epston, 1990), and systemic family therapy (Minuchin & Fishman, 1981).

The general rules and guidelines of brief therapies are as follows:

* People operate out of their internal maps and not out of sensory experience.
* People make the best choice for themselves at any given moment.
* The explanation, theory, or metaphor used to relate facts about a person is not the person.
* Respect all messages from the client.
* Teach choice; never attempt to take choice away.
* The resources the client needs lie within his or her own personal history.
* Meet the client at his or her model of the world.
* A person *cannot not* communicate.
* If it's hard work, reduce it down.
* Outcomes are determined at the psychological level. (Cade & O'Hanlon, 1993, p. 10)

In brief therapy, the counselor focuses the therapeutic conversation on exceptions to the rules of the student, provides positive reframes for negative behaviors and thoughts, focuses on the payoff for continuing the behavior, and at times, prompts the client to practice making changes through prescriptions or directives. The following serves as a guide to what the counselor may say to the student in terms of specific skills used in brief therapy.

Mary: I am really upset with the way that my mom and dad have been fighting lately.

Counselor: Who among all of your friends and family is aware of how sensitive you are to your parents need to get along? [Current focus, reframes upset to be a concern for others' welfare, asks what the potential payoff is for the behavior.]

Mary: I guess my mom knows how upset I get when they fight, and how when they fight I just lock myself in my room and don't eat or talk to anyone.

Counselor: Ok, so if I understand the sequence, your parents fight, you get upset, then you isolate yourself, stop eating and talking with others, and then what happens? [Asks about the sequence of behaviors that cause the unwanted behavior of isolation.]

Mary: Then my mom usually talks to me. A day or two later and she makes me feel better, and then a little bit later, my dad will come and talk to me.

Counselor: So the sequence is ended by mom making things better. Has there ever been a time when mom didn't come and talk to you and you stopped isolating yourself from others at home and at school by yourself? [Counselor asks about exceptions to the rule of always having mom stop the isolation.]

Mary: Yeah, a few weeks ago, I was really upset, and Mrs. Newsome noticed, and we talked about things, and before my mom came back and apologized, I felt better.

Counselor: Ok, so, now here's the tough question: What prevents you from talking with others when you are upset? [Asks if the student is able to do more to get herself out of the isolation habit.]

Mary: Well, I guess there is nothing that is preventing me except myself.

In this example, the counselor helps Mary recognize that she has the skills to get herself out of her own self-imposed isolation. Through the exchange, Mary has the chance to learn that she *can* remove herself from isolation without the help of her mother.

Cognitive Behavioral Therapy (CBT)

In cognitive behavioral therapy (CBT), the counselor tries to get the client to recognize that the client controls his own feelings, thoughts, and behaviors, helping the student take responsibility for his own life. For example, a counselor using CBT may ask a student who is complaining of being depressed to consider what it is about the depression that might be proving useful for the student. In other words, why has the student decided to maintain the behavior and cognitive position to be depressed?

Counselor: So what brings you back this week?

Kevin: I am really having a lot of trouble with Mrs. Smith. She has it in for me.

Counselor: So, if I hear you correctly, Mrs. Smith has the desire to see you fail in life.

Kevin: Yeah, she makes things a lot harder for me than anyone else.

Counselor: So you believe that things should not be hard for you, that you should always be asked to do the same as others, never any more.

Kevin: Yeah, right.

Counselor: Well if that's true, then does it stand to reason that your basketball coach should not ask you to score more points than your teammates? Should he expect you to steal the ball from the other team no more than anyone else does?

Kevin: That sounds kinda silly when you say it that way.

Counselor: Okay, then does it make sense to you that sometimes you should be asked to do more than others?

Kevin: Yeah, I guess.

Counselor: So, you *do* have control over how you think about what Mrs. Smith is asking of you, and you actually do have a choice as to how you are behaving, right?

Person-Centered Therapy (Rogerian Therapy)

Person-centered therapy is often called Rogerian therapy, in deference to the importance of the work of Carl Rogers, considered a pioneer in the area of nondirective counseling techniques during the 1950s and 1960s.

Person-centered, or Rogerian, therapists work from the premise that the student already possesses the answers to his own problems and that effective counseling can aid in helping the client access previously unknown or untapped resources. Using this approach, the counselor maintains a nonjudgmental, genuine stance and uses nondirective responses.

Meghan: I am really mad at her.

Counselor: You are really upset and angry with her.

Meghan: Yeah, it makes me feel really bad when she says those things.

Counselor: You feel bad when others make those comments.

Meghan: Yeah, how do they know what it's like for me to have only one parent?

Counselor: It is hard to have only one parent.

THE ROLE OF SCHOOLS IN SUPPORTING PHARMACOLOGICAL THERAPIES— MEDICAL MODEL INTERVENTIONS

Probably since people first walked the earth, human beings have been trying to alleviate pain through medical remedies (e.g., plant leaves, tree sap, Benadryl). In modern American culture there is a strong bias toward medicating illness, disease, discomfort, and imbalance (Bauer, Ingersoll, & Burns, 2004; Safer, 1997). As a consequence, many children take medication.

Students should always take medications under the direction and supervision of a trained medical professional (e.g., psychiatrist). The prescription should only be given after a thorough evaluation has been conducted. The medication regimen should be part of a comprehensive plan for wellness that includes counseling. Most of these medical interventions take the form of psychotropic medications, examples of which include Ritalin (or methylphenidate), haloperidol, lithium, and risperidone.

The school then must play a significant role in the management and outcome of these pharmacological agents on its students. For example, the school nurse may dispense the medications. Of course, some students, under the direction of the physician or psychiatrist, may take medication at home. Whatever the case, however, both the school and certain

professionals working in the school setting must be aware of medications the student is taking and their potential side effects.

School personnel help a student who has been prescribed medications in many ways. The school can provide both documented and anecdotal evidence of student behavior to the family and doctor, as well as help articulate a plan for continued monitoring and follow-up throughout the time the student is on medications. If the student is to take medications during school hours, the school can arrange for the school nurse or another trained professional to observe the student taking his medications.

The school can also implement certain pragmatic policies that can both maximize the effectiveness of the medication and minimize potential problems. These efforts include developing a written policy regarding the use of medications in the school, creating a permission slip that provides information regarding each student's medication plan, developing procedures for receiving and monitoring prescription refills, creating a secure repository within the school for the storage of medications, and establishing a clear plan to deal with the side effects of any medications.

FIGURE 13–4 Medical Model Interventions
Copyright © 2005 Lisa Walker

ESTABLISHING LINKAGES

It is, of course, very important to develop and maintain the connections between the school and the outside service agency professionals. Developing and maintaining collaborative relationships with these professionals

FIGURE 13–5 Establishing Linkages
Copyright © 2005 Lisa Walker

is critical to successful delivery of service to students with EBD.

Using outside agencies requires referrals. However, a number of questions must be considered *before* any referral is made. What is the appropriate referral for this particular student? How will he be helped by the agency/individual? What is the financial liability of the school in making a particular referral?

Certainly, school personnel must get the parents of minors involved and educate them about what the school is thinking from the onset. Parents have the right to this information not only according to the law, but according to the helping professional's ethical codes as well.

Once the school has decided to refer the student to outside services, and the family has approved that referral (or in many cases made contact with the outside providing agency themselves), the school will need to provide accurate and thorough notes on the case. This documentation may include teacher comments; grades; attendance records; disciplinary records; school counselor, social worker, or psychologist case notes; and/or other ancillary information. Before this information can be released to the agency, the student and his family must be made aware of information that will be shared. Sometimes school-to-agency referrals fail because the information that was shared was incomplete, inaccurate, or was not discussed with the student. In order for outside agency personnel to be of maximum usefulness to both the student and the school, they need as much information as is possible (within legal and ethical frameworks).

MANAGING CONFIDENTIALITY AND RELEASES OF INFORMATION

Both parents and the student have a right to know when and what information will be shared with others (Fischer & Sorenson, 1996). In some cases, they may have the right to determine what information is shared, and with whom. The rights of children and parents concerning school and medical records are protected by two federal laws: the Family Educational Rights and Privacy Act (FERPA) (20 U.S.C. § 1232g; 34 CFR Part 99) and the Health Insurance Portability and Accountability Act of 1996 (HIPAA) (PL 104–191; 45 CFR Part 160 and 164). Public schools and local agencies need to establish policies and procedures that address confidentiality and releases of information in a manner that is consistent with these federal laws and regulations. In addition,

your state and school district should specify how these rights will be protected for students receiving special education services as part of the procedural safeguards statement. There may be negative legal ramifications if proper procedures are not followed explicitly.

Confidentiality

For teachers, discussing the behaviors and attitudes of a student is a common and necessary activity. Teachers regularly share information, tips, and techniques for working with students. However, casual sharing of information is not necessarily appropriate when the student is seen by the school counselor, social worker, or psychologist. Consequently, teachers sometimes feel they are being questioned or interrogated by counselors and other mental health providers, but are not having information cycled back to them. This may be especially frustrating to the teacher who made the original referral. In order to minimize this potential problem, school teachers and administrators need to be aware of the rules and ethical guidelines regarding confidentiality that are practiced by helping professionals within the school.

In general terms, the school counselor is prohibited from sharing information that he has discussed with students in group, individual, or family therapy sessions (Herlihy & Corey, 1996). The intent of this restriction is to protect the counselor-student relationship. Frustrating as it may be, teachers cannot be privy to such information. In fact, if the school counselor were to share such information, he would be open both to sanctions from his ethics board(s) and legal proceedings from the student and family involved in the case (Anderson, 1996).

For example, Johnny, a seventh grade student, is referred to the school counselor by his math teacher, Mrs. Jones, for falling asleep in class. During the subsequent counseling sessions the counselor learns that Johnny is up late almost every night trying to help his mom (who is working 60 hours a week) get his five younger siblings to bed. Three of the children are under the age of 4. Johnny's sleep is irregularly interrupted each night because he has to get up at all times of the night to assist his mother.

Although it may seem that it would be most helpful if all the teachers and professionals in the building understood Johnny's predicament, sharing such information by the school counselor (without the permission of the client) would violate her ethical code. It would also put the school at risk for litigation from the student's mother. Given all of that, however, the most important reason that such information should not be shared with the teacher or anyone else is that it *would* hurt the trust and confidence Johnny has placed in the school counselor.

Releases of Information

There are, of course, ways to legally and ethically share information acquired through the helping relationship. To do this, school personnel must get a **release of information** signed by both the student and the parent/guardian of the student (if the student is a minor). The release of information must specify what will be shared, with whom it will be shared, and the reason it will be shared (Fischer & Sorenson, 1996). The release of information is a critical document the school should use on a regular basis for conversations between professionals in the school and outside agencies.

LOOKING BEYOND SCHOOL WALLS

Schools have begun to develop more pragmatic in-house programming to help students (e.g., comprehensive guidance programs). However, when such efforts are not enough, schools must move beyond their walls and involve mental health practitioners who specialize in treating clients with specific concerns. Such all-encompassing initiatives serve schools, their constituents, and the greater community in meeting the challenges associated with providing a strong, comprehensive, effective educational program for every student.

Unfortunately, for some schools and school districts across the country, gaining access to needed mental health care services is difficult at best (Scholzman, 2003). Lack of access may be especially true in poor school districts, where money and community resources are very limited (Scholzman). Such conditions often leave school personnel and administrators overwhelmed, overburdened, and discouraged (Scholzman). Conversely, however, high socioeconomic status alone does not automatically ensure the existence of adequate mental health treatment. Sometimes, irrespective of socioeconomic factors, ideological and/or turf issues may be so extreme and extensive that they mitigate against effective collaboration with resources outside the school.

Developing constructive collaborations between schools and outside agencies can be taxing and difficult (Adelman & Taylor, 2003). Even though there is a considerable need for such partnerships, these entities may, at times, have trouble connecting on mutual ground. For more than a century, schools and community agencies have developed and existed in somewhat separate and parallel worlds. Rarely have these entities worked closely at developing and maintaining strong, collaborative relationships. In some rare cases, however, such collaborations have had at their core a sense of mutually agreed upon goals and a sufficient formal agreement regarding the mechanisms that lead to fulfillment of such goals (Adelman & Taylor). Where these core elements are missing, partnerships and professional connections are likely to evaporate, sometimes resulting in strong resentments and bridge burning.

FIGURE 13–6 Looking Beyond School Walls

Copyright © 2005 Lisa Walker

FIGURE 13–7 Constructive Collaborations
Copyright © 2005 Lisa Walker

Programs that offer a school-to-community connection for mental health services provide school personel with alternatives, community agencies with referrals, and most importantly, students with more appropriate mental health interventions. Consequently, the community as a whole becomes stronger, healthier, more closely connected, and truly collaborative.

Dating from the 1980s and finding their niche in the 1990s, expanded school mental health programs are one way for schools and community agencies to partner (Weist & Christodulu, 2000). In such programs, schools are linked directly to health departments, mental health centers, and other social services that provide services such as assessment modalities, case management techniques and strategies, treatment options, and preventative programming (Weist & Christodulu, 2000). Such programming can be met through six distinct efforts, specifically:

1. Proactive service delivery
2. Collaborative, nonhierarchical treatment efforts
3. Increased numbers of mental health staff
4. Reliance on developmentally appropriate and empirically based interventions, services, and programming independent of diagnosis
5. Continual growth and development of collaborations with community mental health providers
6. An integrative system of care and wellness (Weist & Christodulu, 2000)

Lawson (1999) articulates the need for schools to become more full service in an effort to prevent, treat, and minimize mental health concerns. He suggests that schools should provide proactive mental health care, partner with community agencies, and collaborate with other professionals in an effort to provide wrap-around services to students and their families. Such efforts should not duplicate the work of others or fragment already existing programs and services, but rather they should integrate multiple services into the school (Lawson).

The typical full-service school houses several different initiatives. These initiatives may be highlighted to a greater or lesser extent depending on the needs of the school. Traditionally, however, these programs are geared toward after-school, weekend, and summer offerings and are designed for all community residents: family support services, including parent education and training programs; coordinated, integrated services for students; and school reform activities and initiatives (Lawson, 1999).

Weist and Schlitt (1998) report that almost every state and more than 1,000 schools across the country engage in school-based health care systems. In those efforts, growing emphasis has been placed on both psychological and psychosocial needs of children, as well as their mental health concerns. Utilizing professionals from the fields of medicine (nurses, psychiatrists, medical doctors, and other mental health practitioners), youth development teams and public health officials are collaborating to help create and maintain comprehensive services to better meet student needs. Such efforts present a complexity beyond the normal realm for school officials. Connections and collaborations must be created and maintained, while existing alliances are developed and expanded. These efforts take time, energy, resources, and of course, money.

Weist and Schlitt (1998) further report that there is help available to develop and maintain such school-based intervention programs. Assistance can come from multiple sources, including foundations, state and federal grants, and professional organizations.

Understanding and maintaining collaborative relationships between agencies and schools requires skill, effort, and common goals. Otherwise, turf issues and problems can ensue (Flaherty et al., 1998).

DEALING WITH TURF ISSUES

One unavoidable issue in such collaboration is that in acting to help students, school personnel may experience

FIGURE 13–8   Dealing with Turf Issues
Copyright © 2005 Lisa Walker

significant overlap in their professional boundaries and expectations. Problems may occur, for example, when the school counselor and/or school social worker disagree with the recommendation of the school psychologist. Another fairly common problem occurs when a teacher and administrator recommend that a student be removed from class while the school counselor and school social worker hold that such an action is not in the student's best interest. Such overlap can be particularly problematic if not handled directly and quickly. Students need school personnel to act in their best interests and should not be snared in political games and quagmires. School personnel should keep in mind that the ability to engage in true professional dialogue and sometimes effect compromises may result in better service delivery to the student.

Consider the following example. Ms. Rivera wants Sarah out of her class because Sarah has a poor attitude toward class and has demonstrated actions of disrespect for the teacher. Mr. Davidson (the school counselor), on the other hand, is aware of significant home issues that are affecting Sarah's classroom behavior. Although Mr. Davidson may not really be aware of the effect Sarah's disruptive behavior periodically has on the classroom atmosphere, he holds that removal from the classroom setting would be extremely detrimental to Sarah's development and that such expulsion may cause her to regress rather than gain greater and more positive insight into her own behavior. Mr. Guerrero, the principal, is concerned about other students in the classroom and is aware that Sarah probably will not pass eighth grade and move on to high school if she is removed from the class. However, he is unaware of the effect Sarah's feelings of projection* toward the teacher are having on

the problem. There seem to be a number of turf issues here. So, how can compromise be effected?

In this case, a number of possible actions could serve the student and the school while improving the classroom atmosphere. First, the school counselor and administrator might take time from their busy schedules to observe Sarah in the classroom. This approach may help them better understand the behavior in context, or she may show more positive behavior in the classroom, or the teacher may feel more supported. The student might choose to complete her work outside of the classroom once or twice a week. Finally, the teacher may modify her classroom presentation and/or atmosphere *within reason* to more effectively and positively affect the experience the student is currently having. In this way, the teacher's turf (classroom) is maintained; the school counselor's turf (psychological ramifications) is maintained; and the school administrator's turf (functioning of the school) is maintained.

CHAPTER SUMMARY

- Schools across the country are under considerable pressure to "Leave No Child Behind," to meet state and federal mandates regarding student performance, and to deal with the increased incidence of mental health and psychological issues surfacing in their students. Schools must develop and maintain positive collaborations with community resources to serve the mental health needs of their students. Failure to create such relationships leaves some students behind as they deal with, in isolation, significant psychological impairments and mental health issues.

*Projection: when an unwanted characteristic or emotion is attributed to someone else in order to deny its existence in oneself (Gladding, 2001).

CHECK YOUR UNDERSTANDING

1. *True or False*. Schools do not have to do anything for kids that experience mental health concerns unless directed by a medical doctor.
2. *True or False*. Overall, there are more concerns with mental health issues in schools today than 70 years ago.
3. Name at least four mental health professionals (either within the school or outside the school walls) and describe what they do.
4. *True or False*. Individual counseling can be thought of in terms of being either talk or play therapy.
5. *True or False*. Family therapy occurs when the student talks to a mental health professional about his/her family.
6. Briefly describe how a cognitive-behavioral counselor works with a client.
7. *True or False*. If a school refers a student for outside services such as counseling, the school is automatically responsible to pay for those services.
8. *True or False*. When making a referral to an outside agency, the school must get permission from both the student and his parents or guardians (if the student is a minor).
9. In expanded school mental health programs, schools are linked to whom or what.
10. When schools collaborate effectively with other agencies, typically, what things are in the agreement?

APPLICATION ACTIVITIES

1. Review the vignette at the beginning of this chapter, and use it as the basis for discussing these questions:

   * Is this typical adolescent behavior? Why or why not?
   * Based on what you know about Amy, is this behavior typical for this student?
   * Does it appear that a mental health or physical issue may be causing her behaviors? Why or why not?
   * As a teacher of students with EBD, what should you do next to help Amy?

2. Research the Family Educational Rights and Privacy Act (FERPA) (20 U.S.C. § 1232g; 34 CFR Part 99) and the Health Insurance Portability and Accountability Act of 1996 (HIPAA) (PL 104–191; 45 CFR Part 160 and 164). Discuss the implications of both for interagency collaboration between schools and community medical and mental health practitioners.
3. Research your local community's mental health agencies and providers. Determine what services they offer, their hours of operation, payment plans, etc.
4. Individually or in small groups, contact an area school district for information regarding how they collaborate and consult with area mental health providers.
5. In small groups, research (using the Internet) schools that have developed useful and helpful school-community agency collaborations.

CHAPTER 14

SCHOOL-BASED CRISIS INTERVENTION

CHAPTER PREVIEW

CONNECTING TO THE CLASSROOM: *A Vignette*

Angelika stood in the middle of the classroom, hands clenched into fists on her hips. "You teachers are all the same," she yelled. "You never listen to my side of it, you just want to get me suspended." Ms. Severns stood about five feet away from Angelika. She looked and sounded serious, but calm. "Angelika," she said, "I will be happy to listen to your side of the story as soon as you can sit down and talk to me quietly." Angelika stalked down the aisle toward the front of the room, knocking papers off desks and onto the floor. "Angelika," Ms. Severns said, "Can you walk to your safe spot, or do you need assistance?" Angelika was now standing near the chalkboard; Ms. Severns had moved to a position near the classroom door and the telephone. Angelika shouted, "It's all Cassandra's fault! When I see her next hour, I'm going to kick her butt!" Ms. Severns lifted the telephone, activated the intercom, and announced "Care Team to Room 112" over the school public address system. The rest of her students had practiced for this eventuality, and they were prepared. They stood, gathered their belongings and walked quietly out the door and down the hall to the library. Because of the Care Team announcement, the librarian was standing in the door ready to receive them. Meanwhile, the other members of the Care Team were walking quickly down the hall toward Ms. Severns' classroom.

Defining Crisis Intervention

Crisis—A critical incident or pivotal situation in which there is a high potential of harm to students or others. A crisis situation has three components: (1) the actual trigger or precipitating event, (2) the perception, reaction, or response of one or more individuals to that event, and (3) the coping skills of the individuals involved.

School-Based Crisis Intervention—A systematic convergence of resources designed to interrupt or divert the crisis incident, minimize potential risk of harm, and return the situation to the functional level that was present prior to the crisis.

Crisis Intervention Plan—A deliberate set of procedural steps that defines the roles and responses of individuals during a crisis, guide the decisions and actions of faculty and others during a crisis situation, and provide resources for postcrisis debriefing and follow-up.

CREATING A SAFE, COMPASSIONATE COMMUNITY

Although we can take rightful pride in our accomplishments on behalf of U.S. youths, we can and must do more. The world remains a threatening, often dangerous place for children and youths. And in our country today, the greatest threat to the lives of children and adolescents is not disease or starvation or abandonment, but the terrible reality of violence.
—Donna E. Shalala, Secretary of Health and Human Services (U.S. Department of Health and Human Services, 2001, p. i)

Our challenge is to understand how to prevent and decrease the prevalence and incidence of children and youth that display behaviors that foster antisocial lifestyles. By presenting behaviors that are dangerous to themselves, other students, teachers, families, and community members, these youth disrupt teaching and learning in schools, create inhospitable neighborhoods, upset family structures and functioning, and ultimately become involved in the criminal justice and/or mental health system. (Sprague et al., 2001, p. 496)

A great deal of statistical and anecdotal evidence supports the conclusion that children are being unfairly suspended and arbitrarily kicked out of school for incidents that could have been very easily handled using alternative methods. As a result, everyday Zero Tolerance Policies force children to be suspended or expelled for sharing Midol, asthma medication (during an emergency), cough drops, and for bringing toy guns, nail clippers, and scissors to school. (Advancement Project/ Harvard Civil Rights Project, 2000, Take no prisoners, para. 2)

School discipline has in general become a hotbed for litigation and debate. While questionable discipline practices that exclude students from school settings are used with students across ethnic groups, they are especially problematic for African American students who continue to be disproportionately subjected to corporal punishment, suspension, and expulsion. (Townsend, 2000, Abstract)

In the wake of a rash of school shootings during the 1990s, increased public attention focused on school-related violence and crime. The media, policymakers, educators, and community leaders have explored the underlying reasons for youth violence, and proposed a variety of solutions designed to improve the safety of schools and the community. However, the research base is not sufficiently robust to lead to consensus among educators about *how* to approach these issues, and certainly not strong enough to guide effective national policy making.

Despite the lack of data, policies were made, programs were designed, and interventions put in place. The national database on school safety appears to demonstrate that the wave of school violence peaked in 1993 and has been decreasing in frequency since that time (DeVoe et al., 2003). (See Figure 14-1 for school crime and safety data.) The specific causes for the increase—and the subsequent decrease—are not known. Myles and Simpson (1998) propose three hypotheses for the apparent increase in student aggression and violence:

1. Exposure to increased societal aggression and violence desensitizes children, who come to see those behaviors as acceptable.

- In a 1-year period, 22 school-associated violent deaths involved students (16 homicides and 6 suicides), compared to 2,124 total homicides and 1,922 total suicides of children and youth ages 5 to 19 in the United States during the same period.
- In 2001, students ages 12 to 18 were victims of 161,000 serious violent crimes at school compared to 290,000 nonlethal violent crimes away from school (i.e., rape, sexual assault, robbery, and aggravated assault).
- Younger students (ages 12 to 14) were more likely to be victimized at school than older students (ages 15 to 18); however, away from school the reverse was true.
- Between 7% and 9% of students in grades 9–12 reported being threatened or injured with a knife on school property.
- The percentage of students who reported fighting on school property declined from 16% to 13% between 1993 and 2001; fights outside school decreased from 42% to 33%.
- Among 12- to 18-year-old students, reports of bullying increased to 8% from 5% in 1993. Males were more likely to be bullied than females (9% vs. 7%).
- Twenty percent of all public schools experienced at least one violent crime; 71% reported at least one violent incident.
- A larger proportion of violent crimes occurred in secondary and urban schools than in suburban or elementary buildings.
- Forty-six percent of schools reported property crimes or thefts.
- Fifty-four percent of schools reported serious disciplinary actions, including: suspensions of 5 days or more (83%), expulsions (11%), and transfers to specialized schools (7%).
- Two percent of schools reported serious disciplinary action for use of a firearm or explosive device, while 4% reported incidents involving possession of those items.
- Four percent of public school teachers were physically attacked by students (135,000 teachers) and 9% were threatened with injury (305,000).
- Twelve percent of students indicated that someone at school had used hate-related language against them (i.e., based on race, religion, ethnicity, disability, gender, or sexual orientation); 36% reported seeing hate-related graffiti at their school.
- Twenty percent of students reported the presence of street gangs in their school.
- Twenty-nine percent of secondary students reported someone had offered, sold, or given them illegal drugs on school property.

FIGURE 14–1 U.S. School Crime and Safety Indicators

Source: DeVoe et al. (2003) *Indicators of school crime and safety: 2003* (NCES 2004–004/NCJ 302368). Washington, DC: U.S. Departments of Education and Justice.

Note: This report presents data on crime at school from the perspectives of students, teachers, principals, and the general population from an array of sources—the National Crime Victimization Survey (1992–2001), the School Crime Supplement to the National Crime Victimization Survey (1995, 1999, and 2001), the Youth Risk Behavior Survey (1993, 1995, 1997, 1999, and 2001), the School Survey on Crime and Safety (2000), and the School and Staffing Survey (1993–1994 and 1999–2000).

2. Decreased use of institutional treatment models for seriously emotionally disturbed and violent children and youth has resulted in increased numbers of those students attending public schools, which do not have the resources to deal with this population.

3. Increased inclusion of children at risk for violence in general education classrooms that are staffed by teachers who lack the skills to work with them effectively.

There is an emerging agreement among professionals who work with children with EBD about how best to work with these most difficult-to-manage and potentially dangerous children and youth. This chapter will review the multiple risk factors identified as predictive of aggression and violent behavior, summarize the programming recommendations of leading professional voices in the EBD field, provide a sample of one staff training curriculum that addresses the need for specialized intervention skills for potentially violent children and youth, and discuss strategies for debriefing students in the aftermath of school violence or other traumatic events.

Multiple Risk Factors

Chapter 8 examined the individual, family, school, and community factors that characterize students at high risk for aggression and violence (see Figure 8–1). Individuals who commit violent acts appear to take two different developmental paths to get there—one that emerges early in childhood, and one that does not manifest until adolescence. However, in spite of convincing data about risk and resilience factors, it is still impossible to predict which high-risk youngsters will commit acts of violence in later years.

The Differential Impact of Race and Ethnicity

Previous chapters have discussed the disproportionate rates of referral and placement of minority youth—particularly African American males—in special education programs. Not surprisingly, similar patterns are seen in teacher office referrals for disruptive behavior, and in differential disciplinary action resulting from those office referrals (Skiba, Michael, Nardo, & Peterson, 2002; Townsend, 2000).

Studies have found that disciplinary decisions made by principals are not always policy or research based and are sometimes capricious and counterintuitive (Morrison, Anthony, Storino, & Dillon, 2001; Skiba & Peterson, 2000). One such study that examined disciplinary referrals and actions found no evidence that racial disparities in school punishment were caused by higher rates of misbehavior by African American students (Skiba et al., 2002). In addition, the study found that the types of infractions students were referred to the office for differed by race: "White students were significantly more likely to be referred to the office for *smoking, leaving without permission, obscene language,* and *vandalism.* In contrast, black students were more likely to be referred to the office for *disrespect, excessive noise, threat,* and *loitering*" (p. 334).

Townsend (2000) hypothesizes that one reason for higher rates of office referrals and disciplinary actions is essentially due to cultural misunderstanding. Students from a minority culture may exhibit verbal and nonverbal communication styles that differ from that of the teacher and the majority culture. Exuberance, slang, and emotionality on the part of youth might then be incorrectly perceived as hostile or disrespectful by teachers or administrators who are unfamiliar with the student's cultural norms.

The Need for Early Intervention Services

The children and youth likely to encounter serious negative outcomes later in their lives need supports and intervention services early on within school and community settings to reduce, buffer, and offset early risk. (Sprague & Walker, 2000, p. 369)

Entrance into school has been associated with increased risk for the display of aggressive behavior. (Van Acker & Talbott, 1999, Intervention in early childhood, p. 12)

The cost of early intervention cannot compare to the lifelong costs of a student's untreated pathology (including law enforcement, incarceration, violence, and crime). (Stewart, 2001, p. 79)

Special education advocates have consistently supported the notion of early intervention. It would seem to be cost effective to intervene early, both in terms of the societal price of treating or incarcerating these children later in life, and in terms of the human cost in loss of potential. However, students with EBD have consistently been referred for special education services later in their school careers, often after experiencing several years of school failure and demonstrating behaviors that become increasingly chronic over time. Stewart (2001) says that by deferring intervention until middle and high school, the educational system is:

- Offering too little, too late by sending the student into a specialized treatment program after the developmental window for optimally effective intervention has passed.
- Passing the buck by sending the student to juvenile justice and corrections institutions.
- Discarding the student into society through suspension and expulsion. (p. 78)

The Need for Multifaceted Interventions

Many of the school-based secondary prevention efforts are designed to work with students whose history includes fighting and discipline problems. However, many students who engage in dramatic acts of school violence are not those who had an obvious, chronic history of aggression or behavior problems in school (Bender, Shubert, & McLaughlin, 2001). Therefore, they may not have been identified or referred for services, including special education, counseling, anger management, or social-skills training. Conversely, the typical administrative responses to noncompliance or aggressive behavior (e.g., detention, suspension, expulsion) have been ineffective for students with chronic behavior problems (Gable & Van Acker, 2000). As a result, it appears that neither the chronic offenders nor the isolated loners have been targeted or treated effectively.

A report from the U.S. Department of Health and Human Services (2001) pointed out the minimal availability of well-designed studies of prevention programs. Further, they pointed out that many of the programs that have been rigorously evaluated have been found to be not only ineffective, but actually harmful for participants.

The following section provides three research-based recommendations from well-known researchers and practitioners in the field of EBD and a summary statement from the 2001 U.S. Department of Health and Human Services report. While there is no single "magic bullet" intervention or curriculum, the best approach to violence prevention appears to be proactive, multitiered, and multifaceted, and should involve schools, families, and community stakeholders.

Sprague and Walker (2000) propose a general set of guidelines for school-based violence prevention efforts: "(1) Intervene as early as possible. (2) Address both behavioral risks and strengths. (3) Involve families as partners in the intervention. (4) Match the strength of the intervention to the antisocial behavior" (p. 374).

Guetzloe (1999) frames the discussion of services for violence-prone youth in terms of the three-tiered mental health model. Primary prevention would provide universal or schoolwide nonviolence interventions for all students (e.g., positive school discipline plan, high academic expectations, comprehensive guidance program, and teaching conflict resolution skills). More intensive secondary prevention efforts would be focused on early identification of, and therapeutic interventions for, students with aggressive and violent tendencies.

> Within the schools, we must use strategies that have been proved to be effective such as (a) early identification of and intervention with children with emotional and behavioral problems; (b) appropriate education and treatment for children with such problems; (c) provision of sufficient and effective mental health professionals in the school; (d) greater involvement of students and parents in school activities; (e) use of a crisis team for decision-making; (f) use of behavioral and cognitive-behavioral interventions; (g) involvement of students in helping others through community-service projects; (h) family therapy; and (i) working toward a weapon-free environment. (Guetzloe, 1999, p. 24)

Van Acker and Talbott (1999) provide a set of recommendations for addressing the school context or culture in which violence takes place. They propose eight necessary ingredients:

1. Philosophical changes in attitudes and approaches to the education of at-risk students, so that aversive consequences that push students away from school are replaced with those that promote improved relationships between the school and the child and enhance the probability of social and academic success.
2. The improvement of support systems involving the school, the family, and the community.
3. The development of instructional programs and strategies that promote both academic and social learning goals.
4. Increased teacher education to provide teachers with the knowledge and skills necessary to change both attitudes toward, and interaction with, challenging students.

5. Improved and increased levels of support for teachers as they attempt to provide instruction to challenging students.
6. The development of alternative and nonaversive consequences for aggressive and violent behaviors . . . that provide students with increased knowledge and skill in the use of prosocial problem solving strategies.
7. The development of improved systems of screening to identify children who are at risk of developing chronic aggressive and violent behavior.
8. Improved communication between home, school, and community to provide intervention and accountability across contexts. (Van Acker & Talbott, 1999, p. 18)

Responses in Law and School Policy

Young and colleagues (2002) characterize the school-based violence-reduction activities developed during the 1990s as falling into four general categories: (1) **education**—providing general mental health and conflict resolution information to all students; (2) **environment/technology**—security measures that "offer protection without requiring human behavior change" (p. 107); (3) **recreation**—based on the theory that active involvement in sports and after-school activities keep students out of trouble; and (4) **regulation**—essentially containment, tougher policies, and consequences. However, some of the measures developed during the 1990s don't address the underlying causes of school violence or provide services for the students who may need them most. For example, increasingly, schools use profiling and checklists of warning signs. However, these tools do not differentiate between students with chronic behavior problems and at risk for delinquent acts from those "invisible" students who are alienated and detached from their peers and the school community at large (Bender et al., 2001). Therefore, students whose characteristics are similar to several of the students who shot classmates during the 1990s would not be identified as needing intervention.

Another group of students may be excluded from services provided by special education because of the social maladjustment clause in the current federal definition of emotional disturbance (Council for Children with Behavioral Disorders and the Council of Administrators of Special Education, 1995; Stewart, 2001).

Two policy initiatives that have gained national attention are "zero tolerance" (i.e., one strike and you're out) and enabling the justice system to try increasingly younger juveniles as adults. However popular these initiatives have become, research has not demonstrated their efficacy in reducing youth violence. A national report published by the Harvard University Civil Rights Project found that strict zero tolerance "is contrary to the developmental needs of children, denies children educational opportunities, and often results in the criminalization of children" (Advancement Project, 2000, executive summary, para. 1). They reported that more than 3.1 million children were suspended and 87,000 were expelled in 1998, many for relatively minor, nonviolent offenses. Similarly, a U.S. Department of Health and Human Services report (2001) labeled the movement to try youths as adults a "misguided policy" that resulted in inefficient use of public resources and was counterproductive. They called the theory that "getting tough with juvenile offenders by trying them in adult criminal courts reduces the likelihood that they will commit more crimes" a myth (HHS, 2001, p. ix).

Preventing Violence at the School and Program Level: Implications for Teacher Training

Chapters 4, 5, and 6 covered the best practices for schoolwide, classwide, and individual student behavioral interventions. Most students with EBD benefit from highly structured classrooms, with explicit functional norms and logical, consistent consequences for misbehavior. However, teachers who will work with potentially violent and aggressive students need training in skills that go beyond the usual behavior management repertoire: conflict resolution, verbal de-escalation, and safe techniques for physical restraint (Guetzloe, 2000). Programs should offer both systematic and incidental teaching of prosocial behaviors and conflict resolution skills (Guetzloe, 2000; Van Acker & Talbott, 1999), as well as have a team of individuals trained to intervene quickly and safely in crisis situations. Crisis teams should have basic skills and knowledge needed to address aggressive and potentially violent student behavior. These skills include an "understanding of crisis theory and intervention; how to identify potential crisis situations; knowledge of non-aversive behavior management techniques in a crisis situation; and the ability to establish short- and long-term intervention plans to address recurrent acts of aggression" (Gable & Van Acker, 2001, p. 12).

CRISIS INTERVENTION TECHNIQUES

EBD teachers need to be familiar with a variety of techniques for intervening with students in the midst of

what would be called a crisis. This section will discuss verbal de-escalation techniques, physical assistance and intervention, post-crisis teaching, and helping students who have experienced violence or trauma.

Verbal De-escalation of Individual Students

Teachers working with students who are verbally and physically aggressive need to be able to appear calm, yet authoritative, in the midst of chaos. The skills for avoiding and deflecting power struggles covered in Chapter 8 are appropriate for this population of students as well. For many students who become agitated, skillful verbal de-escalation can very effectively defuse them at an early stage in the crisis cycle.

Physical Assistance for Individual Students

Physical intervention should only be used as a last resort, and when a student is threatening actual physical harm to self or to others. Physical restraint is used only to keep the individual student from harming self or others; it should never be used to punish or humiliate students who have been disrespectful or noncompliant.

One adult can rarely physically intervene with one student safely, even if the student is relatively young and small. It is advisable to always have two adults present in classrooms that contain potentially violent students (Guetzloe, 2000). Safe physical intervention with larger or older students requires a well-trained, coordinated crisis management team. The crisis team may include general and special educators, as well as administrators and other school personnel. All members should participate in a systematic training that is consistent with school board discipline policy and procedures. Several training and consulting firms offer programs specifically designed for school crisis teams. Developers of one such program, Crisis Alleviation Lessons and Methods (CALM), have provided an overview of two of their training modules for this chapter in Box 14–1.

Seizing the Teaching Moment After an Incident

One of the most critical elements of postincident debriefing is conducting a problem-solving session with the aggressive student. This would be a good time to use the SOCCSS strategy (see Chapter 7) or cognitive behavioral techniques (see chapters 10 and 12). A copy of a sample "think sheet" is provided in Figure 14–2 . It includes data concerning the circumstances in which

BOX 14–1

PERSPECTIVE: JON BAIR B.S.E., M.H.A. AND FRED OVERTON R.N., C
Overview of the CALM* Program

The need for an organized response to crisis escalation in the classroom is obvious. All one has to do is view the nightly news to hear of the difficult situations faced by many educators today. Often, these teachers have not been trained adequately to meet the challenge of dealing with potentially aggressive behavior. Many schools take a hands-off approach, hoping to limit their liability while failing to address the problems experienced in many classrooms. Unfortunately, when there is no plan in place for dealing with the disruptive—and even assaultive—behavior of a small number of students, the educational needs of all students suffer, not to mention "burnout" or even physical harm suffered by teachers.

The CALM program emphasizes: building the therapeutic relationship, active listening, early verbal de-escalation, self-protection, emotional boundaries, control and restrain techniques, postcrisis review, and crisis-response planning. This section will cover two pillars of the CALM program, the Seven Keys to Effective Limit Setting and the Eight Stages of Escalation.

Seven Keys to Effective Limit Setting

Setting limits is a commonly used tool in classrooms, as well as other environments. Simply stated, limit setting is a matter of making the student or other individual aware of your expectations and the consequences of meeting or not meeting those expectations. In order for limits to be effective, they must be properly presented. Limits should be:

1. **Simple**—When in crisis mode, even the most intelligent people deal with information best when it is presented in a simple or basic manner. Limits should be presented in easy-to-understand terms. Avoid abstract principles and metaphors.

2. **Reasonable**—Limits should be reasonable in two ways. First, it is important to choose battles wisely. Deciding which behaviors must be addressed in a time of crisis can be difficult for the individual teacher. In some instances, the decision will depend on organizational policy. A common criterion for intervention is whether the behavior presents a danger or interferes with the rights of others. Second, the consequence portion of the limit needs to be appropriate to the situation. If the consequences are punitive or unreasonable they can contribute to the escalation of a crisis.

3. **Enforceable**—Any consequences used in limit setting must be immediately enforceable. Consequences should be short term, and appropriate to the age and cognitive abilities of the student. An example of an unenforceable limit would be, "I will not dismiss you until your work is neat, legible, and complete." While this language may be effective with some students, other

*The Crisis Alleviation Lessons and Methods (CALM) Program is a systematic approach for crisis de-escalation and intervention, developed in 1999 in response to the needs of an acute care psychiatric hospital. Since that time it has been incorporated into staff training in a variety of settings, including residential treatment centers, outpatient clinics, medical hospitals, juvenile detention centers, nursing homes, and public schools. For more information, contact:

Crisis Management Solutions, Inc.
PO Box 245
Windsor, MO 65360
www.thecalmprogram.com

strong-willed or oppositional individuals will take the teacher to task and go on strike. It is important to remember that as much as we want to, we cannot control the behaviors of others.

4. **Presented as an option**—Giving the student choices puts her in control. For best results, the most desirable option should be presented first, with the more negative option presented last. Include consequences for positive as well as negative behaviors. Presenting more than two options can become confusing and frustrating.

5. **Presented in privacy**—Think of a time you were criticized in front of coworkers, classmates, friends, or family members. Nobody likes to be criticized in front of his or her peer group. Unfortunately, this is easy to forget when we are the one in a position of power or control. Many children, especially teens, are very sensitive about respect. It is preferable to approach them quietly at their desk instead of addressing them in front of peers.

6. **Time limited**—The amount of time students are allowed for making their choice should be limited. When the time limit is up, the decision will be made for the student by the adult. *Note:* This does not apply when setting limits to dangerous behaviors that need to stop immediately.

7. **Individualized**—Appropriate limits vary based on a number of student factors: mental age, cognitive ability, attention span, chemical influences, thought process, and impulsivity.

The Eight Stages of Crisis Escalation

Understanding the complexities of crisis escalation is not dissimilar to following the process of human development as a whole. First, there are predictable stages that a person in crisis goes through. Second, the body provides certain autonomic responses based on the crisis level. However, unlike the stages of human development, which typically occur in a certain sequential order, students passing through the stages of crisis escalation can—and often do—jump from stage to stage or skip a stage altogether. Therefore it is much less important to understand the typical sequence of the stages in crisis escalation than to recognize the behavioral signs that indicate which stage a student is experiencing. Identifying the stage of escalation helps the teacher to target and maximize the effectiveness of strategies or interventions that can de-escalate the student and prevent further escalation. It is important to note that the teacher's goals are to interrupt the crisis cycle in the earliest possible stage, and to reduce the degree of crisis escalation from a dangerous level to a learning or student-empowering level. It is neither possible nor always desirable to eliminate crises from occurring.

For illustration purposes and to demonstrate a progression in acuity, the stages are identified in eight progressive forms. The table below demonstrates how levels increase in intensity and potential for physical injury.

Stages	Intervention
1) Information seeking	Provide the student with information
2) Noncompliance	Set limits
3) Challenging	Remain focused Set limits
4) Threatening	Call for assistance
5) Emotional outburst	Provide privacy Allow venting Consider time limit
6) Acting out toward self	Determine potential for injury Consider physical intervention

7) Acting out toward others	Physical intervention
8) De-escalation	Provide privacy Process event Teach and learn

Stage 1: Information Seeking

As students' anxiety level increases, they often will try to gather information to reassure or comfort themselves. At times, the questions may seem irrelevant to the situation at hand. Questions may be repeated over and over.

Intervention: Provide the student with information.

It is important to remain patient with the student in this stage. Answer questions calmly and rationally. Although it may seem that the student knows the answer to a question, remember that students in crisis are not always able to process information well.

Stage 2: Noncompliance

Students in crisis display noncompliance in many ways, including: ignoring limits, walking away, doing the opposite of what is asked, or saying "no" to teacher requests. When students become noncompliant they are beginning to move into an irrational mode of thought.

Intervention: Set limits.

State and enforce limits in a calm, rational manner, rather than emotionally. Use limits to manage *behavior*, not individuals.

Stage 3: Challenging

At this stage, students move from refusing to follow directions to challenging authority. Statements and questions such as, "You can't tell me what to do, you're not my Mom!" and "Who put you in charge?" are examples of challenging verbal behavior.

Intervention: Remain focused and set limits.

Challenging behavior can easily lead to power struggles. Neither the teacher nor the student wins in the case of a power struggle. Limits should be set and enforced calmly.

Stage 4: Threatening

A wide variety of threatening situations may occur in the classroom setting. The most obvious, of course, is a threat of physical violence. However, threats to file a lawsuit, to report you to the school board, or to call upon a powerful relative may also be threatening behavior. Any time someone attempts to control another person through intimidation, they are threatening.

Intervention: Call for assistance.

In any situation that involves threatening behavior, it is important to have more than one adult present. In the case of threats of litigation or other retaliatory action, additional staff should be present to witness both the threat and the adult's response. If the threat concerns potential harm to the student or others, and the student continues to escalate beyond this stage, you will need a team to handle the situation safely.

Stage 5: Emotional Outbursts

At this stage, students display a seemingly uncontrollable eruption of emotion, sometimes referred to as "breaking down" or "going off." In young children, this stage is typically called a tantrum. Students in this stage of crisis may weep, scream, yell, or stomp their feet. They may engage in minor damage to property (e.g., ripping up papers, knocking books to the floor). Sometimes this outpouring of emotion can be a positive experience, allowing students to express long-repressed feelings that need to be released.

Intervention: Provide privacy; allow venting; consider time limit.

To maintain dignity, separate the student in crisis from the rest of the class. Once in a more private location, allow the student to express feelings without judgment. Although many students will exhaust themselves fairly quickly and begin calming down once removed from the original crisis situation, some may need the adult to establish a time limit (e.g., "I will give you about three more minutes to pull yourself together, blow your nose, splash some water on your face, and get ready to return to the classroom").

Stage 6: Acting Out Toward Self

Acting out toward self can describe a wide variety of behaviors. For example, punching the wall carries the potential for injury; therefore, it is considered acting out toward self. If students demonstrate more dangerous forms of self-damaging aggressive behavior (e.g., taking a handful of pills or cutting their wrists), they are also acting out toward themselves.

Intervention: Determine potential for injury; consider physical intervention.

If the student is engaging in a seemingly harmless behavior like slapping the wall with an open hand or picking at a scab, then continue verbal de-escalation interventions. However, if the student is doing something that may cause serious harm or self-damage, then you must physically intervene to maintain the safety of the student. If you are unable to assess the potential for injury, then assume that the potential is great and a physical intervention plan should be initiated. *Note: In the CALM program, teachers and staff learn self-protective, nonaggressive methods for physical intervention that minimize the danger to the student or to the adults. Physical interventions should only be used as a last resort to prevent injury, and only used by trained staff members in accordance with school district or agency policies and procedures.*

Stage 7: Acting Out Toward Others

At this stage, students have become physically aggressive and are acting out toward others in a potentially violent manner. This behavior may vary in severity from horseplay to throwing things at others, or striking others with objects, hands, fists, feet, or other body parts.

Intervention: Intervene physically.

Unlike Stage 6, teachers cannot wait to intervene when a student is acting out toward others. You must act on the assumption that the potential for injury is great, and utilize physical intervention for the safety of all involved. This can be a very difficult situation to manage if there is more than one student acting out toward others. Physical intervention should not begin until there are sufficient crisis response team members present to deal with all the students involved in the aggressive activity.

Stage 8: De-escalation

This is the most often overlooked stage of crisis escalation. De-escalation occurs when the student begins to regain control. Reaching the de-escalation stage is the goal of each and every one of our de-escalation efforts.

Intervention: Provide privacy; process event; teach and learn.

Initially, provide privacy and time for the student to consider what has happened and how they would like to change their behavior. Next, process the event; the appropriate time for approaching the student to process what has happened will vary from student to student. Processing may involve other members of the faculty, school counselors, social workers, administrators, parents, or even a juvenile officer. Depending on the severity of the incident, the process may need to occur before the student returns to the classroom. During this postcrisis review, discuss problem behaviors and plan for future problematic situations. It is important to discuss potential consequences for future positive behaviors, as well as for negative behavior. While this process may be partially dependent on the disciplinary process, it should be conducted separately. The de-escalation phase is a time to recognize shortcomings and build on strengths, not a time to lecture or attempt to intimidate a student into "straightening up and flying right."

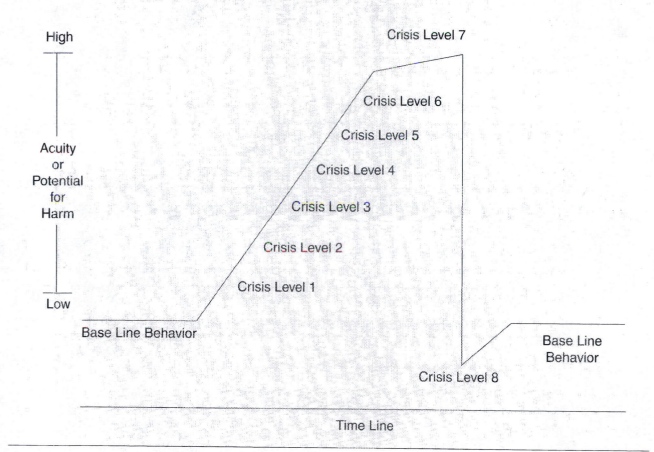

THINK SHEET

Name _____   **Date** _____

Where were you when you got in trouble? (check one)

Classroom	_____	Restroom	_____	Outside/on grounds	_____
Gym	_____	Hall	_____	Lunch room	_____
Office	_____	Group room	_____	Other	_____

What happened? (check all that fit your situation)

Somebody teased me. _____
Somebody took something of mine. _____
Somebody told me to do something. _____
Somebody did something I didn't like. _____
Somebody said something I didn't like. _____
Somebody started fighting/arguing with me. _____
I did something that got me in trouble. _____   What? _____

Who was the problem with? _____

How did you handle yourself? (circle one)

1	2	3	4	5
Poorly	Not very well	OK	Good	Great

How angry were you? (circle one)

1	2	3	4	5
Not angry at all	A little angry but OK	Pretty angry	Very angry	As angry as I can get

---

S   SITUATION — Describe what happened.

O   OPTIONS — List at least three things <u>you</u> could have done differently.
   1.
   2.
   3.

C   CONSEQUENCES — What would have happened if you had chosen the other options?
   1.
   2.
   3.

S   SOLUTION — NOW: What can you do to make things better right now? (Restitution?)

                    NEXT TIME: What can you do next time to make things turn out better for you?

If someone else could help you, name that person and say how they could help _____

Attach a copy of the behavior contract you and staff developed to address this behavior.

FIGURE 14–2   Think Sheet

Things You Can Do for Yourself or Others

- Talk about your feelings and what has happened. (It's okay to talk about wishing things were different.)
- Cry alone or with a friend.
- Express your feelings in concrete ways: write about it, draw or paint, create something that will help you release your feelings.
- Do something physical (sports, working out, go off by yourself and yell or scream, chop wood, pound on an old pillow or cushion).
- Eat healthy (small, nutritious snacks are okay if meals are a problem).
- Get plenty of rest. If you have trouble sleeping, do something relaxing or soothing (listen to quiet music, reading, drawing/doodling). (If you think you are sleeping too much, be sure to exercise.)
- If you need to take a break from dealing with stress and can't physically get away, stand up, walk around, stretch, concentrate on breathing deeply. If you can get away, go do something with friends, watch TV, play video games, take a walk, read a book, watch a funny movie.

Things Adults Can Do to Help

- Recognize that youth can have strong feelings about what has happened even if they did not know the person well. A current crisis can bring up feelings of previous crises or loss. Do not discount the feelings or their intensity.
- Be a good listener. Let the youth express whatever he is feeling. Convey understanding and respect for everything shared, even if you as an adult would interpret the situation differently.
- Be nonjudgmental. Reflect back what you are hearing versus making judgments such as: "You shouldn't be thinking such thoughts," "It's against the teachings of your religion to feel this way," or "It would embarrass me (or your family, etc.) if people knew you felt this way."
- Be supportive. Be reassuring without trying to fix the situation. Helpful comments are ones that check out what you are hearing or provide empathy such as: "I hear that this really hurts," or "I'm sorry." Do not make statements like: "Things aren't really that bad," or "Get over it."
- Be available for physical support. Some youth will be receptive to an arm around their shoulder or a hug; others may not. If in doubt, ask.
- Recognize that youth usually go through some amount of time during which they feel numb and/or experience confusion. They may not track things as they normally do. Give gentle reminders to help them refocus; be patient.
- Be alert for warning signs [listed below]. Do not feel embarrassed about seeking help for your youth or your family. All of us need an objective person to talk things out with from time to time.

Normal Feelings When You Are Grieving

- Denial: This couldn't possibly have happened. This isn't happening to me.
- Anger: How could this happen? How could they do this? It's not fair. Why is the world like this? Why do bad things happen?
- Bargaining: If only she could be here with me, I would be good for the rest of my life.
- Depression: This hurts so bad I can't stand it. I will feel this way forever.
- Panic: I have to do something to fix this.
- Guilt: If I had done/said something differently, this would not have happened. It's my fault. I should have known.
- Worry: If I plan things carefully enough, I can at least make sure nothing makes me feel like this again (or happens like this again).
- Numbness: Why am I feeling nothing when other people are so upset? It's like this is happening to someone else.
- Confusion: Why can't I think straight? Why is my head spinning?

Warning Signs That You or Someone Else May Need Help

- Sudden drop in grades
- Difficulty concentrating
- Loss of interest in friends and normal activities
- Changes in sleeping (more or less) or eating (more or less)
- Experimenting with drugs or alcohol
- Running away or thinking about it
- Increased risk-taking behavior (example: driving too fast)
- Giving away possessions
- Wanting to escape a situation that seems impossible
- Wanting to be with a person who died
- Wanting to get even or punish yourself or others
- Thinking or saying things like: I wish I were dead. You're going to be sorry you treated me like this. I'm tired of this. If this happens (or doesn't happen), I will hurt or kill myself

FIGURE 14–3   Sample Handout for Crisis Counseling

the incident occurred and an abbreviated version of the SOCCSS strategy.

Helping Students Affected by Violence or Trauma

Another element of school violence that often becomes part of the crisis team's responsibility is organizing counseling or debriefing interventions for students, school personnel, and parents who witnessed or were otherwise affected by a traumatic event. Figure 14-3 provides a sample handout for use in working with adults or students.

CHAPTER SUMMARY

* Increasing attention has been paid in recent years to increased youth violence in the community at large and at school. The three-level prevention model presented in previous chapters provides tools and strategies that allow teachers and administrators to create caring communities at the school and classroom level that decrease the likelihood of problem behaviors. Tertiary prevention and individualized intervention strategies for students with common types of behavior have also been discussed in previous chapters. This chapter discussed the strategy for developing effective, multifaceted and multitiered programs for students with aggressive and violent tendencies, including EBD. The excerpt provided from the CALM program identified the usual progression of stages students experience during a crisis cycle, and matched adult intervention strategies with each level of escalation.

CHECK YOUR UNDERSTANDING

1. *True or False.* Based on risk factors, kindergarten teachers can predict which students will become aggressive adolescents.

2. *True or False.* School violence has actually been declining over the past decade.
3. *True or False.* African American males are subject to more disciplinary actions in schools because they commit more serious rule infractions than other students.
4. *True or False.* Physical interventions are warranted whenever a student is disruptive or disrespectful to an adult.
5. *True or False.* The U.S. Department of Health and Human Services supports legislation allowing younger juveniles to be tried as adults.
6. Identify the four general types of school violence prevention activities, according to Young and colleagues.
7. Summarize the skills needed by teachers who work with potentially aggressive or violent students.
8. According to the CALM program, what are the eight stages of crisis escalation?
9. Describe effective limit setting.
10. Describe a process for debriefing after a student involved in a crisis situation has de-escalated and regained control.

APPLICATION ACTIVITIES

1. Locate the full text of the U.S. Department of Health and Human Services report cited in this chapter. Discuss the data and recommendations in small groups.
2. Contact a local school district and ask for a copy of their discipline policies and procedures concerning use of physical interventions, as well as a copy of their crisis intervention plan. Find out what type of training they provide for their crisis intervention team.
3. Role-play crisis situations at CALM levels 1–3. Practice the appropriate teacher responses provided.

APPENDICES

CASE STUDY 1

Reactive Attachment Disorder of Infancy or Early Childhood

Lynda Nelson Day

PERSONAL INFORMATION

Josie celebrated her third birthday last week. She is of a biracial ethnic background. She lives in a midsize city in the Midwest. She was previously enrolled in an early intervention program in which the therapists provided services in Josie's Early Head Start classroom. Margo, Josie's mom, must now decide if she wants her daughter to transition to the early childhood special education program for 3- and 4-year-old special needs children, or to continue only with her day care providers.

EARLY EDUCATION/INTERVENTION HISTORY

An ongoing concern for Margo is Josie's behavior. Her daughter qualified for the early intervention program because of her developmental delays in language and social skills. Although Margo believes her daughter's social development has improved slightly, her lack of social interactions and the sporadic episodes of outrageous behavior are a worry. Margo wonders whether sending Josie to the early childhood special education class might cause her problems to worsen when she is with other children who also have behavior problems; she may retreat further into her shell, or she may model some of the outlandish behaviors of the other children. School personnel have suggested a conference with Margo to discuss this concern; however, she would have to take time away from work to attend a meeting. Presently, she cannot ask for more time off since she has had considerable time off whenever the various day care and after school care providers call to request that she come and get Josie's siblings because of their problem behaviors. Instead of being docked from work

to care for her children, Margo must now locate other day care facilities that are close to where she works.

FAMILY HISTORY

Josie's family consists of her biological parents, two older sisters, and a younger brother. Her older sisters are 4 1/2 years and 6 years old. Josie's brother soon will be 18 months. He was recently diagnosed with autistic-like tendencies. Dan, Josie's biological father, is not regularly in the home due to his job. Dan works as a union laborer for a company that has job sites all over the country; therefore he is gone for long periods of time and not very involved in making educational decisions. Whenever Dan is at home, he spends very little time with the children. Josie receives the least of his attention, due perhaps to her lack of responsiveness when Dan attempts to interact with her. Although Dan's income is considered good for his type of work and he has health insurance for the children, Margo also needs to work in order for the family to have a steady stream of income.

Josie was born one month premature, but it was a normal pregnancy and delivery. However, at birth Josie was diagnosed with a severe case of jaundice that required her to stay in the hospital for an extra 6 days for treatment. In addition, she had minor respiratory problems due to her prematurity and consequently was treated in the NICU at a local hospital. When brought home from the hospital, Josie experienced great difficulty in establishing a regular pattern of sleeping and eating. This lack of routine seemed to be exacerbated by irregular caregiving. Margo returned to work 2 weeks after giving birth. Her irregular work schedule required her to rely on various extended family members and friends to care for the infant Josie. Many of these folks, while accepting the responsibility of helping care for Josie, did not have the parenting skills for dealing with a premature, fussy infant, or the time to take care of her on a regular basis.

At the community well-baby clinic, doctors expressed concerns about Josie's lack of growth. By 18 months, Josie was significantly below the growth charts for weight and height for her age. Due to their concerns about failure to thrive and irregular parenting, doctors referred Margo to the local social services agency for child neglect several times during Josie's first year. Social services threatened to have Josie placed out of the home. Each time Margo agreed to change her ways, but soon returned to her inadequate parenting patterns. At age 3, Josie still experiences irregular sleeping and eating routines.

Some of Josie's problems are thought by her case manager to be the result of being cared for by many different caregivers who do not respond to her physical and social-emotional needs in a consistent manner. Margo reports that Josie is a difficult child to know and to nurture. For example, she cries inconsolably and refuses to let any adult comfort her. Sometimes Josie will want to be near Margo, but as soon as Margo reaches out to physically comfort her daughter, Josie will turn away. According to the reports from her caregivers over the past 2 years Josie has exhibited some disturbing behaviors. She has been very resistant to toilet training. It is not uncommon for her to smear her feces on the walls, herself, and anything nearby. Caregivers also report that occasionally Josie has destroyed her toys or those of her siblings. These behaviors have been sporadic. Margo has responded either by not showing a concern (her attempt to ignore) or giving her daughter spankings. She reports that neither seems to help.

Josie has a limited expressive vocabulary. At age 3 she is not saying more than single words. She does know the basic words to get her needs met, such as: "pee," "McDonalds," "no," etc. However, the professionals who have evaluated Josie believe her receptive vocabulary to be closer to her chronological age.

Josie initiates very limited social interactions with adult family members and her primary caregivers. She carries a Raggedy Ann doll with her at all times. Whenever someone attempts to take her doll, Josie will throw a major temper tantrum so that it becomes much easier to let her continue holding her doll.

When Josie was 2, a social worker who was investigating the family's situation suggested that Margo enroll Josie in the Early Head Start program. While Josie was enrolled in this program, her teacher contacted the early intervention program for developmentally delayed children. Josie qualified because of delayed language and inappropriate social behaviors. Two mornings a week, Josie goes to the local Early Head Start program and once a week on a rotating schedule she has the services of either a speech/language clinician or a social worker. During her time with the early intervention social worker, Josie is seen in a playroom and observed playing. The social worker has attempted to work with Margo, giving her suggestions for ways to interact with Josie in the family setting, but she has not felt very successful, as Margo has been unable to follow through. The early intervention services with the speech/language clinical are provided at the Head Start classrooms to keep with the best practice of providing intervention services in natural settings.

RECENT DIAGNOSTIC RESULTS

When Josie was around 30 months of age, a licensed clinical social worker conducted a diagnostic evaluation to prepare for Josie's transition out of the early intervention program. The social worker conducted a family interview with Margo and Josie's grandmother (who has been doing most of the caring for Josie during the past 3 months). The social worker explained the Ages and Stages Questionnaire (ASQ), and left the checklist forms for both adults to complete and bring to the scheduled Play-Based Transdisciplinary Assessment. The Play-Based Transdisciplinary Assessment included a team of professionals interacting with Josie and her mother while in a familiar play setting. The Peabody Picture Vocabulary Test was also scheduled to be administered to estimate Josie's receptive language skills.

Josie's mother and grandmother filled out the 36 Month–3 Year ASQ checklists, and Josie's grandmother returned them to the early childhood special educator when she brought Josie to the local school district's special education office for completion of the evaluation. Each question was answered and the results demonstrated that areas of communication, problem solving, and personal-social were all below the cutoff scores. However, for the gross motor and fine motor sections, Josie's scores fell at and above the cutoff scores, respectively.

Josie and her grandmother met with the assessment team members prior to conducting the Play-Based Transdisciplinary Assessment. (Margo, at the urging of the assessment team, had asked for time off work in order to be part of the Play-Based Transdisciplinary Assessment, but at the last minute her supervisor said she could not take time away from work.) The team members at the assessment consisted of a clinical social worker (the same one that has been working with Margo through the early intervention program), an occupational therapist, a speech and language clinician, an early childhood special educator, and a school psychologist. Team members took turns in facilitating Josie's play. The session lasted approximately an hour, with structured and unstructured play stages. It was videotaped so team members could review the session to complete their diagnostic findings.

After the assessment, the team completed the printed summary sheets in each of the areas: cognitive, social-emotional, communications and language, and sensorimotor. A brief summary of the team's findings include that Josie is below her expected developmental levels in problem-solving approaches. She appears to rely on a repetitive approach, with minimal evidence of advanced planning. Whenever she does try to problem solve, her activities are more limited to visual scanning or physical searching. She is limited in her discrimination and classification skills and her sequencing ability. However, she can do elementary one-to-one correspondence with familiar pictures.

Her dramatic play is limited by her frequently inappropriate use of objects. She preferred inanimate objects (e.g., trucks, blocks) over the use of unfamiliar dolls or stuffed toys. She seems to have a preference for simple repetitive but inappropriate use of many familiar objects that you would expect a typically developing 3-year-old to know. She did verbally indicate she wanted her favorite doll to stay with her throughout the play session. Although her doll was present, Josie did not interact with it.

In the social-emotional aspects of the assessment, Josie engaged in an approach-avoidance behavior pattern with her grandmother. She had very little to do with her grandmother, ignoring her verbal and nonverbal efforts to come and play. When the play facilitator tempted Josie into situations to gauge her affect and level of reaction to emotions, Josie was slow to respond and tended to be more responsive to the facilitator's verbal encouragements, as opposed to her tactile or kinesthetic encouragements. Josie demonstrated difficulty with any kind of turn-taking behaviors across the adult facilitators. Overall, the findings of Josie's social-emotional development show a child with limited interactive skills, particularly with humans.

In the area of communications and language, findings show that Josie's primary method of communication is use of eye gaze and physical manipulations, but minimal verbalizations. Although there were limited examples to judge, Josie's oral motor development appeared to be on track. The majority of her speech production was categorized as: requesting objects, commenting on objects, and protesting. She seemed to attend to the facilitator who was speaking to her only when she wanted to. Josie's articulation errors were evaluated to be developmental, but she displayed understanding and use of language slightly below her expected chronological age.

Finally, in the area of sensorimotor skills, Josie engaged in age-appropriate skills and showed advanced development for some activities. These included climbing, kicking, and reaching skills. Compared to her overall demonstration of sensorimotor skills, Josie exhibited weakest skills in the area of motor planning. However, that area was judged to be near her chronological age.

The final assessment scheduled was the Peabody Picture Vocabulary Test, Third Edition (PPVT-III); however, it was dropped from the current assessment. The norm groups for this test begin at 2 years, 6 months, which would place Josie close to the beginning of the age groups. Adequate assessment information about Josie's language skills was obtained through the interviews and observation components of the current assessment; thus, the assessment team decided to evaluate Josie with the Vineland Social-Emotional Early Childhood Scales at a later time if more normative data is required.

DIAGNOSIS AND SUMMARY

The assessment team believes Josie meets most of the criteria for reactive attachment disorder of infancy or early childhood listed in the Diagnostic Statistical Manual IV-TR (APA, 2000); however, the assessment team recommends qualifying Josie for the special education early childhood program with the noncategorical diagnosis of a young child with a developmental delay. The local public school district operates a half-day, 5-day-a-week special education preschool program for 3- and 4-year-olds. The school district policy is to include the enrollment of normally developing children into the classroom as a means of introducing the children with delayed development to age-appropriate-developing peer models. This has been a successful strategy for all the children. The early childhood teachers will use peer-mediated, social-interaction strategies to improve Josie's social and language skills.

All teachers and therapists will initially spend one-on-one time with Josie, to help her feel emotionally comfortable and accepting of them. Josie will work with the same adults, rather than having her work with volunteers and other infrequent adults in the classroom until she is more open to new persons.

Establishing routines in the classroom is especially important for Josie. The consistency that routines provide will benefit Josie psychologically. She will come to recognize that she can rely on adults to take care of her physical and emotional needs.

Teachers will monitor Josie's play in the classroom and playground through daily observations. The teacher will use the information to establish facilitation strategies to encourage more age-appropriate levels of play.

The speech and language therapist will provide the teachers and Josie's mother with suggestions to work on improving Josie's language development.

The assessment team feels that, at this time, using strategies in the natural environments is preferable to scheduling individual therapy sessions. However, they recommend that Josie's mother be referred to professional family counseling with the initial goal focused on improving parenting skills. The early childhood special education team will offer Margo encouragement to follow through with this recommendation. Additionally, they will provide support and encouragement for her to attend the monthly parent meetings that they schedule for the children's families.

Given Josie's young age, it is too soon to predict the outcome for her, but the assessment team feels that an early intervention approach that focuses on best practices of empowering the child's family, building upon the child's strengths, providing educational intervention in all developmental domains, and working as a transdisciplinary assessment and treatment team will give Josie the best opportunity for potential change.

CASE STUDY 2

Dual Diagnosis: Mental Retardation and Mental Illness

Jerry Neal

PERSONAL INFORMATION

Spencer is a 10-year-old male in fourth grade who lives with both of his biological parents and one older sister in a suburban section of a large Midwestern city. His mother is an office assistant for a local attorney, and his father is self-employed (he owns a small-engine repair shop). Spencer has been receiving services in a self-contained classroom for students with severe mental retardation and autism since he was in the first grade. All academic course work is delivered through the self-contained class instructor. Because of his behavioral outbursts, tantrums, and extreme aggression toward others, Spencer does not participate with nondisabled peers in any activity, such as recess, lunch, or other nonacademic subjects. He has been assigned a one-on-one paraprofessional who assists him with all of his lessons and personal needs including toileting assistance, and implements his behavioral intervention plan. Although Spencer has been taking Ritalin for 2 years in an attempt to control his extreme hyperactivity and lack of attention to schoolwork, he continues to have little control over his impulsive behavior, is constantly restless, and displays socially inappropriate behaviors throughout the school day. During the past 2 years, his parents have also reported an increasing number of bowel and bladder "accidents" by Spencer at home during daytime hours.

SCHOOL HISTORY

Spencer's district did not offer early childhood services, and his parents were unable to find a preschool that would agree to take him. Therefore, Spencer first came to the attention of teachers at his school when he was in the morning kindergarten class at his neighborhood school. The kindergarten teacher was unable to control his vocal and physical outbursts, and was unsuccessful at teaching Spencer basic pre-academic concepts (colors, shapes, letter recognition, numerals, following simple directions, etc.). She reported in her initial referral for assessment that Spencer's extreme behavior made it impossible to maintain an environment conducive to learning for the other children in the class. A multidisciplinary team conducted an evaluation of Spencer during the third month of his kindergarten year of school. This team consisted of the school psychological examiner, elementary guidance counselor, speech/language pathologist, social worker, mental retardation program instructor, behavior disorders program instructor, building principal, special education administrator, the kindergarten teacher, and both of Spencer's parents. An independent clinical psychologist was also retained by the school district to conduct an extensive psychological examination of Spencer that was beyond the capabilities of the local diagnostic staff.

The multidisciplinary team developed an evaluation plan designed to identify Spencer's strengths and weaknesses in school and determine whether his disruptive behaviors were due to an underlying mental or psychological condition. The team sought to answer two questions. First, were the academic and behavioral problems exhibited by Spencer caused by a recognizable disability under IDEA? Second, if these problems were caused by a disability, what were the implications of this disability on Spencer's current and future social, behavioral, and academic functioning? With those two questions in mind, the team conducted a multifaceted, multidimensional evaluation over the course of 3 weeks.

The team developed the evaluation report, a written summary of the diagnostic results, and presented it to Spencer's parents during the summative multidisciplinary team meeting at the school. These results culminated in a statement describing the existence and nature of his disability. The team determined that Spencer manifested both moderate mental retardation of idiopathic (undetermined) origin, as well as mental illness (childhood disintegrative disorder) according to the classifications of the *Diagnostic and Statistical Manual of Mental Disorders, Fourth Edition, Text Revision (DMS-IV-TR)* (APA, 2000).

At his parents' request, Spencer continued to receive services in a regular education classroom for the remainder of his kindergarten year. However, his continual disruption of the classroom and general lack of academic and social gains, even with a one-on-one aide, continued to be very unsettling to classmates and to his teacher. Because of Spencer's failure to demonstrate progress in general education, at the beginning of first grade, the school placed him in a pull-out resource room setting with students who had similar educational needs. This also proved unsuccessful. Spencer failed to demonstrate progress on his IEP goals and continued to be a very disruptive influence on his peers.

During the middle of first grade, the multidisciplinary team, including Kristol and David, Spencer's parents, agreed that a more restrictive placement would be in the best interests of both Spencer and his classmates. He still attends his neighborhood school, but has been receiving instruction in a self-contained classroom for students with developmental disabilities and autism since that time.

PRESENT LEVEL OF EDUCATIONAL PERFORMANCE (PLEP)

Academic

Spencer has only rudimentary skills in all academic areas. In mathematics he is able to understand the concept of more/less, can count to 50 without error, identifies coin values (penny, nickel, dime, quarter), and can do simple addition and subtraction of numerals with the aid of manipulatives such as blocks, beads, or a counting frame. In reading, Spencer has learned the letters and their corresponding sounds and has acquired a sight word vocabulary of approximately 100 words, mostly words of a functional nature (exit, boys, girls, danger, stop, parents' names, address, etc.). He cannot yet read basic sentences with comprehension. Spencer has learned to write his first name legibly, but cannot write his last name unless prompted by his teachers. He speaks in complete simple sentences, but uses immature grammatical structure and vocabulary (e.g., "My foots hurts," "He gots a ball," "That a book"). Articulation is poor for his age, and Spencer often makes reversals and substitutions in conversational speech ("gwank" for "drank," "wots" for "lots").

Social/Emotional/Behavioral

Spencer does not typically socialize with the other children. His fourth-grade peers have often tried to initiate interactions with him in the classroom and on the playground, but his unruly nature and rather bizarre mannerisms and verbalizations tend to keep most other children at a distance. Spencer has a habit of continually sucking on his thumb, with his index finger curled around the bridge of his nose. When asked why he sucks his thumb by peers and adults, his usual response is, "It's chocolate: wanna try it?"

He still has periods when he soils himself, and when he is in the restroom, a flushing toilet frightens him. He often will turn to other children or adults present and ask, "A monster in there?"

Spencer tends to sit by himself, and talks to himself in muted tones throughout the school day. Occasionally, he will begin to laugh out loud as if he has just heard a joke. He will turn away from his paraprofessional when asked to focus on the task at hand and yell loudly, "NO! NO! NO! Won't do it!"

Spencer impulsively strikes out at other children or adults for no apparent reason. During such times, it has been necessary for the teacher or paraprofessional to physically restrain Spencer so that he does not injure others or himself. On at least two occasions during the past year, his tantrums have gotten so physically out of control that school security personnel had to be called in to protect others from harm. His parents are called to the school at least every other week to take him home due to his out-of-control behavior. His father is generally the one to pick him up in these instances, since his mother cannot leave her work, and the father's repair shop is located at home.

Spencer consistently has refused to get on the bus that takes him to school, and his father has taken it upon himself to personally drive the 2-mile trip to deliver Spencer to his school each day. Although the district is willing to reimburse them for mileage, his parents decided not to bother with the paperwork. On several occasions, Spencer has gotten to the school door only to scream that the "monsters are in there" and that he was not going inside. In these instances, his father explains to Spencer's paraprofessional, who always escorts Spencer to his classroom, that Spencer is "having a bad day" and proceeds to take Spencer home for the day.

Daily Living Skills

A large portion of Spencer's school day is spent acquiring skills that he will need when he is not in a school environment. Spencer and his peers who have similar needs have been working on how to dress appropriately for changing weather conditions and select clothing that matches these conditions. Spencer is able to put on his own clothes, and deals effectively with buttons, snaps, and belt buckles. He cannot yet tie his own shoes and must rely on Velcro or slip-on shoe styles. He has learned to make simple meals and snacks with some prompting and assistance (microwave popcorn, peanut butter sandwiches, canned soup), but lack of memory and off-task behavior have limited his culinary skills. He is learning to tell time from a digital clock and is often asked by his paraprofessional when it will be time for certain daily events to take place, such as recess, lunch period, or speech. He cannot tell time at all from a traditional analog timepiece, and this has been a concern for his parents this year. Recognizing coin values and counting change has also been a focus this year.

FAMILY HISTORY

Spencer lives with his mother, father, and one older sister in a modest home in a suburban area. His mother has a clerical background while his father has held several jobs as an automobile mechanic until he began his own small-engine repair service shortly after Spencer was born. His sister, Karla, is in the ninth grade, makes good grades in school, participates in band and choir, and is a junior varsity cheerleader.

No one in the immediate family has a history of difficulty in school or emotional problems. An interview with Spencer's mother revealed that no problems were encountered during the full-term pregnancy, but complications did occur during the actual birthing process. These complications included: prolonged labor (18 hours), forceps delivery, and possible fetal anoxia due to twisted umbilical cord. Spencer's parents began to notice shortly after birth that Spencer was different than what they had experienced with his older sibling. He did not have regular sleep patterns, was not feeding well (abnormal gag reflex), did not respond immediately to verbal or physical stimulation, and cried uncontrollably even if all of his physiological needs had been met. At 6 months, Spencer's parents contacted his pediatrician with their concerns and explained that he was apparently not attaining normal developmental milestones. The pediatrician, although expressing some sympathy with the parents' concerns, adopted a "wait and see" attitude, instructing that Spencer be brought to her office again in 6 months for the annual well baby checkup.

At age 1, Spencer was examined by his pediatrician, who agreed that Spencer had some possible developmental delays and referred the family to the child development center operated by a not-for-profit agency in their community. For the next 4 years, Spencer and his family attended weekly training and therapy sessions designed to give Spencer the skills necessary to enter public school and lessen the effect of the increasingly obvious challenges that he would have to overcome. A family support group was available to assist the family in understanding the stresses and difficulties that the family would face immediately and in the future, and to offer suggestions concerning how to obtain services and make financial arrangements for Spencer's continuing therapies. Preschools in the local community refused to accept Spencer as a student as he was not toilet trained, had little understandable language, and had a "violent disposition."

RECENT EVALUATION RESULTS

This year, Spencer's parents asked the school if they could get an independent educational evaluation (IEE) of their son, rather than having a series of assessments conducted by the staff of the school district as part of his scheduled re-evaluation. Because of the variety of problems being manifested by Spencer, many of which were becoming more of a concern every day, school district officials and Spencer's parents decided that he should be taken to the local university child study clinic where a comprehensive diagnostic evaluation could be completed at the school district's expense. Evaluations were conducted with Spencer during a week-long stay at the university child study clinic. Evaluation results were as follows.

Wechsler Intelligence Scale for Children, Third Edition (WISC-III) (Wechsler, 1991)

The WISC-III results included a verbal scale IQ of 53, a performance scale IQ of 49, and a full scale IQ of 50 (mean = 100, standard deviation = 15). Spencer had no significant strengths on any of the 13 subtests of the WISC-III and was particularly deficient in similarities, picture arrangement, symbol search, and coding, in which he did not answer any items correctly. These scores place Spencer well below his chronological age cognitively, and fall within the intellectually deficient range of cognitive ability (more than three standard deviations below the mean)

AAMR Adaptive Behavior Scale-School, Second Edition (ABS-S2) (Lambert, Nihira, & Leland, 1993)

The ABS-S2 is divided into two parts and is designed to assess the child's independent living skills and social behavior. Spencer's classroom teacher completed the assessment, as she was most familiar with Spencer's abilities in each of the areas measured by the ABS-S2. Results in the independent living domains indicated low scores in all areas, particularly responsibility, socialization, and self-direction. Particular areas of concern in the social behavior domains included social behavior, stereotyped and hyperactive, social engagement, and disturbing interpersonal behavior. All of these areas yielded scores that were below the 1st percentile rank.

Test of Language Development-Primary, Third Edition (TOLD-P3) (Newcomer & Hammill, 1997)

This assessment of language development was normed for children between the ages of 4 and 9. However, because of Spencer's clear difficulty in the area of language, the diagnostic team determined that this version of this device, rather than the age-appropriate Test of Language Development-Intermediate (TOLD-I:3), would be more appropriate and provide more suitable programmatic information. Spencer had no areas of linguistic strength based on the nine subtests of the TOLD-P·3. His weakest areas were those of word articulation (2nd percentile), grammatic completion (2nd percentile), picture vocabulary (5th percentile), and relational vocabulary (< 1 percentile). Spencer's actual percentile ranks, if based on the norms for his specific age group, would be considerably less than these scores.

Woodcock-Johnson III Tests of Achievement (WJ-III) (Woodcock, McGrew, & Mather, 2001)

Spencer completed the WJ-III standard battery only (mean = 100, standard deviation = 15), as his attention span prohibited completing both the standard and extended batteries of the assessment device. Of the 12 subtests of the standard battery, Spencer's highest scores were on story recall (standard score 68), understanding directions (standard score 65), letter-word identification (standard score 63), and story recall-delayed (standard score 60). All other subtests placed him at or below a standard score of 55. Of particular concern were his scores on calculation, applied problems, spelling, math fluency, and reading fluency, all of which placed Spencer at a kindergarten level of functioning. He scored zero on writing fluency as he refused to write any letters or words as directed by the examiner.

Classroom Observations

Another special education teacher observed Spencer in his classroom environment on five occasions, 2 hours each time, for a total of 10 hours of structured and unstructured activity time. A momentary time sampling procedure was used for these observations, and indicated that Spencer was on task for only an average of 20% of the time he was observed. The remainder of the time was spent out of seat (22%), engaged in self-stimulation or daydreaming (40%), or having tantrums/disturbing others (18%). During three of the five observation periods, Spencer had to be physically restrained by his teacher so that he would not harm other children.

ACCOMMODATIONS/MODIFICATIONS ATTEMPTED TO DATE

- Verbal redirection to stay on task: Unsuccessful.
- Assigned a "study buddy": Unsuccessful, as Spencer attacked the classmate assigned to him.
- One-on-one paraprofessional: Moderately successful, but tantrums by Spencer ensue if the paraprofessional divides her attention with the other children in the classroom.

- Token economy: Somewhat successful. Spencer was given a "work card" containing 50 blank squares. The teacher or paraprofessional marked an "X" in a square when Spencer completed a task, complied with a request, or was otherwise "caught being good" (e.g., attending to task, not disturbing others, staying in his seat, etc.). Spencer could trade in a completed card for free time, an assortment of tangibles that he liked (granola bars, old photographs, stickers, etc.), or a visit to the art room where he could work on finger painting or clay sculpturing. Consistent compliant behavior was still elusive.
- Time-out: Unsuccessful. Spencer had even stronger tantrums in the time-out area, usually resulting in loss of bowel or bladder control, and causing further disruption of the classroom routine.
- Physical restraint: Unsuccessful, usually resulted in further escalation.
- Shortened school day: Somewhat successful. Although Spencer's parents and the rest of the IEP team agree that a shortened school day is not an ideal or long-term solution, they have agreed to limit his attendance to three hours in the morning. He will have a 1:1 paraprofessional and continue to use his token economy, both at home and in the classroom. His IEP goals will be adjusted for this more limited time period and will be focused on preferred activities. If Spencer's tantrums and aggression remain stable, and if his time on task increases, his school day will be lengthened incrementally every 30 days.

CASE STUDY 3

Asperger's Disorder

Theresa L. Earles-Vollrath

PERSONAL INFORMATION

Jarrett J. Jackson is a 12-year-old male in the seventh grade at a public middle school in a large suburban school district. He attends general education classes for all academic areas but receives 45 minutes of direct services daily from staff in the learning center to assist him with work completion and filling in his daily planner. In addition, Jarrett meets with a social worker one time per week for 60 minutes, and an autism specialist attends monthly meetings with his educational team to provide training, to participate in problem-solving sessions, and to assist in implementing the behavior intervention plan.

SCHOOL HISTORY

Jarrett was referred to the child study team at the public elementary school he attended during his fifth grade year. The child study team was comprised of the school principal, a school psychologist, two general education teachers, and the learning center teacher. In addition, other support staff, such as the autism specialist, the social worker, the behavior specialist, the speech and language pathologist, and the occupational therapist, were consulted or served as team members when deemed necessary.

Jarrett's classroom teacher made the referral to the child study team because of Jarrett's noncompliance with teacher directions and frequent arguments with school staff. While Jarrett demonstrated knowledge in the content area by his participation in class discussions, he received Ds and Fs due to poor work completion.

Jarrett also reports that he has obsessive thoughts about racial symbols such as skinheads, the Confederate flag, and the KKK. These obsessive thoughts seem to be becoming stronger and more prevalent because Jarrett attempted to infuse these topics into classroom discussions and approached his peers using the topics as conversation starters.

Mr. and Mrs. Smith, Jarrett's stepfather and mother, chose to have Jarrett evaluated by a team at a local university during the initial stages of the referral process. Upon completion of the evaluation, Jarrett was diagnosed as having Asperger's disorder in accordance with the *Diagnostic and Statistical Manual of Mental Disorders,* Fourth Edition, Text Revision (DSM-IV-TR) (APA, 2000).

PRESENT LEVEL OF EDUCATIONAL PERFORMANCE

Behavior

Jarrett's teachers report that his refusals to comply with directions are affecting his grades and his progress in the general education curriculum. According to data collected during classroom observations, Jarrett complies with 85% of teacher directions that request him to complete a verbal activity, 70% of teacher directions that require him to complete a performance activity, and 45% of teacher requests that require a written response. Jarrett's teachers expect students to be compliant with 95% to 100% of adult requests.

Social Skills

Jarrett's inability to appropriately initiate conversations limits his ability to interact with others as needed to progress in the general curriculum. Both his teachers and his peers report that Jarrett initiates conversations by using phrases such as "Do you want to join my World Wide Wrestling club?", or "There's a KKK meeting tonight, wanna come?" In addition, when a group of students are standing in the school common area, he will push his way to the middle of the group and announce that he has pornographic magazines in his locker if they would like to meet him after school to view them.

Teachers collected probe data over a two-week period. This data indicated that Jarrett appropriately initiated conversations with his peers during an average of 25% of the opportunities, as compared to a control subject's ability to initiate conversations appropriately during an average of 80% of the opportunities.

Work Completion

An analysis of classroom data indicates that Jarrett completes and turns in approximately 50% of his assignments. Teachers report that he is more likely to complete assignments that require Internet searches, that allow him to select the topic of his choice, or that require a verbal presentation of information. Jarrett is less likely to complete written assignments, specifically those that require him to analyze and synthesize information or make inferences regarding what a character may be feeling or thinking. Data indicates that Jarrett's peers complete and turn in approximately 94% of the work assigned.

Grades and Attendance

Jarrett's grades have declined over the years. His grades are higher in courses that utilize computer or math skills. Jarrett also likes science courses that incorporate astronomy. Jarrett has the most difficulty in courses such as physical education, English, or literature. Currently, Jarrett has Ds and Fs in a majority of his courses due to poor work completion. Jarrett's attendance is good. He misses an average of 5 days per school year.

FAMILY HISTORY

Jarrett lives at home with his stepfather, his mother, and his older sister and her daughter. The stepfather works as an account executive and his mother does not work outside of the home. Jarrett's sister, Isabelle, is in the process of filing for divorce. She and her daughter are residing with Jarrett and his family until she can get a job and locate an apartment. Jarrett spends one weekend a month with his birth father. His birth father is currently unemployed. Jarrett reports that a typical weekend with his birth father consists of watching *World Wide Wrestling* and going "dumpster digging" to search for pornographic magazines.

The Smiths are supportive of their son. They attend school functions, parent conferences, and actively participate in monthly meetings with his educational team and in IEP meetings. During meetings Mrs. Smith will periodically make statements regarding the team's understanding of her son's disability. She also states that Asperger's disorder causes Jarrett's behaviors; therefore, he cannot be expected to meet teacher expectations and follow school rules. Members of the school team are concerned with these statements. While they believe that having Asperger's disorder explains why Jarrett exhibits some of his behaviors, they believe that with proper instruction, modifications, accommodations, and a behavior intervention plan, he can meet teacher expectations, follow school rules, and have a successful educational experience. Jarrett's birth father does not currently participate in Jarrett's educational experiences.

According to parent reports, a majority of the early developmental milestones were achieved except in the area of language. His parents report: "Jarrett did not start talking until he was 2 years old; however, when he did start talking, he began speaking in five- and six-word sentences and used big words." Jarrett's sister, Isabelle, states that he was always talking and reading about flags, the presidents, and space. She states that when he was 5 years old, she could name a country and Jarrett could verbally describe the corresponding flag. In addition, if she gave him a year (e.g., 1941), Jarrett could state the name of the president who was in office during the specified year.

Mr. and Mrs. Smith state that it was difficult for them when Jarrett was diagnosed with Asperger's disorder; however, they were somewhat relieved that it was not their parenting that caused his behaviors. Mr. and Mrs. Smith and Isabelle also report that they better understand Jarrett's behavior based upon information that they have read regarding Asperger's disorder.

Jarrett was recently placed on medications in an attempt to address his obsessive thoughts and his non-compliant behavior. Currently he takes 80 mg of Prozac and 40 mg of Adderall daily. Parent and school reports indicate that the medications seem to be working.

RECENT DIAGNOSTIC INFORMATION

After Jarrett was diagnosed with Asperger's disorder, his parents requested that the school conduct a full evaluation. The school administered several assessment measures, including the Weschler Intelligence Scale for Children, Third Edition (WISC-III) (Weschler, 1991), the Woodcock-Johnson III Tests of Achievement (2001), and the Tops-Adolescent: Test of Problem Solving Skill, Revised (1994). The WISC-III is an intelligence test that measures the cognitive abilities of students ranging in age from 6 through 16 years, 11 months. The WISC-III is comprised of two scales, the verbal subtest and the performance subtest, which yield three IQ scores: verbal IQ, performance IQ, and full scale IQ (mean = 100; standard deviation = 15). Jarrett's results on the WISC-III yielded a verbal score of 113, a performance score of 131, and a full scale IQ score of 123. Jarrett demonstrated strengths in the areas of information, arithmetic, digit span, block design, and object assembly. While within the average range of performance, he exhibited relative weaknesses in the areas of comprehension, coding, and similarities.

The Woodcock-Johnson Psycho-Educational Battery, Revised Tests of Achievement (1989) (WJ-R) is an individually administered assessment measure. The results of the WJ-R indicated strengths in the area of letter-word identification, calculation, and science. Jarrett's scores on the passage comprehension, applied problems, and dictation portions of the measure fell within the average range of functioning. Jarrett refused to complete the writing samples subtest.

The Test of Problem Solving Skill, Revised (TOPS-R) (1994) is an assessment instrument that evaluates ability to problem solve and use language-based critical thinking skills for students ages 6 years through 11 years, 11 months. The measure includes 14 picture scenarios and a total of 72 questions that relate to the scenarios. Jarrett received a standard score of 75 on the TOPS-R (mean = 100, standard deviation = 15).

CLASSROOM OBSERVATION/FUNCTIONAL ASSESSMENT DATA

The assessment team conducted classroom observations over a period of two weeks and collected data on Jarrett's compliance with verbal directions and the type of task he was being asked to complete (written, verbal, performance, other). Data indicated that Jarrett complied with 85% of teacher directions that requested him to complete a verbal activity, 70% of teacher directions that

required him to complete a performance activity, and 45% of teacher requests that required a written response.

An interview with Jarrett confirmed the information gained during the observations, as well as provided additional information regarding his noncompliant behavior. During the interview, Jarrett stated that he did not like to complete written assignments. He also stated that his teachers make repeated requests for him to redo his work because it is too difficult to read. As the interview progressed, Jarrett shared information regarding his obsessive thoughts. He stated that he sometimes does not hear the teachers' directions because he can't stop thinking about shaving his head and joining the KKK. He also stated that he wants to develop a *World Wide Wrestling* program in his backyard and spends class time creating it in his mind.

ACCOMODATIONS/MODIFICATIONS ATTEMPTED TO DATE

* Verbal reminders from teacher to complete assignment planner: Not successful.
* Verbal reminders from a one-on-one paraprofessional to complete assignment planner: Not successful.
* Study hall to assist with work completion: Not successful. Much of the work that Jarrett was asked to complete during study hall was labeled by his teachers as "homework." Jarrett refused to complete this work during study hall because he believed that "homework" was to be completed at home, not at school.
* Behavior contract in which Jarrett earned points for completing his planner prior to the end of class. At the end of the week, Jarrett traded his points for extra computer time: Not successful.
* During classes in which a paraprofessional was available, a behavior system was implemented to reinforce compliance with teacher directions. A piece of tape was placed on Jarrett's desk prior to his arrival in class. When Jarrett followed a direction within 30 seconds, the paraprofessional marked a "+" on the piece of tape. If Jarrett did not follow the direction within 30 seconds, a "/" was placed on the piece of tape. With 10 minutes remaining at the end of class, the paraprofessional counted the number of "+" recorded on the piece of tape. If there was 1 more "+" than "/," Jarrett was allowed to go to the counselor's office and play a video game until the bell sounded. This intervention was successful; however, it could only be implemented in three of

his seven courses due to limited availability of a paraprofessional.

TRANSITION INFORMATION

Student Interests

* Space and astronomy
* *World Wide Wrestling*
* Presidents of the United States
* Flags
* Reading
* Computers
* Comic books
* Surfing the World Wide Web
* Video games

Dislikes

* Written work
* Sports

Future Educational Outcomes

Jarrett would like to go to college.

Employment and Career Development

Jarrett would like to be an astronaut.

Jarrett's IEP team agrees that he will continue to participate in mainstream academic and exploratory classes. Based on his test scores and aptitude in these math and science college preparatory high school courses, a career connected with science or the space program would not be unreasonable aspirations. However, to assist with his social skill development and provide the support needed to complete assignments, Jarrett will participate in a weekly social skills group led by the school counselor and will receive special education services in the resource room during the last class period each day.

CASE STUDY 4

Bipolar Disorder

Jerry Neal

PERSONAL INFORMATION

Carlotta is a 16-year-old female who has just completed the 10th grade at a residential program for youth with psychiatric disorders. She attends a self-contained educational program for students with emotional disorders on the grounds of the residential facility and has little contact at school with students who do not have special needs. Carlotta wants to please adults, but is extremely demanding of their time. She is verbally and physically abusive to those around her, both peers and adults. Understandably, people tend to avoid Carlotta after they have experienced her verbal tirades and abusive demeanor. She has been involved in a number of physical altercations with students and faculty members and had two incidents of sexual harassment in which she "inappropriately touched a male peer without his permission." The last allegation resulted in a 5-day school suspension. Upon her return, school administrators recommended that Carlotta's school day be shortened to 4 hours because most of her disciplinary incidents occurred after the lunch break. The IEP team was reconvened to review and update her current educational placement, but since her mother did not attend that meeting to represent Carlotta, the team decided that she should remain in her current educational placement until her IEP is due for annual review in September.

Carlotta has been diagnosed with a variety of psychiatric disorders over the last 7 years, including depression, bipolar disorder, and post-traumatic stress disorder. Carlotta's mother has a history of mental disorders, including bipolar disorder, and does not take her medication on a consistent basis. As a result, her mother often spends time in a psychiatric hospital and does not take an interest in Carlotta's life. Her mother is unable to hold down a job for any length of time and has been receiving Social Security disability benefits as her primary source of income for the past 3 years. Carlotta has two older sisters who live independently of their mother, and neither has expressed an interest in getting involved with Carlotta due to her unstable personality and general "craziness." Although Carlotta's biological father has never been involved in her life, he occasionally sends her a gift at Christmas. Carlotta has been in foster care since the age of 9 as a result of allegations of abuse and neglect against her mother; however, parental rights have not been severed. The family court permits Carlotta's mother to have supervised visits with her on a weekly basis. However, a verbally abusive phone call from her mother 9 months ago left Carlotta in a highly agitated state, and there has been no contact between them since that time.

SCHOOL HISTORY

Carlotta has lived in a series of foster homes for the past 7 years; her frequent changes in placement have been a result of her aggressive and disruptive behavior. As a result, Carlotta has transferred in and out of approximately 10 schools in that time period. During her fifth-grade year, Carlotta's teacher referred her for special education evaluation. The referral noted classic symptoms of emotional disturbance and behavioral disorders including: inability to learn; inability to establish and maintain satisfactory relationships with peers or adults; intense mood swings; noncompliance; disregard for authority; general depression or extreme agitation; and excessive absences from school. The multidisciplinary team determined that her problems were not simply a result of her erratic school attendance, however. They diagnosed her as behaviorally disordered (the IDEA label at that time in her district) late in her fifth-grade year and Carlotta began receiving services in a self-contained classroom for children whose behaviors were threatening to others or impeded the learning of classmates. Each of several subsequent schools that she attended during the next 3 years provided her special education services in settings designed to take into account her emotional, as well as academic, needs.

During her eighth-grade year, the junior high Carlotta was attending implemented a highly regarded program for troubled youth that included individual and group therapies, art and music therapies, and individual tutoring for academics. Carlotta's behavior seemed to improve somewhat but she continued to have episodes of self-isolation that would be followed by emotional outbursts in which she harmed other students physically. The school was concerned that Carlotta's behaviors were not coming under control; instead, as she grew in size, her aggression toward others grew as well.

During the last weeks of the eighth-grade year, Carlotta and one of her foster siblings were involved in a serious physical altercation at home. After she was reprimanded by her foster parents, Carlotta ran away from home. Police found her 3 days later living with two other teen runaways in an abandoned house. She was sent to a juvenile detention facility and remained there for 1 month, after which she was placed by the family court in her current psychiatric residential program. A complete reevaluation of Carlotta was ordered by the medical staff of the residential program. This evaluation resulted in a diagnosis of bipolar disorder (rapid cycle according to DSM-IV-TR [APA, 2000]) with psychotic features and oppositional defiant disorder (ODD). The medical staff prescribed antidepressant and antipsychotic medications; however, the medication that seemed to be most effective in controlling her bipolar cycles (Lithium) was discontinued after she began developing toxic side effects of the medication.

PRESENT LEVEL OF EDUCATIONAL PERFORMANCE (PLEP)

Academic

Carlotta performed at the 35th percentile, which is below proficiency, in all academic areas on the last state-mandated achievement test required by the No Child Left Behind Act.

Carlotta seems to have reading skills that are at or near grade level. Although her oral skills in reading seem to be adequate, she sometimes falters with comprehension tasks, particularly those that require higher-order skills such as synthesizing or analyzing information that is presented in content areas such as science or social studies. She is also unable to respond to questions requiring empathy or insight.

Carlotta's writing skills are also adequate and her English II teacher reports that she has good mastery of writing mechanics. However, that instructor reports that the content of Carlotta's written assignments are frequently rife with sexual imagery, violence, death, and perhaps veiled suicidal messages. Mathematics is the area that gives Carlotta the most trouble. She received a D in Algebra I this year, but her algebra instructor noted that she seldom turns in assignments or fully completes those that are submitted. Carlotta seems to have developed an external locus of control in some regard about math, and other subjects as well. For example, she has often remarked that, "I try to do the work, but when I don't understand something and ask for the teachers' help they don't know how to do the stuff either. They make me dumber than I already am!"

Social/Emotional

Carlotta does not get along well with any of the other students at her school, and has no known friends there. Others tend to avoid her due to her explosive and unpredictable temperament. She resents the staff and instructors keeping her isolated from male students, but if she is in the presence of males, she makes obscene gestures to them and lewd verbal comments as well.

Her verbal abuse of staff is constant, except when she is receiving nonjudgmental, one-on-one assistance.

Carlotta explodes when redirected by staff members and negative consequences imposed on her result in an escalation of noncompliant and avoidant behaviors, as well as increased verbal abuse and threats. She frequently states that she will "run away as soon as I get enough money together." Carlotta usually gets along adequately with one staff member at a time, but turns on them when they demand that she comply with rules and policies of the school. She attempts to pit one staff member against another in order to get what she wants.

Verbal praise seems to have no immediate effect on her behavior. The reinforcers that tend to work most consistently include food, getting her hair or nails done, and one-on-one time with staff of her choosing.

Daily Living Skills

Personal hygiene was initially a problem for Carlotta, particularly caring for her hair, which is rather long and appeared unkempt much of the time. The staff implemented a structured behavior modification program to get her to voluntarily shower, wash her hair, and do her personal laundry.

Carlotta has outbreaks of acne, which may be due to her medications. A dermatologist prescribed topical medications for the condition, and Carlotta applies it diligently without reminders from staff or instructors.

Her physical appearance is no longer a cause for concern. She irons her own clothes, makes her bed, and now keeps her room in good order. Staff has remarked that Carlotta is very much like their own teenagers in terms of daily living skills, and this is not an area for concern.

FAMILY HISTORY

Carlotta is the youngest of three daughters. Her two older sisters are adults who are married and live in cities across the state from each other. Each of the sisters has a different biological father, and none was ever married to the mother. The whereabouts of Carlotta's biological father currently are unknown. He and Carlotta's mother seldom saw each other after Carlotta was about 3 years old, and Carlotta's mother has had many live-in boyfriends since that time.

The state's Department of Social Services has documentation of mother's verbal and emotional abuse, neglect, physical abuse including rubbing Carlotta's skin with harsh chemicals to get rid of "dark spots," and wielding a knife and pointing it at Carlotta on several occasions. Because of Carlotta's current extremely sexualized behavior, sexual abuse at an early age is suspected but has not been verified by the state authorities.

Carlotta's mother worked sporadically at several part-time jobs but was never able to hold down steady employment for long due to an ongoing mental illness (bipolar disorder) for which she takes prescribed medications. The mother has had numerous psychotic episodes since Carlotta was a young child, and has been in and out of psychiatric hospitals for the last 15 years. With no one to provide her with a stable home environment, Carlotta was placed in foster care at the age of 9, and has lived in several foster families for the past 7 years. She has been moved out of most of these because of her attacks, both verbal and physical, on the foster parents or on other children in those residences. She has run away from the foster care facilities on three occasions. As such, the foster care system has labeled her as "incorrigible." She has also been placed in juvenile justice care facilities on a short-term basis for shoplifting and vandalism at ages 12 and 14, and for 30 days after her last elopement. There has been no contact with her sisters for the past 3 years, or with her mother for the last 9 months.

RECENT EVALUATION RESULTS

A multidisciplinary team conducted Carlotta's latest educational reevaluation in March. This was a 3-year evaluation done in accordance with the provisions of the Individuals with Disabilities Education Act (IDEA). As per the regulations governing IDEA, the multidisciplinary team convened to determine what assessments, if any, would be needed to ascertain if Carlotta was still a child with a disability and therefore still eligible for special education and related services. The team developed an evaluation plan and it was signed by her court-appointed advocate. The assessment results were as follows.

Wechsler Intelligence Scale for Children, Third Edition (WISC-III) (Wechsler, 1991)

This intelligence test was last administered to Carlotta 3 years ago. Because she was well within the normal limitations cognitively on that instrument (verbal IQ 97, performance IQ 94, full scale IQ 95), the team decided that it was not necessary to administer another intelligence test to her at this time for reevaluation.

Woodcock-Johnson III Tests of Achievement (WJ-III) (Woodcock, McGrew, & Mather, 2001)

Carlotta took the complete Woodcock-Johnson III, standard and extended batteries, which consists of 22 academic achievement subtests. Each subtest yields a mean standard score of 100. She performed at or above grade level on all subtests of the WJ-III, with the following exceptions: calculation (standard score 84), math fluency (standard score 83), applied problems (standard score 80), quantitative concepts (standard score 85), writing samples (standard score 82), and academic knowledge (standard score 84). These results correlate with the lower grades that she is currently earning in both her Algebra I course and her English II course.

Informal Reading Inventory

This assessment was administered to address the concerns expressed by Carlotta's English II teacher pertaining to higher-order thinking skills and reading comprehension. Oral reading was at grade level (grade 10), and she read orally at about 115 words per minute with 98% accuracy, indicating very good word-attack skills. Her comprehension skills revealed inconsistent results. An analysis of her comprehension errors revealed that she consistently is able to identify main ideas, and provide facts and details from various content areas (94%). However, she had considerable difficulty with prediction (45%), analysis and synthesis (25%), drawing conclusions (10%), and making inferences (0%).

Informal Math Inventory

A variety of math probes and error analyses were administered to Carlotta. According to these results, she appears to know all of her math facts involving all operations with whole numbers that require addition, subtraction, multiplication, and division, and is quite fluent in this area. However, she complained and became visibly frustrated in doing the computations that involved fractions, decimals, and percents. She was able to simplify, add, subtract, multiply, and divide fractions correctly, forgetting only once to invert the second numeral in one division problem. She correctly answered problems involving decimals and percents, rounding to three decimal places, but missed those problems that required her to change a common fraction to a decimal fraction or compute percentages. Carlotta was adept at solving simple substitution-type algebra problems (linear equations), but was unable (refused) to complete any higher-order problems

that were presented to her. She remarked several times during the later portions of the math assessment, "I can already do those! They're stupid, and I am not doing them unless I get some credit for it."

Oral and Written Communication Assessments

Oral communication, both receptive and expressive, has not been observed as a deficit area for Carlotta. As such, the evaluation plan indicated that no additional information in this area was warranted. An examination of the written language samples from the English II classroom and from the Woodcock-Johnson III assessment revealed that Carlotta performs somewhat below average compared to her peers in the area of written expression.

Although her actual handwriting is mostly legible, there is some variation in her handwriting in terms of spacing and size of letters. In longer samples, such as entries in her English II journal, the writing tended to become larger and messier as she wrote, so that by the end of an entry, each letter was filling two ruled lines.

The content of her journal consisted mostly of complaints about mistreatment by teachers and staff, intricate plans about "how to get even" with this person or another, and extremely depressing thoughts about what awaited her in her life on the "outside."

Sentence construction was irregular and paragraphs consisted principally of sentences that were loosely connected to each other in content and context. Spelling seems to be adequate as does punctuation, but her sentence construction consists largely of declarative statements with few descriptive words. Profanities were interspersed in most of the samples that were examined.

Social/Emotional

The evaluation team interviewed Carlotta's residential unit therapist concerning Carlotta's current mental health status. The therapist indicated that very little had changed in terms of the course or symptoms of Carlotta's bipolar disorder. She continues to take her prescribed antidepressant and antipsychotic medication with minimal impact on her frequent cycling or on the volatility of her emotional outbursts.

Carlotta' group therapy was discontinued due to her disruptive influence. If not redirected, Carlotta continues to spend most of her weekly individual therapy time complaining about the behavior of staff, teachers, and peers. She demonstrates minimal insight into her own feelings or behaviors, and expresses little interest in developing better coping skills.

Carlotta's compliance with rules and staff requests has improved on the residential unit over the past few weeks. Her therapist reports this was a result of the addition of an individualized behavior contract she made with Carlotta. Each week that Carlotta earns at least 80% of her token economy points on the unit, she gets to go on an outing with staff to get her hair done or to eat at a Chinese restaurant. Although staff initially complained about the time and expense involved in the contract, they now believe the improvement in compliance has been worth the effort.

Given Carlotta's chronic mental illness and her status as a ward of the family court, she is not considered a good candidate for family reunification or another foster placement. The treatment team has begun discussing moving Carlotta to a transitional independent living program (e.g., a small group home or apartment).

Classroom Observations

One of the staff psychologists at Carlotta's residential placement conducted informal, unstructured observations of Carlotta in several of her classes over a period of 1 week. The psychologist made anecdotal records of these observations. These records indicate in general that Carlotta:

- Does not remain focused on a single task for more than about 3 to 5 minutes
- Makes rude, inappropriate comments at least every other minute
- Mutters to herself
- Has emotional outburst with no apparent trigger or stimulus
- Is verbally abusive to instructors and peers
- Makes lewd comments to males when seated nearby

- Works better in isolation (10 minutes on task in study carrel)
- Frequently seeks the attention of instructors
- Asks for repetition of directions or teacher's remarks
- Makes excuses for not turning in assignments
- Becomes belligerent and verbally abusive when redirected

ACCOMMODATIONS/MODIFICATIONS ATTEMPTED TO DATE

- Preferential seating away from male classmates: Successful only for a limited time. She continued to make lewd comments and gestures to males seated across the room.
- Assigning Carlotta a peer tutor: Successful only if she likes the peer tutor. Most tutors protest having to work with Carlotta given her hostile attitude and verbal abuse.
- Shortening written assignments: Successful for limited time. She continued to complain that the homework was too much for her.
- Providing timely positive reinforcement for appropriate responses and behavior: Successful if the reinforcement involved food or a promise for individual attention at a later time.
- Providing study carrel or isolated work area: Successful. Kept her on task and out of mischief with other students.
- Providing her the opportunity to use a computer for written assignments rather that writing them manually: Successful, but she tended to want to play games on the computer rather than use it for schoolwork.

PUBLICATION INFORMATION FOR SELECTED ASSESSMENT MEASURES

Assessment Measure	Publication Information
Achenbach System of Empirically Based Assessment (ASEBA)	Nelson-Thomson Learning, ASEBA 1 South Prospect St. Burlington, VT 05401-3456 802-264-6432 www.aseba.org
AD/HD Comprehensive Teacher's Rating Scale (ACTeRS)	MetriTech, Inc. 4106 Fieldstone Rd. Champaign, IL 61822 800-747-4868 www.metritech.com
ADHD Rating Scale-IV	Guilford Publications Dept. 5X 72 Spring St. New York, NY 10012 800-365-7006 www.guilford.com
ADHD Symptom Checklist-4 (ADHD-SC4)	Checkmate Plus PO Box 696, Dept. D Stony Brook, NY 11790-0696 800-779-4292 www.checkmateplus.com
ADHD Symptoms Rating Scale (ADHD-SRS)	Wide Range, Inc. 15 Ashley Pl., Ste. 1A Wilmington, DE 19804-1314 800-221-9728 www.widerange.com
Adult Attention Deficit Disorders Evaluation Scale, Home Version (A-ADDES)	Hawthorne Educational Services 800 Gray Oak Dr. Columbia, MO 65201 800-542-1673 www.hes-inc.com
Attention Deficit Disorders Evaluation Scales (ADDES-3)	Hawthorne Educational Services 800 Gray Oak Dr. Columbia, MO 65201 800-542-1673 www.hes-inc.com
Attention Deficit Disorders Evaluation Scale: Secondary-Age Student (ADDES-S)	Hawthorne Educational Services 800 Gray Oak Dr. Columbia, MO 65201 800-542-1673 www.hes-inc.com
Attention-Deficit/ Hyperactivity Disorder Test (ADHDT)	PRO-ED Publications 8700 Shoal Creek Blvd. Austin, TX 78757-6897 800-897-3202 www.proedinc.com

BASC Monitor for ADHD	(Kamphaus & Reynolds, 1998) American Guidance Service 4201 Woodland Rd. PO Box 99 Circle Pines, MN 55014-1796 800-328-2560 www.agsnet.com
Behavior Assessment System for Children (BASC)	(Reynolds & Kamphaus, 1992) American Guidance Service 4201 Woodland Rd. PO Box 99 Circle Pines, MN 55014-1796 800-328-2560 www.agsnet.com
Behavioral and Emotional Rating Scale: A Strength-Based Approach to Assessment (BERS)	(Epstein & Sharma, 1998) PRO-ED Publications 8700 Shoal Creek Blvd. Austin, TX 78757-6897 800-897-3202 www.proedinc.com
Behavior Dimensions Rating Scale	Nelson-Thomson Learning, ASEBA 1 South Prospect St. Burlington, VT 05401-3456 802-264-6432 www.aseba.org
Behavior Rating Profile-2nd edition (BRP-2)	(Brown & Hammill, 1990) PRO-ED Publications 8700 Shoal Creek Blvd. Austin, TX 78757-6897 800-897-3202 www.proedinc.com
Brown ADD Diagnostic Form	Psychological Assessment Resources, Inc. PO Box 998 Odessa, FL 33556 800-899-8378 www3.parinc.com
Brown Attention-Deficit Disorder Scales (Brown ADD Scales)	The Psychological Corporation 19500 Bulverde Rd. San Antonio, TX 78259 800-211-8378 www.harcourtassessment.com
Burks' Behavior Rating Scales (BBRS)	(Burks, 1997) Western Psychological Services 12031 Wilshire Blvd. Los Angeles, CA 800-648-8857 www.wpspublish.com
Child Behavior Checklist (CBCL)	(Achenbach, 1991–1994) University Medical Education Associates University of Vermont, ASEBA 1 South Prospect St. Burlington, VT 05401-3456 802-264-6432 www.aseba.org

Children's Aggression Scale—Parent Version (CAS—P)	Halperin, J. M., McKay, K. E., & Newcorn, J. H. (2002) Development, reliability and validity of the Children's Aggression Scale—Parent Version. *Journal of the American Academy of Child and Adolescent Psychiatry, 41*(3), 245–252.
Children's Aggression Scale—Teacher Version (CAS—T)	Halperin, J. M., McKay, K. E., Grayson, R. H., & Newcorn, J. H. (2003). Reliability, validity, and preliminary normative data for the Children's Aggression Scale—Teacher Version. *Journal of the American Academy of Child and Adolescent Psychiatry, 42*(8), 965–971.
Conners' ADHD/DSM-IV Scales (CADS)	(Conners, C. K., 1997) Multi-Health Systems, Inc. PO Box 950 North Tonawanda, NY 14120-0950 800-456-3003 www.mhs.com
Conners' Ratings Scales—Revised (CRS—R)	(Conners, C. K., 1997) Multi-Health Systems, Inc. PO Box 950 North Tonawanda, NY 14120-0950 800-456-3003 www.mhs.com
Conners' Adult ADHD Rating Scales (CAARS)	(Conners, C. K.; Erhardt, D., & Sparrow, E., 1999) Multi-Health Systems, Inc. PO Box 950 North Tonawanda, NY 14120-0950 800-456-3003 www.mhs.com
Eyberg Child Behavior Inventory (ECBI)	PAR, Inc. 16204 North Florida Ave. Lutz, FL 33549 http://www3.parinc.com/
Revised Behavior Problem Checklist (RBPC)	(Quay & Peterson, 1987) Herbert C. Quay Ph.D. PO Box 248074 University of Miami Coral Gables, FL 33124
Scales of Independent Behavior—Revised (SIB—R)	(Bruninks et al. 1997) Riverside Publishing 425 Spring Lake Dr. Itasca, IL 60143-2079 800-323-9540 www.riverpub.com
Social Emotional Dimension Scale (SEDS)	(Hutton & Roberts, 1986) PRO-ED Publications 8700 Shoal Creek Blvd. Austin, TX 78757-6897 800-897-3202 www.proedinc.com

Social Skills Rating System (SSRS)	(Gresham & Elliott, 1990) American Guidance Service 4201 Woodland Rd., PO Box 99 Circle Pines, MN 55014-1796 800-328-2460 www.agsnet.com
Spadafore ADHD Rating Scale (S-ADHD-RS)	Academic Therapy Publication 20 Commercial Blvd. Novato, CA 94949-6191 800-422-7249 www.academictherapy.com
Sutter-Eyberg Student Behavior Inventory Revised	Psychological Assessment Resources PO Box 998 Odessa, FL 33556 800-899-8378 www3.parinc.com
Teachers Report Form (TRF)	(Achenbach, 1991) University of Vermont Department of Psychiatry 1 South Prospect St. Burlington, VT 05401-3456 802-264-6432 www.aseba.org
Test of Variables of Attention (TOVA)	Universal Attention Disorders 4281 Katella Ave. #215 Los Alamitos, CA 90720 800-729-2886
Walker-McConnell Scale of Social Competence and School Adjustment	(Walker & McConnell, 1995) PRO-ED Publications 8700 Shoal Creek Blvd. Austin, TX 78757-6897 800-897-3202 www.proedinc.com

Council for Exceptional Children (CEC) Knowledge and Skill Base for All Entry-Level Special Education Teachers of Students with Emotional and Behavioral Disorders*

Standard/Competency	Related Textbook Content
Standard #1: Foundations	
CC1K1: Models, theories, and philosophies that form the basis for special education practice.	• Emergence of conceptual models (CH1)
CC1K2: Laws, policies, and ethical principles regarding behavior management planning and implementation.	• CEC Code of Ethics (Fig 1–1) • Discipline-related issues (CH1) • Punishment and negative interaction (CH6) • Discipline and students with disabilities (CH14)
CC1K3: Relationship of special education to the organization and function of educational agencies.	• Ongoing issues and challenges (CH1) • School reform and students with EBD (CH4)
CC1K4: Rights and responsibilities of students, parents, teachers, and other professionals, and schools related to exceptional learning needs.	• Legal entitlements in special education (CH1) • Putting collaboration in context (CH12)
CC1K5: Issues in definition and identification of individuals with exceptional learning needs, including those from culturally and linguistically diverse backgrounds.	• Overrepresentations of ethnic and low-English proficient students in special education (CH1) • Assessing students from diverse backgrounds (CH2) • Impact of gender, ethnicity, and SES on referral for and assessment of disruptive behaviors (CH8)
CC1K6: Issues, assurances, and due process rights related to assessment, eligibility, and placement within a continuum of services.	• Educational legislation directly affecting special education (CH1) • IDEA requirements (Fig 3–1 through 3–5) • Determining placement (CH3)
CC1K7: Family systems and the role of families in the educational process.	• Consultation with families (CH12) • Family therapy (CH13)
CC1K8: Historical points of view and contribution of culturally diverse groups.	• Developing cultural competence (CH12, Fig 12–2)
CC1K9: Impact of the dominant culture on shaping schools and the individuals who study and work in them.	• Developing cultural competence (CH12, Fig 12–2)
CC1K10: Potential impact of differences in values, languages, and customs that can exist between the home and school.	• Developing cultural competence (CH12, Fig 12–2) • The differential impact of race and ethnicity (CH14)
BD1K1: Educational terminology and definitions of individuals with EBD.	• Education of students with EBD (CH1, Fig 1–4 and 1–5)
BD1K2: Models that describe deviance.	• Emergence of conceptual models (CH1)
BD1K3: Foundations and issues related to knowledge and practice in EBD.	• Best practices for addressing problem behavior (CH6)

*Note on coding: CC in the number code indicates a Common Core item; BD indicates an EBD item; K indicates a Knowledge item; S indicates a Skill item.

BD1K4: The legal, judicial, and educational systems serving individuals with EBD.	<ul><li>Legal entitlements in special education (CH1)</li><li>Quality program indicators (Table 5–1)</li><li>Co-occurrence of disruptive problems in school with drug use and juvenile delinquency (CH8)</li><li>Responses in law and school policy (CH14)</li><li>Discipline and students with disabilities (CH14)</li></ul>
BD1K5: Theory of reinforcement techniques in serving individuals with EBD.	<ul><li>Positive behavior supports (CH4)</li><li>Creating a positive classroom learning environment (CH5)</li><li>Intervention techniques designed to teach, increase, or maintain desirable behaviors (CH6)</li></ul>
BD1K6: Principles of normalization and concept of least restrictive environment for individuals with EBD in programs.	<ul><li>Placement issues (CH1)</li><li>Determining placement (CH3)</li><li>The use of least-intrusive interventions (CH5)</li></ul>
CC1S1: Articulate personal philosophy of special education.	<ul><li>Application activities (CH6)</li></ul>

Standard #2: Development and Characteristics of Learners

CC2K1: Typical and atypical human growth and development.	<ul><li>Disorders of attention (CH7)</li><li>Disruptive behavior disorders (CH8)</li><li>Pervasive developmental disorders (CH9)</li><li>Anxiety and mood disorders (CH10)</li><li>Other disorders of childhood and adolescence (CH11)</li></ul>
CC2K2: Educational implications of characteristics of various exceptionalities.	<ul><li>Disorders of attention (CH7)</li><li>Disruptive behavior disorders (CH8)</li><li>Pervasive developmental disorders (CH9)</li><li>Anxiety and mood disorders (CH10)</li><li>Other disorders of childhood and adolescence (CH11)</li></ul>
CC2K3: Characteristics and effects of the cultural and environmental milieu of the individual with exceptional learning needs and the family.	<ul><li>The increasingly challenging school environment (CH4)</li><li>The school community as a positive climate for learning (CH4)</li><li>Social implications and the role of parent training (CH8)</li><li>Parent training and support (CH8)</li><li>Creating environmental supports (CH10)</li><li>Consultation with families (CH12)</li></ul>
CC2K4: Family systems and the role of families in supporting development.	<ul><li>Social implications and the role of parent training (CH8)</li><li>Parent training and support (CH8)</li><li>Consultation with families (CH12)</li><li>Family therapy (CH13)</li></ul>
CC2K5: Similarities and differences of individuals with and without exceptional learning needs.	<ul><li>Education of students with EBD (CH1, Fig 1–4 and 1–5)</li><li>Determining eligibility for special education services (CH2)</li></ul>
CC2K6: Similarities and differences among individuals with exceptional learning needs.	<ul><li>Disorders of attention (CH7)</li><li>Disruptive behavior disorders (CH8)</li><li>Pervasive developmental disorders (CH9)</li><li>Anxiety and mood disorders (CH10)</li><li>Other disorders of childhood and adolescence (CH11)</li></ul>
CC2K7: Effects of various medications on individuals with exceptional learning needs.	<ul><li>The role of medication in the treatment of ADHD (CH7)</li><li>The role of medication in the treatment of disruptive behaviors (CH8)</li><li>The role of medication in the treatment of PDD (CH9)</li><li>The role of medication in the treatment of anxiety and mood disorders (CH10)</li></ul>

	* Efficacy of psychotropic drugs in children (Fig 10–10) * The role of schools in supporting pharmacological therapies—medical model interventions (CH12)
BD2K1: Etiology and diagnosis related to various theoretical approaches in the field of EBD.	* Emergence of conceptual models (CH1) * Determining eligibility for special education services (CH2) * ADHD—Etiology (CH7)

Standard #3: Individual Learning Differences

CC3K1: Effects an exceptional condition(s) can have on an individual's life.	* Disturbing outcomes for students with EBD (CH4) * ADHD characteristics across the life span (CH7) * Planning for transition and community living (CH9)
CC3K2: Impact of learners' academic and social abilities, attitudes, interests, and values on instruction and career development.	* Adolescent issues and individual transition planning (CH3) * ADHD characteristics across the life span (CH7) * Curriculum enhancement and interest areas (CH9)
CC3K3: Variations in beliefs, traditions, and values across and within cultures and their effects on relationships among individuals with exceptional learning needs, family, and schooling.	* Knowing yourself (CH12) * Knowing your collaborative partners (CH12) * Developing cultural competence (CH12)
CC3K4: Cultural perspectives influencing the relationships among families, schools, and communities as related to instruction.	* Knowing yourself (CH12) * Knowing your collaborative partners (CH12) * Developing cultural competence (CH12)
CC3K5: Differing ways of learning of individuals with exceptional learning needs, including those from culturally diverse backgrounds, and strategies for addressing these differences.	* Identifying student learning traits (CH2) * Structuring the educational environment: Effective instructional techniques and inclusive strategies (CH5) * Coteaching, team teaching, and class-within-a-class model (CH12)

Standard #4: Instructional Strategies

BD4K1: Sources of specialized materials for individuals with EBD.	* Resources for FBA (Fig 3–6) * Sample assessment measures for ADHD (Fig 7–3) * Sample assessment measures for disruptive behaviors (Fig 8–7) * Bullying prevention resources (Fig 8–10) * Educational resources for anxiety and mood disorders (Fig 10–11)
BD4K2: Advantages and limitations of instructional strategies and practices for teaching individuals with EBD.	* Characteristics of an effective program for all students (CH4) * Creating a positive classroom learning environment (CH5) * Intervention techniques designed to teach, increase, or maintain desirable behaviors (CH6) * Intervention techniques designed to decrease or eliminate undesirable behaviors (CH6) * Forming and facilitating psychoeducational groups (CH6) * Classroom intervention strategies (CH9) * Selected interventions for students with anxiety and mood disorders (CH10)

BD4K3: Resources and techniques used to transition individuals with EBD into and out of school and postschool environments.	• Adolescent issues and individual transition planning (CH3) • ADHD characteristics across the life span (CH7) • Planning for transition and community living (CH9) • Consultation with other teachers (CH12)
BD4K4: Prevention and intervention strategies for individuals at risk of EBD.	• Characteristics of an effective program for all students (CH4) • Creating a positive classroom learning environment (CH5) • Intervention techniques designed to teach, increase, or maintain desirable behaviors (CH6)
BD4K5: Strategies for integrating student-initiated learning experiences into ongoing instruction for individuals with EBD.	• Therapeutic expressive activities (CH6) • Cognitive behavioral interventions (CH7) • Enhancing communication and social/emotional growth (CH9)
CC4S1: Use strategies to facilitate integration into various settings.	• Consultation with other teachers (CH12)
CC4S2: Teach individuals to use self-assessment, problem-solving, and other cognitive strategies to meet their needs.	• Cognitive behavioral interventions (CH7) • Cognitive behavior management techniques (CH8) • Cognitive behavioral therapy (CH10, CH12)
CC4S3: Select, adapt, and use instructional strategies and materials according to characteristics of the individual with exceptional learning needs.	• Identifying student learning traits (CH2) • Identifying instructional accommodations and modifications (CH3) • Planning for academic success (CH5) • Forming and facilitating psychoeducational groups (CH6) • Classroom intervention strategies (CH7–11) • Assignment modifications (CH9)
CC4S4: Use strategies to facilitate maintenance and generalization of skills across learning environments.	• Lesson planning (CH5) • Grouping students (CH5) • Teach social skills (CH5) • Direct instruction of social skills (CH9)
CC4S5: Use procedures to increase the individual's self-awareness, self-management, self-control, self-reliance, and self-esteem.	• Positive behavioral supports (CH4) • Cognitive behavioral interventions (CH7) • Use cognitive behavioral management techniques (CH8) • Cognitive behavioral therapy (CH10, CH12)
CC4S6: Use strategies that promote successful transitions for individuals with exceptional learning needs.	• Adolescent issues and individual transition planning (CH3) • ADHD characteristics across the life span (CH7) • Planning for transition and community living (CH9) • Consultation with other teachers (CH12)
BD4S1: Use strategies from multiple theoretical approaches for individuals with EBD.	• Best practices for preventing problem behaviors (CH5) • Best practices for addressing problem behaviors (CH6)
BD4S2: Use a variety of nonaversive techniques to control targeted behavior and maintain attention of individuals with EBD.	• Best practices for preventing problem behaviors (CH5) • Best practices for addressing problem behaviors (CH6)

Standard #5: Learning Environments and Social Interactions

CC5K1: Demands of learning environments.	• The increasingly challenging school environment (CH4) • Viewpoints on effective classrooms (CH5)
CC5K2: Basic classroom management theories and strategies for individuals with exceptional learning needs.	• Best practices for addressing problem behaviors (CH6)

CC5K3: Effective management of teaching and learning.	• Structuring the physical environment: Organizing for student success (CH5) • Structuring the instructional environment: Effective instructional techniques and inclusive strategies (CH5) • Best practices for addressing problem behaviors (CH6)
CC5K4: Teacher attitudes and behaviors that influence behavior of individuals with exceptional learning needs.	• The role of positive student-teacher interactions (CH5)
CC5K5: Social skills needed for educational and other environments.	• Teach social skills (CH5) • Direct instruction of social skills (CH9)
CC5K6: Strategies for crisis prevention and intervention.	• Self-damaging behaviors (CH11) • Suicidal behaviors (CH11) • Crisis intervention techniques (CH14)
CC5K7: Strategies for preparing individuals to live harmoniously and productively in a culturally diverse world.	• Creating a positive classroom learning environment (CH5) • Developing cultural competence (CH12)
CC5K8: Ways to create learning environments that allow individuals to retain and appreciate their own and each others' respective language and cultural heritage.	• Creating a positive classroom learning environment (CH5) • Developing cultural competence (CH12)
CC5K9: Ways specific cultures are negatively stereotyped.	• Creating a positive classroom learning environment (CH5) • Developing cultural competence (CH12)
CC5K10: Strategies used by diverse populations to cope with a legacy of former and continuing racism.	• Creating a positive classroom learning environment (CH5) • Developing cultural competence (CH12)
BD5K1: Advantages and disadvantages of placement options and the continuum of services for individuals with EBD.	• Determining placement (CH3)
BD5K2: Functional classroom designs for individuals with EBD.	• Structuring the physical environment: Organizing for student success (CH5)
CC5S1: Create a safe, equitable, positive, and supportive learning environment in which diversities are valued.	• Creating a positive classroom learning environment (CH5)
CC5S2: Identify realistic expectations for personal and social behavior in various settings.	• Proactive behavior management (CH5)
CC5S3: Identify supports needed for integration into various program placements.	• Identifying instructional accommodations and modifications (CH3) • Consultation with other professionals (CH12)
CC5S4: Design learning environments that encourage active participation in individual and group activities.	• Structuring the physical environment: Organizing for student success (CH5)
CC5S5: Modify the learning environment to manage behaviors.	• Structuring the physical environment: Organizing for student success (CH5) • Antecedent instruction-related strategies (CH6) • Classroom organization: Providing support with structure (CH7)
CC5S6: Use performance data and information from all stakeholders to make or suggest modifications in learning environments.	• Identifying instructional accommodations and modifications (CH3) • Evaluating progress (CH3) • Selecting the right intervention (CH6)
CC5S7: Establish and maintain rapport with individuals with and without exceptional learning needs.	• The role of positive student-teacher interactions (CH5) • Build therapeutic relationships with students (CH8)
CC5S8: Teach self-advocacy.	• Teach social skills (CH5) • Cognitive behavioral interventions (CH7) • Implement a bullying reduction program (CH8)

CC5S9: Create an environment that encourages self-advocacy and increased independence.	* Creating a positive classroom learning environment (CH5)
CC5S10: Use effective and varied behavior management strategies.	* Best practices for preventing problem behavior (CH5) * Best practices for addressing problem behavior (CH6)
CC5S11: Use the least intensive behavior management strategy consistent with the needs of the individual with exceptional learning needs.	* Use of least-intrusive interventions (CH5) * Selecting the right intervention (CH6)
CC5S12: Design and manage daily routines.	* Establishing rules and routines (CH5) * Classroom organization: Providing support with structure (CH7) * The highly structured educational environment (CH9)
CC5S13: Organize, develop, and sustain learning environments that support positive intracultural and intercultural experiences.	* Creating a positive classroom learning environment (CH5) * Developing cultural competence (CH12)
CC5S14: Mediate controversial intercultural issues among students within the learning environment in ways that enhance any culture, group, or person.	* Creating a positive classroom learning environment (CH5) * Developing cultural competence (CH12)
CC5S15: Structure, direct, and support the activities of paraeducators, volunteers, and tutors.	* Working with paraprofessionals (CH12)
BD5S1: Establish a consistent classroom routine for individuals with EBD.	* Establishing rules and routines (CH5) * Classroom organization: Providing support with structure (CH7) * The highly structured educational environment (CH9)
BD5S2: Use skills in problem solving and conflict resolution.	* Teach social skills (CH5) * Problem solving (CH7) * Use cognitive behavior management techniques to teach conflict resolution and anger management skills (CH8) * Direct instruction of social skills (CH9) * Seizing the teaching moment after an incident (CH14)

Standard #6: Language

CC6K1: Effects of cultural and linguistic differences on growth and development.	* Developing cultural competence (CH12, Fig 12–2) * The differential impact of race and ethnicity (CH14)
CC6K2: Characteristics of one's own culture and use of language and the ways in which these can differ from other cultures and uses of languages.	* Developing cultural competence (CH12, Fig 12–2) * The differential impact of race and ethnicity (CH14)
CC6K3: Ways of behaving and communicating among cultures that can lead to misinterpretation and misunderstanding.	* Developing cultural competence (CH12, Fig 12–2) * The differential impact of race and ethnicity (CH14)
CC6K4: Augmentative and assistive communication strategies.	* Enhancing communication and social/emotional growth (CH9)
CC6S1: Use strategies to support and enhance communication skills of individuals with exceptional learning needs.	* Enhancing communication and social/emotional growth (CH9)
CC6S2: Use communication strategies and resources to facilitate understanding of subject matter for students whose primary language is not the dominant language.	* Developing cultural competence (CH12, Fig 12–2) * The differential impact of race and ethnicity (CH14)

CC7K1: Theories and research that form the basis of curriculum development and instructional practice.	* Emergence of conceptual models related to EBD (CH1) * Characteristics of effective programs for all students (CH4) * Quality program indicators (Table 5–1)
CC7K2: Scope and sequences of general and special curricula.	* Curriculum-based measures (CH2) * Benchmarks (CH3)
CC7K3: National, state or provincial, and local curricula standards.	* Curriculum-based measures (CH2)
CC7K4: Technology for planning and managing the teaching and learning environment.	* Structuring the physical environment: Organizing for student success (CH5) * Structuring the instructional environment: Effective instructional techniques and inclusive strategies (CH5)
CC7K5: Roles and responsibilities of the paraeducator related to instruction, intervention, and direct service.	* Working with paraprofessionals (CH12)
BD7K1: Model programs that have been effective for individuals with EBD across the age range.	* Characteristics of an effective program for all students (CH4) * Quality program indicators (Table 5–1)
CC7S1: Identify and prioritize areas of the general curriculum and accommodations for individuals with exceptional learning needs.	* Identifying instructional accommodations and modifications (CH3)
CC7S2: Develop and implement comprehensive, longitudinal individualized programs in collaboration with team members.	* Writing the IEP and BIP (CH3) * Setting annual goals and defining measurable objectives and benchmarks (CH3) * Evaluating progress (CH3)
CC7S3: Involve the individual and family in setting instructional goals and monitoring progress.	* Vignette and application activity (CH3) * IDEA IEP team requirements (Fig 3–4)
CC7S4: Use functional assessments to develop intervention plans.	* Functional behavioral assessment (CH3)
CC7S5: Use task analysis.	* Setting annual goals and defining measurable objectives and benchmarks (CH3)
CC7S6: Sequence, implement, and evaluate individualized learning objectives.	* Setting annual goals and defining measurable objectives and benchmarks (CH3) * Evaluating progress (CH3)
CC7S7: Integrate affective, social, and life skills with academic curricula.	* Teach social skills (CH5) * Enhancing social, emotional, and behavioral growth (CH7) * Enhancing communication and social/emotional growth (CH9)
CC7S8: Develop and select instructional content, resources, and strategies that respond to cultural, linguistic, and gender differences.	* Creating a positive classroom learning environment (CH5) * Developing cultural competence (CH12)
CC7S9: Incorporate and implement instructional and assistive technology into the educational program.	* Enhancing communication and social/emotional growth (CH9)
CC7S10: Prepare lesson plans.	* Lesson planning (CH5)
CC7S11: Prepare and organize materials to implement daily lesson plans.	* Structuring the physical environment: Organizing for student success (CH5) * Lesson planning (CH5)

CC7S12: Use instructional time effectively.	* Scheduling and time management (CH5)
CC7S13: Make responsive adjustments to instruction based on continual observations.	* Lesson planning (CH5) * Student monitoring (CH5)
CC7S14: Prepare individuals to exhibit self-enhancing behavior in response to societal attitudes and actions.	* Teach social skills (CH5) * Problem solving (CH7) * Use cognitive behavior management techniques to teach conflict resolution and anger management skills (CH8) * Direct instruction of social skills (CH9)
BD7S1: Plan and implement individualized reinforcement systems and environmental modifications at levels equal to the intensity of the behavior.	* The use of least-intrusive interventions (CH5) * Antecedent instruction-related strategies (CH6) * Reinforcement strategies (CH6)
BD7S2: Integrate academic instruction, affective education, and behavior management for individuals and groups with EBD.	* Teach social skills (CH5) * Problem solving (CH7) * Use cognitive behavior management techniques to teach conflict resolution and anger management skills (CH8) * Direct instruction of social skills (CH9) * Seizing the teaching moment after an incident (CH14)

Standard #8: Assessment

CC8K1: Basic terminology used in assessment.	* Assessment: Definitions and basic assumptions (CH2) * Definitions of assessment terminology (Fig 2–1) * Types of assessment (CH2) * IDEA 2004 evaluation procedures (Fig 2–6)
CC8K2: Legal provisions and ethical principles regarding assessment of individuals.	* Determining eligibility for special education services (CH2) * Standards and ethics of assessment (CH2)
CC8K3: Screening, prereferral, referral, and classification procedures.	* IDEA 2004 evaluation procedures (Fig 2–6) * Steps in the assessment process (CH2) * Determining eligibility for special education services (CH2)
CC8K4: Use and limitations of assessment instruments.	* Types of assessment (CH2) * Basic assumptions (CH2)
CC8K5: National, state or provincial, and local accommodations and modifications.	* Identifying accommodations and modifications (CH3)
BD8K1: Characteristics of behavioral rating scales.	* Behavior rating scales and inventories (CH2) * Commonly used behavior rating scales and checklists (Fig 2–2)
BD8K2: Policies and procedures involved in the screening, diagnosis, and placement of individuals with EBD including academic and social behaviors.	* IDEA 2004 evaluation procedures (Fig 2–6) * Steps in the assessment process (CH2) * Determining eligibility for special education services (CH2)
BD8K3: Types and importance of information concerning individuals with EBD available from families and public agencies.	* Interview techniques (CH2) * Using multiple information sources (CH2) * Establishing the present level of performance (CH3)
CC8S1: Gather relevant background information.	* Interview techniques (CH2) * Using multiple information sources (CH2) * Establishing the present level of performance (CH3)

CC8S2: Administer nonbiased formal and informal assessments.	* Types of assessment (CH2) * The assessment process (CH2) * Application activities (CH2)
CC8S3: Use technology to conduct assessments.	* Types of assessment (CH2) * The assessment process (CH2) * Application activities (CH2)
CC8S4: Develop or modify individualized assessment strategies.	* Types of assessment (CH2) * The assessment process (CH2) * Application activities (CH2)
CC8S5: Interpret information from formal and informal assessments.	* Types of assessment (CH2) * The assessment process (CH2) * Application activities (CH2) * Case studies (Appendix A)
CC8S6: Use assessment information in making eligibility, program, and placement decisions for individuals with exceptional learning needs, including those from culturally and/or linguistically diverse backgrounds.	* Types of assessment (CH2) * The assessment process (CH2) * Application activities (CH2) * Case studies (Appendix A)
CC8S7: Report assessment results to all stakeholders using effective communication skills.	* Application activities (CH2, CH3) * Communicating effectively (CH12) * Case studies (Appendix A)
CC8S8: Evaluate instruction and monitor progress of individuals with exceptional learning needs.	* Evaluating progress (CH3) * Application activities (CH2, CH3)
CC8S9: Create and maintain records.	* Application activities (CH2, CH3)
BD8S1: Prepare assessment reports on individuals with EBD based on behavioral-ecological information.	* Application activities (CH2, CH3)
BD8S2: Assess appropriate and problematic social behaviors of individuals with EBD.	* Application activities (CH2, CH3) * Case studies (Appendix A)
BD8S3: Monitor intragroup behavior changes from subject to subject and activity to activity applicable to individuals with EBD.	* Application activities (CH2, CH3) * Case studies (Appendix A)

Standard #9: Professional and Ethical Practice

CC9K1: Personal cultural biases and differences that affect one's teaching.	* Knowing yourself (CH12)
CC9K2: Importance of the teacher serving as a model for individuals with exceptional learning needs.	* The role of positive teacher-student interactions (CH5)
CC9K3: Continuum of lifelong professional development.	* Application activities (CH1, CH2, CH4)
CC9K4: Methods to remain current regarding research-validated practice.	* Application activities (CH1, CH2, CH4) * Characteristics of effective programs for all students (CH4)
BD9K1: Organizations and publications relevant to the field of EBD.	* Application activities (CH1, CH2, CH4)
CC9S1: Practice within the CEC Code of Ethics and other standards of the profession.	* CEC Code of Ethics (Fig 1–1) * Application activities (CH1, CH2)

CC9S2: Uphold high standards of competence and integrity and exercise sound judgment in the practice of the profession.	* CEC Code of Ethics (Fig 1–1) * Application activities (CH1, CH2)
CC9S3: Act ethically in advocating for appropriate services.	* CEC Code of Ethics (Fig 1–1) * Application activities (CH1, CH2)
CC9S4: Conduct professional activities in compliance with applicable laws and policies.	* CEC Code of Ethics (Fig 1–1) * Discipline-related issues (CH1) * Punishment and negative interaction (CH6) * Discipline and students with disabilities (CH14)
CC9S5: Demonstrate commitment to developing the highest education and quality-of-life potential of individuals with exceptional learning needs.	* CEC Code of Ethics (Fig 1–1) * Application activities (CH1, CH2)
CC9S6: Demonstrate sensitivity for the culture, language, religion, gender, disability, socioeconomic status, and sexual orientation of individuals.	* Developing cultural competence (CH12, Fig 12–2)
CC9S7: Practice within one's skills limit and obtain assistance as needed.	* Basic assumptions (CH2) * Standards and ethics of assessment (CH2) * Knowing when to refer (CH6)
CC9S8: Use verbal, nonverbal, and written language effectively.	* Communicating effectively (CH12)
CC9S9: Conduct self-evaluation of instruction.	* Lesson planning (CH5)
CC9S10: Access information on exceptionalities.	* Application activities (CH1, CH2) * Resources for FBA (Fig 3–6) * Sample assessment measures for ADHD (Fig 7–3) * Sample assessment measures for disruptive behaviors (Fig 8–7) * Bullying prevention resources (Fig 8–10) * Educational resources for anxiety and mood disorders (Fig 10–11)
CC9S11: Reflect on one's practice to improve instruction and guide professional growth.	* Collaborative consultation skills and competencies (CH12)
CC9S12: Engage in professional activities that benefit individuals with exceptional learning needs, their families, and one's colleagues.	* Application activities (CH1, CH2)
BD9S1: Participate in activities of professional organizations relevant to the field of EBD.	* Application activities (CH1, CH2)

Standard #10: Collaboration

CC10K1: Models and strategies of consultation and collaboration.	* Putting collaboration in context (CH12) * Overview of collaborative consultation (CH12)
CC10K2: Roles of individuals with exceptional learning needs, families, and school and community personnel in planning of an individualized program.	* Consultation with other professionals (CH12) * Consultation with families (CH12) * Collaboration with other agencies in the community (CH12)
CC10K3: Concerns of families of individuals with exceptional learning needs and strategies to help address these concerns.	* Consultation with families (CH12)
CC10K4: Culturally responsive factors that promote effective communication and collaboration with individuals with exceptional learning needs, families, school personnel, and community members.	* Developing cultural competence (CH12)

BD10K1: Services, networks, and organizations for individuals with EBD.	• Collaborating with other agencies in the community (CH12) • School partnerships with mental health and medical professionals (CH13)
BD10K2: Parent education programs and behavior management guides that address severe behavioral problems and facilitate communication for individuals with EBD.	• Social implications and the role of parent training (CH8) • Parent training and support (CH8) • Consultation with families (CH12)
BD10K3: Collaborative and consultative roles of the special education teacher in the reintegration of individuals with EBD.	• Roles of the special educator (CH12)
BD10K4: Role of professional groups and referral agencies in identifying, assessing, and providing services to individuals with EBD.	• Collaborating with other agencies in the community (CH12) • School partnerships with mental health and medical professionals (CH13)
CC10S1: Maintain confidential communication about individuals with exceptional learning needs	• Establishing rules and safety (CH6) • Confidentiality (CH12)
CC10S2: Collaborate with families and others in assessment of individuals with exceptional learning needs.	• Functional behavioral assessment (CH3) • Consultation with families (CH12)
CC10S3: Foster respectful and beneficial relationships between families and professionals.	• Consultation with other professionals (CH12) • Consultation with families (CH12)
CC10S4: Assist individuals with exceptional learning needs and their families in becoming active participants in the educational team.	• Functional behavioral assessment (CH3) • Consultation with families (CH12)
CC10S5: Plan and conduct collaborative conferences with individuals with exceptional learning needs and their families.	• Consultation with families (CH12)
CC10S6: Collaborate with school personnel and community members in integrating individuals with exceptional learning needs into various settings.	• Consultation with other professionals (CH12) • Collaborating with other agencies in the community (CH12) • School partnerships with mental health and medical professionals (CH13)
CC10S7: Use group problem-solving skills to develop, implement, and evaluate collaborative activities.	• Collaborative consultation skills and competencies (CH12)
CC10S8: Model techniques and coach others in the use of instructional methods and accommodations.	• Coteaching, team teaching, and the class-within-a-class model (CH12)
CC10S9: Communicate with school personnel about the characteristics and needs of individuals with exceptional learning needs.	• Collaborative consultation skills and competencies (CH12)
CC10S10: Communicate effectively with families of individuals with exceptional learning needs from diverse backgrounds.	• Developing cultural competence (CH12)
CC10S11: Observe, evaluate, and provide feedback to paraeducators.	• Working with paraprofessionals (CH12)
BD10S1: Teach parents to use appropriate behavior management and counseling techniques.	• Social implications and the role of parent training (CH8) • Parent training and support (CH8) • Consultation with families (CH12)

Source: Council for Exceptional Children. (2003). *What every special educator must know: Ethics, standards and guidelines for special educators* (5th ed.). Arlington, VA: Author.

Praxis™ Content	Related Textbook Content
Category 1: Factors Other than Direct Instruction that Influence the Education of Students with Behavioral Disorders/Emotional Disturbance (20% of exam)	
Basic concepts, including characteristics of students with behavioral disorders/emotional disturbance, such as psychological characteristics (for example, neuroses, psychoses, anxiety, depression); affective characteristics (for example, social-emotional development, interpersonal skills); adaptive/maladaptive behavioral characteristics (for example, self-injurious behavior, eating disorders, substance abuse, aggression, social maladjustment, conduct disorders, delinquency); the relationship between behavior disorders/emotional disturbance and distractibility, hyperactivity, and impulsivity; and causation and prevention (for example, environmental factors, cultural factors, genetic factors, neurological factors)	● Number and characteristics of students being served under IDEA (CH1) ● Population description and major features of ODD, CD, DBD–NOS, IED (CH8); autistic disorder, Rett syndrome, CDD, Asperger's disorder, PDD–NOS (CH9); anxiety disorders and depression (CH10) ● Tourette's disorder, schizophrenia and psychotic disorders, eating disorders, self-damaging behaviors, suicidal behaviors, adolescent issues (CH11) ● ADHD (CH7) ● Etiology of ADHD (CH7); risk factors and predictors of disruptive behavior (CH8); etiology of anxiety disorders and depression (CH10); etiology and risk factors for Tourette's disorder, schizophrenia, eating disorders, and suicidal behaviors (CH11)
Definitions/terminology related to behavioral disorders/emotional disturbance (for example, federal definition [IDEA]; professional organizations' definitions [DSM CEC])	● Educational legislation (CH1, Fig 1–4, Fig 1–5) ● Determining eligibility (CH2, CH3) ● DSM-IV-TR eligibility criteria (CH7–11)

Praxis™ Content	Related Textbook Content
Category 2: Delivery of Services to Students with Behavioral Disorders/Emotional Disturbance (80% of exam)	
Conceptual approaches (medical, psychodynamic, behavioral, sociological, cognitive, and eclectic)	● Emergence of conceptual models (CH1, Fig 1–3)
Professional roles/issues/literature, such as public attitudes toward individuals with behavioral disorders/emotional disturbance; the teacher's role as promoter of advocacy (for example, helping parents become advocates for their children, developing student self-advocacy, advocating for students' families and for educational change); the teacher's responsibility in cases of suspected abuse or neglect; the use of professional literature/organizations and formal published research for improving classroom practice and reflecting on one's own teaching; influences of teacher attitudes and expectations on student achievement and behavior; and ways to work with health-related service and social service providers	● Ongoing issues and challenges (CH1) ● School reform and students with EBD (CH4) ● Creating a positive classroom learning environment (CH5) ● Social implications and the role of parent training (CH8) ● Developing systems of care (CH12) ● Roles of the special educator (CH12) ● Consultation with families (CH12) ● School partnerships with mental health and medical professionals (CH13)
Assessment, including how to modify, construct, or select and conduct nondiscriminatory and appropriate informal and formal assessment procedures; how to interpret standardized and specialized assessment results; how to use evaluation results in IEP/ITP development; and how to prepare written reports and communicate findings to others	● Types of assessment (CH2) ● IDEA assessment requirements (Fig 2–6) ● Translating assessment data into instructional practice (CH3)
Placement and program issues, including ways to apply a continuum of alternative placements and related services (for example, early intervention, support systems, least restrictive environment, REI (regular education initiative), mainstreaming, integration, and inclusion); how to participate in the IEP/ITP	● Determining placement (CH3) ● Assessing students from diverse backgrounds (CH2) ● Identifying instructional accommodations and modifications (CH3)

processes in a manner that is responsive to cultural and community influences; how to identify, develop, or adapt and use appropriate instructional materials; how to work with classroom personnel and external resources; how to display awareness of students' abilities and aptitudes and use appropriate alternative methods for instruction, evaluation, and grading (for example, through peer-group tutoring and instructional techniques)	• Structuring the physical environment: Effective instructional techniques and inclusive strategies (CH5)
Curriculum and instruction, including determining current levels of performance, determining instructional needs, identifying appropriate related services and modifications of standard educational practice, establishing effective data collection; preparing legally correct IEP/ITP instructional goals and objectives; selecting chronologically and developmentally age-appropriate instructional activities and materials; using appropriate planning and sequencing of instructional strategies; using data-based decision-making to select from varied teaching strategies and methods, including direct instruction, cooperative learning, task analysis, diagnostic-prescriptive methods, and applied behavior analysis; and using varied instructional formats and components, including motivation, modeling, drill and practice, demonstration, corrective feedback, and reinforcement with individuals and with small and large groups, as appropriate	• Determining need for special education and related services (CH3) • Identifying instructional accommodations and modifications (CH3) • Behavior rating scales and inventories, direct observation (CH2) • Functional behavioral assessment (CH3) • The use of least-intrusive interventions (CH5) • Structuring the physical environment: Effective instructional techniques and inclusive strategies (CH5) • Proactive behavior management (CH5) • Intervention techniques designed to teach, increase, or maintain desirable behaviors (CH6) • Intervention techniques designed to decrease or eliminate undesirable behaviors (CH6) • Classroom intervention strategies (CH7) • General strategies for managing students with disruptive behavior problems (CH8)
How to manage the learning environment, including using behavior management, behavior analysis (such as identification and definition of antecedents, target behavior, consequent events); data-gathering procedures; selecting and using behavioral interventions (for example, approaches to changing behaviors, such as behavioral, cognitive behavioral, and affective, degrees of intrusiveness); using classroom organization/management; providing the appropriate physical-social environment for learning (such as expectations, rules, consequences, consistency, attitudes, lighting, seating, access, strategies for positive interactions); planning transitions between lessons and activities; grouping students; and maintaining effective and efficient documentation (such as parent/teacher contacts and legal records)	• Identifying positive behavioral supports (CH2) • Functional behavioral assessment (CH3) • The use of least-intrusive interventions (CH5) • Structuring the physical environment: Effective instructional techniques and inclusive strategies (CH5) • Proactive behavior management (CH5) • Intervention techniques designed to teach, increase, or maintain desirable behaviors (CH6) • Intervention techniques designed to decrease or eliminate undesirable behaviors (CH6) • Classroom intervention strategies (CH7–11) • General strategies for managing students with disruptive behavior problems (CH8)

Source: Educational Testing Service. (n.d.). *Test at a glance: Special education: Teaching students with behavioral disorders/emotional disturbance (0371)*, 48–50. Available online at http://ftp.ets.org/pub/tandl/0371.pdf. Reprinted by permission of Educational Testing Service. Permission to reprint PRAXIS materials does not constitute review or endorsement by Educational Testing Service of this publication as a whole or of any other testing information it may contain.

ANSWERS TO CHECK YOUR UNDERSTANDING QUESTIONS

Chapter 1

Answers: (1) false (2) true (3) legislative: enacts or makes law; executive: carries out or administers the law; judicial: holds hearings, interprets, and applies the Constitution and law (4) d (5) b (6) b (7) c (8) answers may vary but should include the slow development of the programs and mandates for children with disabilities, aspects of the equal protections from the civil rights movement, significant litigation and legislation (9) a (10) c

Chapter 2

Answers: (1) true (2) false (3) answers may vary; acceptable answers include teacher, parent, or caregiver; other professionals involved with the student; peers, etc. (4) direct observation (5) to reduce subjectivity (6) false (7) false (8) diagnostic probes and dynamic assessment (9) clarifying the referral question(s), using multiple information sources, developing a list of preliminary strengths and concerns, selecting/designing the assessment package, collecting and analyzing data, and synthesizing and interpreting results (10) true

Chapter 3

Answers: (1) false (2) true (3) false (4) a (5) d (6) transition planning beginning 16 (7) answers will vary (8) each public agency shall ensure all alternative placements listed in the definition of special education be available for students with EBD (9) answers may vary, but should include target behavior, antecedents/triggers/circumstances, consequences/reinforcers, hypothesis (10) short-term objective measures a discreet skill component and is usually thought of in steps/benchmark measures a milestone in development and is usually thought of in terms of time

Chapter 4

Answers: (1) true (2) true (3) schoolwide, classwide, individual; examples will vary (4) answers will vary—educational attainment, employment, social relationships (5) succinct, few in number, positively worded (6) answers will vary (7) answers will vary—hallway, restroom, cafeteria, bus, auditorium, playground (8) see citation in text (9) answers will vary (10) consider classroom and/or individual interventions

Chapter 5

Answers: (1) false (2) classwide prevention strategies, answers may vary (3) positive communication (4) a (5) explicit instruction (6) social skills (7) the teacher is constantly aware of where all students are in the classroom and what they are doing (8) how did the student perform relative to progress on the IEP goals and objectives/what modifications would make the lessons more effective (9) dignifying errors is an effective way to respond to incorrect answers without triggering a negative emotional response (10) answers will vary

Chapter 6

Answers: (1) false (2) increases (3) answers will vary (4) contingency contract (5) answers will vary (6) answers will vary (7) restitution (8) six (9) answers will vary (10) answers will vary

Chapter 7

Answers: (1) false (2) false (3) false (4) a (5) c (6) a (7) dietary interventions, biofeedback, perceptional integration, chiropractic manipulation (8) true (9) see strategy (10) answers will vary

Chapter 8

Answers: (1) answers will vary, but should correspond to Figure 8.1 (2) answers will vary, but should correspond to Figure 8.2 (3) answers will vary, but should correspond to the major points in Figures 8.3 and 8.4 (4) answers will vary (6–10) answers will vary

Chapter 9

Answers: (1) autism is sometimes referred to as a spectrum disorder as children with this diagnosis vary in severity of symptoms such as ranges in IQ, language abilities and social skills, age of onset, and associations with other disorders (National Research Council, 2001) (2) true (3) the fundamental characteristic associated with the diagnosis of Rett's Disorder is the loss of previously acquired functional hand use. Purposeful hand use is replaced by continuous stereotypical hand wringing/hand-washing or hand-to-mouth movements (4) the distinction relates to the age of onset of the disability. That is, children diagnosed with autistic disorder display symptoms of pervasive developmental disorder prior to three years of age. In contrast, children with CDD have a period of normal growth and development prior to manifesting social interaction, communication, and behavioral impairments (5) A. DSM-IV-TR diagnostic criteria for a diagnosis of Asperger's disorder require that no significant delay in cognition be present, while a majority of students with autistic disorder have IQs that fall within the range of mental retardation. B. In contrast to autistic disorder, there are no significant delays in early language development among children and youth with Asperger's disorder (6) false (7) discriminative stimulus, response, consequence, intertrial interval, and sometimes a prompt (8) visual schedules allow students with autism to anticipate upcoming events and activities, develop an understanding of time frames, and facilitate the ability to predict change (Brown, 1991; Twachtman, 1995). In addition, schedules can be utilized to stimulate communicative exchanges through the discussion of past, present, and future events (Twachtman, 1995) and to teach new skills such as cooking skills and self-care and grooming skills (9) theory of mind is the inability to understand the feelings, beliefs, and perspectives of others. This deficit may lead the individual to make socially inappropriate statements, and therefore peers and adults may view the student as being rude or odd (10) answers will vary, any of the therapies listed in Table 9.7

Chapter 10

Answers: (1) true (2) false (3) false (4) true (5) false (6) false (7) true (8) true (9) answers will vary, should be based on chapter content (10) answers will vary, should be based on chapter content

Chapter 11

Answers: (1) false (2) true (3) answers will vary, should be individualized, nonaversive (4) true (5) false (6) answers will vary, should be individualized, nonaversive, include medication management (7) answers will vary (8) true (9) answers will vary (10) answers will vary

Chapter 12

Answers: (1) false (2) answers will vary, see Figure 12.1 (3) answers will vary, see Figure 12.1 (4) answers will vary, see Figure 12.1 (5) false (6) answers will vary (7) answers will vary, ex: "Tell me what Janine typically does after she gets home from school" (8) answers will vary, ex: "When you tattle, it makes the other students angry, and then I have to stop teaching to deal with the fuss" (9) answers will vary (10) answers will vary

Chapter 13

Answers: (1) false (2) true (3) answers will vary for description. Professionals are: school counselor, school psychologist, psychiatrist, clinical psychologist, psychiatric nurse, and clinical social worker (4) true (5) false (6) answers will vary: should include the following, taking responsibility for thoughts and actions, client has decisions to make about the problem, and the problem or thoughts about the problem are a choice made by the client (7) false (8) true (9) general answer is community mental health agencies. Specific answer is health departments, mental health centers, other social service agencies (10) mutually agreed upon goals and a sufficient formal agreement regarding the mechanisms that will lead to fulfillment of such goals

Chapter 14

Answers: (1) false (2) true (3) false (4) false (5) false (6) educational, environmental/technological, recreation, and regulation (7) answers will vary (8) answers will vary (9) answers will vary (10) answers will vary

ABC worksheets. A tool often used in functional behavioral assessment (FBA) to place target behavior (B) in a context that includes antecedents (A) and consequences (C) to assist in determining the function of behavior.

Accommodations. Adjustments to instructional activities or settings designed to reduce barriers for individuals with disabilities and provide equal access to curriculum and services.

Activity completion signals. An instructional strategy to provide students with ASD information that will help them anticipate the end of one activity and transition smoothly to the next.

Adequate Yearly Progress (AYP). A Requirement of *No Child Left Behind*; the measurement by which schools are held accountable for academic progress made by all students, including those with disabilities.

Alternative placement. A term used in *IDEA* disciplinary procedures to describe a placement other than the least restrictive environment where a student with a disability might be placed for the safety of self or others while continuing to receive educational services related to both the general education curriculum and IEP goals.

Analogue assessment. A process of systematically manipulating antecedents and consequences to determine the effect on a target behavior; often used as part of the FBA process to verify the functional hypothesis.

Anecdotal record. A direct observation technique where the observer takes general notes to describe incidents or behaviors in concrete, factual terms.

Anorexia nervosa. A *DSM-IV-TR* diagnostic category characterized by avoidance of weight gain and controlling food intake; may be associated with life-threatening complications, and is fatal in approximately 10% of cases.

Anxiety disorders. The most common mental illnesses in the United States, affecting approximately 13% of school age children and adolescents; those most commonly affecting students include generalized anxiety disorder, obsessive-compulsive disorder, post-traumatic stress disorder, reactive attachment disorder, separation anxiety disorder, social phobia, and selective mutism.

Applied behavior analysis (ABA). A systematic behavioral science method of assessment and intervention that focuses on the search for the relationship between behavior and its causes.

Art therapy. The use of art-based activities to provide an opportunity for artistic expression, communication, and therapy.

Asperger's disorder. Also called Asperger Syndrome, a *DSM-IV-TR* diagnostic category characterized by qualitative impairments in social interaction and restricted and unusual patterns of interest and behavior.

Assessment. A process designed to collect and analyze data for decision-making purposes.

Attention deficit hyperactivity disorder (ADHD). A *DSM-IV-TR* diagnostic category characterized by symptoms of attention, hyperactivity, and impulsivity.

Attention signals. A variety of verbal and nonverbal cues teachers use to gain or focus student attention.

Autistic disorder. A *DSM-IV-TR* diagnostic category characterized by impaired social interaction and communication, and a restricted repertoire of interests and activities.

Autism spectrum disorders (ASD). Increasingly, a term special educators and other professionals use to refer to students identified as meeting criteria for *DSM-IV-TR* pervasive developmental disorders, including Autism and Asperger's Disorder.

Autogenic relaxation therapy. A type of relaxation therapy that has been successful at reducing anxiety symptoms; it combines relaxation with autosuggestions.

Behavior cue cards. A management strategy that provides a visual reminder of expectations or target behaviors.

Behavior rating scales. Instruments designed to formally organize and quantify intuitive or perceptual information about student behaviors.

Behavioral momentum. An antecedent instructional strategy that pairs preferred and nonpreferred activities, increasing the likelihood of student compliance.

Bibliotherapy. The use of literature-based activities to provide student guidance and support.

Bipolar disorder. A *DSM-IV-TR* diagnostic category characterized by alternating episodes of depression with episodes of elevated mood or mania.

Brief therapy. A counseling approach that involves a short-term set of interventions designed to assist students in addressing current life issues.

Bulimia. A *DSM-IV-TR* diagnostic category characterized by a cycle of compulsive diet and inhibition (i.e., bingeing and purging).

Bullying. A negative pattern of behavior characterized by deliberate aggression and a real or perceived imbalance of power between aggressor/bully and victim(s).

Chaining. An instructional technique that uses task analysis to break a complex behavior into its component parts, then teach and reinforce each step sequentially; the instructional sequence may be taught forward or backward.

Childhood Disintegrative Disorder. A *DSM-IV-TR* diagnostic category characterized by behavior patterns that resemble autistic disorder, but with at least two years (but fewer than ten) of apparently normal development prior to marked regression of skills and diagnosis.

Circle of Friends. A strategy designed to support the inclusion of individuals with disabilities in social activities involving their nondisabled peers.

Clarifying question. An effective communication technique designed to elicit additional information from a speaker, often with the purpose of checking understanding.

Clinical psychologists. Mental health professionals, generally with a doctorate in psychology, trained to evaluate, diagnose, and treat individuals with mental illness.

Clinical social workers. Mental health professionals who often hold a master's degree and are licensed to work with individuals and families.

Closed questions. An effective communication strategy designed to elicit specific or quantitative information; a question with a limited or predetermined set of responses.

Cognitive behavioral interventions. Strategies that address students' thinking processes as well as behavior, with the long-term goal of teaching self-management; techniques include self-talk or instruction, self-monitoring or recording, self-evaluation, self-reinforcement, and problem solving.

Cognitive behavioral therapy. A counseling approach where the counselor works with clients to recognize that they can control their own feelings, thoughts, and behaviors, helping students to take responsibility for their own lives.

Collaboration. A process whereby two or more professionals work together to achieve a mutually agreed upon goal.

Collaborative consultation. A process that brings together individuals with varied expertise to engage in problem solving.

Comic-strip conversations. Similar to social stories, a cartoon-like, pictorial representation of a conversation designed to assist students with ASD in understanding social expectations.

Compulsions. Meaningless, repetitive behaviors or mental acts performed to reduce anxiety or stress; one of the clinical criteria for obsessive-compulsive disorder.

Conceptual models. The philosophical approaches to the education of students with EBD, including behavioral, biophysical/medical, ecological/environmental, humanistic, psychodynamic/psychoanalytic, psychoeducational, social learning and cognition.

Conduct disorder (CD). A *DSM-IV-TR* diagnostic category characterized by repeated violation of major social rules or norms; may be either overt or covert, with onset in childhood or adolescence.

Consequence. In behavior management, the stimulus that occurs after the target behavior and influences the likelihood that it will occur again; in DTI, the third component of a trial which may involve a reinforcer or an error correction procedure.

Consultation. A process where a professional provides assistance to another, with the intended goal of providing assistance to a third party—in special education, most often the special educator working with a general educator to help a student with a disability being served in an inclusive classroom.

Contingency contract. Sometimes called behavior contract; a formalized if/then statement that prescribes what consequence will occur when a student performs a specific target behavior.

Continuum of services. The range of placement and service options that should be available to students with disabilities, generally described from least to most restrictive.

Cooperative learning. A strategy for grouping students to complete assignments interdependently.

Crisis. A critical incident or pivotal situation in which there is a high potential for harm to students or others.

Crisis intervention plan. A deliberate set of procedural steps to (a) define the roles and responsibilities of individuals during a crisis, (b) guide the decisions and actions of faculty and others during a crisis situation, and (c) provide resources for post-crisis debriefing and follow-up.

Criterion-referenced test. Determines whether or not a student meets a specific, preset criteria or mastery level established by the test developer, national standards, or state or local education agencies.

Curriculum-based measures (CBM). Assessment of a student's abilities or behaviors relative to a specific curriculum or scope and sequence of skills.

Depression. The *DSM-IV-TR* diagnostic categories characterized by unipolar, depressed mood; for school-aged children and youth, includes both Dysthymic Disorder (or dysthymia) and Major Depressive Disorder.

Diagnostic teaching. The systematic manipulation of instructional material and conditions to determine the most effective way to teach a target skill to a specific student; also called diagnostic probes and dynamic assessment.

Direct observation. The process of collecting data by observing the student in natural settings that may be structured and designed to quantify specific behaviors, or less structured and designed to describe the ecology of student behavior.

Discrete trial instruction (DTI). A highly structured teaching strategy applying the principles of ABA to teach skills and behaviors to students with disabilities (most commonly autism) through repeated trials.

Discriminative stimulus. An antecedent that serves as a cue for a target behavior to occur, resulting in reinforcement; in

DTI, the first step of an instructional trial—the instruction or request.

Disruptive behavior disorder—not otherwise specified (DBD-NOS). A *DSM-IV-TR* diagnostic category characterized by clinically significant behavior that appears oppositional/defiant or conduct disordered, but that does not meet the criteria for either ODD or CD.

Duration recording. A direct observation technique designed to determine how long a target behavior lasts from onset to completion.

Dysesthesia. Sometimes associated with self-injurious behavior, particularly after spinal cord injuries; involves feeling pain in the absence of painful stimuli.

Dysthymic disorder (or dysthymia). A *DSM-IV-TR* diagnostic category characterized by chronic and persistent depressed mood.

Echolalia. Speech that involves repetition of words or phrases previously heard; may be immediate, delayed, or mitigated.

Error-correction procedure. In DTI, part of the consequence step of the trial—the assistance provided to the student after an incorrect or no response designed to elicit a correct response.

Extinction. Also called planned ignoring; identifies the antecedents and consequences that have previously reinforced undesirable behavior and withdraws them; most commonly involves withholding attention.

Evaluation. The process of analyzing data to make informed judgments.

Etiology. The study of causation, attempts to discover why things occur; in the case of EBD identifying what biological variables and environmental conditions predict specific problems or diagnoses.

Explicit curriculum. The instructional content, social context, and expectations of the school environment are explicit and provided in writing for all students and stakeholders.

Family therapy. The counselor or mental health professional works with at least two members of a family at the same time.

Feedback. Providing students with information on their performance; may include praise, acknowledgement of effort, or constructive corrective information.

Formal assessment. Refers to administration of published tests that have specific rules for administration, scoring, and interpretation.

Formative data. Information that is collected over time, designed to document student progress or growth of knowledge and skills.

Free appropriate public education (FAPE). A key feature of *IDEA*, the standard which schools and teachers must provide for all students, including those with disabilities.

Frequency count. A direct observation technique where the observer counts the number of times a target behavior occurs within a given period of time.

Functional behavioral assessment (FBA). Part of the assessment process for students with EBD; designed to determine under what conditions target behaviors are most/least likely to occur and to guide development of effective interventions; required by *IDEA* as part of student disciplinary procedures involving a change in placement.

General education curriculum. Students with disabilities are to be held to high academic expectations, including having access to the same curriculum taught to nondisabled students to the maximum extent possible.

Generalized anxiety disorder (GAD). A *DSM-IV-TR* diagnostic category characterized by chronic, excessive worry or anxiety about several different things.

Gestural prompt. In DTI, the teacher provides gestural assistance to elicit a correct student response; prompt may take the form of nodding, pointing, pantomime, etc.

Graphic organizers. Also known as concept maps, a pictorial way of organizing information into a structured, simple-to-read visual display.

Group counseling. The mental health provider works with students who have similar concerns in small groups, rather than individually.

Hidden curriculum. The school's instructional content, social context, and expectations that are NOT explicit, are often unwritten and unspoken, frequently are misunderstood and violated by students with ASD and EBD.

Highly qualified teacher. A provision of *No Child Left Behind* intended to assure that all students receive instruction from individuals appropriately trained to teach them.

Home base. A safe spot where the student may go when they feel anxious to de-escalate and prevent behavioral outbursts; sometimes used proactively at the beginning and end of the day and called "triage."

"I" messages. An effective communication technique that acknowledges the needs of the speaker and the impact of the other individual's behavior without casting blame.

Individualized Education Program (IEP). A description of the needs of a student with a disability, the instructional goals based on those needs, and the services that will be provided to that child as part of providing a free, appropriate public education (FAPE).

Individualized Family Services Plan (IFSP). A description of the needs of a young child with a disability, the goals based on those needs, and the services that will be provided to the child and family as part of a free, appropriate public education (FAPE).

Individualized Transition Plan (ITP). The part of the IEP that addresses postsecondary needs and goals; required by age 16 by *IDEA*.

Informal assessment. A less formalized process of gathering information about student performance; may include both published and teacher-developed measures.

Intermittent explosive disorder (IED). A *DSM-IV-TR* diagnostic category generally diagnosed in adults; characterized by infrequent, unexpected outbursts of disruptive behavior that result in serious harm to people or property.

Inter-trial interval (ITI). The fourth step of DTI, in which there is a 3–5 second pause following the consequence, but before the next discriminative stimulus.

Interview. A purposeful conversation designed to gather information; as part of special education assessment, generally examining a student's history or present level of performance.

Journal writing. A instructional strategy that can be used for a variety of purposes including dialogue, reflection, and problem solving.

Latency recording. A direct observation technique similar to duration recording, where the observer measures the amount of time between two behaviors of interest (e.g., between a teacher's request and the student's behavioral response).

Least intrusive interventions. Strategies and interventions that impose the minimum amount of control necessary to direct student behavior, providing the least possible interruption to the flow of instruction.

Least restrictive environment. Students with disabilities must be educated in the least restrictive environment in which their individual needs can be met, and with their nondisabled peers to the furthest extent possible.

Major depressive disorder. A *DSM-IV-TR* diagnostic category characterized by unipolar episodes of depression.

Manifestation determination. A process established in *IDEA* discipline procedures that may result in a change of placement whereby the team determines whether the behavior that prompted the disciplinary action was caused by—or directly related to—the student's disability.

Measurement. A variety of formal and informal activities designed to describe individual performance in quantifiable terms.

Mentoring. An intervention that pairs an at-risk student with an adult or high-status peer model to provide support and positive influence.

Modeling. An instructional technique that provides an exemplar from which a student can learn or imitate a desired behavior.

Modeling prompt. In DTI, the teacher provides a demonstration of the target behavior in an effort to elicit a correct student imitative response.

Modifications. Adjustments to instructional curriculum that allow students with disabilities to participate in general education settings, but with different goals, materials, or standards than their nondisabled peers.

Music therapy. The use of music and musical activities to provide student support, opportunities for creative expression and communication, and therapy.

Needs assessment. As it applies to transition planning, a formal or informal process designed to identify the knowledge and skills a student needs to meet postsecondary and life goals.

Negative reinforcement. The removal of an aversive stimulus or consequence that results in increasing the likelihood that the student will perform a target behavior.

Normed. A test that has been administered to a large group of individuals to examine their performance and determine the standard to which future test-takers will be compared.

Norming group. Individuals participating in the process of establishing reference scores for a test, general categorized by demographic variables including age, grade level, gender, ethnicity, geographical region, socioeconomic status, and disability.

Obsessions. Persistent and intrusive thoughts, ideas and impulses; one of the criteria for obsessive-compulsive disorder.

Obsessive-compulsive disorder (OCD). A *DSM-IV-TR* diagnostic category characterized by persistent and intrusive thoughts, often feeling driven to perform ritualistic, purposeless tasks.

Open-ended questions. An effective communication technique designed to elicit general or qualitative information; a question with no predetermined response.

Opportunities to respond (OTR). A measure of active student engagement in instruction; the rate at which students have a chance to share information or answer questions.

Oppositional defiant disorder (ODD). A *DSM-IV-TR* diagnostic category characterized by recurrent negative or hostile behavior toward authority figures.

Outcomes-based measurement. Describes assessment that is meaningful and directly related to information needed to guide student instruction and achieve specified student behavioral goals.

Overcorrection. A behavior reduction strategy that requires student effort as a penalty for misbehavior; may include positive practice and/or restitution.

Paraphrasing. An effective communication technique designed to rephrase information provided by another person to check understanding or to clarify.

Paraprofessionals. Also called paraeducators and instructional assistants, these individuals work with—and under the supervision of—certified educators to assist in delivery of services to students, including those with special needs.

Peer rating scale. A type of sociometric measure that provides students with an opportunity to rate or rank their peers on a list of skills, behaviors, or characteristics.

Person-centered (or Rogerian) therapy. The counselor works with students from a nonjudgmental stance, using nondirective responses to help students recognize they already know how to solve their own problems.

Pervasive developmental disorder—not otherwise specified (PDD-NOS). A *DSM-IV-TR* diagnostic category with characteristics similar to autism, but with later onset, atypical symptomology, or symptoms that do not fully meet the criteria for a diagnosis of autism or another developmental disorder.

Pet therapy. The use of animal-assisted activities to provide support and skill development opportunities.

Physical prompt. In DTI, the teacher provides physical assistance to elicit a correct student response; the prompt may take the form of a touch on the hand, hand-over-hand guidance, etc.

Picture exchange communication system (PECS). An icon-based augmentative communication system often used with students with ASD and other communication disorders.

Play therapy. A systematic, interactive process that a therapist employs with a child to promote positive developmental growth and address problems using toys and games to act out student concerns or problems.

Portfolio assessment. A form of authentic assessment in which artifacts demonstrating skill and knowledge are collected and displayed, generally with reflective essays.

Positive behavioral supports (PBS). A systematic set of strategies designed to assist students in development of skills and behaviors that will allow them to be successful in a variety of settings.

Positive practice. Provides students with an opportunity to practice an expected or desired behavior as a consequence of performing the behavior incorrectly.

Post-traumatic stress disorder (PTSD). A *DSM-IV-TR* diagnostic category; the condition develops after an individual is exposed to a terrifying and often potentially life-threatening situation.

Power cards. A type of behavior cue card personalized for a student with ASD and based on their special interests.

Pragmatic language. The ability to use and respond to social language.

Praise. Both an effective communication technique and a form of social reinforcement; should be an honest expression of appreciation for effort and/or accomplishment.

Prescriptive measurement. Evaluation designed to be translated directly into classroom instruction (e.g., goals, objectives, lesson plans).

Primary prevention. Activities designed for the general population, designed to provide information that may prevent the later development of a disease, condition, or problem.

Priming. An antecedent instructional strategy that introduces elements of an activity ahead of time to increase student competence and comfort.

Probes. A brief, informal set of questions or activities designed to demonstrate student mastery or nonmastery of specific information or skills, or to test hypotheses concerning learning or reinforcement preferences.

Procedural due process. Parents of students with disabilities have specific rights regarding participation in decisions regarding their child's evaluation, placement, and education; includes the right to appeal IEP team decisions.

Progressive muscle relaxation. A type of relaxation training that has been found effective at reducing anxiety symptoms; involves systematically tensing, then releasing major muscle groups in a specific sequence.

Prompt. In DTI, an optional fifth component that provides instructional cues or assistance as needed to elicit a correct response; may be verbal, gestural, modeling, or physical.

Proximity control. A classroom management strategy where the teacher actively monitors student behavior while remaining nearby.

Psychiatric nurses. Registered nurses with additional specialized training in mental health issues; often serve as liaison between patients and psychiatrists.

Psychiatrists. Medical doctors with specialized training in diagnosing and treating mental illness; may provide therapy and/or prescribe and monitor medications.

Punishment. A behavioral technique that decreases the future recurrence of undesirable behavior by applying a consequence perceived to be negative by the student.

Reactive attachment disorder. A *DSM-IV-TR* diagnostic category characterized by markedly disturbed and developmentally inappropriate social relatedness before age 5; inhibited and disinhibited subtypes both have been associated with severe abuse and neglect, or lack of appropriate care during early childhood years.

Reactive depression. A transient, temporary feeling of sadness after an unpleasant experience or loss; generally last only a few hours or days.

Reflecting. An effective communication technique that involves paraphrasing what you have heard as well as describing the affect or underlying feelings of the speaker.

Reinforcement. Delivery of a consequence (C) that increases the likelihood that a target behavior (B) will recur in the presence of a given antecedent (A).

Related services. A component of a free, appropriate public education (FAPE) for many students with disabilities; may include counseling, psychological, or social work services for students with EBD.

Release of information. A document, signed by the student and parent or guardian, allowing school personnel to contact outside agencies and mental health professionals to request or share information.

Reliability. Used to describe the extent to which a test would yield the same results in subsequent administrations; a measure of trustworthiness.

Response cost. A behavior reduction strategy where a student loses something previously earned or anticipated as a consequence of an inappropriate behavior.

Restitution. A behavioral strategy designed to reduce future inappropriate behaviors by requiring the individual to correct the damage they have done and make amends.

Rett's disorder. A *DSM-IV-TR* diagnostic category characterized by loss of previously acquired skills following a period of apparently normal development; a progressive neurological disorder.

Role playing. An activity that allows students to practice newly acquired social skills or problem solving strategies in a simulated setting.

Scatterplot. A data collection tool often used in functional behavioral assessment (FBA); designed to identify patterns of behavior during an observation, or a series of observations.

Schizophrenia. A *DSM-IV-TR* diagnostic category characterized by persistent delusions, paranoid and/or bizarre beliefs; rarely occurs in children and adolescents.

School-based crisis intervention. A systematic convergence of resources designed to interrupt or divert a crisis incident, minimize potential risk of harm, and return the situation to the functional level that was present prior to the crisis.

School counselor. Usually the most accessible mental health professional to students with EBD and their teachers; often provides individual and group guidance, as well as consultation.

School psychologist. Mental health professional employed by schools to assess students, assist with diagnoses, and consult with faculty about individual students.

Secondary prevention. Strategies that target individuals considered at risk, providing information designed to minimize the potential impact of risk factors or interrupt development of an emerging condition or problem.

Selective mutism. Formerly called elective mutism, a *DSM-IV-TR* diagnostic category characterized by the refusal to speak in social situations despite the ability to understand and produce language.

Self-injurious behavior (SIB). Also referred to as self-damaging behavior, thought to be a response to or a coping mechanism for anxiety or depression; may have serious consequences, but most often nonlethal.

Separation anxiety disorder. A *DSM-IV-TR* diagnostic category characterized by extreme or prolonged difficulty separating from parents or caregivers.

Shaping. An instruction strategy that requires task analysis and the reinforcement of successive approximations of a target behavior to reach a specified objective.

Social autopsies. A problem-solving strategy to assist students in identifying, understanding, and correcting their social errors.

Social competence. Involves the perception of peers and adults that an individual possesses necessary social skills and uses them appropriately in social situations.

Social phobia. Also called social anxiety disorder (SAD), a *DSM-IV-TR* diagnostic category characterized by significant and persistent fear of embarrassment in situations involving social interaction or performance.

Social skills. Those specific interpersonal skills and behaviors that are valued by peers and adults in natural environments, including school settings.

Social stories. An instructional strategy that involves development of illustrated stories depicting students engaging in desirable behaviors; often used to teach and reinforce rules and routines.

Sociogram. A type of sociometric measure that visually represents student relationships, choices, and perceptions about peers.

Sociometric measures. Behavioral data collection strategies that examine how the student is viewed by peers or self on a set of variables; includes sociograms and peer rating scales.

Standardization. Process of test construction that allows student raw scores and responses to be statistically manipulated, producing scores that conform to specific, predetermined scales of measurement.

Student learning traits. Individual characteristics that provide information about how students acquire and use information.

Student response. The second step in a DTI trial, the student's behavior immediately following the discriminative stimulus.

Summative data. Information collected at the end of an instructional period to determine student mastery of knowledge and/or skills.

Supported employment. Placement of students with disabilities in community-based jobs with support from a coach or other trained individuals.

System of care. An approach to service delivery in which schools work collaboratively with other community agencies and stakeholders to develop services that "wrap around" students with EBD.

Talk therapy. A therapeutic discussion between the student and counselor focusing on the student's issues or concerns.

Task analysis. An instructional strategy that involves breaking a complex or multi-step task into its discrete parts.

Tertiary prevention. Often called treatment, focused individualized activities designed to limit the impact and development of an existing condition or problem.

Testing. The process of administering a structured set of questions/items designed to elicit specific responses from individuals or groups.

Therapeutic activities. Activities that promote students' emotional well-being, coping skills, and self-concept.

Therapy. A clinical process that involves evaluation, treatment planning, treatment activities, and documentation of progress; generally performed by an individual with specialized training, licensure, and/or certification.

Time-out. A behavior reduction strategy that removes the student temporarily from the opportunity for reinforcement.

Time sampling. A direct observation technique where the observer uses a grid or table that divides the entire observation period into shorter increments, noting whether a target behavior is observed during those intervals.

Token. A generalized reinforcer (e.g., good behavior points) that can be exchanged later for a back-up reinforcer (e.g., 10 extra minutes of computer time).

Token economy. A system of dispensing and redeeming tokens for back-up reinforcers, often using a menu/pricing format.

Tourette's disorder. Also known as Tourette's syndrome, a *DSM-IV-TR* diagnostic category characterized by multiple motor and vocal tics; typically a chronic condition.

Validity. The extent to which a test measures what it claims to measure and yields results that match the concepts or constructs around which it was designed.

Verbal prompt. In DTI, the teacher provides verbal assistance to elicit a correct student response; prompt may take the form of additional instructions, a question, a word, a part of the word, etc.

Verbal reprimands. When used appropriately, the teacher provides a brief, positively worded correction statement (e.g., Please return to your seat.); should be used infrequently, especially in front of peers.

Visual supports. A set of commonly used instructional strategies for students with ASD, designed to help students make sense of surroundings, predict activities and events, anticipate change and understand expectations; includes visual schedules, mini schedules, and task organizers.

Warm-up activities. An antecedent instructional strategy designed to decrease resistance and task avoidance prior to a nonpreferred activity.

Zero reject. No school-aged child, regardless of disability, may be excluded from a free, appropriate education; a basic tenet of *IDEA*.

REFERENCES

Chapter 1

Alexander, K., & Alexander, M. D. (2001). *American public school law*. Belmont, CA: Wadsworth Publishing Company.

Allee, T. (2002, June). Enabled or disabled. *The Director, 19*(4), 1–2.

Americans with Disabilities Act of 1990, 42 U.S.C.A. § 12101 *et seq.*

Brown v. Board of Education, 347 U.S. 483 (1954).

Bush, G. W. (2004, December). *President's remarks at the signing of H.R. 1350.* (Press Release.) The White House, Office of the Press Secretary, Washington, DC. Retrieved January 3, 2005, from http://www.whitehouse.gov/news/releases/2004/12/print/20041203-6.html

Education Amendments of 1974, P.L. 93–380, 88 Stat. 580.

Education for All Handicapped Children Act of 1975, 20 U.S.C. § 1401 *et seq.*

Education for all handicapped children—Implementation of part B of the education of the handicapped act. (1977, August). *Federal Register, 42.*

Education of the Handicapped Amendments of 1986, 20 U.S.C. § 1401 *et seq.*

Ewing, N. J. (2001). Teacher education: Ethics, power, and privilege. *Teacher Education and Special Education, 24*(1), 13–24.

Forness, S., & Knitzer, J. (1992). A new proposed definition and terminology to replace "serious emotional disturbance" in the Individuals with Disabilities Education Act. *School Psychology Review, 21*(1), 12–20.

Goodman, L. V. (1976). A bill of rights for the handicapped. *American Education, 12,* 6–8.

Individuals with Disabilities Education Act of 1990, 20 U.S.C. § 1401.

Individuals with Disabilities Education Act of 1997, P.L. 105–17.

Individuals with Disabilities Education Improvement Act of 2004, P.L. 108–448.

Jones, N. L., & Aleman, S. R. (1997). *The 1997 IDEA amendments: A guide for educators, parents, and attorneys.* Horsham, PA: LRP Publications.

Kauffman, J. (2004, January). Panel discussion at Think Tank VII, a meeting of the Midwest Symposium for Leadership in Behavior Disorders, Kansas City, MO.

McIntire, J. (2000, January-February). President's comments. *CASE, 41*(4), 2–3.

Meyen, E. L. (1978). *Exceptional children and youth: An introduction.* Denver, CO: Love Publishing Company.

Mills v. Board of Education of the District of Columbia, 348 F.Supp. 866 (D.D.C. 1972).

National Association of State Directors of Special Education (NASDSE). (1997, June). *Comparison of key issues: Previous law and P.L. 105-17 (1997 IDEA Amendments).* Alexandria, VA: Author.

National Center for Educational Statistics (NCES). (2003). *Digest of educational statistics, 2002.* Washington, DC: Author, Institute of Educational Sciences, U.S. Department of Education.

No Child Left Behind Act of 2001, P.L. 107–110.

Patton, J. M., & Townsend, B. L. (2001). Teacher education, leadership, and disciplinary practices: Exploring ethics, power, and privilege in the education of exceptional African American learners. *Teacher Education and Special Education, 24*(1), 1–2.

Pennsylvania Association for Retarded Citizens (PARC) v. Commonwealth of Pennsylvania, 343 F. Supp. 279 (E.D. Pa. 1972).

Peper, C. B., Martin, K., Jensen, Maichel, W. R., & Hetlage, R. D. (1998, Winter). *Special education and the law.* St. Louis, MO: School Law Department of Peper, Martin, Jensen, Maichel, & Hetlage, attorneys at law.

Rehabilitation Act of 1973, Section 504, 29 U.S.C. § 794.

Rothstein, L. (1990). *Special education law.* New York: Longman.

Trohanis, P. L. (2002, August). *Progress in providing services to young children with special needs and their families.* (NECTAC Notes, No. 12). Chapel Hill: The University of North Carolina, FPG Child Development Institute, National Early Childhood Technical Assistance Center.

Turnbull, H. R. (1993). *Free appropriate public education: The law and disabilities* (3rd ed.). Denver, CO: Love Publishing Co.

Turnbull, H. R. & Turnbull, A. (1978). *Free appropriate public education: Law and implementation.* Denver, CO: Love Publishing Co.

U.S. Department of Education. (January, 2001). Executive Summary of the *No Child Left Behind Act.* Retrieved December 1, 2003, from http://www.ed.gov/nclb/overview/intro/execsumm.html

U.S. Department of Education (2000). *Twenty-third annual report to Congress on the implementation of the Individuals with Disabilities Education Act.* Washington, DC: U.S. Department of Education.

Yell, M. L. (1998). *The law and special education.* Upper Saddle River, NJ: Merrill/Prentice Hall.

Chapter 2

Brown, W. H., Odom, S. L., & Buysee, V. (2002). Assessment of preschool children's peer-related social competence. *Assessment for Effective Intervention, 27*(4), 61-71.

Bullock, L. M., Wilson, M. J., & Campbell, R. E. (1990). Inquiry into the commonality of items from seven behavior rating scales: A preliminary examination. *Behavioral Disorders, 15*(2), 87-99.

Council for Exceptional Children (CEC). (2003). *What every special educator should know* (5th ed.). Arlington, VA: Author.

Downing, J. A., & Smith, A. H. (1999). *Counselor cadre training curriculum: Updating your clinical and consultative skills.* Unpublished manuscript.

Drotar, D. (2002). Behavioral and emotional problems in infants and young children: Challenges of clinical assessment and intervention. *Infants and Young Children, 14*(4), 1-5.

Feuerstein, R. (1979). *The dynamic assessment of retarded performers: Learning potential assessment device.* Baltimore: University Park Press.

Hammill, D. D., Brown, L., & Bryant, B. R. (1992). *A consumer's guide to tests in print.* Austin, TX: Pro-Ed.

Hosp, J. L., Howell, K. W., & Hosp, M. K. (2003). Characteristics of behavior rating scales: Implications for practice in assessment and behavioral support. *Journal of Positive Behavior Interventions, 5*(4), 201-208.

Individuals with Disabilities Education Act of 1990 (P. L. 101-476), 20 U.S.C. § 1400 *et seq.*.

McLoughlin, J., & Lewis, R. (2001). *Assessing students with special needs* (5th ed.). Upper Saddle River, NJ: Merrill/Prentice Hall.

Merrell, K. W. (2001). Assessment of children's social skills: Recent developments, best practices, and new directions. *Exceptionality, 9* (1 & 2), 3-18.

Murphy, L. L., Plake, B. S., Impara, J. C., & Spies, R. A. (Eds.). (2002). *Tests in print VI.* Lincoln, NE: Buros Institute of Mental Measurements, University of Nebraska Press.

Myles, B. S., & Adreon, D. (2001). *Asperger syndrome and adolescence: Practical solutions for school success.* Shawnee Mission, KS: Autism Asperger Publishing Company.

Myles, B. S., Constant, J. A., Simpson, R. L., & Carlson, J. K. (1989). Educational assessment of students with higher-functioning autistic disorder. *Focus on Autistic Behavior, 4*(1), 1-15.

The National Council of Teachers of Mathematics. (2000). *Principles and standards for school mathematics.* Reston, VA: Author. Available from: http://www.nctm.org/standards/

Plake, B. S., Impara, J. C., & Spies, R. A. (Eds.). (2003). *The fifteenth mental measurements yearbook.* Lincoln, NE: Buros Institute of Mental Measurements, University of Nebraska Press.

Plasencia-Peinado, J., & Alvarado, J. L. (2001). Assessing students with emotional and behavioral disorders using curriculum-based measurement. *Assessment for Effective Intervention, 26*(1), 59-66.

Salvia, J., & Ysseldyke, J. (2001). *Assessment* (8th ed.). Boston: Houghton Mifflin.

Sweetland, R. C., & Keyser, D. J. (Eds.). (1984-1994). *Test critiques, volumes I-X.* Austin, TX: Pro-Ed.

Townsend, B. L. (2002). Testing while Black: Standards-based school reform and African American learners. *Remedial and Special Education, 23*(4), 222-230.

Waterman, B. B. (1994). *Assessing children for the presence of a disability.* National Information Center for Children and Youth with Disabilities News Digest No. 23. Accessed December 23, 2005, from http://www.nichcy.org/pubs/newsdig/nd23.pdf

Chapter 3

Asmus, J. M., Vollmer, T. R., & Borrero, J. C. (2002). Functional behavioral assessment: A school based model. *Education and Treatment of Children, 25*(1), 67-90.

Axelrod, S. (2003, August). *Using trigger analysis to teach self control.* Paper presented at the National Autism Conference and Pennsylvania Autism Institute, State College, PA.

Byrnes, M. A. (2000). Accommodations for students with disabilities: Removing barriers to learning. *NASSP Bulletin, 84*(613), 21-27.

Carr, E. G. (1977). The motivation of self-injurious behavior: A review of some hypotheses. *Psychological Bulletin, 84,* 800-816.

Cessna, K. K., & Skiba, R. J. (1996). Needs-based services: A responsible approach to inclusion. *Preventing School Failure, 40*(3), 117-123.

Conroy, M. A., & Davis, C. A. (2000). Early elementary-aged children with challenging behaviors: Legal and educational issues related to IDEA and assessment. *Preventing School Failure, 44*(4), 163-168.

Doggett, R. A., Edwards, R. P., Moore, J. W., Tingstrom, D. H., & Wilczynski, S. M. (2001). An approach to functional assessment in general education classroom settings. *School Psychology Review, 30*(3), 313-328.

Drasgow, E., & Yell, M. L. (2001). Functional behavioral assessments: Legal requirements and challenges. *School Psychology Review, 30*(2), 239-251.

Drasgow, E., Yell, M. L., Bradley, R., & Shriner, J. G. (1999). The IDEA Amendments of 1997: A school-wide model for conducting functional behavioral assessments and developing behavior intervention plans. *Education and Treatment of Children, 22,* 244-266.

Drasgow, E., Yell, M. L., & Robinson, T. R. (2001). Developing legally correct and educationally appropriate IEPs. *Remedial and Special Education, 22*(6), 359-373.

Dunlap, G., & Kern, L. (1993). Assessment and intervention for children within the instructional curriculum. In J. Reichle & D. Wacker (Eds.), *Implementing augmentative and alternative communication: Strategies for learners with severe disabilities* (pp. 215-237). Baltimore: Paul H. Brookes.

Dunlap, G., Kern, L., dePerczel, M., Clarke, S., Wilson, D., Childs, K. E., White, R., & Falk, G.D. (1993). Functional analysis of classroom variables for students with emotional or behavioral disorders. *Behavioral Disorders, 18,* 275-291.

Ervin, R.A., Radford, P. M., Bertsch, K., Piper, A. L., Ehrhardt, K. E., & Poling, A. (2001). A descriptive analysis and critique of the empirical literature on school-based functional assessment. *School Psychology Review, 30*(2), 193-210.

Gable, R. A., Quinn, M. M., Rutherford, R. B., Howell, K. W., & Hoffman, C. C. (1998). *Addressing student problem behavior—Part II: Conducting a functional behavioral assessment* (3rd ed.). Washington, DC: Center for Effective Collaboration and Practice.

Gable, R. A., Quinn, M. M., Rutherford, R. B., Howell, K. W., & Hoffman, C. C. (2000). *Addressing student problem behavior—Part III: Creating positive behavioral intervention plans and supports.* Washington, DC: Center for Effective Collaboration and Practice.

Gartin, B. C., & Murdick, N. L. (2001). A new IDEA mandate: The use of functional assessment of behavior and positive behavior supports. *Remedial and Special Education, 22*(6), 344-349.

Hallenbeck, B.A., Kauffman, J. M., & Lloyd, J. W. (1993). When, how, and why educational placement decisions are made: Two case studies. *Journal of Emotional and Behavioral Disorders, 1,* 109-117.

Individuals with Disabilities Education Act Amendments of 1997, P.L. 105-17.

Individuals with Disabilities Education Act of 1990, 20 U.S.C. § 1400 *et seq.*

Individuals with Disabilities Education Act Regulations, 34 C.F.R. § 300.1 *et seq.*

Jolivette, K., Barton-Arwood, S., & Scott, T. M. (2000). Functional behavioral assessment as a collaborative process among professionals. *Education and Treatment of Children, 23,* 298-313.

Kaplan, J. S. (2000). *Beyond functional assessment: A social-cognitive approach to the evaluation of behavior problems in children and youth.* Austin, TX: Pro-Ed.

Kennedy, C. H. (2002). Toward a socially valid understanding of problem behavior. *Education and Treatment of Children, 25*(1), 142-153.

Kerr, M. M., & Nelson, C. M. (2002). *Strategies for addressing behavior problems in the classroom* (4th ed.). Upper Saddle River, NJ: Merrill/Prentice Hall.

Lewis, T. J., & Sugai, G. (1996). Functional assessment of problem behavior: A pilot investigation of the comparative and interactive effects of teacher and peer social attention on students in general education settings. *School Psychology Quarterly, 11,* 1-19.

Nelson, J. R., Roberts, M. L., Mathur, S. R., & Rutherford, R. B. (1999). Has public policy exceeded our knowledge base? A review of the functional behavior assessment literature. *Behavioral Disorders, 24,* 169-179.

Peterson, S. M. P., Derby, K. M., Berg, W. K., & Horner, R. H. (2002). Collaboration with families in the functional behavior assessment of and intervention for severe behavior problems. *Education and Treatment of Children, 25*(1), 5-25.

Quinn, M. M. (2000). Functional behavioral assessment: The letter and the spirit of the law. *Preventing School Failure, 44*(4), 147-151.

Quinn, M. M., Gable, R. A., Rutherford, R. B., Nelson, C. M., & Howell, K.W. (1998). *An IEP team's introduction to functional behavioral assessment and behavior intervention plans.* Washington, DC: The Center for Effective Collaboration and Practice.

Reid, R., & Nelson, J. R. (2002). The utility, acceptability, and practicality of functional behavioral assessment for students with high-incidence problem behaviors. *Remedial and Special Education, 23*(1), 15-23.

Ryan, A. K. (2001). *Strengthening the safety net: How schools can help youth with emotional and behavioral needs complete their high school education and prepare for life after school.* Burlington, VT: School Research Office, College of Education and Social Services, University of Vermont. Retrieved August 18, 2002, from http://cecp.air.org/safetynet/safetyweb.html

Scott, T. M., & Nelson, C. M. (1999). Using functional behavioral assessment to develop effective intervention plans: Practical classroom applications. *Journal of Positive Behavioral Interventions, 1,* 242-251.

Shearin, A., Roessler, R., & Schriner, K. (1999). Evaluating the transition component in IEPs of secondary students with disabilities. *Rural Special Education Quarterly, 18*(2), 22-35.

Shellady, S., & Stichter, J. P. (1999). Training preservice and inservice educators to conduct functional assessments: Initial issues and implications. *Preventing School Failure, 43*(4), 154-159.

Sterling-Turner, H. E., Robinson, S. L., & Wilczynski, S. M. (2001). Functional assessment of distracting and disruptive behaviors in the school setting. *School Psychology Review, 30*(2), 211-226.

Walsh, S., Smith, B. J., & Taylor, R. C. (2000). *IDEA requirements for preschoolers with disabilities: Challenging behavior.* Arlington, VA: Council for Exceptional Children Division for Early Childhood in cooperation with the ASPIIRE IDEA Partnership Project.

Yell, M. L., & Katsiyannis, A. (2000). Functional behavioral assessment and IDEA '97: Legal and practice considerations. *Preventing School Failure, 44*(4), 158-162.

Chapter 4

Albert, L. (1996). *Cooperative discipline.* Circle Pines, MN: American Guidance Service.

Brophy, J. (1988). Research linking teacher behavior to student achievement: Potential implications for instruction of Chapter 1 students. *Educational Psychologist, 23*(3), 235-286.

Brophy, J. & Good, T. L. (1986). Teacher behavior and student achievement. In M. C. Wittrock (Ed.), *Handbook of Research on Teaching* (pp. 328–375). New York: MacMillan.

Carr, E. G., Dunlap, G., Horner, R. H., Koegel, R. L., Turnbull, A. P., Sailor, W., et al. (2002). Positive behavior support: Evolution of an applied science. *Journal of Positive Behavior Interventions, 4*(1), 4–16, 20.

The Center for Innovation in Special Education (CISE). (2002). *Missouri positive behavior support initiative, module 1*. Columbia, MO: Author.

Center for the Study and Prevention of Violence, Blueprints Project. (2003). Website: http://www.colorado.edu/cspv/blueprints/index.html. Accessed June 29, 2003.

Center for the Study and Prevention of Violence. (1998a). *Dare program*. CSPV Position Summary PS-001. Retrieved July 29, 2003, from: http://www.colorado.edu/cspv/publications/factsheets/positions/pdf/PS-001.pdf

Center for the Study and Prevention of Violence. (1998b). *Positive peer culture programs*. CSPV Position Summary PS-003. Retrieved July 29, 2003, from: http://www.colorado.edu/cspv/publications/factsheets/positions/pdf/PS-003.pdf

Center for the Study and Prevention of Violence. (2000). *Student profiling*. CSPV Position Summary PS-004. Retrieved July 29, 2003, from: http://www.colorado.edu/cspv/publications/factsheets/positions/pdf/PS-004.pdf

Chesapeake Institute. (1994, September). *National agenda for achieving better results for children and youth with serious emotional disturbance*. Washington, DC: Department of Education, Office of Special Education and Rehabilitative Services, Office of Special Education Programs. Retrieved February 1, 2003, from: http://cecp.air.org/resources/ntlagend.asp

Glickman, C. D. (2003). Symbols and celebrations that sustain education. *Educational Leadership, 60*(6), 34–38.

Gottfredson, G. D., & Gottfredson, D. C. (2001). What schools do to prevent problem behavior and promote safe environments. *Journal of Educational and Psychological Consultation, 12*(4), 313–344.

Hawkins, J. D., Farrington, D. P., & Catalano, R. F. (1998). Reducing school violence through the schools. In D. S. Elliott, B. Hamburg, & K. R. Williams (Eds.), *Violence in American schools: A new perspective* (pp. 188–216). New York: Cambridge University Press.

Horner, R. H., & Sugai, G. (2000). School-wide behavior support: An emerging initiative. *Journal of Positive Behavior Interventions, 2*(4), 231–232.

Jolivette, K., Stichter, J. P., Nelson, C. M., Scott, T. M., & Liaupsin, C. J. (2000). *Improving post-school outcomes for students with emotional and behavioral disorders* (ERIC/OSEP Digest E597). Arlington, VA: ERIC Clearinghouse on Disabilities and Gifted Education. (ERIC Document Reproduction Service No. ED447616)

Kartub, D. T., Taylor-Greene, S., March, R. E., & Horner, R. H. (2000). Reducing hallway noise: A systems approach. *Journal of Positive Behavior Interventions, 2*(3), 179–182.

Lewis, T. J., Colvin, G., & Sugai, G. (2000). The effects of pre-correction and active supervision on the recess behavior of elementary students. *Education and Treatment of Children, 23*(2), 109–121.

Lewis, T. J., Powers, L. J., Kelk, M. J., & Newcomer, L. L. (2002). Reducing problem behaviors on the playground: An investigation of the application of schoolwide positive behavior supports. *Psychology in the Schools, 39* (2), 181–190.

Lewis, T. J., & Sugai, G. (1999). Effective behavior support: A systems approach to proactive school-wide management. *Focus on Exceptional Children, 31*(6), 1–17.

Lewis, T. J., Sugai, G., & Colvin, G. (1998). Reducing problem behavior through a school-wide system of effective behavioral support: Investigation of a school-wide social skills training program and contextual interventions. *School Psychology Review, 27* (3), 446–459.

Lewis-Palmer, T., Sugai, G., & Larson, S. (1999). Using data to guide decisions about program implementation and effectiveness: An overview and applied example. *Effective School Practices, 17* (4), 47–53.

Markey, U., Markey, D. J., Quant, B., Santelli, B., & Turnbull, A. (2002). Operation positive change: PBS in an urban context. *Journal of Positive Behavior Interventions, 4* (4), 218–230.

Nelson, J. R., & Martella, R. (1998). The effects of teaching school expectations and establishing a consistent consequence on formal office disciplinary actions. *Journal of Emotional and Behavioral Disorders, 6* (3), 153–161.

Nelson, J. R., Martella, R. M., & Marchand-Martella, N. (2002). Maximizing student learning: The effects of a comprehensive school-based program for preventing problem behaviors. *Journal of Emotional and Behavioral Disorders, 10* (3), 136–148.

Office of Special Education Programs (OSEP). (1998). *Students with Emotional Disturbance Module*, prepared by the Center for Effective Collaboration and Practice. Available online: http://cecp.air.org/resources/20th/intro.asp

OSEP Center on Positive Behavioral Interventions and Supports. (2000). Applying positive behavior support and functional behavioral assessment in schools. *Journal of Positive Behavior Interventions, 2*(3), 131–143.

Quinn, M. M., Osher, D., Hoffman, C. C., & Hanley, T. V. (1998). *Safe, drug-free, and effective schools for ALL students: What works!* Washington, DC: Center for Effective Collaboration and Practice, American Institutes for Research. Retrieved July 23, 2003, from: http://cecp.air.org/resources/safe&drug_free/main.htm

Schaps, E. (2003). Creating a school community. *Educational Leadership, 60* (6), 31–33.

Stephens, R. D. (1998). Safe school planning. In D. S. Elliott, B. Hamburg, & K. R. Williams (Eds.), *Violence in American schools: A new perspective* (pp. 253–289). New York: Cambridge University Press.

Sugai, G., & Horner, R. H. (2002). Introduction to the special series on positive behavior support in schools. *Journal of*

Emotional and Behavioral Disorders, 10(3), 130-135. Available online through Academic Search Premier, AN 7313579.

Sugai, G., Sprague, J. R., Horner, R. H., & Walker, H. M. (2000). Preventing school violence: The use of office discipline referrals to assess and monitor school-wide discipline interventions. *Journal of Emotional and Behavioral Disorders, 8*(2), 94-101. Available online through Academic Search Premier, AN 3183610.

Taylor-Greene, S. J., & Kartub, D. T. (2000). Durable implementation of school-wide behavior support: The high five program. *Journal of Positive Behavior Interventions, 2*(4), 233-235.

Townsend, B. (2003). Leave no teacher behind: A bold proposal for teacher education. *International Journal of Qualitative Studies in Education, 15*(6), 727-738.

Turnbull, H. R., Wilcox, B. L., Stowe, M., Raper, C., & Hedges, L. P. (2000). Public policy foundations for positive behavioral interventions, strategies, and supports. *Journal of Positive Behavior Interventions, 2*(4), 218-230.

Turnbull, H. R., Wilcox, B. L., Stowe, M., & Turnbull, A. P. (2001). IDEA requirements for use of PBS: Guidelines for responsible agencies. *Journal of Positive Behavior Interventions, 3*(1), 11-18.

Utley, C. A., Kozleski, E., Smith, A., & Draper, I. L. (2002). Positive behavior support: A proactive strategy for minimizing behavior problems in urban multicultural youth. *Journal of Positive Behavior Interventions, 4*(4), 196-207.

White, R., Algozzine, B., Audette, R., Marr, M. B., & Ellis, E. D., Jr. (2001). Unified discipline: A school-wide approach for managing problem behavior. *Intervention in School and Clinic, 37*(1), 3-8.

Wyne, M. D., & Stuck, G. B. (1982). Time and learning implication for the classroom teacher. *The Elementary School Journal, 83*(1), 67-75.

Chapter 5

Berliner, D. C. (1984). The half-full glass: A review of research on teaching. In P. L. Hosford (Ed.), *Using what we know about teaching* (pp. 7-31). Alexandria, VA: Association for Supervision and Curriculum Development.

Beyda, S. D., Zentall, S. S., & Ferko, D. J. K. (2002). The relationship between teacher practices and the task-appropriate and social behavior of students with behavioral disorders. *Behavioral Disorders, 27*(3), 236-255.

Bloom, R. B. (1979). *The psychoeducational approach to the teaching of emotionally disturbed children: An instructional manual to accompany the American University/Rose School teacher training videos.* Columbus, OH: Ohio State Department of Education.

Brophy, J. (1988). Research linking teacher behavior to student achievement: Potential implications for instruction of Chapter 1 students. *Educational Psychologist, 23*(3), 235-286.

Brophy, J. (1998). Classroom management as socializing students into clearly articulated roles. *Journal of Classroom Interaction, 33*(1), 1-4.

Brophy, J., & Good, T. L. (1986). Teacher behavior and student achievement. In M. C. Wittrock (Ed.), *Handbook of research on teaching* (pp. 328-375). New York: MacMillan.

Browning, L., Davis, B., & Resta, V. (2000). What do you mean "think before I act"? Conflict resolution with choices. *Journal of Research in Childhood Education, 14*(2), 232-238.

Carpenter, S. L., & McKee-Higgins, E. (1996). Behavior management in inclusive classrooms. *Remedial and Special Education, 17*(4), 195-203.

Chesapeake Institute. (1994, September). *National agenda for achieving better results for children and youth with serious emotional disturbance.* Washington, DC: Department of Education, Office of Special Education and Rehabilitative Services, Office of Special Education Programs. (ERIC Document Reproduction Service No. ED376690)

Choate, J. S. (2000). *Successful inclusive teaching: Proven ways to detect and correct special needs* (3rd ed.). Needham Heights, MA: Allyn and Bacon.

Christenson, S. L., Ysseldyke, J. E., & Thurlow, M. L. (1989). Critical instructional factors for students with mild handicaps: An integrative review. *Remedial and Special Education, 10*(5), 21-31.

Curwin, R., & Mendler, A. (1988). *Discipline with dignity.* Alexandria, VA: Association for Supervision and Curriculum Development.

D'Zamko, M. E., & Raiser, L. (1986). A strategy for individualizing directed group instruction. *Teaching Exceptional Children, 18*(3), 190-195.

Englert, C. S. (1984). Measuring teacher effectiveness from the teacher's point of view. *Focus on Exceptional Children, 17*(2), 1-16.

Evertson, C. M. (1986). Do teachers make a difference? Issues for the eighties. *Education and Urban Society, 18*(2), 195-210.

Freiberg, H. J. (1998). Measuring school climate: Let me count the ways. *Educational Leadership, 56*(1), 22-26.

Good, T. L. (1984). *Teacher Effects.* Columbia, MO: University of Missouri.

Gresham, F. M. (2002). Social skills assessment and instruction for students with emotional and behavioral disorders. In K. L. Lane, F. M. Gresham, & T. E. O'Shaughnessy (Eds.), *Interventions for children with or at risk for emotional and behavioral disorders* (pp. 242-258). Boston: Allyn & Bacon.

Gresham, F. M., Sugai, G., & Horner, R. H. (2001). Interpreting outcomes of social skills training for students with high-incidence disabilities. *Exceptional Children, 67*(3), 331-344.

Gunter, P. L., Coutinho, M. J., & Cade, T. (2002). Classroom factors linked with academic gains among students with emotional and behavioral problems. *Preventing School Failure, 46*(3), 126-132.

Hardman, E., & Smith, S. W. (1999). Promoting positive interactions in the classroom. *Intervention in School and Clinic, 34*(3), 178–180.

Hunter, M. (1994). *Mastery teaching.* Thousand Oaks, CA: Corwin Press.

Johns, B. H., Crowley, E. P., & Guetzloe, E. (2002). *Effective curriculum for students with emotional and behavioral disorders.* Denver, CO: Love Publishing Co.

Johnson, D. W., & Johnson, R. T. (1999). Making cooperative learning work. *Theory into Practice, 38*(2), 67–73.

Kavale, K. A., & Forness, S. R. (1996). Treating social skill deficits in children with learning disabilities: A meta-analysis of the research. *Learning Disabilities Quarterly, 19*(1), 2–13.

Kea, C. (1988). *Analysis of critical teaching behaviors employed by teachers of students with mild handicaps.* Unpublished doctoral dissertation, University of Kansas, Lawrence, KS.

Knitzer, J., Steinberg, Z., & Fleisch, B. (1990). *At the schoolhouse door: An examination of programs and policies for children with behavioral and emotional problems.* New York: Bank Street College of Education.

Leachman, G., & Victor, D. (2003). Student-led class meetings. *Educational Leadership, 60*(6), 64–68.

Lewis, T. J., & Sugai, G. (1999). Effective behavior support: A systems approach to proactive school-wide management. *Focus on Exceptional Children, 31*(6), 1–17.

Lotan, R. A. (2003). Group-worthy tasks. *Educational Leadership, 60*(6), 72–75.

Mayer, G. R., Mitchell, L. K., Clementi, T., Clement-Robertson, E., Myatt, R., & Bullara, D. T. (1993). A dropout prevention program for at-risk high school students: Emphasizing consulting to promote positive classroom climates. *Education and Treatment of Children, 16*(2), 135–146.

McCaslin, M., & Good, T. L. (1998). Moving beyond management as sheer compliance: Helping students to develop goal coordination strategies. *Educational Horizons, 76*(4), 169–176.

Nelsen, J., Lott, L., & Glenn, H. S. (2000). *Positive discipline in the classroom* (3rd ed.). Rocklin, CA: Prima Publishing.

Polloway, E. A., Cronin, M. E., & Patton, J. R. (1986). The efficacy of group versus one-to-one instruction: A review. *Remedial and Special Education, 7*(1), 22–30.

Potter, S., & Davis, B. H. (2003). A first-year teacher implements class meetings. *Kappa Delta Pi Record, 39*(2), 88–90.

Quinn, M. M., Kavale, K. A., Mathur, S. R., Rutherford, R. B., Jr., & Forness, S. R. (1999). A meta-analysis of social skill interventions for students with emotional and behavioral disorders. *Journal of Emotional and Behavioral Disorders, 7,* 54–64.

Schaps, E. (2003). Creating a school community. *Educational Leadership, 60*(6), 31–33.

Scott, T. M., & Nelson, C. M. (1998). Confusion and failure in facilitating generalized social responding in the school setting: Sometimes 2 + 2 = 5. *Behavioral Disorders, 23*(4), 264–275.

Shores, R. E., Gunter, P. L., & Jack, S. L. (1993). Classroom management strategies: Are they setting events for coercion? *Behavioral Disorders, 18,* 92–102.

Shores, R. E., & Wehby, J. H. (1999). Analyzing the classroom social behavior of students with EBD. *Journal of Emotional and Behavioral Disorders, 7*(4), 194–199.

Sindelar, P. T., Rosenberg, M. S., Wilson, R. J., & Bursuck, W. D. (1984). The effects of group size and instructional method on the acquisition of mathematical concepts by fourth grade students. *Journal of Educational Research, 77*(3), 178–183.

Slavin, R. (1992). Putting research to work: Cooperative learning. *Instructor, 102*(2), 46–47.

Smith, D. D., & Rivera, D. P. (1995). Discipline in special education and general education settings. *Focus on Exceptional Children, 27*(5), 1–14.

Stevens, B. (Ed.). (1985). *School effectiveness: Eight variables that make a difference.* Lansing, MI: Michigan State Board of Education.

Stevens, R. J., & Rosenshine, B. V. (1981). Advances in research on teaching. *Exceptional Education Quarterly, 2*(1), 1–9.

Sutherland, K. S., & Wehby, J. H. (2001). Exploring the relationship between increased opportunities to respond to academic requests and the academic and behavioral outcomes of students with EBD. *Remedial and Special Education, 22*(2), 113–121.

Sutherland, K. S., Wehby, J. H., & Gunter, P. L. (2000). The effectiveness of cooperative learning with students with emotional and behavioral disorders: A literature review. *Behavioral Disorders, 25*(3), 225–238.

Traynor, P. L. (2002). A scientific evaluation of five different strategies teachers use to maintain order. *Education, 122*(3), 493–510.

Wehby, J. H., Symons, F. J., Canale, J. A., & Go, F. J. (1998). Teaching practices in classrooms for students with emotional and behavioral disorders: Discrepancies between recommendations and observations. *Behavior Disorders, 24,* 51–56.

Wood, M. M., Long, N. J., & Fecser, F. (2001). *Life space crisis intervention: Talking with students in conflict* (2nd ed.). Austin, TX: Pro-Ed.

Chapter 6

Aiex, N. K. (1993). *Bibliotherapy* (Report No. EDO-CS-93-05). Bloomington, IN: ERIC Clearinghouse on Reading English and Communication. (ERIC Document Reproduction Service No. ED357333)

Anderson, S., Henke, J., McLaughlin, M., Ripp, M., & Tuffs, P. (2000). *Using background music to enhance memory and improve learning.* Unpublished master's action research project, Saint Xavier University/IRI Skylight.

Berman, D. S., & Davis-Berman, J. (2000). *Therapeutic uses of outdoor education* (Report No. EDO-RC-00-5). Charleston, WV: ERIC Clearinghouse on Rural Education and Small Schools. (ERIC Document Reproduction Service No. ED448011)

Brophy, J. (1996). *Working with shy or withdrawn students* (Report No. EDO-PS-96-14). Urbana, IL: ERIC Clearinghouse on Elementary and Early Childhood Education. (ERIC Document Reproduction Service No. ED402070)

Budge, D. (1998). Music rings mental bells. *Times Educational Supplement,* Issue 4288, 26.

Cade, T., & Gunter, P. L. (2002). Teaching students with severe emotional or behavioral disorders to use a musical mnemonic technique to solve basic division calculations. *Behavioral Disorders, 27*(3), 208-214.

Carlson, J. K., Hoffman, J., Gray, D., & Thompson, A. (2004). A musical interlude: Using music and relaxation to increase reading performance. *Intervention in School and Clinic, 39*(4), 246-250.

Chandler, C. (2001). *Animal-assisted therapy in counseling and school settings* (Report No. EDO-CG-01-05). Greensboro, NC: ERIC Clearinghouse on Counseling and Student Services. (ERIC Document Reproduction Service No. ED459404)

Chernoff, N. W., & Watson, B. H. (2000). *An investigation of Philadelphia's Youth Aid Panel: A community-based diversion program for first-time youthful offenders.* Philadelphia: Public/Private Ventures.

Cobine, G. R. (1995). *Effective use of student journal writing* (Report No. EDO-CS-95-02). Bloomington, IN: ERIC Clearinghouse on Reading English and Communication. (ERIC Document Reproduction Service No. ED378587)

Downing, J. A. (2002). Individualized behavior contracts. *Intervention in School and Clinic, 37*(3), 168-172.

Downing, J. A., & Smith, A. H. (1999). *Counselor cadre training curriculum: Updating your clinical and consultative skills.* Unpublished manuscript.

Dunn-Snow, P., & D'Amelio, G. (2000). How art teachers can enhance artmaking as a therapeutic experience: Art therapy and art education. *Art Education, 53*(3), 46-53.

Fliegel, L. S. (2000). An unfound door: Reconceptualizing art therapy as a community-linked treatment. *American Journal of Art Therapy, 38*(3), 81-89.

Forgan, J. W. (2002). Using bibliotherapy to teach problem solving. *Intervention in School and Clinic, 38*(2), 75-82.

Gladding, S. T. (1992). *The expressive arts in counseling* (Report No. EDO-CG-92-3). Ann Arbor, MI: ERIC Clearinghouse on Counseling and Personnel Services. (ERIC Document Reproduction Service No. ED350528)

Gladding, S. T. (1994). *Effective group counseling* (Report No. EDO-CG-94-02). Greensboro, NC: ERIC Clearinghouse on Counseling and Student Services. (ERIC Document Reproduction Service No. ED366856)

Gossen, D. C. (1992). *Restitution: Restructuring school discipline.* Chapel Hill, PA: New View Publications.

Gossen, D. C. (1998). Restitution: Restructuring school discipline. *Educational Horizons, 76*(4), 182-188.

Gossen, D. C. (2004). *It's all about we: Rethinking discipline using restitution.* Saskatoon, SW: Chelsom Consultants Ltd.

Gunter, P. L., & Coutinho, M. J. (1997). Negative reinforcement in classrooms: What we're beginning to learn. *Teacher Education and Special Education, 20*(3), 249-264.

Gunter, P. L., & Shores, R. E. (1994). A case study of the effects of altering instructional interactions on the disruptive behavior of a child identified with severe behavior disorders. *Education and Treatment of Children, 17*(4), 435-444.

Gunter, P. L., & Shores, R. E. (1995). On the move: Using teacher/student proximity to improve students' behavior. *Teaching Exceptional Children, 28*(1), 12-14.

Harding, J. W., Wacker, D. P., Barretto, A., & Rankin, B. (2002). Assessment and treatment of severe behavior problems using choice-making procedures. *Education and Treatment of Children, 25*(1), 26-46.

Hardman, E., & Smith, S. W. (1999). Promoting positive interactions in the classroom. *Intervention in School and Clinic, 34*(3), 178-180.

Henley, D. R. (1999). Facilitating socialization within a therapeutic camp setting for children with attention deficits utilizing the expressive therapies. *American Journal of Art Therapy, 38*(2), 40-50.

Hippie, T. W., Comer, M., & Boren, D. (1997). Twenty recent novels (and more) about adolescents for bibliotherapy. *Professional School Counseling, 1*, 65-67.

Hoffman, J. (1995). *Rhythmic medicine: Music with a purpose.* Leawood, KS: Jamillan Press.

In Sync. (2001). *Current Science, 87*(7), 1.

Jackson, J. T., & Owens, J. L. (1999). A stress management classroom tool for teachers of children with BD. *Intervention in School and Clinic, 35*(2), 74-78.

Jenkinson, E. (1994). *Writing assignments, journals, and student privacy* (Report No. EDO-CS-94-01). Bloomington, IN: ERIC Clearinghouse on Reading English and Communication. (ERIC Document Reproduction Service No. ED365989)

Kauffman, J. M., Mostert, M. P., Trent, S. C., & Hallahan, D. P. (2002). *Managing classroom behavior: A reflective case-based approach.* Boston: Allyn & Bacon.

Kazdin, A. E. (2001). *Behavior modification in applied settings* (6th ed.). Belmont, CA: Wadsworth.

Kerka, S. (1996). *Journal writing and adult learning* (Report No. EDO-CE-96-174). Columbus, OH: ERIC Clearinghouse on Adult Career and Vocational Education. (ERIC Document Reproduction Service No. ED399413)

Kern, L., Choutka, C. M., & Sokol, N. G. (2002). Assessment-based antecedent interventions used in natural settings to reduce challenging behavior: An analysis of the literature. *Education and Treatment of Children, 25*(1), 113-130.

Kerr, M. M., & Nelson, C. M. (2002). *Strategies for addressing behavior problems in the classroom* (4th ed.). Upper Saddle River, NJ: Merrill/Prentice Hall.

Kramer, P. A. (1999). Using literature to enhance inclusion. *Contemporary Education, 70*(2), 34-37.

Kramer, P. A., & Smith, G. G. (1998). Easing the pain of divorce through children's literature. *Early Childhood Education Journal, 26*(2), 89-94.

Kwekkeboom, K. L. (2003). Music versus distraction for procedural pain and anxiety in patients with cancer. *Oncology Nursing Forum, 30*(3), 433-440.

Landreth, G., & Bratton, S. (1999). *Play therapy* (Report No. EDO-CG-99-1). Greensboro, NC: ERIC Clearinghouse on Counseling and Student Services. (ERIC Document Reproduction Service No. ED430172)

Lou, M. F. (2001). The use of music to decrease agitated behaviour of the demented elderly: The state of the science. *Scandinavian Journal of Caring Sciences, 15*(2), 165.

McCaslin, M., & Good, T. L. (1998). Moving beyond management as sheer compliance: Helping students to develop goal coordination strategies. *Educational Horizons, 76*(4), 169–176.

McComas, J. J., Goddard, C., & Hoch, H. (2002). The effects of preferred activities during academic work breaks on task engagement and negatively reinforced destructive behavior. *Education and Treatment of Children, 25*(1), 103–112.

McDaniel, C. (2001). Children's literature as prevention of child sexual abuse. *Children's Literature in Education, 32*(3), 203–224.

McQuillan, K., & DuPaul, G. J. (1996). Classroom performance of students with serious emotional disturbance: A comparative study of evaluation methods for behavior management. *Journal of Emotional and Behavioral Disorders, 4*(3), 162–170.

Mills, B. C. (1996). Effects of music on assertive behavior during exercise by middle-school-age students. *Perceptual & Motor Skills, 83*(2), 423–426.

Myles, B. S., Moran, M. R., Ormsbee, C. K., & Downing, J. A. (1992). Guidelines for establishing and maintaining token economies. *Intervention in School and Clinic, 27*(3), 164–169.

Myles, B. S., Ormsbee, C. K., Downing, J. A., Walker, B. L., & Hudson, F. G. (1992). Guidelines for selecting literature for and about students with learning differences. *Intervention in School and Clinic, 27*(4), 215–220.

National Consortium on Alternatives for Youth at Risk. (1994). PayBack I-77. (Report No. CG-024-149). Sarasota, FL. Available through ERIC Document Reproduction Service No. ED387713.

Nessel, P. A. (1998). *Teen court: A national movement.* Technical Assistance Bulletin #17. Chicago: American Bar Association, Division for Public Education.

Nessel, P. A. (1999). *Teen courts and law-related education* (Report No. EDO-SO-99-2). Bloomington, IN: ERIC Clearinghouse for Social Studies/Social Science Education. (ERIC Document Reproduction Service No. ED429031)

Orr, T. J., Myles, B. S., & Carlson, J. K. (1998). The impact of rhythmic entrainment on a person with autism. *Focus on Autism & Other Developmental Disabilities, 13*(3), 163–166.

Outward Bound. http://www.outwardbound.com

Quinn, M. M., Osher, D., Warger, C., Hanley, T., Bader, B. D., Tate, R. et al. (2000). *Educational strategies for children with emotional and behavioral problems.* Washington, DC: American Institutes for Research, Center for Effective Collaboration and Practice.

Shores, R. E., Gunter, P. L., & Jack, S. L. (1993). Classroom management strategies: Are they setting events for coercion? *Behavioral Disorders, 18*, 92–102.

Smith, F. (2001). Just a matter of time. *Phi Delta Kappan, 82*(8), 572–576.

Sridhar, D., & Vaughn, S. (2000). Bibliotherapy for all. *Teaching Exceptional Children, 33*(2), 74–82.

Staton, J. (1987). *Dialogue journals.* Urbana, IL: ERIC Clearinghouse on Reading and Communication Skills. (ERIC Document Reproduction Service No. ED284276)

Stringer, S. J., Reynolds, G. P., & Simpson, F. M. (2003). Collaboration between classroom teachers and a school counselor through literature circles: Building self-esteem. *Journal of Instructional Psychology, 30*(1), 69–76.

Stroud, J. E., Stroud, J. C., & Staley, L. M. (1999). *Adopted children in the early childhood classroom* (Report No. EDO-PS-99-2). Champaign, IL: ERIC Clearinghouse on Elementary and Early Childhood Education (ERIC Document Reproduction Service No. ED426819)

Sullivan, A. K., & Strang, H. R. (2002). Bibliotherapy in the classroom; using literature to promote the development of emotional intelligence. *Childhood Education, 79*(2), 74–80.

Ullman, E. (2001). Art therapy: Problems of definition. *American Journal of Art Therapy, 40*(1), 16–26. Reprinted from the *Bulletin of Art Therapy*, 1961.

Wade, R. K. (1997). Lifting a school's spirit. *Educational Leadership, 54*(8), 34–36.

Walker, J. E., Shea, T. M., & Bauer, A. M. (2004). *Behavior management: A practical approach for educators* (8th ed.). Upper Saddle River, NJ: Merrill/Prentice Hall.

Wilcox, E. (2000). Music, brain research, and better behavior. *Education Digest, 65*(6), 10–15.

Wise, K. (2001). Structured athletics for challenged children. *The Exceptional Parent, 31*(5), 20–24.

Wolverton, L. (1988). *Classroom strategies for teaching migrant children about child abuse.* Las Cruces, NM: ERIC Clearinghouse on Rural Education and Small Schools. (ERIC Document Reproduction Service No. ED293681)

Yazzie, R. (2000). Navajo justice. *Winds of Change, 15*(4), 84–90.

Chapter 7

American Psychiatric Association. (2000). *Diagnostic and statistical manual of mental disorders* (4th ed., text revision). Washington, DC: Author.

Barabasz, A., & Barabasz, M. (2000). Treating AD/HD with hypnosis and neurotherapy [1]. *Child Study Journal, 30*(1), 25–42.

Barkley, R. A. (1990). *Attention-deficit hyperactivity disorder: A handbook for diagnosis and treatment.* New York: Guilford.

Barkley, R. A. (1991). *Attention-deficit hyperactivity disorder: A clinical workbook.* New York: Guilford.

Barkley, R. A. (1995). Is there an attention deficit in ADHD? *The ADHD Report, 3*(4), 1–4.

Barkley, R. A. (1998). How should attention deficit disorder be described? *Harvard Mental Health Letter, 14*(8), 8.

Bauermeister, J. J., Matos, M., Reina, G., Salas, C. C., Martinez, J. V., Cumba, E., et al. (2005). Comparison of the DSM-IV combined and inattentive types of ADHD in a school-based sample of Latino/Hispanic children. *Journal of Child Psychology and Psychiatry and Allied Disciplines, 46*(2), 166–179.

Bussing, R., Schuhmann, E., Belin, T. R., Widawski, M., & Perwien, A. R. (1998). Diagnostic utility of two commonly used ADHD screening measures among special education students. *Journal of the American Academy of Child and Adolescent Psychiatry, 37*(1), 74–82.

Bussing, R., Zima, B. T., & Belin, T. R. (1998). Variations in ADHD treatment among special education students. *Journal of the American Academy of Child and Adolescent Psychiatry, 37*(9), 968–976.

Center for Mental Health in Schools at UCLA. (1999). *Attention problems: Interventions and resources.* Los Angeles, CA: Author.

Children and Adults with Attention Deficit/Hyperactivity Disorder (CHADD). (2000). AD/HD and co-existing disorders. Accessed February 18, 2002, from: www.chadd.org/fs/fs5.htm.

Downing, J. A., & Smith, A. H. (1999). *Counselor cadre training curriculum: Updating your clinical and consultative skills.* Unpublished manuscript.

DuPaul, G. J., Eckert, T. L., & McGoey, K. E. (1997). Interventions for students with attention-deficit/hyperactivity disorder: One size does not fit all. *School Psychology Review, 26*(3), 369–381.

Fachin, K. (1996). Teaching Tommy: A second-grader with attention deficit hyperactivity disorder. *Phi Delta Kappan, 78*, 437–441.

Faraone, S. V. (2000). Genetics of childhood disorders: XX, ADHD Part 4: Is ADHD genetically heterogeneous? *Journal of the American Academy of Child and Adolescent Psychiatry, 39*(11), 1455–1457.

Faraone, S. V., Biederman, J., & Monteaux, M. (2000). Toward guidelines for pedigree selection in genetic studies of attention deficit hyperactivity disorder. *Genetic Epidemiology, 18*(1), 1–16.

Forness, S. R., & Kavale, K. A. (2001). ADHD and a return to the medical model of special education. *Education and Treatment of Children, 24*(3), 224–247.

Goldstein, A. P., Sprafkin, R. P., Gershaw, N. J., & Klein, P. (1980). *Skillstreaming the adolescent: A structured learning approach to teaching prosocial skills.* Champaign, IL: Research Press.

Gureasko-Moore, D. P., DuPaul, G. J., & Power, T. J. (2005). Stimulant treatment for attention-deficit/hyperactivity disorder: Medication monitoring practices of school psychologists. *School Psychology Review, 34*(2), 232–245.

Hallowell, E. M., & Ratey, J. J. (1995). *Driven to distraction: Recognizing and coping with attention deficit disorder from childhood through adulthood.* New York: Pantheon Books.

Hoagwood, K., Kelleher, K. J., Feil, M., & Comer, D. M. (2000). Treatment services for children with ADHD: A national perspective. *Journal of the American Academy of Child and Adolescent Psychiatry, 39*(2), 198–206.

LeFever, G. B., Villers, M. S., Morrow, A. L., & Vaughn, E. S. III. (2002). Parental perceptions of adverse educational outcomes among children diagnosed and treated for ADHD: A call for improved school/provider collaboration. *Psychology in the Schools, 39*(1), 63–71.

Mental health: A report of the surgeon general. (1999). Accessed December 21, 2005, from: http://www.surgeongeneral.gov/library/mentalhealth/home.html

National Institutes of Health. (2003). *Attention Deficit Hyperactivity Disorder.* NIH Publication 3572. Accessed January 14, 2006, from http://www.nimh.nih.gov/publicat/adhd.cfm

National Institutes of Health. (1998). *Diagnosis and treatment of attention deficit hyperactivity disorder (ADHD), NIH Consensus Statement.* Bethesda, MD: Author.

Pelham, W. E., Jr., Wheeler, T., & Chronis, A. (1998). Empirically supported psychosocial treatments for attention deficit hyperactivity disorder. *Journal of Clinical Child Psychology, 27*, 190–205.

Posavac, H. D., Sheridan, S. M., & Posavac, S. S. (1999). A cueing procedure to control impulsivity in children with attention deficit hyperactivity disorder. *Behavior Modification, 23*(2), 234–253.

Reid, R., Riccio, C. A., Kessler, R. H., DuPaul, G. J., Power, T. J., Anastopoulos, A. D., et al. (2000). Gender and ethnic differences in ADHD as assessed by behavior ratings. *Journal of Emotional and Behavioral Disorders, 8*(1), 38–48.

A review: The search for a genetic basis for ADHD simplified. (2000). *The Brown University Child and Adolescent Behavior Letter, 17*(5), 1–3.

Rief, S. F. (1993). *How to reach and teach ADD/ADHD children.* West Nyack, NY: Center for Applied Research in Education.

Robin, A. L. (1992). CHADD 4th annual conference transcript, pp. 84–93. Chicago, IL: October 15–17, 1992.

Roosa, J. (1995). Cited in Myles, B. S., & Adreon, D. (2001). *Asperger syndrome and adolescence: Practical solutions for school success.* Shawnee Mission, KS: Autism Asperger Publishing Company.

Ross, E. C. (2001). *Where we stand: Access to medication as a component of multi-modal treatment.* CHADD Public Policy Brief. Accessed January 15, 2006, from http://www.chadd.org/pdfs/access_to_medication.pdf

Sciutto, M. J., Nolfi, C. J., & Bluhm, C. (2004). Effects of child gender and symptom type on referrals for ADHD by elementary school teachers. *Journal of Emotional and Behavioral Disorders, 12*(4), 247–253.

Smith, A. L. (2000). School psychologists and attention-deficit/hyperactivity disorder: A survey of training, knowledge, practice, and attitude. *Dissertation Abstracts International Section A: Humanities and Social Sciences, 60*(11-A), 3906.

Sterman, M. B. (2000). EEG markers for attention deficit disorder: Pharmacological and neurofeedback applications. *Child Study Journal, 30*(1), 1–23.

Thompson, A. M. (1996). Attention deficit hyperactivity disorder: A parent's perspective. *Phi Delta Kappan, 77,* 433–436.

Trollor, J. N. (1999). Attention-deficit hyperactivity disorder in adults: Conceptual and clinical issues. *Medical Journal of Australia, 171,* 421–425.

Trout, A. L., Reid, R., & Schartz, M. (2002, February). *Self-regulation and ADHD.* Poster presentation at Symposium for Leadership in Behavior Disorders, Kansas City, MO.

University of Kansas Center for Research on Learning. (2004). *Strategic Instruction Model Products.* Accessed January 14, 2005, from http://www.ku-crl.org/products/index.html

Webb, J., & Latimer, D. (1993). *ADHD and children who are gifted.* (Report No. EDO-EC-93-5). Reston, VA: ERIC Clearinghouse on Disabilities and Gifted Education. (ERIC Document Reproduction Service No. ED358673)

Wechsler, D. (1991). *Wechsler intelligence scale for children* (3rd ed.). San Antonio, TX: Psychological Corp.

Yell, M. L., Busch, T., & Drasgow, E. (2005). Cognitive behavior modification. In T. J. Zirpoli. (Ed.), *Behavior management: Applications for teachers* (4th ed.) (pp. 227–266). Upper Saddle River, NJ: Prentice Hall.

Young, K. R., West, R. P., Smith, D. J., & Morgan, D. P. (1991). *Teaching self-management strategies to adolescents.* Longmont, CA: Sopris West.

Chapter 8

Abikoff, H., & Klein, R. G. (1992). Attention-deficit hyperactivity and conduct disorder: Comorbidity and implications for treatment. *Journal of Consulting and Clinical Psychology, 60*(6), 881–892.

Adams, M. (n.d.) *Solutions to oppositional defiant disorder.* Retrieved June 12, 2003, from http://www.guidance-facilitators.com/odd2.html

American Medical Association (AMA). (2002). *Bullying behavior among children and adolescents: Report 1 of the Council on Scientific Affairs.* Retrieved January 21, 2004, from http://www.ama-assn.org/ama/pub/article/2036-6398.html

American Psychiatric Association (APA). (2000). *Diagnostic and statistical manual of mental disorders* (4th ed., text revision). Washington, DC: Author.

Atkins, M. S., McKay, M. M., Talbot, E., & Arvanitis, P. (1996). DSM-IV diagnosis of conduct disorder and oppositional defiant disorder: Implications and guidelines for school mental health teams. *The School Psychology Review, 25*(3), 274–283.

Bahl, A. B., Spaulding, S. A., & McNeil, C. B. (1999). Treatment of noncompliance using Parent Child Interaction Therapy: A data-driven approach. *Education and Treatment of Children, 22*(2), 146–156.

Brendtro, L., & Long, N. (1995). Breaking the cycle of conflict. *Educational Leadership, 52*(5), 52–56.

Brook, J. S., Whiteman, M. M., & Finch, S. (1992). Childhood aggression, adolescent delinquency, and drug use: A longitudinal study. *Journal of Genetic Psychology, 153*(4), 369–384.

Burke, J. D., Loeber, R., & Birmaher, B. (2002). Oppositional defiant disorder and conduct disorder: A review of the past 10 years, part II. *Journal of the American Academy of Child and Adolescent Psychiatry. 41*(11), 1275–1293.

Campbell, M., Adams, P. B., Small, A. M., Kafantaris, V., Silva, R. R., Shell, J., et al. (1995). Lithium in hospitalized aggressive children with conduct disorder: A double-blind and placebo-controlled study. *Journal of the American Academy of Child and Adolescent Psychiatry, 34*(4), 445–453.

Center, D., & Kemp, D. (2003). Temperament and personality as potential factors in the development and treatment of conduct disorders. *Education and Treatment of Children, 26*(1), 75–88.

Centre for Community Child Health & Ambulatory Paediatrics, Royal Children's Hospital, Melbourne, for the Victorian Government Department of Human Services. (n.d.) Conduct Disorder and associated challenging behaviours in children: Fact sheet for health professionals. Retrieved January 4, 2006, from http://www.nevdgp.org.au/info/std_misc/Conduct_Disorder_children.htm

Clark, C., Prior, M., & Kinsella, G. J. (2000). Do executive function deficits differentiate between adolescents with ADHD and Oppositional Defiant/Conduct Disorder? A neuropsychological study using the Six Elements Test and Hayling Sentence Completion Test. *Journal of Abnormal Child Psychology. 28*(5), 403–414.

Collett, B. R., Ohan, J. L., & Myers, K. M. (2003). Ten-year review of rating scales. VI: Scales assessing externalizing behaviors. *Journal of the American Academy of Child and Adolescent Psychiatry, 42*(10), 1143–1170.

Coy, K., Speltz, M. L., DeKlyen, M., & Jones, K. (2001). Social-cognitive processes in preschool boys with and without Oppositional Defiant Disorder. *Journal of Abnormal Child Psychology, 29*(2), 107–119.

Elliott, D. S., Hamburg, B. A., & Williams, K. R. (Eds.). (1998). *Violence in American schools.* Cambridge, UK: Cambridge University Press.

Eyberg, S. M., & Robinson, E. A. (1983). Dyadic parent-child interaction coding system: A manual. Psychological Documents, 13, Ms. No. 2582. San Rafael, CA: Social and Behavior Sciences Documents, Select Press.

Fay, J. (n.d.) *Parenting with Love and Logic.* Available from www.loveandlogic.com

Filcheck, H. A., McNeil, C. B., & Herschell, A. D. (2001). Types of verbal feedback that affect compliance and general behavior in disruptive and typical children. *Child Study Journal, 31*(4), 225–248.

Gresham, F. M., Lane, K. L., & Lambros, K. M. (2000). Comorbidity of conduct problems and ADHD: Identification of "fledgling psychopaths." *Journal of Emotional and Behavioral Disorders, 8*(2), 83–93.

Guetzloe, E. (1992). Violent, aggressive, and antisocial students: What are we going to do with them? *Preventing School Failure. 36*(3), 4–9.

Guetzloe, E. (1997). The power of positive relationships: Mentoring programs in the school and community. *Preventing School Failure. 41*(3), 100-104.

Guetzloe, E. (1999). Violence in children and adolescents—A threat to public health and safety: A paradigm of prevention. *Preventing School Failure, 44*(1), 21-24.

Guetzloe, E., & Rockwell, S. (1998). Fight, flight, or better choices: Teaching nonviolent responses to young children. *Preventing School Failure. 42*(4), 154-159.

Hall, N., Williams, J., & Hall, P. (2000). Fresh approaches with oppositional students. *Reclaiming Children and Youth, 8*(4), 219-226.

Hamburg, M.A. (1998). Youth violence is a public health concern. In D. S. Elliott, B.A. Hamburg, & K. R. Williams (Eds.), *Violence in American schools* (pp. 31-54). Cambridge, UK: Cambridge University Press.

Heinrich, R. R. (2003). A whole-school approach to bullying: Special considerations for children with exceptionalities. *Intervention in School and Clinic, 38*(4), 195-205.

Hewitt, M.B. (1999). The control game: Exploring oppositional behavior. *Reclaiming Children and Youth, 8*(1), 30-33.

Hoff, K. E., & DuPaul, G. J. (1998). Reducing disruptive behavior in general education classrooms: The use of self-management strategies. *The School Psychology Review, 27*(2), 290-303.

Huizinga, D., Loeber, R., Thornberry, T. P., & Cothern, L. (2000). Co-occurrence of delinquency and other problem behaviors. *Juvenile Justice Bulletin, U.S. Department of Justice Office of Justice Programs, Office of Juvenile Justice and Delinquency Prevention.* From http://www.eric.ed.gov/ERICDocs/data/ericdocs2/content_storage_01/000000b/80/24/91/b8.pdf

Jensen, P. S., Hinshaw, S. P., Kraemer, H. C., Lenora, N., Newcorn, J. H., Abikoff, H. B., et al. (2001). ADHD comorbidity findings from the MTA Study: Comparing comorbid subgroups. *Journal of the American Academy of Child and Adolescent Psychiatry, 40*(2), 147-158.

Kafantaris, V., Campbell, M., Padron-Gayol, M. V., Small, A. M., Locascio, J. J., & Rosenberg, C. R. (1992). Carbamazepine in hospitalized aggressive conduct disorder children: An open pilot study. *Psychopharmacology Bulletin, 28*, 193-199.

Kann, R., & Hanna, F. (2000). Disruptive behavior disorders in children and adolescents: How do girls differ from boys? *Journal of Counseling and Development, 78*(3), 267-274.

Kazdin, A. E. (Ed.). (1985). *Treatment of antisocial behavior in children and adolescents.* Homewood, IL: Dorsey Press.

Kazdin, A. E., & Wassell, G. (2000). Therapeutic changes in children, parents, and families resulting from treatment of children with conduct problems. *Journal of the American Academy of Child and Adolescent Psychiatry. 39*(4), 414-420.

Kempf, J. P., DeVane, C. L., Levin, G. M., Jarecke, R., & Miller, R. L. (1993). Treatment of aggressive children with clonidine: Results of an open pilot study. *Journal of the American Academy of Child and Adolescent Psychiatry, 32*, 577-581.

Kern, L., Choutka, C. M., & Sokol, N. G. (2002). Assessment-based antecedent interventions used in natural settings to reduce challenging behavior: An analysis of the literature. *Education and Treatment of Children, 25*(1) 113-130.

Klein, R. G., Abikoff, H., Klass, E., Ganeles, D., Seese, L. M., & Pollack, S. (1997). Clinical efficacy of methylphenidate in conduct disorder with and without attention deficit hyperactivity disorder. *Archives of General Psychiatry, 54*, 1073-1080.

Kumpfer, K. L. (1996). *Strengthening America's families: Promising parenting strategies for delinquency prevention user's guide.* Rockville, MD: U. S. Department of Justice, Office of Juvenile Justice and Delinquency Prevention.

Lahey, B., Loeber, R., Quay, H. C., Applegate, B., Shaffer, D., Waldman, I., et al. (1998). Validity of DSM-IV subtypes of conduct disorder based on age of onset. *Journal of the American Academy of Child and Adolescent Psychiatry. 37*(4), 435-452.

Lavigne, J.V., Cicchetti, C., Gibbons, R. D., Binns, H. J., Larsen, L., & Devito, C. (2001). Oppositional defiant disorder with onset in preschool years: Longitudinal stability and pathways to other disorders. *Journal of the American Academy of Child and Adolescent Psychiatry, 40*(2), 1393-1400.

Loeber, R., Burke, J. D., Lahey, B. B., Winters, A., & Zera, M. (2000). Oppositional defiant and conduct disorder: A review of the past 10 years, part I. *Journal of the American Academy of Child and Adolescent Psychiatry, 39*(12), 1468-1484.

Loeber, R., Green, S. M., Lahey, B. B., & Kalb, L. (2000). Physical fighting in childhood as a risk factor for later mental health problems. *Journal of the American Academy of Child and Adolescent Psychiatry, 39*(4), 421-428.

Loeber, R., & Stouthamer-Loeber, M. (1998). Juvenile aggression at home and at school. In D. S. Elliott, B.A. Hamburg, & K. R. Williams (Eds.), *Violence in American schools* (pp. 31-54). Cambridge, UK: Cambridge University Press.

Lowry, R., Sleet, D., Duncan, C., Powell, K., & Kolbe, L. (1995). Adolescents at risk for violence. *Educational Psychology Review, 7*, 7-39.

Maag, J. W. (2000). Managing resistance. *Intervention in School and Clinic, 35*(3), 131-140.

Marks, D. J., McKay, K. E., Himelstein, J., Walter, K. J., Newcon, J. H., & Halperin, J. M. (2000). Predictors of physical aggression in children with attention-deficit/hyperactivity disorder. *CNS Spectrums, 5*(6), 52-57.

Marwick, C. (1992). Guns, drugs threaten to raise public health problem of violence to epidemic. *Journal of the American Medical Association, 267*(22), 2993.

McCabe, K. M., Hough, R., Wood, P.A., & Yeh, M. (2001). Childhood and adolescent onset conduct disorder: A test of the developmental taxonomy. *Journal of Abnormal Child Psychology, 29*(4), 305-316.

Mental health: A report of the Surgeon General. (1999). U.S. Department of Health. Accessed December 31, 2005, from: http://www.surgeongeneral.gov/library/mentalhealth/home.html

Mishna, F. (2003). Learning disabilities and bullying: Double jeopardy. *Journal of Learning Disabilities, 36*(4), 336–347.

Mooney, P., Epstein, M. H., Reid, R., & Nelson, J. R. (2003). Status of and trends in academic intervention research for students with emotional disturbance. *Remedial & Special Education, 24*(5), 273–287.

Moore, L. A., Hughes, J. N., & Robinson, M. (1992). A comparison of the social information-processing abilities of rejected and hyperactive children. *Journal of Clinical Psychology, 21*(2), 123–131.

Moss, H. B., Baron, D. A., Hardie, T. L., & Vanyukov, M. M. (2001). Preadolescent children of substance-dependent fathers with Antisocial Personality Disorder: Psychiatric disorders and problem behaviors. *American Journal on Addictions, 10*(3), 269–278.

Nansel, T. (2003). Bullies found to be at risk for violent behavior. *Inside School Safety, 8*(2), 1–4.

National Advisory Mental Health Council Workgroup on Child and Adolescent Mental Health Intervention Development and Deployment. (2001). *Blueprint for change: Research on child and adolescent mental health.* Washington, DC: http://www.nimh.nih.gov/publicat/nimhblueprint.pdf

Olweus, D. (1993). *Bullying at school: What we know and what we can do.* Oxford, UK: Blackwell Publishing Ltd.

Olweus, D. (2001). Peer harassment: A critical analysis and some important issues. In J. Juvonen & S. Graham (Eds.), *Peer harassment in school: The plight of the vulnerable and victimized* (pp. 3–20). New York: Guilford Press.

Olweus, D., Limber, S., & Mihalic, S. F. (1999). *Blueprints for violence prevention, book nine: Bullying prevention program.* Boulder, CO: Center for the Study and Prevention of Violence.

Quinn, K. B., Barone, B., Kearns, J., Stackhouse, S. A., & Zimmerman, M. E. (2003). Using a novel unit to help understand and prevent bullying in schools. *Journal of Adolescent & Adult Literacy, 47*(7), 582–591.

Quinn, M. M., Osher, D., Warger, C., Hanley, T., Bader, B. D., Tate, R., et al. (2000). *Educational strategies for children with emotional and behavioral problems.* Washington, DC: American Institutes for Research, Center for Effective Collaboration and Practice.

Reid, R., Casat, C. D., Norton, J., Anastopoulos, A. D., & Temple, E. P. (2001). Using behavior rating scales for ADHD across ethnic groups: The IOWA Conners. *Journal of Emotional and Behavioral Disorder, 9*(4), 210–218.

Rifkin, A., Dicker, R., Karajgi, B., Perl, E., Boppana, V., Hasan, N., et al. (1997). Lithium treatment of conduct disorders in adolescents. *American Journal of Psychiatry, 154*(4), 554–555.

Shaffer, D., Fisher, P., Dulcan, M. K., Davies, M., Piacentini, J., Schwab-Stone, M. E., et al. (1996). The NIMH Diagnostic Interview Schedule for Children version 2.3 (DISC-2.3): Description, acceptability, prevalence rates, and performance in the MECA Study. *Journal of the American Academy of Child and Adolescent Psychiatry, 35*(7), 865–877.

Simmel, C., Brooks, D., Barth, R. P., & Hinshaw, S. P. (2001). Externalizing symptomatology among adoptive youth: Prevalence and preadoption risk factors. *Journal of Abnormal Child Psychology, 29*(1), 57–69.

Sprague, J., & Walker, H. (2000). Early identification and intervention for youth with antisocial and violent behavior. *Exceptional Children, 66*(3), 367–379.

Stahl, N. D., & Clarizio, H. F. (1999). Conduct disorder and comorbidity. *Psychology in the Schools, 36*(1), 41–50.

Strain, P. S., & Timm, M. A. (2001). Remediation and prevention of aggression: An evaluation of the Regional Intervention Program over a quarter century. *Behavioral Disorders, 26*(4), 297–313.

Van Acker, R., & Wehby, J. H. (2000). Exploring the social contexts influencing student success or failure: Introduction. *Preventing School Failure, 44*(3), 93–97.

van der Wal, M. F., de Wit, C. A. M., & Hirasing, R. A. (2003). Psychosocial health among young victims and offenders of direct and indirect bullying. *Pediatrics, 111*(6), 1312–1317.

Walker, H. M., & Golly, A. (1999). Developing behavioral alternatives for antisocial children at the point of school entry. *Clearing House, 73*(2), 104–106.

Walker, H. M., & Severson, H. (1990). *Systematic screening for behavior disorders (SSBD).* Longmont, CO: Sopris West.

Walker, H. M., & Sylwester, R. (1998). Reducing students' refusal and resistance. *Teaching Exceptional Children, 30*(6), 52–58.

Webster-Stratton, C. (1996). Early-onset conduct problems: Does gender make a difference? *Journal of Consulting and Clinical Psychology, 64*(3), 540–551.

Werry, J., & Quay, H. (1971). The prevalence of behavior symptoms in younger elementary school children. *American Journal of Orthopsychiatry, 4*(1), 136–143.

Woolsey-Terrazas, W., & Chavez, J. A. (2002). Strategies to work with students with oppositional defiant disorder. *CEC Today, 12.*

Chapter 9

Alberto, P. A., & Troutman, A. C. (2003). *Applied behavior analysis for teachers* (6th ed.). Upper Saddle River, NJ: Prentice Hall.

American Psychiatric Association (APA). (2000). *Diagnostic and statistical manual of mental disorders* (4th ed., text revision). Washington, DC: Author.

Attwood, T. (1998). *Asperger's syndrome: A guide for parents and professionals.* London: Jessica Kingsley Publishers.

Autism Society of America. (n.d.). *Asperger syndrome.* Retrieved January 12, 2005, from: http://www.autism-society.org/site/PageServer?pagename-Aspergers

Bambara, L. M., & Koger, F. (1996). *Opportunities for daily choice making.* Washington, DC: American Association on Mental Retardation.

Barnhill, G. P. (2000). *Attributional style and depression in adolescents with Asperger's syndrome.* Doctoral dissertation, University of Kansas.

Barnhill, G., Hagiwara, T., Myles, B. S., & Simpson, R. L. (2000). Asperger syndrome: A study of the academic profiles of 37 children and adolescents. *Focus on Autism and Other Developmental Disabilities, 15*(3), 146-153.

Baron-Cohen, S., Leslie, A., & Frith, U. (1985). Does the autistic child have a theory of mind? *Cognition, 25*, 37-46.

Bieber, J. (Producer). (1994). *Learning disabilities and social skills with Richard LaVoie: Last one picked . . . first one picked on* [videotape]. (Available from Public Broadcasting Service Video, 1320 Braddock Place, Alexandria, VA 22314)

Biklen, D. (1990). Communication unbound: Autism and praxis. *Harvard Educational Review, 60*(3), 291-314.

Bolick, T. (2001). *Asperger syndrome and adolescence: Helping preteens and teens get ready for the real world.* Gloucester, MA: Fair Winds Press.

Brown, F. (1991). Creative daily scheduling: A non-intrusive approach to challenging behaviors in community residences. *Journal of the Association for Persons with Severe Handicaps, 16*(2), 75-84.

Brown, F., Belz, P., Corsi, L., & Wenig, B. (1993). Choice diversity of people with severe disabilities. *Education and Training in Mental Retardation, 28*, 318-326.

Centers for Disease Control and Prevention. (2004). *How Common is Autism Spectrum Disorder?* Retrieved January 15, 2006, from http://www.cdc.gov/ncbddd/autism/asd_common.htm

Cohen, D. J., & Volkmar, F. R. (Eds.). (1997). *Handbook of autism and pervasive developmental disorders.* New York: John Wiley & Sons.

Corbett, J. (1987). Development, disintegration and dementia. *Journal of Mental Deficiency Research, 31*(4), 346-356.

Dalrymple, N. J. (1993). *Helping people with autism manage their behavior.* Bloomington, IN: Institute for the Study of Developmental Disabilities.

Earles, T. L. (1998). *An analysis of the variables that predict outcome scores on the Psychoeducational Profile–Revised.* Unpublished doctoral dissertation, University of Kansas, Lawrence.

Earles-Vollrath, T. L., Cook, K. T., & Ganz, J. B. (2006). *Visual supports and visually-based strategies for students with Autism Spectrum Disorders.* Austin, TX: Pro-Ed.

Earles-Vollrath, T. L., Cook, K., Robbins, L., & Ben-Arieh, J. (2006). Instructional strategies to facilitate successful learning outcomes for students with autism. In R. L. Simpson & B. S. Myles (Eds.), *Educating children and youth with autism: Strategies for effective practice* (2nd ed.). Austin, TX: Pro-Ed.

Edelson, S. M. (1995). *Auditory integration training: Additional information.* Retrieved April 20, 2004, from http://www.autism.org/ait2.html

Ehlers, S. & Gillberg, C. (1993). The epidemiology of Asperger syndrome: A total population study. *Journal of Child Psychology and Psychiatry, 34*, 1327-1350.

Forest, M., & Lusthaus, E. (1989). Promoting educational equality for all students: Circles and maps. In S. Stainback, W. Stainback, & M. Forest (Eds.), *Educating all students in the mainstream of regular education* (pp. 43-57). Baltimore: Brookes.

Frederickson, N., & Turner, J. (2003). Utilizing the classroom peer group to address children's social needs: An evaluation of the circle of friends intervention approach. *The Journal of Special Education, 36*(4), 234-245.

Frost, L., & Bondy, A. (1994). *The picture exchange communication system training manual.* Newmark, DE: Pyramid Educational Products.

Gagnon, E. (2001). *POWER CARDS: Using special interests to motivate children and youth with Asperger syndrome and autism.* Shawnee Mission, KS: Autism Asperger Publishing Company.

Ganz, J. B., & Simpson, R. L. (2004). Effects on communicative requesting and speech development of the Picture Exchange Communication System in children with characteristics of autism. *Journal of Autism and Developmental Disorders, 3*(4) 395-410.

Gillberg, C. (2002). *A guide to Asperger syndrome.* Cambridge, UK: Cambridge University Press.

Gray, C. (1994). *Comic strip conversations.* Arlington, TX: Future Horizons.

Gray, C. (1995). *Social stories unlimited: Social stories and comic strip conversations.* Jenison, MI: Jenison Public Schools.

Gray, C. (2000). *Writing social stories with Carol Gray: Accompanying workbook to video.* Arlington, TX: Future Horizons, Inc.

Greenspan, S., & Wieder, S. (1998). *The child with special needs: Encouraging intellectual and emotional growth.* Reading, MA: Addison-Wesley.

Hagberg, B., & Witt-Engerstrom, I. (1986). Rett syndrome: A suggested staging system for describing impairment profile with increasing age towards adolescence. *American Journal of Medical Genetics, 24* (Suppl. 1), 47-59.

Heflin, L. J., & Simpson, R. L. (1998). Interventions for children and youth with autism: Prudent choices in a world of exaggerated claims and empty promises. Part I: Intervention and treatment option review. *Focus on Autism and Other Developmental Disabilities, 13*(4), 194-211.

Hodgdon, L. A. (1995). *Visual strategies for improving communication: Practical supports for school and home.* Troy, MI: Quirk Roberts Publishing.

Kanner, L. (1943). Autistic disturbances of affective contact. *The Nervous Child, 2*, 217-250.

Kaufman, B. (1976). *Son-Rise.* New York: Harper & Row Publishers.

Kientz, M., & Dunn, W. (1997) A comparison of the performance of children with and without autism on the sensory profile. *American Journal of Occupational Therapy, 51* (7), 530-537.

Lord, C., & Venter, A. (1991). Outcome and follow-up studies of high-functioning autistic individuals. In E. Schopler & G. B. Mesibov (Eds.), *High-functioning individuals with autism* (pp. 187-199). New York: Plenum.

MacDuff, G. S., & Krantz, P. J. (1993). Teaching children with autism to use photographic activity schedules: Maintenance and generalization of complex response chains. *Journal of Applied Behavior Analysis, 26*(1), 89–97.

Maurice, C., Green, G., & Fox, R. (2001). *Making a difference: Behavioral intervention for autism.* Austin, TX: Pro-Ed.

McGee, J. J. (1985). Gentle teaching. *Mental Handicap in New Zealand. 9*(3), 13–24.

Miltenberger, R. G. (2004). *Behavior modification: Principles and procedures* (3rd ed.). Belmont, CA: Wadsworth/Thomson Learning.

Moore, S. T. (2002). *Asperger syndrome and the elementary school experience: Practical solutions for academic and social difficulties.* Shawnee Mission, KS: Autism Asperger Publishing Company.

Myles, B. S., & Adreon, D. (2001). *Asperger syndrome and adolescence: Practical solutions for school success.* Shawnee Mission, KS: Autism Asperger Publishing Company.

Myles, B. S., & Simpson, R. L. (2003). *Asperger syndrome: A guide for educators and parents* (2nd ed.). Austin, TX: Pro-Ed.

Myles, B. S., & Southwick, J. (1999). *Asperger syndrome and difficult moments: Practical solutions for tantrums, rage and meltdowns.* Shawnee Mission, KS: Autism Asperger Publishing Co.

National Research Council. (2001). *Educating children with autism.* Washington, DC: National Academy Press.

Prizant, B. (1983). Language acquisition and communicative behavior in autism: Toward an understanding of the "whole" of it. *American Speech-Language-Hearing Association. 48*, 286–296.

Prizant, B., & Rydell, P. J. (1984). Analysis of functions of delayed echolalia in autistic children. *Journal of Speech and Hearing Research. 27*, 183–192.

Reichelt, K., Sagedal, E., Landmark, J., Sangvik, B., Eggen, O., & Scott, H. (1990). The effect of gluten-free diet on urinary peptide excretion and clinical state in schizophrenia. *Journal of Orthomolecular Medicine. 5*(4), 223–239.

Renner, L. (2000). *Asperger syndrome and autism: Comparing sensory processing in daily life.* Unpublished master's thesis, University of Kansas.

Rimland, B., Callaway, E., & Dreyfus, P. (1978). The effects of high doses of vitamin B6 on autistic children: A double-blind crossover study. *American Journal of Psychiatry. 135*(4), 472–475.

Roosa, J. (1995). Cited in Myles, B. S., & Adreon, D. (2001). *Asperger syndrome and adolescence: Practical solutions for school success.* Shawnee Mission, KS: Autism Asperger Publishing Company.

Rutter, M., Bailey, A., Bolton, P., & Le Couteur, A. (1994). Autism and known medical conditions: Myth and substance. *Journal of Child Psychology & Psychiatry & Allied Disciplines. 35*(2), 311–322.

Simpson, R. L., deBoer-Ott, S., Griswold, D., Myles, B. S., Byrd, S., Ganz, J. B., et al. (2005). *Autism spectrum disorders: Interventions and treatments for children and youth.* Thousand Oaks, CA: Corwin Press.

Simpson, R. L., & Zionts, P. (2000). *Autism: Information and resources for professionals and parents* (2nd ed.). Austin, TX: Pro-Ed.

Sitlington, P. L., Clark, G. M., & Kolstoe, P. O. (2006). *Transition education and services for adolescents with disabilities* (4th ed.). Needham Heights, MA: Allyn & Bacon.

Szatmari, P., Bartolucci, G., & Bremner, R. (1989). A follow-up study of high-functioning autistic children. *Journal of Autism and Developmental Disorders. 19*, 213–225.

Tallal, P., & Merzenich, M. (1997). *FastForWord.* Oakland, CA: Scientific Learning Corporation.

Taylor, G. (1997). Community building in schools: Developing a circle of friends. *Educational and Child Psychology. 14*(3), 45–50.

Tsai, L. (2001). *Taking the mystery out of medications in autism/Asperger syndromes: A guide for parents and non-medical professionals.* Arlington, TX: Future Horizons.

Tsai, L. Y. (2003). *Briefing paper. Pervasive developmental disorders.* Washington, DC: National Dissemination Center for Children with Disabilities.

Twachtman, D. D. (1995). Methods to enhance communication in verbal children. In K. A. Quill (Ed.), *Teaching children with autism: Strategies to enhance communication and socialization* (pp. 133–162). Albany, NY: Delmar Publishing Inc.

Volkmar, F. R., & Cohen, D. J. (1989). Disintegrative disorder of "late onset" autism. *Journal of Child Psychology and Psychiatry and Allied Disciplines. 30*(5), 717–724.

Volkmar, F. R., Klin, A., Marans, W., & Cohen, D. J. (1997). Childhood disintegrative disorder. In D. J. Cohen & F. R. Volkmar (Eds.), *Handbook of autism and pervasive developmental disorders* (2nd ed.) (pp. 47–59). New York: John Wiley & Sons.

Welch, M. G. (1988). Mother-child holding therapy and autism. *Pennsylvania Medicine, 91*(10), 33–38.

Westling, D. L., & Fox, L. (2004). *Teaching students with severe disabilities* (3rd ed.). Upper Saddle River, NJ: Pearson Education, Inc.

Wilde, L. D., Koegel, L. K., & Koegel, R. L. (1992). *Increasing success in school through priming: A training manual.* Santa Barbara, CA: University of California.

Wing, L. (1981). Asperger's syndrome: A clinical account. *Psychological Medicine, 11*, 115–129.

Chapter 10

Amari, A., Slifer, K. J., Gerson, A. C., Schenck, E., & Kane, A. (1999). Treating selective mutism in a paediatric rehabilitation patient by altering environmental reinforcement contingencies. *Pediatric Rehabilitation, 3*(2), 59–64.

American Academy of Child and Adolescent Psychiatry (AACAP). (1998). *Children who won't go to school* (Facts for Families No. 7). Retrieved February 3, 2006, from: http://www.aacap.org/publications/factsfam/noschool.htm

American Academy of Child and Adolescent Psychiatry (AACAP). (2000). *The anxious child* (Facts for Families

No. 47). Retrieved February 3, 2006, from: http://www.aacap.org/publications/factsfam/anxious.htm

American Academy of Child and Adolescent Psychiatry (AACAP). (2002a). *Bipolar disorder in children and teens* (Facts for Families No. 38). Retrieved February 3, 2006, from: http://www.aacap.org/publications/factsfam/ bipolar. htm

American Academy of Child & Adolescent Psychiatry (AACAP). (2002b). *Helping teenagers with stress* (Facts for Families No. 66). Retrieved February 3, 2006, from: http://www.aacap.org/publications/factsfam/66.htm

American Psychiatric Association (APA). (2000). *Diagnostic and statistical manual of mental disorders* (4th ed., text revision). Washington, DC: Author.

Anderman, E. M. (2002). School effects on psychological outcomes during adolescence. *Journal of Educational Psychology, 94*(4), 795–809.

Arnold, P. D., & Richter, M. A. (2001). Is obsessive-compulsive disorder an autoimmune disease? *Canadian Medical Association Journal, 165*(10), 1353–1358.

Birmaher, B., Ryan, N. D., Williamson, D. E., Brent, D. A., Kaufman, J., Dahl, R. E., et al. (1996). Childhood and adolescent depression: A review of the past 10 years. Part 1. *Journal of the American Academy of Child and Adolescent Psychiatry, 35*(11), 1427–1439.

Boris, N. W., Hinshaw-Fuselier, S. S., Smyke, A. T., Scheeringa, M. S., Heller, S. S., & Zeanah, C. H. (2004). Comparing criteria for attachment disorders: Establishing reliability and validity in high-risk samples. *Journal of the American Academy of Child and Adolescent Psychiatry, 43*(5), 568–577.

Boris, N. W., & Zeanah, C. H. (1999). Disturbances and disorders of attachment in infancy: An overview. *Infant Mental Health Journal, 20*(1), 1–9.

Calamari, E., & Pini, M. (2003). Dissociative experiences and anger proneness in late adolescent females with different attachment styles. *Adolescence, 38*(Summer), 287–303.

Cheek, J. R., Bradley, L. J., & Reynolds, J. (2002). An intervention for helping elementary students reduce test anxiety. *Professional School Counseling, 6*(2), 162–164.

Daviss, W. B., Mooney, D., Racusin, R., Ford, J. D., Fleischer, A., & McHugo, G. J. (2000). Predicting posttraumatic stress after hospitalization for pediatric injury. *Journal of the American Academy of Child and Adolescent Psychiatry, 39*(5), 576–583.

Department of Health. (2003). Safety review of antidepressants used by children completed. [Press Release]. Retrieved August 25, 2004, from: http://www.dh.gov.uk/PublicationsAndStatistics/PressReleases/PressReleasesNotices/fs/en?CONTENT_ID=4064098&chk=CzFJcI

Eaton, W., Buka, S., Addington, A. M., Bass, J., Brown, S., Cherkerzian, S., et al. (2004). *Risk factors for major mental disorders: A review of the epidemiologic literature.* Department of Mental Health, Bloomberg School of Public Health, Johns Hopkins University and Departments of Society, Human Development and Health & Epidemiology, Harvard School of Public Health. Retrieved July 30, 2004, from: http://appsl. jhsph.edu/weaton/MDRF/main.html

Evans, A. S., & Frank, S. J. (2004). Adolescent depression and externalizing problems: Testing two models of comorbidity in an inpatient sample. *Adolescence, 39*(153), 1–18.

Evans, J. R., Velsor, P. V., & Schumacher, J. E. (2002). Addressing adolescent depression: A role for school counselors. *Professional School Counseling, 5*(3), 211–220.

Field, T., Diego, M., & Sanders, C. E. (2001a). Adolescent depression and risk factors. *Adolescence, 36*(143), 491–498.

Field, T., Diego, M., & Sanders, C. E. (2001b). Exercise is positively related to adolescents' relationships and academics. *Adolescence, 36*(141), 105–110.

Field, T., Diego, M., & Sanders, C. E. (2002). Adolescents' parent and peer relationships. *Adolescence, 37*(145), 121–130.

Flood, W. A., & Wilder, D. A. (2004). The use of differential reinforcement and fading to increase time away from a caregiver in a child with Separation Anxiety Disorder. *Education and Treatment of Children, 27*(1), 1–8.

Foley, D., Rutter, M., Pickles, A., Angold, A., Maes, H., Silberg, J., et al. (2004). Informant disagreement for separation anxiety disorder. *Journal of the American Academy of Child and Adolescent Psychiatry, 43*(4), 452–460.

Food and Drug Administration (FDA). (2004). FDA updates its review of antidepressant drugs in children. Retrieved August 26, 2004, from: http://www.fda.gov/bbs/topics/ANSWERS/ 2004/ANS01306.html

Frommberger, U. H., Stieglitz, R. D., Nyberg, E., Schlickewei, W., Kuner, E., & Berger, M. (1998). Prediction of a posttraumatic stress disorder by immediate reactions to trauma: A prospective study in road traffic accident victims. *European Archives of Psychiatry and Clinical Neuroscience, 248*(6), 316–321.

Garland, E. J. (2004). Facing the evidence: Antidepressant treatment in children and adolescents. *Canadian Medical Association Journal, 170*(4), 489–491.

Geller, B., & Luby, J. (1997). Child and adolescent bipolar disorder: a review of the past 10 years. *Journal of the American Academy of Child and Adolescent Psychiatry, 36*(9), 1168–1176.

Giddan, J. J., Ross, G. J., & Sechler, L. L. (1997). Selective mutism in elementary school: Multidisciplinary interventions. *Language, Speech, and Hearing Services in Schools, 28*, 127–133.

Gil-Rivas, V., Greenberger, E., Chen, C., & Montero y López-Lena, M. (2003). Understanding depressed mood in the context of a family-oriented culture. *Adolescence, 38*(149), 93–109.

Ginsburg, G. S., & Drake, K. L. (2002). School-based treatment for anxious African-American adolescents: A controlled pilot study. *Journal of the Academy of Child and Adolescent Psychiatry, 41*(7), 768–775.

Goldbeck, L., & Schmid, K. (2003). Effectiveness of autogenic relaxation training on children and adolescents with behavioral and emotional problems. *Journal of the American Academy of Child and Adolescent Psychiatry, 42*(9), 1046–1054. **Note**: The ART manual is available from the journal Web site at http://www.jaacap.com in conjunction with this article.

Hall, S. E. K., & Geher, G. (2003). Behavioral and personality characteristics of children with reactive attachment disorder. *Journal of Psychology, 137*(2), 145–162.

Harris, G. (2004, June 2). Antidepressant seen as effective in treatment of adolescents. *The New York Times.* Downloaded from nytimes.com 06/02/04.

Harris, G. E. (2003). Progressive muscle relaxation: Highly effective but often neglected. *Guidance and Counselling, 18*(4), 142–148.

Hazler, R. J., & Denham, S. A. (2002). Social isolation of youth at risk: Conceptualizations and practical implications. *Journal of Counseling and Development, 80*(4), 403–409.

Hazler, R. J., & Mellin, E. A. (2004). The developmental origins and treatment needs of female adolescents with depression. *Journal of Counseling and Development, 82*(1), 18–24.

Jensen, P. S., Bhatara, V. S., Vitiello, B., Hoagwood, K., Feil, M., & Burke, L. B. (1999). Psychoactive medication prescribing practices for U.S. children: Gaps between research and clinical practice. *Journal of the American Academy of Child and Adolescent Psychiatry, 38*(5), 557–565.

Kehle, T. J., Madaus, M. R., & Baratta, V. S. (1998). Augmented self-modeling as a treatment for children with selective mutism. *Journal of School Psychology, 36*(3), 247–260.

Kennedy, B. L., & Schwab, J. L. (2002). Work, social and family disabilities of subjects with anxiety and depression. *Southern Medical Journal, 95*(12), 1424–1427.

Kopp, S., & Gillberg, C. (1997). Selective mutism: A population-based study: A research note. *The Journal of Child Psychology and Psychiatry and Allied Disciplines, 38,* 257–262.

Last, C., Hansen, C., & Franco, N. (1998). Cognitive-behavioral treatment of school phobia. *Journal of the American Academy of Child and Adolescent Psychiatry, 37*(4), 404–411.

Layne, A. E., Bernstein, G. A., & Egan, E. A. (2003). Predictors of treatment response in anxious-depressed adolescents with school refusal. *Journal of the American Academy of Child and Adolescent Psychiatry, 42*(3), 319–326.

Maag, J. W. (2002). A contextually based approach for treating depression in school-age children. *Intervention in School and Clinic, 37*(3), 149–155.

Marcotte, D., Fortin, L., Potvin, P., & Papillon, M. (2002). Gender differences in depressive symptoms during adolescence: Role of gender-typed characteristics, self-esteem, body image, stressful life events, and pubertal status. *Journal of Emotional and Behavioral Disorders, 10*(1), 29–42.

Masellis, M., Rector, N. A., & Richter, M. A. (2003). Quality of life in OCD: Differential impact of obsessions, compulsions, and depression comorbidity. *Canadian Journal of Psychiatry, 48*(2), 72–77.

McKay, J. S. (2003). Caretaker bias in the study of young children [Letter to the editor]. *Journal of the American Academy of Child and Adolescent Psychiatry, 42*(11), 1267.

Miller, S. A., & Church, E. B. (2002). Easing the transition from home to school. *Scholastic Early Childhood Today, 17*(1), 33–34.

Milne, L. C., & Lancaster, S. (2001). Predictors of depression in female adolescents. *Adolescence, 36*(142), 207–223.

National Alliance for the Mentally Ill (NAMI). (2006). *Anxiety disorders in children and adolescents.* Retrieved February 5, 2006, from: http://www.nami.org/helpline/anxiety.htm

National Alliance for the Mentally Ill (NAMI). (2006). *Child and adolescent OCD fact sheet.* Retrieved February 5, 2006, from: http://www.nami.org/helpline/ocd.htm

National Alliance for the Mentally Ill (NAMI). (2006). *Facts about childhood-onset bipolar disorder.* Retrieved February 6, 2006, from: http://www.nami.org/helpline/bipolar-child.html

National Clearinghouse on Child Abuse and Neglect Information. (2001). *Understanding the effects of maltreatment on early brain development.* Washington, DC: National Clearinghouse on Child Abuse and Neglect Information, Administration for Children and Families, U. S. Department of Health and Human Services. Retrieved August 24, 2004, from: http://nccanch.acf.hhs.gov/pubs/focus/earlybrain.cfm

National Institute of Mental Health. (1999a). *Anxiety disorder research at the National Institute of Mental Health* (NIH Publication 99-4504). Bethesda, MD: Author.

National Institute of Mental Health (NIMH). (1999b). *Facts about obsessive-compulsive disorder* (Publication OM-99-4154). Bethesda, MD: Author.

National Institute of Mental Health (NIMH). (2000a). *Bipolar disorder research at the National Institute of Mental Health* (NIH Publication 00-4502). Bethesda, MD: Author.

National Institute of Mental Health (NIMH). (2000b). *Generalized anxiety disorder: A real illness* (NIH Publication 00-4677). Bethesda, MD: Author.

National Institute of Mental Health (NIMH). (2000c). *Post-traumatic stress disorder: A real illness* (NIH Publication 00-4675). Bethesda, MD: Author.

National Institute of Mental Health (NIMH). (2001a). *Facts about anxiety disorders* (NIH Publication OM-99-4152). Bethesda, MD: Author.

National Institute of Mental Health (NIMH). (2001b). *Reliving trauma: Post-traumatic stress disorder* (NIH Publication 01-4597). Bethesda, MD: Author.

National Institute of Mental Health (NIMH). (2001c). *Step on a crack . . . obsessive compulsive disorder* (NIH Publication 01-4598). Bethesda, MD: Author.

National Institute of Mental Health (NIMH). (2002). *Facts about post-traumatic stress disorder* (NIH Publication OM-99-4157). Bethesda, MD: Author.

Nauta, M. H., Scholing, A., & Emmelcamp, P. M. G. (2003). Cognitive-behavioral therapy for children with anxiety disorders in a clinical setting: No additional effect of a cognitive parent training. *Journal of the American Academy of Child and Adolescent Psychiatry, 42*(11), 1270–1278.

Rapoport, J. L. (1990). The waking nightmare: An overview of obsessive compulsive disorder. *Journal of Clinical Psychiatry, 51*(Suppl), 25–28.

Rasid, Z. M., & Parish, T. S. (1998). The effects of two types of relaxation training on students' levels of anxiety. *Adolescence, 33*(129), 99–101.

Reber, K. (1996). Children at risk for reactive attachment disorder: Assessment, diagnosis and treatment. *PROGRESS: Family Systems Research and Therapy, PGI*, 83-98.

Roland, E. (2002). Bullying, depressive symptoms and suicidal thoughts. *Educational Research, 44*(1), 55-67.

Schlozman, S. C. (2002a). An explosive debate: The bipolar child. *Educational Leadership, 60*(3), 89-90.

Schlozman, S. C. (2002b). The jitters. *Educational Leadership, 59*(4), 82-83.

Schlozman, S. C. (2002c). Quit obsessing! *Educational Leadership, 59*(5), 95-97.

Schlozman, S. C. (2002d). When illness strikes. *Educational Leadership, 60*(1), 82-83.

Smyke, A. T., Dumitrescu, A., & Zeanah, C. H. (2002). Attachment disturbances in young children I: The continuum of caretaking casualty. *Journal of the American Academy of Child and Adolescent Psychiatry, 41*(8), 972-982.

Snyman, M. V., Poggenpoel, M., & Myburgh, C.P.H. (2003). Young adolescent girls' experience of non-clinical depression. *Education, 124*(2), 269-288.

Spengler, P., & Jacobi, D. (1998). Assessment and treatment of obsessive-compulsive disorder in college age students and adults. *Journal of Mental Health Counseling, 20*(2), 95-112.

Substance Abuse and Mental Health Services Administration (SAMHSA). (2003a). *Anxiety disorders* (Publication KEN98-0045). Washington, DC: National Mental Health Information Center—Center for Mental Health Services, Substance Abuse and Mental Health Services Administration, U.S. Department of Health and Human Services.

Substance Abuse and Mental Health Services Administration (SAMHSA). (2003b). *Children's mental health facts: Children and adolescents with anxiety disorders* (Publication CA-0007). Washington, DC: National Mental Health Information Center—Center for Mental Health Services, Substance Abuse and Mental Health Services Administration, U.S. Department of Health and Human Services.

Thomsen, P. H., Rasmussen, G., & Andersson, C. B. (1999). Elective mutism: A 17-year-old girl treated successfully with citalopram. *Nordic Journal of Psychiatry, 53*(6), 427-429

U.S. Department of Health and Human Services. (1999). *Mental health: A report of the surgeon general.* Rockville, MD: Author.

Valleni-Basile, L. A., Garrison, C. Z., Waller, J. L., Addy, C. L., McKeown, R. E., Jackson, K. L., et al. (1996). Incidence of obsessive-compulsive disorder in a community sample of young adolescents. *Journal of the American Academy of Child and Adolescent Psychiatry, 35*(7), 898-906.

Verduin, T. L., & Kendall, P. C. (2003). Differential occurrence of comorbidity within childhood anxiety disorders. *Journal of Clinical Child and Adolescent Psychology, 32*(2), 290-295.

Videon, T. M. (2002). The effects of parent-adolescent relationships and parental separation on adolescent well-being. *Journal of Marriage and the Family, 64*(2), 489-503.

Wilkinson, G. B., Taylor, P., & Holt, J. R. (2002). Bipolar disorder in adolescence: Diagnosis and treatment. *Journal of Mental Health Counseling, 24*(4), 348-358.

Wilson, S. L. (2001). Attachment disorders: Review and current status. *Journal of Psychology, 135*(1), 37-51.

The World Health Organization. (2006). Depression. Retrieved February 20, 2006. From: http://www.who.int/mental health/management/depression/definition/en/print.html

Zeanah, C. H. (1996). Beyond insecurity: A reconceptualization of attachment disorders of infancy. *Journal of Consulting and Clinical Psychology. 64*(1), 42-52.

Zeanah, C. H., & Smyke, A. T. (2003). Reply to "Caretaker bias in the study of young children" [Letter to the editor]. *Journal of the American Academy of Child and Adolescent Psychiatry, 42*(11), 1268.

Zeanah, C. H., Smyke, A. T., & Dumitrescu, A. (2002). Attachment disturbances in young children II: Indiscriminate behavior and institutional care. *Journal of the American Academy of Child and Adolescent Psychiatry, 41*(8), 983-989.

Chapter 11

American Academy of Child & Adolescent Psychiatry (AACAP). (1998a). *Teen suicide* (Facts for Families No. 10). Retrieved January, 2006 from: http://www.aacap.org/publications/factsfam/suicide.htm

American Academy of Child and Adolescent Psychiatry (AACAP). (1998b). *Teenagers with eating disorders* (Facts for Families No. 2). Retrieved January 7, 2006, from: http://www.aacap.org/publications/factsfam/eating.htm

American Academy of Child and Adolescent Psychiatry (AACAP). (1998c). *Teens: Alcohol and other drugs* (Facts for Families No. 3). Retrieved January 7, 2006, from: http://www.aacap.org/publications/factsfam/teendrug.htm

American Academy of Child and Adolescent Psychiatry (AACAP). (1999). *Self-injury in adolescents* (Facts for Families No. 73). Retrieved January 7, 2006, from: http://www.aacap.org/publications/factsfam/73.htm

American Academy of Child and Adolescent Psychiatry (AACAP). (2000a). *Schizophrenia in children* (Facts for Families No. 49). Retrieved January 7, 2006, from: http://www.aacap.org/publications/factsfam/schizo.htm

American Academy of Child and Adolescent Psychiatry (AACAP). (2000b). *Tic disorders* (Facts for Families No. 35). Retrieved January 7, 2006, from: http://www.aacap.org/publications/factsfam/tics.htm

American Academy of Child and Adolescent Psychiatry (AACAP). (2002). *Gay and lesbian adolescents* (Facts for Families No. 63). Retrieved January 7, 2006, from: http://www.aacap.org/publications/factsfam/63.htm

American Psychiatric Association (APA). (2000). *Diagnostic and statistical manual of mental disorders* (4th ed., text revision). Washington, DC: Author.

Anderson, R. N., & Smith, B. L. (2003). Deaths: leading causes for 2001. *National Vital Statistics Report, 52*(9), 1-86.

A new cognitive model. (2004). *Eating Disorders Review, 15*(2), 5.

Ayyash-Abdo, H. (2002). Adolescent suicide: An ecological approach. *Psychology in the Schools, 39*(4), 459-475.

Bostic, J. Q., Rustuccia, C., & Schlozman, S. C. (2001). The suicidal student. *Educational Leadership, 59*(2), 81-90.

Carroll, L., & Anderson, R. (2002). Body piercing, tattooing, self-esteem, and body investment in adolescent girls. *Adolescence, 37*(147), 627-637.

Centers for Disease Control (CDC). (2004a). *Suicide* (Fact Sheet). Retrieved August 28, 2004, from: http://www.cdc.gov/ncipc/factsheets/suifacts.htm

Centers for Disease Control (CDC). (2004b, June 11). *Morbidity and Mortality Weekly Report, 53*(22). Retrieved August 26, 2004, from: http://www.cdc.gov/mmwr/PDF/wk/mm5322.pdf

Davies, M., Howlin, P., Bernal, J., & Warren, S. (1998). Treating severe self-injury in a community setting: Constraints on assessment and intervention. *Child Psychology and Psychiatry Review, 3*(1), 26-32.

Diego, M. A., Field, T. M., & Sanders, C. E. (2003). Academic performance, popularity, and depression predict adolescent substance use. *Adolescence. 38*(149), 35-42.

Field, T., Diego, M., & Sanders, C. E. (2001). Adolescent suicidal ideation. *Adolescence. 36*(142), 241-248.

Gerson, J., & Stanley, B. (2003, December). Suicidal self-injurious behavior in people with BPD. *Psychiatric Times, 20*(13) 59-60.

Harrison, T. W. (2003). Adolescent homosexuality and concerns regarding disclosure. *Journal of School Health. 73*(3), 107-112.

Kaplan Seidenfelf, M. E., Sosin, E., & Rickert, V. I. (2004). Nutrition and eating disorders in adolescents. *The Mount Sinai Journal of Medicine, 71*(3), 155-161.

Matthews, W., & Wallis, D. N. (2002). Patterns of self-inflicted injury. *Trauma, 4*(1), 17-20.

McVey, G., Tweed, S., & Blackmore, E. (2004). Dieting among preadolescent and young adolescent females. *Canadian Medical Association Journal, 170*(10), 1559-1561.

Munson, B. L. (2005). About Tourette's syndrome. *Nursing, 35*(8), 29.

National Alliance for the Mentally Ill (NAMI). (2001a). *Early onset schizophrenia.* Retrieved January 7, 2006, from: http://www.nami.org/helpline/earlyonsetschizophrenia.htm

National Alliance for the Mentally Ill (NAMI). (2001b). *Teenage suicide.* Retrieved January 7, 2006, from: http://www.nami.org/helpline/teensuicide.html

National Alliance for the Mentally Ill (NAMI). (2004). *Tourette's syndrome.* Retrieved January 7, 2006, from: http://www.nami.org/helpline/tourette.html

National Eating Disorders Association. (2002). What's going on with me? Evaluating eating and exercise habits. Seattle, WA: Author. Retrieved January 7, 2006, from: http://www.nationaleatingdisorders.org/p.asp?WebPage_ID=286&Profile_ID=41155

National Institute of Mental Health (NIMH). (2001). *Eating disorders: Facts about eating disorders and the search for solutions* (Publication 01-4901). Bethesda, MD: Author.

National Institute of Mental Health (NIMH). (2003a). *Facts about childhood-onset schizophrenia* (Publication 04-5124). Bethesda, MD: Author.

National Institute of Mental Health (NIMH). (2003b). *In harm's way: Suicide in America* (Publication 03-4594). Bethesda, MD: Author.

Palmer, S. (2002). Suicide reduction and prevention: Strategies and interventions. *British Journal of Guidance and Counselling, 30*(4), 341-352.

Perosa, L., & Perosa, S. (2004). The continuum versus categorical debate on eating disorders: Implications for counselors. *Journal of Counseling and Development, 82*(2), 203-206.

Portes, P. R., Sandhu, D. S., & Longwell-Grice, R. (2002). Understanding adolescent suicide: A psychological interpretation of developmental and contextual factors. *Adolescence, 37*(148), 805-814.

Prestia, K. (2003). Tourette's syndrome: Characteristics and interventions. *Intervention in School and Clinic, 39*(2), 67-71.

Rogers, J. R., Lewis, M. M., & Subich, L. M. (2002). Validity of the suicide assessment checklist in an emergency crisis center. *Journal of Counselling and Development, 80*(4), 493-503.

Ruddell, P., & Curwen, B. (2002). Understanding suicidal ideation and assessing for risk. *British Journal of Guidance and Counselling, 30*(4), 363-372.

Schlozman, S. C. (2002a). Feast or famine. *Educational Leadership, 59*(6), 86-87.

Schlozman, S. C. (2002b). Why "just say no" isn't enough. *Educational Leadership, 59*(7), 87-89.

Stayer, C., Sporn, A., Gogtay, N., Tossell, J., Lenane, M., Gochman, P., et al. (2004). Looking for childhood schizophrenia: Case series of false positives. *Journal of the American Academy of Child and Adolescent Psychiatry, 43*(8), 1026-1029.

Steiger, H. (2004). Eating disorders and the serotonin connection: State, trait, and developmental effects. *Journal of Psychiatry and Neuroscience, 29*(1), 20-29.

Stice, E., & Whitenton, K. (2002). Risk factors for body dissatisfaction in adolescent girls: A longitudinal investigation. *Developmental Psychology, 38*(5), 669-678.

Stone, J. A., & Sias, S. M. (2003). Self-injurious behavior: A bi-modal treatment approach to working with adolescent females. *Journal of Mental Health Counseling, 25*(2), 112-125.

Subramaniam, M., Chong, S., & Pek, E. (2003). Diabetes mellitus and impaired glucose tolerance in patients with schizophrenia. *Canadian Journal of Psychiatry, 48*(5), 345-347.

Substance Abuse and Mental Health Services Administration (SAMHSA). (1998a). *Eating disorders* (Publication KEN98-0047). Washington, DC: National Mental Health Information Center—Center for Mental Health Services, Substance Abuse and Mental Health Services Administration, U.S. Department of Health and Human Services.

Substance Abuse and Mental Health Services Administration (SAMHSA). (1998b). *Schizophrenia* (Publication KEN98-0052). Washington, DC: National Mental Health Information

Center—Center for Mental Health Services, Substance Abuse and Mental Health Services Administration, U.S. Department of Health and Human Services.

Tanofsky-Kraff, M., Yanovski, S. Z., Wilfley, D. E., Marmarosh, C., Morgan, C. M., & Yanovski, J. A. (2004). Eating-disordered behaviors, body fat, and psychopathology in overweight and normal-weight children. *Journal of Consulting and Clinical Psychology, 72*(1), 53–61.

Treating bulimia nervosa with topiramate. (2004). *Eating Disorders Review, 15*(2), 4–5.

Videon, T. M. (2002). The effects of parent-adolescent relationships and parental separation on adolescent well-being. *Journal of Marriage and the Family, 64*(2), 489–503. Retrieved July 31, 2004, from EBSCOhost.

Vogel, J. S., Hurford, D. P., Smith, J. V., & Cole, A. (2003). The relationship between depression and smoking in adolescents. *Adolescence, 38*(149), 57–74.

Vogel, L. C., & Anderson, C. J. (2002). Self-injurious behavior in children and adolescents with spinal cord injuries. *Spinal Cord, 40*(12), 666–668.

White Kress, V. E. (2003). Self-injurious behaviors: Assessment and diagnosis. *Journal of Counseling and Development, 81*(4), 490–496.

Chapter 12

Aldinger, L. E., Warger, C. L., & Eavy, P. W. (1991). *Strategies for teacher collaboration.* Ann Arbor, MI: Exceptional Innovations.

Arguelles, M. E., Hughes, M. J., & Schumm, J. S. (2000). Co-teaching: A different approach to inclusion. *Principal, 79*(4), 48, 50–51.

Bernal, C., & Aragon, L. (2004). Critical factors affecting the success of paraprofessionals in the first two years of career ladder projects in Colorado. *Remedial and Special Education, 25*(4), 205–213.

Broer, S. M., Doyle, M. B., & Giangreco, M. F. (2005). Perspectives of students with intellectual disabilities about their experiences with paraprofessional support. *Exceptional Children, 71*(4), 415–430.

Chesapeake Institute. (1994, September). *National agenda for achieving better results for children and youth with serious emotional disturbance.* Washington, DC: Department of Education, Office of Special Education and Rehabilitative Services, Office of Special Education Programs. Retrieved February 1, 2003, from: http://cecp.air.org/resources/ntlagend.asp

Chopra, R. V., & French, N. K. (2004). Paraeducator relationships with parents of students with significant disabilities. *Remedial and Special Education, 25*(4), 240–251.

Chopra, R. V., Sandoval-Lucero, E., Aragon, L., Bernal, C., De Balderas, H. B., & Carroll, D. (2004). The paraprofessional role of connector. *Remedial and Special Education, 25*(4), 219–231.

Cook, L., & Friend, M. (1996, September). Co-teaching: What's it all about? *Teaching Exceptional Children, (CEC Today Supplement), 29*(1), 12–13.

Covey, S. (2004). *7 habits of highly effective people.* New York: Simon and Schuster.

Dissinger, F. K. (1988). *The identification of critical elements of the Class Within a Class alternative service delivery model and the development of a teacher training package based on the critical elements identified.* Unpublished doctoral dissertation, University of Kansas, Lawrence.

Duckworth, S., Smith-Rex, S., Okey, S., Brookshire, M. A., Rawlinson, D., Rawlinson, R., et al. (2001). Wraparound services for young schoolchildren with emotional and behavioral disorders. *Teaching Exceptional Children, 33*(4), 54–60.

Fisher, D., Frey, N., & Thousand, J. (2003). What do special educators need to know and be prepared to do for inclusive schooling to work? *Teacher Education and Special Education, 26*(1), 42–50.

French, N. K. (2003). Paraeducators in special education programs. *Focus on Exceptional Children, 36*(2), 1–16.

French, N. K. (2004). Introduction to the special series. *Remedial and Special Education, 25*(4), 203–204.

Friend, M. (2005). *Special education: Contemporary perspectives for school professionals.* Boston: Allyn & Bacon.

Friend, M., & Cook, L. (2003). *Interactions: Collaboration skills for school professionals.* Boston: Allyn & Bacon.

Giangreco, M. F. (2003). Working with paraprofessionals. *Educational Leadership, 61*(2), 50–53.

Giangreco, M. F., & Broer, S. M. (2005). Questionable utilization of paraprofessionals in inclusive schools: Are we addressing symptoms or causes? *Focus on Autism and Other Developmental Disabilities, 20*(1), 10–26.

Giangreco, M. F., Edelman, S. W., & Broer, S. M. (2001/2002). *A guide to schoolwide planning for paraeducator supports.* Burlington, VT: University of Vermont, Center on Disability and Community Inclusion. Retrieved September 30, 2005, from: http://www.uvm.edu/~cdci/parasupport/guide.html

Giangreco, M. F., Edelman, S. W., & Broer, S. M. (2003). Schoolwide planning to improve paraeducator supports. *Exceptional Children, 70*(1), 63–79.

Hanson, M. J., & Lynch, E. W. (1990). Honoring the cultural diversity of families when gathering data. *Topics in Early Childhood Special Education, 10*(1), 112–131.

Hanson, M. J., & Lynch, E. W. (1992). Family diversity: Implications for policy and practice. *Topics in Early Childhood Special Education, 12*(3), 283–304.

Hernandez, M., & Hodges, S. (2003). Building upon the theory of change for systems of care. *Journal of Emotional and Behavioral Disorders, 11*(1), 19–26.

Idol, L., Nevin, A., & Paolucci-Whitcomb, P. (1995). The revised collaborative consultation model. *Journal of Educational and Psychological Consultation, 6*(4), 347–361.

Idol, L., Paolucci-Whitcomb, P., & Nevin, A. (1995). The collaborative consultation model. *Journal of Educational and Psychological Consultation, 6*(4), 329–346.

Irmsher, K. (1996). *Communication skills* (ERIC Digest 102). Eugene, OR: ERIC Clearinghouse on Educational Management. (ERIC Document Reproduction Service No. ED390114)

Johnson, L. J., Zorn, D., Tam, B. K. Y., Lamontagne, M., & Johnson, S. (2003). Stakeholders' views of factors that impact successful interagency collaboration. *Exceptional Children, 69*(2), 195–209.

Keefe, E., & Moore, V. (2004). The challenge of co-teaching in inclusive classrooms at the high school level: What the teachers told us. *American Secondary Education, 32*(3), 77–88.

Keefe, E., Moore, V., & Duff, F. (2004). The four "knows" of collaborative teaching. *Teaching Exceptional Children, 36*(5), 36–42.

Lucas, J. (2004, September). Stretching and expanding: The changing role of special educators. *Missouri Innovations in Education, 32*(1). Retrieved December 28, 2004, from: http://www.cise.missouri.edu/publications/innovations/september-2004/lucas.html

Mattessich, P. W., & Monsey, B. R. (1993). *Collaboration: What makes it work*. St. Paul, MN: Amherst H. Wilder Foundation.

McConnell, M. E., & Townsend, B. L. (1997). How do you keep going? *Intervention in School and Clinic, 33*(2), 125–127.

National Center for Education Statistics. (1995). *Statistics in brief: Public school student, staff, and graduate counts by state, school year 1993–1994* (NCES Publication 95-213). Washington, DC: Author.

National Center for Education Statistics. (2005). *Public elementary and secondary students, staff, schools, and school districts: School year 2002–03* (NCES Publication 2005-314). Washington, DC: Author.

Nevis, E. C., DiBella, A. J., & Gould, J. M. (1994). *Understanding organizations as learning systems*. Accessed January 14, 2006, from: http://www.solonline.org/static/research/workingpapers/learning_sys.html

Osher, D., & Hanley, T. V. (2001). Implementing the SED national agenda: Promising programs and policies for children and youth with emotional and behavioral problems. *Education and Treatment of Children, 24*(3), 374–403.

Robinson, S. M. (1989). *Collaborative consultation teacher training project manual*. Kansas City, KS: University of Kansas Medical Center, Department of Special Education.

Rosenblatt, A., & Woodbridge, M. W. (2003). Deconstructing research on systems of care for youth with EBD: Frameworks for policy research. *Journal of Emotional and Behavioral Disorders, 11*(1), 27–37.

Santos, R. M., & Reese, D. (1999). *Selecting culturally and linguistically appropriate materials: Suggestions for service providers* (Report No. EDD-PS-99-6). Champaign, IL: ERIC Clearinghouse on Elementary and Early Childhood Education. (ERIC Document Reproduction Service No. ED431546)

Shaw, C. C. (1997). *Critical issue: Educating teachers for diversity*. North Central Regional Educational Laboratory (NCREL). Accessed December 29, 2004, from: http://www.ncrel.org/sdrs/areas/issues/educatrs/presrvce/pe300.htm

Turnbull, A. P., & Turnbull, H. R. (2001). *Families, professionals, and exceptionality: Collaborating for empowerment* (4th ed.). Upper Saddle River, NJ: Merrill/Prentice-Hall.

Turnbull, A. P., Turnbull, H. R., Shank, M., & Leal, D. (1999). *Exceptional lives: Special education in today's schools* (2nd ed.). Englewood Cliffs, NJ: Merrill/Prentice-Hall.

Walker, J. S. (2001). Caregivers' views on the cultural appropriateness of services for children with emotional or behavioral disorders. *Journal of Child and Family Studies, 10*(3), 315–331.

Walsh, J., & Jones, B. (2004). New model of cooperative teaching. *Teaching Exceptional Children, 36*, 14–20.

Walther-Thomas, C., Korinek, L., & McLaughlin, V. L. (1999). Collaboration to support students' success. *Focus on Exceptional Children, 32*(3), 1–18.

Weiss, M. (2004). Co-teaching as science in the schoolhouse: More questions than answers. *Journal of Learning Disabilities, 37*, 218–223.

Werts, M. G., Harris, S., Tillery, C. Y., & Roark, R. (2004). What parents tell us about paraeducators. *Remedial and Special Education, 25*(4), 232–239.

Wunder, M., & Lindsey, C. (2004, April). The ins, outs of co-teaching. *Missouri Innovations in Education, 31*(4). Retrieved December 28, 2004, from: http://www.cise.missouri.edu/publications/innovations/april-2004/lindsey.html

Chapter 13

Adelman, H. S., & Taylor, L. (2003). Commentary: Advancing mental health science and practice through authentic collaboration. *The School Psychology Review, 32*(1), 53–56.

Anderson, B. (1996). *The counselor and the law* (4th ed.). Alexandria, VA: American Counseling Association.

Axline, V. M. (1969). *Play therapy*. New York: Ballantine Books.

Baker, S. B., & Gerler, E. R., Jr. (2004). *School counseling for the twenty-first century* (4th ed.). Upper Saddle River, NJ: Merrill/Prentice Hall.

Bauer, A., Ingersoll, E., & Burns, L. (2004). School counselors and psychotropic medication: Assessing training, experience, and school policy issues. *Professional School Counseling, 7*(3), 202–211.

Brammer, L. M., Abrego, P. J., & Shostrum, E. L. (1993). *Therapeutic counseling and psychotherapy* (6th ed.). Upper Saddle River, NJ: Prentice Hall.

Cade, B., & O'Hanlon, W. H. (1993). *A brief guide to brief therapy*. New York: W. W. Norton & Company.

Capuzzi, D., & Gross, D. R. (1992). *Introduction to group counseling*. Denver, CO: Love Publishing Company.

Compton, B. R., & Galaway, B. (1999). *Social work processes* (6th ed.). Pacific Grove, CA: Brooks/Cole.

Corey, G. C. (2001). *Theory and practice of counseling and psychotherapy* (6th ed.). Belmont, CA: Wadsworth/Thomson Learning.

Corey, M. S., & Corey, G. C. (2003). *Becoming a helper* (4th ed.). Pacific Grove, CA: Brooks Cole.

de Shazer, S. (1985). *Keys to solution in brief therapy*. New York: W. W. Norton.

Downing, J. A. (2004). Related services for students with disabilities: Introduction to the special issue. *Intervention in School and Clinic, 39*(4), 195–208.

Fischer, L., & Sorenson, G. P. (1996). *School law for counselors, psychologists and social workers* (3rd ed.). White Plains, NY: Longman Publishers.

Flaherty, L. T., Garrison, E. G., Waxman, R., Uris, P., Keys, S. G., Glass-Seigel, M., et al. (1998). Optimizing the roles of school mental health professionals. *The Journal of School Health, 68* (10), 420–424.

Haley, J. (1986). *Problem solving therapy*. San Francisco: Josey-Bass.

Herlihy, B., & Corey, G. (1996). *ACA ethical standards casebook* (fifth ed.). Alexandria, VA: American Counseling Association.

Gladding, S. T. (2001). *The counseling dictionary: Concise definitions of frequently used terms*. Upper Saddle River, NJ: Merrill/Prentice Hall.

Ivey, A. E., & Ivey, M. B. (2003). *Intentional interviewing and counseling: Facilitating client development in a multicultural society* (5th ed.). Pacific Grove, CA: Brooks Cole.

Katsiyannis, A. (1990). Provision of related services: State practices and the issue of eligibility criteria. *The Journal of Special Education, 24,* 246–252.

Landreth, G. (1991). *Play therapy: The art of the relationship*. Bristol, PA: Accelerated Development, Inc.

Lawson. H. A. (1999). Two mental health models for schools and their implications for principals' roles, responsibilities, and preparation. *NASSP Bulletin, 83*(611), 8–27.

Maag, J. W., & Katsiyannis, A. (1996). Counseling as a related service for students with emotional or behavioral disorders: Issues and recommendations. *Behavioral Disorders, 21*(4), 293–305.

Minuchin, S., & Fishman, H. C. (1981). *Family therapy techniques*. Cambridge, MA: The President and Fellows of Harvard College.

Missouri Department of Elementary and Secondary Education. (1998). *Comprehensive guidance: The box*. Jefferson City, MO: Instructional Materials Laboratory.

Myrick, R. D. (2003). *Developmental guidance and counseling: A practical approach* (4th ed.). Minneapolis, MN: Educational Media Corporation.

National Information Center for Children and Youth with Disabilities. (2001, September). Related services (2nd ed.). *News Digest, ND16.* Retrieved August 21, 2003, from www.nichcy.org

Nugent, F. A. (1994). *An introduction to the profession of counseling* (2nd ed.). New York: Macmillan College Publishing Company, Inc.

Rodman, J., Weill, K., Driscoll, M., Fenton, T., Alpert, H., Salem-Schatz, S., & Palfrey, J. S. (1999). A nationwide survey of financing health-related services for special education students. *Journal of School Health, 69* (4), 133–139.

Rogers, C. (1951). *Client-centered therapy*. Boston: Houghton Mifflin Company.

Ruiz, A. (1990). Crisis and resolution. *Journal of Multicultural Counseling and Development, 18,* 29–40.

Safer, D. J. (1997). Changing patterns of psychotropic medications prescribed by child psychiatrists in the 1990s. *Journal of Child and Adolescent Psychopharmacology, 7*(4), 267–274.

Scholzman, S. C. (2003). Innovative models for school consultation. *Educational Leadership, 60* (6), 87–89.

Sue, D. W., & Sue, D. (2003). *Counseling the culturally diverse: Theory and practice* (4th ed.). New York: John Wiley and Sons, Inc.

Thompson, R. A. (2002). *School counseling: Best practices for working in the schools* (2nd ed.). New York: Brunner-Rutledge, Inc.

Walsh, M. (1999). Educators say ruling could drain budgets. *Education Week, 18* (26), 1–2.

Webb, N. B. (1999). *Play therapy with children in crisis: Individual, group and family treatment* (2nd ed.). New York: The Guilford Press.

Weist, M. D., & Christodulu, K. V. (2000). Expanded school mental health programs: Advancing reform and closing the gap between research and practice. *The Journal of School Health, 70*(5), 195–200.

Weist, M. D., & Schlitt, J. (1998). Alliances and school-based health care. *The Journal of School Health, 68*(10), 401–403.

White, M., & Epston, D. (1990). *Narrative means to therapeutic ends*. New York: W. W. Norton & Company.

Yalom, I. (1995). *The theory and practice of group psychotherapy* (4th ed.). New York: BasicBooks, Inc.

Young, M. (1998). *Learning the art of helping: Building blocks and techniques*. Upper Saddle River, NJ: Prentice Hall.

Chapter 14

Advancement Project/Harvard Civil Rights Project. (2000, February). *Opportunities suspended: The devastating consequences of zero tolerance and school discipline.* Cambridge, MA: Author.

Bender, W. N., Shubert, T. H., & McLaughlin, P. J. (2001). Invisible kids: Preventing school violence by identifying kids in trouble. *Intervention in School and Clinic, 37*(2), 105–111.

Council for Children with Behavioral Disorders and the Council of Administrators of Special Education. (1995). *A joint statement on violence in the school.* Reston, VA: Council for Exceptional Children.

DeVoe, J. F., Peter, K., Kaufman, P., Ruddy, S. A., Miller, A. K., Planty, M., et al. (2003). *Indicators of school crime and safety: 2003* (NCES 2004-004/NCJ 302368). Washington, DC: U.S. Departments of Education and Justice.

Gable, R. A., & Van Acker, R. (2000). The challenge to make schools safe: Preparing education personnel to curb student aggression and violence. *The Teacher Educator, 35*(3), 1–18.

Guetzloe, E. (1999). Violence in children and adolescents—A threat to public health and safety: A paradigm of prevention. *Preventing School Failure, 44* (1), 21–24.

Guetzloe, E. (2000). Teacher preparation in the age of violence: What do educators need to know? *The Teacher Educator, 35*(3), 19–27.

Morrison, G. M., Anthony, S., Storino, M., & Dillon, C. (2001). An examination of the disciplinary histories and the individual and educational characteristics of students who participate in an in-school suspension program. *Education and Treatment of Children, 24* (3), 276–293.

Myles, B. S., & Simpson, R. L. (1998). Aggression and violence by school-age children and youth: Understanding the aggression cycle and prevention/intervention strategies. *Intervention in School and Clinic, 33*(5), 259–264.

Skiba, R. J., Michael, R. S., Nardo, A. C., & Peterson, R. L. (2002). The color of discipline: Sources of racial and gender disproportionality in school punishment. *The Urban Review, 34* (4), 317–342.

Skiba, R. J., & Peterson, R. L. (2000). School discipline at a crossroads: From zero tolerance to early response. *Exceptional Children, 66,* 335–346.

Sprague, J., & Walker, H. (2000). Early identification and intervention for youth with antisocial and violent behavior. *Exceptional Children, 66* (3), 367–379.

Sprague, J., Walker, H., Golly, A., White, K., Myers, D. R., & Shannon, T. (2001). Translating research into effective practice: The effects of a universal staff and student intervention on indicators of discipline and school safety. *Education and Treatment of Children, 24*(4), 495–511.

Stewart, J. (2001). Preventing violent behavior. *Educational Leadership, 58* (5), 78–79.

Townsend, B. (2000). Disproportionate discipline of African American learners: Reducing school suspensions and expulsions. *Exceptional Children, 66* (3), 381–391.

U.S. Department of Health and Human Services (HHS). (2001). *Youth violence: A report of the surgeon general—Executive summary.* Rockville, MD: Author.

Van Acker, R., & Talbott, E. (1999). The school context and risk for aggression: Implications for school-based prevention and intervention efforts. *Preventing School Failure, 14* (1), 12–20.

Young, E. M., Autry, D., Lee, S., Meesemer, J. E., Roach, P. S., & Smit, J. C. (2002). Development of the Student Attitudes toward School Safety (SATSSM) instrument. *Journal of School Health, 72*(3), 107–114.

Appendices

American Psychiatric Association. (2000). *Diagnostic and statistical manual of mental disorders* (4th ed., text revision). Washington, DC: Author.

Bowers, L., Huisingh, R., Barrett, M., Orman, J., & LoGiudice, C. (1991). *TOPS—Adolescent: Test of Problem Solving.* Eastmoline, IL: LinguiSystems.

Bricker, D., & Squires, J. (1999). *Ages and stages questionnaires: A parent-completed child-monitoring system* (2nd ed.). Baltimore, MD: Paul H. Brookes Publishing Co.

Lambert, N., Nihira, K., & Leland, H. (1993). *AAMR adaptive behavior scale-school* (2nd ed.). Austin, TX: Pro-Ed.

Linder, T. (1993). *Transdisciplinary play-based assessment and intervention: Child and program summary forms.* Baltimore, MD: Paul H. Brookes Publishing Co.

Newcomer, P. L., & Hammill, D.D. (1997). *Test of language development-primary* (3rd ed.). Austin, TX: Pro-Ed.

Squires, J., Potter, L., & Bricker, D. (1999). *The ASQ user's guide for the ages and stages questionnaires: A parent-completed, child-monitoring system* (2nd ed.). Baltimore, MD: Paul H. Brookes Publishing Co.

Wechsler, D. (1991). *Wechsler intelligence scale for children* (3rd ed.). San Antonio, TX: The Psychological Corporation.

Woodcock, R. W., McGrew, K. S., & Mather, N. (2001). *Woodcock-Johnson III tests of achievement.* Itasca, IL: Riverside Publishing.

NAME INDEX

SUBJECT INDEX

AACAP. *See* American Academy of Child
    and Adolescent Psychiatry (AACAP)
A-ADDES. *See* Adult Attention Deficit
    Disorders Evaluation Scale, Home
    Version (A-ADDES)
AAMR Adaptive Behavior Scale-School,
    Second Edition (ABS-S2), 299
ABA. *See* Applied behavior analysis (ABA)
ABC Observation Form
  completed, 53
  sample, 52
ABCs of behavior management, 100
ABC worksheets, 50
Absenteeism, students with EBD and, 69
ABS-S2. *See* AAMR Adaptive Behavior
    Scale-School, Second Edition
    (ABS-S2)
Abuse
  educator guidelines for children with
    histories of, 205–206
  reactive attachment disorder and,
    208–209
Academic goals, individual transition
    planning and, 63
Academic outcomes, students with
    EBD and, 69
Academic skills, developing, in students
    with Autism Spectrum Disorders,
    174–177
Academic success, planning for, 90–91,
    94
Accommodations, identifying, 61
Achenbach System of Empirically Based
    Assessment (ASEBA), 149, 309
Achievement, 152
Achievement tests, 23
ACTeRS. *See* AD/HD Comprehensive
    Teacher's Rating Scale (ACTeRS)
Acting out toward others, CALM
    program and, 286
Activity-completion signals, for
    students with Autism Spectrum
    Disorders, 179
Acute stress disorder, 199
ADA. *See* Americans with Disabilities
    Act (ADA)

ADDES-S. *See* Attention Deficit
    Disorders Evaluation Scale:
    Secondary-Age Student (ADDES-S)
ADDES-3. *See* Attention Deficit
    Disorders Evaluation Scales
    (ADDES-3)
Adequate yearly progress (AYP), 9
  placement issues and, 15
AD/HD Comprehensive Teacher's
    Rating Scale (ACTeRS), 309
ADHD Rating Scale-IV, 309
ADHD-SC4. *See* ADHD Symptom
    Checklist-4
ADHD-SRS. *See* ADHD Symptoms
    Rating Scale (ADHD-SRS)
ADHD Symptom Checklist-4, 309
ADHD Symptoms Rating Scale
    (ADHD-SRS), 309
ADHDT. *See* Attention-Deficit/Hyper-
    activity Disorder Test (ADHDT)
Adlerian family therapy, 267
Adolescent Health Project, 214
Adolescent issues, individual transition
    planning and, 62–64
Adoptable children, reactive
    attachment disorder and, 208
Adult Attention Deficit Disorders
    Evaluation Scale, Home Version
    (A-ADDES), 309
Advance organizer, in lesson plan, 90,
    91, 92, 93
Affective disorders, 198
African American students, 69
  differential disciplinary action and, 280
  overrepresentation of, in category of
    EBD, 151
  overrepresentation of, in special
    education, 15
Age, suicide and, 237
Ages and Stages Questionnaire (ASQ),
    294
Aggression in students, increase in,
    278–279
Agoraphobia, 199
Agoraphobia without history of panic
    disorder, 199

Alaska Native students, overrepresenta-
    tion of, in special education, 15
Alpha statements, 154
Alternative placement, discipline and, 16
Alternative teaching, 255
Alternative therapies
  examples of, 193–194
  for students with anxiety and mood
    disorders, 221
  for students with Autistic Spectrum
    Disorders, 191–192
Altruism, 152
American Academy of Child and
    Adolescent Psychiatry (AACAP),
    134, 210, 218, 219, 223, 228, 235
American Academy of Pediatrics, 134
American education, students with
    disabilities and, 4–7
American Indian students, overrepre-
    sentation of, in special education
    classes, 15
American Psychiatric Association
    (APA), 125, 148, 171
Americans with Disabilities Act (ADA),
    6, 7
Amygdala, fear and, 204
Analogue assessment, 58
Anecdotal record, 29
Anger management skills, for students
    with disruptive behaviors,
    155–156
Annual goals, setting, 59–60
Anorexia nervosa
  description of, 231
  DSM-IV-TR diagnostic criteria for, 232
Antecedent instruction-related
    strategies, desirable behaviors and,
    100
Antecedents, 100
  manipulation of, 101
Antidepressants, cautionary note on
    use of, 222–223
Antisocial behavior, school contextual
    factors contributing to, 153
Anxiety disorder due to general
    medical condition, 199